# PETTICOATS AND PREJUDICE

# Petticoats and Prejudice

## Women and Law in Nineteenth-Century Canada

CONSTANCE BACKHOUSE

Published for The Osgoode Society
by Women's Press

©The Osgoode Society 1991
Printed in Canada

**Canadian Cataloguing in Publication Data**

Backhouse, Constance, 1952–
Petticoats and prejudice: women and law
in nineteenth century Canada

Includes bibliographical references and index.
ISBN 0-88961-161-0

1. Women — Legal status, laws, etc. — Canada
— History — 19th century. 2. Sex discrimination
against women — Law and legislation — Canada
— 19th century. I. Title.

KE509.B3 1991     346.7101'34     C91-094011-8

Cover illustration from *The Delineator*, 1901,
courtesy of the personal collection of the author.

Editing: P.K. Murphy
Copy editing and proofreading: W. Herrington
Indexing: Beth McAuley
Cover design: L. Gustafson
All rights reserved. No part of this book may be used or reproduced in
any manner whatsoever without written permission except in the case
of brief quotations embodied in critical articles and reviews.
For information address: Women's Press, 517 College Street, Suite 233,
Toronto, Ontario, Canada M6G 4A2


This book was produced by the collective effort of Women's Press.
Women's Press gratefully acknowledges financial support from
The Canada Council and the Ontario Arts Council.
2  3  4  5     1995 1994 1993 1992

*For my grandmother,*
*Zofia Wziatkowska Czechowski, my only living female relative to*
*experience part of the nineteenth century in person.*

# Contents

## PART IV: WOMEN'S WORK IN THE PAID LABOUR FORCE

# Foreword

## THE OSGOODE SOCIETY

The purpose of The Osgoode Society is to encourage research and writing in the history of Canadian law. The Society, which was incorporated in 1979 and is registered as a charity, was founded at the initiative of the Honourable R. Roy McMurtry, former Attorney-General for Ontario, and officials of the Law Society of Upper Canada. Its efforts to stimulate legal history in Canada include the sponsorship of a fellowship, a research support program, and work in the field of oral history and legal archives. The Society publishes (at the rate of about one a year) volumes of interest to the Society's members that contribute to legal-historical scholarship in Canada, including studies of the courts, the judiciary, and the legal profession, biographies, collections of documents, studies in criminology and penology, accounts of great trials, and work in the social and economic history of the law.

Current directors of The Osgoode Society are Jane Banfield, Brian Bucknall, Archie Campbell, J. Douglas Ewart, Martin Friedland, Howard Hampton, John Honsberger, Kenneth Jarvis, Allen Linden, James Lisson, Colin McKinnon, Roy McMurtry, Brendan O'Brien, Peter Oliver, James Spence, and Richard Tinsley. The annual report and information about membership may be obtained by writing The Osgoode Society, Osgoode Hall, 130 Queen Street West, Toronto, Ontario, Canada, M5H 2N6. Members receive the annual volumes published by the Society.

Over the past decade, Professor Constance Backhouse of the Faculty of Law, University of Western Ontario, has been publishing pioneering articles on the place of women in nineteenth-century Canadian society as reflected in law and legal institutions. These articles, which cover a wide range of topics, deal with numerous cases, both Canadian and foreign, through both legal and historical analysis. By contrast, each chapter of *Petticoats and Prejudice* highlights only a few of the more significant cases in each subject area. The resulting work, the first comprehensive book in the field of Canadian women's legal history, is marvellously readable. Covering issues such as marriage, divorce, separation, child custody, seduction, rape, infanticide, abortion, prostitution, and labour law, the book also addresses the battle for women's admission to the practice of law. In doing so, it makes an outstanding contribution to our understanding of a range of critical issues in nineteenth-century Canadian history. *Petticoats and Prejudice* is a pioneering effort that will be read with pleasure and profit by all.

R. Roy McMurtry
*President*

Peter N. Oliver
*Editor-in-Chief*

*February 1991*

# Acknowledgments

This book was conceived in 1978, when Morton Horwitz of Harvard Law School prompted me to select the law of child custody as my LL.M. thesis topic. I had always been interested in history and had spent a frustrating three years as a law student who found contemporary legal materials dry, uninviting, and nowhere near as intriguing as historical writings. I pursued graduate legal training in part to develop a wider understanding of law through history.

The field of women's studies was still young back then, and it took an advisor who was something of a visionary to suggest combining feminist analysis with legal research. Certainly I do not think I would have thought of it without Professor Horwitz's prompting. During the course of our work together, he encouraged me to think well beyond the scope of my thesis. Before I left Harvard, we had mapped out a prospectus for a full-length, ten-chapter book on women and the law in nineteenth-century Canada. Professor Horwitz advised writing one chapter a year, and predicted that in ten years I would have completed the book.

This seemed a reasonable, even sedate, agenda and I took up residence in London, Ontario, as a newly hired member of the law faculty at the University of Western Ontario in 1979. Aided by a research grant from the Social Sciences and Humanities Research Council of Canada, which enabled me to take a full year's leave during 1982–83, I kept on course tolerably well for the first years. The birth of my children, Diana and Mark in 1985 and 1986, and my initiation into the wonders of colicky babies and intractable infant ear infections, wreaked havoc with my carefully laid schedule. I have always found it surprising how many authors write glowingly in the forewords to their books of the support and assistance offered by their children. Honesty requires me to note that without my kids, whose diversionary capacity had its delightful aspects as well as its exhausting ones, this book would have appeared much sooner. It would take another year's leave in 1989–90, generously funded by the Social Sciences and Humanities Research Council of Canada and The Osgoode Society, to complete the manuscript.

Throughout the years I worked on this book I published a series of academic articles on women's legal history in various legal and historical periodicals.[1] One way of writing this book would have been to pull this already-published work together into a comprehensive, revised whole. Certainly there is much that I would like to alter from my earlier writings. As the field of secondary research in legal history has widened, as I have become more knowledgeable about my sources, I have changed a number of the ideas I set out in the original pieces. With substantial revisions, I could have built upon my initial work to write a full-scale academic treatise on women's legal history.

But I knew when I started writing in 1989 that I wanted this book to be framed differently from the scholarly articles I had published over the years. I wanted to reach beyond the small circle of legal history scholars, to describe the world of women in the nineteenth century to a general audience. If I have succeeded in this task, much credit is due to Leah Cohen, my co-author in *The Secret Oppression: Sexual Harassment of Working Women*, who shared her skill and knowledge while we worked together on that book.[2] Where my material bogs down the responsibility rests with me.

So many people have helped me with this book over the past twelve years that I hardly know where to begin thanking them. Much of the most painstaking research was done by research assistants, whose work was generously financed by the Law Foundation of Ontario and The Osgoode Society: Stephanie McCurry, Kate Hughes, Rosemary Coombe, Elaine Deluzio, Elizabeth Seto, Catherine Fedder, David Maslak, Martha Healey, Laurie Catherine Wright, Sandra Smith, Helen Pelton, Rico Toffoli, and Annamaria Feltracco. The more senior of these are now law professors and lawyers. Of the more junior, I expect to hear great things shortly. Their combined energy, wisdom, patience, and insight have strengthened the foundation of this book.

I am particularly indebted to Sylvio Normand, Marie-Aimeé Cliche, and Victor Nabhan for their assistance with Quebec sources, to David Bell and Brian Munro on New Brunswick sources, and to DeLloyd Guth and Indiana Matters on British Columbia sources. Ontario Archivists Catherine Shepard, Garron Wells, and Alex McEwen provided invaluable advice. University of Western Ontario Law Librarians Pat McVeigh, Marianne Welch, Margaret Banks, and George Robinson gave their time and knowledge unstintingly, regularly giving me research advice that went far beyond what any faculty member has the right to anticipate. Jean Fisher, Teresa Bourne, Jean Tasker, and Beryl Theobald helped with countless secretarial and administrative tasks. And I will be ever grateful to Fran Meyer, who photocopied more research materials and manuscript pages than I care to admit requesting.

The list of those who reviewed portions of my research in its earlier stages, or offered stimulating criticisms and shared sources, is long. Twelve years is a long period over which to have built up such academic debts. To all of the following, I offer my thanks and my hopes that I may some day be able to return the favours: Beth Atcheson, Moira Armour, Fred Armstrong, Norma Basch, Blaine Baker, Sharon Batt, David Bell, Paula Bourne, Christine Boyle, John E.C. Brierley, Ruth Compton Brouwer, Richard Chused, Marie-Aimée Cliche, Curtis Cole, Jim Connor, Nancy Cott, Nathalie Des Rosiers, Nancy Erickson, Anne Rochon Ford, Ben Forster, Hamar Foster, Burton Glendenning, Philip Girard, Lorraine Greaves, Michael Grossberg, DeLloyd Guth, Roger Hall, Dirk Hartog, Susan Houston, Louis Knafla, Kathleen Lahey, Svetlana MacDonald, Jean Matthews, John McLaren, Wendy Mitchinson, Mary Jane Mossman, Sylvio Normand, Joy Parr, Jim Phillips, Dana Richardson, R.C.B. Risk, Theresa Roth, Diana Russell, Marylynn Salmon, Laurel Sefton MacDowell, Jennifer Stoddart, Mary Stokes, Carolyn Strange, James Snell, Jon Swainger, Michele Thivierge, Barbara Todd, Eric Tucker, Margot Warren, Wendy Williams, and Sylvia Van Kirk.

I owe special gratitude to David Flaherty, who has inspired a generation of new Canadian legal historians to explore hitherto uncharted waters. As the editor of the first two Osgoode Society volumes, *Essays in the History of Canadian Law*, he provoked many of us to begin publishing our first historical research. A colleague at the University of Western Ontario, David has guided me toward a greater appreciation of the study of legal history, and my work would be poorer without his influence. Peter Oliver, the Editor-in-Chief of The Osgoode Society, and Jim Phillips and Susan Houston, who served as academic referees for The Osgoode Society, have also been extraordinarily helpful. I am equally indebted to

Ann Decter of Women's Press and P.K. Murphy, my editor, for their work. I can only hope that my text does justice to their thought-provoking comments. The Osgoode Society provided research funds in the very early stages of my work, as well as honouring me with the Osgoode Fellowship for 1989–90. The role of The Osgoode Society in advancing and encouraging scholarship on legal history is remarkable and unprecedented, and I have benefited enormously from it over the years.

To the two people who have most influenced my work over the past twelve years, sharing the rocky ups and downs of research, writing, and revisions, I offer heartfelt thanks. Diana Majury and Bruce Feldthusen listened for hours, joining me in my elation when I was delighted over my work, and putting up with me gracefully when I was not. To them, I say, at last, twelve years later, it is done!

Constance Backhouse
London, Ontario
*26 July 1990*

# Introduction

This book explores the legal status of women in nineteenth-century Canada by examining individual women who were swept up into the legal process as litigants, accused criminals, or witnesses. The format highlights the relationship between women and law through a detailed account of the situation of a few women, selected because their experience was representative of many. I am indebted to members of my feminist reading group, "The Hags and Crones" in London, Ontario, who inspired me to consider this framework in 1982. Curious about my research, some of the members of the group challenged me with locating new nineteenth-century Canadian "heroines" along the way. They wanted me to bring history alive through the accounts of individual women who had striven for change, who had suffered and sometimes triumphed in their efforts to improve the society around them.[1]

Unsure about how to define "heroine," I turned to various dictionaries for assistance. Traditional dictionaries such as the *Oxford* refer readers to the male-centred "hero," defined as an "illustrious warrior," "a man admired for achievements and noble qualities." *Vogue* magazine, a more unconventional, if more female source, describes a "heroine" as "infinitely alluring, a shade tragic" and "hero" as "valiant and honorably bold." The women who featured prominently in nineteenth-century law — improperly married wives, victims of seduction and rape, perpetrators of infanticide and abortion, prostitutes, petitioners for divorce and child custody, and waged labourers — fit neither definition. They were not warriors active in military manoeuvres, and any admiration they may have received from a paternalistic society was grudgingly qualified at best. Nor were they *Vogue's* damsels in distress, imprisoned in castle turrets and rescued by handsome princes.[2]

Even Cheris Kramarae and Paula A. Treichler's *A Feminist Dictionary*, published in 1985, provides little help. The entry for "hero," from Charlotte Perkins Gilman (a turn-of-the-century American feminist, writer, and lecturer), is at least more amusing: "the strong, square determined jaw. He may be cross-eyed, wide-eared, thick-necked, bandy-legged — what you please; but he must have a more or less [protuding] jaw." The feminist dictionary contains no entry for "heroine."[3]

Perhaps this is a word that some feminists are trying to forget. And there is much in the traditional construction of "heroine" to suggest it would be better left to wither and die. Saccharine femininity and the glorification of characteristics prized by men seem to have seriously infected the concept. And even where feminists have intentionally searched for heroines of the past, class power and racism tend to get in the way. Where women's historical achievements have been acclaimed, the primary focus has fallen upon those whose lives resembled famous men: typically white, well-educated, middle- and upper-class, gentile women.

But I have always been partial to the reclamation of words. The feminist movement could forge a new definition of "heroine," one much richer, fuller, and more reflective of the diversity of women's lives. Shorn of its classist, racist, and patriarchal connotations, there is much to recommend in the rehabilitation of "heroine" to describe many different kinds of women who show resistance, courage, persistence, and fortitude in the face of oppression. To my mind, each of the women whose stories follow lends new meaning and dimension to the word "heroism."

Some, like Euphemia Rabbitt, who courageously resisted a vicious rape attempt, and Clara Brett Martin, who successfully challenged an all-male legal profession to secure entry, were widely admired in their own time. But as feminists well know, successes are limited and setbacks not unknown. Not all of the heroines I have included were victorious, even in their own eyes. Ellen Rogers, a prostitute who believed that all women should be protected by law from sexual assault, was viciously maligned and ridiculed for her ideas. Her struggle to assert her claim to human dignity in front of a courtroom of buffoons was heroic. Nellie Armstrong, whose attempt to wrest the custody of her young children from her estranged and violent husband went down to defeat, presents an image of an independently minded woman too often hidden from historical records.

Some of the women whose stories are included sought to use law as a tool for their own vindication. Esther Arscott, a prostitute who sued the city mayor and Crown attorney for unlawfully confining her, is one. Others, like Lucinda Camp, asserted legal claims through family members. Her father's action for seduction extracted financial compensation from the man who seduced her. Some women are noteworthy mainly for their silence throughout lengthy legal proceedings in which male litigants, witnesses, lawyers, judges, and jurors deliberated over their fates. Before the coroner's jury considering whether to accuse her of infanticide in the death of her newborn child, Anna Balo made only the brief retort: "Nothing to say." The perspective of Mary Gorman, a recidivist prostitute caught up in the treadmill of police court trials, was obliterated in the rapidity with which she was sentenced to yet another term in jail. These women may look like classic victims, but their very survival in the face of such dramatic interventions in their lives exemplifies heroism. They may not have been leading the battle charges, as the *Oxford* editors presume male heroes do, but they acted valiantly and survived the excesses of male-orchestrated disruptions to their lives. These women received few accolades from a patriarchal society, but they stand as foresisters to remember.

Some of the women, Emily Stowe, Agnes Machar, Carrie Derick, and Clara Brett Martin, are already well known to readers of Canadian women's history. Widely acclaimed, prominent advocates for women in their day, they have already been recognized as feminist heroines. Some would suggest that modern-day feminists have glorified their achievements, making them into role models or symbols of wisdom, insight, and inspiration for the current generation. But there were wide gaps in their understanding of class relations, racism, and ethnocentrism and the role these also play in discrimination against women.

Historians have traditionally been reluctant to affix labels such as "racist," "anti-Semitic," and "classist" upon figures from the nineteenth century, arguing that people are the product of their society and environment. I do not pretend to be neutral, however, and have departed from this historical convention, choosing to use some of these labels where I consider the legal records warrant. In doing so, I do not mean to attempt to distance myself artificially from their behaviour, or to suggest that I might have behaved differently had I stood in their place. However, class discrimination, anti-Semitism, racism, and other forms of bias have had an undeniable impact on the lives of the people who have been their target. Even in the nineteenth century, some people recognized the injustice of such practices and sought to eliminate them. There were choices to be made, and women such as Stowe, Machar, Derick, and Martin sometimes made the wrong ones. Their failures to make feminism inclusive of all women's interests are centrally important to any full analysis of their places in feminist history. We can learn much from their errors, many of which continue to plague us today.

Yet I would not be so hasty as to bar these women from their places as heroines. There ought to be some room for such women within our evolving, rehabilitated concept of "heroine." They too waged battles to advance women's cause, and paid a price for challenging portions of the patriarchal system, however limited their goals and however partial their vision of feminism.[4] A new generation of feminists may criticize our efforts and find us similarly wanting, in part for errors that we ought to have recognized ourselves, and in part for failure to move in directions that we can only faintly imagine.

This is still another way in which feminist definitions of "heroine" should depart from male models. Demanding perfection as a precondition fails to recognize the complexity of human behaviour, setting up an artificial, rigid vision of a heroine as omniscient and faultless. We might work toward a more humble sense of human error, a more grounded set of expectations about human failings and deficiencies. Scrutinizing the ways in which some of our foresisters failed to recognize and even furthered discrimination against women of diverse races, religions, and class may assist us in developing a heightened appreciation of gaps in their, and our own, understanding of fairness and equality. Dissecting the biases of our ancestors may assist us in beginning to transcend the defensiveness that so often rears its head upon any assertion of racism and class bias today.

I have organized the stories of these women into ten chapters, which encompass an eclectic but fairly comprehensive mix of topics. I have selected these topics over the past decade, partly out of a sense that these areas of law most affected women, and partly out of my own interests. Loosely grouped under Part I, "The Regulation of Marriage, Courtship, and Sexual Violence," I have dealt with the law's treatment of bi-racial and multicultural marriages, as well as underage marriages conducted in secret. Also included in this section is the law of seduction, in which fathers sued their daughters' seducers for financial compensation, and the law of rape. Part II deals with the legal intrusion upon women's attempt to regulate their fertility, through infanticide and abortion. Part III explores aspects of family law, including divorce, separation, and child custody. Part IV examines women's work in the paid labour force. It includes prostitution, which was attacked through criminal law, and describes the legal regulation of other occupations such as shop-clerking and factory work. It also recounts the prohibition of women from certain occupations, as miners, as waitresses in bars, and as street newspaper vendors. Lastly, the campaign waged to admit women to the profession of law is recounted through the story of Clara Brett Martin, Canada's first woman lawyer.

This still omits many significant areas. The scope of the present study was already so large that I could not include important fields such as breach of promise to marry, bigamy, marriage contracts, criminal conversation, loss of consortium, married women's property, a husband's financial obligations to provide "necessaries" for his wife, wills, dower, child adoption and welfare, vagrancy, obscenity, incest, domestic murder, theft, arson, and assault. All of these issues are rich in sources for the legal historians of women, and I hope they will be explored in depth by others in future.

I have also attempted to provide a balanced geographic representation, although the concentration of population and legal activity in central Canada has meant that Ontario is overrepresented. I have tried to include materials relevant to Quebec wherever possible, particularly where the Quebec law differed from the law in other jurisdictions. However, Quebec legal history is less charted than other areas within the secondary literature, and the Quebec discussion in my book is not as complete as I would have liked.

White, middle-class, apparently heterosexual women are prominent in many of the cases described, particularly in the chapters dealing with marriage, abortion, divorce, child custody, and lawyering. These women and their families had access to the knowledge and resources needed to seek redress from legislatures and courts. Their concerns were deemed worthy of consideration by the white, predominantly middle- and upper-class males who created and administered the legal system. Despite their relative privilege, these women often experienced discriminatory treatment in law.

But my goal was not to recount only the story of white, middle-class women. When I began this research in 1978, I assumed that I would discover cases involving women of colour, women of the First Nations, and working-class women. I did unearth some cases and included them in the texts of the academic articles I was writing. More than ten years later, I have reviewed some of my earlier publications through a more critical race- and class-conscious lens and also realize that the conception of my study was not well suited to inclusivity.[5]

Studying the legal records of a white supremacist, patriarchal regime is not well calculated to unearthing much of relevance about the lives of women of the First Nations and women of colour in the nineteenth century. Some women do turn up, but they do so in stereotypical ways. Women of the First Nations show up, as in the case of Susanne "Pas-de-nom," when they fit clichés. An "Indian princess," she was deemed worthy of keen consideration by an all-white male judiciary that studiously considered the legality of her marriage to a white man. Angelique Pilotte, a domestic servant, was noticed because she was accused of having contravened the white man's criminal law against infanticide. Euphemia Rabbitt was a woman who successfully fought off a rapist. If she had not been married to a white man, however, it is unlikely that her case would have warranted the legal attention it received. Women of the First Nations who fought white men and women for their children, their relatives, their land, and their status, did not find their actions recorded by white legal scribes.

Women who contributed to the development of First Nations' customary law will never be found in the documents left by white recorders. Murray Sinclair, an Ojibwa judge in Winnipeg, has urged historians to give credence to the oral histories of the First Nations, arguing that the written word "is not necessarily any more accurate a record of historical events than an oral history." A complete reformulation of what women's legal history encompasses is necessary to capture this past.[6]

Similarly, none of the case studies included in this collection involve Black women. Black women do not appear in the records I researched. Nonetheless, Black slaves had begun to be transported to Canada in the mid-1600s. Black people, including women, had escaped slavery and had begun to come to Canada in the early 1800s, after Lieutenant-Governor John Graves Simcoe banned the importation of new slaves into Upper Canada in 1793. Slavery itself would continue until 1833. There are a number of immigrant women present: Euphemia Rabbitt (the victim of an attempted rape, who was described as partly Italian), Anna Balo (a Finnish immigrant convicted of infanticide), Soy King (a Chinese teenager subjected to a custody battle), and Mary Gorman (an Irish immigrant convicted of prostitution). The legal records often portray immigrant women in subordinate, victimized roles. A full account of the role of Black and immigrant women would be found only through intricate reformulation of their community, local, and religious operations.

Working-class, white women are marginally more obvious in conventional legal and historical sources, particularly where their sexuality contravened white, patriarchal prescriptions. Certainly they show up in abundance in jail register records on prostitution. Cases of seduction and infanticide often centred on the experience of poor women. But their experience is often told through the eyes of others: their fathers in the case of seduction, neighbours and employers in the case of infanticide, and middle-class novelists and lobbyists in the case of the regulation of working conditions. With cautious analysis, however, these accounts can still serve to illuminate some of the experience of working-class women under nineteenth-century law. The situation of disabled women is less clearly depicted, although aspects of the lives of some emerge from the litigation between Alberta and Alfred Abell, who operated a boarding school for deaf children. Without question, the rhetoric around the advocacy of protective labour legislation, where the prospect of giving birth to disabled children was touted as horrific and cause for national alarm, reflects an intense nineteenth-century phobia of disability.

The most glaring omission is the absence of lesbian women from the stories that follow. Some of the women I discuss may have been lesbian, but the historical record treats them all as heterosexual. Undoubtedly lesbians found themselves intertwined with law in nineteenth-century Canada. But the discipline of history has tended to ignore lesbianism and male homosexuality, claiming that sources that reveal sexual non-conformity have been destroyed, hidden, and generally restricted from use. The stigmatization that still attaches to same-sex sexual orientation prevented many men and women from disclosing their sexual preferences historically and intimidates some researchers even today.[7]

This book, then, serves as a beginning. It recaptures what life was like for some of the women who lived in Canada in the nineteenth century. Its angle of vision is through legal records, which provide vivid snapshots of the conditions under which women struggled, rebelled, and eventually accommodated themselves. I have chosen the title *Petticoats and Prejudice* because of the marked preoccupation over women's dress in the nineteenth century and because of the many ways in which the symbolic importance of female fashion found its way into legal files. Petticoats, whether the "cedar bark" variety attributed to Cree women by Henriette Forget, or the elegant undergarments worn by Alberta Abell beneath her "black velvet coat and satin dress," were the hallmark of femininity in the nineteenth century. To wear them was to encounter differential treatment and prejudice within the irrefutably male legal system.

# 1

# The Ceremony of Marriage

In 1803 in Rivière-aux-Rats, near Lake Athabaska, Susanne "Pas-de-nom" and William Connolly were married *à la façon du pays* (according to the fashion of the country). She was just fifteen, the daughter of a prominent Cree chief. She seems to have been a spirited, resourceful young woman. William Connolly was seventeen, a white man on his first fur-trading expedition in the service of the North-West Company. He had a reputation as a kind and honest person who was ambitious, proud, and "hot-tempered" at times. By all accounts the two were very much in love.[1]

Their marriage, which would later provoke unprecedented legal scrutiny, was a by-product of the fur trade. First, William Connolly would have secured the consent of her father and mother. According to Joseph Mazurette, who later testified in court about First Nations' marriage customs, would-be suitors who ignored this requirement did so at their peril: "Il y aurait du danger d'avoir la tête cassée, si l'on prend la fille dans ce pays, sans le consentement des parents"; ("You risk having your head broken if you take a girl without her parents' consent"). After securing consent, William Connolly would have offered her parents valuable presents such as game, horses, canoes, furs, and dry goods. Noel Annance, another contemporary expert on First Nations' customs, emphasized the importance of these gifts:

The chief or father will never give his consent to give away his daughter to any man, as a wife, without these marriage rites.... They consider it to be a disgrace for any girl, without her father, or her mother, or brother, having received this token of marriage, to live with any man.

Cree custom also required the husband to promise the future produce of his hunt to his wife's parents until he had proved himself capable of supporting his family and the first child was born. Equally important, Susanne Connolly's consent would have been a necessary prerequisite to the marriage.[2]

William Connolly may have visited the Cree encampment to smoke calumet, as this was often used to seal the alliance. Although detailed records of the ceremony have not survived, accounts of Cree traditions indicate that the daylong ceremony would have begun with the elders preparing the groom for marriage. William Connolly would have been ritually cleansed with the smoke of burning sweet grass. He would then have offered a special marriage pipe to one of his new relatives or to an elder, and all present would have smoked the pipe to purify their minds and bodies. The chief, Susanne Connolly's father, would have draped a marriage blanket around the couple's shoulders, and they would have eaten food from a single plate to mark their willingness to share everything in the future. A wedding feast would have followed, completed by a ceremonial circle dance symbolizing friendship and the cycle of existence. Had the ceremony been between two Cree people, this would have concluded the marriage. Most marriages were expected to be permanent and monogamous, although the most proficient male hunters occasionally took several wives, who were often sisters. All marriages could be terminated by a simple separation.[3]

Because William Connolly was white, there were some additional steps required to complete the marriage according to white fur-traders' custom. The young couple would have been escorted to the fur-traders' fort. There Susanne Connolly would have undergone a ritual marking her passage between Cree and white cultures. The other women of the fort would have removed the traces of the Cree celebration. Her leather garments, embroidered with beadwork and coloured threads in floral designs, would have been exchanged for a shirt, short gown, petticoat, and leggings. Finally, William Connolly would have conducted his bride to his quarters and thenceforth they would have been considered husband and wife.[4]

Susanne Connolly had been born about 1788 in the rich fur district of

William Connolly, Chief Factor of the Hudson's Bay Company.

Athabaska, in what is now northern Alberta and Saskatchewan. By the early nineteenth century the Cree occupied the largest geographic territory of any of the First Nations, reaching from Labrador to the Rockies. The legal records tell us little of her maternal background, despite the fact that many of the First Nations traditionally were matrilineal, following lines of descent from their mothers. Instead, the records note only that she was the daughter of a wealthy and influential chief of the powerful Cree nation. Her name comes down to us as Susanne Pas-de-nom, a name that would have been invented by the French traders, missionaries, or legal officials. Since the Cree took the custom of naming even more seriously than did the Europeans, it is unlikely they would have used the label "no-name" to describe anyone. More plausibly, the whites who later traced her lineage could not or did not try to elicit her Cree name. At times, they referred to her only as Susanne *Sauvagesse*.[5]

William Connolly had been born in Lachine, Lower Canada, and raised there by parents of Roman Catholic, Irish descent. In 1801 at the age of fifteen, he signed on as a clerk with the North-West Company. He was immediately dispatched to the distant post of Rat River in Athabaska country for his first tour of duty. There he met Susanne and romance soon followed. Trade considerations may also have played some role in the attachment, since he would later admit to relatives that he had been having some difficulty in his trading until he arranged to marry the daughter of a prominent Cree chief.[6]

The marriage seems not to have solved all of young William Connolly's problems. His relationship with Susanne Connolly's father is reported to have been initially stormy, involving some violent episodes. Ultimately the two men resolved their difficulties and William Connolly's fur-trading career blossomed. He moved successively from Rat River to Île à la Crosse, Cumberland House, Fort Chippewayan, Rainy Lake, Lake of the Woods, York Factory, Norway House, Great and Little Slave Lake. By 1817 he had been promoted to senior clerk, and one year later he became a chief trader. With the union of the North-West Company and the Hudson's Bay Company in 1821, his fortunes continued to increase and he was appointed Chief Factor. Throughout this period Susanne Connolly appears to have played a prominent role as her husband's partner. Accompanying him on all of his travels, she would have provided extensive diplomatic and interpretative skills as well as invaluable assistance in the preparation of furs, the netting of snowshoes, foraging and the securing of small game. Virtually all who knew them described their relationship as both monogamous and very loving. Their fidelity to each other was widely acknowledged as inviolable.[7]

Six or seven children were born to William and Susanne Connolly over a twenty-eight-year period. In their traditional culture, women of the Cree nation tended to give birth to an average of four children. However, those who married white fur traders found that their male partners had different expectations, which often resulted in families of eight to twelve children. Undoubtedly this created additional health complications for many of the women, as well as increased child-care responsibilities. The fragility of infant life was a day-to-day concern as well, as dramatically illustrated by a catastrophe that struck the couple relatively early on in their marriage. One of Susanne and William Connolly's children died tragically while still very young, when her dress caught fire from a spark from the open hearth in the mess hall at York Factory. Although a Cree nursemaid tried to rescue her by rolling her in a rug and carrying her out to the snow, the child did not survive.[8]

The problems that would ultimately lead to the destruction of their marriage first surfaced in 1812. William Connolly was in the habit of journeying back to Montreal occasionally, and that winter he returned east with his eldest son, John, in order to have him baptized by the Roman Catholic Church and to make arrangements for his education. In itself, this was indicative of the increasing intrusion of white culture into traditional indigenous ways. White fathers had initially been content to leave the education of their bi-racial children to the elders of the mother's people. Now some, like William Connolly, began actively to promote the acculturation of their offspring within white religious and educational structures. Many First Nations' mothers experienced great anguish over the prolonged separation and inevitable estrangement from their children that followed.[9]

William and John Connolly spent the winter of 1812 in Quebec with William Connolly's sister, Mrs. Delamar, who was also hosting Julia Woolrich, Connolly's second cousin. Julia Woolrich was the daughter of a prosperous Montreal merchant and was described as an "accomplished" and "highly respectable" woman, of "cultivated intellect and feminine virtues." William Connolly appears to have found himself drawn back into the white world of his childhood, and highly attracted to his sociable cousin. Various accounts indicate that he and Julia Woolrich became engaged that winter. His Lower Canadian relatives, in any event, were given to understand that when Connolly finally returned to the east, he would marry Julia Woolrich and set up permanent residence with her in Montreal.[10]

Nothing further appears to have ensued until 1831, when he left the fur country for good and moved with Susanne Connolly and their children out of the North-West, first to Saint-Eustache, Lower Canada, and then settling in Montreal. By all indications, at least at the outset he intended to bring his Cree family into white society. He had two of his youngest daughters, Marie and Marguerite, baptized in the Roman Catholic Church, and spoke to the priest about formalizing his marriage. Reports are that Susanne Connolly seems to have been generally accepted by white people and acknowledged as Connolly's wife.[11]

What changed William Connolly's outlook can only be the subject of conjecture. Without warning on 16 May 1832, he married Julia Woolrich in a Roman Catholic ceremony, fulfilling an engagement promise nineteen years old. Julia Woolrich was now thirty-six, long past the usual age for women to make their first marriage. She apparently was well aware of Susanne Connolly's claims on Connolly, but may have reassured herself because he had obtained a dispensation from the bishop on the grounds that the Cree marriage was not valid and could be superseded by their Roman Catholic ceremony.[12]

His repudiation of Susanne Connolly was indicative of the sweeping changes that had begun to alter the face of fur-trading society. As agriculture came to challenge the dominance of the fur trade, white officials began to discount the usefulness of the First Nations as allies, and policies were developed to expropriate their lands and restrict them to reserves. The introduction of Protestant and Roman Catholic clergy to the North-West brought demands for Christian marriage rites and an attack on the old custom of marriage *à la façon du pays*, now decried as sinful and immoral. Increasing white dominion would characterize the 1830s, and status-conscious traders pursued marital liaisons with white women, often forsaking earlier alliances with First Nations' mates.[13]

Hudson's Bay Company Governor George Simpson provided one of the most visible examples in his repudiation of various relationships with First Nations' women. He married his eighteen-year-old white cousin, Frances, and sought to instil racist views among his colleagues. Referring variously to his First Nations' female partners as "my article," "my japan helpmate," and "the commodity," Simpson developed a notorious reputation for his cavalier treatment of First Nations' women. Connolly had been known to look somewhat askance at Simpson's actions. But Simpson, in a letter to his friend, John George McTavish, dated 2 December 1832, wrote:

You would have heard of Connolly's marriage — he was one of those who considered it a most unnatural proceeding "to desert the mother of his children" and marry another; this is all very fine, very sentimental and very kind hearted 3000 miles from the civilized world but is lost sight of even by Friend Connolly where a proper opportunity offers. [14]

Susanne Connolly's initial reaction to the wedding is reported to have been anger. She seems to have been kept ignorant of the plan and was still in Montreal on the day William Connolly and Julia Woolrich wed. Several observers noted that Susanne Connolly was furious about her husband's desertion and marriage to another woman. Others noted that she maintained great dignity, even to the point of expressing her disdain for the situation. Mr. Larocque, who conversed with Susanne Connolly shortly after the wedding, recounted:

She laughed and talked about it, and said that she, Julia Woolrich, had only got her leavings. [Susanne Connolly] was a Cree woman I believe. I understand and speak the language well. I had occasion to see her often at this time, and had frequent conversations with her about William Connolly's marriage with Julia Woolrich. *She did not seem to care much about it.* She had some hopes that Connolly would have married her; and I think if he had not fallen in with Julia Woolrich that he would have married her. *But she seemed not surprised at his marrying a white woman.* But among other things she said "he will regret it bye and bye."[15]

Julia Woolrich and William Connolly set up residence in Montreal "in great style," but Connolly's last years in the fur trade were not ones of contentment. Julia Woolrich is said to have greatly disliked the travel to the posts. Her health deteriorated and she yearned for the amenities of the city, frequently forcing her husband to return to Montreal. One of Connolly's business partners was moved to complain that William Connolly was so dominated that he was "under petty coat government." Governor Simpson disapproved of Connolly's frequent absence from the posts, and he was pushed into early retirement.[16]

For his part, William Connolly seems to have retained his emotional attachment to Susanne Connolly and their children and kept up contact with them. Some of the children remained very fond of their father, and corresponded with him affectionately over the years. He initially continued to visit Susanne Connolly after his marriage to Julia Woolrich, and on one occasion Susanne Connolly came to visit him at his Montreal home, causing Julia Woolrich great distress. Perhaps in consequence, in 1840, he finally made arrangements to have Susanne Connolly and her younger children shipped off to the convent of the Grey Nuns in St. Boniface in the Red River settlement. He wrote to Governor George Simpson, thanking him for providing for their safe passage, noting: "They will be much happier there than here, and their removal has taken a heavy weight off my mind." Here Susanne Connolly lived from 1841 until her death in 1862. Throughout her stay she was financially supported by William Connolly, and upon his death in 1848, by Julia Woolrich.[17]

By the time of his death William Connolly had amassed a considerable estate, with assets such as bank stocks, shares in the profits of the Hudson's Bay Company, grist and saw mills in Hemingford, houses in Kingston, and extensive acreage throughout Quebec. All of this he willed to Julia Woolrich and the two children who had been born of the second marriage. Two years after Susanne Connolly's death in 1864, her eldest son, John, decided to contest the will. John Connolly, who had been brought so many years before to Montreal for an eastern education, was now a middle-aged man. He brought an action claiming entitlement to his father's estate. The main focus of the litigation would be the validity of Susanne and William Connolly's marriage.[18]

The case, which quickly became a *cause célèbre*, attracted public attention across the Dominion and internationally. In part, this was due to the size of the estate, reputed to be "of greater value than has ever previously, in one action, been in litigation before the courts in this country." In part, the case attracted interest because it asked whether Christian, European marital rites would be demanded of peoples of the First Nations, or whether Canadian courts would honour First Nations' traditional practices. "The questions involved strike at the very root of our social system," the Montreal *Herald* would later announce.[19]

The effects of white settlement on the cultures of the First Nations had been catastrophic. The pressure to trap animals for export to European markets had begun to displace traditional subsistence hunting and harvesting, leading to enforced dependence on whites. Peoples of the First Nations had no immunity to European diseases such as smallpox, tuberculosis, measles, and influenza, and whole communities were devastated. Many whites had concluded that the First Nations were doomed to extinction. While some embraced this as a goal, others looked back longingly to the "nobility" of pre-contact life among the First Nations. The *Connolly* case would operate as a testing ground to determine how the law would respond.[20]

Much of the argument heard by the Superior Court of Lower Canada in 1867 was framed within a narrow Euro-Canadian analysis, using language and concepts that were fundamentally hostile to the First Nations. Alexander Cross, the lawyer acting for Julia Woolrich's children, would insist that the Cree were no more than "barbarians" with "infidel laws." A Scottish immigrant who had gained fame for his military service in putting down the Lower Canadian Rebellion of 1837–38, Cross made no bones about his view of the Cree ceremony. "The usages and customs of marriage observed by uncivilized and pagan nations, such as the Crees" could not be recognized as giving validity to marriage "even between the Indians themselves" much less "between a Christian and one of the natives."[21]

There were two arguments being made here. First, Alexander Cross was attacking the legality of marriages made entirely within the First Nations. Second, he was contesting the validity of marriages between a person of the First Nations and a Christian of European descent, celebrated according to the customs of the First Nations. On the first point, Cross was arguing against the bulk of nineteenth-century English law, which tended to maintain a respectful distance from indigenous marital customs in colonial jurisdictions. In West Africa, "Mohammedan marriages" between "Mohammedan natives" were recognized as lawfully valid, and in South Africa separate provision was made for validating marriages between Blacks. In India, English law regarding marriage was not formally extended to Hindus, Sikhs, Jains, or Buddhists, and the rules prohibiting bigamy were not applied to the Buddhist sects that recognized male polygamy.[22]

But Cross was on stronger legal ground with his second point about mixed marriages. British legal treatises would express similar concerns about whether legal status should be accorded to marriages between a Christian and a member of various sects such as the Hindu, Mohammedan, Buddhist, Sikh, Jain, or Parsi religions. Claiming that it was doubtful whether such marriages were valid, some texts would caution that these conjugal unions should be solemnized according to Christian rites.[23]

The case was heard at first instance by Samuel Cornwallis Monk, who had been appointed to the Superior Court of Lower Canada in 1859, following an illustrious career as a criminal lawyer. John Connolly may have wondered what he was up against. Monk could not have been further removed from Cree culture. He had been born thousands of miles from the Athabaska country, in Halifax, of a long line of United Empire Loyalist lawyers and judges. He was married to a woman of his own class, the daughter of the Honourable P.D. DeBastzch, a member of the Legislative Council of Lower Canada. Like Susanne and William Connolly, he was the parent of six children; similarly, one daughter had predeceased him. His reputation as a judge was of "vast legal knowledge," "graceful elocution," and "a high sense of justice."[24]

Monk seems to have immersed himself in the controversial precedent-setting case. In an exhaustive and lengthy judgment, he went to great lengths to canvass Roman, canon, English, Irish, and First Nations' law. He mistakenly concluded that the Cree were largely indistinguishable from other First Nations. Cree law was, he reported, "not exceptional, but entirely in harmony with, and comfortable to the general usages of the barbarians over the entire continent of North America." Citing American texts and the testimony of various fur traders who had given evidence, Monk characterized "Indian marriage" as distinctly lacking in "rites or ceremony." His ethnocentric perspective was an insuperable impediment to understanding a Cree marriage. Since it did not resemble the Christian exchange of sacred vows with which he was familiar, he saw it as a simple, somewhat backward custom.[25]

Yet despite his equation of Cree culture with "barbarianism," Monk was prepared to allow that Cree law was the governing force at Rivière-aux-Rats in 1803. "Indian political and territorial rights, laws, and usages remained in full force," he concluded. Summing up the practicalities of the situation with a colourful turn of phrase, Monk emphasized that it strained credulity to think that William Connolly could have "[carried] with him this common law of England to Rat River in his knapsack."[26]

Alexander Cross had hoped that his denunciation of polygamy, occasionally practised within the Cree nation, would have deterred Monk from this ruling. "The connection of the plaintiff's parents was fugitive, temporary, dissolvable at pleasure, and had none of the legal or religious characteristics of marriage," Cross had argued. Monk clearly was troubled by this, and referred to polygamy as "an infidel and unchristian abuse," but noted that William Connolly himself had never practised polygamy while among the Cree.[27]

Monk tried to put himself into Connolly's shoes, looking back to the situation in 1803:

A mixture of barbarism and peculiar civilization ... prevailed in the Athabaska country in 1803.... At such a place, surrounded by such influences and such unfavourable circumstances, if Mr. Connolly, whose moral character seems to have been without reproach, desired, whether from feeling or interested motives, to take this Indian maiden to his home, he had one of three courses to pursue; that was, to marry her according to the customs and usages of the Cree Indians — to travel with her between three and four thousand miles, in canoe and on foot, to have his marriage solemnized by a priest or a magistrate — or to make her his concubine. I think the evidence in this case will clearly show which of these three courses he did adopt, and which of them, during a period of twenty-eight years, he honourably and religiously followed.[28]

It seems that it was not out of any particular appreciation of, or respect for, Cree culture that Monk made the decision he did. It was rather out of regard for William Connolly's reputation, at least as Monk perceived it.

Alexander Cross would not give up easily, however. He tenaciously argued that since the court was prepared to grant validity to the Cree marriage, it should also recognize Cree divorce. Connolly's decision to cast Susanne Connolly aside was merely a manifestation of Cree custom, where marriages could be repudiated at the will of the parties. Here Monk would have felt himself on firm and familiar ground, as he concluded that whether or not Connolly could have dissolved his marriage in Cree country, when he returned east that right ceased. Just as Connolly could not lug the common law to Rat River in a knapsack, "much less could he bring back to Lower Canada the law of repudiation in a bark canoe."[29]

Perhaps the most remarkable of Cross's arguments was that Connolly's second marriage had been validated by Susanne Connolly's "acquiescence": she had never formally challenged Julia Woolrich's position. Indeed, Cross asserted, in her old age she had accepted financial support from Julia Woolrich. Cross placed great weight upon the evidence that Susanne Connolly had smiled when she learned of the betrayal. Much court time would be taken up analysing the enigmatic smile, which Monk characterized as "true Indian apathy."[30]

Monk noted:

It is proved that when Susanne heard that Connolly had deserted her and married another woman, she smiled; what she meant to express or to convey, by that smile, does not appear. The smile of a woman may express a variety of emotions: it would not, perhaps, be considered a very reliable indication of feeling in an Indian woman, or in any other; but it may fairly be presumed that Mrs. Connolly (Susanne) did not mean to express approval or satisfaction, for she added "that Miss Woolrich would have only her leavings...."

In this passage, Monk revealed his own belief in the vast gap between the world of men and women and between the Cree and whites. The inscrutability of the group cast as "other" would defy Monk in his inquiry into the meaning of Susanne Connolly's behaviour. In the result, he concluded that none of Susanne Connolly's actions — the smile, the failure to contest Connolly's decision, the acceptance of financial support from William Connolly and Julia Woolrich — amounted to acquiescence or constituted a bar to the present litigation.[31]

After dismissing all of Cross's contentions, Monk finally accepted John Connolly's claim, although not without expressing his sincere apologies to Julia Woolrich:

The Court itself could have testified to the high and accomplished character; to the cultivated intellect and feminine virtues of the amiable lady whose name and position figure so conspicuously in this unhappy case. She passed among many as the lawful and honoured wife of William Connolly. She was so reputed. She was respected and beloved by those who knew her best; but behind and beyond all this, there have arisen other claims and other interests.

The obscure and stigmatized offspring of William Connolly and his Indian wife has come forward, after many years, to vindicate his mother's memory and honor, and his own rights as their lawful child. The law is with him.... I am bound, however painful it may be, to declare that the second marriage was and is an absolute nullity.[32]

The indefatigable Alexander Cross refused to concede defeat and launched an appeal. When the Court of Appeal ruled to uphold Monk's decision, Cross began to file the necessary papers to take the case to the Privy Council in London, England. By this point, however, the principals seem to have run out of steam. An out-of-court settlement was reached before the Privy Council could determine the matter, and Monk's decision was left intact.[33]

The litigation may have eaten substantially into John Connolly's share of Connolly's estate. None of Susanne Connolly's other children supported him in the action, although Amelia, one of the elder daughters, seems to have been gratified about the outcome. In 1828 she had celebrated a marriage à la façon du pays with a white North-West clerk, James Douglas. When he was later named Governor of the Crown Colony of Vancouver Island in 1859, she became its First Lady. Despite considerable racism in British Columbian society, Amelia Connolly Douglas's role as First Lady was widely acclaimed. Perhaps influenced by her mother's situation, she had her Cree marriage to James Douglas formally sanctioned by the Church of England in 1837. John Connolly's legal victory benefited her directly, for she received a legacy from the settlement of the estate. The decision also ended doubts about her legitimacy, which had been a source of some gossip in British Columbia circles for years. Sir James Douglas wrote to one of John Connolly's lawyers after the trial:

I have to thank you for a copy of the Montreal Transcript, containing the judgment on the Connolly case — John is a noble fellow and has bravely won his rights...; but to me the most pleasing part is, that he has vindicated *his* mother's good name; and done justice to the high-minded old lady, now at rest in the peaceful grave, — and worthy of a kinder husband than poor Connolly.[34]

Susanne Pas-de-nom Connolly may have been vindicated by the courts, but events of a larger scale were overtaking the peoples of the First Nations. The Confederation of the central and eastern provinces in 1867

Amelia Connolly Douglas, First Lady of British Columbia.

set the stage for rapid political expansion across the continent to the Pacific. In 1869 the Hudson's Bay Company made arrangements to cede Rupert's Land to the new Dominion. A well-founded fear escalated among the First Nations and the Métis that the new Canadian government would not respect their rights. In late 1869, the charismatic leader of the Métis, Louis Riel, defied the easterners by seizing Fort Garry and setting up a provisional government. A military expedition was quickly despatched, and in early 1870 Riel was forced to flee to the United States in defeat.[35]

Without consultation with the First Nations or the Métis, the federal government reformulated the Indian Act in 1869 to provide that any woman of the First Nations who married a non-First Nations man would lose her "Indian status," as would her descendants. The pressure of white immigration upon First Nations' lands was such that the government was increasingly trying to tie the peoples of the First Nations to reserves, and even these areas would shrink rapidly. The ultimate goal was complete assimilation into Euro-Canadian culture. One step toward this was to deny their culture and to deny land entitlements to women of the First Nations who "married out." Protests from peoples within the First Nations, many of whom had traditionally followed matrilineal practices, went ignored.[36]

In this increasingly white-supremacist environment, the question of First Nations' marriages was catapulted once more into the courts. In 1881 a series of Quebec judges embarked upon a six-year inquiry into the validity of a marriage that had been celebrated in fur-trade country in 1788 or 1789 between Angélique Meadows and Alexander Fraser. The court records refer to Angélique merely as an "Indian woman," providing no national designation beyond this very broad description. To the judges, "Indian" had become an all-encompassing, generic term.[37]

We know little about Angélique Meadows except that she married a white fur trader, Alexander Fraser, "according to the usages and customs of the Northwest Territory, where they so lived and cohabited together." The testimony about the marriage ceremony conflicted, although most witnesses described her as having covered him with a "blanket" to indicate her desire to join with him. George April, a friend of Fraser's, testified that Fraser had also told him that upon the occasion of a marriage, there would be feasting and ceremonial dancing. Apparently this was not Angélique Meadows's first marriage, since she had previously been married to another fur trader named Letang. Four or five children were born to Angélique and Alexander Fraser, several of whom he brought back to Lower Canada for baptism.[38]

By 1806 Alexander Fraser had amassed a considerable fortune, and he retired from the North-West Company. He returned east with Angélique Meadows and the children, settling at Rivière-du-Loup in Lower Canada. The family lived together for a short while in the expansive, seigneurial house. Alexander Fraser subsequently built a smaller, separate house for his wife and her children nearby, where he went often to visit her. Witnesses recalled that Angélique Meadows preferred her own little house to the *cabat* (commotion?) of the world, and told of seeing her "in her house, smoking her pipe and seated on the hearth." Alexander Fraser would continue to support her financially, but he soon took up with two house servants in succession, Pauline Michaud and Victoire Asselin, with whom he had at least seven more children. Angélique Meadows died in 1833, and was buried in a Roman Catholic cemetery, which registered her solely as "Angélique, sauvage, native des pays du Nord-Ouest." Decades later, Alexander Fraser's grandchildren began to litigate over his estate, thus calling into question the validity of Angélique Meadows's marriage.[39]

The key decision would be rendered by the Court of Queen's Bench in Appeal on 8 May 1885. Samuel Cornwallis Monk was still on the bench, and he ruled, as he had in the *Connolly* case, that the marriage was valid. He had not changed his opinion of First Nations' customs, which he referred to variously as "uncivilized," "peculiar," and "simple." However, he continued to recognize such marriages as legally binding. He may have felt strengthened in his position because Alexander Fraser had supported his wife and the children financially, had baptized the children using the surname "Fraser," and had publicly acknowledged Angélique Meadows as his wife. The evidence about Angélique Meadows's previous marriage he hurriedly dismissed: "I think we may admit that she was a widow, when Fraser married her; otherwise we would have to add crime to crime...." The final thread in his argument was that Alexander Fraser had never purported to remarry either of the domestic servants with whom he later cohabited. "It is impossible to say that Fraser repudiated his Indian wife, as Connolly did," concluded Monk.[40]

But times had changed. In 1884 Louis Riel had returned from exile to help Gabriel Dumont lead a second rebellion in the spring of 1885. Poundmaker and Big Bear, chiefs renowned as warriors and respected throughout the Territories, joined forces with the Métis to try to drive out the whites. Armed troops marched in from the east, and after several military engagements, Riel was taken prisoner to be held for trial in Regina. There he, along with eight other First Nations' men, would be hanged for high treason in November. It would cost the federal government five million dollars to take control of the situation once more. Tensions were palpable, reverberating all the way to the eastern courts. Samuel Monk may have been unwavering in his views of the validity of First Nations' marriages, but he could no longer carry the majority of the judges with him. Now he wrote only to dissent.[41]

The irony is that it was Alexander Cross who wrote the majority decision in Angélique Meadows's case. In 1877 Cross had left behind an extensive and remunerative practice to join Monk on the Quebec Court of Queen's Bench. Cross, who had failed to convince Monk as an advocate at the bar, would turn the tables on him in 1885. Cross's memory of the bitter defeat in the Connolly case was long: "To my mind [the Connolly] decision was unsatisfactory, and I think it is well the subject should be further ventilated, to satisfy the doubts that have been entertained, as to the soundness of that decision."[42]

Cross wrote extensively of what he took to be critical distinctions between First Nations' customs and Christian marriage. He dismissed the former as follows: "In countries inhabited by savage tribes, there is generally little consistency, or uniformity, in the regulation of that intercourse, and it is, for the most part, very unceremonious." He found his own culture to be eminently preferable:

Civilization introduces obligatory duties, for the protection of women and children. In Christian countries, the relation of husband and wife is distinguished by an amplification of reciprocal, obligatory duties and consequences, as affecting property ... forming a striking contrast to the relations of male and female in savage life, where perpetuity of union and exclusiveness is not a rule, at least not a strict rule.

Marriage, as understood by Christians, is the union for life of one man with one woman, to the exclusion of all others; any intercourse without these distinctive qualities cannot amount to a Christian marriage.[43]

The incorporation of Christian principles was a prerequisite, as far as Cross was concerned. While he would admit that he was not suggesting that parties to a marriage had necessarily to be Christians, they did have to intend to contract to marital obligations "in the christian sense." Unless peoples of the First Nations submitted to "civilized law," the union amounted to nothing more than an arrangement made by "savages in a state of nature." In this, Judge Cross stepped far beyond the scope of the case before him, which involved a mixed marriage, to pronounce upon the legality of marital customs within the First Nations themselves. Just as he had done in argument in the *Connolly* case, Cross attacked the autonomy of First Nations' marriages.[44]

Cross also noted with disdain that the "sauvagesse" had admitted she had another husband prior to Alexander Fraser. He was not satisfied that Letang was dead, adding: "It is a well known fact that polygamy prevails among the pagan Indians." Cross was equally unimpressed with Alexander Fraser. The eldest son of Malcolm Fraser and Marie Allaire, Alexander Fraser was illegitimate. "He appears to have preferred having all his children in the same rank, in this respect, as himself," claimed Cross. If Alexander Fraser had wished legality for his marriage, Cross concluded, then he should have made a voyage to civilization, imported an ordained clergyman, or at the very least solemnized the marriage upon returning to a "civilized" country. Otherwise the relationship would be more properly characterized as concubinage than marriage.[45]

Cross's perspective seems to have coincided nicely with the views of the majority of the other white men on the bench. Together they dismissed the validity of the mixed marriage celebrated according to First Nations' customs, leaving Monk as the lone dissenter. The Supreme Court of Canada reviewed the case one year later, and although it did not rule specifically on the marriage, preferring to deal with side issues such as the rules regarding the revocation of legacies, neither did the Supreme Court justices upset the Quebec appeal decision. The larger question, of the validity under Canadian law of the marriage customs practised between First Nations' men and women, was yet undetermined. Alexander Cross's comments on these matters went beyond what was necessary to decide the case before him, and were thus legally classifiable as comments *in obiter*, and beside the point. A decision three years later, by the Supreme Court of the North-West Territories, expressly validated marriages celebrated "according to Indian custom" between "Indians" regardless of their lack of conformity with English rules. Unaccountably, the North-West Territories Supreme Court made no mention of the *Fraser* discussion.[46]

However, the fate of First Nations' customs would be dealt a legal death blow in 1899, when a man of the Blood nation was charged with polygamy under the Criminal Code. The accused man, Bear's Shin Bone, had entered into a marriage with two women of the Blood nation: Free Cutter Woman and Killed Herself. Both women were living with him as his wives. The marriages had been celebrated "according to the marriage customs of the Blood Indians," which explicitly permitted some men to take more than one wife. Bear's Shin Bone was arrested and held over for trial on the charge of violating section 278 of the Canadian Criminal Code prohibiting polygamy.[47]

Justice Charles Borromée Rouleau delivered a terse one-paragraph judgment for the Supreme Court of the North-West Territories in Calgary on 9 May 1899. He convicted the prisoner, holding definitively that the marital customs of the Blood nation were contrary to the Code. Judge Rouleau's decision implicitly recognized the validity of Bear's Shin Bone's first marriage, at the same time that he pronounced criminal sanctions upon the second. First Nations' marriages between First Nations' peoples were accorded legal respect only so far. Where indigenous customs violated central beliefs of Christian, Euro-Canadian society, they would be condemned. Marital monogamy would be imposed upon First Nations' peoples through the full force of the criminal law. Although the records do not show the sentence served, upon conviction Bear's Shin Bone stood at risk of five years' imprisonment or a fine of five hundred dollars.[48]

At least among white leaders of the community, contemporary opinion was squarely in agreement with this approach. One year after the decision in *Bear's Shin Bone*, Henriette A. Drolet Forget, a white woman from Regina, wrote about the superiority of her culture, particularly as it related to marriage practices and women. Forget was the honorary president of the Daughters of the Empire and an active member of the National Council of Women of Canada, a group of middle- and upper-class women who sought to improve the status of their sex. She was also the wife of the Honourable Amédée E. Forget, a man who was both Lieutenant-Governor of the North-West Territories and the Indian Commissioner. Perhaps it was her husband's latter position that led her to believe she was qualified to speak on such matters.[49]

Writing for the National Council of Women of Canada, Forget was scathing in her attack on First Nations' marriage customs. She misconstrued the significance of the gifts that a First Nations' suitor would present to the woman's parents. Forget also seems to have been unaware that the woman's mother was equally involved in this tradition. "The maidens were sold by their paternal relatives," she asserted, "to become the wives of those who proffered the greatest number of horses in exchange. The prices ranged from two horses to twenty, according to the attractions of the bride." She did not see that the transfer of gifts from the bridegroom to the bride's family would represent an honouring of the bride's parents, a symbol of the debt both young people owed to the former generation.[50]

Henriette Forget also failed to recognize the intricacies of First

Nations' customs, mistakenly advising that "the marriage ceremony was as meagre as the bride's dress — among some tribes nothing but a cedar-bark petticoat." She saved special denunciation for the practice of polygamy, which she described in an exaggerated manner as "the general practice." "The richer an Indian was (his wealth being horses), the more wives he sought, or rather bought," she noted. "Divorce was as easy as marriage," she added, and "a man, tired of his wife, could easily sell her to someone else."[51]

Henriette Forget had no monopoly on surprise at the customs of other cultures. In one fascinating account, John McLean, who lived for nine years among the Blood nation in the North-West Territories, described the hilarity with which First Nations' peoples sometimes viewed white marriage customs:

"How many horses did you give for your wife?" said Eagle Arrow to me. "I did not give any," said I. So I had to tell them the old story of how I got my wife. They listened very attentively, occasionally nudging each other, and laughing at the strange customs of the white man. Again I related the story of the years of courtship, the struggles of the youthful heart in mustering courage to ask the young lady's consent, the seeking of the approval of the young lady's father and mother, the marriage ceremony, presents given by friends, the feast, and last, but not least, the bridal gifts of household articles, given by the young lady's mother. When I had reached this part of my story they lost control of themselves, and roared with laughter. Eagle Arrow was able, after a moment, to ejaculate, "Her mother paid you for taking her!" and again were they convulsed with laughter.[52]

But the growing power imbalances between whites and First Nations' peoples meant that the former were increasingly imposing their dictates upon the latter. The close of the nineteenth century witnessed a marked departure from the early decades where white fur traders such as William Connolly had adapted themselves to the rules and practices of the host society. Striking what she may have thought of as a note of optimism for her readers, Henriette Forget prophesied that the customs of the First Nations were coming to an end. Of the 46,289 "Indians" living west of Ontario, Forget estimated that only 10,061 remained "pagans." The efforts of the missionaries, the wise actions of the benevolent government, the rise of Industrial Schools to train the youth, were all paying off handsomely. She concluded triumphantly:

Horses, cattle, or other wealth are still sometimes given in exchange for a wife, but polygamy exists no longer, except among a few of the least civilized tribes. Most marriages are now sanctified by a religious ceremony, and just as the agricultural pursuits of the men are leading them to substitute houses for tepees (tents), so the cedar bark petticoat is being supplanted by the neat dress of modern make.[53]

MIXED MARRIAGES AND PARENTAL CONTROL IN QUEBEC

First Nations' marriage customs would not be the only nineteenth-century matrimonial practices to bring discomfort to the legal authorities. Simmering linguistic and religious tensions also characterized the relations between the French Roman Catholic and English Protestant communities of central Canada. Two solidified communities, separate in language, religion, economic and social milieu, faced each other with suspicion and distrust. On rare occasions young people in love would sometimes try to bridge these chasms. The law was one avenue that their distressed relatives could call upon to resolve the familial hostilities that often would result. As such, legal records sometimes capture the essence of the cultural conflict. The Mignault–Hapinian marriage litigation is one case.

Zoé Mignault was born in May 1845 to a Roman Catholic, francophone family. Her father, an upper-middle-class gentleman, described himself as a *bourgeois* of the city of Montreal. His business affairs often took him to the state of New York, and at times he moved his family with him to reside there. Zoé seems to have found American culture captivating, and she soon became bilingual. By 1863, the family was again ensconced in Montreal. Zoé Mignault was now eighteen years old, still categorized as *une fille mineure*, "a minor." Throughout the latter half of the nineteenth century, it was customary for Quebec couples to wait until their mid-twenties before marrying. However, Zoé Mignault was of an age to begin taking special interest in male suitors. One in particular seems to have struck her fancy. He was Frederick Hapinian (also known as Hapeman), a young anglophone who was also a minor, just up from the United States. The records reveal little about Hapinian, although some things are indisputable. He was not as financially well-off as Zoé Mignault, not a Roman Catholic, and he had never been baptized.[54]

Unbeknown to her family, she developed a strong affection for Frederick Hapinian, who seems to have returned her interest with much ardour. The two "kept company" and then resolved to wed, but knew that her father would vociferously oppose the union. It was rare for

Roman Catholics to marry outside their religion. In some jurisdictions as few as 5 per cent of the marriages involved Catholic–Protestant unions. And having never been baptized within any church, Frederick Hapinian would have been viewed as fundamentally suspect in religious matters. Class differences would have posed equally substantial barriers to marriage. Consequently, the couple plotted to marry secretly. Frederick Hapinian arranged to obtain a marriage licence from the civil authorities. Zoé Mignault attempted to disguise her identity, signing the licence rather elaborately as "Susan Sarah Agnes Mignault." They set 24 December as their wedding date, apparently relying on the commotion of the holiday season to camouflage their actions.[55]

Frederick Hapinian called on Zoé Mignault that afternoon, and the two of them went off for a drive in his horse-drawn sleigh. Sleighing was a popular recreation among the courting set of Montreal, and no one would have been concerned about seeing the couple, wrapped up in warm robes and blankets, out for an afternoon's excursion. It would not have been proper, of course, to have ventured out without a chaperone, and her brother had been brought along to serve the purpose. Shortly after they embarked, they sent the young boy off to the post office on an errand and drove to the private residence of Reverend Bonar, a minister of the American Presbyterian Church. They assured Bonar that they were of age, and showed him the marriage licence. Two witnesses (unidentified) were called in to watch. Suspecting nothing, Bonar performed the marriage rites.[56]

The records do not reveal much about the ceremony. But secret marriages were a matter of great public excitement and interested observers could content themselves by imagining the event in vivid detail. Perhaps it would have been something along the lines portrayed by Rosanna Leprohon in her widely read novel *Antoinette De Mirecourt: A Canadian Tale*, which would be published to great acclaim in Montreal one year later in English, and the year after that in French. Antoinette De Mirecourt, the novel's heroine, is a wealthy Quebec heiress. Not yet eighteen, she has a "slight, exquisitely-formed figure," a "lovely, expressive face," and "rich waves of hair." The novel begins as she departs from her father's peaceful village home in Valmont to spend the winter with her socialite cousin, Montrealer Lucille D'Aulnay. Her father bids her well, advising her to enjoy herself "to her heart's utmost desire," but warns her also to "watch well over her affections and bestow them on none of the gay strangers who might visit at her cousin's house."[57]

Antoinette De Mirecourt's father had long intended to set up an arranged marriage for his daughter with a loyal family friend, Louis

Beauchesne. Instead, she meets and falls in love with a Protestant British Army officer, Major Audley Sternfield. Leprohon goes to some care to describe Sternfield, who is apparently an "Apollo" of sorts. He is "a tall and splendidly-proportioned figure — eyes, hair and features of faultless beauty, joined to rare powers of conversation, and a voice whose tones he could modulate to the richest music."[58]

Antoinette De Mirecourt realizes that her father is unlikely to approve her choice of suitor, and seeks Madame D'Aulnay's intervention. The heated argument that follows constituted a clear portrayal of linguistic and religious divisions in the Quebec community. The control that fathers expected to play over their daughters' marriage arrangements is also unmistakable. De Mirecourt begins:

"Tis of no use, Lucille. Soft words and pleading looks will not prevent me saying what I have to say; and again, I repeat, I hope that my daughter has not forgotten herself so far as to enter into any secret love-engagement with those who are aliens alike to our race, creed and tongue."

"But if she should have done so, dearest uncle — if she should have met with some noble, good man, who, apart from the objection of his being a foreigner, should have proved himself worthy in all other things of inspiring affection —"

"Then, Madame D'Aulnay," he interrupted, striking the table so violently that the vases and other ornaments on it shook again, "the first thing she has to do is to forget him; for never, never will she obtain either my consent or my blessing."[59]

Antoinette De Mirecourt agonizes over her plight, finally resolving to marry Sternfield without her father's blessing. The couple conclude that no Catholic priest would dare marry them privately and secretly. Instead, they select a British chaplain, Dr. Ormsby, although the pious young woman shrinks from the idea of a marriage service without proper religious benediction. Dr. Ormsby agrees to marry them secretly in Madame D'Aulnay's drawing room.

A ferocious winter storm rages the entire day of the ceremony, forebodingly setting the stage for Antoinette De Mirecourt's undoing. Leprohon captures the anxiety of the group as she describes the event in detail:

The clergyman, a young, intellectual-looking man with dark, earnest eyes ... stole an earnest, scrutinizing glance towards Antoinette, beside whose chair Sternfield was already bending. Neither the pink hue of her dress, the heated atmosphere of the drawing-room, nor yet the presence of her lover, had brought color to her cheek, or animation to her eye.

Mrs. D'Aulnay turned quickly to the door, which she noiselessly fastened, and then moved to the table near which the remainder of the party were now standing. In a few moments, those solemn words, "They whom God hath joined let no man put asunder," rang in their ears, and Antoinette de Mirecourt and Audley Sternfield were man and wife.[60]

Whether any of this corresponded to Zoé Mignault's situation we can only surmise. But novelist Leprohon was a native Montrealer, from a wealthy Roman Catholic family, and she seems to have had her pulse on the public's fascination with bicultural marriages, especially where these were embarked upon by young people contrary to the views of their elders. It was not without reason that Leprohon would subtitle her novel "Secret Marrying and Secret Sorrowing." The story was meant to serve as a lesson to impetuous youths not to disregard their parents' wishes. Marriage was far more than a romantic union of two lovers: it was equally important that the match be a prudent one, according to family interests. In this Leprohon reflected very traditional views about who should control the decision to marry.[61]

In Leprohon's culture, parents would arrange marriages for all classes of women — peasants, the bourgeoisie, and the aristocracy. Social, economic, and kinship criteria underlay the choice of marriage partner far more than the prospect of romantic attraction or emotional satisfaction. Catholic marriage manuals that circulated in nineteenth-century Canada admonished young people to follow the edicts of their elders. "Parents have at heart the interests of their children, and know better than they do the means by which they can be promoted. Children should, therefore, follow their advice, rather than blind inclination, in an affair so important and on which their happiness for time and eternity is so dependent," insisted one Montreal text of the time.[62]

Yet as society became more industrialized and urbanized, young people would have greater access to occupational and financial autonomy, as well as to geographic and social mobility. The traditional parental supervision over courtship began to weaken as young men and women strained to appropriate more control over their marital futures. They wanted to select their spouses on the basis of romantic desire, even where such choices conflicted with their family's sense of proper alliances. Young women such as Zoé Mignault and her fictional counterpart, Antoinette De Mirecourt, would increasingly disobey their elders.[63]

**ELOPEMENT A LA MODE.**

From Toronto *Grip*, 12 March 1887.

Leprohon's story registered her disapproval of this trend. Consequently, her plot holds misfortune after misfortune for poor Antoinette De Mirecourt. The two fictional lovers have no opportunity to savour their new status. Antoinette De Mirecourt insists upon denying her husband any marital intimacy whatsoever until her father has been informed. And months pass as they try to determine how to resolve matters with her father. Ultimately, the author reveals Sternfield to be a swaggering braggart, a man who could bring Antoinette little happiness. The marriage is finally disclosed publicly on Sternfield's deathbed, after he has been fatally injured in a duel. Only Antoinette De Mirecourt's subsequent delirium and brain-fever induces her father to forgive her.

Although the plot line may seem improbable, this fictional account is not entirely far-fetched. Secret marriages could wreak scandal and havoc for the individuals and families involved. The Mignault–Hapinian match is a good case in point. Like their fictional counterparts, Zoé Mignault and Frederick Hapinian would initially resolve not to disclose their marriage. While the couple had been willing to contravene Monsieur Mignault's wishes in the marriage, they were not prepared to face his wrath immediately. Frederick Hapinian drove Zoé Mignault home right after the ceremony, and neither breathed a word about the change in their situation.

Her father suspected nothing for quite some time. It is not clear when or how Monsieur Mignault discovered the true state of affairs, but when he did he exploded with anger. Like his fictional counterpart, De Mirecourt, he would not be placated or induced to accept his daughter's decision. Frederick Hapinian was not only a virtual stranger to him, but — and unpardonably — he was of a different economic status, creed, tongue, and nation. Furious over his daughter's decision to select her husband for emotional reasons only, Mignault believed that affinity of religion, language, and class were factors of far greater importance. The family was the crucible of Québécois culture, the preservatory of time-honoured values, religion, and language. Too much was at stake to permit foolhardy young people to choose their own partners. It was incumbent on parents and their priests to exercise a powerful influence upon the marital selection of their offspring.

Monsieur Mignault immediately retained a prominent lawyer, Louis Amable Jetté. Jetté was the son of a Quebec merchant who had been educated at L'Assomption College in Lower Canada. Called to the bar in 1857, he had established his practice in Montreal. The first step that Mignault and Jetté took was to launch a legal action against Reverend Bonar. The basis for their claim was Zoé Mignault's age. She had been only eighteen years old at the time of the marriage. It was possible for women to marry after they reached the age of twelve; men were kept waiting until the age of fourteen. But French civil law was very strict about parental consent. Determined to foster parental control, French law forbade the marriage of women under the age of twenty-five or men under thirty against the will of their parents. Zoé Mignault had been legally underage, and could not marry without parental consent.[64]

Furthermore, there had been no publication of banns. And, equally discreditable, the ceremony had been conducted in English. Bonar had married Zoé Mignault to Frederick Hapinian, an "aventurier sans resources aucunes et sans religion," a penniless adventurer, who had no religion. Mignault charged that he had been "injured in his feelings and affections" and "the future of his daughter irrevocably compromised." For this out-rage, he demanded five hundred pounds in damages.[65]

Reverend Bonar defended himself, arguing that he had been ignorant that either party was underage and that he had solemnized the marriage in good faith. Zoé Mignault was a "well-formed woman" and by all appearances she had been the age she pretended. The marriage licence was in order. He had had no suspicion that there was any impediment to the match. Furthermore, he noted, since the marriage had never been followed by cohabitation, neither Mignault nor his daughter had suffered any real damage.

Zoé Mignault appears to have been cowed by the whole situation. She supported her father in court, testifying that she was tricked into the marriage. She stated that when she was taken to Reverend Bonar, she "stood up and something was said," but that she had "no intention of getting married." Judge William Badgley of the Quebec Superior Court, who was charged with hearing the case, was sceptical of her tale, which he tagged "a very unlikely story." As for the contention that she might not have understood the English ceremony, Badgley dismissed this argument summarily: "Rev. Mr. Bonar read something out of a book, which she must have comprehended, as she was familiar with the English language read to her, and after it was all over she was told that she was married."

William Badgley was descended from a long line of British fur dealers and Montreal merchants. Called to the bar of Lower Canada in 1823, he had practised law in Montreal until ill-health forced him to travel to Europe for a change of pace. There, in 1834, at the age of thirty-three, he met and married Elizabeth Wallace Taylor, the eldest daughter of Colonel J.W. Taylor of the East India Company. He returned to Montreal with his new wife that year and embarked upon an illustrious career as a lawyer, politician, and judge. Elizabeth and William Badgley had six children. By the time Badgley heard the *Mignault* case, he was sixty-four years old. Most of his children would have been grown and married. His vantage point would have caused him to sympathize more with a father's perspective than with that of a young suitor or bride.[66]

The law was clear, according to Badgley. Minors had to obtain the consent of their parents. French civil law stood out as particularly onerous in this regard. While the rest of the English-speaking common law provinces had set the age limit at twenty-one years, in Quebec parental consent was required until a woman reached twenty-five and a man thirty. In cases where the mother and father disagreed, the decision of the father prevailed. Although there is no record of what Zoé Mignault's mother thought, the disapproval of Monsieur Mignault would have been more than sufficient to bar the marriage. There was some possibility for a court to overrule a father's refusal, where this was an abuse of good faith. However, Quebec courts utilized this power very sparingly, intervening only in extraordinary cases. In any event, Zoé Mignault and Frederick Hapinian had taken no steps to overcome her father's disapproval.[67]

Badgley did express some sympathy for Reverend Bonar, whom he found innocent of any deliberate misbehaviour. Bonar was "misled," duped by the lies that Frederick Hapinian and Zoé Mignault had told him. Nevertheless, he "did not make sufficient enquiry before hand," said Badgley, and thus ran afoul of the law. Following a precedent set eight years earlier, he held that "a clergyman who celebrates the marriage of a minor, without the consent of her parent or guardian, is liable in damages." Badgley seems to have agreed with Bonar's contentions that Mignault was making a bit too much of his damage claim, however, and he awarded only one hundred dollars.[68]

Mignault was not content to rest with his initial victory, and had his lawyer, Jetté, seek to annul the marriage. Once more bringing an action before the Superior Court, they would argue that the marital contract was a nullity for several reasons. The absence of parental consent was first on the list. The foundation of public order rested on laws that ensured that families would be intimately involved in decisions significantly affecting their honour, income, and future lineage. To permit couples to make their own matches without parental supervision would be folly.[69]

Mignault and Jetté would also argue that the marriage licence had been obtained fraudulently. The parties had lied about their ages, and there had been no publication of banns to alert the community to the betrothal. What was more, they would again assert, Zoé Mignault had not been acting on her own true wishes.

Malgré les protestations et résistances de sa fille mineure, et tandis qu'elle était éloignée et hors de la protection de son père, le Défendeur, tant par ses sollicitations que par ses menaces, et par dol, fraudes et artifices, la força à consentir à l'épouser...; (In spite of the protestations and resistance of his daughter, and while she was far away from the protection of her father, the defendant forced her to consent to marry him, by earnest entreaties and threats, and by fraud and artifice).

Young Frederick Hapinian, it appears, was not represented by counsel, called no witnesses, and may not have defended the action at all. In any event, he offered no contradictory version of the betrothal or wedding.

The judge assigned to hear the case was William Badgley, who had ruled for Mignault the year before. This might have seemed promising, but there would be a major hurdle to overcome. Mignault was also seeking to have his daughter's mixed marriage annulled because of his insistence that Québécois Catholics should marry within their own community. Badgley, in contrast, had an avowed preference for things British and Protestant. One of the last of the old-style Lower Canadian Conservatives, Badgley was preoccupied with anglicizing Quebec, in order to protect "the interests of those of British origin." He had been one of the staunchest proponents for the union of Upper and Lower Canada, purportedly to redress what he saw as an imbalance between the French and English in Quebec. An active member of his own church, he was devoted to the propagation of Protestant education. He worked extensively on the development of the Protestant McGill College, where he had served as the first Dean of the Law Faculty. Mignault and Jetté would have a difficult task presenting their case in the courtroom of Mr. Justice Badgley.[70]

Jetté's main argument, however, would be unequivocally based on Roman Catholic religious doctrine. The major impediment to the validity of the marriage, asserted Jetté, was Frederick Hapinian's status as a stranger, an "infidel" according to the Roman Catholic Church. Mignault and Jetté introduced testimony from Édouard Charles Fabre, the Canon of the St. James's Cathedral of Montreal who would be named the first Archbishop of Montreal some years later. Fabre told the court that he had examined the young man, who had insisted that he had "no religion." Frederick Hapinian had maintained that he was certain he had never been baptized. Fabre informed those present that it was not possible to marry an infidel to a believer, or a baptized person to one not baptized, without a dispensation from the Ecclesiastical Superiors. Such dispensations were only granted when the petitioners were properly able to explain their motives, to assure the faith of the Catholic party, and to promise to raise their offspring in the Catholic faith. In this situation, there had been no application for dispensation. Jetté wrapped up his case by insisting that it was not competent for a Protestant minister to marry a Roman Catholic according to the rites of the Protestant church.[71]

After the Conquest, the English had begun making sporadic attempts to assimilate the French. But the realities of the situation had forced the English to recognize the existing language and religious affiliations of the

French. The Quebec Act of 1774 had promised the Canadian people the right to French institutions, language, civil law, and the free exercise of Roman Catholicism. The enclave of francophone *habitants*, seigneurs, clergy, and small traders within a vast English colonial empire soon began to voice a nationalist perspective. In 1837, Louis-Joseph Papineau mounted a popular but unsuccessful rebellion in an attempt to defend French Canadian language, religion, and laws through the establishment of a French Canadian republic.[72]

Lord Durham, sent out from England to examine the situation, made matters worse when he asserted that any agenda for change must have the assimilation of the "obviously inferior" *canadiens* as a goal. Equally offensive to French Canadian nationalism was the Act of Union in 1841, which granted equal representation to Upper Canada (population 450,000) and Lower Canada (population 650,000) in an explicit effort to "swamp the French." French Canadian historians and poets objected to these cultural aspersions and fought to vindicate Quebec separatism.[73]

The Roman Catholic Church asserted the primacy of the church over the state. In 1866 Monseigneur Louis François Richer Laflèche, the Vicar-General of Trois Rivières, published his *Quelques considérations sur les rapports de la société civile avec la religion et la famille*, a thorough argument for the subordination of the temporal state to the spiritual power of the church. The church's duty to teach the law of God put it in closest touch with the source of that law. An obvious component of this formulation was the need for the church to possess complete control over the sacrament of marriage in Quebec: "not only when the contracting parties [were] both Roman Catholics; not only in mixed marriages, when one [was] a Roman Catholic, and the other a Protestant; but also over the marriages of heretics." The church contested the very authority of the civil courts. It was for the church, and not the state, to make laws concerning marriage. Some would contend that all matrimonial cases ought to be taken before ecclesiastical judges.[74]

The civil courts had trod carefully upon the sentiments of the Québécois in these matters. At times, judges had referred questions involving the validity of Roman Catholic marriages to the Bishops for adjudication. Upon the receipt of these decisions, the civil judges often gave them legal and binding effect. But this formula had only been followed when all of the parties were Roman Catholic. Jetté might have thought that Frederick Hapinian's "heretic" status would disqualify this case from a resolution of that sort. Or perhaps he was aware of Badgley's pronounced Protestant leanings and decided not to ask for adjudication by the Bishops. He deferred to Badgley for a decision, although he took care to put Fabre on the stand to pronounce on the Roman Catholic view.[75]

After hearing all of the evidence, Badgley issued a terse two-page judgment on 30 May 1866. Presaging his conclusion, the thoroughly bilingual judge delivered his opinion in French, reciting the facts and the arguments that had been set forth by Mignault, Fabre, and Jetté. Then, without elaboration or explanation, he rendered his decision. Mignault had proven his case, with evidence of:

[le] défaut de consentement du Demandeur, du défaut des publications des banns requises par la loi; du dol, fraudes, artifices et menaces employées par le Défendeur pour obtenir le consentement de Zoé Mignault, et enfin, l'empêchement dirimant existant entre Zoé Mignault et le Défendeur...; (the lack of consent of the Petitioner, the failure to publish the banns required by law, the fraud, artifices and threats used by the Respondent to obtain Zoé Mignault's consent, and finally, the nullifying impediment that existed between Zoé Mignault and the respondent ... ).

Badgley had neatly catalogued the arguments, placing the lack of parental consent at the head of a long list. Contrary to the earlier decision, he also adopted the Mignault version of the facts surrounding the wedding. Zoé Mignault was depicted as a coerced and unwilling victim. Badgley tacked on a reference to the religious impediment, although only obliquely and without identifying it specifically. Perhaps it was easier to adopt the Roman Catholic perspective if it hadn't been labelled as such. Perhaps he had been convinced by the forcefulness with which the francophone Roman Catholic community was prepared to defend its future. Perhaps his decision had been easier because Frederick Hapinian was not a Protestant, but an atheist. Perhaps it helped that he had already ruled that the Protestant minister contravened the law in marrying the two. And there was the perspective of paternal control to be upheld, a premise that was important to Badgley. Faced with a confrontation between a young couple bent upon marrying for love and parents who sought to restrict them to suitable economic and social matches, Badgley's preference would have been toward the parents.

William Badgley declared the marriage to be null and void, and restored Zoé Mignault and Frederick Hapinian to a single state. He ordered the two to cease representing themselves as husband and wife, and forbade them to keep company together, "sous les peines de droit" (under penalty of law). The principle of parental control was enshrined in the

Quebec law of marriage, overriding whatever independent impulses young lovers might have wished to exercise.

One year after the *Mignault* decisions, the Quebec Legislature would revise its requirements for parental consent in marriage. While it is unlikely that the legislative amendment was directly related to that case, it seems that the Quebec legislators were responding to the changing social milieu. From 1866 on, the age at which men and women from Quebec could wed without parental consent was twenty-one. Other provinces would also begin to reduce the marital age of consent, with Ontario reducing its age of consent to eighteen in 1894.[76]

In Zoé Mignault's time, few women would have dared to consider marrying without obtaining formal parental permission. Parental control was so important that the law stood ready to bolster it by shoring up the rights of parents across linguistic and religious lines. But as the changes in legislation indicate, young people were slowly winning greater independence in courtship. The diaries and letters of middle- and upper-class women, filled in the first part of the century with references to parental approval or disapproval of their suitors, would in the latter decades rarely contain any mention of the dreaded parental veto. The accelerating pressures of urbanization and industrialization would fundamentally weaken the hold of parents upon their offspring as the nineteenth century drew to a close. This would come too late to assist Zoé Mignault. Her choices were dramatically confined by the values and beliefs of her father and the legal structures that stood ready to enforce his decision.[77]

# 2

# Seduction

Amelia Hogle and Philip Ham conducted their courtship in the Midland District of eastern Ontario during the mid-1820s. Philip Ham had begun to "pay his addresses" to Amelia Hogle, a schoolmate of his who lived on a neighbouring farm, when he was twenty-one and she was sixteen. The word flew and soon the two families and the neighbouring community began to consider him Amelia Hogle's suitor. The community considered the match a good one involving two families that were old friends.[1]

Most heterosexual courtships in nineteenth-century Canada took place within well-defined social settings. Church services and religious functions, house parties, skating, sleighing, picnics, concerts, plays, and summer excursions provided opportunities for socializing between marriageable young men and women. But the pre-eminent location for couples to socialize was the family home, where romance blossomed under the scrutiny of close relatives. The Hogle–Ham courtship seems to have been typical, for it was at the Hogle home that most of the contact took place.[2]

Philip Ham's circumstances were such as to "induce a reasonable expectation in the family and among their friends and neighbours that a marriage would take place." Nevertheless, no betrothal occurred. There was no promise of marriage even after it became clear in the late summer of 1824 that nineteen-year-old Amelia Hogle was pregnant. Family, community, and church members often intervened in such cases to put pressure on recalcitrant young men to wed their pregnant lovers. It was not unheard of for some nineteenth-century Canadian fathers to stand guard over wedding services, shotgun in hand. Here, however, there was no such parental intervention, and no one shamed Philip Ham into legitimating his sexual relationship with Amelia Hogle.[3]

Women who became pregnant out of wedlock are reported to have been something of a rarity in nineteenth-century Canada. Estimates suggest that illegitimacy affected no more than 5 per cent of all nineteenth-century births. As long as marriage occurred before childbirth, sexual indiscretion generally posed few insurmountable problems. "Knowing looks, private chastisement, brief local notoriety, and some embarrassment" might follow, but there would be little permanent damage. Pregnant women who did not marry breached fundamental social taboos. Childbirth outside of marriage was viewed as proof of incontrovertible personal depravity.[4]

But young Philip Ham refused to marry Amelia Hogle, and the Hogle family rallied to her support. She was permitted to stay in the family home for the duration of the pregnancy and after the birth of her child. It was widely understood that destitution was the most likely end when family members shunned or ostracized an unmarried, pregnant woman. To forestall this, the nineteenth-century rural white family commonly would take in errant daughters and their illegitimate offspring. But the families often assumed that the male seducer should bear some of the costs. And they frequently turned to the law to ensure redress.[5]

Sebastian Hogle, Amelia Hogle's father, went first to make inquiries of Christopher Alexander Hagerman, a thirty-three-year-old lawyer with a lucrative Kingston law practice. Sebastian Hogle chose well. Hagerman was a man famous for his "natural eloquence," passionate oratory, and "air of bravado." He would eventually earn the title of "the Thunderer of Kingston." Observers said that "bashfulness would never stand in the way" of the tall, rugged, handsome Hagerman.[6]

Hagerman advised the Hogles that an action for seduction was the best route to take. The tort of seduction was based on a centuries-old, common law rule that allowed an employer to sue someone who had injured his or her servant. The law treated a servant as a valuable property owned by the master. Where a master lost the services of the employee because of the wrongful act of an aggressor, compensation was available. As early as the seventeenth century, fathers had begun to use the action to avenge the seduction of their daughters. In his capacity as a master

Depiction of a "Seduced Daughter,"
from *Canadian Illustrated News* (Montreal), 17 January 1880.

entitled to the domestic services of his daughter, a father would sue the seducer "just as he would have been entitled to sue a neighbour who had lured away from his estate a particularly talented stable-boy," according to one legal authority.[7]

Embedded in this thinking was the belief that certain individuals could hold property interests in others. By the nineteenth century the popularity of the action had waned in the area of employment as a modernizing economy was beginning to favour a more contractual, individualized framework for the labour market. But the lawsuit remained popular within the family, as countless fathers sought pecuniary compensation for the seduction of their daughters, perhaps consciously or unconsciously asserting parental property interests in the sexual behaviour of their female offspring. And they felt thoroughly within their rights to call upon the law in doing so.[8]

Trial in the *Hogle* case would begin at the next Assizes for the Midland

District, held in Kingston. The Assizes were circuit courts with the juris-diction to hear both civil and criminal cases. Typically, one Supreme Court judge would preside, often with a jury to assist. On the first day of trial, Christopher Hagerman called Amelia Hogle to the stand as the first witness. The first thing Hagerman would have to prove would be that Amelia Hogle's father had been dependent on her services. As a legal scholar would later describe it:

The law gives no remedy to the parent for the mere seduction of his daughter, however wrongfully it may have been accomplished. Incontinence on the part of a young woman cannot be made the foundation of an action against the young person who has tempted her and deprived her of her chastity; but if she is living with her parent at the time of the seduction, and the seduction is followed by pregnancy and illness, whereby the parent is deprived of the filial services there-tofore rendered to him, an action is maintainable against the seducer.[9]

In a typical nineteenth-century farming family, a daughter would have been intimately involved in the productive work of the household. From the age of six, she would have been looking after children younger than herself. From the age of eight to twelve, she would have done laundry, swept, set the table, cleaned the dishes, and apprenticed as a cook. Although sex-role divisions generally kept young girls from labour-ing in the fields, many would have done some outside work, such as hoeing and harvesting in market gardens. Farm children were expected to repay their parents for their upkeep by working for the family until the age of eighteen to twenty. It was a simple matter for Hagerman to obtain evidence that Amelia Hogle provided important and essential services to her father.[10]

The next element of the case would be to prove that Philip Ham had "debauched" Amelia Hogle, that in the legal language of the day, he had had "carnal knowledge" of her. These sexual relations had to be illicit, that is, intercourse out of wedlock. Here there was no dispute that Philip Ham had had sexual intercourse with Amelia Hogle. Both admitted it. Furthermore, Amelia Hogle would testify that she had become pregnant and had "borne a child to the defendant." Hagerman put the question to his witness: Had she ever "dispensed her favours to others than the defendant"? She responded firmly: "Never."[11]

Lastly, Hagerman would have to prove that Sebastian Hogle, Amelia Hogle's father, had experienced real losses as a result of the defendant's actions. The type of damages generally sought were limited. Fathers could claim their "loss of services" for the time during which their daughters were incapacitated from pregnancy and childbirth. In this case, Sebastian Hogle would claim that Amelia Hogle had been "ill about three weeks." Fathers could also claim the costs of providing nursing and medical care during their daughters' confinement. More significantly, they could also seek compensation for their "wounded feelings" and the "moral injury" that had been inflicted upon their families.[12]

The narrow proscription of damages was the result of the origin of the action. It was peculiarly a master's or father's legal injury that was at stake. The quantification of harm was based upon his perspective. It was not possible to claim for the continuing losses that would be experienced by an unwed mother. Amelia Hogle's costs in raising a child, her diminished expectations for the future, her pain and suffering were all out of reach in a seduction action. A woman might have a legal remedy for a breach of promise of marriage suit, or a paternity proceeding against the father of the child, but these were separate and unrelated actions and could not be considered during the seduction trial. And often the circumstances of the seduction were such that these alternate claims were unavailable.[13]

It was a strange feature of the law that it permitted fathers to sue where the seduced woman's action was barred. Various legal and medical groups suggested that the right of action properly belonged to the seduced woman, who was truly the injured party. In Quebec, where the rules surrounding "dommages pour séduction" (damages for seduction) arose from French civil law, women frequently would sue in their own names. For the claim to be successful, however, Quebec women had to meet particular evidentiary requirements. Quebec women had to prove that the seduction had been accomplished by misrepresentation, fraud, or trickery. Prior to the enactment of the Quebec Civil Code in 1866, it was presumed that a woman seduced out of wedlock had succumbed under a promise of marriage, which would constitute clear-cut evidence of fraud. Requirements for proof were tightened in the second half of the century, as Quebec judges began to exhibit more suspicion that women might have agreed to sexual relations of their own free will. And after 1866 it also became clear that either a woman or her father could sue for seduction in Quebec. But in the common law provinces, the seduction action was entirely out of reach to women.[14]

In 1852, however, Prince Edward Island enacted a landmark statute permitting actions for seduction to be brought in the name of the woman seduced. This was rather a startling initiative, since the P.E.I. Legislature was not known for its pro–women's rights stance. In 1832 Prince Edward Island had been one of the first colonial jurisdictions to prohibit women from exercising the franchise. Perhaps, in 1852, the legislators took their lead from some of the American states, which by this time had begun to permit women to sue independently for seduction. The women of Prince Edward Island made little headway, however, because two years later the Supreme Court of Prince Edward Island practically nullified the legislation. A surprising judicial ruling held that before the seduced woman could be permitted to sue in her own name, she would have to prove that at the time of the seduction she had had a parent, master, or guardian who would have been entitled to maintain the action at common law.[15]

Other common law jurisdictions were even more inflexible. Apart from the North-West Territories (then including Alberta and Saskatchewan), which finally transferred the right of action to the seduced woman in 1903, none budged on this issue. Chief Justice Brenton Halliburton of the Nova Scotia Supreme Court would articulate some of the rationale in 1838:

An action for seduction, unaccompanied by a promise of marriage, will not certainly lie at the suit of the female; the law has so settled it, and perhaps wisely, and I am content to take the law as I find it.... It might be a want of that strict care we are bound to have over the public morals, if we were to allow a female to come into court, and without setting forth any extenuating circumstances, shew she had permitted herself to be seduced, and claim damages against her seducer.[16]

Whether a more widespread and effective legislative shift on the right of action would have proved much of a boon to women is an open question. From our vantage point, it seems that it would have been galling to have had to depend upon one's father to instigate legal proceedings and frustrating to see damages claimed as a father's loss. But shifting the right of action to the woman concerned might have caused more harm than good. As Chief Justice Halliburton had suggested, to the nineteenth-century mind it would have been contradictory to permit women to recover directly for sexual injury. However, in the Upper Canada of 1825, there was no question that the right of action lay squarely with Sebastian Hogle, the father of the seduced woman. He had set out all of the essential elements in the claim: illicit intercourse, loss of services, costs of confinement, and moral injury to the family.[17]

Philip Ham would vigorously defend himself through the services of his lawyer, Jonas Jones. A gentleman farmer from a privileged Upper Canadian background, Jones had developed a flourishing legal practice in Brockville. Famous for his single-minded sexual pursuit of women in his younger days, Jones may have felt personally drawn to the situation of a client forced to defend himself against a charge of illicit intercourse. Jonas Jones conceded that Philip Ham had admitted the sexual connection. But the fault, he would claim, lay with the Hogles. The "indiscrete" Amelia Hogle had "tempted" Philip Ham "many times ... before he gave way to his passions." She was set up as a temptress, while the man was depicted as unable to bridle his strong sexual urges. Furthermore, Jones would charge, Sebastian Hogle had knowingly allowed Philip Ham and Amelia Hogle to "sit up whole nights in a bed room."[18]

With this, Jones unmasked to the court a practice that had traditionally been known as "bundling." This custom had been widespread among the poorer classes in Europe and the American colonies in the eighteenth century. Young people were allowed to continue their courting into the small hours of the night, unimpeded by direct adult supervision. All-night conversations were frequently accompanied by physical exploration, although sexual interplay was expected to halt prior to intercourse.[19]

Women had generally favoured bundling, a practice over which they had a fair degree of control. Male suitors might plead ardently for such access, but it was the woman who ultimately decided whether to grant the request. Bundling also offered the woman a certain measure of protection. When sexual intimacy took place in her parents' house, with her parents' knowledge, a young man could be held accountable for his actions. In the atypical situation where he abused his privileges and pregnancy resulted, moral convention had traditionally precipitated a speedy marriage. But bundling was on the wane. In England and America it was disappearing under pressure from evangelical religious reformers. As the custom came under attack, the community pressures that had held young people to a strictly regulated code of sexuality weakened. The number of cases resulting in unwed pregnancies increased.[20]

Evidence that bundling had existed in the province of Upper Canada had surfaced one year earlier in Niagara, during the August Assizes. There, as in the *Hogle* case, the strictures of bundling had been disobeyed, pregnancy had resulted, and the male suitor had refused to honour his obligation. That case had prompted a diatribe in the press, which claimed the custom to be a "disgrace to the country." The inroads of evangelical ministry were also evident. The reporter covering the case for the *Colonial Advocate* voiced his regret that neither the young woman nor her family had "been under the influence of a gospel ministry, had lived under the example of an evangelical priest." Had stronger religious influences prevailed, he was convinced "that the disclosures she made, which are a disgrace to the country ... would never have shocked the ears of a Niagara audience." Jones may have intended to shock the court with the evidence of bundling in the Midland District, since he would have been aware that in urban settings such familiarity would never have been permitted among the propertied classes. Jones would make much of this point later, insisting that Mr. Hogle's laxness should bar his claim for damages.[21]

Hagerman would attempt to counter this evidence by focusing upon the class of the litigants. Pointing out that the Hogle residence was a simple structure, he would emphasize that it was divided into two apartments: a room and a kitchen. "What has been called a bed room of the young woman is, properly speaking, the only apartment in the house into which a visitor can be shewn. Gentlemen, you know the country — the poor man cannot have a long suite of apartments; if there be a bed in his only one, is it an indication of vice?"[22]

The other line of attack that Jones would use would be to undermine Amelia Hogle's credibility with the jury. Jones called as a witness a man named Impey. Impey swore that Amelia Hogle was "not so immaculate as she pretended to be." He personally had had sexual intercourse with Amelia Hogle, he alleged. Even more damaging, Impey would state that in an unguarded moment, Amelia Hogle had admitted to him that her child was "probably not the child of the defendant." Jones made much of this, arguing that Philip Ham should not be liable for any damages at all.[23]

Lastly came the all-important addresses to the jury. The lawyers' exchanges were so impassioned that the Kingston *Chronicle* and the *Upper Canada Herald* published them in full. Christopher Hagerman would lead off first, for the Hogles:

May it please your Lordship, Gentlemen of the Jury:

The action ... is one which, I am happy to say, is rare in this Province, and was never before brought in this District: It is, Gentlemen, that of a father seeking redress for the ruin of his only remaining daughter & claiming from you some compensation for the greatest injury a Parent can sustain.

Gentlemen, my client is an old man, nearly seventy years of age, fast descending in the vale of years, and must, in the course of nature, shortly visit that country "from whose bourne no traveller returns." During his long and chequered life he has sustained a character free from stain and from reproach: and, till the hour that gave his daughter to the embraces of a villain, looked with proud satisfaction to his happy family.

That family, gentlemen, consisting at one period, of eleven children, he reared with all the care of a fond and affectionate father. He gave them an education suitable to his station in life, and saw his cares rewarded by the respectable marriage of his other daughters. This one alone remained — she was the youngest — the hope and stay of his declining years; and her settlement in life seemed the principal tie that bound him to existence.

But, gentlemen, those hopes were blasted. The foul seducer came — what was it to him that he was to destroy so much happiness — what to him to crush a young and tender flower — what to him to rob it of its sweets, and, having robbed it, "threw it like a loathsome weed away."

For more than three years, I say, has the Defendant been intimate with the Plaintiff's daughter; and, till more than two of these had passed in fruitless endeavours to rob her of her innocence, the breath of calumny never shed its influence on the face of her fair fame. But, gentlemen, the arts of the seducer — the weakness of the seduced — the hope of marrying the man she loved, lulled to repose the voice of honor — and, in an evil hour, she consented.[24]

On the matter of Sebastian Hogle's allegedly lax parental supervision, Hagerman would counter:

I have heard, gentlemen, that the Defendant places his hopes of escape on the practice of allowing young men and women to set up at nights and keep company together. Gentlemen, is it in a Court of Justice we are to get a code of morality — and is it the seducer that is to teach it? I am not an advocate for the practice but it is the custom of the country — not of this country only — but of many others. Let not my client suffer for following a custom so general — and let not the seducer escape for taking advantage of the confidence reposed in him.[25]

Hagerman would outdo himself in the summing up:

Gentlemen, I have done. The eyes of your Country are upon you. Let your verdict, this day, prove that the hearth of the poor man is as sacred as that of the rich man, and that he who violates the purity of his dwelling, will find from you his merited punishment. He may, like the Defendant, glory in his villainy, and boast to his companions the conquests he has made...; but let him learn that retributive justice will one day overtake him, and that he is not to judge the sentiments of others by the baseness of his own.

Gentlemen, recollect that by your evidence this day, you may save many a father a broken heart, and if, Gentlemen, which I cannot think will be the case, you give the Plaintiff trivial damages, you may one day, which may God prevent, feel the effects of your folly. A daughter, or a sister, or the daughter or sister of a relation, may share a similar fate. You will then say, had we, when we had it in our power, made an example in the first instance, we might now have averted disgrace and dishonour.[26]

Jonas Jones would respond in kind. Addressing veiled compliments to his adversary, he labelled Hagerman's eloquence mere emotionalism:

Gentlemen of the Jury:
You must have been highly entertained, Gentlemen, by the eloquent address of the Learned Counsel for the Plaintiff; the over-powering effect of which, on your feelings, it is my duty to endeavour to remove. I have practiced many years at this bar, and I must say that it is, without question, the best address ever heard. But, Gentlemen, let me point out to you the necessity of separating that part of it addressed to your feelings from the real and actual state of the case.[27]

Jones challenged the custom of bundling, which he implied was the real cause of the illicit sexual relations:

You do not need to be told, Gentlemen, of the custom of some people in this country of allowing their daughters, in a separate room, to sit up whole nights together, with young men. [...] Think ... Gentlemen, of the situation of the Defendant; he had access to Plaintiff's house at all times and at all hours; he was allowed, with the knowledge of her father, to sit up with his daughter in her bed room all night; and when we reflect on the infirmities of human nature, can we be so much astonished at the result.[28]

Jones would concede, with Hagerman, that the case was precedent-setting. But he would urge quite a different resolution:

Gentlemen, you have heard the Learned Counsel declare that this is the first action of the kind brought in this District, but not the first cause of it. What is this but to say that they are waiting to find how much you will give, and then inundate our Courts with actions of this kind. Will you encourage litigation? Will you stir up the dying embers of family contention? It will be for you to say, I leave the case to your impartial decision, with every confidence that you will do it justice.[29]

The all-male jury was sent off to decide whom to believe, how far the indiscretion of Sebastian Hogle might limit his claim, and to settle the amount of damages owed, if any. Upon return the jury announced that they believed Amelia Hogle's version. They disregarded the defendant's claims and Impey's evidence. They may have thought that Impey's aspersions on Amelia Hogle's character had further injured the Hogles. They brought back a verdict for the plaintiff and awarded Sebastian Hogle the unprecedented sum of two hundred and fifty pounds.

In so doing, the *Hogle* jury began what would form a pattern that spanned the century. Canadian jurors would consistently show themselves to be sympathetic toward the fathers of seduced women. In later years, the action would grow to be one of the most common lawsuits in the country, with plaintiffs winning their cases before juries as often as 90 per cent of the time. The damage awards would continue to be substantial, frequently running to hundreds of dollars. The awards bore little relation to the actual value of lost household services, since juries consistently concluded that the amounts necessary to compensate for dishonour and distress far outdistanced the original basis of the action.[30]

Not all who observed this phenomenon thought it fair. The editors of the *Upper Canada Law Journal* thought it distinctly prejudicial to the interests of justice:

The defence of such an action ... is peculiarly difficult. The action is easily brought, easily proved, and most difficult to meet. Should the seduced be a person of doubtful character, the defendant, with a view to impeach her credibility or lessen damages, may be tempted to put witnesses in the box. This, however, as the law stands, is an experiment fraught with danger. The jury perhaps, more influenced by the tears of the young woman or the eloquence of her counsel than by the evidence of her accusers, may disbelieve the testimony of the latter, and, because of the supposed attempt to "blacken her character," swell the damages.[31]

The overworn refrain of the chivalrous jury stretched the truth. If it were the situation of the woman that had motivated the jury, they would have been as supportive of rape victims as they were of victims of seduction. But as we shall see in the area of rape law, nineteenth-century jurors would be anything but chivalrous to assaulted women. All-male juries may have felt some degree of sympathy toward the seduced daughter, but their compassion here was primarily for the father, a man who was seeking to avenge his family's honour. Their empathy lay with him, and it would be him they would seek to compensate. The young victim of seduction was simply the vehicle of her family's loss.

The danger of attempting to defame the victim's character was more accurately portrayed. This was a double-edged legal sword, which could pay off handsomely in the right case. Lawyers regularly tried to introduce evidence of the woman's sexual behaviour and reputation in seduction trials, but the process was complicated. A young woman's reputation for promiscuity with the defendant, or anyone else for that matter, did not bar her father's action, since the central issue was the loss experienced by her father. By law, the woman was considered a form of property, and her consent to sexual relations was irrelevant. She could not give what she did not own.[32]

However, evidence of the seduction victim's lack of chastity could significantly lessen the amount of damages her father would be entitled to receive. The thinking was that an "immoral" daughter had contributed less to the domestic happiness of her father prior to the seduction, and the amount of compensation he deserved should be thereby reduced. The logic of permitting a reputation for immorality to reduce damages when outright consent to sexual relations did not was ironic but clear. A piece of property could neither give nor withhold consent to sexual intercourse, but property could easily be valued according to whether it had been damaged prior to the event in question. Future lawyers would occasionally convince juries to reduce the amount awarded to sums as low as ten dollars, and even twenty-five cents, in situations where the reputation of the victim had been sullied and the jury wished to ridicule the plaintiffs. But where the jury believed the evidence about the woman's reputation was falsified, they could decide to inflate the damages. And contrary to the views of the law editors, they would have been entitled to do so. Their award was intended to compensate a father for the family's loss of reputation. Insofar as the defendant wrongfully enhanced that loss with bogus testimony about a woman's sexual behaviour, he ought to have been required to pay.[33]

In *Hogle*, the evidence was muddled. Impey had claimed that Amelia Hogle had not confined her "indiscretion" to Philip Ham. Amelia Hogle had denied this, although apparently Jones had shaken her somewhat on cross-examination. The legal report suggests that Amelia Hogle may have reluctantly admitted to having sexual relations with Impey, although only *after* the seduction at issue. What went through the jurors' minds as they sifted through these accounts will never be known. They may have concluded that Impey was an unsavoury character, who had exploited

Amelia Hogle's precarious situation after her demise at Philip Ham's hands. The Hogles' lawyer had phrased it as "a case of two libertines supporting each other in their base practices." Or the jurors may have believed Amelia Hogle's examination-in-chief, where she denied all sexual encounters except those with Philip Ham. In any event, they seem to have thought that Impey's evidence justified a marked inflation of the award.[34]

The size of the award may also have been related to the jury's assessment of Amelia Hogle's physical attractiveness and feminine demeanour. Newspaper reporters of the day often remarked that juries tended to measure their awards according to their impressions of the wronged woman. Plaintiffs' lawyers were at pains to escort their clients' daughters into the courtroom in such a manner that their beauty was modestly, but prominently displayed. Where a seduction victim was sensationally beautiful, her beauty could escalate the damages dramatically. Perhaps the jurors were driven to generosity because they thought that a prize property had been despoiled.[35]

Whatever the explanation, the substantial award of two hundred and fifty pounds in this case provoked the wrath of Philip Ham, who immediately retained the services of another lawyer, John Solomon Cartwright. Cartwright was newly called to the bar that year. Born in Kingston, he had been educated at the Midland District Grammar School. Just twenty-one years old, he was said to be a man with a passion for high living: horses, gambling, good food and wine. He had no difficulty indulging his tastes, for he had inherited a substantial fortune from his father, a United Empire Loyalist who was a spectacularly successful businessman. This would have been one of Cartwright's first cases, and he would have been determined to make an impression.[36]

Cartwright would file with the Court of King's Bench for an order to set aside the original Assize verdict and grant a new trial on the "grounds of public policy and morality." "The £250 were not so easily raised as £5000 were in England," he declared. The local economy was notorious for a marked scarcity of money or property that could be converted into money. "The jury," charged Cartwright, must have been "influenced by undue motives." Seeking to establish their altruism, Cartwright and Philip Ham would profess to be concerned about morality generally, and warned that the verdict boded ill for the future:

[S]hould the court permit damages to follow conduct of this sort, it would soon be flooded with these actions. [P]arents of loose morals, looking forward to the remuneration, would be careless of their daughters' virtue, and would even use means to entrap inexperienced young men.[37]

Cartwright would also maintain that Sebastian Hogle was the author of his own misfortune. By permitting his daughter to be "frequently alone" with the defendant, Sebastian Hogle had been guilty of "great indiscretion," which had made him a *particeps criminis* and should bar his claim. It was outrageous to be rewarding fathers "for their indiscreet carelessness of their daughters' virtue," concluded Cartwright.[38]

The Hogles also switched lawyers, a decision that was likely to have been taken on Hagerman's advice. Their new counsel was James Buchanan Macaulay, a thirty-two-year-old Toronto barrister, and brother-in-law to Hagerman. Intermarriage among the small and cohesive legal community was common; Cartwright would wed Macaulay's sister six years later. Macaulay had been admitted to the bar for only three years, and he was known as a "shy, retiring man, hesitant of speech." However, he had all the right connections for professional success. The son of well-to-do British immigrants, his "impeccable social standing" had allowed him to rub shoulders since birth with the foremost political, judicial, and legal figures of the day. That May, he would be appointed to the Executive Council, a bastion of the Family Compact.[39]

Macaulay would try to point to the good reputation of the plaintiffs in the community. "The plaintiff has been proved to be of respectable character as well as his family," he noted. Then he added somewhat sheepishly, "except in this instance." Sebastian Hogle had accepted Philip Ham as an honourable suitor, and he had permitted him "such freedoms in his house and family as are usually permitted under such circumstances." Stressing that the courting practices of the farming classes were different from the wealthy, Macaulay explained:

[T]he custom of allowing young persons to see each other in bed rooms and alone, and at late hours, though not agreeable to more refined notions, was predicated upon the confidence which the inhabitants of the country placed in each other, and the few instances in which that confidence had been violated shewed that it had not often been misplaced.

Wishing to emphasize the reason for this behaviour, Macaulay insisted that "in this respect something must be allowed to the situation of the young yeomanry of the country, who were labouring in the field during the day, and had little opportunity of being introduced to each other but at night." In this, Macaulay was simply elaborating upon the argument concerning the class of the litigants first raised by Hagerman at trial.[40]

Cartwright would remonstrate that the custom of allowing young men and women to remain together in bedrooms overnight was "immoral in the extreme." Dismissing traditional rural courting practices, he urged that the force of law be brought into play. The time had come, he declared, for the courts to "mark this custom with their animadversion."[41]

The case was heard by the full bench of judges sitting at York (Toronto) in the fall of 1825. William Campbell, a sixty-six-year-old Scottish immigrant who had been appointed to the bench in 1812, delivered the final decision. He had spent most of the fall on a whirlwind tour of the western circuit of the province, hearing criminal and civil trials from Sandwich (Windsor) to Niagara (Niagara-on-the-Lake). Returning to York in late September, he learned of his elevation to the position of Chief Justice on 17 October 1825.[42]

Campbell's first impressions of Amelia Hogle were not flattering. To her he attributed "inexperience and weakness," although he conceded that "[y]oung unmarried inexperienced female[s]" were "peculiarly exposed" to "excitements and temptations ... especially when approached, as they frequently are, by seducers under the mask of honourable addresses." Campbell would be more harsh in his criticism of Sebastian Hogle:

I consider it ... the indispensable duty of a parent to use all possible care and vigilance, and, if necessary, to exercise his authority to prevent a daughter from being exposed to such temptation, much less to be left alone in bedrooms, or any other rooms or places at unseasonable hours, and for whole nights with an individual of the other sex.

A parent knowingly allowing such opportunities betrays not only a foolish and ridiculous confidence and want of common prudence and circumspection, but also such a degree of culpable negligence as in effect amounts to criminal connivance, and therefore, renders his right of action extremely doubtful; but at all events diminishes his claim to damages in an action of this kind for an injury, which has been the natural consequence of his entire neglect of a most sacred duty as a parent, and the dictates of ordinary prudence as a man of common sense.[43]

Campbell also made short shrift of Macaulay' argument about the need to permit young people time to socialize. Whatever may have been the custom of the farming classes, the legal authorities were scandalized by the "intimate intercourse and nightly visits." As far as Campbell was concerned, young people already had all sorts of opportunities for heterosexual interaction:

... the parties have been intimately acquainted from infancy; they have been brought up in the same neighbourhood, and have had daily opportunities of forming a thorough estimate of the good and bad qualities of each other; and, in short, all of those circumstances, the knowledge of which is usually considered necessary to enable young persons and their respective parents to decide on the propriety of the intended match.... [N]othing was wanting for all the purposes of honourable courtships, but the usual proposal of marriage.[44]

Campbell's views would be echoed by Judge Levius Peters Sherwood who issued a concurring opinion in the case. The Quebec-born lawyer had become well known as a pillar of the York establishment, and he had been appointed to the King's Bench of Upper Canada that year. According to observers, he cut a very imposing figure, with his "dignified form and grey locks of flowing hair." Rather surprisingly, Sherwood noted in his decision that if Philip Ham had proposed marriage to Amelia Hogle, no one would have been very alarmed about the overnight visits: "Had [a proposal of marriage] clearly appeared, the plaintiff's want of care would, in a great measure have been excused, and the verdict would have probably remained as it is." Perhaps Sherwood thought that the morality of the labouring classes was less scrupulous than he would have expected in his own circles. Yet even he would not countenance the customary intimacy in other than betrothed couples.[45]

What was at stake was the enforcement of proper codes of sexual conduct. No one could have been clearer than Sherwood about where the emphasis should lie. "It is of the greatest importance to society," he wrote, "that females should be brought up in habits of virtuous and chaste demeanour." Men, the seducers, were to benefit indirectly. The behaviour of women, Sherwood noted soberly, "will always have a decisive influence in correcting any licentious deportment in the other sex." Known as a conservative in politics and law, Sherwood was adamant about maintaining sharply differentiated responsibilities for heterosexual behaviour, with women tagged as the "gate-keepers" of morality.[46]

Although the Court of King's Bench would rule that the trial jury had awarded excessive damages, the judges expressed some caution about overstepping their authority here. Campbell quoted extensively from English judgments in which courts had refused to overrule jury assessment of damages, even where these had seemed excessive. "This is a doctrine to which I cannot subscribe," cautioned Campbell. Where the amount of damages was so high as to suggest that the jury must have acted "under the influence of either undue motives, or of gross error, or of misconception of the subject," he thought it was the duty of the court to overturn the award. Disavowing any intention to encroach upon the jurisdiction of the jury, he nevertheless ordered the verdict expunged, and directed a new trial be held. There is no record that a second trial was held, and the likelihood is that the Hogles simply got tired of the wrangling and the legal fees and abandoned the claim.[47]

So began what would become a constant theme in seduction litigation. Juries would regularly rule for the plaintiffs, and defendants would then appeal to the full bench of judges to set aside the verdict. On balance, their success at this stage was well known. The judges overturned about half of these verdicts on points of law.[48]

Why there was such a difference in outlook between judges and juries is not clear. Perhaps juries, a group slightly more representative of the community, were more aware of the family loss associated with seduction. Juries would have been more likely to identify with a grieving father than judges, who came from a class in which the prospect of litigating over seduction was far more remote. Upper- and middle-class families almost never sued for seduction. That they did not may indicate that their daughters were more tightly chaperoned and thus not exposed to the same danger of seduction. On the other hand, it may have meant that fathers with greater financial means chose not to sully their reputations further through public litigation.[49]

Few of the judges were very forthcoming about why they so commonly overturned jury verdicts. William Henry Draper, Chief Justice of Upper Canada, was an exception. Although most of his opinions on seduction were delivered in the 1860s, and may not be fully representative of the perspectives of judges throughout the nineteenth century, the explicitness of his decisions warrants their further examination. As Judge Sherwood had, Draper would place the emphasis for sexual decorum upon women. He believed that the real culprits were the women, but lawsuits for seduction did little to punish women for their immoral behaviour. Draper, whose oratorical skills had earned him the nickname "Sweet William," stated in an 1862 decision:

... actions of seduction are becoming far too frequent, and, in not a few instances, shew such a total want of moral principle among the so-called victims of seduction, as to make one fear that the prospect of publicly avowing their own frailty on the trial where large damages may be recovered, does not make them sufficiently careful of exposing themselves to temptation.... Nor is that public confession always attended with that sense of shame and disgrace which ought to attend the consciousness of yielded virtue, either in the mind of the fallen one, or of the community around her.[50]

An Englishman who had spent his early years at sea with the East India Company, Draper had achieved fame and fortune as a lawyer and politician in Upper Canada. Realizing a lifelong ambition with his appointment to the judiciary in 1847, he rose to prominence on the bench, where he was promoted to Chief Justice of the Court of Common Pleas in 1856, Chief Justice of the Court of Queen's Bench in 1863, and Chief Justice of the Court of Error and Appeal in Ontario in 1869. Exhibiting a deep-seated distrust of women, Draper would insinuate, often within the context of specific cases, that women had a propensity to lie, scheme, and extort:

Verdicts for the plaintiff (verdicts for the defendant are rare) certainly fail to prevent seduction, or to operate as a warning against yielding to it; and the case leads to the conclusion that the female seduced would not have yielded her chastity if the seducer would not have been a good matrimonial connexion, or a good mark for damages if he could not be coaxed or frightened into marriage.[51]

Draper never directed such viciousness at the plaintiffs, the fathers. He never accused them of conniving to mulct innocent men. His venom was entirely gender-specific. This anti-female perspective was shared by other members of the legal community. W.H. Chewett, the editor of the Toronto *Local Courts and Municipal Gazette*, used particularly memorable phrasing in 1866: "[T]here is, we think, a prevailing impression that in its present shape an action for seduction is no adequate means of preventing the immorality which it is intended to check, whilst it is in numerous cases an engine of oppression in the hands of a corrupt or designing woman."[52]

It is no doubt possible that some women may have engaged in heterosexual intercourse in the belief that this would lead to marriage. But Draper and Chewett were suspicious of something more. They apparently believed that the prospect of damages in a seduction action enticed some women into having heterosexual intercourse itself, a claim that would have been astonishing to most seduced women and their families. The assertion is simply illogical, given the extremely restrictive nature of the damages, which in most cases excluded the costs of maintaining the illegitimate child and the loss of prospects of its mother. Furthermore, it was the father who pursued the defendant and collected the compensation. No doubt women may have sometimes benefited from the awards. But it is far-fetched to suggest that women were consciously scheming to engage in illicit sexual relations and pregnancy, lured to their demise by the prospect of an elusive, incomplete, indirect damage claim.

Draper and his fellow judges also frequently expressed their concern about the impact on the public of seduction trials. The *Hogle* case may have provided an opportunity for the judiciary to lecture the rural populace about proper sexual practices, but by and large, the courtroom audiences were there for entertainment, not edification. Draper would complain in 1863: "The trials themselves do harm, as every one who has witnessed them frequently must admit, when he calls to mind the ill-suppressed disturbance among the audience when any thing particularly flagrant is detailed in evidence, or pressed upon witnesses under examination." The ignominy of presiding over a tittering crowd of spectators transfixed by every lurid detail may have been yet another reason why the judges so disliked the action.[53]

### THE CASE OF LUCINDA CAMP:
### VIOLENT SEDUCTION OF A DOMESTIC SERVANT

Not every seduction action arose out of a courtship. In fact, many women reported that their seduction had been more akin to rape. Frequently these were poor women who had hired out as domestic servants. One of the best illustrations was the case of *Camp v Blows*, heard in 1888 in Hamilton.[54]

Robert Charles Camp, the plaintiff, was a labourer. He resided in the township of Beverly, on the limestone ridge of the Niagara Escarpment near Hamilton. Camp lived close to the village of Lynden, which the press would christen "a small but wicked place" where the morals were "anything but exemplary." He would claim that his twenty-year-old daughter, Lucinda Camp, had been seduced by Russell G. Blows, a farmer living in the neighbourhood. Lucinda Camp had been hired by the Blows family for the summer of 1886 as a live-in domestic servant. For her labour, she was paid seventy-five cents a week, most of which she probably turned over to her parents.[55]

Domestic service was the largest single occupational category for Canadian women at this time, although lamentations about the shortage of servants were heard frequently throughout the century. Statistics from 1891 show that 41 per cent of all working women were employed in this line of work. Some, like Lucinda Camp, were neighbour girls who had been bound out temporarily to farming families. Their employers required assistance because of illness, new births in the family, or the harvest, and could afford to pay cash for the service. The help often worked jointly with their employers and ate at the family table. With urbanization, it would become more common for young women to travel to the growing cities and take work in middle-class homes, where the power relations of class and ethnicity would leave them far more isolated and subject to even greater risk of economic and sexual exploitation. If they lost their jobs, they lost their homes, and in contrast to Lucinda Camp, they no longer had family nearby to intervene.[56]

The most backbreaking household chores were delegated to domestic workers: the heaviest housework, cleaning floors, grates and stoves, washing clothes, cooking for the family and other hired help, and assisting with any dairy and poultry enterprises. The following description of women's labour gives some idea of the many tasks of a rural household:

They grew their own hops to make their own rising to make their own bread. They saved ashes to make their own lye to boil with collected fat to make their own soap. They made their own candles. They spun wool, they made clothes, cutting up old garments for patterns. They had complete responsibility for the dairy, the milking, the butter-making and the cheese-making. They took part in the butchering of the beasts, in the making of sausages, the smoking of hams, the salting of pork. They did great laundries, which they finished, in spite of protective bandages, with bleeding wrists....

The vegetable garden too was the woman's care, as well as the putting down of berries, pickles, fruits and preserves; the making of substitutes for teas and coffee from dandelion roots, sumach leaves and parched grain; the dying of wool and knitting; the care of poultry; the dressing and curing of fish and game.[57]

Many servants came from families where poverty was so acute that they placed themselves out simply to be fed. These women worked for room and board alone, indentured for years with the promise of "two suits of apparel" as the only reward for their labour at the end of the apprenticeship. When the scarcity of female labour forced employers to pay cash, wages were generally half those paid to male servants. A general female servant in eastern Canada could earn eight to fourteen dollars per month, and from ten to twenty dollars per month in the west by the turn of the century. The vulnerability of domestic servants to sexual exploitation was also widely understood. The culprits were typically their masters, or male relatives of their master, or hired men working within the same or nearby households. The long hours of work and lack of privacy were such that female servants were almost continuously accessible. Many found that seduction and an ensuing pregnancy were twin perils of the job.[58]

Robert Camp first learned of Lucinda Camp's seduction when she returned home from the Blows' residence and told him she was not going to work for Russell Blows any more. She was apparently very angry, and vowed that she "would make Russell Blows smart." Robert Camp also recalled that Lucinda Camp was embarrassed about her situation. "It was quite a while before we could make her tell what was up," he noted. What he learned would prompt him to launch court proceedings immediately, claiming two thousand dollars in damages.[59]

Fortunately for the Camps, there had been some changes in the law of seduction since the time of *Hogle* v *Ham*. In 1825, Mr. Hogle had had to establish that he relied upon his daughter's services in order to prove his claim for damages. If this rule had still applied, Robert Camp would have had no grounds for his suit. The master entitled to sue for Lucinda Camp's loss of services would have been the seducer, Russell Blows. Lucinda Camp's father could not have shown that he depended on his daughter for domestic duties, since he had sent her out to work for wages. The fact that she was probably sending home her wages, in lieu of her labour, would have escaped legal notice. The tort of seduction, as originally constructed, held no promise for working-class families.

The barriers to working-class recovery of damages had been recognized increasingly as the nineteenth century wore on. It came to be seen as unjust to extend legal protection to rich men while denying redress to poor men who had to send their children out unprotected to earn their living among strangers. Pressure began to mount for legislative reform. In the wake of the 1837 Rebellion with its class-conscious discourse and demands, the Legislature of Upper Canada moved to correct this deficiency. The Seduction Act of 1837 stepped in to eliminate the requirement for the proof of service entirely. Fathers were thereafter to be entitled to sue "notwithstanding such unmarried female was at the time of her seduction serving or residing with any other person, upon hire or otherwise...."[60]

The legal reform was widely agreed to be a good one. Judge Jonas

Jones of the Upper Canada Queen's Bench would note in 1843 that "the great mischief intended and relieved against by the statute ... was the seduction of unmarried females by their masters." Judge John Wilson of the Court of Common Pleas would stress the class dimension in 1869:

The struggles of the earlier settlers for existence, frequently compelled the younger members of a family to leave home and engage in domestic service.... Nor was it unusual for the younger members of families from the British Isles, both male and female, to precede their parents and settle here, betaking themselves to domestic service till they had bettered their condition and acquired experience of the country.... [T]hey were under their condition a class, where the common law was no remedy for them.[61]

The *Upper Canada Law Journal* would also agree that the extension of the action to the working classes was beneficial. "The daughter may be the chief source of support of a widowed mother or aged father," it stated in 1862; "her ruin while in service may be starvation to her parents." Praising the achievement of Canada in this field, the article noted that law in England and the United States was "powerless to afford redress." Manitoba would pass an almost identical statute in 1892 after a much criticized judicial verdict in 1890 denied the claim of a parent whose daughter was engaged as a domestic servant outside the family home. The North-West Territories followed suit in 1903. Somewhat inexplicably, New Brunswick legislators did not change their legislation, despite the urging of its Supreme Court judges in 1858.[62]

The legislative revisions appear to have produced the desired effect, and the seduction action became very much a working-man's lawsuit. Most of the fathers who launched seduction actions would be from the skilled and unskilled working class. Many were labourers, like Robert Camp, although others listed more skilled occupations such as carpentry, house-framing, and caretaking. Nor did the claims cross class boundaries significantly as far as the defendants were concerned. The seducers represented a relatively prosperous cross-section of the working classes, typically somewhat wealthier than the plaintiffs. Most were listed as farmers or farmers' sons, like Russell Blows. There were some merchants, but others gave their occupations as printers, upholsterers, engine drivers, solderers, market gardeners, cabinet-makers, fishermen, and blacksmiths.[63]

The working-class fathers of seduced women seem to have had little hesitation about seeking redress in a legal forum. The class barriers that might have been expected to deter poor people from pursuing the unfamiliar terrain of civil courts do not seem to have held here. The frequency with which working-class families resorted to seduction litigation indicates that this was an area of the law that they regarded as their own. Lucinda Camp had come home pregnant, vowing to "make Russell Blows smart," and her family's immediate response was to translate her anger and grief into a father's lawsuit. The high degree of success achieved at seduction trials would have fed into the popularity of the action as information spread throughout the working-class community via relatives and neighbours.

Robert Camp's first task was to select a lawyer. He settled upon Henry Carscallen, a local Hamilton lawyer who practised with the firm of Carscallen and Cahill. The Camps may have learned of Carscallen from previously satisfied clients or from the press, which was always full of references to the eloquence of the local bar. Although lawyers' fees were often beyond the means of working-class people, the cost does not seem to have been a barrier to actions for seduction. The bar may have had special fee structures to accommodate the financial needs of the plaintiffs. Carscallen may have offered his services at a nominal rate, hoping to recover his full fees upon a successful outcome at trial. The writ was issued on 29 November 1886.

The case proved to be a difficult one, dividing jurors and requiring an unusual amount of time to resolve. The first trial began on 12 September 1887, before John Douglas Armour. After hearing the evidence and the final addresses of the lawyers, the jury retired to consider their verdict. But by 11 p.m. they still had not reached a decision. The foreman reported that they were split and unable to reach a unanimous verdict. The jurors were interrogated by the judge, but they saw no prospect of agreeing, and were discharged. Some plaintiffs might have stopped at that point, defeated by the extended and uncertain legal process. But Robert Camp had the case set down to be heard again in the Winter Assizes of 1888.[64]

Hugh MacMahon was presiding over the Court of Queen's Bench in Hamilton that session. At 10:30 a.m., on 11 January 1888, the third day of the sitting, *Camp* v *Blows* was called. Lucinda Camp was Carscallen's first witness, but no record survives of her testimony. All too often, it seems, legal records tell the stories of women through the testimony of men. But perhaps it was inevitable that in a seduction action, the father's narrative would outlive the daughter's. Robert Camp informed the court that his daughter had been seduced by Russell Blows in July 1886, and that she had given birth to a male child on 21 April 1887. Robert Camp stated that

Russell Blows and his wife, Elizabeth, had hired Lucinda Camp to assist with the domestic responsibilities around the farm. One night Russell Blows excused himself from his wife's company, ostensibly because he and Elmer Blaasdel (presumably a live-in hired hand) were travelling to Brantford the next day. Russell Blows told his wife that he was planning to sleep with Blaasdel that night, so they could get off to an early start in the morning. Robert Camp continued:

Instead of going to sleep with [Elmer Blaasdel], he goes into my daughter's bedroom and gets in bed with her. She made a rumpus to get out and Mrs. Blows came up and caught them in the bedroom.

Carscallen intervened at that point to ask if Blaasdel had been there and had seen what had transpired. Camp answered: "He worked there. He was in the house. He heard the racket." Elmer Blaasdel would have made a first-rate witness for the Camps, but the records show that he was not called. Perhaps he had left the jurisdiction, or he feared retaliation from his employer, Russell Blows.

Elizabeth Blows had also witnessed the scene, and Robert Camp testified that it had prompted "a terrible racket" between husband and wife the next morning. Elizabeth Blows had threatened to leave her husband and to tell Lucinda Camp's mother what had occurred. Russell Blows had retorted that if she did, she would just be making "a fool of herself." The couple may have resolved their differences, or perhaps Elizabeth Blows felt obliged to support her husband in the face of a civil lawsuit, for she would later deny all of Camp's testimony, firmly backing her husband in his defence at trial.

The evidence up to this point was unclear about whether Russell Blows had had intercourse with Lucinda Camp. Carscallen's questioning of Robert Camp would soon dispel all uncertainties on this point. This exchange followed, with Camp leading off:

Some days after, I can't say how long, [Lucinda] went to the barn to feed the pigs. They were in the barn in a little pen and it was about 3:00 in the afternoon. She expected Russell was out at the plowing. When she went to the barn he was in there and he closed the door. She had a pair of new drawers on that were torn off her back.
Q. Did they do anything there?
A. That was the time it was done. When [Russell] got through he said, "I suppose you will tell your Pa and Ma." She said yes she would. He said he would

deny it. That is all I know about it. She says the child belongs to Russell Blows and nobody else.

Q. Did your daughter tell you those were the only two occasions he had to do with her?

A. Those were the only occasions she told me about.

Q. And she didn't leave there until some days after that.

A. She left a few days after it was in the barn, 2 or 3 days.

The vulnerability of a young girl sexually pursued by her employer would have been obvious. Lucinda Camp had been accosted at night and in the middle of the day, in her own bedroom and out in the barn, in front of potential witnesses and alone without anyone who could come to her aid. The level of physical violence that attended the assault would have added to her apprehension and terror. But the reporter who wrote up the case for the Toronto *Daily Mail* did not mention this and described Lucinda Camp as "a rather weak-minded girl."[65]

It was not uncommon for seduction cases to involve extensive physical violence, tantamount to rape. Generally the courts paid scant attention to evidence of sexual assault in seduction actions. Rape did not increase the damages awarded, regardless of the physical suffering entailed. It was just one more illustration of the law's indifference to the circumstances surrounding the seduction. At issue was a father's loss, an injury he would have suffered whether his daughter had been raped or whether she had freely consented to the sexual relationship.[66]

One judge strayed a bit from the accepted practice of ignoring evidence of assault. James Vernall Teetzel of the Ontario Court of Common Pleas penned an unusual decision just after the turn of the century. In 1905, rather than using the information to raise the amount of damages awarded, Teetzel used it to dismiss an action for seduction. He was at pains to distinguish seduction and rape. He wrote: "In order to constitute seduction, the defendant must use insinuating arts to overcome the opposition of the seduced, and must by wiles and persuasions without force, debauch her." Emphasizing that "the action of seduction [was] predicated upon the consent of the party seduced," he concluded that "any damages resulting to her from acts which would amount to rape, although pregnancy might follow, would be personal to her and would not accrue to her father."[67]

This was a departure from earlier jurisprudence, which had never attempted to define seduction itself. The courts had viewed the methods — whether physical coercion, emotional pressure, deception, or trickery

— by which the seducer accomplished his goal as irrelevant. It was also an unnecessary new distinction, since the core of the seduction action was a father's loss of services and family honour, losses that would have been sustained whether intercourse was accomplished through artifice or force. Not surprisingly, the ruling was rapidly overturned for this reason in Divisional Court.[68]

What is interesting about the ruling is that a much younger Teetzel had served as defence counsel to Russell Blows. He may have found the 1888 case intriguing. Although he did not argue to bar Camp's action because of the evidence of sexual assault, this lawsuit may have set him to thinking about new strategies for protecting male seducers. Instead, representing the firm of Osler, Teetzel, Harrison & Osler, the thirty-five-year-old Teetzel would take a more conventional approach to the evidence. Considered a "phenomenal verdict-getter," Teetzel set out to sway the jury against the Camps. His first focus would be on Lucinda Camp's reputation, and he intimated that it was much tarnished as he cross-examined Robert Camp. The range of his attack is apparent from this exchange:

Q. Do you remember after [Lucinda] came back from Blows', she was taking some medicine?
A. No.
Q. Didn't you give her some medicine?
A. No, I never did.
Q. Were you not present in the house one time a few weeks after she came home from Blows', when she was being punished by you or your wife?
A. No sir, not in my presence.
Q. Did you ever hear of her being given some lye and salts?
A. No sir.
Q. Did she ever have a baby before?
A. No sir.
Q. Had a miscarriage?
A. No sir, she never did.
Q. Never had any conversation in your place about having intercourse with other young men?
A. No sir.[69]

The references to medicine, lye, and salts were meant to insinuate that Lucinda Camp and her father had resorted to an old folk remedy in an attempt to terminate the unwanted pregnancy. Queries about previous pregnancies, miscarriages, and sexual liaisons were meant to sully Lucinda Camp's reputation, lowering her in the eyes of the court and reducing her father's claim to damages. The question about parental chastisement would have raised some important questions about the Camps' response to Lucinda Camp's situation. Teetzel would have wanted the jury to infer that Lucinda Camp's parents disbelieved her version of the events and felt she was to blame. Far more interesting, however, is the implication that even families that rallied to the legal defence of unwed daughters could have directed some of their rage at the women. Lucinda Camp might have been permitted to remain in her home, but her lot may have been less than comfortable.

Teetzel's main line of defence would be Russell Blows's denial of the entire story. Russell Blows was a young man of twenty-three, who had been married for two years. He told the court that he had known Lucinda Camp for six or seven years because they lived near one another. Blows admitted that he had hired Lucinda Camp during July and August in 1886, but denied that sexual intercourse had taken place. He professed to be dumbfounded by the legal action against him, and speculated that Lucinda Camp was trying to cover up another liaison.

He testified that the first time he heard of Lucinda Camp's pregnancy was when she came to the house to tell him and his wife that "she was 'in a family way' and that a man named Sam Woods was the father." Teetzel probed further:

Q. How did you come to ask her if she was with Sam Woods?
A. I didn't come to ask her, she told herself.
Q. Just volunteered the statement that she was with Sam Woods and was in the family way?
A. Yes.

Although much was made of this Sam Woods, he was never called as a witness or produced for cross-examination.

The dredging up of an alternate candidate to blame was a commonplace strategy among defence lawyers. The same tack had been taken in the *Hogle* case. It fit well with prevailing beliefs about women and their propensity to falsify sexual claims. The editors of the *Upper Canada Law Journal* articulated the conventional wisdom in an 1862 column. In most cases, they surmised, the seduced woman was merely trying to salvage what she could out of a difficult situation:

When a woman is deprived of her virtue her moral character is generally shaken. Perhaps, she has nothing left but to make as good a speculation on her altered circumstances as will admit. Her real seducer it may be is a young man of buoyant expectations but no substance. Her speculation is much more likely to pay if she can only get a jury to believe that a man of property, who perhaps innocently was once or twice in her company about the time of her seduction, is her seducer. If a married man, so much the better — he is the more likely to pay handsomely in order to prevent the exposure of a trial, however innocent he may be of the charge. [...] The temptation is great, and we fear that some women are bad enough to give way to that temptation. When chastity goes truth frequently follows. When marriage is out of the question, a good round sum of money is not to be despised.[70]

Whether the views of these legal editors reflected the wider views of the larger legal community is another question. But no one wrote back to dispute the comments.

Although Carscallen would have little opportunity to attack the defendant's insinuations about Woods, he did have an opportunity to cross-examine Russell Blows, and he made a skillful job of it, as this extract shows:

Q. Did you ever have your hand inside [Lucinda's] dress on her bosom?
A. No.
Q. But you had on the outside?
A. Once in 20 years.
Q. How often had you your arm around her?
A. Maybe a couple of times while she was there.
Q. And why should you be putting your arm around your servant girl in the house?
A. Because in walking around she would catch me when I was sitting down. She would scuffle.
Q. Do you think it is correct for a married man to scuffle with a hired girl?
A. I don't know that it makes much difference.
Q. How long was it you had connection with her in the barn?
A. I didn't have connection with her in the barn.
Q. Never had sexual intercourse with her any place?
A. No.
Q. Funny how she got a baby and it looks just like you. She is accusing you wrongly is she?
A. Yes.

Under Carscallen's barrage, Russell Blows had conceded "scuffling" with Lucinda Camp. His irreverent attitude toward extramarital, sexual by-play was now openly displayed before the jury.

Both lawyers seem to have dug in their heels. Each piled witness upon witness in an attempt to shore up his client's version of the case. Although no details of the testimony survive, the Camps called six more people to the stand. The Blows called eleven witnesses in addition to Russell and Elizabeth Blows. Presumably most of these were neighbours and friends who testified to the character of the plaintiff, his daughter, and the defendant. The extent of the evidence was such that the trial was forced to continue into another day. This was most unusual, since judges in this era usually dispensed with many trials in one day.

The jury charged to decide the case was composed of twelve men. Typical jurors for the time would have been white, reasonably affluent property-holding males from the region. Women were barred from jury service, and although there were some signs that they were organizing to demand the right to vote by this period, there is no record of women claiming the right to sit on juries. The *Camp* jury brought in their verdict at 8:10 p.m., two hours after they had retired. Following the usual jury pattern in seduction cases, J.W. Jardine of Saltfleet, the foreman, announced they had found for the plaintiff. Blows's testimony had done him in. But the jury had not been prepared to award Robert Camp the full amount he had claimed. In their estimation, the injury he had suffered was worth only five hundred dollars in damages. The bulk of the award may have been for the "moral" injury rather than loss of services, since the market value of Lucinda Camp's services had only been seventy-five cents per week.[71]

This was a bit below average for seduction awards at this time, and may have represented the jurors' views that Lucinda Camp's sexual reputation was questionable. Nevertheless, five hundred dollars represented a considerable sum, especially to a labourer's family. Russell Blows was also required to pay the Camps' legal costs, a customary order that would have assisted in placing such litigation within reach of the working class. The costs of this action, with its double trial, were particularly high, amounting to $290.11, according to the bills submitted by Carscallen.[72]

One sad feature of this otherwise relatively successful verdict is Lucinda Camp's exclusion from the case. Her rape and subsequent pregnancy formed the basis for the action. But the lawsuit was designed to ensure that it was purely a contest between two men. When it came down to the trial, the evidence of Lucinda Camp's suffering was only a footnote in an otherwise lengthy discourse between men. The inquiry was whether Russell Blows had infringed upon a property interest belonging to Robert Camp.

## THE CRIMINALIZATION OF SEDUCTION

Trials such as *Camp* v *Blows* reflected the changing world of the white working-class family. Robert Camp was caught between two eras: the traditional, firmly hierarchical society in which a father had held patriarchal authority over inferior family members, and the modernizing society in which young persons would leave to seek independent, waged labour outside the family unit. Lucinda Camp may have held a paid job, but her work kept her in close proximity to her family. When she needed help, she could return to the patriarchal home. Increasingly, working-class women found themselves drawn further away, geographically and culturally, from their family units.

As large numbers of women moved from the countryside to take employment in urban areas, the working-class family was subjected to increasing strain. Fathers, the traditional patriarchs, were losing their hold on their daughters as many working-class families became dislocated physically and socially. New sources of leisure were transforming heterosexual courting patterns. By the last quarter of the nineteenth century, couples had moved from sleigh rides and dances within the formal oversight of family and community to the amusement parks, nickelodeons, and smoke-filled dance halls of the city.[73]

Fathers had retained the right to sue their daughters' seducers, but distance began to intervene. If Lucinda Camp had been working far away in a city such as Ottawa or Winnipeg, her father might not have been able to launch a seduction action so easily. Increasingly, seduced women found themselves propelled into the new cities, alone and unprotected, without access to paternal backing. For the growing numbers of female immigrants from England, Ireland, Germany, Austria, Russia, and Scandinavia, these problems would be even more magnified. Reformers hastily began to create protective mechanisms such as employment agencies, protective unions, travellers' aid stations, and working girls' leisure clubs. And they came to reflect increasingly on the deficiencies in the law of seduction.[74]

An obvious avenue for legal reform would have been to have recognized the growing independence (and isolation) of working-class women by granting them the autonomous right to sue for seduction in their own names. Reformers could have pointed to the Prince Edward Island experiment of mid-century as precedent. Yet this path would not be followed for the duration of the century. Instead of granting the female victim access to the seduction complaint, social reformers went in the opposite direction. They would attempt to transpose the problem of seduction from the family to society as a whole. Their goal was to make seduction a crime. They wanted to add the force of national criminal law to the more private, civil action.

John Charlton surfaced as the most vociferous proponent of the campaign for criminalization. A New Yorker who had moved to Canada at the age of twenty, Charlton was a lumber merchant who became a politician. In 1872 he was first elected to Parliament as the Liberal member for Norfolk North. He held the seat continuously until 1904. Although issues such as tariffs and commercial union with the United States would occupy a great deal of his time, his major passion was the need to protect women and children from sexual exploitation. A religious man of Presbyterian background, Charlton described himself as "driven to take up this question ... by the strongest sense of public duty."[75]

In 1882 he introduced a bill into the federal House of Commons to a storm of controversy. In it he proposed to bring the force of the criminal law against teachers who seduced their female pupils. He also proposed to criminalize the acts of men who seduced women by the promise of marriage. Moving to the temper of the times, Charlton would argue that seduction was a social, not a purely familial, problem: "The degradation of women is a crime against society. Vice in the shape of social immorality is the greatest danger that can threaten the State."[76]

Given the exclusion of women from direct participation in politics, it is not surprising that a man would be the chief proselytizer of legislative reform. Charlton purported to speak for "thousands of ladies" on whose behalf he presented petitions urging swift passage of the bill, but that would be the last reference in the legislature to the feminine voice. Women could not vote nor sit as elected representatives in Parliament. And the legal treatment of seduction had historically been very male-centred. Charlton pitched his pleas in the House of Commons to men as the fathers and brothers of potential victims of seduction:

I am unable to understand how a father, whose daughter is the pride of his life, the hope of his family, beautiful and beloved — how a brother whose sister fills the horizon of his hope, who is all that is lovely in womanhood — I say, Mr. Speaker, I cannot understand how either that father or that brother can vote against this Bill....

John Charlton and his wife, Ella Gray Charlton.

The prospect of criminalization would send a clarion message of legal censure to would-be seducers and protect young women whose families would not or could not provide support.[77]

The bulk of the male commentators would condemn the bill. Goldwin Smith, a prominent Canadian writer and social critic known for his antipathy to women's rights, was one of the first to attack. He decried the move toward criminalization. Seduction was not "a crime in the legal sense," insisted Smith, "much less is it a crime in one party alone." For Smith, the main problem lay in exonerating seduced women as "guiltless victims," "creature[s] devoid of sense and will." Focusing on the hoary old theme of women's propensity for maliciousness in matters of sexuality, Smith complained: "Any woman who can entrap a foolish youth will be able to compel him to marry her on pain of being put into the dock." Within the legislature, the attack would be no less severe. The Prime Minister, Sir John A. Macdonald, proffered the absurd proposition that "if [the bill] should pass, we will drive a great many young men out of this country." Charlton rejoined: "If we are to lose the vigorous, healthy, active young men of this country because they commit crimes of this kind, I say let them go."[78]

The Conservative Minister of Justice, Sir Alexander Campbell, opposed any extension of legal remedies for seduction. Despite his long years at the bar, he told the House of Commons he could not remember a case of seduction "which commanded the sympathy which an honest man would naturally feel for a betrayed girl." In contrast, he insisted, "these are cases of mutual and equal guilt, or cases where strong passion has carried away one or the other, or both of the parties." Bolstering his opinion, Campbell cited several letters from "two of the most eminent judges in Canada," neither of whom he identified, calling for the defeat of the bill. These apparently unsolicited judicial perspectives characterized the proposal as "a burlesque on discriminating justice." Wrote one:

I can hardly conceive any more dangerous step that could be taken in the present complicated state of society than to bring such matters within the scope of criminal legislation.... As an old Judge, alas, of many years' experience in trying civil and criminal cases, I look with undisguised alarm at the probable effects of such legislation on the world as it now is around us; but to my mind the greatest objection to the proposal (as I understand it), it is only a crime for punishment in the man and not in the woman....

Women should be made to understand that they must guard their own honour and chastity. As the law now is, they are too frequently the seducers and tempters, and then obtain, or their parents for them, damages. Give them the additional terrors of a criminal prosecution and the effect on public morals will be indeed edifying.[79]

The judicial hostility toward seduction actions expressed in this passage is a faithful echo of the voice of William Henry Draper. And the views of the judges apparently had great force. According to the *Canada Law Journal* "some of our judges ... have, by their remarks in Court, helped to lead astray public thought on this matter."[80]

Senator Alexander W. Ogilvie of Quebec argued that the bill would lift responsibility from women, where it properly belonged. "I do not think we can legislate people into virtue and morality. [T]his Bill is an insult to the morality of the sex in Canada. A virtuous woman as a rule can protect her own honour." Ogilvie wished to fix women with the responsibility for heterosexual sexual relations. His views were emphasized by his use of the phrase "the sex" to characterize the female populace, as if only one sex bore the burden of sexuality.[81]

Senator Thomas R. McInnes of British Columbia was worried about the potential for extortion. Providing a vivid hypothetical example for his fellow senators, he cautioned:

Take for instance a young man of fifteen or sixteen who is sole heir to a large property, and a designing girl of nineteen or twenty seduces him and then takes an action against him for seduction.... [T]he boy would have no alternative but to leave the country or be imprisoned in the penitentiary, or what is worse, to condone the offence by marrying her.

He added: "I have a couple of sons ... and we do not want to see them marry characters of that kind and bring them to our homes to be treated as we should treat daughters-in-law and members of our families."[82]

Charlton seems to have been surprised at the level of animosity expressed toward his proposal. He confessed in the House of Commons that he had been "subjected to many gibes and some abuse." The personalization of the abuse bothered him deeply. "I have been characterized as the apostle of cant," he complained; "I have been accused of legislating for the purpose of creating brazen females." Charlton did not retreat, however, and various Protestant religious groups rallied behind him, supporting the act as part of a wider and growing campaign to eradicate prostitution and the sexual exploitation of young women and children. It would take

four years and many successive drafts before the federal Parliament finally created the crime of seduction in 1886. The legislation as finally passed
was significantly less comprehensive than originally intended.[83]

The "Charlton Seduction Act" made it a crime to seduce and have
"illicit connection" with any girl between the ages of twelve and sixteen
of "previously chaste character." Unmarried women under the age of
eighteen were also covered if they were of previously chaste character and
the seduction took place "under promise of marriage." The age ceilings
were a compromise and had been considerably higher in earlier drafts of
the bill. The maximum penalty for these offences was two years. The
legislators dealt with their fear of false complaints by insisting that in
every case there must be corroborating evidence, something in addition to
the woman's own word. L.H. Davies, member of Parliament for Queen's,
Prince Edward Island, had objected to this last provision. Describing it as
a "monstrous" attempt to "nullify the Bill," he had argued: "We know
that practically, it would be impossible to get this corroborating evidence
in ninety-nine cases out of a hundred." Undeterred, his colleagues included the safeguard.[84]

The forces seeking reform were not satisfied, for they lobbied to increase the age limitations to twenty-one. The opposition to this was
remarkably intense. According to *The Legal News*:

Women under 21 are often more mature than those of the opposite sex whom
they allure.... A woman of 20 may figure as the prosecutor of a verdant youth of
17 or 18.

There was a case of rape a few days ago before our Courts, in which the
complainant was a girl of only 13. Yet it appeared on cross-examination that she
was a consenting party to the connection; the prosecution was an afterthought;
and the medical evidence indicated that she had lost her virginity at a period
long antecedent to the date of the alleged crime.

Such girls ripen fast in profligacy, and they would have ample time before
the age of 21 to entrap a victim with the convenient aid of the Seduction Act. It
might possibly be difficult to prove the previous unchastity, yet in reality they are
the women "whose lips drop as a honeycomb and whose mouth is smoother
than oil."[85]

Despite such remarkable outpourings, in 1887 Parliament raised the age
limit to twenty-one for seduction under promise of marriage, so long as
the seducer himself was over twenty-one.[86]

During the last decade of the nineteenth century, legislation covering the crime of seduction continued to expand. In 1890 the law would reach out to encompass guardians who seduced their wards and employers or supervisors in factories, mills, and workshops who seduced young female employees. And in 1892, the seduction of female ship-passengers by ship-masters, officers, or other seamen would be added. The focus on female wage-earners and immigrants voyaging to Canada revealed deep concerns about the potential for sexual exploitation among those groups. But even these amendments did not pass without misogynist repartee inside the halls of the legislature.[87]

The reformers never budged from their opinion that these measures did not go far enough. The decade of the 1890s would see the flowering of the National Council of Women of Canada (NCWC) and of a variety of Local Councils that acted as member chapters to the national affiliate. The Councils were composed largely of middle- and upper-class women who sought to exert influence upon social issues. Their frame of reference was largely that of "maternal feminism," a desire to speak from the perspective of women to protect "homes and nation." Maternal feminism was premised on women's responsibility as guardians of the home. The intent was not to disrupt this role, but to expand upon it by arguing that women possessed special sensitivities and nurturing abilities that could be used to great advantage as a feminizing influence for society generally. The members of the NCWC vociferously criticized the criminal law of seduction in 1896.[88]

Lady Ishbel Marjoribanks Gordon, Countess of Aberdeen, the wife of the Governor-General of Canada and President of the NCWC, wrote to the Minister of Justice in February 1896. On behalf of the Council she protested the presence of the words "of previous chaste character" in the seduction law. She wrote: "We are informed, although I am not in a position to vouch for the exact cases, that under this section, offenders have escaped punishment who have seduced a girl who was known to have been assaulted as a little child, and therefore not held to be of 'previously chaste character.'"

Lady Julia Drummond was also a staunch proponent of the movement to delete all reference to "previous chaste character." The President of the Local Council in Montreal, she spoke at length about the matter at the 1896 meeting:

In the class of life where such offences are most frequent, girls thus defiled are not likely to be able to substantiate a good character nor to disprove the charge of a "bad" one; and, therefore, we may say with truth, that this character clause

A meeting of the National Council of Women of Canada at Rideau Hall, Ottawa;
Lady Aberdeen at centre.

makes almost all the difference, that in fact it qualifies away [any] ostensible
protection afforded by this law....

But our House of Commons looks at it from another standpoint. It says that
this character clause is essential for the protection of the man. [...] No, it is that
having yielded to temptation, having finished her ruin, a ruin to which no law
needs to add its penalty, he may stand before a jury whose sympathies are
invariably with their sex, and plead her guilty, to cover, to condone, to justify his
own.[89]

Drummond's appraisal of the leanings of male juries was quite different
from that commonly expressed among the legal fraternity, where complaints about misplaced juror chivalry were standard.

Mrs. Foster Avery, also in attendance at the 1896 Montreal meeting, agreed that the character clause was insurmountable. Casting aspersions of her own upon male credibility, she noted: "It is simply impossible for a young girl, under such circumstances, to prove previously chaste character, because it is always easy for the kind of men who are liable to be indicted for this offence to get a friend or friends to prove that this girl has been previously unchaste." Pointing out another discrepancy, she queried: "Now why should it be placed upon a woman to prove her previously chaste character when we do not question the man as to his previous character?"[90]

The Honourable A.R. Dickey, the federal Minister of Justice, promptly wrote back to Lady Aberdeen. The status of the key members of the NCWC was enough to cause even the most chauvinist politician to respond with politeness. But Dickey would ignore the substance of the request. He wrote:

It is not thought wise to strike out the words "of previously chaste character." It must not be forgotten that after the age of fourteen a girl might acquire vicious habits, and in that case some such protection as these words provide would seem to be necessary. The case suggested of a character acquired before the age of fourteen is likely to be very rare in practice. It is almost impossible for a lawyer to understand how any Justice could have held that a girl who had been assaulted as a little child had lost her previously chaste character, under this section. Such a decision is so monstrous and so clearly against the meaning of the Statute that one cannot anticipate a repetition of it. Indeed the very occurrence of it seems to be doubtful.[91]

Dickey responded summarily and a touch condescendingly to the other proposal of the NCWC as well, that the employment seduction section be expanded to include women who worked in domestic service:

While theoretically girls in domestic service may stand in need of such protection as this, no case which would need protection has occurred actually so far as the Department of Justice can ascertain. To include girls of that class would moreover be a departure from the principle upon which this Section was founded. It was to meet the new conditions arising in modern life of young girls going out into the world and taking employment under the control of men. The case of domestic service is different in principle. Employment of that kind has been going on during all the ages. The work takes place in the vast majority of cases not under the control of men in any way.[92]

Lady Julia Drummond, President of the Local Council
of Women in Montreal, and her daughter.

Although there would be nothing the members of the Council could do about Dickey's position, they continued to agitate for reform well into the twentieth century. The women also criticized the tone of some of the parliamentary debates, particularly the references to the tendency of women to make false complaints. Lady Drummond was perhaps the most adamant on the point:

Nor can we but believe that the blackmail [sic] which is feared is exposure of actual wrong, for the fact is notorious that false charges of this kind are of very rare occurrence....

It is very necessary to have patience in this cause, a cause which is especially the woman's cause, whilst the laws which relate to it being made by men, and by men alone, must in the very nature of things be partial laws, but it is hard sometimes not to lose patience, and I confess that when the old word "blackmail" is advanced as a reason for robbing the girl of 14 or 15 of adequate protection ... I confess for one that my patience is hardly worthy of the name.[93]

There was one thing on which supporters and opponents alike could agree. John Charlton, the women of the NCWC, and Alexander Campbell would all concede that most victims of seduction would be too ashamed to initiate criminal prosecution. "The girls have a terror of the courts of justice and of being questioned there," stated Mrs. Marion Bryce of the Winnipeg Local Council in 1896. "It is almost impossible to get them induced to prosecute." Testifying in a criminal trial about such intimate sexual matters would have compounded the problems faced by an unwed mother. Her sexual background would have been subject to scrutiny by a defence lawyer eager to unearth evidence of her "previously unchaste character." The circumstances of her fall would have been publicly displayed to a crowded courtroom and through the eyes of the press to the community at large. The notoriety would have been exceedingly unpalatable.[94]

There are few reports of criminal prosecutions under the new act in the remaining years of the nineteenth century. In one of the reported cases, a jury convicted Donald Walker of Medicine Hat, Alberta, of seducing Fanny Ford Small under promise of marriage. Alberta Judge Hugh Richardson overturned the verdict, following the pattern of a judge overruling a jury verdict in civil law. Although the evidence showed that Fanny Ford Small was under twenty-one, of prior chaste character, and that the two had been engaged at the time of the seduction, Richardson would conclude that there had been no proof that the seduction had been accomplished by means of a promise of marriage. The hurdles to be cleared before a conviction could be registered were to prove a serious impediment to further prosecution.[95]

John Charlton had been successful in his quest to criminalize seduction. "My name will be remembered by the Charlton Act," he wrote in his memoirs; "I have been the author of several statutes, but this Act is the only one of great importance." But in the end it was really a hollow victory. There was no incentive for seduced women or their families to seek the intervention of criminal law. Even with a successful outcome, there would be no compensation or vindication. For unlike the traditional seduction action, where at least there had been some modicum of restitution for the injured, the criminal law focused on punishment and deterrence, with the only sanctions being fines and imprisonment. The new battery of criminal provisions may have reflected an emerging awareness of the social ramifications of seduction, but the reforms held little of substance for seduced women.[96]

# 3

# Rape

"Shocking Brutality" and "Horrible Outrage on a Woman" claimed the Toronto newspaper headlines of a gang rape that had taken place on Monday evening, 13 December 1858. Calling the event an "atrocity" unprecedented in the city's history, reporters insisted the events would have been more expected in the sinful city of New York. It was, wrote the Toronto *Leader*, "a state of things as existing in our midst which could not be surpassed by the most barbarous people in the world."[1]

Ellen Rogers and Mary Hunt were the rape victims whose home had been violently broken into by a gang of fifteen drunken young men. Each woman had been physically assaulted and raped by four or five of the youths. The young men had then burglarized the house, making off with cash and jewellery. What would have made the case even more salacious was that the two women were said to have been living in a "house of bad repute," and were described as "not of very good character."[2]

Ellen Rogers was a married woman whose husband had left her almost a year earlier. In his absence she kept company with George Irwin, a professional gambler. He would often spend the night at her Sayer Street home, but on the evening in question he was working late and had not yet arrived. Ellen Rogers's Sayer Street residence was located in a working-class neighbourhood between Agnes Street and Osgoode Street, just around the corner from Osgoode Hall. She also owned a house on

Edward Street, west of Yonge. Both houses appear to have been used as brothels. Although her birthplace is not known, Ellen Rogers is reported to have been a francophone who spoke English poorly.[3]

Mary Hunt was boarding at Ellen Rogers's Sayer Street residence, where she had been staying since her release from a one-month stint in jail some weeks earlier. She was a prostitute who had been arrested after she "had some words with a girl on the streets." It is not clear whether Mary Hunt was working as a prostitute for Ellen Rogers, but she was known to have been doing "housework and sewing" in exchange for her room and board. She too had a male companion, John McCallum, who would visit her at the Sayer Street house most evenings. He was present on the night of the rapes, but he was unsuccessful in his attempts to stop the youths.[4]

Both women put up a fight against their assailants, exhibiting extraordinary courage in the face of such a large number of violent men. Inevitably, they were overpowered. As soon as she could, Ellen Rogers escaped and went immediately in search of a constable. Several police officers arrived on the scene while the men were still milling around the place. The women urged the police to make arrests immediately, but Constable Dunlop sent the young men home and told the women they should get warrants in the morning.[5]

Both Ellen Rogers and Mary Hunt took their complaints to a Toronto magistrate the next morning. At this time, most criminal proceedings were initiated by private citizens, usually by those who had been the victims of a crime. Fledgling police forces would have been unequipped to handle much more than preliminary investigation and arrests. The Toronto constabulary had increased from eight men in 1843 to fifty in 1858, but the professionalization of the police force would take until the 1880s. The laying of charges was a fairly heavy responsibility for private citizens to bear, but it also permitted considerable freedom for individuals to activate the criminal law. Without that autonomy, this case might never have come to court.[6]

Most of the rape charges that came to court in the nineteenth century involved young, unmarried women still living with their fathers, or married women who lived with their husbands. In many cases the parents or the husband seem to have been the instigators of the charge. It was rare to find independent women launching a rape prosecution, and even more unusual where such women were involved in sexually explicit occupations. But Ellen Rogers and Mary Hunt were extraordinary women, as their behaviour during the legal proceedings would demonstrate. They had an unrelenting belief in their own right to privacy and bodily integrity, and they were willing to insist on the full activation of the law.[7]

This is the information that Ellen Rogers laid before the magistrate, as published in full by the Toronto *Leader*:

I live on Sayer Street, between Osgoode and Agnes Streets. On the night of Monday last ... about midnight, there being then no other person in the house except Mary Hunt, as I was sitting up at work, though in my night-clothes, a crowd of young men came to the door and demanded admittance, which I refused, and then they threatened to burst open the door, if I did not open it.

I told them I had no girls there and was sick myself, and could not allow them in. They then burst open the front door, and a number rushed in. I ran upstairs to get out of their way, and at my bedroom door I saw a number of them (twelve as I counted them) who rushed upstairs after me.

Mary Hunt was at this time locked in her own room, and I cried out to her for assistance. She jumped out of bed and opened the door, but on seeing so many rioters she became frightened and ran back to her own room.

One of them, named Robert Gregg ... here caught hold of me, and wanted me to go into another room. I refused and he then pulled me onto his knees, on a chair, at the foot of the bed, upon which four or five other rioters had got and were holding down Mary Hunt. Gregg and another then dragged me from that room into another, while a third person locked the door on the inside.

Gregg then ordered me to strip **** [the newspaper interjected here that this portion was "unfit for publication"]. I refused and he then threw me down on the bed, ****. He then stripped himself and began his violence. I screamed when he called out to the other man, "strike her," "choke her, the d--d French ---," and he held me by the throat, **** he succeeded in forcibly violating my person.

Then Gregg held me by the neck while the other fellow effected the same object. After this the man who had the door locked, and who stood on the outside, got into the room and forced me in the same way, and then another man did the same, making in all four men who violated my person. While this was going on in my room, I heard the scream of Mary Hunt from another room, crying out, "They are murdering me!," "Ellen, come help me!" etc. etc.

The moment I was released from the violence of these men I ran out, almost naked, to the Avenue Saloon, where I put on a petticoat. On my return I found that they had broken in my cupboard and stolen nearly four dollars in money therefrom and did other damage.

The name of the person who held me **** while Gregg committed the first violation of my person is — Hughes, and the other three persons whom I now see in custody, viz., William Ross, Alexander Doig and John Hellam, were among the rioters who broke into my house and assaulted Mary Hunt and myself that night.[8]

Mary Hunt's information was similar, although she would note that John McCallum had been present and had tried unsuccessfully to come to her aid:

I lately boarded in the house of Ellen Rogers, on Sayer Street. About mid-night on Monday last, just as I and Ellen Rogers had retired to our respective bed rooms, we heard knocks and kicks at the front door. Ellen Rogers went down stairs, and I heard her ask who was there, and if it was George. George was the person who lives with her. To this a reply came from the outside, "No, it is a friend." She asked "What do you want?" and the reply was, "We want to get in."

She told them they could not come in, as there was no one they could see. I called to her not to let them in. She opened the back-door to afford her a chance of escaping. I "hollered" from up stairs, upon which a young man named John McCallum came in from a neighbouring house and entered my room, the door of which I locked.

The party outside burst the door open and rushed up stairs. Mrs. Rogers called out to me to open my door, and I did so and let her in, when five or six men entered the room and threw themselves across me on the bed, and afterward dragged me into another room.

Gregg laid hold of Ellen Rogers, and asked her to go out into the hall with him. She refused, and then he and another man named Hughes, (not yet in custody) dragged Ellen Rogers into another room.

Those who stayed in the room were trying to throw me on the bed, when John McCallum tried to protect me. Ross knocked him down, and he and the others kicked him and beat him. Ross then ordered me to go down stairs and get him a drink of water. After some objections I went down stairs, and as soon as I got down, Ross dragged me into the sitting-room, put out the candles, fastened the door, and tried to violate my person.

I resisted when he drew a knife from his right-hand vest pocket, and threatened to "stick" me if I did not submit. I called out to Mrs. Rogers, "He is going to stick me." Ross succeeded in forcing me, and when he had done so, he went out, and another of the party came in, he also violated my person.

Three others came in afterwards, and did the same thing. The last one who did so was Hellam. When this was done, Ross came again into the room, and forcibly took the rings from my fingers, and also the rings from my ears.

Gregg was the leading person in the party. He dragged Rogers away with him when he left the room. Mrs. Rogers escaped from the house after the violence. After she was gone the rioters searched all over the house. I saw one of them take some money, about four dollars, from the cupboard. The man who did so is not in custody.[9]

Four of the men, Robert Gregg, William Ross, Alexander Doig, and John Thomas Hellam, were arrested and taken into custody. George Hughes, the only other young man identified, had escaped and was never brought to trial. On Friday, 17 December, the hearing began in front of Toronto's police magistrate, George Gurnett. Gurnett was a lay magistrate with no formal legal training. An active city politician, he had variously served as alderman, mayor, and district clerk of the peace before he was appointed Toronto's first police magistrate in 1850. He may not have been unfamiliar with prostitutes, since he had been defeated in his mayoralty candidacy of 1841 by rumours that he was renting a house to a brothel keeper.[10]

The notoriety the case received in the press had piqued the curiosity of the public, bringing crowds of people down to the courtroom to watch the proceedings. By Saturday, the Toronto *Leader* would describe the scene:

The court was crowded to excess. So thick did they pour in, that before long, notwithstanding the great coldness of the day, the windows had to be opened, in order to afford some purification of the thick atmosphere within. Head over head might be seen on the far wall of the building, outside the bar, and every available hole and corner found an occupant.

The location of the courtroom, in a room at City Hall overlooking the main fruit and vegetable market, added to the commotion.[11]

Mary Hunt was sworn in, and she related the events that had led to the charges. James Boulton, the defence lawyer for Gregg, Ross, and Hellam, would be determined to undermine Mary Hunt's credibility. First he tried unsuccessfully to contest her identification of the four men charged:

Q. How many came into the room after Ross went out?
A. Four others.
Q. Did they all come in together or one at a time?
A. One at a time.
Q. If there was no candle lighted how would you know the parties?
A. There was a coal fire in the stove, and I could perceive their faces.[12]

"Scene in Police Court" from
*Canadian Illustrated News* (Montreal), 28 August 1875.

Mary Hunt's quick response to defence lawyer Boulton's challenge would have chagrined him. Things had generally not been going well for him. Several days earlier he had been defending a man charged with murder at a coroner's inquest. Dr. Norman Bethune, one of the medical witnesses, had accused Boulton of napping through the trial and of "conducting the investigation very indifferently on behalf of his client." The press had covered the exchange fully, and Boulton's client had been found guilty and jailed to await trial. Boulton would have been eager to redeem himself. This cross-examination offered a golden opportunity. The courtroom audience was boisterous, and Boulton played to the crowd's perverse sense of humour. Focusing on Mary Hunt's reputation as a prostitute, Boulton began:

*Q.* Are you a very quiet person generally?
*A.* I am sometimes not very quiet. (Laughter)

Q. Were you drunk on this occasion?

A. I was not.

Q. How many years have you been engaged in your present line of business?

A. I don't think I am bound to tell that. [After some discussion and delay, Mary Hunt eventually admitted to two years.]

Q. Two years since you went astray?

A. Yes, two years since I went astray.[13]

Boulton and Mary Hunt then entered into a discussion about John McCallum's role that evening. Despite the fact that she had already admitted to "sexual impropriety," Mary Hunt seems to have been determined to cling to her statement that McCallum had been an innocent passer-by who just happened to come to her rescue.

Q. Was McCallum in the room before Ross came into the house?

A. He was not.

Q. Was it necessary that McCallum should have his coat off, and his pants and his shoes, to defend you?

A. He had only his coat off.

Q. What did he take off his coat for?

A. He took it off, and placed his back to the door.[14]

These last exchanges had no bearing on whether the rape had occurred. James Boulton was attempting to emphasize Mary Hunt's reputation for sexual promiscuity. Her character would be what was at stake, not the deeds of the men charged with rape. Nineteenth-century judges and juries seem to have been almost pathologically driven in their quest to assess the reputation of raped women. Women who were known to drink alcoholic beverages, frequent taverns, or indulge in extramarital sex were virtually guaranteed legal rebuff when they complained of violent rape. In the language of the courts, they lacked credibility. The legal system would restrict the protection of rape law to virtuous women who lived their lives in modesty and above reproach.[15]

There was a second defence lawyer present in the courtroom that day. S.B. Campbell was representing Doig. His turn at Mary Hunt came next:

Q. What resistance did you make?

A. (hesitating) — When I made an effort to scream, Ross put his hand on my mouth. When he took his hand off my mouth, I did not scream; I hollered to Mrs. Rogers. The candle was out, but there was a fire in the stove. I opened the stove door, when Ross left me, with my skirt, for the purpose of seeing the faces of the others as they came in.

Q. Oh! I see you have got it to fit. I was wondering where the light came from. Did you expect the others to come in?

A. Doig came in next. He was the worse of liquor. He came in and took hold of me, but I was too strong for him. He went to the door and said to those outside that I was too strong for him, but they said go back and try again. He came into the room and put his hands behind my back and threw me on the floor. He then forced me. I got away from him the first time he came in.

Q. Did you lie still on the floor?[16]

At this point, Mary Hunt seems to have had enough. Instead of answering, she stood up and tried to leave the witness stand. Ordered to return and answer the question, she did so reluctantly, stating, "I tried to get away. I could not open the windows to scream for help, as they were nailed down." But S.B. Campbell would not quit. The cross-examination got nastier and nastier. Mary Hunt made several attempts to leave the stand during the next segment of the cross-examination. This extract is from the press report:

Q. I ask you this. Did you make any resistance with your hands when they were attempting to violate you?

A. I did.

Q. You say you could overcome Doig when he came the first time into the room, how was it that you were unable to do so a second time?

[The witness did not reply to the question.]

Q. Have you ever tried to settle this matter for a sum of money?

A. I never have.

Mr. Campbell: I have sufficient testimony of a respectable character to prove that you did; evidence that cannot be gainsayed.

[At this time the witness appeared to be very reluctant to answer any further questions.]

Q. Is Irwin known as your "fancy" man?

A. (with great pertness and levity) — No Sirree!

[A loud laugh from the audience following this remark, His Worship said he would have the enquiry conducted in future with closed doors, as there had been most unseemly conduct during the investigation. He considered the case was one of a very grave character, and ought not to be treated with levity.]

Q. I ask you how you know there were from ten to fifteen persons in the room?

A. I will not answer the question, I have told you before.

[She here left the stand, but was again put back by Sergeant Hastings. She then exclaimed "I will not answer you any more questions."]

Q. You will have to be committed to jail then. Did McCallum come in during or after the knocking commenced at the door?

A. He came in during the knocking.

Q. Is there a yard at the back of the house?

A. Go up there and see. (Laughter) I have been here long enough. (Laughter)

Q. Did McCallum tell you that there were "rowdies" at the door, when he came into your room?

A. I will not tell you. (Laughter) I won't answer any more questions to any one. I am not going to stand here all day answering questions. (Laughter)[17]

Mary Hunt's resistance on the stand mirrored her courageous fight to stop the rapists on the night in question. That she was able to muster such strength in front of a jeering, insolent crowd is truly a tribute to her character.

Ellen Rogers would be subjected to similar treatment. At one point, she objected to James Boulton's cross-examination. According to the Toronto *Daily Globe*, she replied in a "loud pert tone":

I am neither English nor Irish, and do not know the language. If you wish me to answer your questions, I will do so in French. (Laughter) It is hard to be bothered in this manner after being used so bad.

Q. Oh! You can speak English well enough when you like. How long have you known any of the prisoners at the bar?

A. Six or seven months.

Q. Were these men in the habit of visiting at the house?

A. All the prisoners, with the exception of Doig, had visited me at my other house. I never saw Doig before that night. On the occasions I refer to, they conducted themselves in a disorderly manner.[18]

Boulton stopped her here, before she could give the details of the disorderly behaviour of his clients on former occasions. Later, information would surface that crowds of young men had terrorized Ellen Rogers at her other house, forcibly breaking their way in as many as twelve or thirteen times, and as often as twice a week. Climbing in through windows or breaking through door panels, they would detain the women "till all hours," often making off with money and goods. None of them had ever physically attacked Ellen Rogers before, but their growing sense of bravado and immunity had finally escalated to rape. The marauding male gangs were out of control.[19]

John McCallum was called to the stand next. Initially he would maintain that he had come up to Mary Hunt's room only in answer to her screams for help. "I stripped off my coat, waistcoat and hat in order to make them believe that I was looking for the place," he offered rather lamely. Yet when faced with an increasingly derisive courtroom audience, McCallum would stand steadfast in his defence of the two women:

I placed my back against the door, but when they pushed against it too strongly, I was forced to let it open. The room at once crowded up, and I thought there would never be an end to them. (Laughter) Says I to myself "my end is come at last." (Laughter)

The men then tumbled into the bed where Mary Hunt was lying and began to treat her roughly. I tried to protect her and I got a kick in the shoulder, which no one would like to get. (Laughter) It was Ross that kicked me.

The girl then got out of bed, and the fellows took her down stairs against her will, after which I heard her screams in the sitting room. That is all I know about Mary Hunt. Ellen Rogers was dragged into another room. Gregg was the principal party who did this. She resisted in going into the room, but they dragged her in spite of all she could do. Three or four of the parties remained in the room with me, but I do not know who they were.

When I came down I saw Mary Hunt lying on the sofa pale and apparently exhausted. All the fellows ran away when they saw the policeman coming.[20]

S.B. Campbell then tried to take McCallum apart in cross-examination:

Q. Was it starlight?
A. I didn't look up. (Laughter)
Q. Was it raining?
A. I believe it was, now that you have reminded me of it.
Q. Was there anything peculiar about that night?
A. Didn't see anything new about it. (Laughter)
Q. Were you wet or dry that night?
A. That's a question. (Laughter)
Q. Were you drunk or not?
A. That's my business.
Q. Were you drunk or sober?
A. I was as sober as I am this minute. When up stairs I had my boots off. I had

two shirts on last Monday night, one red and one white. The white one outside the red.

Q. How did you take that white shirt off?

A. (Hesitatingly) I was so put about that I didn't know what I was doing. That's all I'm going to tell you now — look out. (Laughter)

Q. Did you take your neck-tie off?

A. Well, I did.

Q. That's good, so far. Did you take the white shirt off?

A. I did not.

Q. Were your trousers off?

A. No.[21]

After this exchange, S.B. Campbell would go through a long series of questions about what had happened after the two women were removed from the room. To the continuing punctuation of laughter from the audience, John McCallum began to get completely mixed up. He would testify at one point that he had been left alone in the room, and later that four or five of the men had stayed in the room with him. Campbell exclaimed that the great discrepancies in the evidence of the witness left it without a shred of credibility.[22]

Finally Constable Dunlop was called to testify. He stated that when he arrived at the house, fifteen or sixteen men were coming out. Upon entering, he had seen Mary Hunt sitting on the sofa. Constable Dunlop was highly sceptical of her story:

Mary Hunt appeared when I first saw her, as if she had just got out of bed. She had a petticoat on. She had not the appearance of having been recently ill-used.

Q. What did she say to you?

A. She only told me she had been "pulled about."

Q. What did the young men do when you told them to go home?

A. They went away. They did not appear as if afraid that I would arrest them. I saw nothing to indicate that there had been any row in the sitting room. I did not look at the door to see if it was broken. If Hunt had told me all about the violence committed, I would have tried to arrest some of the men. I think if the women had screamed for help, they would have been heard in the houses adjoining. Hunt did not appear as if she had been crying.[23]

Mary Hunt's reluctance to confide in the constable would have been influenced, in part, by the strained relations between the police and prostitutes. She had just been released from jail for causing a disturbance. And one wonders how Constable Dunlop would have preferred Mary Hunt to look. John McCallum had described her as "lying on the sofa, pale and exhausted." Perhaps Constable Dunlop wanted something more — torn clothing and visible physical injury. Nineteenth-century courts were very reluctant to convict unless the rape victim had put up a discernible show of resistance.[24]

Despite the testimony of Constable Dunlop, Magistrate George Gurnett seems to have been as impressed with the determination of the women as he was by the insinuations and hair-splitting of the defence counsel. His role was not to deliver a final verdict, but to determine whether there was sufficient evidence to put the matter over for a full-fledged trial at the forthcoming Winter Assizes. Lay magistrates seldom dismissed charges at this stage. Without giving any reasons, Gurnett committed all four of the accused men to trial, setting their bail at fifty pounds each.[25]

Both Ellen Rogers and Mary Hunt had also been confined to jail throughout the hearing. Rumours were rife that friends and relatives of the accused men were attempting to bribe the two women to drop the charges. The press reported that the women were ordered confined to custody to prevent the compromising of justice. That Ellen Rogers and Mary Hunt were associated with prostitution lowered their status to the point that they could be treated in much the same manner as the accused men.[26]

Chief Justice John Beverley Robinson opened the Winter Assizes in Toronto a few weeks later on 12 January 1859. At the opening of the court, it was customary for the judges to make a formal speech in which they would frequently comment, for the general edification of the community, on the cases set to come before them. Robinson spoke at length about the Sayer Street affair:

There are four persons charged with rape and house-breaking. With regard to the rape, if it should turn out that, knowing this house to be disorderly, those persons broke into the house with any intention to gratify their passion by the commission of a crime of that kind, it would be no mitigation of their crime, that in getting in there they found only disreputable females. They cannot be molested thus because of their being such. Otherwise there would be but little chance of their reformation.

The commonest prostitute in the world has the same protection in law as the most virtuous. The guilt of the parties committing the crime would not therefore be lightened in such an event. It would only necessitate a keener inspection of the case by the jury.[27]

At first reading, these opening remarks would appear to be quite promising. Here we have the Chief Justice of the Court of Queen's Bench stating that all women, regardless of their status or reputation, deserve protection from sexual assault. His statement also had some backing in the accepted legal rhetoric of the day. Sir William Blackstone, long considered the foremost text-writer on English common law, had written along these lines in the late eighteenth century. Dealing specifically with the question of whether a prostitute or "common harlot" could be raped, Blackstone stated that it was a felony "to force even a concubine or harlot: because the woman may have forsaken that unlawful course of life."[28]

The catch was the qualification in Blackstone's comment. There was to be a clear separation between reformed prostitutes and unrepentant, abandoned women who would still flout the sexual mores of the community. Blackstone did not mean to suggest that courts should be concerned to protect sexually unconventional women from rape because of their inherent right to be free from criminal assault. Compassion would be extended only insofar as the "harlot" was attempting to rehabilitate herself. Robinson's lecture, which on the face of it seems to offer legal protection to all women, also posed reformation as the rationale.

Prostitutes lived on the margins, never quite encompassed within the circle of legal protection. And there was always that chronic suspicion of their veracity. As Robinson had cautioned, the jury should be instructed to give the testimony of such witnesses "a keener inspection." The law of rape had always required corroboration, evidence beyond the affirmative oath of the woman herself. Medical evidence or testimony from family and friends typically functioned to lend strength to the account of the woman herself. Here there should have been little difficulty. The two women could corroborate each other's evidence, and John McCallum had been practically an eye-witness to the rapes. Yet Robinson's admonition to higher vigilance had sounded an ominous note.[29]

Archibald McLean was assigned to preside over the trial. McLean had been appointed to the bench in 1837, leaving behind a flourishing legal practice in Cornwall and a political career as a Tory member of the assembly. Contemporaries described him as a "commanding presence, tall, straight, and well formed in person, with a pleasant, handsome face." He looked "every inch a man and a gentleman." A member of the Family Compact, McLean was noted for his pro-British leanings. He had a particular fondness for the highly demarcated class structure of British tradition. McLean's interest in preserving class differentiation would shape the way in which he heard the testimony of these two rape victims. As prostitutes, Ellen Rogers and Mary Hunt would have fallen within the lowest gradation that could be assigned to Victorian women.[30]

John Hillyard Cameron, QC, the lawyer appointed to represent the Crown, gave the opening address. Crown attorneys were usually appointed, as a form of political patronage, to prosecute criminal Assize cases on an *ad hoc*, part-time basis. Cameron was a prominent Conservative who had served as an elected politician and as an influential backroom political advisor. A well-educated and gifted criminal lawyer, Cameron was also highly qualified as a prosecutor. But Cameron was famous for his insensitivity to French Canadian interests. Ellen Rogers's language difficulties would surface again at this trial, but Cameron would not insist upon interpreter services.[31]

Cameron's strategy for the prosecution would be to emphasize the "disreputable" backgrounds of the two women himself, hoping to blunt the edge of the defence. He would concede that "the evidence of an abandoned female would be generally received with considerable suspicion." He would then attempt to use this to his advantage, arguing that it provided a practical safeguard against prostitutes complaining except in the very worst situations. "The very fact of the female having been of loose character would, in itself, afford some sort of guarantee that she would not make such a charge without sufficient grounds." It was an interesting gamble that Cameron took. Only time would tell if it would pay off.[32]

The first rape charge tried was the one against Robert Gregg, the ringleader. Passionately, clearly, and courageously, Ellen Rogers and Mary Hunt testified in horrifying detail to the multiple rapes. Unequivocally they corroborated each other's story and identified Robert Gregg, who was sitting in the dock, as the culprit. James Boulton, Gregg's defence counsel, had transferred the case to Henry Eccles, QC, a lawyer who had articled for him some years earlier and then gone on to surpass him in reputation. Eccles was a very imposing character, renowned for his ability to simplify issues to a jury. His strategy would be to play upon the deep-seated fears of nineteenth-century male judges and jurors that rape victims were given to fabricating complaints about rape. Many reasons were conventionally offered for this. Maliciousness and vengeance topped the list, but William Henry Draper had also speculated in 1855 that women caught in the act of extramarital sex might lie to protect themselves. "A detected adulteress might, to save herself, accuse a paramour of a capital felony," he said, adding: "The accusation of rape is one easily made, and even if in some respects hard to be proved, yet still harder to be defended and rebutted by the party accused, however innocent he may be." Eccles's line of attack would be a variation on the theme of fabrication. He would insinuate that the two women were trying to bribe their assailants and that the rape complaint was tied to an elaborate plan of extortion.[33]

Eccles began by asking Ellen Rogers if she had ever sought to claim money from the accused men or from their families. Ellen Rogers denied having asked for or taken any money. But she said that she had twice been asked to do so. In the first instance, she claimed that Mr. and Mrs. Andrew Gregg, Robert's father and mother, had come to her house offering to "settle the matter." Secondly, a man named Constable D. Jones, apparently the brother-in-law of Alexander Doig, had spoken to her and Mary Hunt in the chief's office at the police station. According to Ellen Rogers, "Mr. Jones offered ... to give us money if we would say Doig was not there. He also offered to convey us out of town in his buggy. If I would say that I was not positive about Doig, he would give me a sum of money, and take Mary Hunt and myself out of the city." In neither case, she stressed, had she agreed to the suggestions.[34]

Under cross-examination Mary Hunt described herself as having been a little more favourably inclined to accept the proposals. She admitted to Eccles that she knew Jones as a constable, and that she had spoken to him and to Hellam's brother after the hearing in police court. "I told him and Hellam's brother that I was willing to leave town," she stated, "only I did not want to put my bailsman in for the money." Running away may have seemed very tempting to Mary Hunt. Unlike Ellen Rogers, she was not deeply rooted in the Toronto community. She had spent much of the past several years working in the United States, and the prospect of returning there may have been very inviting.[35]

Eccles next called Constable D. Jones to the stand. Jones testified that Mary Hunt had confided in him that the story she had told in police court was false. She had lied, according to Jones, as part of a "plan to get money out of the 'boys.'" Furthermore, added Jones, Ellen Rogers and her boyfriend, George Irwin, had threatened Mary Hunt with arrest "for stealing money from a man in the house" if she did not side with them. George Hellam, John Hellam's brother, was sworn and he corroborated Jones's version of the facts.[36]

Andrew Gregg, Robert's father, also took the stand. A boot and shoe-maker by trade, he would deny ever having spoken to Ellen Rogers. Instead, he told the court:

On the day after the alleged outrage, I went near to Rogers' house with my wife and a carpenter to see if the door had been broken. The carpenter examined the door, but neither my wife nor myself went into the house. I did not offer any money to anyone to settle the affair. [George] Irwin came up next morning, before they went to the Police Court, and asked $300 to settle it and get the women out of town.... I refused to give them a copper.[37]

Later, the carpenter, Thomas Coyne, would testify that he had gone to see Ellen Rogers at the request of Mrs. Andrew Gregg, Robert's mother. Apparently Mrs. Gregg had been most apologetic for her son, and had offered to repair anything that had been damaged.[38]

Which version of the events is accurate will likely never be known. Constable Jones, George Hellam, and Andrew Gregg were interested parties who would have had considerable motivation to falsify their evidence to protect family members. And George Irwin's involvement in this was another wild card. He may indeed have been trying to extort money from the families of the accused men. Whether he did so under the direction or control of Ellen Rogers or Mary Hunt would, significantly, have been a separate question.

It is also important to note that the prospect of receiving compensation for criminal injuries was quite an accepted part of mid-nineteenth-century mores. Traditionally, criminal prosecutions had been initiated and pursued by private parties, most frequently by persons who had been victimized by criminal acts. There were costs involved in taking such cases to trial, costs that would usually be borne by the private prosecutor who would obtain compensation after a successful conviction. This state of affairs encouraged some extortionate prosecutors to institute proceedings in order to be bribed to drop them. Charges associated with prostitution and gambling were notoriously subject to this type of abuse. Even prosecutors who began the criminal process with honest intentions sometimes succumbed to bribery, especially if they were poor, or feared that their witnesses might prove corruptible. By the mid-nineteenth century the Crown was increasingly stepping in to conduct criminal prosecutions, but Ellen Rogers would have been familiar with the syndrome of accused persons buying off their victims.[39]

Henry Eccles's address to the jury would focus on the disparate positions of the accusers and the accused. Brandishing a sheaf of papers in front of the jury, he claimed that Robert Gregg and his father had given him a list of more than twenty witnesses, "some of whom were to testify to the bad character of the women, and others to the good character of the prisoner and his family." He told the jurors that he had decided to call none of them. "The women themselves admitted their degraded position," he stated, "and with respect to the prisoner, his respectable appearance and that of his father was quite sufficient for the purposes of this trial."[40]

It could not have been clearer. This was a contest between two very different classes of people. On the one hand, there sat Ellen Rogers and Mary Hunt, with their socially debased occupation and "sullied reputations." On the other sat Robert Gregg, son of a respectable, skilled labourer, backed by his male friends and family. In case the jurors had missed the point, Eccles repeated:

Any man is liable to be prosecuted at any time by women of this character. They might come forward whenever they pleased, and say that they had been violated. And where was the protection in such an event? Nothing but the security of the jury![41]

Eccles reiterated Chief Justice Robinson's rhetoric that all women, regardless of reputation, should be protected from rape. "Let a woman be ever so depraved, she was as well to be protected by the law as the most exemplary character," he said. "But," he added, "I would urge that although she was entitled to the protection of the law, she was not entitled to credit, and no jury would convict upon the bare statement and assertions of a woman, who, while telling her story, admitted that she was of the lowest grade of character."[42]

The belief that sexual "impropriety" in women was linked to untruthfulness pervaded the trial. Chief Justice Robinson, in his opening address, had urged the jury to make a "keener inspection" of the evidence because of the occupation of the victims. Henry Eccles insisted that Ellen Rogers's testimony was completely discreditable because of her "character." Even the prosecutor, John Hillyard Cameron, offered his view that the evidence of an "abandoned female" was suspicious. This theory would be fully entrenched in law by the Supreme Court of Canada in 1877 in the Quebec case of *Laliberté* v *The Queen*. There the judges would conclude that prosecutors should be given free rein to question rape victims about their prior sexual history. Evidence of extramarital heterosexual relations was "manifestly calculated to affect the character, and as a consequence, the credibility of the prosecutrix in a case of rape," they concluded. None of the lawyers or judges would elucidate the rationale for the belief that so profoundly discriminated against sexually unconventional women.[43]

Defence lawyer Eccles's last and perhaps most telling point in the

Sayer Street trial was that rape was punishable by death. This had been the penalty set in England, under common law and by statute, and transported to the North American colonies. In 1841 the Legislature of Upper Canada had reaffirmed this rule by enacting a statute that provided that "every person convicted of the crime of rape shall suffer death as a felon." By contrast, England had experienced a wave of reform sentiment with political battles raging over the large number of capital crimes. By the 1830s the English Parliament had begun to remove the death penalty from many crimes. In 1861 the penalty for rape would be added to the list, reduced from a capital sentence to life imprisonment.[44]

The mood in Canada was less hospitable to sentencing reform, and throughout the nineteenth century the Canadian jurisdictions held onto the capital penalty for the crime of rape. In 1873 Parliament would add imprisonment from seven years to life as an alternate punishment, but the politicians would specifically retain the death penalty as well. Racism proved to be one of the key motivating features for the retention of the capital punishment in rape. According to Prime Minister John A. Macdonald, in a letter written in 1868:

We still have retained the punishment of death for rape.... We have thought it well ... to continue it on account of the frequency of rape committed by negroes, of whom we have too many in Upper Canada. They are very prone to felonious assaults on white women: if the sentence and imprisonment were not very severe there would be a great dread of the people taking the law into their own hands.

The assumption that Black men are prone to rape white women would not have been peculiar to the Prime Minister. A mainstay of the ideology of white supremacy, this thinking led to thousands of lynchings in the American South and has continued to be a rallying cry for white supremacists. The rape of Black women by white men would go unexplored. Both during slavery and after emancipation in the American South, the rape of Black women would be a horribly effective means of keeping Blacks of both sexes "in their place."[45]

Not all convicted rapists sentenced to execution were hanged. Many applied for pardons, and many received them. There had been no hangings of rapists in central Canada for decades. Cameron stressed to the jury that in a case such as this, the death sentence "would hardly ever be carried into effect." Yet the threat would have lurked in the jurors' minds.[46]

Cameron seems to have been on the defensive when it came time for his address to the jury. He repeated that "violence committed on the persons of those girls came as much under the eye of the law as if perpetrated on the most chaste and virtuous persons." Yet he seems almost immediately to have backed down, suggesting to the jury that if they should decide not to find Robert Gregg guilty of rape, they might still find him guilty of the lesser and included offence of common assault. It was a common tactic to charge with or to convict rapists of lesser offences such as indecent assault, assault with intent to commit rape, or common assault in situations where it seemed unlikely that the prosecution could secure a conviction for rape. Because rape convictions were so hard to come by it would have seemed better to convict the accused of something, even a lesser crime, than to let them off completely. Cameron appealed to the jurors to send a message to the groups of youngsters disturbing the neighbourhoods. He urged the jury, "for the peace of society," to convict the men at least of common assault.[47]

The jurors were sent off to deliberate, and they returned in short order. The foreman announced to the packed courtroom that they had found Robert Gregg (and by implication Ross Hellam, and Doig, who had been charged as his accessories) not guilty. Noted the *Globe*: "The announcement of the verdict was received with loud cheering and other demonstrations of pleasure by the audience. It was sometime before order was restored...."[48]

This may have been an unusual case, but it was not an atypical verdict. Prosecutions for rape in Ontario rarely resulted in convictions in the nineteenth century. But the facts did little to stop the outpouring of anti-female sentiment seen so frequently in the writings of Canadian lawyers. The topic of false complaints and unfounded convictions haunted the male legal community. In 1866 the editors of the *Upper Canada Law Journal* would write:

[B]ut every man is fully alive to the risk he runs from the fact that, if a woman takes it into her head to charge him with an indecent assault, the chances are ten to one that he will be found guilty, no matter how strong may be the proofs of his innocence, or how weak the evidence against him. To be accused of such an offence is to be condemned. The chivalrous male juror feels that woman, as the weaker vessel, requires special protection; and his notion of specially protecting her is to accept, in the face of all evidence, whatever charges she may like to bring against her male oppressor.[49]

This was the same sort of fear-mongering that the legal community spread about the law of seduction. There the statistics bore out their claims, at least in part. Male jurors could identify with a father's rage over the loss of his daughter's chastity. Balancing a father's demand for compensation against a male seducer's freedom of action, they were inclined to sympathize with the former. But where the contest was squarely between a woman and a man, sympathy suddenly evaporated. Where the struggle was between a woman's right to be free from sexual violence and a man's freedom to sow a few wild oats, the jurors sided with the latter.

But the Sayer Street case was not yet over. Cameron may have failed to score a conviction for rape, but he was not ready to concede entirely. He directed the court officials to arraign the four men for burglary, breaking and entering. Cameron seems to have been determined to convict the men of something, and the matter of the stolen money gave him an alternate way of proceeding. Ellen Rogers was called back to the stand. Angered and frustrated by the earlier verdict, she exhibited enormous courage. Speaking through tears, she conveyed her pain, her outrage, and overriding everything, her strong sense of her entitlement to dignity and rightful treatment. Glimpses of this can be found in the coverage from the Toronto *Leader*:

[Ellen Rogers] came into the witness box crying; and, on being sworn, said she didn't think there was any use in her being called on to give any evidence, as lawyers and witnesses had all spoken of her as being unworthy of belief. She was very angry at this; and said she didn't care about giving any more evidence. If, she said, I am unfortunate, surely I am not to be murdered by any set of men. In conclusion she said she didn't care about saying anything at all. She was threatened with being committed to jail, but said she didn't care.

At length, by advice of Mr. Cameron, His Lordship allowed witness to make her own statement. She accordingly addressed the jury for about ten minutes, detailing the circumstances in broken English.... She spoke with excessive rapidity and a great deal of vehemence, and at the close of her address, resumed her crying.

Witness was then examined and deposed that $4 were taken from the cupboard by the parties breaking into the house that evening. The examination having been closed, witness talked at a frightful rate for about five minutes, and then left the box.[50]

Hampered by the barrier of language, jeered by an obnoxious and unruly crowd of observers, Ellen Rogers would have needed every ounce of bravery she had to persist in standing up for herself. She equated her violent rape at the hands of drunken, insolent men with murder: "If I am unfortunate, I am not to be murdered by any set of men." Mary Hunt had shouted something similar that night in December: "Ellen, come help me! They are murdering me!" The enormity of the crime of rape, the devastating impact that it has on women's freedom and self-esteem, and the anguish of the rape victim is all summed up in Ellen Rogers's remarkable fortitude.

Few seem to have heard her that day. The Toronto *Globe* referred to her impassioned statements as a "harangue," noting coldly, "it was with the greatest difficulty that she could be made to hold her tongue." It took the jury less than ten minutes to reach another set of "not guilty" verdicts. The crowd was silent, but only because the judge had warned that he would not tolerate another outbreak of cheering. Judge McLean spoke to the prisoners before discharging them, warning them in a kindly tone to stay away from disreputable houses such as Ellen Rogers's in future. And according to the Toronto *Leader*, "the immense crowd, which had filled the gallery and body of the Court all day, mov[ed] off, apparently very well pleased with the result of the trials." As for Ellen Rogers, she seems to have packed up her belongings and left town.[51]

### ATTEMPTED RAPE AND MURDER AT SLATE CREEK, BRITISH COLUMBIA, 1897

Some forty years later, Euphemia Rabbitt would rival Ellen Rogers for courage. When attacked by a violent neighbour who was attempting to rape her, she fought back, cutting short her assailant's attack with a rifle-shot to his arm and side. When he died one day later of his wounds, she was placed on trial for murder. She had the dubious distinction of being the second woman ever to be tried for murder in British Columbia.[52]

Euphemia Rabbitt lived with her husband, Thomas, in Slate Creek, a rather sparsely settled area of southern British Columbia near Kamloops. The Shuswap tribe of the Salish nation were the original people of this region. Thomas Rabbitt, after whom Rabbitt Mountain was named, was one of the earliest white settlers, although the province remained predominantly inhabited by peoples of the First Nations until the 1880s. Gold-seekers moved into the region in the 1850s, and Thomas Rabbitt set up a store and roadhouse catering to the large numbers of itinerant men who had come to pan for gold.[53]

Conditions were rough in the early years. By the 1880s, observers noted that although there were "twenty-two saloons and twenty-two whores" and thousands of men living in pitched tents, there were no schools, churches, roads, or streets to speak of. The miners would gather in the bars to "drink, gamble and chew the fat," and inevitably there were confrontations, fighting, and some gun play. Rabbitt's bar became a stopping-place for miners and prospectors going up to the headwaters of the Tulameen. Activity became even more brisk after the last spike was driven in the Canadian Pacific Railway in 1885. As many as two thousand unemployed men moved into the region looking for gold. By 1893 Kamloops had become a regional metropolis of six thousand people, but many of the miners were starving along the creeks and living on deer meat.[54]

When most of the placers had played out, Thomas Rabbitt gave up his store and bar and took up ranching. He married Euphemia Rabbitt, a woman who traced her heritage both from Italian immigrants and the First Nations. The Kamloops *Daily Standard* would note with emphasis in all of its press coverage that she was "of Italian descent, with a little Indian blood in her veins." Euphemia Rabbitt bore three children in quick succession, adding extensive child rearing to the already-demanding tasks of a rancher's wife.[55]

James Hamilton, the man Euphemia Rabbitt would kill, was an Irish immigrant who had travelled to British Columbia as part of a construction crew for the CPR. After the completion of the railway, he had taken up residence in Otter Creek and had turned to mining, as a ground sluicer on Slate Creek. He soon met Thomas Rabbitt, and the two men struck up a friendship that would last ten years. James Hamilton fell upon hard times in the winter of 1896–97, and Thomas Rabbitt took him into his home as a lodger.[56]

In February of that winter, Thomas Rabbitt was away from home one night when James Hamilton made his first overture to Euphemia Rabbitt. After she had gone to bed, he made "improper proposals," which Mrs. Rabbitt rebuffed. "I told him not to attempt to take liberties with me or there would be trouble," she would later state. James Hamilton seemed embarrassed, and sheepishly apologized the next morning. Euphemia Rabbitt was not appeased. She did not want to tell her husband the details of what had occurred, since she feared "trouble" would ensue. However, when he returned she asked him to make James Hamilton leave, because he was "getting too bold around the house."[57]

Thomas Rabbitt ordered James Hamilton out of the house, and there was no further interaction until the spring. In May 1897, when Euphemia Rabbitt was out working in her garden, James Hamilton approached her again. "He came crawling on his hands and knees to me in the field," she exclaimed. "I ran to the house and barred the door." This incident she related in full to her husband. Euphemia Rabbitt was so alarmed and frightened that Thomas Rabbitt took his neighbour, William J. Kyle, down to James Hamilton's cabin to have a word with him. They threatened him with arrest, and ordered him to leave within forty-eight hours. James Hamilton was quite belligerent and is said to have retorted: "I've made it hot for you and I'll make it hotter before I'm through." However, he seems to have thought better of his threats, and the situation calmed down for the summer.[58]

Violence erupted in the late afternoon on Saturday, 18 September. Thomas Rabbitt had gone off to Otter Flat to collect the monthly mail. Euphemia Rabbitt was working in her vegetable garden when she looked up to see James Hamilton approaching. She ran for the house, but James Hamilton caught her, wrestled with her, and threw her to the ground. "He raised my skirts, he tried to unbutton his suspenders," she would later tell the court. "I shouted all I could, calling on Mickey, my little boy [aged five]. My knees were scratched, my dress all torn, my shoes torn off. I was screaming for help all the time."[59]

With a flash of inspiration, Euphemia Rabbitt shouted out that a man was coming down the hill. James Hamilton turned to look around, and she managed to dash back to the safety of her home. She immediately grabbed a 45-calibre Winchester rifle, but when she looked out, James Hamilton was no longer to be seen. Taking the rifle with her, Euphemia Rabbitt ran down to the river, where William Kyle lived. From the moment she had escaped from James Hamilton, Euphemia Rabbitt had kept shouting for help. When her neighbour came out to see what the commotion was about, she handed the rifle to him, reproaching him for not having come to her aid sooner. According to William Kyle, she was very excited, her hair was loose, and her dress was torn and covered with mud.[60]

Euphemia Rabbitt's response to the attempted rape was almost classic in terms of how nineteenth-century jurists believed a proper woman should behave. Women were supposed to put up extraordinary resistance in the face of force and violence. The Ontario case of *R. v Fick* in 1866 had set the standard. Adam Wilson of the Court of Queen's Bench had stipulated there that "the woman [must have] been quite overcome *by force or terror, she resisting as much as she could,* and resisting *so as to make the prisoner see and know that she really was resisting to the utmost.*" In the same case, Chief Justice William Buell Richards made an even more remarkable statement. Phrasing it as a matter of *jurors' rights,* he told the jury that it "had a right to expect some resistance on the part of the woman."[61]

This was surely a total reversal of roles. What was before the court

## MURDEROUS OUTRAGE ON A LADY

Nineteenth-century artist's depiction of a violent rape
in the *Illustrated Police News* (London), 1870.

was the question of a woman's right to be free from sexual assault.
Instead, the judges had dramatically altered the terrain so that it appeared
that the raped woman was seeking some sort of favour from the male
jurors, who were to grant it only if she had satisfied all of the conditions
they were entitled to expect. Yet the legal commentators were fully in
agreement. Edward East, a prominent English text-writer on criminal law,
insisted that once attacked, women were expected to put up an outcry, to
notify the nearest available person of the outrage, and to seek immediate
assistance. All of this Ellen Rogers and Mary Hunt had accomplished as
well, but the key difference was that Euphemia Rabbitt was widely
viewed as a respectable woman. The Kamloops *Daily Standard* described
her as a "good wife and mother," and Alexander Swan, a mine manager
in the district, would testify that he had known the woman for six or
seven years, and that she was known for her "good moral reputation."[62]

But it never came down to a trial against James Hamilton on the charge of attempted rape. As Euphemia Rabbitt stood with William Kyle on the banks of the Tulameen River, James Hamilton loomed over the hill again. According to Kyle, Hamilton looked like "a wild beast." William Kyle shouted to him to stay back, but Hamilton appeared undeterred. Kyle repeated his warning: "For God's sake, go back; if you come any further you will be shot." But Hamilton is said to have merely retorted: "If Rabbitt is keeping a whore house, I want my share of it." Then he threatened to "shut Euphemia's wind off if she did not quit hollering."[63]

This was too much for Euphemia Rabbitt. She caught hold of the rifle, took aim, and fired twice. Hamilton was only ten or twelve paces away, and the bullets entered his right arm and side, puncturing his lung and liver. Hamilton staggered on, stopped to try to pick up a stone, and then fell backwards. William Kyle went immediately to his aid. With the assistance of a neighbouring miner named Ole Benson, they moved Hamilton to a neighbour's cabin and tried to patch up his wounds. Dr. A.M. Sutton was sent for, from the nearby town of Nicola, but Hamilton died the next morning.[64]

Hugh Hunter, the constable at Granite Creek, was called in, and he notified the coroner. The office of the coroner was an English legal institution that had been transported to the colonies as an adjunct to the more formal law courts. Coroners were men who were appointed to investigate situations of violent or apparently unnatural death. In order to determine the cause of death, coroners swore in a panel of local male jurors to view corpses and to hear evidence from medical experts and other witnesses. The hearing was usually less formal and the testimony more candid than what would transpire in court. The process was called a "Coroner's Inquest." Findings were forwarded to the Crown attorney, and where there was evidence of foul play, a justice of the peace would order the suspect taken to jail to await trial.[65]

Coroner John Clapperton and a coroner's jury of seven men (four local miners, a storekeeper, a surveyor, and a minister) gathered at the Rabbitt's ranch on 21 September 1897. Dr. Sutton conducted a post-mortem examination of the body and pronounced that the rifle-shots had been the cause of death. Both Euphemia Rabbitt and William Kyle gave sworn statements as to what had occurred. Ole Benson testified that Hamilton had joked about his importuning of Euphemia Rabbitt, saying he was just "having some fun with the missus." Commented Benson: "I have known the deceased since 1887. Have always considered he was a little off on the woman question. He was fond of them." William Kyle agreed. "He [Hamilton] was erratic and most abominable in his speech, especially about women," he stated.[66]

It took the coroner's jury only one hour to arrive at their verdict:

We, the jury empanelled to enquire into the matter of the death of James Hamilton after hearing and duly considering the evidence in this case, do find that James Hamilton came to his death by a gun shot wound, said gun being in the hands of Mrs. Euphemia Rabbitt. And it is our opinion and belief that Mrs. Rabbitt shot the said James Hamilton in self-defence.

Despite the coroner's finding of self-defence, the case had to be set over for trial. Euphemia Rabbitt was brought before two justices of the peace (Dr. Sutton and Coroner Clapperton), who conducted a swift preliminary inquiry. Then she was ordered to stand trial at the forthcoming Kamloops Assizes.[67]

Public sympathy was mounting for Euphemia Rabbitt, and the press pursued the story with gusto. Evidencing some partiality to the accused woman, the Kamloops *Inland Sentinel* noted: "Our Nicola correspondent states that much sympathy is expressed for Mrs. Rabbitt owing to her painful position." The Victoria *Daily Colonist* was even more open about its support for Euphemia Rabbitt:

From Granite Creek comes news of how a plucky woman, Mrs. Thomas Rabbitt, in defence of her honor shot and killed a man who had attacked her. It was on the afternoon of Saturday the 18th inst., that the shooting took place, and although Mrs. Rabbitt is now under arrest and will be tried at the assizes at Kamloops on October 4, there seems not the least doubt, as far as can be gathered from the story of the tragedy, that she will be fully acquitted on the ground of justifiable homicide.[68]

After Constable Hunter delivered Euphemia Rabbitt to the Kamloops jail, the Kamloops *Daily Standard* sent a reporter to interview her. The paper meant to set an upbeat tone for the pending trial:

Mrs. Rabbitt is a nice-looking woman of about 25 years of age, and has some Indian blood in her veins. Endowed with youth and good looks, she seems to be of a gentle disposition and is very courteous. Her awful position does not seem to weigh much on her nor does she seem in the least bit worried....

She was comfortable and very happy at being allowed to retain her baby, a bright little girl of eleven months.... It is a great happiness to have her little one with her in her trouble. Her little girl is a fine, bright child, with merry, good-na-tured eyes and dark auburn hair. She says only a few words, but seems, like her mother, to look out on the bright, rather than on the dark side of life.[69]

The anomaly of confining a respectable woman to a crowded jail cell was obvious to all observers. There were thirty-eight people in the Kamloops jail that fall, many serving sentences for crimes such as house-breaking, robbery, assault, drunkenness, and indecent assault. Constable Hunter intervened and Euphemia Rabbitt was permitted to sleep with her infant daughter upstairs, so that she was not "obliged to mix with the other inhabitants."[70]

For his part, Thomas Rabbitt also travelled to Kamloops, where he secured the services of a local lawyer, W.H. Whittaker, to defend his wife. Whittaker, realizing the importance of the case, called upon a prominent Vancouver lawyer, Charles Wilson, QC, to assist him. The Fall Assizes opened in Kamloops on 4 October, and the Crown prosecutor immedi-ately moved to have Euphemia Rabbitt's case transferred to Vernon. "Public opinion was so strongly excited in regard to the case at Kam-loops," argued the Crown, "that an impartial trial might not be secured." Given the obvious sympathy of the press in such distant cities as Victoria, the move to nearby Vernon would seem futile. But in any event the change in venue was granted.[71]

On 11 October 1897, the trial got under way in Vernon, before Mon-tague William Tyrwhitt Drake, an English barrister who had tried his hand at placer mining in British Columbia in the early 1860s, and then resumed the practice of law in Victoria. Drake had been appointed to the Supreme Court of British Columbia in 1889. Wilson and Whittaker fol-lowed their client to Vernon, and Allan Macdonald, a Vernon lawyer, represented the Crown. The evidence unfolded much the way it had at the coroner's inquest. The argument of the defence was that Euphemia Rabbitt had been in fear of her life when she shot James Hamilton. Charles Wilson, the defence lawyer, would prove particularly adept at stressing this theme.[72]

Wilson's cross-examination of William Kyle provides a good case in point. He questioned Kyle about James Hamilton's reputation regarding women. Kyle replied that in all the time he had known Hamilton "he had heard the deceased speak of women in general only in the vilest terms." Kyle was also pressed to describe James Hamilton's physical stature. William Kyle emphasized that he "was a large man, weighing possibly 220 pounds and being over six feet in height." Asked whether he and

Euphemia Rabbitt could have protected themselves without a rifle, Kyle did not hesitate in his reply: "He was a powerful man and it would take three ordinary men to cope with him. It was not possible to have protected ourselves without a weapon."[73]

Alexander Swan, the mine manager, gave similar evidence. James Hamilton was "a very powerful man," who generally spoke of Euphemia Rabbitt "in a disgusting manner." Indeed, Swan had heard Hamilton say "he would get that woman some day." Ole Benson was also cross-examined about James Hamilton's character. Hamilton had "what was known as a cold laugh," testified Benson, and he had talked about his exploits with Euphemia Rabbitt as "having some fun across the river with her." Benson also stated that he had nursed Hamilton through his dying moments, at which time Hamilton had confessed that although Euphemia Rabbitt was the cause of all the trouble, he "would forgive her."[74]

In his address to the jury, Charles Wilson would insist that Euphemia Rabbitt had been "compelled to act as she did in order to save her own life." He "did not wish to speak ill of the dead," Wilson stressed, "but in this case he found it was a necessity." He catalogued the "frequent insults" that Hamilton had offered to Mrs. Rabbitt, and argued that "it would have been useless for her to attempt a proper chastisement, when the man's muscular development was taken into consideration." Emphasizing the last words of the deceased, in which he expressly forgave the accused woman, Wilson urged the jury to render a finding of justifiable homicide.[75]

Allan Macdonald's case seems to have gone quite badly. Even his own witnesses had provided testimony central to the defence of the prisoner. Public sentiment was squarely on Euphemia Rabbitt's side. Shrewdly, he concluded that the trial was coming down to the question of whether women should be allowed to kill in defence of their honour. The crucial element, of course, was whether a woman was reputed to be honourable to start with. The available evidence had suggested that Euphemia Rabbitt was considered to be a chaste and proper woman. Lacking direct testimony to contradict this supposition, Macdonald did the best he could. He "did not question Mrs. Rabbitt's chastity," he told the jury, "but he thought it rather strange that so many improper proposals had been made and Mr. and Mrs. Rabbitt had not sent the deceased away."[76]

This was a gamble. The evidence was clearly against him. Euphemia Rabbitt had asked her husband to throw James Hamilton out of their home after his first sexual advance, and he had done so. Thomas Rabbitt had confronted Hamilton in his cabin some months later, threatening to have him arrested and insisting that he should leave the area for improperly propositioning Euphemia Rabbitt. And perhaps most persuasively, she had time and again physically repelled and eluded the violent sexual attacks of a powerful, six-foot-tall, 220-pound man. But Macdonald would have wanted to instil a lingering doubt in the minds of the jurors. Prevailing Victorian mythology held that women were responsible for maintaining the sexual mores of the community. Male lust was an inescapable, enduring feature of life, and it was women who were expected to take measures to prevent setting it off, and to contain it when it erupted. What was it about Euphemia Rabbitt, Macdonald wanted the jury to think, that caused a man like James Hamilton to become so fixated with her?[77]

Then it was Judge Drake's turn to read the charge to the jury. He began by explaining the different classes of murder:

If the shooting was done by the prisoner from ill will and with intent to kill him, it will be murder.

Death by accident is manslaughter.

If the shooting was not done from ill will but done in self-defence and to protect herself from death or serious bodily injury intended towards her by the deceased, or from a reasonable apprehension of it induced by the conduct of deceased, though the latter may not in fact have intended death or serious injury—

If the shooting was done under such a degree or alarm and bewilderment of mind caused by the conduct of the deceased as to deprive the prisoner for the time of her reason and self-control —

If the shooting was in self-defence after an attack of the deceased, endangering life and limb — or reasonably apprehended by the prisoner as likely to do so, in either case the prisoner has the right to acquittal.

Summing up, Judge Drake would say that "he could not see that it was murder in this case," but he left it to the jury to decide whether it was manslaughter or whether there should be an acquittal.[78]

Despite Judge Drake's stated opinion, the jury was still free to explore whether a finding of murder was possible. G.W. Burbidge, the author of a leading Canadian treatise on criminal law, had written in 1890 that "malice aforethought" was an essential ingredient in murder. He defined "malice aforethought" as "an intention to cause the death of, or grievous bodily harm to any person," or "knowledge that the act which causes death will probably cause the death of, or grievous bodily harm to some person." On the face of it, Euphemia Rabbitt seems to have had sufficient malice aforethought to fit this definition. Thus in spite of the judge's opinion, a finding of murder would not have been completely out of line. This would have exposed her to the prospect of capital punishment. The only remaining question would have been whether the argument of self-defence might have been determined in her favour, thus negating a murder conviction.[79]

The prospect of a conviction for manslaughter was also open for consideration. Burbidge had defined manslaughter as "unlawful homicide without malice aforethought." The maximum penalty for this offence was life imprisonment. Murder could be reduced to manslaughter where the homicide was acted out "in the heat of passion, caused by provocation." Interestingly, assault and battery were examples of provocation that had long been accepted by Canadian courts. S.R. Clarke, a Canadian legal authority on criminal law, provided the following as a typical example of provoked manslaughter: "Where, upon a sudden quarrel, two persons fight, and one of them kills the other, or where a man greatly provokes another by some personal violence, etc., and the other immediately kills him."[80]

A verdict of manslaughter would have been a logical finding upon these facts. Euphemia Rabbitt could easily point to the attempted rape as sufficient provocation. That she did not kill Hamilton at the exact moment of the attempted rape could have presented difficulty. She had waited to get a rifle, and then shot her assailant subsequent to the attack. Thus she had not killed him immediately upon provocation. But the jurors could have looked upon Hamilton's behaviour as one continuing attack, thus constituting provocation at the moment of the shooting.

The only thing that could have saved Euphemia Rabbitt from a finding of murder or manslaughter was the concept of self-defence. S.R. Clarke described the law of self-defence as follows:

Where the homicide is committed in prevention of a forcible and atrocious crime, as for instance, if a man attempts to rob or murder another and be killed in the attempt, the slayer shall be acquitted and discharged.

Where a man kills another, upon a sudden encounter, merely in his own defence, or in defence of his wife, child, parent, or servant, and not from any vindictive feeling, which is termed homicide *se defendendo*, or in self-defence ... [it shall be] excusable homicide.[81]

The result of a successful plea of self-defence was a complete discharge for the prisoner. This may have been what the jurors fastened upon, because it took them only twenty minutes to return a verdict of "justifiable homicide," dismissing all charges against Euphemia Rabbitt. Reaction from the courtroom was much more muted than it had been in the Sayer Street trial. "There was a slight demonstration by the prisoner's friends as soon as the verdict was rendered, which called forth a rebuke from His Lordship." The press heralded the victory with banner headlines of "Mrs. Rabbitt Acquitted" and "Mrs. Rabbitt Freed," adding that "considerable satisfaction" was felt at the result. Euphemia Rabbitt was set free to return home to her husband and children at Slate Creek.[82]

It had been a remarkable trial. Evidence had unfolded of the indisputable resourcefulness and bravery of a woman who had used every means at her disposal to stop a malicious assailant bent upon raping her. Had James Hamilton effected his object, and completed the rape, the case might have been treated differently. There would have been all those thorny questions about consent to deal with. Allan Macdonald, the Crown prosecutor, would have had so much more to work with, potentially able to insinuate that the long-standing relationship and the history of prior sexual advances between the parties intimated a measure of willingness to engage in sexual relations. Perhaps Euphemia Rabbitt's mixed ancestry would have been invoked as a predisposing factor implying sexual availability. Nineteenth-century literature written by white males frequently emphasized the sexuality of women from the First Nations.[83]

The message was plainly explicit. As the case of Ellen Rogers and Mary Hunt shows, women who were raped could expect little sympathy from criminal courts. Sceptical lawyers, judges, and jurors pored over every detail of their background and actions, striving to ensure that only the most "deserving" women were granted protection. For women whose sexual lives were condemned by nineteenth-century mores, this meant that they would never obtain legal protection from rape, regardless of what the rhetoric of law professed. But women who, against all odds, successfully defended themselves against sexual assault captured the respect of the community. Even where resistance resulted in the death of the attackers, these women were viewed with admiration and sympathy. On occasion they also inspired a stirring sense of pride. Euphemia Rabbitt, the focus of public congratulation and adulation, was a prime beneficiary of such ideology.

# 4

# Infanticide

One long, hot day in early August 1817, the body of a male infant was discovered in Chippawa, Upper Canada. It was unearthed from a very shallow grave near the home of Mary and John Ussher. The Usshers were white settlers in a racially mixed community. Peoples of the Algonquian-speaking Ojibwa, Ottawa, and Algonkian nations were confronted with an influx of Loyalist refugees who had begun to overrun their hunting grounds by the late eighteenth century. Despite the fact that infanticide was reportedly less common within the First Nations than in European cultures, suspicion settled upon twenty-year-old Angelique Pilotte, a First Nations' woman who was probably Ojibwa.[1]

Angelique Pilotte worked as a "waiting woman" for Miss Elizabeth Ann Hamilton, a white woman from Drummond Island, Michigan. Originally from Michilimackinac (Mackinac Island, Michigan), Angelique Pilotte had joined Elizabeth Hamilton's service that year. When her mistress left Michigan to travel to the Ussher home for a three-week visit, Angelique Pilotte was brought along to attend to Hamilton's personal needs. Little else is recorded about Angelique Pilotte's background. But her employment status is indicative of a woman with few prospects. She may have been an orphan or have come from a disrupted family, since jobs as domestic servants to whites were not much sought after by women from the First Nations. The pay was negligible, usually even lower than that offered to white domestic servants, and the subordination in status would have been demeaning. The people of the First Nations preferred to have kept, where possible, to their own communities. The thrust of white people's efforts to "civilize" (that is, colonize) women of the First Nations was to turn them into domestic servants.[2]

The first person to cast an accusing finger at Angelique Pilotte was her own mistress, Elizabeth Hamilton. The white woman initially checked her suspicions with the Usshers' servant, Mary McQueen. The latter had been assigned to share a bed with Angelique Pilotte for the duration of the visit. Mary McQueen is reported to have said that Angelique Pilotte had appeared to be sick and had risen from the bed two or three times during the night of 29 July. Upon learning this, Elizabeth Hamilton and Mary Ussher had promptly searched through Angelique Pilotte's belongings and linen. They discovered "an Infant's shift" among her clothes.

The two women confronted Angelique Pilotte on the morning of 9 August. She broke down and confessed to being the mother of the child. Later that day, "in a state of extreme convulsion" she was taken before two white justices of the peace, Samuel Street and Thomas Clark. They bound her over for trial on the charge of infanticide, and Angelique Pilotte was delivered to the newly built jail in the capital city of Niagara (now Niagara-on-the-Lake).[3]

Infanticide was an unsavoury but surprisingly common feature of life in nineteenth-century Canada. The bodies of newborn infants were frequently discovered inside hollow trees, buried in the snow, floating in rivers, at the bottom of wells, under floorboards, under the platforms of railway stations, in ditches, in privies, in stove pipes, and in pails of water. Fifty or more bodies were found by the coroner in the 1860s in each of Toronto and Quebec City alone. Not all of the bodies would have been discovered, and even when they were, it would often be impossible to determine who was responsible.[4]

Those who were caught were usually young, unmarried, working-class women. Frequently, like Angelique Pilotte, they were domestic servants who had attempted to hide their pregnancy and childbirth. These attempts at concealment would have been motivated by fear. Giving birth to an illegitimate child would have resulted in disgrace, termination of employment, and severely diminished job prospects. The harsh economic and social realities left these women with almost no options.

Most would have had to carry out their concealment plans with extraordinary courage and determination. They would have had to keep up normal appearances in front of employers and acquaintances despite any pregnancy-related illnesses, disguising their growing bulk with layers of clothing and excuses. They would have had to secure some degree of privacy in which to give birth unobserved, serve as their own midwife, and do away with the child and its body before discovery. Afterward, many tried to continue with their daily routine as if nothing had happened. Those who slipped up in completing the hurdles would be caught and swept up into the criminal justice system.

Angelique Pilotte's failure to dispose of the infant's body was her first mistake. But her inability to allay the suspicions of her white mistress was her final undoing. She was confined to jail for the rest of the summer to await the opening of the Niagara Assizes on 8 September 1817. The statute under which Angelique Pilotte was charged was entitled "An act to prevent the destroying and murthering of Bastard Children." First enacted in France in the mid-sixteenth century, this draconian law had spread to England in 1623, and entered colonial jurisprudence in New France in 1722. By the early nineteenth century it had been extended to apply in Lower Canada, Nova Scotia, New Brunswick, Prince Edward Island, Newfoundland, and Upper Canada.[5]

The statute set out some rather exceptional rules for trials where women were charged with infanticide. In such cases there was to be a presumption of guilt, rather than innocence. Prosecutors were relieved from having to prove that the mother had murdered her illegitimate infant. All that was required was evidence that the mother had given birth, that the child had died, and that the mother had attempted to conceal its death. At this point there was an automatic presumption of guilt. The mother was to be put to death as a murderer, no matter how credible and convincing her testimony might be to the contrary.

All-male legislatures had adopted these extraordinary rules because of their anxiety that women who committed infanticide were eluding criminal conviction. They feared that authorities were failing to obtain convictions for murder because there were few witnesses to the births. If they were caught, the terrified mothers would claim that the child was stillborn or that it had died right after birth. Since so many babies died at birth from natural causes anyway, prosecutors were sorely pressed to dispute this.

With the passage of the legislation, the situation was reversed. That an infant had died where the mother had been trying to conceal the childbirth would henceforth be sufficient to merit capital punishment. Courts were instructed to convict unless the accused woman could provide some other person as a witness to her innocence. This witness would have to testify that he or she had seen the mother give birth and that the child had been stillborn. Since the purpose of concealment would have been undone by inviting a witness to attend the birth, it would have been clear to the legislators that, if the courts applied the new law as it was written, few women accused of this crime would be able to meet this burden of evidence.[6]

William Campbell was the Scottish-born judge presiding over the Niagara Assizes, the same Campbell who would respond so unsympathetically to Amelia Hogle's seduction case eight years later. Henry John Boulton, a young English-born barrister who had been called to the bar the year before, prosecuted the case for the Crown. A jury of twelve men was selected. Trial was set to begin when Campbell noticed that Angelique Pilotte was without legal representation.[7]

It would take until 1836 before accused persons were granted the full right to defence counsel. And even then prisoners without the means to pay could find themselves out of luck. A prisoner without funds was totally reliant upon the charity of a barrister. A tradition had arisen, however, that the judge would appoint someone to act as counsel where a poverty-stricken accused person was on trial for a capital offence. Any barrister so appointed would have the right to decide whether or not to work for free.[8]

On the day of the trial, 9 September 1817, William Campbell appointed Bartholomew Crannell Beardsley to act for Angelique Pilotte. Beardsley had been one of the founding members of the Law Society of Upper Canada. Born in New York, he had practised law in New Brunswick and Upper Canada, developing an extensive reputation as a criminal lawyer. He may have been drawn to Angelique Pilotte's case out of a sense of compassion. He would have been familiar with familial and marital relations that transgressed societal norms. His father, John Beardsley, had been forced to resign his post as a military chaplain in 1801 because at least one of his five marriages had been denounced as bigamous. Whatever Beardsley's sympathies, Angelique Pilotte seems to have had no conception of the role of defence counsel. The rather late appointment of Beardsley certainly did little to advance her case. Beardsley could not elicit any information from her. She watched in complete silence as the case unfolded before her that day.[9]

The white criminal justice system would have been foreign to Angelique Pilotte. The English adversary process, with its reliance on cross-examination to elicit the truth, was quite at odds with systems of justice within the First Nations, which preferred to resolve disputes by permitting everyone a say, without detailed rebuttal or testing, working toward the ultimate goal of consensus. But none of the whites would question whether they had jurisdiction to extend the force of their criminal law to an Ojibwa woman.[10]

There was very little direct or even circumstantial evidence to tie Angelique Pilotte to infanticide. Mary McQueen, the Usshers' servant, could state only that Angelique Pilotte's illness had taken her from bed several times that night. No one else had observed or heard anything. Mary Ussher would recall a "Strange Noise," which might have been the crying of an infant, on the night in question. At the time, she had imagined this to be the noise of a cat. The case for the prosecution rested largely upon Angelique Pilotte's confession. Thomas Clark, one of the justices of the peace who had examined her originally, took the stand to read the contents of the confession into the record. Thomas Clark told the court that Angelique Pilotte's confession had been "freely made, neither threats nor promises being used to induce or influence her."

The power of those who had secured the confession — white, upper-class women and men of prominence — over the young Ojibwa domestic servant who had given it, would not have been a matter for comment. Furthermore, it would become increasingly apparent as the century wore on that First Nations' people accused of crimes often made long and damaging confessions, without much overt pressure. They may have been attempting to speak their piece, as they were accustomed to doing within their own justice systems.[11]

Nor does it seem to have been thought a problem that Angelique Pilotte had been accused and questioned without anyone beside her to act as her counsel, agent, or even as a friend. That she was in a state of "extreme convulsion" when she provided the information would be viewed only as a further indication of guilt, not as a factor urging restraint in the reception of such evidence. Seemingly untroubled by these matters, Thomas Clark explained to the court that Angelique Pilotte's problems had begun in France. She had been travelling in Europe as a domestic servant to a white woman from Drummond Island, Michigan. "An unhappy connection" with a friend of her employer, a British officer named Lieutenant Luckman of the 81st Foot, had left Angelique Pilotte pregnant and unmarried. On top of that, her mistress died suddenly, and Angelique Pilotte was forced to return home alone. She obtained another domestic position, with Elizabeth Hamilton, by disguising her pregnant condition.

According to the confession, the onset of Angelique Pilotte's labour occurred on the evening of 29 July 1817. Rising from her bed, Angelique

Pilotte had gone out to a nearby field and given birth to a male infant around 2 a.m. on the morning of 30 July 1817. She conceded that the child had been born alive, but said it was sickly and did not cry out at all. "[It] moved its little legs, but did not move its arms," she had stated.

After lying next to the infant for an hour or so, she returned to the house, as she was feeling very ill herself. She left the baby "upon the grass then moving his legs but not crying," she said. When she returned to the field several hours later, the child was "still moving its legs." She wrapped a "cloth very tight about the child" and left it behind the stable. During the day of 30 July, Angelique Pilotte seems to have been up and about, carrying out her domestic duties without incident. Fearful of the discovery of the infant's body, she returned to the stable some time during the middle of the next night, and buried it in a shallow grave in the open field.

The confession had established every point required under the statute. Angelique Pilotte had admitted concealing her pregnancy, giving birth to a live infant, and the dead infant's body had been duly unearthed. Technically speaking, the cause of death was legally irrelevant unless there was evidence from witnesses other than the mother. The prosecution could have rested its case there, but rarely did Crown counsel feel confident enough to do so. There seems to have been some lingering worry about the heavy-handedness of the legislation. Courts were a bit hesitant to apply it without a sense of certainty that the accused woman was truly to blame for the death of her infant.[12]

Henry John Boulton was a cautious man. He probed further. His most telling questions to Thomas Clark would concern Angelique Pilotte's direct admission of guilt. Clark testified that he and Samuel Street had asked Angelique Pilotte why she had wrapped the infant so tightly in the cloth. According to Clark, she had replied that she had done this "for the purpose of choaking it." After that critical admission, Boulton called additional medical evidence. Elizabeth Hamilton, Mary Ussher, and Mary Margaret Clark took the stand in sequence to testify that they had "privately examined" Angelique Pilotte and concluded that "she had lately been delivered of a Child." It would not have been unusual for lay neighbourhood women to have made medical diagnoses of pregnancy. The medical profession was as yet underdeveloped and far from establishing the sort of monopolistic control it possesses today.

Yet there was some role for physicians. John Roberts, a local surgeon, was called to the stand to testify to the state of the infant at birth. The body "was perfect in form," he noted, "and had every appearance of mature birth." Furthermore, Roberts stressed that a child so "tightly pinned up ... must necessarily soon be smothered." Under cross-examination, defence lawyer Beardsley would get the surgeon to concede that it was usual for babies to cry after birth. Angelique Pilotte's child had never uttered a sound. Beardsley also got Roberts to admit that the infant's death might have been caused by "the want of proper assistance at time of delivery." Indeed, the child might have died from birth defects. But this would have been legally irrelevant. Under the statute, without witnesses, the cause of death was totally without import.

Some of the most damning testimony came from Angelique Pilotte's mistress, Elizabeth Hamilton. She did not challenge the conventional wisdom of her class — that the working classes were of a different and diminished capacity and attitude. Distancing herself from Angelique Pilotte, she launched a deliberate attack on her servant, whose extreme vulnerability could not have been more apparent. She spoke at length about Angelique Pilotte's character, testifying that her servant "border[ed] on Idiotism." Angelique Pilotte, she told the court, was "so Simple and ignorant as not to know right from Wrong, nor that she thought it a crime to Kill her own child."[13]

The evidence was more than enough to permit a finding of guilt, and the jury brought in its verdict accordingly. The jurors coupled their decision with a "strong recommendation for mercy." William Campbell pronounced a sentence of death. As the Niagara *Spectator* and the Kingston *Gazette* duly reported, Angelique Pilotte was "sentenced to be taken to the prison from whence she came, and from there to the place of execution and Thursday next, the 11th [of September], there to be hanged by the neck till she be dead, and her body to be delivered over for dissection."[14]

Criminal punishment was remarkably brutal in this era. Mary Swayne, who was convicted of bigamy in the same court session as Angelique Pilotte, was sentenced to be burned on the hand and imprisoned three months. Mary Murray, convicted of grand larceny, was sentenced to be publicly displayed in the pillory for one hour, hands and head imprisoned immovably in a wooden structure while spectators were invited to commit whatever indignities they wished upon her. Then she was to be banished from the province forever. But the manner proscribed for Angelique Pilotte's death stands out as particularly horrifying in a time when many believed that any interference with the dead body constituted an abominable and terrifying intrusion.[15]

Beardsley scrambled to muster his energy for another round of argu-

The illustration "L'Enfant Trouvé" (The Foundling),
from *Le Monde Illustré* (Montreal 1887), depicts prevailing
Christian mythology of infant death.

ments right after sentence was passed. Declaring that he had not had sufficient time to prepare the case adequately, the defence lawyer obtained a respite of the execution until 4 October and pulled together a petition for mercy, which he submitted on 15 September 1817. It seems that Beardsley had finally convinced Angelique Pilotte to talk to him. Possibly someone from the Ojibwa community had been called in to act as a go-between. The petition asserted Angelique Pilotte's innocence, arguing that the trial had adduced a great deal of incorrect information.

The birth of the child, according to the petition, had taken place before Angelique Pilotte and her mistress had ever arrived at the Usshers' in Chippawa. It was during the latter days of the voyage to Chippawa that Angelique Pilotte had gone into labour. Admitting that she had concealed the birth, Angelique Pilotte was adamant that the infant had been stillborn. Fearing the wrath of her mistress, she swore that she had stolen ashore one night in late July and buried the dead child.

This version of events differed drastically from the evidence put forth at the trial. Yet it accorded with the testimony of Elizabeth Hamilton and Mary Clark. The two white women had reiterated for the court that Angelique Pilotte had consistently maintained that her baby had been stillborn. Apart from the confession, nothing in the evidence at trial challenged or detracted from the contents of the petition. And given the circumstances under which the confession was extracted, its reliability is certainly subject to serious criticism. The major question was whether the authorities would believe and act upon the petition.

Beardsley had drafted the petition with some ambivalence on the question of how to treat Angelique Pilotte's status as an Ojibwa woman. On the one hand, with ethnocentric bias, he would excuse her behaviour by arguing that she had never been exposed to the beneficial influences of white, European civilization. She was a "poor girl," he wrote, with "no education whatever, nor the slightest instruction in the Principles of Christian Religion." On the other hand, he drew attention to the specific "customs and maxims" of First Nations' cultures in the matter of childbirth. It was the "invariable custom of Indian women to retire and bring forth their children alone, and in secret," he noted. To convict such a woman under a European statute making it a capital offence to conceal childbirth was, he argued, notoriously unfair.

Childbirth within Ojibwa culture was different from European experience. Knowledge about giving birth was much more widely dispersed in a hunter-gatherer society, where isolation and seasonal migrations required individualized ability to cope. A few women were recognized as the most senior and experienced midwives in the area, but all Ojibwa women would have attended births from time to time. In the more settled, agriculturally based European communities, specialization had already begun to intrude upon the level of birthing knowledge available to most women. Delivery continued to take place in the home until well into the twentieth century, but depending upon their ability to pay, European women were coming more and more to rely upon "expert" assistance from midwives or medical doctors.[16]

Most Ojibwa women would also have approached childbirth with a more positive outlook than prevailing European beliefs inspired. White onlookers frequently thought the relative lack of difficulty that First Nations' women experienced during birth worthy of extensive commentary. Andrew Graham, a white fur trader who wrote in the late eighteenth century, stressed how few of the illnesses that "afflict the delicate European" were encountered in First Nations' women giving birth. "Their pains [are] very light and soon over," he noted. Women commonly gave birth while travelling, he recorded, dropping behind and bringing forth "the little stranger ... and carrying it on their backs, proceed[ing] to overtake their companions as if nothing had happened." There are some racist assumptions operating here. The author is disavowing the physical expenditure of energy and pain that First Nations' women would have experienced during labour. But the cultural overlay that imbued childbirth with positive attitudes and a detailed knowledge of the process would have made a difference to many of the women. A pregnant Ojibwa woman would not have made the sorts of arrangements that European women commonly did for an extended period of "confinement and lying-in." Nor would she likely have approached members of the white community, medical or otherwise, for information or assistance. Whether this ought to have culminated in a conviction for concealment where the infant died would have been highly problematic.[17]

Beardsley's petition touched a nerve in the small Niagara community. The twenty members of the grand jury that had committed Angelique Pilotte for trial wrote in collectively. They stated that they were "strongly inclined to give credit" to the assertions in the petition, and recommended mercy. Thomas Clark and a number of other magistrates and "principal Inhabitants" of the area also wrote to urge that Angelique Pilotte be pardoned. The military officers stationed at Fort George (Niagara-on-the-Lake) added their voices as well, petitioning for mercy through their spokesman, Henry William Vavasour of the Royal Engineers. The Ojibwa left no written records of their opinions in this matter.

Why so many prominent white men expended such energy on Angelique Pilotte's behalf is not clear. Many of these men relied upon trading arrangements with the First Nations and they may have been anxious not to jeopardize relations. On the other hand, they may have thought that Angelique Pilotte had not received a fair trial. Some may have been sufficiently knowledgeable about First Nations' customs that they viewed the application of the European law to an Ojibwa woman as anomalous. Many of the men who interceded had extensive links with the Indian Department, while others were married to women of First Nations' descent. Thomas Clark, for example, was married to Mary Margaret Kerr, a granddaughter of the Mohawk woman Mary Brant.[18]

There may also have been some motivation to seek clemency because of the alliances that had been forged during the War of 1812. The Ojibwa, along with peoples of the Iroquois Confederacy, had fought with the British during the War of 1812, hoping to stem the advancing tide of American white settlers. Their contribution was widely credited by Canadian residents as vital to the American defeat. The white settlers did not honour their allies' full, legitimate claims to land entitlements. In the fifteen years after the war, vast tracts of First Nations' lands were transferred to agricultural settlers through seven land treaties. In contrast, conspicuous efforts to exercise leniency on behalf of a young Ojibwa woman may have been more acceptable.[19]

A common white male attitude of the time is revealed in the following passage, which would be published in the Kingston *Chronicle* a few years later:

Our readers will easily believe that we are not afflicted with any Rousseau-like sentimentality for savage life, and may therefore credit us when we say, that the youthful squaw exhibits, in her ordinary appearance, a persuasive gentleness of demeanour, a winning delicacy and very often a beauty of figure and countenance joined to a softness of voice peculiarly pleasing; and that there is about her a quiet submissiveness which, betraying the habitual endurance of oppression, interest us in her fate.

Robert Gourlay, a white, Upper Canadian social activist and reformer who advocated clemency on Angelique Pilotte's behalf, described her in just such terms. Writing to the Kingston *Gazette* in March 1818, he emphasized Angelique Pilotte's passivity and silence in the face of the criminal trial, and urged compassion on the basis of her "whole innocency of appearance."[20]

Blinkered by racism, Judge William Campbell was a proponent of assimilating First Nations' peoples and their customs. He would insist in 1822 that individuals of First Nations' descent who committed crimes against other people from the First Nations must be brought within the purview of English criminal law. In 1826 he would accuse "nine-tenths of the Blacks" in the province of subsisting "primarily by theft." But the community outcry on behalf of Angelique Pilotte would have given him reason to pause.[21]

Furthermore, Campbell would have been aware that the rigid English infanticide statute under which Angelique Pilotte had been convicted had been amended in many jurisdictions. In 1803 the English Parliament had repealed the law, noting that it "had been found in sundry cases difficult and inconvenient to be put into practice." Thus English women charged with the murder of their illegitimate children were again governed by the rules and presumptions of law used in ordinary murder trials. To deal with the difficulties of proof, the new legislation further provided that when a mother was acquitted on the murder charge, a new verdict of "concealment" could be substituted. This new offence had a maximum penalty of two years' imprisonment, a sharp drop from the death penalty seen in the earlier statute.[22]

The jurisdictions of New Brunswick, Lower Canada, and Nova Scotia had already moved to repeal the harsh death penalty for the concealment offence, following the English lead: New Brunswick in 1810, Lower Canada in 1812, and Nova Scotia in 1813. Each adopted provisions almost identical to the 1803 English statute, setting a penalty for the new concealment offence at a maximum of two years. Upper Canada was beginning to look reactionary and uncompromising against this backdrop.[23]

Pardons and commutation of sentence were the prerogative of the Crown, which retained the authority to extend "Royal Mercy" to those convicted of crime. On 18 September, Campbell forwarded the documents concerning the case to the colonial administrator of the province, Samuel Smith. Smith was asked to decide whether Angelique Pilotte was a "fit object for the exercise of the Royal Mercy." Several weeks later, Smith granted a further respite of six months. Noting the "very uncommon Interest the case seems to have excited in all Ranks," Smith forwarded the petitions to Colonial Secretary Lord Bathurst for Royal consideration. Angelique Pilotte was to be "recommended to the mercy of the Prince Regent for a final reprieve." This process of appealing the capital sentence through colonial channels was the normal procedure followed by convicted felons in Canada.[24]

October, November, December, January, February, March, and April dragged by, while Angelique Pilotte remained confined to jail. This in itself posed a considerable risk to her health. It was widely understood that First Nations' prisoners exposed to the disease-ridden inmates of most Canadian jails seldom survived with their health intact. Described in the Kingston *Gazette* as a "poor, neglected wretch" who had experienced "cruel injustice" through her own "ignorance and the inadvertency of others," Angelique Pilotte would not know if she would be granted a reprieve until 13 May 1818. That day she learned that the Prince Regent had reduced her sentence to one year of imprisonment. Angelique Pilotte's case had provided an opportunity for the ostentatious display of both might and mercy.[25]

INFANTICIDE ON A VANCOUVER ISLAND BEACH, 1896

It was Wednesday, 8 April 1896, and the hawkers of the Nanaimo *Free Press* flourished some sensational copy. On page one, tucked between advertisements for "Plain and Fancy Sailor Hats at 50¢, 75¢ and $1.00" and "Odoroma toothpaste," was the following news:

A GRUESOME FIND
Body of a Newly-Born Child
Discovered on the Beach
Last Night.

A number of children inadvertently made a gruesome discovery on the beach near No. 1 [mine]shaft last night in the shape of a dead and newly-born baby, whose body was contained in a rough sack.

The latter was first observed by Aily Matson and Joe Raines, and was lying about six feet away from Mr. S.M. Robins' private boathouse, towards high water mark. The boys at once noticed that the sack was not empty, and with the natural curiosity of youth, proceeded to investigate. One youngster, bolder than the rest, whose name has not yet been ascertained, caught up the sack and dumped out the contents, which, as might be expected, startled him and his companions not a little.

The body was stark naked, the only other article in the sack being, curiously enough, a bright English sixpence, which was loosely attached to the child's neck by a piece of string.[26]

A little girl named Greenwell picked up the silver sixpence, which was lying in one of the wrinkles of the infant's neck. Then the children went running for help. Alexander Matheson, the first adult they found, notified James Crossan, the Chief of Police of Nanaimo, who lived nearby. He hastened to the scene, rolled the infant's body up in a sheet, and carted it home. The body was turned over to John Hilbert's undertaking parlour, and the search was on for the guilty party.[27]

Police Chief Crossan's initial examination of the body revealed that it was a female infant, weighing eight or nine pounds. According to the press, this was an "exceptional size." Most newborns of the time were significantly smaller. Decomposition had not yet set in, and Crossan adduced from the appearance of the potato sack that it had been in the water for several days before the tide washed it up on the beach. There were no obvious signs of violence, although the reporters noted that this was inconclusive. "A newly-born child could be easily disposed of without leaving any surface indications," they wrote.[28]

News of the tragedy spread quickly through the small city, into all corners of the community. Late-nineteenth-century Nanaimo was a city of stark contrasts. Perched on a narrow plain on the east coast of Vancouver Island, it was a thriving, bustling resource town. Coal had been discovered in the 1850s, and the completion of the Esquimalt and Nanaimo Railway in 1886 had spurred its development as an important regional centre. Powerful and confident coal-mining magnates and business entrepreneurs had built grand, stylish residences displaying their wealth. Impoverished working-class employees lived nearby, often in neighbourhoods separated along ethnic or racial lines, in bleak clapboard row houses.[29]

It was the Finnish community in Nanaimo that would offer the first lead in the case. A sizeable group of Finnish immigrants had settled in Nanaimo and the surrounding area by the late nineteenth century. The Canadian government had been aggressive in its efforts to promote immigration, and Finnish men had arrived seeking jobs in mining and lumbering industries. Some brought their wives and families, and the population of Finnish women swelled as young, single women joined the immigration stream as well. Many Finnish women found jobs in the new country, segregated into occupations designated as "female," most frequently in domestic service. Women had been barred by legislation from working in the mines in British Columbia since 1877.[30]

Dubbed the "Finland Colony" by the other inhabitants of Nanaimo, many of the Finns spoke only Finnish, and they are reported to have tended to keep to themselves. Restricted by language barriers and prejudice from well-paid, safe, and secure jobs, they set about establishing a cultural base for their community. They founded the first Finnish Lutheran congregation in 1893 and a Finnish Temperance Society (Aallotar, or Maiden of the Waves) shortly thereafter. They ran their own theatre, music events, and political (predominantly socialist) discussion groups.[31]

Some members of the Finnish community would become actively involved in the hunt to expose the wrongdoer that April. An unnamed male Finn first came forward to see Chief Crossan. He confided his suspicions about a fellow Finn, Anna Balo (or Ballo), who had been living in Nanaimo for the past five years. She had recently been in the family way, he said, and no sooner had she heard of the infant's discovery than she left the city.[32]

Without this tip, suspicion might never have centred on Anna Balo. Most of the women who were charged with infanticide were young, unmarried women, pregnant for the first time. Angelique Pilotte had been typical. In contrast, Anna Balo was forty-four years old, married, and the mother of six children. It was unusual for married women to find themselves confronted with charges of infanticide. This may reflect the fact that they would seem to have been less likely to have been involved in child murder. Unlike single women, they would not have faced life-altering shame at pregnancy. Furthermore, bearing and raising a child within a heterosexual marriage would have been economically much more feasible than trying to do so alone.[33]

On the other hand, the relative absence of accusations against married females may simply reflect the greater difficulties of proof. Married women would rarely need to have concealed the full pregnancy, could have given birth openly, killed the child, and later declared that it had died of natural causes. With the collusion of their husbands, it would have been virtually impossible to obtain a conviction. The newspapers not infrequently reported incidents of "laying over," where infants were smothered or suffocated while sleeping in their parents' beds. Such situations were generally declared "accidental," and criminal charges would not be pressed.[34]

Anna Balo's marital status did not serve as much protection in this instance, however. As the press recounted, "her husband [was] said to have deserted her three years ago." She was a deserted wife trying to cope with six children, and showing visible signs of pregnancy. Neighbours would have done some speculating about who the father was, and the pregnancy would have been a source of embarrassment and some shame. Furthermore, Anna Balo was experiencing acute financial distress. At least one of her sons was helping to support the family by working in the Dunsmuir coal mine, but his earnings were not sufficient. Anna's child-care responsibilities would have obliterated any prospect of her earning wages as a live-in domestic servant. The family's situation was so precarious that the City of Nanaimo had been providing Anna with a small welfare pension of five dollars a week. This in itself would have made her a target for community suspicion.[35]

Police Chief Crossan's informer told him that Anna Balo had abandoned her children and fled north to the nearby town of Wellington. Crossan pursued her that very evening. A day passed before he discovered that Anna Balo had spent the night at the home of another Finn in Wellington. By this time, she had set off again. She walked all the way to Qualicum before the police caught up with her. At this, the press expressed its complete astonishment. "It seems almost incredible, but is none the less a fact, that a woman within a few days of childbirth should have walked all the way from Wellington to Qualicum, a distance of thirty miles, in a little better than a day and a half," noted the Nanaimo *Free Press*. Finnish women were viewed as hardy, physically capable individuals. Like most immigrant women, they would have had demanding workdays, with little opportunity to plead indisposition due to female or other ailments. As a group, they were thought to have exhibited remarkable physical endurance, but this press commentary was somewhat voyeuristic. While the reporter extolled Anna Balo's stoicism and strength, the implication was that she was somewhat inhuman in her capacity to withstand pain.[36]

The police arrested Anna Balo on Friday night, 10 April, at J. Hanna's house in Qualicum. She told the constable that she was on her way to Union, in search of her husband, but she surrendered quietly. Anna Balo was taken by train back to Nanaimo, where she was arraigned in police court the next morning. There she revealed her inability to understand the proceedings in English. "Anna Balo is a foreigner and unable to understand the English language," was the first note inscribed on many of the subsequent depositions. Arrangements were made for an interpreter, and Gus Hill was retained to serve in this capacity. Dr. Robert S.B. O'Brian was sent into the county jail to examine the prisoner that afternoon. "I asked her a few questions and examined her breasts and they had the appearance of a woman that had lately been confined," he would later testify. Almost immediately thereafter, Anna Balo broke down and confessed to being the mother of the dead infant.[37]

Speaking through her Finnish interpreter but without a lawyer, Anna

Balo told Chief Crossan that the child was hers. She had given birth one week previously on 4 April. The child had died almost immediately after its birth, she stressed. Trying to dispose of its body, she had wrapped it in an empty potato sack and deposited it upon the beach of the Nanaimo Harbour. Chief Crossan carefully recorded the confession and then released all of the details to the newspaper reporters who had been awaiting the news.[38]

Meanwhile, the Nanaimo coroner, Lewis Thomas Davis, had obtained the dead infant's body from John Hilbert's undertaking establishment. On Thursday afternoon, 9 April, Coroner Davis opened an inquest before seven jurymen. They took turns viewing the body, and then turned it over to Dr. O'Brian for a post-mortem examination. When the inquest resumed on Thursday, 16 April, Dr. O'Brian was ready with a complete report. Medical jurisprudence had changed greatly since the days of Angelique Pilotte's trial. By the close of the nineteenth century, physicians had developed a sense of their own stature that was significantly inflated from earlier times. Armed with "scientific" principles and methods, they no longer gave terse reports at coroner's inquests. Now they held forth at length and in enormous detail.[39]

Dr. O'Brian's testimony was divided into three parts. First, he described the external features of the dead infant:

It was a female; the body was 21 inches in length; the umbilicus was one inch below the center of the body; the head was 13 1/2 inches in circumference; the chest 12 inches in circumference; the eyes were firmly closed and opaque, either from incomplete absorption of the pupillary membrane or from post mortem change; the ears lay close to the scalp; the scalp was covered with yellow hair, dry over the ears but glutenated over the apex; the inferior maxillary bone was not fully developed; the mouth was empty; the tongue not swollen; there was no sanguineous tumour over the crown of the head; there was no goose skin nor sign of strangulation; the chest was rather flat; the abdomen not distended; the skin of the body was discoloured and destitute of epidermis in patches; the umbilicus had not been tied; it was of rose tint, flabby and not surrounded by a zone of redness; sebaceous matter adhered to the groins and armpits; the nails were fully developed; the body weighed nine pounds.... [40]

The second part of the report, given in equal detail, concerned Dr. O'Brian's examination of the infant's internal organs. The bulk of this evidence would be about the state of the lungs. Although the lungs were only "partially distended," O'Brian noted that when he had immersed them in water, "they floated under all tests." The "water immersion" test had traditionally been used to determine whether the infant had ever drawn breath. If the lungs sank, it was taken to mean that the child had been stillborn. If they floated, the conclusion was that the child had been born alive.[41]

Some concern had been cast over the reliability of the water immersion test, since some doctors had concluded that the simple decomposition of the body could introduce air into the lungs. So Dr. O'Brian added that he had not left the matter to rest there. He had also compressed the lungs firmly, and upon incision he reported that "blood froth escaped." Dr. O'Brian finished up by noting that the lungs had "the characteristic marbled appearance of lungs in which the air cells had been distended by breathing."[42]

The last part of the report contained the conclusions. These the Nanaimo *Free Press* reported in full:

1st.  The child had not quite arrived at full term.
2nd.  The child had breathed.
3rd.  Death occurred during delivery, possibly before full legal birth or
       immediately after.
4th.  There was nothing to prove the cause of death.
5th.  The child had been dead some time before it was immersed in water.
6th.  It had been in the water probably two or three days.[43]

Detailed as the medical report had been, it seems to have raised more questions than it answered. A slightly premature infant had apparently drawn breath and then died, although from what cause the doctor could not ascertain. Whether death had occurred before, during, or after the birth was indeterminable.

Several other witnesses were called at the inquest to testify regarding Anna Balo's actions. Mrs. Anna Sharp was called first. She was a Finnish woman who lived on Pine Street, opposite the Balos. Anna Sharp stated that she had known Anna Balo for the past five years, but that she had "never been on very good terms" with her. There had been a great deal of neighbourhood interest in Anna Balo's situation, according to Mrs. Sharp. Rumours of her pregnancy were rife, and at least some were speculating that she might "take care" of the child at birth.[44]

Anna Balo had become quite reclusive since the fall, and although many of the neighbours were curious, no one was quite certain that she was pregnant. Mrs. Sharp was just one of the local Finnish women who had made a point of visiting Anna Balo to learn more. It was early in March, she told the inquest, and "I went to see Mrs. Balo but she put me out of the house for talking about her, and I never went back again...." Nevertheless, she was able to assure the jurors: "I then saw it with my own eyes that she was pregnant."[45]

Anna Sharp's testimony was meant to hurt Anna Balo. Like the unnamed male Finn who first tipped off the authorities, she was fully prepared, even eager, to implicate Anna Balo in criminal behaviour. Indeed, Anna Balo may have been an outcast within the Finnish community. Deserted and unemployed, that she was forced to take public assistance from civic officials would have emphasized her marginal status. Even the tightly knit Finnish community did not extend sufficient private support to tide her over. Neighbourhood women seem to have been estranged from Anna, gossiping behind her back and visiting her only to confirm their suspicions.

Anna Balo seems to have violated several important norms of her community. First, she had become pregnant and borne a child as a single parent. Her marital status by itself would not have been the problem. Finns attached no great social stigma to being single, and common law marriages were widespread. Some Finns had advocated the abolition of marriage as a precedent for establishing a utopian socialist community. But the evidence of sexual activity outside of a stable family unit would have presented difficulties. Finnish women who worked as prostitutes experienced great social ostracism. And the prospect of giving birth outside of a stable, heterosexual unit would have been viewed as a serious transgression of Finnish norms.[46]

Nor is infanticide reported to have been common among the Finnish population, many of whom had acquired relatively sophisticated knowledge about birth control and abortion. But it was not solely the alleged infanticide that would have alienated the community from Anna Balo. She had also abandoned her other children in her acute distress following childbirth. It is likely that Anna Balo's flight to Qualicum, leaving behind her impoverished children to fend as best they could, shocked the Finnish community as much or more than the discovery of the infant's body that had washed up on the Nanaimo beach.[47]

The next witness called by the coroner was Alexandra Balo, Anna's twelve-year-old daughter. How she felt about testifying is not known, but it is obvious that she was quite ignorant about her mother's status. She told the inquest she did not even know when her mother had been arrested. Under close questioning Alexandra Balo said that her mother had been sick about two weeks ago. "My mother was awfully white," she said, and she "told me that I couldn't go to school because she was sick." Instead, Anna Balo sent her downtown to purchase fifty cents worth of alcohol for medicinal purposes. When she returned, Anna Balo mixed the alcohol with some warm water and sugar and drank it. Young Alexandra Balo had been anxious to get back to school. This time her mother was too weak to argue. "Go if you want to, I can't do anything because I am sick," she said from her bed.[48]

What Alexandra Balo discovered when she returned from school made her decide to stay home for the next week. There was blood on the floor in her mother's bedroom, blood on the bedspread, and blood on some of her mother's dresses. Anna Balo told her to wipe up the blood on the floor, but she got up herself and washed the bedclothes and dresses. Although Alexandra Balo could not be certain, she told the inquest that she thought her mother had left the house for a few hours several days later. "I did not see her take anything with her when she went away," she added. "I am twelve years of age. Mother didn't tell me anything more," she said.[49]

Perhaps the most damning piece of evidence concerned the shiny English sixpence. Alexandra Balo was asked about it at some length, and her reply was devastating. "There was a sixpence in the house which my mother and myself thought was no good," she admitted. "It was kept in the cupboard, and the morning my mother went away I went to look for the sixpence and could not find it." The sixpence coin that had been found on the infant's body was then produced, and Alexandra Balo identified it as the same one.[50]

It is hard to know how Alexandra Balo could have been so certain of the identity of the sixpence coin. Perhaps it was damaged in some way that left it both unusable and easily identifiable. In any event, its identification traced the infant's body to the Balo home. With that, the evidence drew to a close. Anna Balo was asked whether she wished to have the testimony re-read to her, and through her interpreter she said "no." Asked whether she wished to give a formal statement, she replied, again through the interpreter, "Nothing to say."[51]

The coroner's jury retired to consider their findings. Despite the damaging revelations of Anna Sharp and Alexandra Balo, the complexity and contradictions inherent in the medical evidence seem to have been the predominant concern. The verdict would reflect the jurors' uncertainty over the cause of death. "We the Jury find that the child found on the Beach on the 7th of April died during Child Birth," they inscribed on the

The deposition of Alexandra Balo reads, in part:
*c. I also saw blood on the cover (?) that was on the bed.*
*d. There was a sixpence in the house which my mother and myself thought was
no good. It was kept in the cupboard and the morning my mother went away
I went to look for the sixpence and could not find it. Sixpence produced is the
same one. I don't remember the date when my mother went away.*

formal "Inquisition" document. And with that, they adjourned, having neither condemned nor exonerated Anna Balo.[52]

On 16 April Police Magistrate J.H. Simpson committed Anna Balo for full trial at the Spring Assizes. Due to the vagueness of the medical report, the charge was "concealment of a birth" rather than murder or manslaughter. There had been many legislative changes since Angelique Pilotte's trial in the early decades of the nineteenth century. Angelique Pilotte had been charged under the old draconian statute that made it a capital offence for an unmarried woman to conceal a birth. By 1836 this law, with its reverse evidentiary onus, had been repealed in all jurisdictions.[53]

From that date forward, no woman could be put to death for infanticide unless the Crown could prove all of the elements of the formal charge of murder. Instead, a lesser offence of "concealment of a birth" was placed on the books, with a maximum penalty of two years' imprisonment. Additional amendments had also made it possible to charge married women with concealment. Criminal law became the responsibility of the federal government in 1867, and when British Columbia joined Canada in 1871 it inherited this legal framework.[54]

The exact wording of the concealment offence had been spelled out in the Criminal Code of 1892: "Every one is guilty of an indictable offence, and liable to two years' imprisonment, who disposes of the dead body of any child in any manner, with intent to conceal the fact that its mother was delivered of it, whether the child died before, or during, or after birth." Here was a charge that would serve, despite the inability of the medical experts to ascertain the cause of death.[55]

Interestingly, Anna Balo was not charged with another offence that had been added to the Criminal Code in 1892. Where a child died or was permanently injured during birth, the law had begun to question the competence of women to arrange the circumstances of their own labour. "Failing to obtain reasonable assistance during childbirth" was an entirely new crime that reflected the increasing social and medical control that was being exercised over birthing. This was quite a different approach from that of the First Nations, which viewed childbirth primarily as an individualized responsibility. Now the law would force women to seek, on pain of criminal penalty, various sorts of "expert" assistance in labour.[56]

The punishment set out for this new offence was comparatively severe. The penalty was a maximum of life imprisonment, if it could be proved that the mother's intent in not seeking reasonable assistance was that the child should not live. If she intended only to conceal the birth, the penalty was set at a maximum of seven years. In some ways, it is surprising that Anna Balo was not charged with this offence. In answer to a question from one of the jurymen at the coroner's inquest, Dr. O'Brian had stated that he thought "if the woman would have had proper medical attendance the child might have been saved."[57]

If the Crown could prove the intent to conceal the birth, either charge was open to it. Yet Anna Balo was charged only with concealment, the less serious offence. Perhaps the authorities felt that Anna Balo's actions should not place her in jeopardy of serving seven years in prison. Or perhaps the increasingly "professionalized" approach to childbirth that was developing in the more populous regions back east had not yet taken hold on the west coast. Perhaps western legal officials thought that it would have been unreasonable to have expected an impoverished immigrant woman to seek expensive medical assistance during childbirth.

The Deputy Attorney-General, Arthur G. Smith, acted as the Crown attorney in the matter. As he began to prepare the case for trial, he made some handwritten notes on the back of the coroner's deposition documents. Here he worried about his ability to secure a conviction, even in the two-year concealment charge. "We should have some better evidence of the birth," he scrawled. Unless he could pin down Anna Balo as the dead infant's mother, his case would come to nothing. The Deputy Attorney-General had several thoughts on how to secure such evidence. "Can the sack be identified?" he queried. He may have thought that Alexandra Balo's identification of the silver sixpence would be insufficient to tie the body to Anna Balo. He also wanted to locate a new witness, a Mrs. Mattison. Alexandra Balo had revealed at the inquest that Mrs. Mattison, a neighbour, had dropped by the Balo home while Anna Balo was still bedridden, the week after she took sick. Deputy Attorney-General Smith may have thought that Mrs. Mattison would be able to offer some first-hand account of Anna Balo's condition.[58]

The notes also reveal the Crown attorney's serious reservations about Anna Balo's confession to Chief Crossan. This he described as her "supposed confession." Was he worried that a court would decide it had not been made voluntarily? Coming so quickly after the intrusive physical examination Dr. O'Brian had carried out on Anna Balo in jail, it might have struck a jury that the confession was tainted by the events that had preceded it. There were long-standing rules of evidence concerning the acceptability of confessions. Customarily they were treated as inadmissible in court if obtained under coercive circumstances. According to S.R. Clarke's 1872 *Treatise on Criminal Law as Applicable to the Dominion of Canada*, these were important, time-honoured principles of law:

It is a general and well-established principle that the confession of a prisoner, in order to be admissible, must be free and voluntary. Any inducement to confess held out to the prisoner by a person in authority, or any undue compulsion upon him, will be sufficient to exclude the confession.[59]

The Crown attorney anticipated some difficulty in getting Anna Balo's confession into court.

The Spring Assizes opened on 5 May 1896. Montague William

Tyrwhitt Drake, the same judge who would try Euphemia Rabbitt one year later, was presiding. He had a reputation as a dour man, both strict and to the point. Anna Balo, without funds and unfamiliar with legal proceedings, appeared without defence counsel. There is no indication in the court records that anyone advised the accused woman that she should retain a lawyer. Judge Drake seems to have seen no reason to order a court-appointed lawyer for a non-capital offence. Without legal advice Anna Balo would have had no inkling that the Crown perceived its case as weak. After she was arraigned, the prisoner announced that she intended to plead "guilty" to the charge. No one contested the identification of the dead infant as Anna Balo's child. No one took issue with the Crown's position that Anna Balo had flung the child into the Nanaimo Harbour with the intention of concealing her pregnancy and birth from the community at large. The perceived inadequacies of Anna Balo's confession suddenly became irrelevant with her decision to plead guilty as charged.[60]

But Anna Balo's break would come at the time of sentencing, which was handed down in court the next day. His Lordship Judge Drake pronounced as follows:

He considered that a nominal punishment would be sufficient under the circumstances, as beyond the mere concealment of birth there was no suggestion of impropriety. The sentence of the Court was 24 hours' imprisonment, and as this dated from the first day of the Assizes, the prisoner was now discharged.[61]

This was a "nominal" punishment, a slap on the wrist compared to the maximum penalty of two years' imprisonment. Anna Balo's immediate discharge provided a clear signal that legal officials were prepared to tolerate, if not exactly condone, the secret disposal of the bodies of dead infants, and potentially even outright infanticide.

With this decision, Judge Drake was following in the footsteps of a long line of male judges and jurors who had exhibited similar sentiments in other nineteenth-century infanticide cases. In some areas of the country, up to two-thirds of the courts were issuing outright acquittals of women charged with murder or manslaughter, despite overwhelming and gruesome evidence of maternal guilt in many cases. On the lesser charge of concealment, up to nearly half of the women were being discharged and released. If Anna Balo had been legally represented, and if she had pleaded not guilty, the chances would have been good that she would have been acquitted. Lenience in verdicts and sentencing is indicative of a pervasive sense of tolerance and even compassion that the legal system expressed toward women accused of infanticide.[62]

Why were legal authorities so "soft" on these women? First, they seem to have been very sympathetic to the motives that forced women to take the lives of their own offspring. According to the legal authors of an *Upper Canada Law Journal* article in 1862, women frequently committed infanticide out of a "sense of shame" to prevent the "loss of reputation." "The loss of character is the loss of earthly prospects," emphasized the lawyers. "The consequence at times is a life of prostitution, loathsome disease — in a word, a living death."[63]

It was almost as if the male lawyers believed that these women were acting out of a sense of honour, to preserve their reputations and to avoid descent into unimaginably harsh circumstances. They may have been impressed by the courage and resourcefulness that the women exhibited as they struggled to hold their lives together. There was virtually no discussion of mental illness or insanity. Instead, these acts were seen as deliberate and rational steps women took to reassert order upon a situation tragically altered by an illegitimate pregnancy.

Second, the infants who were the victims of these crimes occupied a position of little status in the nineteenth century. Infant mortality rates were relatively high well into the twentieth century, frequently ranging over one hundred deaths for every thousand live births. Infant death was omnipresent, and there was a certain sense of inevitability, even complacency, over its commonness. Many individuals responded to infant death with what would seem to us today to be callous behaviour. One example of this surfaced at a coroner's inquest in Halifax in 1861. Evidence revealed that when the body of an infant was found in an alley behind a rum shop on Water Street, people laughed and joked about the discovery, referring to the body as the "prize in the alleyway."[64]

Prominent medical authorities frequently referred to infants as somewhat less than human. For example, in his *Crime and Insanity* published in England in 1911, Dr. Charles Arthur Mercier stated:

In comparison with other cases of murder, a minimum of harm is done by [infanticide]. The victim's mind is not sufficiently developed to enable it to suffer from the contemplation of approaching suffering or death. It is incapable of feeling fear or terror. Nor is its consciousness sufficiently developed to enable it to suffer pain in appreciable degree. Its loss leaves no gap in any family circle, deprives no children of their breadwinner or their mother, no human being of a friend, helper, or companion. The crime diffuses no sense of insecurity.[65]

In a society in which infants were often treated as subhuman, the victims of infanticide would have been almost beneath notice. These were children that no one wanted to claim. Their mothers could not care for them, and their fathers would not acknowledge them. Nineteenth-century children would assume importance in the eyes of the law when there were disputes between grown adults over their custody. Issues regarding the proper descent of male blood lines and the orderly conveyance of family property to future generations brought children's legal status to the fore. However, the mothers of children who died by infanticide were primarily poor, working-class, unmarried women who had been seduced and abandoned by men who wanted nothing more to do with them. There were no blood lines to protect, and certainly no estates to be concerned about transferring. In Anna Balo's case, that the child was the offspring of a "foreigner" would have consigned it to even greater marginality. These were children that the courts could afford to ignore almost completely.

Finally, the lenience of the courts was at least in part a response to the desperation of most of the women charged with child murder or abandonment. There were simply no options. Child welfare agencies, which might have provided facilities for unwanted children, were still in their infancy. In the meantime, a woman who could not care for her infant faced painfully few alternatives. In some areas, neighbourhood women took unwanted infants into their own homes for a time. They did this as a business, and charged a lump sum or regular fees to the parents. Occasionally they would also place these infants out for private adoption. Censured as "baby farms," these homes came under increasing criticism by the turn of the century for their very high infant death rates. Accusations were regularly voiced that the infants in these homes were deliberately murdered through neglect or drug overdose. But Anna Balo would have been unable to afford the required fees, even if she had been able to find a willing home.[66]

In some of the larger cities, charitable organizations and religious institutions had begun to establish Infants' Homes to look after deserted children. Operating on voluntary contributions, religious donations, and in some cases small government grants, these homes also had infant death rates that were shockingly high. La Creche D'Youville, managed in Montreal by the Grey Nuns, accommodated over fifteen thousand abandoned children between 1801 and 1870. Between 80 and 90 per cent died while under institutional care.[67]

There were no institutionalized resources whatsoever in Nanaimo. In

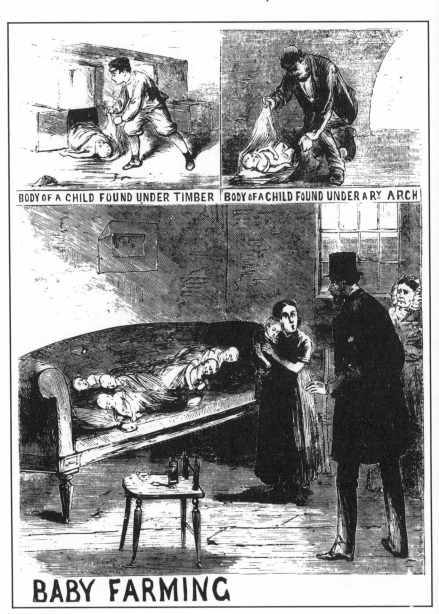

The discovery of infants' bodies and baby-farming
depicted in the *Illustrated Police News* (London), 1876.

the entire province of British Columbia by the end of the nineteenth century there were only three. The closest Infants' Home Anna Balo could have found would have been in Victoria, where the Roman Catholic Orphanage and the Protestant Orphan Home competed for clients. There were considerable tensions between the Finnish Lutheran churches and the more established religions in Canada, and Anna Balo would have been unlikely to have sought assistance from either orphanage. Even if she had wished to try, and had been able to secure transportation with the child to Victoria, it is by no means clear that the child's future would have been significantly different. Women for whom child rearing created impossible demands chose infanticide out of necessity, and the courts by and large respected their decisions.[68]

It is hard to imagine, however, that the women themselves would have been entirely unmoved as they were forced to terminate the lives of their newborn children. It will never, of course, be known whether Anna Balo murdered her infant child, or whether she was just trying to dispose of the body of a child that had died of natural causes at birth. Whatever the truth, she was obviously very distraught when she left the newborn infant on the Nanaimo beach. The shiny English sixpence that she tied around its neck as a blessing stands as eloquent testimony to her grief.

# 5

# Abortion

Emily Howard Stowe is widely remembered today for her role as the first white Canadian woman to practise medicine in Canada. Less is known about her role as one of the first doctors in nineteenth-century Canada to be tried for attempting to procure an abortion. That she became the target of a well-publicized prosecution in Toronto in 1879 was no accident. Her stature as a feminist activist made her a focal point for unprecedented medical and legal scrutiny.[1]

Emily Howard Stowe was born in 1831 in the village of Norwich, southwest of Brantford. Hannah Howard Jennings and Solomon Jennings, her parents, were American Quakers who had immigrated to Upper Canada. Emily Stowe was the eldest of six female children, all of whom were educated at home by their mother, who came from a family of school-teachers. At age fifteen, she took her first teaching job at a one-room, rural school-house in Norwich.[2]

Anxious to pursue her general education further, she applied to study at the University of Toronto some time in the late 1840s or early 1850s. The University Senate apparently considered her application, but rejected it on principle. No woman had yet been permitted to register for study at a Canadian university. Instead, Emily Stowe was steered toward further training in teaching, and in 1854 she graduated from the Normal School in Toronto with a First Class Teacher's Certificate.[3]

Upon her graduation from Normal School, she accepted the position of principal at Brantford Public School, becoming the first woman principal in Canada. She taught there until 1856, when she married John Stowe, an Englishman from Yorkshire. As was customary for middle-class white women, Emily Stowe resigned her teaching post upon marriage. She moved with her husband to Mount Pleasant, a small town just southwest of Brantford where John Stowe practised his trade as a carriage-maker. He built a large home for his bride, and Emily Stowe gave birth to three children in 1857, 1861, and 1863. Tuberculosis eventually forced John Stowe into a sanatorium for extended treatment. His carriage-trade business disintegrated, and Emily Stowe resumed teaching, this time at the Nelles Academy in Mount Pleasant. John Stowe's illness affected her deeply, and she resolved to embark upon a career as a physician.[4]

Although her choice of occupation was unusual for a woman, it had not always been thus. Prior to the nineteenth century, healing had traditionally been a female occupation practised within the home. Medical knowledge had been widely distributed among the population. There were pockets of expertise; certain herbalists, midwives, and lay practitioners ministered to relatives and neighbours in the immediate vicinity. Among the most knowledgeable were members of the religious nursing orders of the Roman Catholic Church, and they practised primarily within the province of Quebec.[5]

The nineteenth century witnessed an organizational upsurge in North America among medical theorists and practitioners, who began to form defined "sects" and compete actively for patients. The most affluent and powerful group called themselves the "regular" doctors. For the first half of the century, their formal training generally consisted of an apprenticeship to a licensed physician for a number of years and successful completion of a licensing examination. At best they studied at one of the few medical schools in Canada, the United States, or England for a brief period. Many preferred to heal by "heroic" measures, which for much of the century consisted of the massive letting of blood, and the prescription of huge doses of laxatives, arsenic, strychnine, and alcohol- and opium-based medications.[6]

In contrast, some of the competing sects used less dangerous treatment. The Thomsonians prescribed mild herbal remedies. The Homeopaths emphasized self-care, minute doses of tinctures and powders, and a moderate regimen including fresh air, pure foods and water, and the avoidance of over-stimulation. The Eclectics adopted a mixture of remedies tailored to the individual patient. Other sects advised dietary

Emily Howard Stowe.

changes and preventive care. And specific groups, such as peoples of the First Nations, preferred their traditional healers.[7]

The "regulars," who would ultimately succeed in asserting dominance in the medical field, were predominantly middle-class, white males with a greater share of political influence and economic resources.

The "irregular" medical sects were more open to women and people of colour, and this distinction became one of the focal points for debate. In 1874, for example, John Stewart of Kingston attacked homeopathy because two of the seven Homeopathic Colleges in the United States were for women, suggesting that homeopathy ought to be confined "to the crones of the Province." In Quebec the situation was further complicated by French–English power struggles, as British-trained physicians secured licensing legislation that elevated them to an élite status over the francophone practitioners.[8]

In the 1860s, when Emily Stowe resolved to become a physician, the regulars and the irregulars were inextricably locked in battle over which group would successfully monopolize the profession of medicine in Ontario. Emily Stowe seems to have recognized that the regular physicians were in the ascendancy in Canada and she chose first to seek "regular" medical training. She applied for admission to the school of medicine at the University of Toronto, which promptly rejected her application on the basis of gender. A prominent medical journal, the *Canada Lancet*, articulated the rationale for barring women: "As wives, mothers, sisters and dainty little housekeepers we have the utmost love and respect for them; but we do not think the profession of medicine, as a rule, a fit place for them." Undeterred, Emily Stowe looked south of the border, where a number of American medical colleges had begun to open their doors to women.[9]

Even in the United States options were limited. Emily Stowe selected a homeopathic medical college in New York City that catered to an exclusively female student body. She placed her family in the care of her sister, Cornelia, and enrolled in the New York Medical College and Hospital for Women, Homeopathic. Dr. Clemence Sophia Lozier, the founder of the school, had established it in 1863 to enable more women to obtain medical training. At the time, the typical American female medical college was run by one of the "irregular" sects, reflecting the somewhat greater openness of these medical groups to women. While Emily Stowe chose to pursue homeopathic training, she never relinquished her desire to compete, on male terms, with the regular physicians back in Canada.[10]

In 1867 at the age of thirty-six, Emily Stowe graduated from the school of medicine, and took up residence with her family in Toronto. There she opened her doctor's office and placed an advertisement in the local papers. Presuming that her patients would be primarily women, Stowe addressed her appeal to them directly: "Mrs. E.H. Stowe, M.D., Physician and Accoucheur, Respectfully announces to her patients, and ladies in general, that she is now permanently located at N. 39 Alma Terrace, Richmond Street. Office Hours from 9 a.m. to 3 p.m."[11]

In 1869 the Ontario Legislature enacted a statute providing the College of Physicians and Surgeons of Ontario with the sole authority to license doctors. While provision was made to ensure homeopathic and eclectic membership on the governing council, the regulars would dominate by force of numbers. One correspondent with the *Canada Lancet* suggested that the integration of the various medical factions would ultimately serve to "hug ... Homeopathy and Eclecticism to death." Some of the regulations passed by the new College, struggling to establish a centrally organized profession, would have a major impact upon Emily Stowe. All doctors trained in the United States were ordered to take a matriculation examination before a Council of the College of Physicians and Surgeons. Before qualifying for licensing, they also had to attend at least one session of lectures at an Ontario medical school.[12]

Emily Stowe applied repeatedly for admission to the Toronto medical school, but the authorities there persistently barred her registration on the grounds of gender. Despite this, she continued to see patients openly, ignoring the statutory penalty of one hundred dollars that had been set for those who practised without a licence. Her practice flourished, and she was soon forced to expand to larger premises at 111 Church Street.[13]

In 1870, the Toronto School of Medicine relented and for one session opened the doors of its medical school to two women: Emily Stowe and Jenny Kidd Trout, a Toronto woman ten years Emily Stowe's junior who was just embarking upon a career in medicine. The two attended classes amid unrelenting, uproarious manifestations of sexual harassment. The anti-female graffiti plastered upon the classroom walls was so vile that the caretakers had to whitewash them four times that session. Students and faculty alike engaged in classroom discussions that deliberately emphasized vulgarity. Filth and garbage were piled upon the women's seats on numerous occasions.[14]

Both women graduated. Jenny Trout went on to further medical training at the Women's Medical College of Pennsylvania, and Emily Stowe returned to her Church Street office. But Emily Stowe refused to submit to the oral and written matriculation examination at the hands of the College of Physicians and Surgeons. It would have been an indignity to submit to additional evaluation from a hostile group of men, and she resolved simply to carry on practice, despite the absence of a licence.[15]

THE TRIAL OF EMILY STOWE, M.D.

A rather bizarre chain of events surrounding the death of Sarah Ann Lovell on 12 August 1879 would provide the perfect forum for a renewed attack upon Emily Stowe's claims to professional status. Sarah Ann Lovell, a nineteen-year-old, unmarried domestic servant, was discovered dead in the bedroom of her mother's Deer Park home that afternoon. Her death was startling. She had been in excellent health and had just returned in high spirits from a morning's outing to Eaton's on Yonge Street to purchase a dress. Her mother, Elizabeth Lovell, was shocked by her daughter's death. She called in Dr. Thomas Armstrong, who had attended Sarah Ann Lovell during an illness several years earlier.[16]

Dr. Armstrong was baffled by the suddenness of the death, and he immediately notified Coroner John McConnell of Thornhill. Dr. McConnell, who had been acting as coroner for several years, had graduated from the medical school of the Toronto University in 1869 and had been in practice for ten years. He commenced an inquest at the Deer Park Hotel that same evening. Dr. Armstrong and Dr. Philbrick were assigned to conduct a post-mortem examination on the body. The two were unable to ascertain the cause of death, although they noted that congestion of the lungs was an immediate factor. Most important, however, they reported that Sarah Ann Lovell's "uterus was large and contained a male foetus of about five months."[17]

Prior to her death Sarah Ann Lovell had been boarding and working for about a year and a half at a hotel on West Market Street, near the St. Lawrence Market. Her employer, Mrs. John Avis, told the inquest that she had discharged her servant when she first suspected the illegitimate pregnancy, several months before the young woman's death. "She asked me to let her go to see a doctor, and as she was not ill I suspected she was pregnant," testified Mrs. Avis.[18]

Further investigation revealed that the physician Sarah Ann Lovell had gone to see was Dr. Emily Stowe, and that she had been taking medication prescribed by the doctor before her death. With mounting interest, Coroner McConnell pursued this lead. Testimony from Augusta Stowe, Emily Stowe's eldest daughter, who was accustomed to assisting her mother when she consulted with patients, confirmed the visit. The twenty-two-year-old Augusta stated that she remembered Sarah Ann Lovell's arrival at her mother's office on 23 May 1879 "very distinctly." "When I opened the door I observed that [the young woman's] eyes were very much swollen as though she had been weeping. When she asked for the doctor, I showed her into the house."[19]

Dr. Emily Stowe was anxious to tell her side of the story, but questions about her medical status preoccupied her questioners. "I have followed my profession in Toronto for eighteen years," she announced, revealing that she understood her medical practice to have begun well before her formal medical training. Then she added: "I graduated in the New York Medical College for Women and attended one course of lectures at the Toronto School of Medicine. I decline to say whether I am a licensed practitioner."[20]

Of her contact with the deceased woman, she spoke at some length:

The late Sarah Ann Lovell called on me on the 23rd of May at my office.... She gave me her name as "Levall" and said she lived on Elm Street.... She said that her menses were interrupted. At one time she told me this was caused by cold; and at another that she thought it was from another cause. I made the usual examination of the breast and satisfied myself that she was *enceinte* [pregnant]. She asked me to give her something to prevent conception, but I refused to do so. She then behaved frantically, and said that she would kill herself, and that if I would not give her something she would go somewhere else.[21]

If the post-mortem examination were accurate, Sarah Ann Lovell would have been a little more than two months' pregnant at the time that she sought Dr. Stowe's assistance. Most nineteenth-century women did not consider conception an established fact until the foetus had "quickened." "Quickening" described the first recognizable movement of the foetus in the womb, generally sometime within the fourth month after conception.[22]

Sarah Ann Lovell would not yet have felt foetal movements. She would not have seen herself as pregnant but as "irregular" and would have been seeking to "bring on a period," something that most women of her era believed to be well within their rights. Initially women would try to restore the menses with hot baths and violent exercises. Next came the consumption of large quantities of purgative drugs and herbs. There were scores of pills and potions widely marketed for these purposes: Dr. Love's "celebrated pills for suppressed menstruation," "Cook's Cotton Root Compound — successfully used monthly by thousands of ladies," Dr. Gordon's "Pearls of Health — They Make Women Regular," Sir James Clarke's Female Pills, and others. While most of these pharmaceutical products were of doubtful efficacy, some were composed of traditionally

recognized herbs and roots that could induce miscarriage in certain circumstances. Designed to produce vomiting, muscular contractions, and
convulsion, they sometimes produced abortion as a side effect. Sarah Ann
Lovell may have tried, presumably without success, any number of these
products.[23]

Under English common law it had never been considered wrongful to
procure an abortion prior to quickening. Nineteenth-century legislation
eventually began to encroach upon this principle, but the new laws seem
to have been somewhat at odds with the views of much of the population.
In 1810 New Brunswick became the first Canadian jurisdiction to pass a
statute that prohibited abortions regardless of their timing. Those done
after quickening attracted the death penalty, but those completed prior to
quickening involved a lesser penalty of imprisonment or fines. Prince
Edward Island passed very similar legislation in 1836.[24]

Abortion legislation was expanded in later decades, extending the
reach of the criminal law still further. In 1841 Upper Canada became the
first jurisdiction to eliminate the quickening distinction entirely, rendering
all abortions regardless of stage subject to a maximum penalty of life
imprisonment. Other provincial legislatures followed suit, and when the
Dominion government gained control over the criminal law upon Confederation, it cemented the far-reaching statutory enactments into federal law.[25]

Developing medical notions about conception provided the lobby
composed of the regular physicians with a technical rationale for the
introduction of much of this legislation. By the nineteenth century some
Canadian physicians had come to believe in the vitality of foetal life from
the moment of conception. The regular physicians seized upon this argument and campaigned vigorously to make abortions illegal. The real
motivation behind the lobby, however, was more complex than would
appear on the surface.[26]

Unlike infanticide perpetrators, who seem to have been typically
working-class and frequently immigrant women and women of colour,
women who sought abortions seem to have been more widely dispersed
throughout the population. Some, like Sarah Ann Lovell, were undeniably
single, working-class women. But others, particularly those who paid
relatively high sums of money to professional abortionists for the procedure, came from the married, middle and upper classes. The doctors who
lobbied for more expansive abortion legislation throughout the nineteenth
century expressed particular alarm about the declining birth rate of the
"respectable classes." Wealthy women were seeking to avoid conception,
they argued, because it was not "fashionable to have a large family."

Bottles of "Sir J. Clarke's Female Periodical Pills," filed as an exhibit in the abortion prosecution of *The Queen* v *Robert Stitt*, Toronto, 21 October 1878.

Although there was no indication that the doctors were lobbying for increased penalties for infanticide, they were unceasing in their denunciation of abortion.[27]

Religious, racial, and ethnic biases reinforced class distinctions. Physicians' journals made reference to the decline of the birth rate among "the better class of inhabitants" and "Protestant families," while the "extraordinary fecundity" of the French Canadians, the Irish, and other non-English immigrants moved the writers to fearful speculation. When women from the "respectable classes" sought to regulate their reproductive abilities, it generated a concern of great magnitude.[28]

In addition, the doctors' lobby reflected inter-sect rivalries. The regular physicians had historically refused to perform abortion, partly because they adhered to the Hippocratic oath, which specifically forbade the practice. While none of the other sects publicly embraced abortion and some of their members openly disagreed with the procedure, their adherents were not wedded to a professional oath censuring it. In the absence of strong anti-abortion laws, those within the irregular sects who would provide abortion services had a definable competitive edge that gained them short-term fees and the possibility of long-term patient–physician relationships. Fulminating in the medical columns of the *Canada Lancet*, regular physicians attacked abortionists as "traffickers in human life," who were "unlicensed and unqualified to practice medicine."[29]

Dr. Alfred A. Andrews, a Windsor, Ontario physician, wrote in the clearest of terms when he entreated his fellow doctors in 1875 to stand firm against the impassioned demands of women seeking abortion:

When we consider the terrible penalties inflicted by society on the female sex for incontinence, we need not wonder at the desperate efforts young girls make to escape them. When you are solicited to interfere for the relief of these poor wretches, pity them, pity them with your whole hearts; ... meet their entreaties with prompt, decided refusal.

[In one of my cases] the poor child (for she was scarcely more than a child) protested that if not relieved, rather than disgrace her recently-married sister and kill her mother, she would conceal her fault and avert exposure by suicide. Thank God, I have no confession to make in this case; I did not yield, but my heart bled when I refused her.[30]

When Sarah Ann Lovell came into Dr. Emily Stowe's office that May afternoon in 1879, a decision would have had to be reached quickly. Should the request be refused? Dr. Stowe could have followed the example of her New York medical instructor, Dr. Clemence Lozier. In December 1869, Dr. Lozier had called the police and laid charges against a couple who had approached her for an abortion. Or she could have followed the lead of Dr. Andrews, and refused to have anything to do with the young woman.[31]

Emily Stowe did not call the police. She did not order Sarah Ann Lovell out of her office. Instead, she provided her young patient with a prescription of hellebore, cantharides, and myrrh that was customarily viewed as potentially effective in promoting menstrual discharge. But she wrote out a dosage level designed to ensure the drugs would have a minimal effect. She prescribed thirty drops, to be taken with sugared water three times a day over the course of ten days. What she intended by this is unclear. If she had determined to provide a placebo, why did she choose a combination of medicines that was commonly regarded as abortion-inducing?[32]

In front of Coroner McConnell, Dr. Stowe pressed the placebo explanation:

[Sarah Ann Lovell] detained me for some time and ultimately I gave her a prescription to get her out of my house.... I state positively that there was nothing in the bottle which could have harmed the girl. I gave her the prescription to prevent her going to another doctor with the object which had induced her to come to me, and also to quiet her mind.... There was nothing in the prescription which could have produced any serious consequences to affect her condition in any way.

She also tried to separate herself from the deceased woman, using language that was decidedly antagonistic toward her former patient. "After the girl left my place I remarked that she was weak-minded to my daughter," noted Emily Stowe.[33]

As Emily Stowe revealed, she had not even thought it necessary to protect Sarah Ann Lovell's privacy. Mrs. John Avis, Sarah Ann Lovell's employer, called upon Dr. Stowe one day after the consultation. In response to Mrs. Avis's questions, Emily Stowe confirmed that she had seen the young woman. She even disclosed the diagnosis of pregnancy. Furthermore, without hesitation she had recommended that Mrs. Avis discharge Sarah Ann Lovell. "I advised her to inform Mrs. Lovell (Sarah Ann Lovell's mother) of her daughter's condition, and get the girl off her (Mrs. Avis's) hands," Emily Stowe testified. Mrs. Avis had promptly complied with this advice.[34]

It is unknown whether Emily Stowe's hostility was real, or whether it was feigned in whole or in part to protect her from the prying eyes of the coroner's jury. Her actions in revealing the pregnancy to her patient's employer indicate that she perceived her loyalty to lie with her class and thus with the prying Mrs. Avis, wife of a hotel owner, rather than with Sarah Ann Lovell, a pregnant domestic servant. She seems to have fully believed that the termination of Sarah Ann Lovell's employment was the proper outcome.

Emily Stowe's middle- and upper-class contemporaries would frequently manifest an inability to see beyond their own needs as employers of domestics. Although she would advocate that domestics be paid "ungrudgingly a fair remuneration," and would fight to upgrade the social recognition accorded to housework skills, Emily Stowe could also turn upon female servants with hostility and condescension. A lecture she would give in 1889 on "Housewifery" made the point only too clearly:

Housewives are reaping what they have sown in the incompetency of those who now place themselves in the labor market as domestics. They are very generally unskilled, untrained, and often unprincipled, and from the lowest grades of society, yet we must hire them, pay them fairly good wages and teach them everything we desire them to do, and the probabilities are that as soon as they have acquired some considerable skill and proficiency they will want to change their employer in order to play off Miss Wiseacre to a new mistress.[35]

What Emily Stowe's views were on abortion is less clear. Her testimony indicated that she had little patience with unmarried domestic servants who sought such remedies. What she might have said to a married, "respectable," middle-class woman seeking to regulate the number of children in her family might have been somewhat different. Heterosexual Canadian women endeavoured to limit the number of their offspring for much of the nineteenth century, using methods such as sexual abstinence, prolonged nursing, coitus interruptus, sheaths, pessaries, douches, and abortion where all else had failed. In response, fertility rates began a long-term decline, dropping approximately 30 per cent across Canada between 1851 and 1891.[36]

Access to information about birth control was difficult to come by, spread mostly by word of mouth. Certainly the medical profession did little to assist inquiring women. The journals of the regular physicians castigated women who sought "to pervert the highest function of woman's nature." Contraception "made marriage a form of prostitution, cheapened sex, dulled sexual enjoyment and so led to unfaithfulness," they argued. What Emily Stowe thought of these sentiments is also unclear. Although not initially trained as a regular physician, she was seeking to make her mark upon the larger medical community. One can only conjecture how much of their perspectives she embraced in the process.[37]

But Emily Stowe was not only a doctor. She was also a feminist, a leading activist on an international plane. She had founded the Toronto Women's Literary Club in 1876, the first known female suffrage organization in Canada. With her nurturing it would grow into the nationally prominent Dominion Woman's Enfranchisement Association by 1889. She travelled extensively in Canada and the United States speaking on women's rights in the fields of education, employment, and property.[38]

As a notable feminist advocate, Emily Stowe might have been expected to have had some personal views on reproduction as well. What evidence remains suggests that Dr. Stowe believed in sexual abstinence except for procreation. On at least one occasion in the mid-1870s, she advocated "anti-sex" sex education, in order to teach young people "all the consequences of the transgression." There is still no evidence that nineteenth-century feminists were publicly demanding access to birth control or abortion. As late as 1900, Emily Murphy, one of Canada's most visible feminists, would deplore all artificial means of birth control as "desperate acts," which could damage health "physically ... or morally and mentally by the degeneracy which such a class of living must certainly bring about." There was no organized birth control movement in Canada until the 1920s and 1930s. Where nineteenth-century feminists spoke of the need for women to control their own bodies, they mounted a campaign for "voluntary motherhood." By this, feminists meant the right of women to insist upon abstinence from heterosexual intercourse to prevent unwanted pregnancies. The right of women unilaterally to refuse their husbands' sexual advances became a key demand. They campaigned to restrict male sexual aggression, not to open up widespread access to non-reproductive sexual intercourse. Thus it is likely that Dr. Emily Stowe was personally not sympathetic to abortion.[39]

Emily Stowe's prominent accusers, however, portrayed her as a deliberate abortionist. One of the key witnesses to display this perspective at the coroner's inquest was Dr. Cornelius James Philbrick. Philbrick was a sixty-three-year-old English physician who had trained in London, Dublin, and Edinburgh before immigrating to Toronto in the 1850s. There he developed a large surgical practice in the Yorkville district. Highly respected by the regular physicians, he had held the position of Professor of Surgery at Trinity College. A rather crusty man, he was also described by one of his peers as "a little eccentric."[40]

Dr. Philbrick had participated in the post-mortem on the body, and he took the stand to testify about the composition of Dr. Stowe's prescription. "Hellebore" and "cantharides," two of the chemicals included, should never have been given to a pregnant woman, he insisted. Because of their potential to produce an abortion, they "could only have been given with that view." As a licensed medical practitioner with over fifty years' experience, Dr. Philbrick would have been confident that his medical views should be conclusive.[41]

At this point Coroner McConnell interrupted to advise Dr. Stowe that she should consider procuring counsel for herself. Emily Stowe shot back that she "did not care to have a counsel but would like to have the opinion of some intelligent physician besides Dr. Philbrick." When Dr. Philbrick raised objections to this, Coroner McConnell called an adjournment. Before the jurymen were dismissed, however, Coroner McConnell circulated several anonymous letters, written in "a scrawling hand-writing," that he had recently received. "This is only one case," warned one letter, which went on to hint broadly that, if subpoenaed to testify, various physicians would be able to "disclose Dr. Stowe's specialty.[42]

The inquest resumed at O'Halloran's Hotel on Yonge Street on 27 August, attended by a growing number of spectators attracted by the spreading notoriety of the case. Emily Stowe had taken Coroner McConnell's advice, and retained the services of Dr. Daniel McMichael, whose law premises in the St. James Buildings were just down the street from her Church Street medical office. Although Daniel McMichael customarily used the designation "Dr.," this was a reference to a doctorate of laws, not a medical degree. Dr. McMichael had distinguished himself one year earlier when he had defended Robert Stitt from Spencerville, Ontario, on an abortion charge, and Emily Stowe may have hoped that his experience in that case would serve her well. She was also extremely fortunate in being able to bring with her several other doctors to testify as witnesses on her behalf: Dr. Henry Wright, Dr. Charles Valance Berryman, and Dr. Uzziel Ogden.[43]

Coroner McConnell does not appear to have been pleased about the prospect of the doctors testifying. Immediately upon taking his seat, he turned to the jury and suggested that he did not think it was really necessary to hear the evidence of any other medical witnesses. Instead, McConnell produced another anonymous letter, which he handed over to the jury. At this Dr. McMichael could restrain himself no longer. Objecting strenuously to the letter, he argued that "no judge would allow the jury to read an anonymous letter." Coroner McConnell's succinct retort was: "Opinions differ."[44]

This prompted an explosion from Dr. McMichael. He demanded to know "how he stood in this case." Would he be permitted to represent Dr. Stowe, or had he come "on a fool's errand"? An enraged Coroner McConnell shouted: "Constable, clear the court." There ensued a delay of two hours, while physicians, jurymen, and the coroner heatedly debated their differences. When the room was once again opened to the public, Coroner McConnell announced that Dr. Stowe would be permitted to call her witnesses.[45]

Dr. Henry Wright spoke first. An Ontario-born physician, his entire training had been through medical apprenticeship to the politically radical Dr. John Rolph, who had been forced to flee to the United States during the Mackenzie Rebellion. In 1837, Dr. Wright had followed his mentor to Rochester, New York, where he continued to pursue his studies under Dr. Rolph's direction. Dr. Wright's ambition had been to attain security within the most powerful medical circles, and upon his return to Ontario he quickly rose through the medical hierarchy to become an established member of the Council of the College of Physicians and Surgeons of Ontario, and a lecturer in medicine at the Toronto University. His support for Emily Stowe may have reflected his awareness of the discrimination she had faced. His son, Frederick, had been studying medicine at the same time as Dr. Stowe.[46]

Reflecting substantial division of opinion even among regular physicians themselves, Dr. Wright would testify that he had examined the prescription that Dr. Stowe had given to the deceased woman and that he "was of the opinion that the medicine, if taken as prescribed, could have no effect whatever on a woman." Hellebore, noted Wright, had been used about one hundred years ago, but had since fallen into disuse. "If taken in large enough doses it might have the effect of causing inflammation of the stomach," he conceded. But even if Sarah Ann Lovell had taken the whole bottle at once in May, he could not see what connection it would have had with her death in August.[47]

Dr. Berryman, who was noted as an expert on medical jurisprudence, would agree. Pointing out that the dosage prescribed was less than the minimum doses ordinarily given, he stated that even if the entire bottle had been emptied in May, he could not conceive how the medicine could cause death unless the patient had been continuously ill. As for Dr. Philbrick's post-mortem report, Dr. Berryman noted scathingly that the description of the stomach "was so indefinite that he could not give an opinion as to the cause of death."[48]

Dr. Uzziel Ogden would be equally sceptical of Dr. Philbrick's testimony. Dr. Ogden had studied medicine at Victoria University in Cobourg, and he had risen to prominence as the chair of Midwifery and Diseases of Women and Children at the Toronto School of Medicine. His support for Emily Stowe may have been traceable to his first wife, who was one of the Nelles's who had lived next to the Stowes in Mount Pleasant, and whose family had owned the Nelles Academy in which Emily Stowe had taught after her husband took ill.[49]

Dr. Ogden suggested that Dr. Stowe's medicine, taken as prescribed, would have no more effect than "so much cold water." Despite this, Ogden observed that he would not have prescribed such medicine to a pregnant woman. "Unscrupulous people might make a handle of it to create false impressions," he cautioned. Why did Dr. Stowe choose the prescription she did? If she had wanted to prescribe a placebo, why not a prescription that was accepted as bearing no abortion-inducing properties?[50]

Coroner McConnell then summed up the evidence for the jury. Before closing he would again remind the jury of the anonymous letters. He had received "about fifty" of them by now, he said, but, perhaps with an eye on Dr. McMichael, he urged the jury "to pay no attention to those letters." Despite the belated caution, McConnell's behaviour was castigated by the local press. The coroner's behaviour was "unfair" wrote the editors of the Toronto *Evening Telegram*, and "directly opposed to the principles of law and justice." Indeed, "people [were] saying that he had attempted to bias the jury against Mrs. Dr. Stowe."[51]

Despite these charges, the coroner's jury delivered its verdict on 27 August. It found that Sarah Ann Lovell "came to her death by means of an irritant poison, taken by herself or at the hands of others unknown to the jury for the purposes of procuring an abortion." The jurors had chosen to believe Dr. Philbrick's assessment of the dangerous properties of the drug. But inexplicably they refused to name Dr. Emily Stowe in their verdict and instead blamed the deceased woman herself or persons unknown. It was a non-committal verdict that satisfied no one.[52]

The behaviour of Coroner McConnell and Dr. Philbrick deeply troubled some observers, at least one of whom published a lengthy criticism in the Toronto *Evening Telegram* several weeks later.

Sir: The first thing that claims our consideration is the duties of coroners. They are evidently appointed for the purpose of guarding the interests of the public, but it does not follow that they should individually or collectively incriminate everyone that may be suspected to have committed a misdemeanour.

In this case Coroner McConnell, who should have acted the part of an impartial judge, persisted in prejudicing Mrs. Stowe's case by taking down the ... points that would tell against her and omitting those that were favourable to her interests, which was manifest in reference to the medical testimony of Drs. Wright, Berriman [sic], and Ogden ... as well as in her own evidence.

Then Dr. Philbrick, an associate coroner ... was most officious in encouraging the belief that Mrs. Stowe was guilty of a misdemeanour.

... These men are appointed for the purpose of performing a most important public duty and they should not be allowed to perch themselves upon their dignity and decline to enlighten us upon these points, or they may be suspected of considering themselves so secure in their positions that they cannot be disturbed.

Their medical testimony also is open to severe criticism, in that they had not used in their own practice the medicines named in the prescription that Dr. Stowe gave and were not conversant with the opinions of the latest medical authorities as to their strength or properties.... [T]he sterling men in the profession can testify to their incompetency in this direction as was done at the inquest....

Although the letter was signed only "An Observer," the medical knowledge possessed by the writer suggests that it may have been written by one of Dr. Stowe's medical witnesses.[53]

Meanwhile, the Crown attorney for the County of York, Frederick Fenton, was considering the case. Since 1857 Ontario had moved beyond the earlier *ad hoc* appointment of prosecutors, now appointing one Crown attorney for each county to oversee all of the prosecutions at the Assizes and quarter sessions. Although still part-time, the position of a professional public prosecutor had taken on an aura of earnestness and responsibility that the new Crown attorneys were anxious to foster.[54]

After a careful review of the documents from the coroner's inquest, on Wednesday, 10 September, Fenton drew up an indictment against Dr. Stowe. The official charge was that she had "administered and caused to be taken by Sarah Ann Lovell, large quantities of certain poisons, to wit, 1/2 oz. tincture of hellebore, and 1/4 oz. tincture of cantharides, and other noxious things, to wit, 1 oz. tincture of myrrh, with intent thereby to procure the miscarriage of the said Sarah Ann Lovell." Gone was any reference to causing the death of the patient. The sole charge was now related to abortion.[55]

Fenton drafted the charge as "administering or causing to be taken," which under the 1869 federal Offences against the Person Act carried a maximum penalty of life imprisonment. He did not choose to try Emily Stowe under the lesser offence of "supplying" poisons for the purpose of procuring miscarriage, an offence that entailed a maximum sentence of only two years. While the latter offence would have been easier to prove, Fenton seems to have wanted to make an example of Dr. Stowe through a high-profile trial.[56]

A warrant was issued for the apprehension of Dr. Stowe, who learned for the first time on 11 September that criminal charges were being pressed. Given her status as a middle-class, "respectable" woman, she was not arrested. Instead, she was permitted to appear voluntarily in court. On Thursday, 11 September 1879, she pleaded "not guilty" to the charge, and was released on bail of eight thousand dollars — four thousand in cash and four thousand in sureties.[57]

Trial began on the morning of 23 September before Judge Kenneth Mackenzie of the County Court. The crowd was large, and the air was filled with anticipation. The Toronto *Mail* captured the mood:

On the opening of the Court of General Sessions yesterday morning, some surprise was occasioned by seeing about twenty-five or thirty ladies tripping into the room and taking seats. The unoccupied jury box to the right was quickly taken possession of by the fair visitors and about fifteen additional ladies found resting places on the lower seats in the body of the court-room.

Various were the conjectures bandied about among the male visitors as to this unusual marshalling in of lady spectators, and many looked upon it as another outward move of the "woman's rights" army. The real motive of the visit, however, was quickly made known. Mrs. Dr. Emily Stowe was about to [be] placed on trial....

The ladies who occupied seats in the Court were the friends of and sympathizers with the accused. During the whole proceedings they were attentive listeners to the arguments of counsel and showed evident signs of approval when the lawyer for the defence succeeded in "bothering" any of the witnesses for the Crown.

During the progress of the trial, which was opened shortly after 11 o'clock, the court-room and the approaches leading thereto were densely crowded with spectators, which fact did not materially improve the already foul atmosphere of the room. At one time Judge McKenzie [*sic*] was considering the advisability of clearing the room of spectators, but instead of doing so, he contented himself with abusing in good round terms the miserable building now doing duty as a court house.[58]

The Toronto *Globe* noted that nearly all of the female spectators were members of the Women's Literary Society. The *Globe* also remarked upon the large number of physicians present, some of whom had been summoned as witnesses and others who were just interested in the outcome of the case. Dr. Stowe was called to plead, and reiterated her "not guilty" claim "in a firm voice." She had been sitting at the front of the room, within the enclosure set apart for the legal profession, but she was instructed to enter the prisoner's dock. As Dr. Stowe complied, her daughter Augusta and her sister (possibly Cornelia) moved to sit on either side of the dock and remained there throughout the trial.[59]

Emily Stowe had two well-known lawyers in court with her that day: D'Alton McCarthy and Nelson Gordon Bigelow. McCarthy, who acted as the lead defence counsel, was generally acknowledged to be one of the pre-eminent lawyers of the era. An Irishman who had been called to the bar in 1858 and a long-standing member of Parliament, McCarthy's highly successful litigation practice ranged throughout the province of Ontario. As Judge Mackenzie motioned for the trial to begin, there was a tussle between Crown Attorney Fenton and Dr. Stowe's lawyers over whether it was permissible to call evidence from the coroner's inquest. Over the objections of McCarthy and Bigelow, the judge gave the go-ahead. Fenton called as one of his first witnesses Coroner McConnell.[60]

Coroner McConnell took the stand and announced ruefully that he had misplaced all of the physical evidence from the inquest. Both Dr. Stowe's written prescription and the empty bottle of medicine were gone, despite Dr. McConnell's search throughout the hotel, his buggy, and his office. Judge Mackenzie admonished the witness for not having given the evidence over to the Crown attorney for safe-keeping. But McConnell shrugged off the criticism, replying: "I thought they were of no further use after the [coroner's] jury had returned a verdict."[61]

Dr. McConnell's medical testimony would duplicate Dr. Philbrick's commentary from the inquest. "Hellebore is a poison," he claimed, "and so is cantharides. Myrrh is poisonous when taken in large quantities. Each of these is an emmenagogue. I would not prescribe any one of these medicines or a combination of them to a pregnant woman, particularly if I knew her object was to procure an abortion." An "emmenagogue" was a medicine thought to promote menstruation, or to restore it if it had been suppressed. As Dr. McConnell saw it, "it was impossible for an emmenagogue to be given to a pregnant woman so as to produce the menstrual discharge without first producing a miscarriage."[62]

Then Dr. McConnell was turned over to D'Alton McCarthy for cross-examination. It was a lengthy exchange that kept the doctor in the witness box for over two hours. McCarthy scored several damaging admissions. The most important of these concerned the coroner's inattentiveness to Dr. Stowe's testimony at the inquest. McCarthy questioned Dr. McConnell closely about whether he had taken careful notes as Dr. Stowe gave her evidence. "I am not a fast writer, but I take down the statements of the witnesses in substance as I understand them," Dr. McConnell responded. "To the best of my ability I did take down every word of what Mrs. Stowe said in evidence." However, the repetition of the question brought a less guarded admission: "Mrs. Stowe spoke for sometime to the jury without being asked any questions, and I did not take down what she said." Questioned further, McConnell admitted that it was during this time that "she may have explained what the maximum and minimum doses of an emmenagogue were."[63]

McCarthy finished off with a series of queries designed to further undermine Coroner McConnell's credibility:

Q. Were you in a fit condition when the jury brought in their verdict?
A. Yes I was.
Q. Had you not been drinking?
A. I had a glass or so of lager.
Q. Oh, a glass or so of grog.
*Mr. Fenton:* He says lager, not grog.
Q. How many glasses — twenty or thirty?
A. No, not more than three.[64]

At this point a drunken male spectator rose from his seat in the courtroom and tried to address the bench and bar. According to the Toronto *Mail*, he was "pounced down on" by half a dozen ushers and "bodily carried from the room." This may have been too much for Judge Mackenzie, who ordered the jury sequestered in the William the Third Hotel, and the trial adjourned until the next day.[65]

The next morning the press noted that although the courtroom was again crowded, there had been a "perceptible falling off in the number of lady visitors," which the reporters attributed to "the foul and unhealthy atmosphere of the crowded room." Dr. Philbrick was sworn as the next Crown witness. Recalling the day of the post-mortem examination, Dr.

Philbrick told the court that "the moment the abdomen was open," he had exclaimed: "My goodness, this woman has taken something to procure an abortion!" According to Philbrick, hellebore and cantharides were "poisonous" and myrrh, when administered to pregnant women, was "noxious." He summed up: "The effect of the prescription would be to produce a miscarriage."[66]

D'Alton McCarthy's cross-examination of Philbrick was heated, and the sparring between the two would be quoted in full in the Toronto *Mail*. McCarthy's main thrust was to characterize Dr. Philbrick as hostile to Dr. Stowe because of her status as a female physician:

Q. Do you take as much interest in every case as you have done in this?

A. I do.

Q. Have you written to the Attorney General in reference to this case since it has closed?

A. I have not.

Q. Have you spoken in pretty strong language of the conduct of Mrs. Stowe in this instance?

A. Yes, I said she was a fool for speaking so much about the matter — that if she had kept her mouth closed, no person would have been any wiser. I gave my testimony before she was suspected —

Q. There, there, that will do. We don't wish to hear you make a speech just yet. Did you have any conversation with a Mr. Englehardt [a member of the coroner's jury] about this case?

A. Not any more than with any other juror.

Q. Did you say that "Mrs. Stowe was a b---h, and that you were an 'old stager' at the business and would have her yet"?

A. No, I never made use of the words. If Mr. Englehardt says so, he must have misunderstood me.

Q. I understand you hold some pretty strong opinions in reference to women practising medicine?

A. No sir, on the contrary. I have given gratuitous assistance scores of times to women practising midwifery.

Q. But you object to their practising outside of that sphere?

A. Oh no, not at all. I don't mind it. You look as if you would make an excellent midwife. (Loud laughter.)[67]

Dr. Philbrick's last remark might have sparked laughter from the physicians in the audience, but D'Alton McCarthy had made his point well. Despite Dr. Philbrick's denials, it would have been clear to many of the observers that he was carrying on a personal vendetta against Dr. Stowe.

D'Alton McCarthy was so sure of his ground that when the Crown closed its case, he did not call one witness. Instead, he moved directly into legal argument. His key point would be that there was no evidence whatsoever that Dr. Stowe had "administered" the drugs or "caused" them to be administered. She had simply given a prescription to Sarah Ann Lovell. This might have amounted to a "delivery," but not to "administering" or "causing" to be administered. Many people did not follow the advice of their physicians, he noted, and recipients of prescriptions might fill them or just tear them up.[68]

Crown Attorney Fenton was very likely ruing the day he had decided to charge Dr. Stowe with "administering" abortion-related drugs rather than "supplying" them. He rose to claim that "no manual delivery was necessary to prove the crime." But his argument was lacklustre and the Crown's case was doomed. Judge Mackenzie concluded that there was no point in asking the jury to render a verdict since there was no legal case to answer. The charge of "administering" or "causing" the drugs to be administered required evidence far beyond the mere supplying of a prescription. "The prisoner was entitled to the benefit of any doubt," noted Judge Mackenzie, and "there was no administering or causing to be taken."

Using Dr. Philbrick's own testimony against him, the judge stated:

Dr. Philbrick had said (using rather strong language) that Dr. Stowe was a fool for if she had kept her tongue quiet they would have had nothing against her. But women would not keep their tongues quiet — (laughter) — but as she had spoken to her own injury, the jury must not forget that she had said that what she had prescribed for the girl was harmless.[69]

Playing to the misogyny of some of the observers in the courtroom, Judge Mackenzie had made the customary dig about women's alleged talkativeness. He had also displayed some uneasiness of his own over the prospect of women practising medicine. During the legal arguments, D'Alton McCarthy had made several references to Emily Stowe, using her medical title of "Doctor." At one point Judge Mackenzie interrupted to note: "When you speak of a doctor, I place in my mind a man." Judge Mackenzie was unlikely to have been a proponent of feminism. But even he was struck by Dr. Philbrick's single-minded venom, and he opted not to use the force of the law to contribute to the attack on Emily Stowe. The judge ordered the jury to acquit the prisoner, and Dr. Emily Stowe was discharged.[70]

The verdict was an unusual one among abortion cases. Abortion trials were a rarity in the nineteenth century, usually occurring only when major medical complications or death resulted. But when these cases were tried, Canadian courts tended to be relatively severe. In contrast to infanticide verdicts, where up to two-thirds of the murder and manslaughter charges could result in acquittals, in some provinces approximately half of the abortion-related charges resulted in guilty verdicts.[71]

In 1875 the Ontario courts had convicted Dr. Sparham of Brockville of murder in connection with an abortion he had performed on Sophia Elizabeth Burnham, who had died shortly after the procedure. The medical evidence had suggested that Sophia's death might have been caused by blood poisoning brought on by smallpox, but the courts disregarded this and convicted Dr. Sparham. Robert M. Stitt of Spencerville, Ontario, was convicted in 1879 of supplying "noxious" drugs to his lover, Mary Collins, in an attempt to procure her abortion. The two bottles of Sir James Clarke's Female Periodical Pills that he had given Mary Collins were sold in drugstores without restriction to all who asked for them, and the medical evidence was far from conclusive that the dosage he advised would have prompted a miscarriage.[72]

Although legal records would tend to underestimate the number of abortionists who did a volume business, revealing only those who were caught and charged, professional abortionists appear to have been few and far between in the nineteenth century. A few male physicians and several laywomen, who charged fees ranging from ten to one hundred dollars, were prosecuted for administering drugs or for introducing various instruments through the cervix into the uterus to disrupt the ovum and cause its expulsion. One case was spawned by a sensational police raid in 1886 upon the Toronto medical office of Dr. Ransom J. Andrews. The seventy-one-year-old physician, whose office correspondence contained hundreds of letters from women seeking abortions, would be convicted of performing an abortion on Jennie Leslie, a woman from Whitby. The Crown's key evidence in this case was the female patient, Jennie Leslie, who was apparently granted immunity from prosecution for testifying. Traditionally, judges had been very cautious about accepting evidence from such witnesses, who were technically classified as "accomplices" to the crime. Here the courts received the testimony with eagerness and convicted without concern.[73]

In 1896 the British Columbia courts would convict Dr. John Kaye

Garrow, apparently another professional abortionist, of manslaughter after his patient, Mary Ellen James, died following an unsuccessful abortion. None of the doctors examined at this trial could swear positively as to the cause of death. One testified he could not tell if there had been a miscarriage or even if Mary Ellen James had been pregnant. Convictions intensified as the century progressed. By the 1890s, four out of six abortion trials resulted in a conviction. Courts appear to have been using loose standards of factual proof and legal analysis, convicting despite evidence that would clearly have permitted acquittals if judges and jurors had been so inclined.[74]

In view of the lenience shown infanticide perpetrators, it is difficult to argue that the guilty verdicts commonly bestowed on abortion-related charges reflected any great sensitivity to the rights of the unborn. Part of the answer may lie with who was on trial in each situation. With infanticide trials, skillful counsel could rouse a great deal of sympathy for the distressed woman in the prisoner's dock. Abortion trials typically focused on the abortionist, not the immediate desperation of an unwillingly pregnant woman.

This may have been why an acquittal was registered in Dr. Emily Stowe's case. Here there *was* a sympathetic female sitting in the dock. For years Dr. Stowe, a woman initially trained as a homeopath, had been contesting the male monopoly over regular medical practice. Throughout her criminal prosecution, her sex had been an obvious focal point. While bemused over the spectacle of a lady physician, many felt that Drs. Philbrick and McConnell had gone too far. The newspaper editors had expressed alarm over the number of anonymous letters attacking Emily Stowe, and the use to which they had been put at the coroner's inquest. D'Alton McCarthy and Judge Mackenzie had made short shrift of Coroner McConnell's slipshod procedure and Dr. Philbrick's obvious partiality. The acquittal registered a significant degree of sympathy for Emily Stowe's precarious position and resistance to the vendetta that some physicians were so clearly waging against her.

Upon the announcement of the verdict, there was great jubilation from at least one side of the crowd in the courtroom. "Mrs. Stowe's friends, both ladies and gentlemen, crowded about her and shook hands with her and with each other, expressing every satisfaction with the result of the trial," noted the *Globe*. The Toronto *Mail*, seemingly anxious to stress the absurdity of women trying to mix in legal matters, added:

One excitable lady endeavoured to ascend the Bench where his Honour was seated, for the purpose no doubt of returning thanks. While on the steps, the lady was interrupted by a constable, who ordered her to retire, which she did very reluctantly, and with a dissatisfied air.[75]

For their part, the physicians in the audience continued to have doubts about Emily Stowe's motives. The medical editors of the *Canada Lancet* would profess surprise at the verdict, noting: "It was a most unfortunate prescription, as Dr. Stowe admitted, taking the most charitable view of the case...." And several days after the trial a curious letter showed up in the pages of the Toronto *Evening Telegram*. Purportedly signed by "ONE WHO DOES NOT BELONG TO THE MEDICAL PROFESSION," it reads like a missive from a professional lobbyist for the regular physicians. Although the author claimed to have nothing against Emily Stowe's acquittal in general, the letter complained that "a feeling of partisanship" had been "displayed at the trial." Then followed the customary attack against unlicensed and irregular medical practitioners:

Those who try to uphold the law and to exclude quacks are always accused of being actuated by bigotry or by selfish motives, but they are discharging a duty of medical police which is essential to public safety.

... if women choose to enter what has hitherto been a male profession, they must submit to male rules and responsibilities, otherwise we shall have a medical anarchy. There are bad women as well as good women in the world.[76]

Nonetheless, in 1879 Emily Stowe's daughter Augusta had been admitted to medical studies at Victoria College in Cobourg, and in 1883 would become the first white woman to graduate from a Canadian medical college. On 16 July 1880, only months after the trial, Dr. Emily Stowe finally obtained her licence to practise medicine in Ontario. Both mother and daughter maintained prominent and visible positions of leadership within the Canadian feminist movement for decades to come.[77]

Whether Emily Stowe was innocent of attempting to procure an abortion upon Sarah Ann Lovell cannot be assessed with certainty. The insinuations of the anonymous letter-writers that Dr. Stowe was a professional abortionist surely ring false. The perspectives of nineteenth-century feminists on reproduction, and Dr. Stowe's avowed desire to secure entry into the professionalizing world of male medicine, render it most unlikely that she would have been setting out to practise as an abortionist. Furthermore, the differences of class and marital status between Stowe and Lovell were such that she was unlikely to have been

Augusta Stowe (later Augusta Stowe-Gullen), daughter of Emily Stowe and the first woman to graduate from a Canadian medical college.

providing abortion services in this specific case. Yet Dr. Emily Stowe didn't turn her patient over to the criminal authorities. Instead, she gave her that "unfortunate prescription," noted for its ability to reintroduce "regularity" to a woman's menses. The dosage prescribed was exceedingly low, but as Dr. McConnell had testified, "those desiring to procure an abortion without injuring the mother would be more likely to use a mild medicine."[78]

The nineteenth century witnessed a rapid expansion in the laws prohibiting fertility control. In the earliest years the common law permitted a great deal of leeway for women seeking early abortions. By the 1870s, in response to the concerted medical lobby, some of the country's leading politicians were vociferously denouncing abortion. Prime Minister John A. Macdonald wrote in 1871: "The practice saps the life blood of a nation and must be put down with a strong hand." By the end of the century all attempts at abortion had been prohibited. With the passage of the Criminal Code in 1892 the sale, distribution, and advertisement of contraceptives were also banned. John Charlton, the member of Parliament for Norfolk North who had lobbied so tenaciously for the criminalization of seduction, was one of the key proponents of the new provision.[79]

This sweeping legal encroachment upon heterosexual women's reproductive rights would bring little public dissent from the leaders of the women's rights movement at the time. Whatever her actions in the Sarah Ann Lovell case, Emily Stowe, one of the key proponents of medical equality for women, offered not a single protest about the need for Canadian women to have access to birth control or abortion. The feminist campaign for "voluntary motherhood" was significantly different in scope, asserting a woman's right to control her own body by setting limits upon the exercise of male sexuality. Many nineteenth-century feminists feared that abortion and birth control would only free men to take greater sexual advantage of women. While there may have been some truth to these fears, the campaign for "voluntary motherhood" was not terribly successful, and within the context of the patriarchal family it provided little solace for Canadian women.[80]

# 6

# Divorce and Separation

ESTHER HAWLEY HAM: A BATTERED WIFE

During the spring of 1813, George Ham swept Esther Hawley off her feet with his romantic ardour, and the two were married on 23 April. The ceremony was performed by Reverend Robert Macdowall, a Presbyterian of the Reformed Dutch Church, in Midland District in the province of Upper Canada. The couple were very much in love, their families appeared to be satisfied with the arrangements, and "every hope was entertained that they would live happily together."[1]

Canadian divorce law differed greatly depending upon the province of one's residence, but for most nineteenth-century heterosexual couples, marriage was a tie for life. Peoples of the First Nations had a more flexible view of conjugal union, but among descendants of European nations living in Upper Canada, divorce was almost unknown. English tradition forbade divorce, although on rare occasions the English Parliament would pass special statutes granting divorces to named individuals. Following this precedent, the Legislature of Upper Canada granted its first divorce in 1839, but by Confederation it had heard only seven petitions in all. In neighbouring Lower Canada, the environment was even less hospitable for those seeking divorce. French law as transported to Quebec had never recognized the concept of divorce. The Civil Code of Lower Canada, enacted in 1865, would state: "Marriage can only be dissolved by the natural death of one of the parties; while both live it is indissoluble."[2]

The Hawleys and the Hams, two farming families, lived only three miles apart in the township of Earnestown, on the St. Lawrence River upstream from Kingston. The Hawleys were staunch adherents of the Church of England, and the Hams were members of the Presbyterian Reformed Dutch Church, but religious differences did not initially appear to be contentious. Although the Hams were not particularly wealthy, George Ham was very ambitious and shortly after the marriage his career began to blossom.

A shoe-maker by trade, twenty-one-year-old George Ham purchased a farm of his own near Bath, to which he and his bride soon moved. Through hard work and good luck he slowly began to amass wealth and standing in the community. He was appointed a magistrate for the area, and in 1824 he would be elected to sit as a member of the Legislature of Upper Canada. Thus it was with some surprise and considerable interest that the community began to learn about marital problems between George and Esther Ham.[3]

The couple had been married less than a year when Esther Hawley Ham gave birth to a child. About three months after the birth she took ill, and left to recuperate at her parents' home. Her husband apparently thought she was malingering. Much to the surprise of her family, George Ham showed up one afternoon and insisted upon her return. "My lady," he announced, "you must make ready and go home with me." Shaking a whip over her head, he commanded her to ride behind him, on his horse. Sheldon Hawley, her father, intervened, cautioning that she should not be moved except in a wagon. George Ham's temper flared. Flourishing his whip over his wife again, he shouted: "My lady, you must get up and come with me, and if you live to have another child by me, I shall discharge the nurse on the third day and make you do all the work of the house — and if you do not get out of bed I will flog you out."

Isabel Hawley, Esther's ten-year-old sister, and her parents witnessed the outburst. Mrs. Hawley was shocked and angered by George Ham's display of temper, and apparently retorted that she "wished her daughter was in her tomb before she married [George Ham]," all the while "shaking her fist" under her son-in-law's nose. Esther Hawley Ham returned home with her husband that day, but whatever remained of marital happiness had been permanently shattered.

The Hawleys were very concerned about their daughter, and their further probing revealed that Esther Hawley Ham had been the victim of both physical and emotional abuse since the fourth month of her marriage. She eventually divulged to her parents that the degree of "personal

FEARFUL WIFE BEATING

Illustration of a husband whipping his wife from
the *Illustrated Police News* (London), 1868.

chastisement" she had been subjected to had rendered her life "almost insupportable." Armed with this information, Sheldon Hawley and his wife marched down to their daughter's farm to retrieve her. Extreme cases of wife battering often elicited community intervention in the nineteenth century. The homes of relatives and neighbours functioned as the equivalent of modern battered women's shelters. Battered women would turn to family and friends for the counselling and peace-keeping services now furnished by marital counsellors, mental health professionals, and the police. In this case Esther Hawley Ham's family came to her rescue.[4]

On the day he removed his daughter from George Ham's home, Sheldon Hawley left his son-in-law with these words: "You damned rascal, you have ill-used my daughter. I was able to support her before she married you, and I am so yet." To neighbours he met on the way home, Mr. Hawley vowed "she shall not live with him again." Thus began a marital separation that would last more than twelve years. Esther Hawley Ham went home to live with her parents, where she washed, sewed, knitted, and did housework for her keep. She brought her child with her, until George Ham's efforts to secure custody were successful nine months later. At the time, as we shall see later, the law gave fathers almost unfettered rights to custody.

The estranged couple had few options. There were no grounds to argue for an annulment of the marriage. The prospect of seeking an individualized divorce statute from the legislature remained open, but neither spouse pursued it. George Ham might have had more luck exploring this avenue than Esther Hawley Ham would have had. Of the five divorces that the Legislature of Upper Canada would ultimately grant before Confederation, not one was on behalf of a woman.[5]

But presumably George Ham had no grounds to seek a legislative divorce. The English tradition, upon which the legislative practice of granting divorces was based, typically provided divorce only to men whose wives had committed adultery. And there was no evidence that Esther Hawley Ham had committed adultery. As it transpired, Esther Hawley Ham might have had more success in proving George Ham's sexual transgressions, but this would have been of little assistance. The English practice dictated a double standard, forcing women to prove not only that their husbands had committed adultery, but also that they had been guilty of some other serious crime such as incest or bigamy.[6]

Many nineteenth-century couples simply decided to live apart, practising a form of "self-divorce." Some reached their own agreements about separation, covering such matters as property division, maintenance, and custody. Where courts refused to enforce such agreements, some couples may have turned to private arbitrators within the community to work out their differences. The high rate of prosecutions for bigamy indicates that many who were not legally entitled to marry again thumbed their noses at the inflexible divorce laws, trying as much as possible to manage their marital affairs outside of the law.[7]

The Hams and the Hawleys seem not to have been able to work out their own private arrangement, although Sheldon Hawley was emphatic that George Ham should, at the very least, be paying for his wife's upkeep. At some point in the mid-1820s, the Hawleys turned for legal advice to Christopher Hagerman, the Kingston lawyer who had acted for the Hogle family in their seduction action of 1825. Hagerman suggested a civil action for alimony, whereby Sheldon Hawley would sue George Ham for the full cost from the date of separation of providing food, clothing, and shelter to Esther Hawley Ham.

This form of action would become the mainstay for middle-class women who did not want or could not obtain a full divorce but who wished to escape abusive marriages. The litigation could be initiated by the wife herself, or as frequently happened, by her father or another male relative. An order for alimony would give the separated couple no opportunity to remarry, but it did provide some legal authorization for the separation, and it settled any outstanding questions about the right to spousal support. Fundamental to the right of action, however, was evidence that would satisfy the court that the wife was fully justified in living apart from her husband.[8]

In this vein, Christopher Hagerman would have advised his client to ensure that there was absolutely no possibility of restoring the marriage. In the fall of 1825, Esther Hawley Ham made several attempts to reconcile with her husband. Taking her sister with her on 24 September, she went to George Ham's home and offered to live with him once more. George Ham was unimpressed, and boasted: "If all be true, I have several children in the country, and I have a sweetheart in Montreal, much prettier than you are." Esther Hawley Ham apparently responded, "George, that is nothing to the purpose, I want to know whether you will live with me or not?" Upon hearing this George Ham delivered the following speech: "*I am independent, king, lord of all!* You must humble yourself very much before I tell you whether I shall live with you or not. I have the whip in my own hand, and I shall use it as I shall think proper."[9]

Esther Hawley Ham departed. But several days later, and again accompanied by her sister, Isabel, she sought the intervention of George Ham's father and mother. Although John Ham entreated his son to take his wife back, George Ham was adamant. In front of Isabel, his mother, and his father, he addressed Esther Hawley Ham as follows: "If you live with me, you must do all the work of my house — and you must do it in style — and if you show a cross look, or a frown, you shall walk. I shall dismiss all my servants, except a man to wait on myself, for I am worthy." While the workload George Ham was assigning was no more than a working-class wife would have been expected to shoulder, for a man of his station and wealth to give such orders would undoubtedly have been viewed as tyrannical. It flew in the face of accustomed class privilege.

Yet Esther Hawley Ham persisted in her expressed wish to return. When she showed up at her husband's home that evening, he sent her

away for a month "to consider the matter." George Ham seemed determined to resist all overtures, for when she returned on 24 October he had
a list of outrageous proposals to put to her:

You shall be confined in a room, and I shall neither eat, drink, nor lodge with
you, and you shall receive no visitors, nor meddle with anything belonging to
me, for the instant you do, I shall show you the door and you walk. You must not
be disappointed if five or six other women may occasionally come into the house.

George Ham would conclude with the most intolerable question of all.
"Have you any objection that another man should sleep in the same
room?" he asked her, insinuating that she was as interested in extramarital heterosexual liaisons as he. Before taking her final leave, Esther
Hawley Ham angrily responded, "This is not receiving me as a wife, nor
treating me as such."

Whether these attempts to restore marital relations were sincere on
Esther Hawley Ham's part is unclear. Her repetitious and diverse efforts
to seek reconciliation after more than a decade of separation had passed
seem somewhat suspicious. That she had ensured her sister's presence
during all of these discussions suggests that she might have had a pending alimony action foremost in her mind. Quite likely she was seeking
helpful evidence for the case, backed up by a reliable eye-witness.
Whatever her purpose, George Ham had provided yet additional material
upon which to base a claim for alimony.

Christopher Hagerman promptly issued a legal claim against George
Ham, seeking damages of one thousand pounds "for meat, drink, washing, lodging and other necessities" provided to Esther Hawley Ham. In
return for granting a husband almost complete control over his wife's
property, the law presumed that he was responsible for maintaining his
wife and children. If the Hawleys could prove that George Ham had
made it impossible for his wife to live with him, and that consequently
her father had been forced to support her for the past twelve years,
Sheldon Hawley could obtain reimbursement for his expenses.[10]

George Ham and his relatives turned out in full force for the trial of
the case at the Midland District Assizes, which began in Kingston in
September of 1826. He was represented by the illustrious Henry John
Boulton, then the Solicitor-General of the province. This was the same
Henry Boulton who had so ably represented the Crown in the infanticide
prosecution against Angelique Pilotte. The thrust of the defence would be
that Esther Hawley Ham had been overreacting, that she was not justified

in living apart from her husband, and that she was guilty of serious indiscretions herself.

Boulton put a number of George Ham's relatives on the stand, several of whom swore that they had been with George Ham when he had first retrieved the ailing Esther Hawley Ham from her father's house. They had "not seen Mr. Ham flourish a whip or say anything angry," they testified. Conceding that George Ham had "a very small whip in his hand," they were nonetheless adamant that he had not shaken it over his wife. Mary Perry, George Ham's sister, told the court that although she had resided with the couple throughout much of their cohabitation, she had never seen her brother strike his wife. Mary Perry put the marital problems up to Esther Hawley Ham's parents, whom she said had pressured a tearful and reluctant Esther to leave her husband against her will. George Ham's father would carry this theme further when he suggested that the major difficulty lay between George Ham and his mother-in-law, Mrs. Hawley, who had been circulating unkind rumours about George Ham's brutality.

Rumours these were, and nothing more, claimed Henry Boulton. "If his client were such a beast — such an absolute brute as they represented him," said Boulton, he would not have agreed to take the case. On the contrary, George Ham was "a respectable man," who had raised himself up from a "poor shoemaker" to "wealth and respectability" through "his own merit and good conduct." As a long-time magistrate, George Ham conducted himself with "decency and propriety." Despite the slanders of the Hawleys, he had been duly elected to Parliament. "Were he such a monster as they would make him to be — yes, if he kept five or six women in Bath, if he really kept a Seraglio like the Grand Turk ... how was it that he is now ... respected by his neighbours?" demanded Boulton.

To strengthen his position further, Henry Boulton tried to discredit Esther Hawley Ham's character. He argued that she had been guilty of teaching her child "improper language." He suggested that Esther intended to cross her husband in matters of religion, proposing to become a Methodist. He insinuated that Esther had been overly familiar with a Dr. Baker, a chair-maker who had resided at her father's home. What was more, he alleged, Esther had sat up one night "sparking" with William Fairfield and Samuel Clark. George Ham had good cause to be both angry and jealous about his wife's actions, claimed Boulton.

Isabel Hawley, the main witness for the Hawleys, vigorously denied these allegations, insisting that her sister had always "conducted herself with propriety." Christopher Hagerman backed her up, arguing that the scandalous insinuations proved nothing other than the "absolute baseness and depravity" of George Ham's mind. The real issue, according to Hagerman, was the level of violence displayed. Isabel painstakingly described the incident with the whip and George Ham's behaviour in response to Esther Hawley Ham's attempts at reconciliation.

The Hawleys were also fortunate in being able to put forth evidence from an acquaintance of George Ham, John Simpson, who appeared to be a somewhat more independent witness. He told the court that he had questioned his friend once about the separation. George Ham had frankly admitted, said Simpson, that "in consequence of some dispute between them, he chastised [his wife] with a riding whip, and she left him." When it came time for legal argument, Henry Boulton would try to minimize Simpson's evidence. Simpson had sworn that George Ham had chastised his wife with a riding whip. But this was not sufficient in Boulton's mind to warrant marital separation. "Fear and terror of life must be proved," he asserted, and "no such terror existed in the present case."

Christopher Hagerman countered that no woman would leave her husband and her child "without some extraordinary cause." And Hagerman also denied that a man was at liberty to chastise his wife. "That was the law of former times," he insisted, "but the day ... was now too far advanced to admit such doctrines." He urged the jury to bring back a verdict that would "prove a salutary warning to all husbands not to ill-treat their wives."

Chief Justice William Campbell was the judge sitting on the case, the same Campbell who had denied the seduction claim of Amelia Hogle and had convicted Angelique Pilotte. Of uncertain health, the next year would be Campbell's last of hearing cases, and he may have been anxious to leave his mark upon the law for posterity. In his address to the jury he set out an extensive analysis of the law as it related to wife battering. The Kingston *Chronicle* would immortalize the comments of the Chief Justice, a man of great prominence who was also the president of the Executive Council and the speaker of the Legislative Council. The paper reported his statements in full. "It was true," began Campbell, "that a chastisement had taken place; but however ungallant such conduct might be considered, yet a man had a right to chastise his wife *moderately* — and to warrant her leaving her husband, the chastisement must be such as to put her life in jeopardy." Apparently prepared to declare chastisement with a riding whip as "moderate" discipline, the Chief Justice wanted the public "distinctly to understand" that the law was "decidedly hostile to the practice of wives running away from their husbands."[11]

Campbell was expressly critical of the intervention of Esther Hawley Ham's parents in their daughter's marital problems. According to the *Chronicle*, Campbell outlined "with great good humour" his notion of the proper parental course of conduct, using a parable to underscore the lesson:

It once upon a time so happened that a person who had some dispute with his wife gave her a moderate chastisement — upon which the fair one ran home, and complained to her father.

The father pretending to be in a desperate rage at the husband said — what! has the scoundrel really had the impudence to beat my daughter — , well says he, I shall be revenged upon him, for I am determined to beat his wife, which he did, and sent her home and was no more troubled with the quarrels of the parties — and Mr. Hawley should have done the same.

Some of the many people who were crowding the courtroom that day would no doubt have found this story humorous and would have fundamentally approved of the hierarchical vision of marriage that Campbell was extolling. Others may have been shocked at the Chief Justice's levity about an acknowledged case of wife battering. Campbell's biographers have noted that his address occasioned some "private twittering among Kingston's female gentlefolk." One wonders what his wife, Hannah Hadley, and his four daughters made of the remarks and the ensuing public notoriety.[12]

Chief Justice Campbell concluded his address to the jury by recommending that "not a farthing of damages ought to be given" to Sheldon Hawley. At most, maintenance for "one month" was all that was owing, cautioned Campbell, and the entitlement even to this was "not certain." The jury of twelve male residents from the surrounding countryside would heed the Chief Justice well. They returned a verdict for two pounds and ten shillings, heaping derision upon Sheldon Hawley's original claim for one thousand pounds.[13]

Campbell's decision in *Hawley* v *Ham* set the stage for a century of Canadian judicial precedent denying women basic protection against ruthless mistreatment. Case after case revealed women brutalized by vicious husbands. They were strangled, beaten with the handles of brooms, scalded with boiling water, threatened with loaded revolvers, kicked, bloodied, bruised, blackened, and blistered. Judge after judge would profess themselves mortified at having to hear testimony about the violence husbands were perpetrating upon their wives. It was not the cruelty itself that bothered them so much, but rather that "transactions of this sort" should be "screened from public gaze."[14]

Where they were forced to confront such cases, the judges searched scrupulously for particulars that would justify a husband's violent response. Many probed for evidence about the battered wife's behaviour or character, speculating that her shortcomings might "excuse considerable severity" on the part of her husband. Ruling that it was all a question of degree, they meticulously weighed the amount and nature of the violence. Before a court would "sanction her leaving her husband's roof," the law laid "upon the wife the necessity of bearing some indignities, and even some personal violence." "Danger to life, limb or health" was necessary to "entitle the wife to relief."[15]

Quebec judges, who were considering actions for *séparation de corps* (separation from bed and board) under the French legal system, ruled similarly to their common law judicial brothers. In a remarkable decision in 1856, Judge Charles-Dewey Day of the Superior Court in Montreal ordered a battered woman to return to her husband. Various acts of brutality had forced Emérance Hervieux to flee for shelter to her brother's home. Some of the beatings had resulted in injuries so severe that her husband had been arrested and criminally prosecuted. The court ordered Madame Hervieux home, concluding that although the violence may have constituted "strong ... moral reasons" for her departure, this did not furnish "a legal defence."[16]

The judges justified their rulings with tributes to the importance of marriage. "The well-being of our whole social system rest[s] upon this foundation of mutual forbearance," insisted Chancellor William Hume Blake in 1852. "Those who enter into that engagement do so for better, for worse. [W]here the result fails to realize all our anticipations, it is our manifest duty to bear and forbear." But the marriage they were eulogizing was a very rigid, overbearing, patriarchal one. Husbands were expected to wield all the power and could behave as they wished, setting their wives' work agendas, refusing them the right to come and go from the family home, stipulating with whom they could socialize, even to the exclusion of their own relatives. "I am independent, king, lord of all!" declared George Ham, and his proclamation was endorsed and strengthened by Chief Justice Campbell, who found the whole situation so amusing that he joked as he delivered his address to the jury.[17]

Wives found their roles rather more circumscribed. They were to be obedient, restrained, forgiving, and passive. Through prudent forbearance and submission they were to accommodate themselves to their husbands' desires. Legally denied any semblance of independence or autonomy, women were admonished to meet temper with meekness and harsh conduct with self-abasement. Most important, patriarchal marriage was predicated upon the silence of women. Institutionalized male supremacy in marriage required that family problems be screened from public gaze. Those who complained too loudly threatened the entire inequitable arrangement with exposure. Esther Hawley Ham and Sheldon Hawley found themselves sharply reprimanded by the judge and jury for daring to assert a more egalitarian model of marriage.

The roots of this patriarchal concept lay buried under the elaborate legal rules that had developed around marriage. The English common law, transported to all Canadian jurisdictions except Quebec, had developed a "doctrine of marital unity." This meant that the very existence of the wife was legally absorbed by her husband. "By marriage, the husband and wife are one person in law" wrote eighteenth-century English jurist Sir William Blackstone, and he left no doubt that the "one person" was the husband. The most significant consequence of this would be its impact upon property. In most marriage ceremonies, the husband solemnly promised to endow his wife with all his worldly goods. The law, however, worked in complete contradiction to this vow.[18]

Upon marriage, a woman forfeited the right to manage all of her real estate under common law, although she did not lose the ownership of the property. All rents and profits from the land flowed by right to her husband during the marriage. Married women were legally incapable of contracting, suing, or of being sued in their own names. Women were only permitted to carry on business separately from their husbands if they had their spouses' consent to do so. Furthermore, all personal property belonging to the wife, including her wages, was transferred absolutely to her husband.

This could result in grave injustice, as starkly evidenced by the case of James and Mary Whibby in 1869 in Newfoundland. James Whibby had abandoned his wife and four children sixteen years earlier, but returned upon his wife's death to lay claim to the wages she had managed to put together from years of labouring as a washerwoman. Newfoundland Chief Justice Sir H.W. Hoyles ruled categorically that James Whibby was fully entitled to Mary's earnings. A few wealthy women were able to protect their property through recourse to highly technical "equitable" exceptions to the common law, but for the bulk of women there was no recourse.[19]

But property rules were only part of the package of common law. Due to the doctrine of marital unity, husbands and wives were barred from suing each other in tort. Violent husbands who injured their wives deliberately or through negligence were completely immune from any lawsuits seeking compensation. The theory was that since the couple was really one person, the law could not permit the husband to sue himself. Furthermore, any damages the wife might have won would immediately have reverted to the husband as property he was entitled to through the marriage.[20]

In Quebec, the rules derived from the *Coutume de Paris*, and after 1865, from the Civil Code of Lower Canada. Quebec women experienced the same legal incapacity upon marriage as women in the rest of Canada. They could not contract, take legal action, or start a business without their husbands' authorization. But they were not subject to the "doctrine of marital unity." French marriage was built upon the legal concept of "community of property." Under this system all of the property that the two spouses obtained after the marriage became their "joint" property. The catch was that the husband alone had the right to administer and dispose of the property. Couples could opt out of this system by signing special marriage contracts permitting a wife to retain control over her own property. The extent to which women managed to bargain such exemptions remains unclear.[21]

The law also created problems for women who suffered violent sexual assault within marriage. Sir Matthew Hale, an eighteenth-century English treatise-writer, had speculated that no husband could be criminally convicted of raping his wife. It was a case of irrevocable contract, according to Hale. "By their mutual matrimonial consent and contract the wife hath given up herself in this kind unto her husband, which she cannot retract." Since a husband and wife were legally one person, the crime of rape between them was taken to be theoretically impossible, no matter how often it may have occurred in real life. When doubts were expressed whether this was the proper legal perspective, the Canadian Parliament rushed through an unequivocal immunity in 1892. Making a mockery of the feminist campaign for "voluntary motherhood," the legislators ruled that no Canadian husband could ever be convicted of raping his wife.[22]

In return for virtually uncontested dominance inside marriage, husbands were legally liable for their wives' debts, torts, and contracts. This, in turn, seems to have provided further justification for rulings such as Judge Campbell's. As William Blackstone saw it:

the husband also (by the old law) might give his wife moderate correction. For, as he is to answer for her misbehaviour, the law thought it reasonable to intrust him with this power of restraining her, by domestic chastisement.... But this power of correction was confined within reasonable bounds....[23]

The legal rules that transferred women's property to their husbands upon marriage had spawned reasoning that began to treat women themselves as property. Wife battering was the logical, inevitable consequence. Dr. Emily Stowe would make the connection explicit in 1893, when she spoke to a large Toronto audience on "Crime, its Cause and Cure." The subordinate status of women was one of the "most prolific causes of crime," she argued. Dr. Stowe denounced what she characterized as "man's persistent assumption of ownership in woman, a barbarism still tenaciously clung to, and heralded in the ceremony at every fashionable wedding."[24]

Such imbalance in the laws of marriage moved many nineteenth-century women to action. Their focus would not be to call for greater access to divorce, but rather to demand fairer relations within marriage. The prevailing perspective of maternal feminism, with its glorification of women's role as wife and mother, disinclined women from encouraging the disruption of the family. Instead, reformers sought to preserve the marital bond by ameliorating some of the marital laws that encouraged exploitation. Elizabeth Dunlop, a woman who would later devote years to working with prostitutes through the Toronto Magdalene (or Magdalen) Asylum, was the leader of one group that demanded reform of the property law affecting married women. Her petition to the Legislature of Upper Canada in 1857 maintained that laws that transferred the property and earnings of the wife to the "absolute power" of the husband "occasion[ed] manifold evils becoming daily more apparent." Training attention upon the particular abuses perpetrated by alcoholic fathers, she deplored the misappropriation of women's wages:

A drunken father ... wrings from a mother her children's daily bread.... She may work from morning until night to see the produce of her labour wrested from her, and wasted in a tavern.... [S]uch cases are within the knowledge of every one.[25]

After 1851, the law of married women's property began to undergo incremental reform. In Quebec the law did not change significantly, but legislators in the other provinces slowly enacted a cross-section of new statutes increasing married women's ability to control their own property. By the end of the century — at least with respect to formal and theoretical rights over property — married women would be on an equal footing with married men. But actual access to resources and wealth remained markedly skewed in favour of men.[26]

Canadian judges did their best to retard any progress, repeatedly dispensing rulings that watered down the new rights and freedoms women had won from the legislatures. And the law journals harped continuously on the dangers of any reform of the common law system. The new married women's property legislation smacked too much of "sentimentalism," charged the lawyers. The reforms tended to "loosen the matrimonial tie," and left women as prey for "designing wolves in sheep's clothing." "All that is now required to cap such legislation is to declare that every woman shall be a man, the provisions of nature to the contrary notwithstanding," criticized the editors.[27]

The law of married women's property changed substantially, but very slowly throughout the nineteenth century. The law regarding marital violence did not. This was not for want of activists seeking reform. One woman, who identified herself only as "M.M.," wrote a letter that was published in *The Novascotian* in 1826. Describing instances of wife battering in England, she outlined one case where a woman had been assaulted with the "butt end of a gig whip, till a great part of her body was beaten to a jelly" and another where a woman had succumbed to insanity after being "horsewhipped." Arguing for laws that would "restrain and check the authority and powers of the husband," she urged: "If a wife act improperly, let the law and not the husband inflict the punishment; it is a legal maxim, that no man should be allowed to take the law into his own hands...."[28]

Another notable set of advocates came from the Woman's Christian Temperance Union. Under the leadership of the powerful Letitia Creighton Youmans of Ontario, the WCTU came to number ten thousand Canadian adherents between 1874 and 1900. Letitia Youmans had been converted to the cause of temperance when one of her Bible-class students from Picton, Ontario, confessed that her father became a wife beater when intoxicated:

"Oh," said one dear young girl (in the strictest confidence), "my heart is just breaking; father is so kind and good to us when he is sober, but liquor makes him a raving maniac. He hurled a burning lamp at mother the other night; sometimes he pursues us with a kettle of boiling water. I fear that sometime he will take our lives."[29]

The nineteenth-century temperance movement presented a strong challenge to the ideology of male supremacy. Much of the WCTU's criticism of alcohol came from its members' abhorrence of male violence against women and children. The image of the beaten wife was prominent in temperance literature, and male brutality was one of the key targets of prohibitionists.[30]

By 1879, the Nova Scotia Society for the Prevention of Cruelty, an all-male organization founded in 1877 to campaign against cruelty to animals, also turned its attention toward wife battering. Undertaking to prosecute wife batterers under criminal law, agents of the Nova Scotia Society were sometimes able to negotiate agreements for maintenance in return for dropping the charges. All of this they accomplished "in the shadow of the law," since the judicial alimony rules remained unchanged throughout the century.[31]

Nineteenth-century Canadian novelist Maria Amelia Fytche, a Maritimer, wrote scathingly in 1895 of the life of a fictional woman who served as a "model wife" within a patriarchal union.

[S]ubmitting herself upon her husband as unto the Lord ... she hung upon his utterances divine; learning in silence with all subjection, and believing that woman shall be saved in childbirth if she continue in faith and charity and holiness with sobriety. Twenty summers of this domestic bliss mingled with twenty winters of discontent, and the child-wife, grown gray in the service, was released from the bondage and called up higher, leaving ten little slaves in her place.[32]

But despite the work of the reformers, the judges remained committed to the male-dominant perspective. Their blatant acceptance of wife battering shored up the patriarchal family with a vengeance.

DIVORCE IN NEW BRUNSWICK, THE DIVORCE CAPITAL OF CANADA

Reverend William Armstrong was the Rector of the St. James Anglican Church in the southern port city of Saint John, New Brunswick. On 22 March 1876 he was called upon to officiate at the wedding of Alberta Lowell Gardner, one of his parishioners, and Alfred Henry Abell, of Moncton, New Brunswick. In the parlance of the day, the groom was "deaf and dumb." The bride's younger sister, Ada Gardner, was also deaf. Before Oralism — the teaching of the deaf to speak rather than to sign — achieved ascendancy in the 1880s, people who were deaf from birth seem

"Le Travail: Tu te plains, mon pauvre mari, de tes dix heures d'ouvrage; voici
quatorze heures que je travaille, moi, et je n'ai pas encore fini ma journée;
(You complain, my poor husband, of your ten hours of work; I have worked for
fourteen hours, and I am still not finished my day)."
*L'Opinion Publique* (Montreal), 2 November 1871.

rarely to have been forced to learn to speak and were often described as
"deaf mutes."[33]

Alfred Henry Abell was a distinguished graduate of the "Institution
for the Deaf and Dumb at Halifax." Under the direction of Principal James
Scott Hutton in Halifax, Alfred Abell had become a fluent signer and
excelled in written English. In October 1873 Abell had returned to New
Brunswick and opened a school for deaf adults in Saint John. Lobbied by
parents who did not wish to send their deaf children all the way to
Halifax, he widened his operation to include children. In November 1873
he opened a boarding school on Peter Street exclusively for deaf children.
Despite some competition between the Halifax facility and the Saint John

school, Abell's business thrived. Formally named the "New Brunswick Deaf and Dumb Institution," it expanded to larger premises on St. James Street.[34]

The conventional wisdom of hearing people held that deaf individuals who wished to marry should choose hearing persons as partners. Charles J. Howe, a strong proponent of Oralism, wrote in 1888:

The best wife for a deaf and dumb man — if he can find one and persuade her to marry him — is a woman who can hear, one who has acquired a ready means of communication with him, sympathizes with his affliction, and so is prepared to take upon herself a larger share than ordinary of the management of their family and joint affairs....

The hearing sisters or daughters of deaf and dumb persons would be most likely to fulfil the necessary requirements.... We can bear testimony that when two are well-matched, intelligent, and of amiable disposition, and especially if they act from Christian principle, they get on together exceedingly well.[35]

When Alberta Lowell Gardner's interest in her sister Ada's situation brought her into contact with Alfred Abell, the latter began to pursue her seriously. Alberta Lowell Gardner was apparently a skilled signer, and was intrigued by the distinguished advocate for the educational rights of deaf persons. She soon found herself falling in love with Alfred Abell. He proposed, she accepted, and the two were married by Reverend Armstrong in the presence of family and friends.[36]

The newlyweds resided in Saint John for approximately two years. During this time the economic pressures of the fledgling business created considerable anxiety. Alfred and Alberta Abell, who served as the Proprietor and the Matron of the Institution respectively, tried to run the facility as a profit-making venture. They collected fees from the parents of the pupils, and solicited charitable contributions from the public to cover additional expenses. But it was exceedingly difficult to make ends meet. In June 1877 the premises were destroyed by the "Great Fire" that razed the finer parts of Saint John. As Alfred Abell scrambled to put together a fund for rebuilding, financial difficulties reached their peak. On 8 January 1878, the President and Directors of the Institution placed a notice in the Saint John *Daily Evening News* that they would no longer "be responsible for any debts contracted except upon the written order of the Secretary-Treasurer."[37]

Nevertheless, the school reopened in September 1879, on the outskirts of Saint John, on Beaconsfield Road in the Fifth Ward of the city of Portland. The new building was to serve as a boarding facility for the students and as the Abell residence. The demand for such services was substantial, and numerous male pupils were promptly despatched to the school. Finances were still tight, however, and by the spring of 1880 the New Brunswick Deaf and Dumb Institution had begun to admit female pupils as well. Ada, Alberta Abell's fifteen-year-old sister, was one of the first.

The initial two years of marriage had proved to be difficult for the Abells. The frenetic ups and downs of the Institution had created an anxiety-ridden environment for the couple. Although they experienced periods of happiness together, the couple also faced "frequent quarrels and strifes." On 20 December 1878, the tensions exploded. As Alberta Abell would later describe it, her husband lost his temper, and beat and "severely bruised and injured" her with "blows, strokes, kicks and slaps." She fled from the house, and took refuge in the home of a neighbour, where she remained until 13 January 1879. That morning she departed for the train station, intending to travel to Moncton to stay with her father. But Alfred Abell had learned of her plans, and he was determined to find his wife and bring her home. He gathered together five of the boys from the school and barricaded the road. They waylaid Alberta Abell's horse-drawn sleigh and seized her, forcibly dragging her back to the Abell house. She screamed for help, frantically waving her handkerchief to attract attention. One outraged witness described it as "a nice escort — six gentlemen to one lady." At the time, however, no one intervened.[38]

Once home, Alfred Abell "stripped" Alberta Abell of her scarf, black velvet coat, satin dress, petticoat, and corsets. He left her standing clad only in her drawers, stockings, and chemise. His plan was to confine her to the house, unable to escape again without proper street attire. To Alberta Abell's extreme embarrassment, at least five of the male students witnessed the whole scene. Her husband then tried physically to make up with her. "I was kissing her as often as I could to awaken in her a feeling of love for me," he would later admit. But she vigorously resisted, so Alfred Abell took her clothes away to burn them, and left his wife locked in her room.[39]

At least one of the witnesses to the scene on the roadway had alerted the police, and three Portland police constables arrived without delay. They released Alberta Abell, who was in tears and clad only in her underwear. She urged the officers to arrest her husband for assault. Alfred Abell communicated with the officers in writing, insisting that he would not give his wife's clothes back "until she was in a better state of mind toward him." He also contested the right of the police to be in his home without a warrant.[40]

Nonetheless, the Portland police officers promptly arrested him, charging him and three of the students with assault. The case came on for trial before the Portland police magistrate on 14 January 1879. The newspapers made much of Alfred Abell's deafness, headlining their coverage with titles such as "Brutal Conduct of Alfred H. Abell and Four Other Mutes to Mrs. Abell" and "An Almost Unprecedented Case of Hardship." The papers also speculated freely about the genesis of the assault. "The wife is a pretty woman," the reporters noted, and the "jealous[y]" of a "deaf mute" was their theory about the motivation behind the crime.[41]

Alberta Abell retained her own lawyers to represent her during the criminal trial. Alfred Augustus Stockton and Charles A. Stockton came from a long line of prominent New Brunswick lawyers. Among the original United Empire Loyalists, the Stockton family had moved from Princeton, New Jersey, to found the city of Saint John, then known as Parr Town. The Stocktons were famous for their family law firms, their outstanding educational record, their political skills, and their extensive community involvement. Alfred Abell retained D.S. Kerr, a lawyer with a reputation for tenacity.[42]

Alfred Abell requested that his brother be sworn to act as his interpreter, but the police magistrate refused. Instead, all questions were put to Abell in writing and he, in turn, would reply in writing. The police magistrate's refusal to allow Abell's brother to act as interpreter led to an excessively lengthy proceeding, and months passed before all of the evidence was in. Even the newspapers began to get impatient with the delays and the incessant arguing of the lawyers.

Detailed coverage resumed, however, when D.S. Kerr tried to plead an old English text written by Bacon to back up his argument that "a man could beat his wife if he beat her reasonably." Charles Stockton immediately rose to rebut this point, claiming that "Mr. Kerr's law was as old as the hills." The Saint John *Daily Sun* quoted:

[Stockton] admitted that there once was a time when a man could do as he liked with his wife, owned her in fact as a planter did his slave, and that there were still barbarians; but said that we here lived in a Christian country and age, and had laws on the statute book which protected a wife from being beaten and ill-treated by her husband. If Mr. Kerr's law was correct he, Mr. Stockton, did not want any female friend of his to live in the country, and he did not want to live in it himself.[43]

This argument is highly reminiscent of the debate between the lawyers in Esther Hawley Ham's case. But in this instance the criminal judge would choose to take a firmer line against wife battering than most of his predecessors. This may have been due to Alfred Abell's deafness. Public opinion seems to have been that Abell was lucky to have a pretty — and hearing — wife and that he ought therefore to prove himself worthy of the marriage by treating her more kindly. On 3 April 1879, the court convicted Alfred Abell of assault, and he was fined fifty dollars and costs. The four students were fined twenty dollars each. None was forced to pay. The magistrate allowed the fines "to stand for their future good conduct."[44]

Immediately after the conviction Alberta Abell left for Moncton, where she took up residence at her father's home. Alfred Abell refused to accept the separation. Promising repeatedly to change his behaviour, he begged his wife to return. In December 1879 Alberta Abell relented and went back to her husband in what would be the first of a series of "reconciliations." This one would be short-lived. On 1 April, Alfred Abell struck his wife in the face with such force that he broke her nose, leaving her unconscious. When she came to, he held his wife prisoner, in the house under lock and key, for days.

When Alberta Abell escaped, she sought refuge once again with her father. While there she gave birth to a son, whom she named "Eddie," on 6 January 1881, approximately nine months after the last assault. When news reached Alfred Abell of the birth, he pursued his wife to Moncton and pleaded with her to return for the sake of the child. Invariably won over by her husband's entreaties, she went back to him, bringing Eddie with her. This time the Abell family would remain together for little more than two months. On 6 June 1881 Alfred Abell beat his wife severely and she fled once more, retreating again to her father's for a few months. In October she struck out on her own and moved to Boston, Massachusetts. Her husband followed her there, and at his "earnest request and solicitation" she returned to the Abell home. She lived with Alfred Abell from 6 July 1882 until 1 February 1883, when what she learned about her husband's conduct forced her out for good.

For the full year, Alfred Abell had been having sexual relations with a number of the young female students in his care. He had raped at least one, Mary Upham. In the case of others, he had apparently used less forcible means. To Alberta Abell's horror, she also discovered that her sister, Ada, had been among Alfred's conquests. During May and June, while Alberta Abell had been living in Boston, her husband and her sister had been having regular sexual relations. This information would finally accomplish what years of violence had failed to do. The day she learned about her sister and her husband, Alberta Abell made an irrevocable break with him. She moved to her father's home, vowing never to return. Four days later she retained Robert Barry Smith, a prominent Moncton barrister and solicitor, to petition for a divorce.

Alberta Abell's decision to seek an absolute divorce differed markedly from Esther Hawley Ham's more cautious one to seek only alimony. In part this reflected prevailing social attitudes toward adultery, which was viewed as significantly more damaging to marriage than mere wife battering. A husband's violence was thought to be but one manifestation of the commonly accepted power imbalance between spouses. Heterosexual liaisons outside of marriage, however, struck right at the heart of the institution. The foundation of nineteenth-century marriage was its potential for reproduction. To violate the vows of monogamy was to breach the original premise of the bargain.

In part Alberta Abell's choice to seek a full divorce also reflected the passage of time. For late-nineteenth-century Canadians, divorces were more accessible than they had been in the earlier decades. But most of all, Alberta Abell's action reflected where she lived. New Brunswick, along with Nova Scotia, was the "divorce capital of nineteenth-century Canada." The legal barriers to divorce in Quebec and Upper Canada had never fully applied in the Maritime provinces. Legislation enacted as early as 1758 in Nova Scotia and in 1791 in New Brunswick offered considerable access to divorce. Prince Edward Island passed similar legislation in 1833, although few of its residents would employ the divorce law in the nineteenth century, and it was spared the reputation that its sister provinces developed.[45]

These Maritime divorce statutes were a complete departure from the historical English legal tradition. Their roots may have originated in the states of New England, some of which had developed similar laws in the eighteenth century. Puritan lawmakers had long advocated the reform of English law, believing that by dissolving dysfunctional unions divorce benefited society and strengthened the family. Many of the Maritime colonists had come from New England, and they may have transported their divorce laws with them.[46]

Initially the Maritime Governors and Councils were authorized to grant divorces. Later, formal matrimonial courts were established to hear petitions for divorce on grounds such as adultery, impotence, frigidity, cruelty, and willful desertion. The situation became complicated when

Confederation turned matters of divorce over to federal jurisdiction in 1867. However, in the absence of any federal legislation, the Maritime provinces continued to dispense divorces as always. By 1890 the Nova Scotia matrimonial court had dealt with between 150 and 200 divorce applications. By 1900 the New Brunswick court had dealt with approximately 130.[47]

For its part, the most that the federal government accomplished was to take over the original parliamentary jurisdiction to pass special statutes of divorce in individualized cases. Citizens of Ontario, Manitoba, and the North-West Territories used this option. But between 1867 and 1900, only sixty-nine such divorces were granted by Parliament. The Canadian Parliament seems to have been awash in anti-divorce rhetoric and sentiments. It had become a matter of national pride to invoke Canada as a country that knew how to value and cherish "the sacred character of the matrimonial tie" and "the purity and sacredness of the family." In contrast, by 1857 England had passed a general divorce statute, substantially loosening the legal barriers to divorce. Prime Minister Sir John A. Macdonald was appalled by the English example: "The number of divorces, the corruption of society, and the number of collusive trials increase to the annually increasing degradation of the public mind." He had nothing but praise, however, for the Canadian system, which he noted offered "considerable impediments to the granting of divorce."[48]

The American states had gone further than England, responding to popular demand for divorce with a series of acts and a remarkably broad range of grounds. In some jurisdictions, vaguely worded clauses even permitted the courts to grant divorce whenever it seemed in the interests of the parties. Canadians reacted to this with shock and dismay. American divorce laws were denounced in Canadian legal journals as "libertinism (falsely called freedom)," and in the Canadian Senate as "ruinous" to the "morals, well-being and the entire social interests of communities."[49]

Some of the fiercest rejection of divorce came from Quebec. There the Civil Code continued to make divorce legally impossible. Some Québécois did apply to Parliament for a special statute, but within the avowedly anti-divorce atmosphere this was an extreme rarity. Quebec politician John Hyacinthe Bellerose castigated divorce as an "unchristian practice" in 1868. Hormisdas Jeannotte rose in the House of Commons in 1894 to assert that "throughout the whole province of Quebec — I say the whole province as nine-tenths of the population are Catholics — every Catholic is opposed to divorce." Quebec women who advocated improvements in the status of women also embraced this aversion to any legal recognition of divorce. Josephine Dandurand would write in 1900:

According to the law, divorce does not exist in Canada. [Parliament] in certain exceptional cases ... grants a special decree; but Catholics do not take advantage of it. Once married, it is understood to be for life. If one has made a mistake, one tries to accommodate one's self to it, and to make the best of it, rather than give way to useless despair.[50]

British Columbia courts laid claim to jurisdiction over divorce in 1877. That province had inherited English law after the divorce reform, and there the courts decided that they had the right to grant divorces under the English act. In British Columbia the applications for divorce were somewhat more sporadic than in the east, however, and the western province never rivalled Nova Scotia or New Brunswick in divorce statistics.[51]

By 1881, when census figures revealed the ratio of divorced to married people in Canada, Nova Scotia and New Brunswick outstripped the rest of the country with figures of 1:2,608 and 1:2,350 respectively. Quebec ran last, at 1:62,334. These statistics did not, of course, reflect the presumably large number of self-divorces, nor the number of couples who travelled to the United States to be divorced.[52]

Horrified by her husband's acts of sexual exploitation, and apparently relying upon the relatively easier access to divorce in her home province of New Brunswick, Alberta Abell instructed Robert Barry Smith to file the necessary documents. Born in Portland, Smith had studied at Mount Allison College in Sackville, New Brunswick, had articled under Alfred Augustus Stockton in Saint John, and had been called to the bar in 1875. He was well known as a criminal defence lawyer and constitutional law advocate. A strong opponent of the prohibition of alcohol, he would appear in front of the Supreme Court of Canada in 1885 arguing the case of liquor dealers against temperance legislation.[53]

The procedure for initiating a divorce application was to file a "libel" with the court, setting forth the grounds that would justify dissolution of the marriage. The libel Smith drafted, filed on 15 February 1883, outlined various incidents of brutality and sexual misconduct by Alfred Abell. He was a person of "lewd and vicious habits and disposition," the document alleged, of "violent temper" and of "vicious life and conversation." Robert Barry Smith was careful to add that Alberta Abell had always lived a "strictly virtuous and moral life" and had never violated her marital vows. Finally, Smith took care to note that immediately upon learning of her husband's adulteries, she had left him and had refused to reside or cohabit with him since. Had she "condoned" her husband's actions, this would have posed a bar to her application.[54]

The New Brunswick divorce statute set out the grounds for divorce as follows: frigidity, impotence, adultery, and consanguinity within the degrees prohibited by English law. Nova Scotia was the only jurisdiction that allowed cruelty as a ground for divorce. In New Brunswick, cruelty and marital violence were not on the list. For this reason, it was curious that Alberta Abell set out, along with the requisite claims of adultery, the numerous assaults to which she had been subjected. Theoretically, she was entitled to allege adultery alone.[55]

Perhaps Alberta Abell and her lawyer were simply exercising caution. Possibly they were concerned that despite the words of the statute, women who claimed adultery alone would meet resistance from divorce courts. Certainly traditional rules had always enshrined a sexual double standard into divorce procedure. In England throughout the nineteenth century men could obtain divorce upon proving simple adultery, but women had to prove adultery plus some additional marital impropriety. The French tradition had been equally imbalanced. In Quebec a man could obtain *séparation de corps* with proof of his wife's adultery. A woman had to prove that her husband was keeping "his concubine in their common habitation."[56]

British Columbia had adopted the discriminatory English law in its entirety. In the North-West Territories, Manitoba, and Ontario, where Parliament ruled on divorce applications, similar impediments confronted women wishing to obtain divorce upon the ground of adultery alone. It was not until 1888 that a woman procured a parliamentary divorce on the basis of simple adultery, and her petition led to an intense legal confrontation over the pros and cons of the sexual double standard. While some argued that the 1888 case had abolished the inequality of treatment, by the turn of the century only three other women had fared as well.[57]

Even those who favoured legal equality for men and women who committed adultery were quick to say that the sexual indiscretions of women were more reprehensible. John Gemmill, the author of the most influential treatise on divorce in the nineteenth century, concluded that wifely infidelities "deserve[d] a heavier chastisement" than identical acts of husbands. While he advocated permitting women to divorce their husbands on the simple ground of adultery, Gemmill was by no means prepared to equate the extramarital sexual relations of the two:

Looking at it from a social, rather than from a moral standpoint, it is true that the wife's infidelity is followed by results of a graver character than those which follow the infidelity of the husband, and it is therefore in the interest of society that one should be punished more promptly and more severely than the other.

The problem was obvious to most observers. Women could become pregnant from extramarital intercourse, and this would confuse the proper descent of blood lines and inheritance.[58]

Against this backdrop of the widespread social and legal sanctioning of a sexual double standard, the Maritime divorce statutes stood out as anomalous. All were apparently "gender-neutral." Enacted in the early days of the colonies, they may have reflected the relatively higher status that women initially enjoyed in the Maritimes. Similar enactments in the United States were often attributed to Puritan or republican sentiments. Whatever the origins of these egalitarian provisions, however, Alberta Abell and her lawyer were clearly apprehensive about relying upon the letter of the law. They backed up their assertions of adultery with detailed and graphic references to the repeated instances of wife assault.[59]

When Alfred Abell learned of his wife's initiative, he sent off a "libel" of his own, alleging that it was he, not Alberta Abell, who should be granted a divorce. He claimed that his wife had been guilty of "adulterous intercourse" with Charles Stockton, one of the Portland barristers who had pleaded Alberta Abell's case on the earlier criminal charge. He alleged that his wife and Charles Stockton had had "carnal knowledge" of each other on 28 January 1883 in Alfred Abell's house and office. Furthermore, he asserted that the son that his wife had borne was really Charles Stockton's issue. Alfred Abell noted that he had begun to suspect that his wife's motives for marrying him had been dishonest. He had been used as a "cloak or shield" to hide her adulterous affair, and she had thought that his being both "deaf and dumb" would save her from exposure.[60]

Whether truthful or not, the public allegations against Charles Stockton would have reverberated throughout the legal and social communities. Alfred Abell would have been aware of this, and he clearly feared repercussions. He was terribly worried that Charles Stockton would use his legal connections to try to influence the outcome of the litigation. "I will have hard [up]hill work with my case," Alfred Abell predicted. In his eyes, Charles Stockton was "a great rogue," who would go to any lengths to turn everyone, including Alfred Abell's own solicitor, against him.[61]

Alfred Abell also disputed his wife's allegations against him, insisting that he had treated her "with kindness," provided her with a "comfortable home," and fulfilled all of his responsibilities as a husband. He was a "person of good temper," "moral and sober conduct," and a man of "virtuous life and conversation," he insisted. Setting himself up as the injured party, he called for a speedy divorce. As he would write to the Registrar of the Divorce Court that June, "I hope to get rid of that vile woman and all lawsuits which are the fruits of the marriage that I get from her."[62]

Alfred Abell retained Charles N. Skinner, QC, a Saint John lawyer and politician, to help him with his divorce application. But he was not entirely happy with Charles Skinner's services. In addition to his fears that the Stockton family was trying to pressure his lawyer, Alfred Abell was disturbed that Skinner was constantly out of the city, on business in Fredericton and New York. Consequently Alfred Abell found himself issuing subpoenas for witnesses and writing up many of the documents. This work would generate a great deal of anxiety over the direction of the forthcoming case. At one point he wrote to Judge Andrew Rainsford Wetmore, who had been assigned to hear the case, asking for legal assistance. Judge Wetmore may have had some inkling that Alfred Abell would spell trouble for him down the road. He replied to the letter carefully, detailing how to issue subpoenas and make application for custody of the child. He also warned Alfred Abell not to write to him again, chiding him to do his business through his solicitor. This would not be the last he heard from Alfred Abell.[63]

Trial began in the Fredericton courthouse on 23 October 1883. It would take ten days before all of the evidence was in. Judge Wetmore, who appeared to be astounded by the length of the trial, filled sixty-three pages of foolscap with closely written notes. The nature of the evidence also bothered Wetmore, who pronounced it to be "of a most disgusting character."[64]

As most of the witnesses were deaf, an interpreter, Alfred R. Woodbridge, was brought in. Woodbridge came from an English family that had a long and distinguished history of working with deaf persons. Relatives had served as principals of schools for deaf children in cities such as Birmingham, England, Halifax, and Fredericton. The accommodation of the deaf witnesses within the courtroom was an indication that, whatever else the parties and their lawyers might disagree about, they seem to have been serious about the legal rights of Alfred Abell. Accommodation may not have been without precedent. In the 1840s and 1850s the impaired hearing of Judge George Frederick Street of the New

Brunswick Supreme Court had led him to employ a lawyer as a full-time transcriber of the evidence.[65]

Yet Judge Wetmore found the accommodation of deaf witnesses a "painful and tedious undertaking" under "most trying and annoying circumstances." His ruling contained a series of subtle but negative references to "deaf mutes," which clearly evidenced his impatience with them. Judge Wetmore ruled decisively for Alberta Abell on 6 November. Whether he would have ruled the same way if Alfred Abell had been a hearing person is impossible to ascertain. At the very least, it would have been a more balanced contest.

Wetmore justified his decision on the ground that Alberta Abell's allegations against her husband had been "positively proved." As for Alfred Abell's witnesses, the judge was highly sceptical: "Their evidence is characterized throughout by such ridiculous extravagance and manifest absurdities as to render it to my mind absolutely incredible." Furthermore, Charles A. Stockton had taken the stand to deny the allegations concerning his relationship with Alberta Abell. According to Wetmore, Stockton had "in the clearest and most satisfactory manner to my mind entirely disproved the committing of any adulterous intercourse." Alberta Abell was granted her divorce, along with her legal costs of one hundred and seventy-five dollars.[66]

Alfred Abell had feared that Stockton's involvement would prejudice the process from the outset, and despairing of fair treatment within the New Brunswick bar, he wrote directly to the Minister of Justice in Ottawa. He did not cite his deafness or the judge's manifest discomfort with it as the ground for complaint:

Saint John, New Brunswick
Canada, 22nd January 1884

To the Minister of Justice
Ottawa, Ontario, Canada

Dear Sir

Please stop the execution of the judgment of Judge Wetmore of the Court of Divorce and Matrimonial Causes until you have investigated the case; the undersigned begs leave to state that he believes the Judge received a bribe and that his judgment is totally false and illogical and illegal; the facts of the evidence do not warrant his conclusions, you may call in from the evidence while shortly I will

Saint John, New Brunswick,
Canada, 22nd January 1884

To The Minister of Justice
Ottawa, Ontario, Canada

Alfred Abell

Dear Sir

Please stop the execution of the judgment of Judge Wetmore of the Court of Divorce, and Matrimonial Causes until you have investigated the case; the undersigned begs leave to state that he believes the Judge received a bribe and that his judgment is totally false and illogical and illegal; the facts of the evidence do not warrant his Conclusions, you may call in from the evidence while shortly, I will furnish you evidence, so that you can see that you have not garbled testimony before you.

The undersigned states only two deaf mute girls appeared as witnesses against him; one of them falsely proved his marriage, she never present at the wedding and other swore other lies and absurdities

both

Portions of Alfred Abell's letter of complaint
to the Minister of Justice, 22 January 1884.

furnish you evidence, so that you can see that you have not garbled testimony before you.

The undersigned states only two deaf mute girls appeared as witnesses against him; one of them falsely proved his marriage, she never present at the wedding and other swore other lies and absurdities both rebutted by their bedmates and other persons and one Mr. Teed exposed partly the tampering of one of them by the plaintiff. Then one lawyer and seven deaf mutes testified to the improprieties of the plaintiff with a wealthy lawyer of St. John and two hearing and speaking persons proved the kind treatment of the plaintiff a beautiful hearing young woman by the defendant a deaf mute.

The Judge was requested by the counsel of the defendant to order the presence of the child of the plaintiff in Court as it is an exact image of the paramour of the plaintiff; but the judge only laughed at him and said he would not look on the child as evidence, a creature of red hair and very fair features, bandy legged and fat bellied while the defendant and his wife are of dark or brunette complexion and dark hair and lean in person....

The Counsel of the defendant, perhaps out of timidity, gave up the case and the defendant has not yet engaged another counsel. The defendant did not think his counsel conducted the case very honestly for him and while he wanted the case then going on unexpectedly rapidly to be postponed for a few days in order to have more witnesses to expose the tampering of one of the witnesses of the plaintiff he was told the Court would not give any postponement. The Counsel said he could not see how the judge could give such a total divorce. However he said if I appeal to the Supreme Court the other Judges would side with Wetmore in five minutes.

If you think the Judge deserves an impeachment in the Parliament you may take steps to have him punished.... It is time to purify the Bench of New Brunswick. I trust you will give the matter your serious attention. I suggest to you that it is a bad policy to appoint defeated lawyer candidates for legislative honors to the Judgship [sic] which position ought to have been conferred on skilful lawyers of good and honest repute.

> All of which is Respectfully Submitted
> Your Humble, Obedient Servant
> Alfred H. Abell
> P.O. Box 26, St. John N.B.

Disparaging the conduct of his own lawyer, alleging that the judge had been bribed, and castigating the federal government for its judicial appointments process was risky to say the least. Given Alfred Abell's own were supported by another lawyer Jeremiah Travis and instead of prosecuting Kerr before a jury he had him tried before the judges and debarred from Court practice for ever. It is time to purify the Bench of New Brunswick I trust you will give the matter your serious attention I suggest to you that it is a bad policy to appoint defeated lawyer Candidates for legislative honors to the judgship which position ought to have been Conferred on skilful lawyers of good and honest repute.

All of which is Respectfully Submitted
Your Humble, Obedient Servant

(Sigd)         Alfred H. Abell
P.O. Box 26. St. John N.B.

Hon. C.N. Skinner 2 c. Counsel for
Defendant gave up the case
another Counsel not engaged yet

R. Barry Smith, Counsel for Plaintiff

Portions of Alfred Abell's letter of complaint
to the Minister of Justice, 22 January 1884.

deafness and his line of work, what seems even more unwise was his decision to plead his case by attacking the credibility of adverse witnesses because they were "deaf mutes."

Judge Wetmore was requested by the Ministry of Justice to reply to the letter. In a rather restrained manner, Wetmore expressly denied the bribery in May 1884. He wrote that his judgment was the result of "careful consideration of all the evidence," and he thought it a matter for some pride that Abell's letter had admitted that the appeal judges would side with the trial ruling. Wetmore took issue with Abell's comments about Charles Skinner, his lawyer: "I did not discover any giving up of his case. On the contrary, C.N. Skinner exhibited the most enduring patience, persevering industry and unquestionable ability." The Ministry of Justice appears to have accepted Judge Wetmore's view that Alfred Abell's charges were completely unfounded, and there was no further activity on the complaint.

As for the sexually abused deaf students, nothing further was done. The exploitation of deaf children appears to have been all too common. In 1902, Albert F. Woodbridge, the Principal of a rival facility, the "Fredericton Institution for the Education of the Deaf and Dumb," would also be charged with immoral conduct with young female pupils. A provincial government inquiry closed the school and Albert Woodbridge, Norman Woodbridge, and George Ernest Powers were all subsequently convicted of criminal charges.[67]

Meanwhile, now a divorcée who had reverted to using her maiden name, Gardner, the former Alberta Abell returned to Moncton. Divorced persons were seen as aberrations in all parts of Canada, and great social stigma marked those whose marriages had been terminated by law. Ostracism was one of the most common reactions of the community. Even wealthy and prominent women found that their positions could not withstand divorce. Addie Chisholm Foster, the wife of Prime Minister Macdonald's Minister of Finance, and President of the WCTU of Ontario, was refused admittance to important social functions in Ottawa because she had divorced her former husband after he deserted her.[68]

Alberta Gardner was neither wealthy nor influential, and she was faced with immediate financial problems on top of ostracism and isolation. She settled into a rented house with her son, and took up dressmaking, an impoverished living at best. She described her situation as "very poor," and at times she and young Eddie went without food. Her brother, a carpenter in Moncton, built her a small four-room house in the family neighbourhood, and although he never quite completed it, she was grateful to have her own roof over her head.[69]

To the further shock of the community, Alberta Gardner bore another child, a second boy, in the spring of 1884. Who the father was, whether Charles A. Stockton or someone else, is not known. Moncton neighbours whispered about the comings and goings of unnamed men "at very late and unseasonable hours." Some speculated that she might have been trying to supplement her income through "illegitimate" activities. Word soon got back to Alfred Abell, who vehemently denied being the father, insisting that there had been no cohabitation since the final separation in February 1883. He claimed that the second child must have been conceived in July 1883, some four months before the divorce decree had been registered. He went back to court, this time with a new lawyer, to seek a reopening of the case.[70]

Alberta Gardner registered her objection as soon as she learned of Alfred Abell's actions. First, she argued that her poverty prevented her from retaining legal counsel to defend herself. Second, although she admitted the birth of the second child, she denied that she had been living immorally. "I have on the contrary endeavoured to live a good life and a proper one, especially since the birth of my son in the spring of 1884," she wrote. There is no record of any further judicial proceeding. Presumably Alfred Abell's application failed, and Alberta Gardner continued her life, with even more precarious finances and even greater social disgrace. Living in one of the divorce capitals of Canada may have given her access to a legal divorce denied other women, and it may have freed her from the violent attentions of her husband. But as the single, female parent of two children, socially ruined and faced with severe economic deprivation, her future was anything but secure.[71]

She was one of relatively few nineteenth-century women who received legal approval for divorce. Esther Hawley Ham, upbraided by the court for failing to keep her marriage intact, was more typical of Canadian women's experience. The law's perspective on marriage was patriarchal and hierarchical, with a double standard that treated female adultery more seriously than male adultery built into the legal framework, in some cases expressly and in others implicitly through the pleadings of lawyers and the decisions of judges. These rules and practices created a setting that tolerated and in some cases encouraged acts of physical and sexual brutality against married women. The relative inaccessibility of divorce, geographically, socially, and economically, further locked many women into inequitable and sometimes abusive family structures.

# 7

# Child Custody

Helen "Nellie" M. Armstrong was desperate. She had separated from her husband, William Armstrong, on 29 January 1895, and had not seen her children for more than eight months. There were four children in all: Frank Byron aged eight, Bessie M. aged six, Sofia Eugene aged four, and William Frederick aged two. Her husband had sent the children out of town, some to his sister's and the others to his brother's home. Nellie Armstrong had written repeatedly to her husband, begging to see the children. She had tracked the children to their temporary dwelling-places, and had gone with the local sheriff to demand to see them. But her husband and his siblings had denied her any access. On 22 October 1895, Nellie Armstrong and her lawyer, H.A. Connell, appeared before Judge Frederic Eustache Barker, a Judge in Equity of the Supreme Court of New Brunswick, in a suit for custody. But as nineteenth-century custody law was heavily weighted in favour of fathers, she would have known it would be an uphill battle.[1]

It had not always been so. Traditionally, the First Nations had allocated most child custody to mothers. As Judge Samuel Cornwallis Monk had noted in the *Connolly* case, "it was the unwritten law of the red man [sic] that [the mother] should herself retain those whom she had borne or nursed." But this understanding had been quickly superseded by the introduction of European laws that favoured fathers' rights. Under English common law, the father had almost exclusive control and custody of all children.[2]

Clara Brett Martin, who would become the first woman lawyer in Canada, described the father's common law custodial rights in the following terms:

[C]hildren belong to the father, — they are his, and his only. The father is the sole guardian of his infant children, and no contract before marriage that the mother is to have the custody and control of the children of that marriage is binding on the husband, nor will the courts enforce it.

A father may bind out his infant children, apprentice them, give them in adoption, educate them how and when he pleases, and in what religion he pleases. He is entitled to all their earnings until they reach their majority. In fact he has control and custody of their persons until they reach that age.

This situation caused Clara Brett Martin to protest that mothers stood "legally in exactly the same position as a stranger."[3]

This was but another aspect of the patriarchal family model that had so rooted itself into nineteenth-century Canadian law. The family functioned under hierarchical structures, and at the pinnacle stood the father. Women were subordinate to men, and children were subordinate to adults. Within this vision, children were, for all practical purposes, regarded as property or as economic assets, which could gainfully contribute to household production or family income through waged labour. Since the male head of the household generally controlled family property, it seemed only logical that he should have sole authority and control over the children.

Theoretically there were some limits upon a father's rights to his children. For centuries judges had the authority under rules of equity to seize custody from a father where he had behaved so outrageously that a child's security was endangered. But the extreme caution with which most courts exercised this power had left paternal custody rights almost unchallenged. As one Manitoba justice, Thomas Wardlaw Taylor, noted in 1893, "the Court is always unwilling to interfere with the common law rights of the father."[4]

However, the nineteenth century was also an era of great change. As more Canadians moved to towns and cities, the family began to be transformed. Work was no longer primarily centred within the household, as it had been in pre-industrial, rural society. Grown men and children increasingly began to labour in factories and offices away from the home. Childhood was assigned enhanced status, as a special phase in life requiring a warm, protected, and prolonged period of nurture. Mothers, left behind at home, were charged with the remaining tasks of taking care of small children and supervising the day-to-day domestic chores. Some have called this isolation of women and young children in the home, stripped of most economic activities, a "domestic void."[5]

The void would not remain for long. Mothers were soon exhorted to meet increasingly high standards for housekeeping, child rearing, and the emotional caretaking of all family members. During the second half of the nineteenth century, some Canadians began to espouse a "cult of motherhood," trying to elevate the role of mothering to unprecedented height. Religious leaders, such as Reverend Robert Sedgewick, who spoke to the Halifax YMCA in 1856, likened the situation of a mother to that of a sculptor, and even of a deity:

What is [the influence of] a mother? It is in this relationship that [women's] power for good is specially manifest, and specially blissful.... It is not too bold a use of the figure to say that [a child] is in her hands as clay in the hands of the potter, that she can mould it at will. The power she can exert for a considerable period is well nigh absolute.... The love of a mother is like the bounty of God.... [6]

Educators such as Principal George Monro Grant of Queen's University furthered these images. Grant spoke to the Montreal Ladies' Educational Association in 1879 and characterized mothers as the rulers of the domestic kingdom, wielding "enormous power in their hands." Focusing on their role as child rearers, he announced:

[Woman's] end and aim is marriage; her kingdom, a happy home; her subjects, little children clinging about her knees.... The great majority of women will be wives and mothers. Their influence in both relations is paramount. In the latter, there is no one to compete with them for the first ten years of the child's life, and in that time more is done towards the formation of character than in all the rest of life.[7]

Women's organizations were among the foremost proponents of this ideology. Many who demanded greater recognition for women did so through the perspective of "maternal feminism." They insisted that women's role as mothers provided them with special insight and wisdom that could profitably be brought to bear upon the public agenda. They sought to transform the nature of household work, to upgrade it, and to demand greater respect for these tasks. Adelaide Hoodless founded the Woman's Institute in 1897 in Stoney Creek, Ontario. Committed to promoting women's work within the home as "household science," the institutes spread like wildfire throughout the country. The National Council of Women of Canada, the YWCA, and the Imperial Order of the Daughters of the Empire began to call for professional training for homemakers.[8]

The emerging and distinct phase of childhood, too, came under increasing scrutiny. The rapid movement toward urbanization had brought growing apprehension about street crime and the proper socialization of the young. In 1890 Dr. Annie Parker, a prominent Toronto suffragist, described children as "embryo citizens." J.J. Kelso, a Toronto *World* reporter and one of the leaders of the child-saving movement in Toronto, argued that to prevent the wholesale expansion of delinquency, the standards of home life should be raised. The need to "mould" children to become upstanding citizens meant great care would be required in setting the proper spiritual, physical, and educational environment. Since fathers were assumed to be away from the home earning the family wage, mothers were exhorted to undertake this responsibility.[9]

Legislators responded slowly and grudgingly to the changing perceptions. The first breakthrough would come in Canada West (Ontario) in 1855. An Act Respecting the Appointment of Guardians and the Custody of Infants authorized judges to award child custody and maintenance to a mother where the court "saw fit." The act only applied to young children, under the age of twelve. And any mother found guilty of adultery was disqualified from the right to custody. This created an obvious imbalance between mothers and fathers, as adulterous fathers suffered no such stricture.[10]

The majority of Ontario judges applied this legislation with hesitation, generally refusing to exercise their discretion in favour of mothers except in the most egregious cases. The father had to have behaved completely outrageously, and the mother's character and reputation had to be able to withstand critical scrutiny from the bench and emerge without the slightest taint of impropriety. Customarily mothers were awarded custody only when they were living under the protection of some other adult male, usually their fathers or brothers. In 1887 the Ontario Legislature amended the law, in order to nudge the judges into less pronounced preferences for paternal custody. The age limit of twelve was removed, and the adultery bar that had affected only women was formally abolished. The judges were instructed to consider "the welfare of the infant," "the conduct of the parents," and "the wishes as well of the mother as of the father" in disposing of custody disputes.[11]

In Quebec, the Civil Code of 1865 specified two stages for judicial decisions about child custody. Where husband or wife applied for *séparation de corps* (separation from bed and board), the provisional care of the children remained with the father, unless the court ordered otherwise "for the greater advantage of the children." Here there was a clear preference for paternal custody rights, at least in the first instance. When the court issued its final ruling on the separation, custody was generally awarded to the victorious party: "The children are entrusted to the care of the party who has obtained the separation, unless the court ... orders, for the greater advantage of the children, that all or some of them be entrusted to the care of the other party, or of a third person."[12]

The latter criteria seemed fairly neutral. Whichever party won the separation proceeding was apparently entitled to custody. However, it was substantially easier for men to obtain separation decrees than for women. And the Quebec judges, like their common law brothers, tended to lean distinctly toward fathers in their application of these standards.[13]

The 1867 Montreal case of *Bisson* v *Lamoureux* was typical. Madame Bisson, the wife, sued for a separation from her husband, Lamoureux, because of physical abuse and abandonment. She proved that her husband was living with another woman. Judge Joseph-Amable Berthelot granted Madame Bisson her separation, but was sceptical about her claim for custody of the children. Monsieur Lamoureux had provided evidence that his wife had also behaved adulterously, which prompted Judge Berthelot to pronounce her guilty of "la mauvaise conduite" (wicked conduct). Seemingly unconcerned about the implications of granting custody to an adulterous father, whom he had earlier branded "disgraceful and immoral," the judge awarded custody to Monsieur Bisson.[14]

For most of the nineteenth century, in the other common law provinces, traditional English rules that heavily favoured fathers' rights to custody also remained in force. Prince Edward Island, Manitoba, and the North-West Territories made no changes to the common law position. On both coasts there would be minor changes in the final years of the century. In 1897 British Columbia authorized judges to award custody to non-adulterous mothers where circumstances rendered such a decision "fit." The "tender years" doctrine was firmly embedded there, for only children under the age of seven were involved. In 1893 the Nova Scotia Legislature enacted legislation very similar to the 1887 Ontario statute. The major distinction was that Nova Scotia continued to deny custody to adulterous mothers, but not to adulterous fathers.[15]

New Brunswick, where Nellie Armstrong was about to begin her custody case, occupied the middle ground in custody legislation. Having passed the Practice and Proceedings in Supreme Court in Equity Act in 1890, the New Brunswick Legislature had begun to improve upon the common law rules. The act authorized New Brunswick judges to award the custody of children under sixteen years of age to their mother. While not as low an age ceiling as in British Columbia, neither was it as encompassing as the Ontario and Nova Scotia statutes, which covered children up to twenty-one years. Nellie Armstrong and her lawyer were wary of the "tender years doctrine," and did not file for custody of all four children despite the statutory ceiling of sixteen years. Nellie Armstrong sought custody only of the two youngest, Sofia and William Frederick. She may have thought that if she confined her petition to the smallest children, the court would be more sympathetic.[16]

The New Brunswick statute was somewhat fairer than its British Columbia and Nova Scotia counterparts in that it did not explicitly disentitle adulterous women to custody. Mothers were permitted to "petition" the court for custody of their children. The statutory standards were vague, but seemingly balanced. The judges were required to "take into consideration the interests of such infant or infants, in deciding between the claims of the parents." Nothing in this statute gave mothers the *right* to custody. All they were granted was the right to petition an all-male court for a custody order. Everything would depend on how Judge Barker chose to exercise his discretion.[17]

On 5 November 1895, Nellie Armstrong, took the stand to state her case. She told Judge Barker that she and William Armstrong had been married in Glassville, New Brunswick, in the County of Carleton on 7 July 1886. Her husband was a well-to-do livestock farmer, who raised poultry, sheep, and cattle. His family came from Lakeville, New Brunswick, approximately twenty miles away. Immediately after the marriage, the couple moved to his family home in Lakeville. There they resided with his fifty-year-old mother, his brother, and two sisters.[18]

Nellie Armstrong told the judge that problems had set in from the beginning. Living within an extended family had posed various tensions. The root of the difficulty seems to have been a disagreement over who should function as the head of the household. William Armstrong, the undisputed male head of the home, had taken charge as the eldest son upon the death of his father. It was the position of mistress that provoked contention.

Mrs. Armstrong Senior seems to have been determined to assert her dominance over household matters, despite the presence of her new daughter-in-law. According to Nellie Armstrong, her mother-in-law would lock the kitchen pantry, the henhouse, and the room with the organ, expressly to keep William Armstrong's young wife out of them. Nellie Armstrong had responded defiantly, refusing to cook if her mother-in-law controlled the larder. Mrs. Armstrong Senior disparaged her daughter-in-law's cooking skills, complaining about her incessantly to neighbours and friends.

There were also arguments about standards of cleanliness. Mrs. Armstrong Senior accused Nellie Armstrong of being "dirty," and William Armstrong's sister complained that since Nellie had arrived "the house was rotten with dirt." The very ownership of cleaning equipment was cause for dispute. On one occasion William Armstrong's sister emptied a full pail of water on the verandah floor, declaring that "it was her scrub pail."

Nellie Armstrong became pregnant shortly after the marriage, and the first son, young Frank, was born in 1887. Three more children followed, with a new birth approximately every two years. Family disputes soon arose over the children. William Armstrong's mother and sister complained that his wife did not dress the children "tidily," or keep them sufficiently clean. At one point, the sister-in-law locked herself up in her room with one of the little boys, refusing to come out for two days and two nights or to let Nellie Armstrong see the child. Eventually, after a series of arguments, Nellie Armstrong left the Armstrong household and returned to her father's home in Glassville.

William Armstrong persuaded his wife to return by promising to convert the house into two separate apartments. He constructed new doors for the back of the house so that there would be two separate entrances, and moved his mother and siblings upstairs, leaving himself, his wife, and the children on the main floor. But as Nellie Armstrong's cross-examination would reveal, even this did not solve the problem:

Q. Well, who had charge of the house when you lived there?
A. His mother.
Q. She had charge of the house, and she also had charge of what was brought in the house for cooking purposes and so on?
A. Yes.

Q. After you went there, didn't you understand she was to take charge?
A. No; I didn't understand it that way at all.[19]

Such evidence was not sufficient to warrant an action for alimony, let alone an application for custody. Conscious of the reluctance with which legal authorities regarded marriage breakdown, Nellie Armstrong and her lawyer introduced additional evidence against her husband. First they charged him with repeated instances of adultery.

Nellie Armstrong testified that she had caught her husband having sexual relations with their domestic servant, Ada Clark, in the carriage house in 1891. During the haying season in 1893, she had found her husband engaged in sexual intercourse with another domestic servant, Eliza Wethers, next to the calves in the barn. That same summer she caught him and Belle Wolch, a third domestic servant, having intercourse in the hallway of the Armstrong house. Nellie Armstrong told the court that she had summarily discharged all three servants, but that her husband was a "man of bad habits" who went "with bad women."

William Armstrong vigorously denied these allegations and charged in turn that he had surprised his wife one evening "lying on the lounge" with Herb Buchanan, the hired man. "She had her dress turned up. I could see her legs," her husband testified. Furthermore, he told the court that she had boasted that she had slept with Henry Parent, another hired hand, and that she had taunted her husband that Parent "was a damned sight better man." William Armstrong reported that he had promptly discharged Henry Parent. Nellie Armstrong angrily denied having committed any sexual improprieties.

Nellie Armstrong and her lawyer also presented evidence about William Armstrong's violent tendencies. She told the court that on various occasions she had been "beaten ... slapped in the face, and choked." At one point her husband had "jerked the chair from under" her, and she had fallen, injuring the back of her head against an iron pipe. At another time, she said, he had beaten her until her face was black and blue, leaving a long nail-scar across her nose. In a fit of jealousy over her alleged sexual involvement with Herb Buchanan, her husband had grabbed her "by the hair of the head with both hands" and thrown her to the floor. When she escaped into the kitchen, she felt "something hanging" down by her head. She discovered it was her hair, "torn out by the roots, hanging down from the pug in the back." In front of an amazed Judge Barker, Nellie Armstrong produced the shock of hair, acknowledging that she had "kept it ever since."

Nellie Armstrong testified that it was not only her husband's violence that she had to withstand. In a fit of anger, his brother, Charles, had come into her pantry and pounded her over the head with a large horse collar. She recounted how she had walked all the way to Centreville to lay criminal charges for assault against her brother-in-law. The incident resulted in considerable litigation, as the dispute mushroomed from an initial conviction in magistrate's court through appeals to the county court, and ultimately to a perjury case heard in Fredericton. Charles Armstrong was put to considerable expense in defending himself, and the animosity between the in-laws and Nellie Armstrong had amplified accordingly. Rumours circulated widely that William Armstrong was the chief financier of his brother's lawsuits.

When Charles Armstrong took the stand to provide his side of the horse-collar incident he would depict Nellie Armstrong as willful and physically violent:

Q. Now, will you be so good as to tell us briefly your version of [this incident].

A. I was standing on the veranda in the morning, and I was looking at a [horse]collar that my brother brought down to Centreville to get fixed ... and I heard somebody from the table back up the chair like that (witness indicates) and I supposed it was my brother, and the first thing I got a shove on the veranda from Mrs. Armstrong.

Q. Enough force to swing you off the veranda?

A. Just swung me off. She then went down into the wood shed, and picked up a paint can, and struck me on the shoulder, then wheeled, and picked up a hardwood chair, and as she threw the chair, I threw the collar. My brother came to the door, and she made a race to scald me, and he said: "Hold the screen door against her," and I did, and then she went to the window and got some boiling hot water, and scalded me....

Q. You didn't strike her at all?

A. No, sir; I didn't. She said: "Damn you, I will scald you," and she did.

Q. Did you say nothing all this time?

A. I said to let her rip. I held the door. She took the tea kettle and put it up against the screen. That didn't suit her, and she raised the window, and put a quart dipper of hot water on me.[20]

His testimony characterizing Nellie Armstrong as a woman who could give as well as she got would have come as a shock. This was far from the idealized domestic mother-image so carefully cultivated by nineteenth-century Canadians. Nellie Armstrong's lawyer, H.A. Connell, made every effort to repair the damage in his cross-examination. His last question was: "Whose statement did the magistrate believe on the hearing — yours or Mrs. Armstrong's?" Charles Armstrong had to concede defeat. He mumbled his response: "Believed her's."

But William Armstrong also gave testimony that cast Nellie Armstrong in the same light. He related the following account of one after-breakfast argument, which began with Nellie Armstrong shouting, "I am done with you after this morning."

With that she went out of the hallway, and picked up a rock, and fired it. It didn't hit me. She ran out doors, and picked up an old can, and she fired it in the room at me. I held [one of our children] all the time. I dodged that. She then grabbed the poker off the woodbox, and broke four holes in the door, and I says "Nellie, don't break the door in." I had the child this time. She ran around, and picked up some soap, and fired it, and it took me in the ear. It would have struck the child if not me.[21]

This was more effective testimony, further strengthened by the fact that Nellie Armstrong had admitted under cross-examination to throwing the soap and threatening her husband with a raised poker. But unlike Nellie Armstrong, neither her husband nor her brother-in-law could muster any evidence that Nellie Armstrong had ever actually seriously hurt them. Her violence was more spectacular than injurious. Nevertheless, William Armstrong's lawyer, Wesley Van Wart, would underscore the significance of the child's presence as he closely questioned Nellie Armstrong:

Q. And had he not one of the little children in his arms ... all the time that you were carrying on this row?
A. No; not all the time.
Q. Was it not part of the time so?
A. Well, I don't just remember.
Q. Will you say he didn't?
A. He had the child in his arms part of the time.[22]

Judge Barker had now heard startling evidence about adulterous goings-on and violent arguments on the part of at least three members of the Armstrong household. He had been visibly shocked by the public display of Nellie Armstrong's clump of hair. But what would really make him take notice were the allegations about obscene language. Nellie

Armstrong complained that ever since her arrival at the Armstrong home, she had been repeatedly insulted by the Armstrong family's outrageous language. To a scandalized court, Nellie Armstrong reported that Mrs. Armstrong Senior, Charles Armstrong, and both her sisters-in-law had referred to her as a "an ogle-eyed whore," "that bitch of Willie's," a "targer," a "ranger," and a "Scotch bitch."

William Armstrong's lawyer would cross-examine Nellie Armstrong extensively on this. First he made her rhyme off the names that the Armstrongs had called her, in order to force her into the unladylike position of having to pronounce such phrases repeatedly. Van Wart then began his counter-attack:

*Q.* [W]ould there be differences between you and Mrs. Armstrong, and you were calling one another names?
*A.* Yes.
*Q.* You have been both a little angry, and the result would be that you would end in calling one another names?
*A.* No, sir; I never called her out of her name; for she was an old lady, and I respected her. I called her Mrs. Armstrong when I spoke to her.
*Q.* Now, Mrs. Armstrong, do you pretend to tell me — what age is Mrs. Armstrong?
*A.* Sixty something, to the best of my knowledge.
*Q.* Do you wish me to believe that she would deliberately come to you and call you these names that you refer to, without any provocation?
*A.* While we were quarrelling she would call those names.
*Q.* During all the quarrel, you would simply call her "Mrs. Armstrong"?
*A.* Yes.
*Q.* Did you ever swear at her?
*A.* Well, I don't remember — I might have said "Damn" or something like that — I don't remember of ever swearing.[23]

In rebuttal, the Armstrongs would retort that Nellie Armstrong was given to considerably stronger language. Charles Armstrong swore that she had often called his mother a "damned old whore." William Armstrong testified that his wife frequently called him a "damned old son of a bitch," and often referred to their domestic servants as "damned whores." John Cody, a labourer in William Armstrong's employ, admitted that he had overheard Nellie Armstrong call out to her husband: "You kiss my ass, you son of a bitch."

Most damagingly, her brother-in-law also accused Nellie Armstrong of teaching her children to use such words. "I have heard her tell her little boy to call [his] papa a 'Damned whore master,'" he told the court. Judge Barker leaned right out of his chair at this point: "You have heard her?" he interjected. "Yes," replied Charles Armstrong solemnly. He would refuse to budge from this, even on cross-examination:

Q. When was it you heard [Nellie Armstrong] tell the little boy to call his papa a "Damned whore master"?
A. Right in his kitchen....
Q. What was the boy's name?
A. Fred.
Q. That was the eldest?
A. Yes. He was able to walk, and could talk too.
Q. Could he talk plainly?
A. Yes.
Q. And you mean to tell us that woman told this little child to call her father a "Damned whore master"?
A. Yes.
Q. Did the child repeat the words?
A. He did.[24]

The first lesson of cross-examination has always been not to ask any questions to which you do not know the answer. Here an astonished H.A. Connell, who simply could not believe his ears at Charles Armstrong's initial testimony, had dug himself in deeper. Now he had to contend with evidence that Nellie Armstrong swore in front of her children, and that the son was only too willing to mimic his mother. H.A. Connell recalled Nellie Armstrong to the stand. She vehemently denied that any such incident had ever taken place. But the damage was done.

Judge Frederic Barker announced he was "shocked" by the tone that prevailed within the Armstrong family. "Foul epithets," "vulgar oaths," "gross, revolting expressions," and "obscene language" reigned in a household "where freedom of speech was without limit." Declaring himself to be quite torn over the proper disposition of this case, he protested, "Where one is driven to decide whether in the interests and welfare of these children they should be entrusted to the care of the father or of the mother, it looks about a choice of evils."[25]

But under the New Brunswick legislation, Judge Barker was required to make a ruling one way or the other. Although nothing in the statute required it, Barker came down squarely in favour of fathers over mothers as a general rule where child custody was concerned: "As to the primary right of the father to the custody of his infant children there can be no doubt." Several months earlier in another case, Judge Barker had stated that the traditional right of fathers to custody could not be defeated unless the "habits and character of the father" were "open to the gravest objection." This interpretation of the law essentially nullified the neutral and balanced wording of the statute, which on its face required only that the "interests of the infants" be considered.[26]

This was a clear throwback to the traditional common law position, and indicated a considerable reluctance to permit the new legislation to undermine a father's authority within the family. In so ruling, Judge Barker sided with the majority of Canadian judges, who were simultaneously laying siege to custody legislation across the country. A few renegade judges had begun to use the new statutes on behalf of women, and their numbers and the strength of their judgments had begun to increase as the decades passed. But by and large the men on the bench were unsympathetic to increased child custody rights for mothers. Most disregarded the new enactments, which were discretionary after all, and applied the old common law as they saw necessary.[27]

Judge Barker did purport to scrutinize the wording of the custody provisions. "Where the contest is between the parents, the Court is bound by the statute to consider the infants' interests — their welfare is, I think, the first principal object to be borne in mind," declared Barker. Quoting from an earlier English case, the judge listed the relevant factors:

The welfare of a child is not to be measured by money only, nor by physical comfort only. The word welfare must be taken in its widest sense. The moral and religious welfare of the child must be considered as well as its physical well-being. Nor can the ties of affection be disregarded.[28]

Comparing William and Nellie Armstrong's conduct against this backdrop, Judge Barker would turn first to the issue of adultery. He admitted that he was completely confused by "the mass of contradictions" in the evidence. He recounted William Armstrong's accusations of his wife's sexual indiscretions with Herb Buchanan. He also admitted that Nellie Armstrong had strongly denied any wrongdoing. Yet he confessed himself inclined to favour her husband's account. Remarkably, Judge Barker offered the vicious hair-ripping assault as proof. If William Armstrong had had no reason to provoke his rage, the judge thought it improbable that he should "tear a quantity of hair from [his wife's] head and otherwise ill-treat her."[29]

The judge found himself unable to ascertain if William Armstrong's sexual liaisons had really occurred. What was more important, declared Judge Barker, was that if William Armstrong had committed adultery, his wife had condoned it. "Her protest is of the mildest character," stated Barker. "No great estrangement resulted.... She continued to share her husband's room as his wife." There had been no hair-ripping here, but for this Nellie Armstrong would be penalized.

Neatly condemning Nellie Armstrong either way, Judge Barker would deny her aspirations for custody:

It is not necessary for the matter in hand that I should determine which of the parties has spoken falsely. It is certain, however, either that Mrs. Armstrong has fabricated these charges and deliberately perjured herself in order to support them, or else she has too free and easy notions of morality generally, and of the marriage tie and marital obligations especially, to make her influence a desirable one for a young child.[30]

The growing glorification of the "cult of motherhood" was tied to a very circumscribed sphere of proper maternal activity. From the pulpit, from the lectern, even from the song books and sheet music popular in the late nineteenth century, came an increasingly narrow and confining image of motherhood. Mothers were acclaimed for their innocence and purity, their natural tenderness and kindness of heart, their selfless long-suffering and moral superiority.[31]

But not all women could, or even wanted, to live up to this ideal. Nellie Armstrong's marriage had thrust her into the middle of a difficult, strife-ridden family. The properly submissive, altruistic wife would have deferred to the situation, or gone home to her own family in silence and in shame. But in complete contrast to the model Victorian wife and mother, Nellie Armstrong was one battered woman who tried to hold her own through shouting matches and fist-fights. If William Armstrong's evidence is to be believed, she responded to her husband's outrageous sexual entanglements with extramarital adventures of her own. What was more, she boasted about them to her husband.

All of this cost Nellie Armstrong dearly. Had she been the model wife and mother, she would still have had a difficult time convincing Judge Barker to override his avowed preference for paternal custody. But where women failed to live up to the stereotype of the noble and nurturing

Sentimentalized version of "Motherly Love"
from *Canadian Illustrated News* (Montreal), 1871.

mother, their claims to greater recognition of their rights within the family were met with distinct hostility. On the surface Nellie Armstrong's and her husband's actions against one another seem relatively balanced. But to Judge Barker, this would make William Armstrong the more responsible parent. "So far as the moral welfare of the child is concerned, it is at least as well assured in the father's custody as in the mother's," he declared.

There is no indication that the incidents of violence were factors in Barker's conclusion. Despite the very considerable evidence of domestic brutality, Judge Barker would give this matter short shrift. His judgment would contain no reference whatsoever to the assaults committed by Charles Armstrong or Nellie Armstrong. William Armstrong's brutal assault upon his wife would be explained away as the natural reaction of a husband who found his wife behaving improperly with a hired man: "The seeming cruelty to his wife is not without some show of justification; for, under such grave provocation, one is not apt to deliberate or measure his conduct, as if under no excitement." Possibly Judge Barker downplayed the evidence of violence against Nellie Armstrong out of a desire to justify his decision to award custody to her husband. Having determined to reject Nellie Armstrong's application, he would have wanted to emphasize the factors that supported his ruling and de-emphasize those that did not. However, his rationalization of male violence placed him squarely within the nineteenth-century judicial norm as another apologist for wife battering.

Only a tiny portion of Barker's judgment would explicitly compare their abilities as parents. It had been clear from the trial that Nellie Armstrong was the primary child rearer in the family, especially since her husband's business had taken him away from home extensively. Nineteenth-century fathers were not expected to supervise the day-to-day activities of their children. But William Armstrong's level of ignorance about fundamental aspects of his offspring's lives was remarkable. Under cross-examination, he had admitted that he didn't even know which bedrooms the children occupied. Nor could he name the various illnesses, even the serious ones, that his children had contracted over the years. "I think it was cold or dysentery or something like that," he speculated when asked about one particularly serious bout of illness.

Most telling of all, upon the final separation in January, William Armstrong had lasted only one week alone with the children. After seven days of washing and cooking, he had frantically contacted his married sister, Eliza Watt, with an urgent plea for relief. Eliza Watt and her husband had taken two-year-old William Frederick back home to Woodstock, New Brunswick, to live with them. Next, William Armstrong had placed Sofia Eugene, the four year old, with his brother, Charles Armstrong, who had moved with Mrs. Armstrong Senior and his sisters to Fort Fairfield, Maine.

This was not a contest between a father and a mother for the right to raise and care for their children. William Armstrong had no intention of taking a hands-on supervisory role. He wanted his legal right to custody affirmed, and with it the right to place his children with whomever he wished. And that is what Judge Barker granted. What would have made the decision even more galling to Nellie Armstrong was that she lost her children to the very in-laws who had been so hateful to her. The "unseemly" behaviour that had disqualified her had been equally exhibited by the Armstrong in-laws, but this had not disentitled them from caring for the children.

Instead, the judge made much of the disparate economic status of husband and wife. Musing that William Armstrong had "ample means for the maintenance and education" of his children, and that the Watts were "also comfortably off," the judge seems to have thought that this should be the decisive factor. Nellie Armstrong had vainly intervened, to remind the court that her father, William Love, was a prosperous farmer and hotel keeper, of "more than comfortable, even independent means," whose property was valued at over ten thousand dollars. William Love had expressly offered to take Nellie Armstrong and her children under his roof, to care for them without cost to William Armstrong.

Nellie Armstrong had also volunteered to support her children, even if she had to go out to a waged position. "I think I could support the baby," she had told the court, "I would work for him; I would do anything for my child's sake." But women's economic opportunities, so vastly inferior to men's, could not help but block their chances for success in custody battles. Nellie Armstrong's finances were a source of concern for the judge: "Mrs. Armstrong is without a home or means of support except such as her father may supply her," he noted. Women who won custody cases were almost always living under the protection of some other male relative, usually a father or brother who promised to support them and the children. But even this would not always be sufficient. For Judge Barker it was Nellie Armstrong's very dependence upon her father that disinclined him to rule in her favour:

[Mr. Love] seems a most respectable looking man, has means, and expresses his willingness to support and educate the child without expense to the father. He is, however, under no obligation or duty to do this as the father is. He is a man over sixty years of age, and so far as ability to contribute to the physical comfort and education of the child, it is not greater than that of his father.[32]

With that Judge Barker dismissed the jubilant Armstrong clan and the grief-stricken Nellie Armstrong and her father. He admonished William Armstrong to ensure that his wife should have some opportunity to see her children, "at least once a fortnight." Then he rose and retired from the courtroom, no doubt relieved that the distasteful proceedings had finally drawn to a conclusion.

A CUSTODY BATTLE IN VICTORIA: THE CASE OF SOY KING

Not surprisingly, the first inroads against parental custody were rarely made against the rights of whites. Instead, a series of legal decisions in the late nineteenth century removed children from the custody of their Chinese and First Nations' parents, who found themselves the target of the new thrust toward granting child custody to religious and charitable organizations. Possibly it was easier for white male judges to justify intruding upon a father's rights over his children when that father was a man of a different race.[33]

On 26 July 1900, Archer Evans Stringer Martin, a white judge of the British Columbia Supreme Court, sat down to rule on a custody matter that had pitted a Methodist missionary group against the Chinese community. Sam Kee, a Chinese man, was fighting to retain control of Soy King, a fourteen-year-old Chinese girl. A naturalized British subject living in Victoria, British Columbia, Sam Kee claimed that Soy King was his adopted daughter. The Rescue Home for Chinese Girls, a Methodist missionary hostel, sought to take custody of Soy King. The white missionary reformers alleged that Soy King was not an adopted daughter, but a "slave girl."[34]

The port city of Victoria was the funnel through which most Chinese people entered Canada in the nineteenth century. It boasted a thriving Chinese community that occupied four city blocks around Fisgard Street, just off the harbour front. Chinese immigrants had begun arriving as early as 1858 from the war-torn, southern Chinese provinces. They worked the mines, laboured at the construction of the railway, and took casual employment in the logging, farming, and canning industries of British Columbia.[35]

The early Chinese population in Canada was primarily male, for the large bulk of the immigrants were forced to come without their wives or families. The cost of immigrating was substantial, and after the federal government slapped a "head tax" of fifty dollars on all Chinese immigrants in 1885, subsequently raised to one hundred dollars in 1900, few women or children could afford entry. Chinese women known to be prostitutes were specifically denied admission under the 1885 statute. Beginning in 1875, the British Columbia Legislature had also passed a series of discriminatory statutes that restricted the employment of Chinese and barred them from voting. White racists provoked riots in the Chinese quarters, one of the most spectacular examples being the violent eruption in Vancouver in 1887. The environment in British Columbia was so hostile that most Chinese men had concluded that Canada was no place for family life.[36]

The presence of fourteen-year-old Soy King in Victoria would have been accounted for by her relationship to Sam Kee, who was most likely a merchant. A small fraction of the Chinese immigrant population was made up of affluent merchants who set up shop in the Chinese districts. Since the Canadian government favoured the admission of entrepreneurs, these were exempted from the discriminatory immigration legislation and not required to pay the head tax. Merchants who could afford to do so brought their wives, children, and female servants with them. In the China of the time, affluent men maintained a large retinue of wives and servants.[37]

Soy King's status within the Kee family is less clear. According to Sam Kee, Soy King had been "confided to his charge" by her father in Canton. Sam Kee had pledged to support and educate Soy King "as his own daughter," and had brought her to Canada in April of 1897. Adoption was fairly widespread in China during the nineteenth century. Extreme poverty often forced families to send their young women to wealthier homes. Elaborate forms of exchange had arisen around adoption procedures, ranging from contracts of betrothal to outright sale. Some of the young women were received into the adopting families as brides-to-be, others worked exclusively as domestic servants, and still others were sold into prostitution.[38]

The white Methodist missionaries recognized no distinctions. In their eyes, all such transfers were outright purchases. Slavery was legal throughout the nineteenth century in China, and the Western missionaries coined the phrase "slave girl" to describe the women who laboured without wages in their adoptive homes. Horrified that some of these adopted women were ultimately traded in prostitution, religious reformers began to proselytize against the practice. One Methodist pamphlet charged that in the 1880s, Canada had received "annually from one to two hundred Chinese women and girls who were enslaved and brought into the country for the vilest purposes."[39]

According to the missionaries, the origin of such treatment lay in the extremely low status of women in China. Reverend Scott Stephen Osterhout described it thus:

Comparatively little value has ever been placed upon the life of a girl in China, one reason given being that the country is overcrowded already with a dense population of many millions and another that the responsibility for ancestral worship descends upon the sons of the family and not upon the daughters. Hence it has come about that the social customs of China in cases of extreme poverty recognize the selling of girls for the payment of debts and to relieve the family of their support. To the purchaser she becomes a slave-girl wife, or, in case of maturity, his adult wife, but, in any case, she is ordinarily subject to considerable abuse and ill-treatment by her master or her mother-in-law.[40]

Eager to recognize the degradation of women in another society, Reverend Osterhout was apparently less anxious to explore the abuse of women within his own.

Reverend John E. Gardner took the leading role in Canadian religious rescue work. Born in China of white missionary parents and fluent in Cantonese, he joined the Metropolitan Methodist Church in Victoria in the 1880s and quickly began working among the Chinese community. He appealed to the women of the Methodist Church for funds to open a Home for Chinese Women, which would operate as a hostel for penitent prostitutes. Anti-Chinese sentiments within the Methodist congregation in Victoria hindered his initial drive, but the Women's Missionary Society of the Toronto Methodist Church ultimately supported him.[41]

In 1888, the Rescue Home for Chinese Girls was formally established at 100 Cormorant Street in Victoria. With the co-operation of the police, Reverend Gardner and the newly appointed white matron, Miss Leake of Parrsboro, Nova Scotia, removed several Chinese prostitutes from the Chinese districts and brought them to the Home. This initiative failed dismally. The women may have been living under exploitative and difficult conditions, but they found the regimen offered by the Christian missionaries even less desirable and quickly returned to their community.[42]

Gardner soon shifted his energies from prostitutes to young domestic servants (or, as he called them, "slaves"). Evangelical missionaries called door-to-door in the Chinese quarter, spreading the news about the Rescue Home and offering to teach English to any young women who wished to learn it. The missionaries conceded that many of the domestic servants were well treated, some considerably better than domestic servants in European homes. But in their view, these young women were not being given much opportunity to obtain an education. Furthermore, it was believed that most of the women would be sold in marriage or prostitution. Chinese women represented a scarce and valuable commodity. Women composed less than 1 per cent of the Chinese population in Canada, and young Chinese women brought prices between five hundred and twenty-five hundred dollars on the North American market.[43]

To attract young Chinese women to the Home, the organizers sponsored a day school, a Sunday school, and for those who wished, complete residential facilities. The curriculum ranged from arithmetic to music, with an emphasis on domestic training and Christian religious instruction. The missionaries, who seem honestly to have sympathized with the situation of Chinese women in Canada, were at the same time deeply racist. Like their white Canadian neighbours, they viewed Chinese people as posing "biological problems" for the white Canadian population. Unlike their neighbours, they did not advocate restrictive immigration and employment laws. Instead, they sought to assimilate the Chinese into the dominant white community through education in Christianity.[44]

The women who slowly began to attend the Methodist classes at the Rescue Home came largely for the instruction in English and had to put up with the bias against their culture in order to obtain the language training that would further their prospects in their new country. Some of the most disaffected would eventually break with their community and live at the Home. Between 1888 and 1902, forty Chinese and eight Japanese girls and women came to stay. The price of residence was conversion to Christianity. Future careers as "Bible women" among Asian peoples in Canada or in Asia awaited those who did not marry the Christianized Asian men hand-picked for them by the missionaries.[45]

Soy King was an early convert. She had run away from Sam Kee's household on 30 June 1900, and had gone immediately to the Rescue Home. Soy King's motivation for leaving is not known. Her voice was silenced in the dispute that erupted almost immediately between the Chinese and the Methodist communities. Numerous visitors besieged the Rescue Home, begging, cajoling, and threatening Soy King to come home. Some may even have offered the new Matron, Ida Snyder, money for Soy

King's release. When the administrators of the Home refused to allow Soy King to leave, Sam Kee sought legal recourse.[46]

Sam Kee's decision to pursue his case in court was courageous. The Canadian legal and judicial system excluded the Chinese from positions as lawyers, jurors, and judges. The Chinese sometimes had difficulty finding lawyers who would act for them. The ability of an all-white legal system to deliver justice to the Chinese was further hampered by racist propaganda circulating throughout nineteenth-century Canadian society. The 1885 Royal Commission on Chinese Immigration heard witnesses argue that Chinese testimony should never be trusted in court. Methodist Reverend Otis Gibson told the Commission that "there is no doubt but that they constantly perjure themselves in our courts." Montague William Tyrwhitt Drake, the white Supreme Court justice who had presided over the cases of Euphemia Rabbitt and Anna Balo, testified: "The Chinese are utterly unacquainted with truth, and it is a universal comment on their evidence that you cannot believe anything they say."[47]

The lawyer that Sam Kee found to represent him was Harry Dallas Helmcken, QC, a man with a short-lived but illustrious career as a Victoria lawyer and politician. Helmcken, the British Columbian–born great-grandson of Susanne Pas-de-nom Connolly, through the line of her daughter, Amelia Connolly Douglas, served as the counsel of record in many of the cases that concerned the Chinese.[48]

Helmcken's first move would be to file a writ of *habeas corpus* with the British Columbia Supreme Court. A legal document often referred to as "the most celebrated writ in the English law," the literal meaning of "habeas corpus" is "you have the body." Where an individual was being detained in custody or illegally restrained of liberty, friends or relatives could issue a writ of *habeas corpus*, forcing the restrainer to bring the person before the court. The court would then scrutinize the situation, and order the release of anyone who was being held improperly.[49]

As procedure required, lawyer Helmcken served the *habeas corpus* papers upon the Matron of the Rescue Home. This was not the first time that the missionaries had been confronted. Several Chinese merchants had preceded Sam Kee in legal action. The administrators of the Home were decidedly bitter about the use of the *habeas corpus* proceeding. As one protested: "Almost as soon as the girls are within the precincts of the Home, a writ of habeas corpus is issued at the instance of their so-called owners, for their appearance in court. Then begins what is often a long and hard-contested legal conflict."[50]

Siding squarely with racists who accused the Chinese of inveterate lying in court, the missionaries charged that "the Chinese owner in every instance is willing to spend money lavishly and does spend it, buying witnesses to give under oath just such evidence as he thinks necessary in order to regain his chattel." As for lawyers who represented the Chinese, the Methodists were scornful about their role:

It seems a great pity that in a land of boasted civilization and Christianity there should be men who belong to a reputable profession such as law, who will lend themselves and their services, for financial gain, to the ignoble work of discovering technicalities in the law which will frustrate the court of justice, often working injury to the innocent and affording advantage to the guilty.[51]

The Methodists promptly retained Thornton Fell to represent their side. Initially refusing to bring Soy King before the court, they moved instead for an opportunity to show cause why the writ should not be issued. In front of Judge Martin, the administrators of the Home argued that Sam Kee was not Soy King's father. Furthermore, they claimed that Soy King's father had never entrusted his daughter to Sam Kee's care, but rather had sold her as a slave. Helmcken admitted that Sam Kee was not Soy King's natural father, but argued that his client stood *in loco parentis*, in the place of the parent, to the girl. Since Soy King's father had committed his daughter to Sam Kee's charge, Helmcken argued that, except for the natural father, Sam Kee was the person authorized to care for her. Judge Martin was clearly reluctant to rule on the legal status of Soy King's adoption. Instead, he examined the case as if Sam Kee were "the representative of the father's authority." He accepted Helmcken's argument that Sam Kee stood *"in loco parentis* to the child committed to his charge and custody."[52]

But that was not the end of the matter. Judge Martin noted that on writs of *habeas corpus* relating to children, the court had to decide whether the child was old enough to decide for him or herself where to live. The age standards were visibly differentiated by sex, with female children being thought to require protection for a longer period. As a general rule, boys were allowed to choose by the age of fourteen, and girls by the age of sixteen. Fourteen-year-old Soy King had advised the court by affidavit, a sworn document, that she wished to remain in the Rescue Home. But she was clearly not of legal age to make her own decision.

Judge Martin then laid out the law for the parties before him:

It appears to have been the invariable practice of the common law courts on an application for *habeas corpus*, to bring up the body of a child detained from the father (and the case would be the same as to a testamentary guardian) to enforce the father's right to the custody, even against the mother, unless ... there be an apprehension of cruelty from the father, or of contamination, in consequence of his immorality or gross profligacy.[53]

The father's rights to custody were obviously still paramount, particularly as compared with the mother's. However, at least on *habeas corpus* applications, the courts had begun to voice some willingness to supervise paternal custody. The new legislative standards requiring judges to consider the "interests" or "welfare" of the child had begun to diminish parental rights generally. As the courts took on the responsibility of dissecting parental behaviour, it was only logical that judges might begin to query whether some children ought to be removed from their family's control altogether and transferred to the care of a charitable institution.[54]

A series of statutes passed toward the end of the nineteenth century had begun to encroach directly on the rights of parents as against those of charitable institutions and foundling homes. The legal system was expanding its reach to deprive "unfit" parents of the custody of their children entirely. In 1884 the Nova Scotia Legislature authorized courts to remove children younger than sixteen from the custody of their parents where they were growing up "without salutary parental control." In turn, these children were to be committed to orphan asylums or charitable institutions. After 1889 New Brunswick police magistrates were given similar jurisdiction. In 1893 the Ontario Legislature authorized officers of any Children's Aid Society to apprehend and take custody of neglected children under fourteen years of age. Manitoba enacted legislation along these lines in 1898.[55]

R.E. Kingsford, a Toronto lawyer and author in 1896 of *Blackstone's Commentaries Adapted to Ontario*, wrote enthusiastically of these developments:

This new branch of jurisprudence is only in its initiatory stages, but already the results are satisfactory. Unworthy parents may be deprived of their children and foster homes may be sought out and children may be sent there by order of a police magistrate.... Children's aid societies in a municipality, when formed, are given extensive powers of interference. Great hopes are entertained that this long-felt want is at last in the way of being supplied.[56]

Such sentiments were just what the Methodist missionaries were relying upon. Their task was to convince the court that Sam Kee was an unfit parent and should not be allowed to raise Soy King. Their argument was that Sam King had failed to maintain and educate Soy King properly. Sam Kee had also been guilty of cruelty toward her, they alleged, and he was a "grossly immoral" man. On the latter count, they introduced an affidavit from Soy King stating that Sam Kee had two wives.[57]

H.D. Helmcken did not dispute the bigamy evidence. The Chinese custom whereby some men maintained multiple wives had been transported to Canada. Knowledge of this began to filter into the white community when the evangelical missionaries went proselytizing door-to-door in the Chinese quarters. They were shocked to discover that among the wealthiest Chinese families, there were two, three, and sometimes four wives for every husband. Helmcken argued in reply that the Rescue Home had no right to charge his client with immorality, when it was they who were unlawfully depriving Sam Kee of his lawful custody.

The standard that Judge Martin had set out was "immorality or gross profligacy." The only evidence before him was the written affidavit that the Rescue Home's lawyer had drafted and in which Soy King stated that Sam Kee maintained two wives. Judge Martin was concerned about the slimness of the evidence, and cautioned counsel that "it would have been more satisfactory to my mind if I had been furnished with fuller information with regard to the domestic relations existing in the applicant's household." Ultimately, however, this would not stop him. Noting "how difficult it is to obtain the testimony of friends or neighbours as to matters of this kind," Martin concluded that he should "accept an uncontradicted statement as being true if there is no ground for suspicion of falsity."[58]

The evidence may have been true. But the alacrity with which the judge dismissed any suspicions about the veracity of the affidavit is remarkable. Judge Martin's decision was rendered at a time in which pervasive racist attitudes depicted Chinese people in stereotyped and highly inflammatory ways. Welcoming them as cheap labourers initially, whites subsequently attacked the Asian immigrants as undesirable and non-assimilable because of their "Oriental pagan vices." British Columbia Chinese were portrayed as sexually depraved opium addicts and compulsive gamblers.[59]

Within this environment it was only too easy for Judge Martin to conclude that Sam Kee was sufficiently immoral and profligate that he should forfeit custody:

In the present case though the evidence of Soy King may not be sufficient to prove that Sam Kee, who says he is a naturalized British subject, is living in a

Entitled "The Heathen Chinee in British Columbia,"
this 1879 cover of the *Canadian Illustrated News* (Montreal)
portrays the racist context behind the Soy King case.

state of bigamy, yet it satisfies me that the atmosphere of his house is, as viewed from the standard of social life in this country, so grossly immoral that there is serious danger to apprehend that Soy King will be morally contaminated by a further residence under his roof.[60]

Judge Martin believed that Soy King's continued exposure to the sexual practices of the Kee household would "contaminate" her. Presumably he foresaw a future as concubine or prostitute, a picture that conformed with widely held white beliefs about the status of most Chinese women. Chinese prostitutes were said to "glory in their shame, and ... to advertise their depravity in all possible ways." The Victoria *Colonist* had complained in 1876 that "Chinese women are in the habit of luring boys of tender age into their dens after dark, and several fine, promising lads have been ruined for life in consequence." The allusion to "ruin" was meant to convey that the boys had been stricken with syphilis. What was not said explicitly, but what was unquestionably understood by all readers, was that the boys were white. Chinese prostitutes were thought to be jeopardizing the morals and health of the white community, and the services of Chinese prostitutes were said to be so cheap that even the youngest boys had ready access to them.[61]

Against this hopelessly racist backdrop, it is small wonder that Judge Martin refused to accede to Sam Kee's request. "It is best for the child that she should remain in the custody of the authorities of the Refuge Home," he ruled, and Matron Ida Snyder bore her young charge back to Cormorant Street. Shortly thereafter she recounted her triumph in her annual report for the Advisory Board of the Home:

We have just got over the excitement of our last rescue case — that of a young slave girl, Toy [sic] King — who sought our protection and whom the law has given us the right to protect. The costs, $120.00, may seem large, and yet can we estimate the value of one human sole [sic] in money? As we hear the house ring with the merry laughter of these rescued ones and see their bright smiling faces, we feel, indeed, that God has used us in this work, and we believe that some day they will sing the song of the redeemed.[62]

The odd judge voiced concern about this pattern. Chief Justice Theodore Davie of the British Columbia Supreme Court noted in 1897 that few of the Chinese girls before the court spoke English. Their affidavit evidence was largely produced by the officials of the Rescue Home, and the judge worried whether the words of the affidavits might "have been put into [their] mouth[s]." Chief Justice Davie also expressed anxiety about the implications of proselytizing Chinese women "to the customs, habits and creed of an alien race":

We must always remember that the law knows no distinction of race or religion, but all stand equal before the law. If we were in China, and the tribunals there were to uphold the right of benevolent Chinese societies to take our children from us, and raise them as Chinamen, we should denounce it as an outrage, but is it not precisely the same kind of an outrage upon the Chinese which is asked recognition in this case?[63]

But Chief Justice Davie's remarks were delivered only in dissent, and his brothers on the bench were predominantly of the view that the environment and surroundings of the Methodist Rescue Home were preferable to those of the Chinese community. Soy King's perspective on this, at the time of the trial and thereafter, is not known. Whether she had been physically mistreated or sexually exploited by Sam Kee, whether she was rebelling against Sam Kee's future plans for her, or whether she independently sought the religious environment that the Home offered, is not recorded.

# 8

# Prostitution

The law has always classified prostitution as criminal behaviour, although it ought more accurately to be regarded as a form of work. The exact nature of this form of women's work is more elusive. Was nineteenth-century prostitution a hazardous, poorly paid pursuit? Or was it a lucrative, exciting, flamboyant occupation? Did women prostitutes function as servants to a sexually coercive culture, contributing to the maintenance of male control and the subordination of women? Or did they represent a group of strong, independent, career women who flouted marriage, the patriarchal family, and restrictive sexual mores?[1]

The answer is complex, not least because prostitution in nineteenth-century Canada was not a rigidly uniform occupation. Some women prostitutes were impoverished, overworked, ravaged by disease and alcoholism, and subjected to unrelenting police harassment. This was particularly true of prostitutes whose race, ethnicity, or religion made them vulnerable to the rampant hostilities of a discriminatory social and legal system. Others used prostitution for empowerment, to achieve positions of material security and social status despite their unconventional businesses. A glimpse into the lives of Mary Gorman, her daughter Mary Ann Gorman, and Esther Forsyth Arscott — all nineteenth-century Canadian prostitutes — provides a study in these contrasts.

## THE GORMANS: DESTITUTE IRISH PROSTITUTES
### IN VICTORIAN TORONTO

Mary Gorman's public notoriety began when she was convicted in 1860 of being "drunk and disorderly" in Toronto. Thirty-nine-year-old Mary Gorman was an Irish-born, illiterate prostitute whose behaviour on the streets had begun to annoy public officials. Fined one dollar with costs or fourteen days by Police Magistrate George Gurnett, she served out her full term in the Toronto City Jail.[2]

The bulk of the prison population in Ontario during the mid-nineteenth century was composed of Irish immigrants, many of whom had fled Ireland during the famines in the late 1840s. Perilously poor and suffering from marked social dislocation, the famine Irish found themselves prosecuted by the police roughly twice as often as their numbers within the total population would warrant. For crimes such as vagrancy, drunkenness, and prostitution, Irish women represented upwards of 90 per cent of the female prisoners in some jurisdictions.[3]

Mid-nineteenth-century Toronto's brothels were widely dispersed across the city on Queen, Richmond, Yonge, Bay, College, Church, Adelaide, Stanley, and Parliament streets. Mary Gorman, however, seems to have practised largely from the streets. Of no fixed address, she was legally defined as a "vagrant" from the "lower rank in life." She had run counter to old English laws, transplanted to Upper Canada in 1800, that sought to punish the impoverished "idle and disorderly."[4]

Mary Gorman's first brush with the law would develop into protracted encounters with the criminal authorities over the next thirteen years. Understaffed nineteenth-century police forces devoted the largest part of their energy to dealing with the most visible members of society's underclass: street-walkers and drunks. Prostitution was illegal throughout the century, but although she was arrested repeatedly, Mary Gorman was rarely charged specifically with prostitution offences. Instead, she was convicted of larceny and of being "drunk and disorderly." Prostitutes frequently found themselves convicted of petty theft and public order offences. Alcohol dependencies were a common occupational hazard, and the public visibility of a working-class prostitute's business made it almost certain that any untoward behaviour she exhibited would disrupt the neighbourhood. Disputes over fees and outright acts of theft often prompted the larceny charges.[5]

Throughout these years the jail keepers would record Mary Gorman's occupation as "prostitute," leading to the speculation that her status as a prostitute had some connection to the behaviour cited in the charges. Disorderly behaviour that might have gone overlooked in other women resulted in criminal charges when committed by a prostitute. On occasion Mary Gorman tried to elude such labelling by passing under the alias of Mary McGarry, but this proved largely unsuccessful.

And it was clear that Mary Gorman was not thriving in the business. Fines of a few dollars were often beyond her means. She would endure thirty-day jail terms at hard labour for want of the money to pay her fine. During these years, "hard labour" for female prisoners could mean anything from washing, scrubbing, and sewing, to picking oakum. Solitary confinement was regularly imposed upon inmates who defied prison authorities. Mary Gorman was unlikely to have chosen to serve out her jail terms if she had not had to. The mid-nineteenth-century Toronto City Jail was an abominable place to be confined.[6]

Jails were poorly heated and ill-ventilated. In December 1865, for instance, Mary Gorman contracted a case of frostbite serious enough to require the attention of the jail surgeon. Communicable diseases including smallpox, dysentery, and influenza flourished. Mary Gorman had both dysentery and influenza while imprisoned in 1865. In addition, she suffered from a serious sprain during her term in April 1866.[7]

In July 1866, a second Gorman arrived at the Toronto jail. That month Mary Ann Gorman, apparently Mary Gorman's daughter, began what would soon surpass her mother's arrest record for vagrancy and prostitution-related offences. Presumably Mary Gorman had given birth to Mary Ann Gorman in 1857 or 1858. Although prostitutes often knew more about contraception than other women, some inevitably became pregnant as a result of the repetitious sexual activity of their work.[8]

How Mary Gorman looked after her child is not clear. The mother was in jail for at least two fourteen-day terms in 1860, fourteen days in 1861, and thirty days in 1863. Between 1864 and 1866 Mary Gorman spent a total of ten months in jail. Possibly she found an older woman running a "baby farm," whom she could pay for the child's upkeep. In these circumstances young Mary Ann Gorman's environment would have been far from tranquil. At the age of nine, Mary Ann Gorman was arrested and charged with "vagrancy." The vagrant was a "status" criminal in nineteenth-century Canada, subject to detention simply because she or he belonged to a wide-ranging class of "undesirables and misfits" who were thought to threaten social order. Sentenced to one month of imprisonment, the nine-year-old child spent from 11 July to 10 August at hard labour in the Toronto jail. Her mother, who had been most recently released from jail on 21 May, was not with her.[9]

Although Mary Ann Gorman did not work as a prostitute in these early years, she had quickly developed alcohol dependencies. Still only nine years old, she was convicted of being "drunk and disorderly" on 20 October 1867. Unable to raise the three dollars to pay her fine, she spent the next thirty days at hard labour. Her mother had been released thirteen days earlier after serving twenty days for the same offence. The next year young Mary Ann Gorman turned to theft to support herself. At the age of ten, she was convicted of larceny three times — on 19 May, 31 October, and 30 December. On the first occasion, Mary Ann Gorman seems to have been involved with a large gang of children, twelve of whom were caught by the police and charged with larceny. According to the press:

A melancholy spectacle was witnessed at our police court yesterday — one, indeed, which we hope to see as seldom as possible. In the prisoners' cells fully one half the parties confined were children ranging from 9 to 14 years of age and of both sexes.

What an amount of crime in its incipient stages these are guilty of it is impossible to tell, but that they are fast paving the way for worse crimes was evident. Of the whole number, two said they had neither father or mother, five had no father, and three of the remainder had no mother. Even at their tender years they charged drunkenness with the crime of depriving them of a home and throwing them on the street.[10]

Mary Ann Gorman was released "on further examination," which meant that she was not sentenced at the time. Often such individuals would be arrested on another charge before they could be sentenced for the initial offence. In fact, she was arrested again before the disposition of the first theft. She would be charged only months later with "stealing a quantity of copper" from Mr. James Morrison. For this Mary Ann Gorman, described in the press as "a very small girl," served thirty days at hard labour. In December of that year she was sentenced to four months at hard labour for "stealing old metal from Mr. James Cooper."[11]

Throughout, Mary Ann Gorman had found intermittent work as a domestic servant, a common occupation for young Irish Catholic women in the decades immediately following the famine. She adopted the alias "Bridget McCarthy," perhaps in order to separate her life of gainful employment from her criminal reputation. But she would be only partially successful in removing herself from the grip of the criminal law.

"No Mother at Home" from the *Canadian Illustrated News*
(Montreal), 31 March 1877.

Despite her claims to the occupation of domestic service between 1866 and 1872, she was convicted once more for vagrancy and twice for being "drunk." On one occasion the press described her as having been on a "Grecian bender." For these crimes she served a total of four months and three days at hard labour.[12]

By the age of fifteen, Mary Ann Gorman had apparently moved into prostitution. The jail authorities would no longer list her as a "servant" in their files. She was now officially labelled a "prostitute." The reasons women entered prostitution never ceased to fascinate nineteenth-century social reformers. Speculation was rife that most were the victims of manipulation from deceitful and cunning individuals who devoted their lives to procuring new objects for the sex trade. Undoubtedly some women were forced into prostitution through trickery and coercion. But others chose it out of economic necessity as one of a very limited array of options.[13]

Mary Ann Gorman may have "inherited" the job. Growing up among prostitutes and their customers, she may have been exposed to sexual activity as an observer or a participant at a very young age. No doubt, as her mother's namesake, she would have been tagged in the larger community with an undeniable reputation. They were often in jail together. On occasion the two were arrested at the same time, suggesting that they may have worked in combination. The daughter's move into prostitution may have seemed both natural and inevitable.[14]

Over the next several years, Mary Ann Gorman practised her trade partly from the streets, and partly from a series of brothels. In 1873 she was working exclusively from Colenzo's "Terrace" on 56 Dummer Street, which was widely renowned as a disreputable brothel in an impoverished Irish tenement area. William Colenzo, the owner of the house, had served time in the Toronto jail as well. There the labourer-builder had been diagnosed with gonorrhoea in 1862–63. The entire area had become so notorious that the grand jury, a group of prominent citizens charged with screening criminal cases and inspecting prisons, had paid a visit to the quarter in 1873 to determine exactly what led to so much immorality and crime. By 1874, Mary Ann Gorman had transferred to Annie Seaton's house on Queen Street West, perhaps in an effort to remove herself from the Irish Catholic ghetto.[15]

The job itself was a demanding one. While higher-priced prostitutes working through established brothels would service four or five customers in an evening, the Gorman women would have required more customers to make ends meet. Poor prostitutes commonly withstood between thirteen and thirty sexual transactions daily. Additional occupational risks included brutal customers, venereal disease, and dependencies on drugs and alcohol as a means of coping with the stress of the work.[16]

Whatever Mary Ann Gorman may have earned through her work, she seems to have retained very little. Pimps and landlords frequently skimmed off a large share of prostitutes' earnings. Her tenuous finances were dramatically demonstrated when it came time to pay the fines ordered against her. On occasion she scraped together sufficient funds to pay fines up to the amount of five dollars, but she would serve as much as six months at hard labour because she did not have $6.25 to purchase her freedom.

Her career not only failed to lead her out of poverty, it also catapulted her into further confrontations with the police. The criminal law had long permitted the arrest of prostitutes solely because of their occupation, without further proof of criminal activity. Classifying prostitutes as "vagrants," various provincial legislatures had enacted statutes specifically authorizing their detention: Nova Scotia in 1759, Lower Canada in 1839, and Canada West in 1858. The legal authorities considered prostitution a "lifestyle" crime, which threatened to undermine morality.[17]

Middle-class women were somewhat more sceptical of the penal approach to prostitution. Some began to organize themselves into charitable groups in various cities to provide alternatives to lock-up in a criminal jail. Mrs. Elizabeth Dunlop, earlier a key proponent for improving the rights of married women to control their property, joined with fifteen other prominent Toronto women in 1858 to incorporate the Toronto Magdalene Asylum. For Elizabeth Dunlop, who would serve as one of the Asylum's directresses and chief fund-raisers, as well as a member of the "visiting committee" for years, the goal was to eliminate prostitution by rehabilitating prostitutes.[18]

The Magdalene Asylum, initially at 112 Richmond Street East, and later on Yonge Street near Yorkville, provided housing to female prostitutes who would agree to reform along specified lines. Would-be residents had to promise to stay for twelve months, during which they pledged to refrain from any alcoholic stimulants and all contact with former friends and associates. Strict rules about dress, hairstyle, gossip, and the use of "insulting" language were also enforced. The residents worked for their keep at washing, knitting, and sewing, as part of a plan to train them as domestic servants. Income earned from their work went to support the maintenance of the Asylum, although the bulk of the costs were met by annual private donations and government grants.[19]

Religious rehabilitation was a dominant feature in the work of the middle-class women reformers. They commonly concluded that deficiencies in religious instruction were in large measure responsible for the "moral" degradation of prostitutes. As a result, they delivered extensive religious training to the residents of the Asylum, through compulsory religious services every morning and night. Simple faith in the power of religion to reclaim prostitutes provided a foundation for the female reform perspective throughout the century. Witness the testimony of a Montreal member of the National Council of Women of Canada in 1896:

I was once one of a few ladies who gained permission to visit a house of ill-fame, and it was the saddest of sights to see the wretchedness in their faces. We were not to talk to them, but only to sing; we sang "Jesus Lover of My Soul," and the keeper of the house, with tears pouring down her face, said, "Don't sing that; I used to hear it at home. I am a lost wretch now, but if you go on I shall lose all the girls I have in the Home."[20]

Prostitutes in general may have been less moved. The bulk of the female philanthropists who ran the Asylum were Protestant, and anti-Irish Catholic sentiments were common among Toronto's Protestants of the time. The compulsory Protestant religious instruction at the Toronto Asylum would have been anathema to what is reported to have been a largely Roman Catholic population of prostitutes.[21]

The number of inmates in the Toronto Asylum was usually small, ranging from twenty to thirty at any one time. Few were "successfully reformed," and most quickly returned to prostitution after leaving. Surviving records do not reveal the names of the inmates, so it cannot be determined whether either of the Gormans spent a session at the Asylum. However, their residence was unlikely. The Protestant proselytizing would have been offensive to the Gorman women and the prohibition on alcohol consumption would have been a problem. Furthermore, Mary Ann Gorman's brief stint as a domestic servant would have hardly convinced her of the merits of training for such an insecure, poorly paid occupation.

Confronted with the seemingly intractable problem of prostitution, which neither charitable organizations nor the harsh criminal law were capable of eliminating, the legislators took a brief fling at an entirely different legal approach. For a short period of five years between 1865 and 1870, the provinces of Canada East and Canada West flirted with a regulatory approach to prostitution. Accepting that prostitution was impossible to stop, the focus shifted to controlling the trade and regulating its negative impact. The Contagious Diseases Act authorized police constables to detain women suspected of prostitution for medical examination. Those found infected with venereal disease could be locked up at certified hospitals for up to three months. Similar legislation was considered, although not enacted, in Nova Scotia.[22]

The intent of the legislators seems to have been to prevent the spread of venereal disease to men of the military. Similar provisions passed in England had spread throughout the colonies, as far as South Africa and Australia. No attempt was made to detain males who might have been infected with venereal disease, since this was viewed as unpopular with the soldiers. Furthermore, the statute authorized detention and forced treatment despite the fact that no effective medical remedy was discovered for venereal disease until the twentieth century.[23]

The statutes provoked great controversy in England, but generated little discussion in Canada. Governmental authorities were lax in their implementation, failing to certify any hospitals as lock-up and treatment facilities. In December 1866 and January 1867, the Toronto *Daily Telegraph* urged enforcement of the new law, arguing that prostitution could never be totally repressed and that the best situation was to control its ill-effects. But without certified facilities, the regulatory attempt was doomed. The legislation expired in 1870 without ever having been activated. The Gormans, who continued to come and go from the Toronto City Jail throughout this period, may have never even known of its existence.[24]

In 1867, one year after Mary Ann Gorman's first arrest, the federal government took jurisdictional control of the criminal law. Two short years later Parliament passed "An Act respecting Vagrants," which confirmed that Canadian prostitutes should continue to be treated as status criminals. The following groups were singled out for arrest and punishment of up to two months in jail:

1) all persons causing a disturbance in the streets or highways by screaming, swearing or singing, or being drunk, or impeding or incommoding peaceable passengers;
2) all common prostitutes, or night walkers wandering in the fields, public streets or highways, lanes or places of public meeting or gathering of people, not giving a satisfactory account of themselves;
3) all keepers of bawdy houses and houses of ill-fame, or houses for the resort of prostitutes, and persons in the habit of frequenting such houses, not giving a satisfactory account of themselves; and
4) all persons who have no peaceable profession or calling to maintain themselves by, but who do for the most part support themselves by the avails of prostitution.[25]

While the legislation seemed harsh in consigning prostitutes to prison solely for their occupation, without further requirement for offensive conduct, it also seemed balanced in that it attacked prostitutes, pimps, and customers equally. In the eyes of the law, living off the avails of prostitution and frequenting brothels had been twinned with the selling of sexual services. This initiative would have been met with great enthusiasm from the women who ran the Toronto Magdalene Asylum. Since 1855 they had been demanding extended incarceration for men involved in prostitution, whom they characterized as "those monster criminals who trade in the debasement, the sufferings, and the ruin of woman."[26]

From 1860 on, the directors of the Asylum had attacked the double standard, campaigning widely for social sanctions against the customers of prostitutes:

The erring female is at once crushed by public sentiment, while the notorious seducer and profligate is received into respectable society, even perhaps although boasting of his crimes.

Were mothers and daughters to frown the well-known seducer or the licentious from their presence, and were the heads of respectable families peremptorily to exclude him from their society, until he repented of his crimes, [the number of fallen women would be greatly diminished].[27]

In 1894 the Ontario Woman's Christian Temperance Union threatened to publish the names of prostitutes' clients so that mothers could protect their daughters from such men. In 1895 Dr. Annie Hamilton, the first female medical graduate of Dalhousie, denounced the double standard from a public platform. Women were "more sinned against than sinning," she declared, since they suffered "the awful consequences of their evil deeds while men escape scot free." Jessie C. Smith, who spoke to the WCTU in Nova Scotia in 1898, insisted that both prostitute and customer were equally involved in the selling of sexual services. She urged her listeners to "get the names of the frequenters and their inmates, and let us, as Christians, do personal work with both classes."[28]

Unfortunately, when it came to enforcement the will to implement the inclusive provisions was lacking. Toronto female prostitutes continued to be charged disproportionately to male customers. In the latter half of the nineteenth century, women prostitutes represented 97.5 per cent of those charged, while the number of male customers registered only a paltry 2.5 per cent. This disparity was further underscored by the fact that on any day, given the workload of most prostitutes, there had to be more customers than prostitutes potentially available for arrest.[29]

Mary Ann Gorman spent nearly the entire year of 1873 imprisoned. Arrested variously for vagrancy, drunken and disorderly behaviour, or for having been found as an inmate in a brothel, she would serve anywhere from a few days to more than a month in jail. She would no sooner be released than she would be arrested once more. It is difficult to imagine how the authorities continued to list Mary Ann Gorman as a prostitute since she had almost no time to practise the trade between jail terms.

Both Mary and Mary Ann Gorman appeared once in front of the Assizes on larceny charges, but the vast bulk of their cases were heard in Toronto Police Court. Dogged by chronic complaints of overcrowding and overpowering stench and noise, the police court moved from City Hall to the Mechanics' Institute building, and finally into premises of its own in February 1876. Large crowds of unruly spectators cheered their heroes and booed their villains. The snickering hostility that had greeted Ellen Rogers and Mary Hunt in 1858 was typical of the response directed toward accused prostitutes. Repeated appearances before such crowds would certainly have brought the Gormans stigma and notoriety both.[30]

The police magistrates who staffed the Toronto Police Court faced hundreds of prostitutes yearly. "Drunk and disorderly" charges accounted for roughly 40 per cent of the cases before them. Turnstile justice is perhaps the best phrase to describe what happened. Legal niceties were seldom cause for concern where as many as eighty cases could be concluded in one day. Colonel George T. Denison, a "military enthusiast" who convicted Mary Ann Gorman a number of times in the 1870s, boasted of completing 250 cases in 180 minutes. Preferring to rule according to "intuition," Denison dismissed legal argument, bragging: "I never follow precedents unless they agree with my views. This is a court of justice, not a court of law."[31]

Nicknamed "the Beak," Denison's conduct of police court was described as follows:

A swift thinker, a keen student of human nature, the possessor of an incisive tongue, he extinguishes academic lawyers, parries thrusts with the skill of a practised swordsman, confounds the deadly-in-earnest barrister with a witticism, scatters legal intricacies to the winds, will not tolerate the brow-beating of witnesses, cleans off the "slate" before the bewildered stranger has finished gaping, shuts the book with a bang, orders adjournment of the court, then, stick in hand, strolls off to lunch at the National Club.[32]

The class differences between Magistrate Denison, lunching at the National Club, and the Gorman women, often without residence or subsistence, were stark. The point was not lost on one Irish woman named "Biddy," a "chronic drunk" who was convicted by Denison later in his career. She is reported to have said: "The only diff'rence between me and Lady O'Flaherty up in Rosedale, is that I have no powdered flunkeys to carry me up to bed whin I'm drunk."[33]

Magistrate Alexander MacNabb, in front of whom both Gorman

Police Magistrate Colonel George T. Denison,
who convicted Mary Ann Gorman in the 1870s.

woman appeared in the 1860s and 1870s, was noted for his irregular
hours and frequent vacations. Completely out of touch with the circumstances of the prostitutes who appeared before him, he often lectured
them on the error of their ways, and urged them to go straight. "How
easy it was to procure situations of domestic service," he would exhort,
"where [women] might live decent lives if they were industrious." The
disparity between MacNabb's independent life and the harsh, unremitting work of nineteenth-century domestic servants seems to have been
beneath his notice. That many prostitutes, like Mary Ann Gorman, were
former domestics who had lost their positions was simply irrelevant. That
notorious prostitutes might have difficulty obtaining domestic employment also went unexplored. Attacked by the Toronto *Globe* for his lenience

in sentencing drunks, Alexander MacNabb also released the Gormans "on further examination" more often than did some of his fellow magistrates. On 6 February 1872 MacNabb discharged Mary Gorman "with a caution" when she said that she "fell down on the sidewalk not ... because she was drunk, but because the sidewalk was slippery."[34]

By the end of 1873, the sentences had begun to lengthen, regardless of the magistrate sitting. Between 1874 and 1878, instead of a few days or weeks, Mary Ann Gorman received terms of up to six months at hard labour. Her crimes had not changed. She was still being arrested for drunkenness, vagrancy, and for being an inmate of a brothel. Her record for theft had increased somewhat, as she was convicted of stealing a silver watch from one Samuel Lee, and eighty-five dollars from John Shannon in Annie Seaton's brothel on Queen Street West. She was also occasionally convicted for assault. But none of these offences was particularly singled out for harsher treatment. The increasing severity of punishment may have been attributable to Mary Ann Gorman's growing recidivism. It may also have been part of a pattern that saw vagrants treated more harshly in periods of economic downturn, in the 1870s particularly. No doubt it was also attributable to a statutory amendment in 1874 that had escalated the maximum sentence for vagrancy from two to six months' imprisonment.[35]

By the 1870s professionalized urban police forces were slowly beginning to replace the more indulgent constables of the earlier era. Clearing the streets of drunks and troublesome prostitutes had always occupied a great portion of police time, but undisciplined officers had not infrequently succumbed to habitual drunkenness and the frequenting of brothels themselves. By the final quarter of the nineteenth century, however, exhorted by the press and the dominant forces of Victorian Toronto, the police sought to forge themselves into an efficient "instrument in curbing the immorality of society." The perceived need for greater authority to detain prostitutes and other vagrants largely prompted the lengthening of the maximum term.[36]

That the Gormans were Irish Catholic may also have been a factor in their repeated arrests and imprisonments. Impoverished Irish immigrants faced severe treatment from the criminal justice system. Disproportionately prosecuted and convicted, the Irish made up nearly 60 per cent of those arrested and incarcerated in Toronto in 1863. Nor would reliance on traditional customs prove a good defence for Mary Ann Gorman. On 7 October 1873 she defended herself by arguing before Alexander MacNabb that she had "been at an Irish wake." She was fined $4.50 and costs or sixty days.[37]

On at least one occasion Mary Ann Gorman's arrest was specifically linked to her being Irish Catholic. On 17 March 1878 an anti-Catholic riot broke out around St. Patrick's Hall and the Queen Street West tavern run by Owen Cosgrove, which had become a popular meeting place for the Irish Catholic community. O'Donovan Rossa, an American Fenian and proponent of a free Ireland, had come to deliver a lecture in Toronto. Angry anti-Catholic Protestant demonstrators rioted, and the police turned out in full force. Mary Ann Gorman was only too familiar to them, and she was taken into custody. Charged with vagrancy, this was one of the few occasions on which she managed to pay her $4.25 fine and obtain release.[38]

Irish Catholics were not the only group to receive harsher treatment under criminal law. In Halifax and Calgary, Black women were considerably overrepresented among the population of convicted prostitutes. On the west coast in British Columbia, Chinese and Japanese women were similarly overrepresented. In part the high number of convictions reflected racial discrimination in the enforcement of prostitution and vagrancy laws. Whether these high rates of convictions may also have reflected the greater activity of these groups in the business of prostitution — segregated as they were from many other fields of employment — is not known.[39]

In some cases, however, the letter of the law itself discriminated against minority groups. During the 1880s the federal Parliament passed a series of laws specifically to deal with the prostitution of "Indian" women. Harsher penalties were prescribed for keepers of brothels employing "Indian" prostitutes, and the evidence required to convict First Nations' women and their customers was lessened. The legal phrase customarily used to describe a brothel, "common bawdy house," was not used where women of the First Nations were concerned. Accordingly it was no longer necessary for the Crown to provide evidence of the reputation or character of the premises. Any house would suffice. Men from the First Nations could be convicted for merely "frequenting" or being "found" on the premises, while other customers had to be proved to be "habitual frequenters."[40]

Quebec prostitutes were also singled out for particular attention. Under special legislation of 1871, the federal government stipulated that Quebec women who had been convicted of vagrancy more than once should serve their sentence in the Quebec female reformatory prison. These women were forced to stay there *a minimum of five years*. Montreal was perceived as a thriving centre for prostitution in 1871, purportedly hosting up to forty-one brothels. Slightly more than half of the prostitutes were thought to be French Canadian, with the rest assumed to be mostly Irish and Scottish immigrants.[41]

In 1891 the federal government expanded its new policy of extending the prison terms for prostitutes who were not of the dominant race, religion, or ethnic group. Roman Catholic women convicted of vagrancy in Nova Scotia were expressly subjected to a minimum term of one year and a maximum term of four years. The general penalty for other women convicted of vagrancy remained a maximum of six months' imprisonment throughout this period.[42]

Roman Catholic women in Nova Scotia were required to serve these longer sentences in the female reformatory operated by the Sisters of the Good Shepherd in Halifax. The religious order that ran the prison devoted itself to providing religious instruction and domestic training for "wayward girls and fallen women." By 1894 fifty inmates, mostly former domestic servants, were serving sentences of one or two years under the direction of twenty-two nuns. Whether the conditions of reformatory life constituted an improvement over conditions in city or provincial jails is not clear. But the substantially longer deprivation of freedom would have rendered most gains illusory.[43]

On 25 July 1873, Mary Gorman was released from the Toronto City Jail for the last time. Aged fifty-two, she would have had little future left in the business of prostitution. She was briefly listed as a roomer in William Colenzo's house on Dummer Street, but by 1874 she had disappeared from sight. Of uncertain health and with a long history of alcohol dependency, she may have died.[44]

Mary Ann Gorman seems to have continued to work as a prostitute, sometimes under the new alias of Margaret Haggerty, until 1 May 1878, when she was released from the Toronto jail for the last time. She missed by two years and three months the opening of the first entirely female prison in Canada: the Andrew Mercer Reformatory for Women. Built with ninety-thousand dollars from the estate of wealthy philanthropist Andrew Mercer, the women's prison on King Street near Dufferin in Toronto was graced with "ornamental towers" to provide a "softer" design than traditional prisons. Large enough to hold 196 women prisoners, the Mercer was run by female staff supervised by Superintendent Mary Jane O'Reilly, an upper-middle-class, Roman Catholic, Irish widow.[45]

Mary Ann Gorman would have been a prime candidate for the Mercer. The majority of its early inmates were young recidivists, many of whom had spent the largest part of their lives in various city jails across

Ontario. Most gave their occupations as prostitutes or as domestic servants. The goals of the Mercer staff were similar to those of the Magdalene Asylum workers: to reform the inmates morally while retraining them at domestic tasks. While the prison setting enabled the staff to compel participation, the success rate of the Mercer was not significantly better than the Magdalene. Still, the environment was somewhat less harsh than in the mixed-sex prisons.[46]

In the last decades of the nineteenth century, provincial legislatures passed a rash of statutes designed to intervene pre-emptively in the lives of women before they became mired in a life of prostitution or crime. Ontario set up an Industrial Refuge for delinquent girls, housed in a separate wing at the Mercer, to accommodate up to fifty girls for terms of five years. Judges were authorized to commit any girl under the age of fourteen who was found "wandering" or not having a "settled place of abode," whose parents were in prison, or who was growing up "without salutary control" due to the neglect, drunkenness, or other vices of her parents. Nova Scotia enacted similar legislation in 1884, and Manitoba in 1898.[47]

This massive intrusion by the state into the affairs of working-class families was sparked largely by fears that the conditions of urbanized living were giving rise to a hardened criminal class that was renewing itself with each generation. Living conditions at the Refuge would have been better than at the Toronto jail, but the rigid class demarcations meant that any occupational training available would have been severely circumscribed. And the individualized focus on moral rehabilitation stubbornly ignored the economic and social factors that propelled so many impoverished, destitute women into confrontation with the police.[48]

In any event, these developments came too late for Mary Ann Gorman. Unaided by the dubious improvements in penology represented by the advent of the Mercer and the Industrial Refuges, she was only twenty years old at her final release from the Toronto jail in 1878. The rest of Mary Ann Gorman's life must remain a matter for speculation. Given her age, death seems an unlikely explanation for her disappearance. For a notorious prostitute with diminished prospects, heterosexual marriage or "respectable" employment in Toronto were similarly unlikely. She may have moved from the jurisdiction, perhaps to attempt to forge a new life or to seek more promising horizons for her occupation.[49]

Prostitution had not proven to be much of an occupation for the Gorman mother and daughter. Destitute, outcast, and desperately dependent on alcohol, for some women prostitution in mid-nineteenth-century Toronto served as a ticket to public exposure, police harassment, and downward social mobility.

ESTHER FORSYTH ARSCOTT:<br>A PROPERTIED BROTHEL OWNER IN LONDON

Esther Arscott's spectacular confrontation with the law began on 24 September 1884. In a surprise and dramatic police raid, four constables broke into her house on 233 Rectory Street in London East. Between twelve and fourteen men and women were handcuffed. After some preliminary skirmishing and negotiation, all of the men and most of the women were allowed to leave. Esther Arscott and two of her employees, Mary Blow and Hattie Robson, were taken to jail.[50]

Esther Arscott was the owner of a thriving brothel that had achieved some prominence as a recognized landmark in the working-class, industrial suburb of London, Ontario. London East was a rough-and-tumble residential area, interspersed with oil refineries, spur lines of the Great Western and Grand Trunk Railways, and the heavy industry of the railway car-yards. Political annexation to the City of London was under serious consideration in 1884, although it would not be accomplished until March 1885. Part of the difficulty lay with the diverse images of London East and the City of London itself. There was an obvious antagonism between working-class London East and the smug, self-satisfied city burghers of the City of London.[51]

London itself was a city of some twenty-six thousand people, which boasted a reputation as a fledgling metropolis and a centre of finance, manufacturing, trade, and culture. London was touted for its affluence and refinement, as this extract from the 1881 *London City Directory* portrayed:

[London] has aptly been named the "Forest City," from the immense number of beautiful trees which adorn the broad boulevarded thoroughfares. [It is situated in the County of Middlesex], one of the largest and wealthiest in the Province.... London is noted for the enterprise of its inhabitants, its beautiful park-like avenues and its handsome and costly public and private buildings.[52]

The clash between the images of the City of London and London East was sometimes vividly demonstrated during the annual fall fair. One of the largest in Ontario, the yearly Western Fair was held at the expansive London Fair Grounds. The popular seasonal event attracted large numbers of fair-goers from the surrounding agricultural County of Middlesex.

Crowds of itinerant men out for a drinking spree and entertainment met up with boisterous groups of women, some of whom were prostitutes from London East seeking customers. Staid Londoners would have watched the ensuing transactions with great alarm.[53]

It seems no accident that Esther Arscott's house was raided on 24 September, one of the very last days of the 1884 Western Fair. And no accident that it was Esther Arscott whose brothel was chosen. The authorities wished to make a prominent example of one of the most notorious women connected with the business of prostitution. Targeting Esther Arscott would be a symbol to other prostitutes and to the wider community of a serious attack on commercialized sexuality. But the authorities had not considered Esther Arscott's determination to fight back.

Forty-two-year-old Arscott, whose maiden name was Forsyth, was English-born but had been residing in London East for some years. Long considered a "notorious character," she had been charged twice, in 1874 and 1877, with keeping a house of ill-fame. The first time she was discharged without penalty. The second time she had been fined $23.90. The brothel keeper had deep roots in the London East community. Many other members of the Forsyth family, including her brother, a labourer named Frederick Forsyth(e), lived in the neighbourhood. An Anglican who was probably of working-class background, she had only rudimentary formal education. Although Esther Arscott would boast to the jail authorities of her ability to read and write, she was apparently illiterate.[54]

At some point between 1877 and 1879, thirty-seven-year-old Esther Forsyth married William Arscott, a tanner and sometime "commercial traveller." A man with considerable real estate holdings in London East, he was ten years younger than his bride. Shortly after their marriage, he was charged with aiding and abetting during an assault and tried in March of 1880. Acquitted of the charge and released from jail, he died not long afterwards in December 1883. Esther Arscott may have discontinued work in prostitution during her marriage, but business seems to have picked up shortly after she became a widow in 1884. Using her home as the base of her operation, she may have decided that returning to brothel keeping was a resourceful response to the financial uncertainty of widowhood.[55]

The records do not reveal whether Esther Arscott engaged in acts of prostitution, or whether she simply served as the manager of the brothel. She was never charged with anything other than "keeping" a bawdy house. Restricting her work to the supervisory aspects of the business would have allowed her to escape some of the more rigorous aspects of the job. Unlike the Gorman women, she seems never to have developed an alcohol dependency. The press reported that Esther Arscott's links with alcohol were primarily financial; she purportedly sold liquor to her patrons without a licence.[56]

The morning after her arrest, Esther Arscott was brought before Charles Lilley, sitting as the Police Court Magistrate. Lilley was a prominent name in London East, and the whole area had been known some years earlier as "Lilley's Corners." Charles Lilley, a well-to-do merchant, was both the Postmaster and Mayor of London East, and he would have been anxious to protect the reputation of his town during the ongoing annexation deliberations. London East was under severe financial constraint, and many citizens believed annexation with London was the only way to save the town from bankruptcy.[57]

Charles Hutchinson of the Hutchinson and McKillop law firm was the prosecuting attorney. Formerly the clerk of the peace for Middlesex County, Hutchinson had been promoted to County Crown Attorney some years earlier. A vociferous advocate for temperance, for years he had been complaining about drunkenness at the race course and about the many licensed taverns in London East. He even decried the use of sacramental wine in religious service.[58]

A prominent proponent of the Charlton Bill to criminalize seduction, Charles Hutchinson was also one of the key forces behind much of the crackdown on prostitution in London. Nineteenth-century charges reached their peak between the mid-1870s and the late 1880s generally, but September of 1884 was a spectacular period in London. The day after the dramatic raid on Esther Arscott's, the police rounded up and arrested the people found in a second brothel at 172 Bathurst Street, run by Elizabeth Kenny. Prostitution was not the only form of "vice" that triggered Charles Hutchinson's wrath. During December 1885 and January 1886, he would conduct a lengthy prosecution against a bill-poster named Frank Kerchmer for displaying indecent pictures in public. The picture of a female trapeze artist "appeal[ed] to the sensual feelings of the young," claimed Hutchinson.[59]

Charles Hutchinson chose to prosecute Esther Arscott for "keeping" a house of ill-fame, the same offence of which she had been convicted previously. "Keeping" had been classified as a "nuisance" under the old English common law, but more specific criminal legislation passed initially in New Brunswick and Nova Scotia had spread to Lower Canada and Upper Canada by the mid-century. The federal Vagrancy Act of 1869

Poster that resulted in Charles Hutchinson's prosecution of Frank Kerchmer for displaying indecent pictures in public, London, Ontario, December 1885–January 1886.

consolidated these provisions, and set out a maximum penalty of fifty dollars, two months' imprisonment, or both. In 1874 the penalty was increased to six months' imprisonment, and in 1881 Parliament clarified that prisoners so convicted could be sentenced to hard labour during their term.[60]

Esther Arscott was convicted of "keeping a common bawdy house," and sentenced to the maximum penalty, six months at hard labour. The two women arrested with Esther Arscott were convicted of being "inmates of a common bawdy house," but were let off much more leniently. Mary Blow was fined twenty dollars and costs, and Hattie Robson ten dollars and costs. Esther Arscott, outraged over her penalty, was denied the option of paying a fine. Even the London *Free Press* labelled the jail term "a smart sentence."[61]

Esther Arscott immediately retained the services of a local London criminal lawyer, Edmund Allan Meredith, who conferred with his client in the London jail and resolved to commence an appeal. But the first matter was to get Esther Arscott out of jail. Meredith applied for bail, but Mayor Lilley set the amounts at five hundred dollars cash, and two sureties of two hundred and fifty dollars each. Esther Arscott instructed Meredith to try to bargain down the bail amounts, perhaps because of an inability to pay, perhaps as a matter of principle. Meredith tried to strike a deal with Charles Lilley and Hutchinson, but after two days of argument, there was still no resolution and Esther Arscott was growing impatient.[62]

Having served as the former Mayor of London from 1882 to 1883, Edmund Meredith was well versed in the personality quirks of municipal politicians. He took the case to another justice of the peace, Squire Murray Anderson. Long active in city government, and himself a former Mayor, Anderson was widely known for his personal hostility toward Mayor Lilley. He immediately agreed to bail in the amount of three hundred and fifty dollars cash, with two sureties of one hundred and fifty dollars each. Esther Arscott furnished these amounts, and she was released from jail on 26 September 1884, two days after the initial arrest. Squire Murray Anderson's "little game" caused "some trouble in magisterial circles," the press reported.[63]

Mayor Lilley and County Crown Attorney Hutchinson took the unprecedented action of putting their case to the people through lengthy appeals that they published in the London *Free Press* the next day. Mayor Charles Lilley wrote:

[L]ast night I heard from several that Esther Arscott who I had the day before convicted for keeping a house of ill fame, from the best of evidence, to six months' imprisonment, had been liberated from jail by ex-Mayor Anderson. My reply to one and all was I cannot believe it, as I had not been served with any papers of the appeal, but on going into the city I found it too true.

Now Mr. Editor, I as Mayor of London East, do all I can to put down crime, fearlessly, without gain, as all costs go to the Corporation [of London East]. The only gain I expect is in doing good and what I consider is my duty as Mayor of London East, and a moral living man; but if I have an ex-Mayor and Mrs. Arscott's money — with all her money and the backing I am sorry to say she has — to fight against, I shall have a hard fight, and it may be necessary for the Corporation to come forward with a will to surpress [sic] crime in London East, but I hope and trust there are enough good living people to assist me in driving every house of ill-fame from London East.

Charles Hutchinson had similar objections:

There can be no doubt that this was a very improper and inconsiderate act on the part of Mr. Anderson.... He should have been doubly cautious, knowing as he admitted, the notorious character of the woman and her house, and as a professing Christian and active member of the Church, he should have been careful not to interfere in the action of the Mayor of the town in his efforts to suppress a nuisance of such vile character.

Squire Murray Anderson labelled Lilley and Hutchinson's claims just so much "twaddle," motivated by an "inordinate desire" to see themselves in print "to the result of dotage." The London *Free Press* left no doubt where it stood on the matter. Its headline accused Anderson of "thwarting" Mayor Lilley's campaign to "suppress crime and vice." The situation "demand[ed] the attention of the Attorney-General," declared the paper.[64]

Angry as they were, Charles Lilley and Charles Hutchinson were also wary of Esther Arscott's considerable perseverance. If they were going to have to go to court to argue against her appeal, they would need some community backing themselves. On 23 October 1884, Mayor Lilley asked the London East Municipal Council for specific instructions to defend the appeal. This was a rather unusual move, since everyone agreed that the County Crown Attorney and the magistrate who decided the case already had the authority to defend against an appeal. But the Mayor was as much a politician as a magistrate, and he wanted popular affirmation for his campaign.[65]

The request was carefully staged. A petition signed by forty-eight citizens was read that night. It begged the council "to take steps to exterminate" Arscott's brothel, because the operation "materially depreciated the value of their property and disgraced the whole neighbourhood." But the Council refused to vote the authorization. Several Council members expressed fear that any interference on their part would mean they would be called upon to pay the costs if the appeal was ultimately successful. They too were very wary of Esther Arscott's formidable reputation and did not want to get involved.[66]

That night the Mayor exploded in the Council chambers, threatening that he would "in future dismiss all such cases when brought before him, no matter if there were 50 houses of ill-fame in the town." The press contributed to the acrimony by printing the views of an unidentified but "prominent London Easter" who expressed stern disapproval of the actions of the Council, suggesting that it "reflect[ed] anything but credit on the councillors."[67]

By November 1884, the London *Advertiser* would note that the Mayor's threat was having a dire impact:

Complaints are daily being made by prominent citizens of the increase in the number of disreputable houses in the town. The gentlemen assert that houses of this character appeared on nearly all the principal streets after the action of the Council in reference to the social evil.

Word had spread to neighbouring towns. According to the Hamilton *Times*, Mayor Lilley's words had given heart to many. Brothel keepers who had "an uneasy time of it" in Hamilton, were looking to the London suburb as a veritable "haven of rest." "London East may now look for a rapid increase of the population," concluded the Hamilton paper. Londoners were outraged when the London *Advertiser* reprinted the remarks in their entirety.[68]

Now Charles Lilley and Charles Hutchinson had to defend the appeal while badgered by concerned property-owners in the area, watched as if through a microscope by reporters, and without the support of the Council of London East. The appeal came on before the Court of General Sessions on 9 December 1884. To the surprise of many, the conviction was upheld, but no reasons were given. Charles Hutchinson and Charles

Lilley made out a warrant for Esther Arscott's arrest. It condemned her to serve the full original sentence, six months at hard labour.[69]

Esther Arscott was picked up and reimprisoned on 18 December. A woman of less self-possession, less resolve would likely have given in. But Esther Arscott contacted her lawyer and began afresh. When Edmund Meredith examined the warrant, he discovered that it sentenced Arscott to the full six months, neglecting to reduce the term to reflect the two days she had served prior to bail. In short order he drew up a writ of *habeas corpus*, seeking to have her brought before a court of law and released because she was being held unlawfully.[70]

The *habeas corpus* action would not be heard until 4 February 1885, and throughout this stretch Esther Arscott waited in jail. Judge Thomas Galt of the High Court heard the argument, which was delivered in Toronto by Edmund Meredith and his more famous younger brother and law partner, Richard Martin Meredith. Impressed by the arguments of Esther Arscott's counsel, Judge Galt immediately ordered her discharge from jail. Charles Hutchinson refused to release her for several hours after he had received the discharge order, but by the next morning the triumphant Esther Arscott "packed up her things and took leave of the jail." But her release was not to be. As the London *Free Press* recounted it:

Just as she stepped out into the Court House hall, Detective Hodge, who stood waiting near the door, stepped forward and arrested her on a new commitment made for the same offence. It seems Mayor Lilley has made up his mind that he can keep it up as long as the game lasts, and as soon as he heard of the order being sent, he made out a new commitment allowing for the time already served, and now Mrs. Arscott is back in jail again. She was very much amazed at the new turn of affairs, and told the officer it was a put up job, but she would soon find a way to settle the question.[71]

By six o'clock that night, the defence lawyers had fired off yet another motion for Arscott's release. Six hours after her recommittal, an apprehensive Sheriff Glass "personally went into the jail and released the woman." But Charles Hutchinson would not give up. He resolved to go before the Court of General Sessions once more, to seek an additional warrant. And Mayor Lilley boasted to the press that "the woman would not be long out of jail."[72]

Meanwhile, Esther Arscott instructed her lawyers to sue Charles Lilley and Charles Hutchinson each for damages of one thousand dollars, on the grounds of false imprisonment. The forty-three-year-old brothel keeper had had enough. If she was going to be put to the expense of defending herself against criminal charges, she would try her hand at using the law for her own ends. The old English Habeas Corpus Act provided that persons who wrongly imprisoned an individual should forfeit the sum of five hundred pounds sterling. Esther Arscott considered that if anyone was entitled to recompense she was. "The recent Arscott case is going to prove a treasure to the lawyers," remarked the *Free Press*.[73]

On 21 February 1885, Charles Hutchinson brought an application before the Court of General Sessions to obtain another warrant for Esther Arscott's arrest. Apparently concerned about making a ruling contrary to Judge Galt's earlier order to release the prisoner, the Court of General Sessions refused the request. But Charles Lilley would not concede defeat. In mid-March, Mayor Lilley began to snoop around Arscott's Rectory Street house, interviewing neighbours and watching for any unusual activity. William Trace, who lived opposite the house, had been one of the signatories to the petition against Arscott. He informed Lilley that Esther Arscott had been conducting business as usual for about two weeks. "Girls or women are there and men frequent the house day and night," he advised. Mayor Lilley sent a letter to Charles Hutchinson, complaining that "all say Mrs. Arscott was keeping her house just as bold as ever...." Hutchinson and Lilley issued another warrant on 18 March 1885, and arrested Esther Arscott again six days later, determined that she should serve out her term. Richard Martin Meredith bailed her out on 2 April and, joined by Britton Bath Osler, QC, made out a second writ of *habeas corpus* on Arscott's behalf.[74]

This unprecedented legal battle would consume the next two years. Arscott was remarkably well advised and represented by a cast of brilliant, leading criminal and civil barristers. Richard Martin Meredith was a prominent London equity lawyer who practised with Meredith, Judd and Meredith in London. He came from a singularly successful family. In addition to his brother Edmund, the criminal lawyer and former mayor, his older brother, William Ralph Meredith, was the leader of the Tory opposition in the Ontario Legislature and would later become the Chief Justice of Ontario. Richard Martin would be appointed to the Supreme Court himself several years after the Arscott litigation.[75]

Britton Bath Osler, QC, who joined Meredith almost immediately for the defence, had practised in Dundas, Hamilton, and Toronto since 1862. Often acclaimed the "foremost criminal lawyer in Canada," he too had a brother, Featherstone Osler, who sat on the Ontario Court of Appeal. D'Alton McCarthy, QC, who would come in on the case later, was the

McCarthy who had served Dr. Emily Stowe so well in her abortion trial of 1879. He was also Osler's partner in the Toronto firm of McCarthy, Osler, Hoskin and Creelman.[76]

Unlike the Gorman women, who never had the defence of a single lawyer, even one far less famous than the Merediths, Oslers, and Mc-Carthys of the bar, Esther Arscott would mount a sophisticated, highly technical legal defence. For the Gorman women, who could rarely pay even the most petty fines, legal counsel was simply out of reach. Esther Arscott, however, was financially secure enough to hire the best. There were class gradations within the ranks of prostitutes themselves. Upper-class prostitutes secured legal assistance from upper-class lawyers.

But it is tempting to speculate further how a brothel keeper, even a relatively rich one, obtained such illustrious representation. Assuming she could pay fully for the service, these were still men who could afford to pick and choose their clients. Richard Martin Meredith described himself as a man with "an inclination to favour the underdog," and perhaps he took on Arscott's case because he was disturbed by the Lilley and Hutchinson vendetta. A more cynical observer might query whether the lawyers involved knew Arscott personally, or had friends who did. Lawyers were occasionally found in brothels when police raids occurred, and this sometimes resulted in differential legal handling. One contemporary reporter described such a case in Toronto during the 1890s:

Fanny Rogers pleaded guilty to a case of illegal liquor selling at her [brothel] on King Street west, and his Worship remanded her for one week, at the request of her counsel.... This is the case where several lawyers were found in the place when it was raided. One of the police said that Miss Rogers was induced to plead guilty so as the legal lights in question would not have to be called by the Crown to testify.[77]

Cold-hearted economic calculation may also have cemented the relationship between well-to-do prostitutes and élite lawyers. Whatever one could say about the Arscott arrests, at the very least they were high profile. Eager squads of reporters followed every development. Citizen groups were mounting extensive petitions. Politicians were at each other's throats. Acting as counsel in such dramatically visible cases enhanced lawyers' reputations, ultimately attracting scores of the more lucrative commercial and industrial business clients.[78]

Not to be outdone, Charles Lilley and Charles Hutchinson retained Allen Bristol Aylesworth, another illustrious Toronto lawyer, to defend against the appeal. Aylesworth was slightly younger than the defence lawyers, and his practice was just beginning to take off. He would be named a QC in 1889, and would go on to argue many appeals before the Privy Council in England. He would also sit as a member of Parliament, a minister of justice in the Laurier government, a senator of the university, and a bencher of the Law Society.[79]

The second *habeas corpus* case came on for hearing before Judge John Edward Rose of the Court of Common Pleas on 29 May 1885. There Messrs. Meredith and Osler delivered an ingenious legal argument. They asked Judge Rose to focus on the exact wording of the section of the Vagrancy Act under which Esther Arscott had purportedly been convicted. The statute penalized "all keepers of bawdy houses and houses of ill-fame, or houses for the resort of prostitutes, and persons in the habit of frequenting such houses, not giving a satisfactory account of themselves." The key phrase was "not giving a satisfactory account of themselves," contended the defence lawyers. The police had never asked Esther Arscott to give an account of herself, and lacking evidence of the insufficiency of her reply, they were not entitled to arrest her.[80]

Aylesworth argued that the phrase "not giving a satisfactory account of themselves" was meant to apply only to frequenters of bawdy houses, who might have a legitimate motive for their presence. Keeping a bawdy house was an offence that offered no defensible explanation, he insisted. But Judge Rose was not convinced. A highly successful commercial lawyer in Toronto, Rose had accepted elevation to the bench only a few years before. His reputation was that of a man of "eminent abilities," with "industrious and pains-taking habits, and a ready faculty of discerning the essential points of a case." In this matter, he was distinctly drawn to Esther Arscott's position. Neither prostitutes, night-walkers, keepers, nor frequenters of bawdy houses were "criminal[s] liable to punishment as such," declared Rose. He conceded that such persons were of a class "against whom society must be protected," but only "when found at such places, and under such circumstances as suggest to the conservators of public peace and morality, suspicion of impropriety of purpose."[81]

The ramifications of Judge Rose's decision were far-reaching. He had considered federal legislation that, on its face, seemed to criminalize the very keeping of a brothel. He had taken issue with the principle behind such a law, declaring that individuals associated with prostitution were not criminals as such. Instead, he insisted upon a very strict application of the law, restricting its ambit to those whose actions were "offensive or dangerous to the public." He issued his decision and discharged Esther Arscott from custody.[82]

Judge Rose's decision took place within a context of some tension between the bench and the legislatures over the proper role of law in dealing with prostitution. Between 1869 and 1892 an explosion of federal enactments had attempted to place sweeping prohibitions on all prostitution activity. Parliament had made it criminal to procure the defilement of women under the age of twenty-one by false pretences, representations, or other fraudulent means. Householders were prohibited from allowing women under the age of sixteen to resort there for the purpose of "unlawful carnal knowledge." It was an offence to entice a woman to a brothel for the purpose of prostitution, or to knowingly conceal her in such a house. It was made criminal to procure women for unlawful carnal connection, or for parents or guardians to encourage the defilement of their daughters. A new offence, "conspiracy to defile," had also been created.[83]

The industriousness of the legislators was a response to a growing outcry from middle-class social reformers against the sexual exploitation of women. John Charlton's persistent campaign for the criminalization of seduction was only one manifestation of this sentiment. D.A. Watt, one of the founders of the Montreal Society for the Protection of Girls and Young Women, lobbied throughout the 1880s and 1890s to criminalize the behaviour of procurers, seducers, and abductors of women and children. Under Watt's influence, three of the leading Protestant churches of Canada, the Presbyterian, the Congregational, and the Methodist, had joined forces to demand greater legal sanctions. A Toronto grand jury emphasized similar sentiments in 1882 when it urged more legislation and more enforcement: "From the vast increase of the social evil the foundation of the social system is being threatened and a lasting blot left upon the fair name of Canada. Let our Judges and Legislators use every means to have it removed."[84]

This campaign was part of an attack on the sexual double standard, which traditionally had consigned women to a narrow range of procreative heterosexual activity inside marriage. In contrast, male sexuality was viewed as natural, more legitimate, and, at times, even uncontrollable. The goal was not to open up vistas for freer sexual activity, but to demand from men the same standard of "purity" that had long been applied to women. The eradication of prostitution, where men had long exercised their rights to "sow a few wild oats," would provide a promising start.[85]

Judge Rose's decision to contain the reach of this legislation was part of a much wider perspective that higher court judges were expressing toward prostitution throughout the nineteenth century. The judges were gravely concerned about the rapid expansion of criminal legislation in the area. Judge Adam Wilson of the Ontario Court of Queen's Bench had written in 1870 that prostitutes were entitled to rights just as other citizens were: "[S]he cannot suppose she is [to be apprehended] for wandering in the streets, though she is a common prostitute, so long as she is conducting herself harmlessly and decently, and just as other people are conducting themselves."[86]

Several Quebec judges had narrowed the scope of the new laws by redefining the word "prostitution." In cases where a mistress had commercial heterosexual relations with only one man, Judges A.A. Dorion and Jonathan S.C. Wurtele concluded separately that this did not constitute "prostitution" in the legal sense. The purpose of the law, they argued, was "the repression of acts which outrage public decency and are injurious to public morals." While a kept woman might violate moral law, her private behaviour "did not outrage public decency nor violate any provision of the criminal law of the land."[87]

The Supreme Court of Canada pronounced the rationale behind these rulings in 1882:

The desire for shutting up houses of ill-fame or disorderly houses in any community, and for the prevention of crimes generally, is highly commendable, and should be seconded by all legal means, and by the aid of all judicial officers of every rank, but it must be done in such a way as not to violate most valuable and important principles and rules of evidence upon which depend the safety of life, liberty and property.[88]

The judges spoke the language of privacy and individual rights. But they did not mean to suggest that women should have unfettered rights to work or to express their own sexuality. Judges were chronically suspicious of working-class women's sexuality, as they so often stated in tort of seduction cases. Their decisions in other areas, such as divorce and custody law, also indicated that they had little respect for women's rights as such.

The prostitution rulings are best understood when juxtaposed with rape decisions. The judges' refusal to convict in cases where the rape victim was not modest, virtuous, and chaste clearly marked off a group of women as outcasts. Sexual contact with these women was condoned for men, even when it took place through physical coercion. Prostitutes were part of this designated group of women, whose sexuality was viewed as publicly available. Ellen Rogers and Mary Hunt had learned this decades earlier at the trial that made a mockery of their rapes. Insofar as the social reformers and legislators were trying to remove prostitutes from the sexual market, the judges were collectively obstructionist. By implication, they seem to have disliked the prohibitive array of statutes, preferring to tolerate prostitution as a "necessary social evil." Prostitution could accommodate unstoppable male sexual needs, while the courts regulated its most unsavoury public aspects.

Elated by her initial victory, Esther Arscott left the London jail and pursued her action for civil damages. Chief Justice Matthew Crooks Cameron considered her claim at the Fall Assizes in London. He reviewed the evidence of the four warrants for her arrest over five months, all arising out of the same charge. The issue was whether the warrants were legally valid, or whether Esther Arscott had been unjustly imprisoned. Concluding that there had been no legal authority to detain her in jail, Cameron awarded "the sum of $2,430, or the equivalent of £500 sterling, with costs" against Charles Lilley and Charles Hutchinson.[89]

The disgruntled Mayor and the Crown Attorney were advised by Lilley's lawyer, Allen Bristol Aylesworth, that "the amount of money at stake is so large, and the questions of law involved so important and so doubtful, that the case should, in my opinion, be carried as far as the Supreme Court, if necessary." On 12 January 1886, they moved to have the judgment set aside. At this point Judge Adam Wilson of the Ontario Court of Queen's Bench seems to have felt that things had definitely gone too far. Ruling against Esther Arscott in March of 1886, he held that damages should never have been assessed against Charles Lilley and Charles Hutchinson.[90]

From there the case went in front of the Ontario Court of Appeal, with the full cast of lawyers once more arguing their respective positions. The two days of hearing devoted to the issues stand in stark contrast to the few seconds of time that the Gorman women generally received in front of police magistrates. Remarking that the "history" of the case was "full of surprises," Judge Christopher Salmon Patterson settled the matter in May 1887. Esther Arscott was not entitled to damages for false imprisonment, he ruled. She had been "convicted and sentenced to six months imprisonment at hard labour, and she has got off without serving her sentence!" he exclaimed.[91]

Patterson was also of the view that Judge Rose's interpretation of the Vagrancy Act was erroneous. Keeping a bawdy house, by the very nature of the act, was a criminal offence. What possible account could a brothel keeper give of herself that would justify such activity? Patterson conceded that prostitutes, night-walkers, and frequenters might all be able to provide satisfactory explanations for their situations, but keepers were of an entirely different order. With this decision Judge Patterson placed something of a halt on the judicial trend of restrictive interpretation of anti-prostitution legislation. But the contours had been set. The scope of the statutes had been severely circumscribed, and this ruling did little to detract from the overall pattern.[92]

On a rather frank note, Judge Patterson added that the expensive and lengthy litigation had not really been justified:

[L]ooking back after the event, it may be thought that the interests of the community would not have suffered, and that possibly the ends of justice would have been substantially served, if the plaintiff had taken the opportunity to do what we are told she has since done, and leave the country before a fresh warrant could overtake her.

Sensing that she had won what legal victories she could, Esther Arscott had taken her leave, probably for the United States.[93]

But Esther Arscott was not one to be run out of town ignominiously. She had left behind family and friends whom she did not care to abandon. Flush with prosperity, she would return to London sometime in the 1890s. There she lived with her new husband, Robert T. Barnes, a man who listed his occupations as a bookkeeper, farmer, foreman, horse dealer, and horse breeder. There is no record of any further legal confrontations.[94]

Esther Forsyth Arscott Barnes died on 2 July 1902, leaving behind a considerable estate. The bulk of it she bequeathed to her second husband: horses, carriages, over three thousand dollars in cash and mortgages, and two brick houses on Rectory and York streets. To her adopted daughter, Mary Howell, she left her brick house on Van Street. For her sister Jane Pashby in Iowa, she willed cash, clothing, and her dinner and tea set of china. Five hundred dollars was saved for Esther Broadbent, a grandniece and presumably a namesake. And her brother Frederick Forsythe was granted the sum of two hundred dollars. A certain sum was also set aside for improving and maintaining the burial plot that she had purchased for herself, beside her first husband, in the Woodland Cemetery in London.[95]

Prostitution had proven to be a profitable choice of occupation for Esther Arscott. She had operated her brothel as a solid and lucrative enterprise, plowing back the returns into real estate investments. The criminal law had intruded upon her venture with excessive zeal in the mid-1880s, but she had used every resource at her disposal, securing important and unprecedented legal victories at several points. Leaving when her string of successes was about to give out, she had returned as a woman of means and influence and lived out the rest of her days in middle-class respectability. A proper tombstone in a well-groomed, wooded London cemetery by the banks of the Thames River marked the demise of a woman who had bested them all.

# 9

# Protective Labour Legislation

THE STORY OF THE FRAIL SHOPGIRL

At "M----'s dry goods store," a well-appointed Montreal emporium frequented by fashionable ladies of leisure in the late nineteenth century, the focus of attention was Esther Ryland, a bright and cheerful shopgirl much sought after by the clientele. One observer would remember:

Esther Ryland was noticed ... on account of her unusually attractive person and elegance of manners; she was a little above the average height, yet graceful and well-formed, with remarkably handsome features, and eyes that sparkled like a pair of diamonds.

Esther was very proud of her attractions, both professionally and otherwise; she did not calculate, however, that the more popular she became the more work she would have to do, and that she would, in time, pay for her popularity with her health, if not her life.[1]

This warning was sounded by Charlotte Fuhrer, a German-born midwife who practised in Montreal between 1859 and 1907. She published her memoirs (apparently part truth, part fiction) in 1881 as *The Mysteries of Montreal: Memoirs of a Midwife*. Charlotte Fuhrer's practiced eye had discerned a potential medical problem that gripped social reformers of the day: the prolonged standing required of shopgirls might wreak havoc with their future motherhood.

At the time described, however, Esther Ryland was being courted by Mr. Quintin, a merchant tailor just set up in business, who sought her hand in marriage. According to Charlotte Fuhrer, Esther Ryland and Mr. Quintin would "stroll together on the long summer evenings, and together they might be seen, fondly looking into each other's faces, as, arm-in-arm, they perambulated the more remote portions of Sherbrooke and St. Denis streets." The strolling soon proved too much for Esther, and she began to plead fatigue.[2]

Mr. Quintin questioned her about her weakness, and Charlotte Fuhrer recounted the following exchange:

Quintin drew forth the avowal that she [Esther Ryland] *had not sat down for a quarter of an hour* during the whole day! It seems it was the busy season at M——'s, and, besides being engaged incessantly in serving customers, Miss Ryland was obliged to shorten her dinner hour, and to hurry back to meet the increased demand.

Quintin was quite shocked at this discovery. Although well aware of the brutal treatment of shopkeepers' assistants, he had never been an interested party, and so had the matter placed before him *in all its horrors* for the first time. He resolved that, come what might, he would emancipate his intended wife from a life of such slavery, and so, having carefully arranged his business and purchased a neat little cottage in Cadieux street, he urged Miss Ryland to consent to marry him without delay, and so avoid her life of thraldom.[3]

They married, but three years passed and the couple was still childless. As Charlotte Furher noted in her memoirs, her suspicions were confirmed that Esther Ryland's waged employment had left her barren. Then suddenly Mr. Quintin called on Charlotte Fuhrer to engage her midwifery services for his wife. When Charlotte Fuhrer met with her, Esther Ryland Quintin broke down:

To my great surprise, she burst into tears, and confessed that she was not *enceinte* [pregnant], or likely ever to become so; that her career in M——'s store, and continued standing for hours together, had rendered her physically unable ever to become a mother.[4]

Mrs. Quintin had been deceiving her husband by feigning pregnancy. She intended to obtain an infant from an unwed mother and pass it off as her own. Charlotte Fuhrer put the deception down to a body and mind ravaged by disease, and refused to become involved. But Esther Ryland

"Her Day of Rest (The Song of the Shop Girl),"
from *Punch*, 8 April 1893.

Quintin would carry off her plan without Charlotte Fuhrer's assistance.

Although the midwife was unsympathetic with Esther Ryland Quintin's reproductive trickery, she was adamant about her opposition to the typical working conditions of shop-clerks. "Dozens of these poor creatures stand day after day," she wrote, "from morn till night, without a moment's rest except at mealtimes; even then the short period allowed them barely suffices to permit of a hasty meal, when they have to hurry back again to undergo another term of misery. A bruise or a blow may be brutal and severe, yet neither is so hurtful, so systematically cruel, as the forcing young girls to stand erect for lengthened periods, without change of posture."[5]

The contention that women were somehow less capable of standing than men was common. In 1875, Dr. Ely Van der Warker of Maine had written on this, in what is perhaps one of the most delightful medical opinions ever recorded:

Woman is badly constructed for the purposes of standing eight or ten hours upon her feet. I do not intend to bring into evidence the peculiar position and nature of the organs contained in the pelvis, but to call attention to the peculiar construction of the knee and the shallowness of the pelvis, and the delicate nature of the foot as part of a sustaining column. *The knee joint of woman is a sexual characteristic.* Viewed in front and extended, the joint in but a slight degree interrupts the gradual taper of the thigh into the leg. Viewed in a semi-flexed position, the joint forms a smooth ovate spheroid. The reason of this lies in the smallness of the patella in front, and the narrowness of the articular surfaces of the tibia and femur, which in man form the lateral prominences, and this is much more perfect as a sustaining column than that of a woman.

The Ontario Bureau of Industries also noted in its annual report in 1885 that women workers were subject to "fainting spells and spasms," apparently as a direct result of prolonged standing.[6]

Midwife Charlotte Fuhrer's concerns were primarily about health and her proposed solution the provision of seating: "Were shopgirls provided with even the commonest of seats, untold numbers of crimes and diseases would be heard of no more." The means of ensuring these reforms lay with the legislature. Charlotte Fuhrer speculated that "if the members of the House of Commons were deprived of their seats even for one session, we would, without further ado, have a Bill enacted making it criminal for shopkeepers to make slaves of their employees, or individuals to patronize such establishments." She would base her pleas on this "story of the frail shopgirl, who from being young and handsome, and the belle of her circle of acquaintances, became a wretched and deceitful woman, diseased both in body and mind, and finally sank into a premature grave."[7]

Charlotte Fuhrer's Montreal, then the acknowledged commercial capital of Canada and rapidly industrializing, was quickly developing a reputation as a consumer's paradise. Department stores boasting dry goods, home furnishings, clothing, sporting goods, housewares, toys, and books sprang up to replace rural general stores and urban specialty shops in the late nineteenth century, revolutionizing the buying habits of middle-class women. A one-price system (subject to sales) replaced the old practice of haggling over the cost of merchandise. Goods were no longer sold on credit, and a new policy of refunds for unsatisfactory produce was inaugurated. Most important, the new department stores provided employment for working-class women. There were some male salesclerks as well, but they worked in the "heavier" departments such as carpets and household furnishings. The women, who were invariably paid less than the men, sold gloves, hosiery, laces, buttons, fancy goods, and ribbons.[8]

Shop-clerking was a job of preference for many young women. Domestic work was believed to be inferior because of its interminable hours, isolation, and close supervision. Factory work, while seen as a step above domestic labour, was considered more arduous and unhealthy. Department stores, designed to appeal to middle-class women customers, were cleaner, more pleasant places to work. The pay may have been marginally lower than for factory work, and the job was no less fatiguing for aching backs and feet, but a salesclerk commanded respect. "Maggie" in the factory became "Miss" in the store. The job offered an opportunity for social interaction, variety, and relative autonomy. The only drawback was the aura of sexuality that attached itself to shopgirls who were "too much in the public eye." As one commentator noted: "The public nature of the store, its sumptuous atmosphere, and its low wages combined … to make the transition from the counter to the bordello all too easy." But there was the opportunity to meet, date, and marry men who worked in the store, or better still, the men that might be met across the counters.[9]

Those selected for these jobs were hired for their manners, their appearance, and their acceptability to the customers. Salesclerks who dressed in a "tawdry, befangled, or eccentric fashion" or who displayed an "untidy, careless toilet" offended class-conscious customers. Department store managers were looking for white Anglo-Saxon women (Canadian-born or second- or third-generation immigrants) who had the social demeanour of their middle-class clientele. Charlotte Fuhrer's careful description of Esther Ryland was no accident. Her "grace" and "elegance of manner" were preconditions for the job. This narrowly prescribed set of manners also marked these working women out for special concern. For the social reformers, compassion was limited by class prejudice and racism. Their fears were for the reproductive capacity of the white Anglo-Saxon race.[10]

But even for this relatively privileged group, working conditions were not good. Jean Thomas Scott, an early graduate of the arts program at University College in Toronto, publicized some of the problems in her thesis, *The Conditions of Female Labour in Ontario*, in 1892. She noted that the typical rate of pay for salesclerks was three to four dollars a week, while the cost of living (rent and meals) came to roughly three dollars a week. Keeping up one's appearance required a significant cash outlay for clothing. Many paid a weekly fee of ten cents to obtain insurance, so that in case of accident or illness some money would be forthcoming. This was "barely living," Scott concluded.[11]

Shopgirls were forced to remain on their feet for as long as twelve hours a day, six days a week. Employee facilities were often spartan — some rickety benches and a table in a basement room — and breaks insufficient. Scott took issue with the short dinner break in particular: "In some cases where the girls find the evening mealtime too short to permit them to go home, they bring a 'lunch' with them and eat it at the store — a method hardly conducive to health."[12]

The night hours were also contentious. "Another objection to the custom of long hours," wrote Scott, "is that the girls have often to find their way home alone at late hours, along lonely streets." As a result, Scott urged that night work be prohibited for women. Female shop-clerks no doubt faced harassment and the possibility of sexual assault on the streets at night, but restricting women from public spaces after nightfall seems a rather punitive response.[13]

### LIZZIE MASON: THE HAGGARD FACTORY-HAND

Factory workers rarely had the leisure time to write memoirs in the nineteenth century. Novelists sometimes attempted to capture their lives in print, although depending on the class and knowledge of the author, the depiction might be accurate or woefully misleading. One of the most interesting accounts of a female factory worker comes from the popular Canadian novel *Roland Graeme: Knight*, published in Montreal and New York in 1892, by middle-class social activist Agnes Maule Machar.

In Agnes Machar's novel, Lizzie Mason works as a mill-hand at Pomeroy and Company's silk and woollen mills in the fictional manufacturing town of Minton. Lizzie Mason, although white, would have had no chance as shopgirl. Most observers found it difficult to describe her without appending the adjective "poor" before her name. Her face is sad and tired; she is a "pale, wistful girl"; her dress is shabby. Many lamented "the poor working-girl — little as there was of beauty in the pale, thin face, without any advantage of dress to make up for the defects of contour and colouring."[14]

Lizzie Mason lives with her mother, "a tired-looking woman, prematurely broken down by ceaseless toil." Their home is a "wretched hovel" owned by the mill owner, on a poor street with "dingy unattractive houses." Although "poor and shabby," middle-class reformers would have classed the family as the "deserving poor": the house is "yet clean and tidy." Lizzie Mason works in the mill at "hard, unremitting, monotonous toil for eleven, twelve, and sometimes thirteen hours a day." Although her wage is not specified, the severe mill manager, Mr. Willett, has cut the wages of nearly all the women, and none complained for fear of discharge. Some of the female mill-hands are subjected to sexual harassment by the mill owner's son, Harold Pomeroy.[15]

Working conditions appear to have been significantly more unhealthy than those faced by Esther Ryland. Under questioning by Nora Blanchard, the young, middle-class central character of the novel, Lizzie Mason reveals her situation in a "matter-of-fact, uncomplaining way":

The needs of the family had made her very anxious to earn a little more, if possible, and she had undertaken a kind of work that commanded higher wages on account of its inconvenience. It was that of spinning silk which had to be kept constantly wet by a spray of water, which, of course, kept the garments of the spinner more or less wet also.

The obvious precaution of providing a water-proof suit, for this work, had not been deemed necessary by Mr. Willett; and Lizzie could not think of affording the outlay. So she worked on all day in damp clothes, running home afterwards, as quickly as she could, to exchange them. While the mild spring weather continued, no great harm resulted; but as often happens in spring, it had become extremely raw and cold. Lizzie, leaving the overheated room in her damp clothing, had taken a chill, which in her weakened constitution had brought on an attack of pneumonia.

Lizzie Mason's pneumonia becomes so severe that she is hospitalized, and although she partly recovers, she is never well enough to go back to work. In a "settled decline," she is not expected to see another summer.[16]

Nora Blanchard is deeply moved, and can not free herself from the vision of Lizzie Mason's workplace: "of droning wheels and flashing shuttles, of long arrays of frames ... and the thought of the girls with feelings and nerves like her own, tending through so many weary hours, these senseless and relentless machines, oppressed her quick sensibilities like a nightmare." This identification with working women would have reflected the feelings of author Machar, who spent much of her life advocating measures she believed would improve the situation of working-class women. Whether Nora Blanchard (or Agnes Machar) could accurately appraise the needs of working-class women is another question.[17]

Factory working conditions were notoriously bad. Industrialization had gained momentum in the 1850s and manufactured goods proliferated to feed the new railway network that had so greatly expanded the Canadian market. By the 1880s scores of new factories using modern machinery clustered around urban centres in central Canada and the Maritimes. An increasingly distinct class of permanent wage-earners emerged around them. A limited number of industries hired women: garment industries, textile factories (cotton, wool, and silk), boot, shoe, tobacco, book-binding, and leather manufacturers, and canning plants for fish, fruit, and vegetables.

Most of the women workers were young and unmarried. (It was extremely difficult for married women to work because most families still produced a certain amount of their food and clothing at home and household work was extremely demanding.) Six days out of seven, the women had to report to the factories by 6:30 a.m. The usual workday was between ten and thirteen hours. A federal Commission of Inquiry appointed by S.L. Tilley, Minister of Finance, reported in 1882 that meal breaks were inadequate and factory-hands often had to eat at their stations for want of proper facilities. The Woman's Christian Temperance Union protested in 1897 that women who did not have lunch-rooms were "known to eat their lunch day after day in all kinds of weather as they walk up and down a back street."[18]

Lunch-rooms were not the only facilities missing from some Canadian factories. Employees needed washrooms that were clean, sanitary, and sufficient in number to accommodate the staff. According to the report of the federal commissioners, in some cases there were no washrooms at all. In others, there were an insufficient number, and these were poorly lit, badly ventilated, and ill-drained. The commissioners were appalled to find that some washrooms were being shared by workers of both sexes. In others, although separated facilities had been set up, "they lie in too close proximity and the divisions in some cases are only inch boards six feet high." The commissioners warned:

The pernicious tendency of this need not be enlarged upon by us.... The above facts in relation to the imperfect sanitary arrangements of some factories cannot be too harshly commented on, and show a callous indifference on the part of the employer toward the physical and moral interests of those under his charge.[19]

Shared washroom facilities may have resulted in intrusions upon privacy. The commissioners may also have been referring to incidents of sexual harassment, assault, or other overtures from male managers and co-workers that had occurred in these washrooms. Perhaps they were anxious about women working outside the home in a culture in which there was widespread sexual aggression against women and children. But the use of the word "moral" is troubling, and suggests that the commissioners feared that the reputation of the women was blighted. Nineteenth-century society stigmatized the female employees exposed to such working environments.

Female factory employees found themselves subjected to the same sexual taint as store clerks. Canadian journalist and social reformer Phillips Thompson pronounced the morals of the women in the textile industry as "bad, very bad. The conduct of the girls is immodest in the extreme.... I do not think there are ten virtuous girls in a hundred. A good looking girl is almost certain to fall." The federal commission reported that they had included within their mandate a search for unwed mothers, prostitutes, and other women of "unchaste" reputation in Canadian factories. These pressures caused factory managers — and other female employees — to victimize sexual transgressors even more. Where such women were revealed, they were promptly dismissed.[20]

Factory employers punished lateness, mistakes, and carelessness with fines deducted from wages. Wages, prior to deductions, varied from one dollar a week to ten dollars, or generally one-third to one-half of what male factory workers were earning. Periods of unemployment were frequent, particularly in winter. Extremes of heat and cold, along with insufficient ventilation, overcrowding, excess dust, high humidity, and lack of sanitary facilities, often made the work disagreeable and dangerous. Hazardous gearing, fly wheels, pulleys, belts, and steam-engines were often completely unguarded. According to the federal commissioners' report, women faced particular risks of injury because of their sex. "Girls in different parts of the country have had their hair caught in the shafting," it noted, "one being completely scalped and the others partially so."[21]

The manufacture of silk was a particularly difficult and unpleasant occupation. Silk worms were killed after they had spun cocoons, and workers would extract the silk by "reeling" or "spinning" it. The cocoons were soaked in tanks filled with nearly boiling water. The spinners constantly had their hands in these boilers, since the temperature of the water had to be controlled exactly. It was up to the individual worker to fire it with more coal or cool it with a bowl of cold water when necessary. The extraction of the extremely fine fibres was a delicate matter requiring concentration, skill, and dexterity. The process required a high level of humidity, so the floors were continuously doused with water and humidifiers kept the atmosphere thick with steam. Agnes Machar's graphic story about Lizzie Mason is far from improbable.[22]

### THE LEGISLATURES AND THEIR INTERVENTION

The extremely poor working conditions of industrial employees inspired a number of Canadians to call for legislation. Dr. Darby Bergin was one of the first. Born in Toronto in 1826, the son of a successful merchant family, he graduated in medicine at McGill University in 1847. Elected to Parliament as the Conservative representative from Cornwall in 1872, he held the seat with only one interruption in service until his death in 1896. His experience of treating typhoid victims among the Irish immigrant community in Cornwall, Ontario, in the early years of his medical practice left him with a profound concern for the working classes.[23]

In 1879, Dr. Bergin introduced his first bill in the House of Commons, arguing for some restrictions on child labour. In 1880, he broadened his proposal to include adult women. At this point the press noted that it disapproved in principle with comparing grown women to children. The editors of the Toronto *Globe* would accept Dr. Bergin's bill insofar as it applied to young children. But they rejected the inclusion of women: "It is of course desirable that women should not overwork themselves, but the less the state interferes between the employers of labour and those of the work people who have attained full growth and intelligence the better."[24]

The decision to tie women and children together was a strategy that deserves close examination. Both groups experienced extensive oppression. Nineteenth-century women and children shared political disenfranchisement, an inferior economic status, vulnerability to sexual and physical abuse. But Dr. Bergin did not justify his bill with reference to similarities in the political, economic, or physical status of women and children. As he pressed his legislative proposals unsuccessfully through the 1880s, the reasoning behind protecting each group would diverge significantly.

Persuaded by some of the newly developing ideas about childhood that were influencing the shape of custody law, Dr. Bergin insisted that waged work interfered with schooling and religious instruction. The proper socialization of children was essential for the future inhabitants of an urban environment that was rapidly increasing in population. Child labour should be restricted or Canada would face "a generation of ignorant children, without any education, without any knowledge of the Christian doctrines ... and so it will go on generation after generation, increasing in ignorance, increasing in degradation, increasing in everything which would be a shame to the country...."

In contrast, adult women were singled out because of potential health problems associated with their reproductive ability. Specifying the potential for damage to "internal organs," Dr. Bergin shocked the legislators by insisting that because "her conformation is entirely different from that of a man," a woman factory worker would almost certainly face "sexual weakness." He quoted from a leading American physician and public health advocate, Dr. Edward Jarvis, whose recent report to the Massachusetts Board of Health had put the matter very clearly:

Amongst the women of factory operatives, much more than among the general population ... deranged states are present, e.g., leucorrhoea, and too frequent and profuse menstruation; cases also of displacement, flexions and versions of the uterus, arising from the constant standing and the constant heat of and confinement in the mills.[25]

The genetic role of women as mothers was critical, according to the 1871 *Report of the Massachusetts Bureau of Labor Statistics*. Revealing a phobic dread of disability, the authors stated:

It is well known that like begets like, and if the parents are feeble in constitution, the children must also inevitably be feeble. Hence, among that class of people, you find many puny, sickly, partly developed children; every generation growing more and more so.

While the physicians spoke of women's health, their central concern was really with reproduction. This signified only too clearly that women's primary role was childbearing. The anxiety was over reproductive capacity, not women's health in its fullest sense. Seen from this perspective, Charlotte Fuhrer's sad tale of Esther Ryland, the shopgirl left barren by her work, reflects a preoccupation with reproductive tragedy. Women were candidates for inclusion under protective labour legislation largely because of concern about the health of their prospective fetuses. The focus of regulation was primarily fetal and the discussion not really about regulating women, but regulating children in their many guises.[26]

Despite Dr. Bergin's pleas to the federal legislators, it would be the provinces that would pass the first statutory enactments. The Ontario Liberal government of Sir Oliver Mowat seized the initiative in 1884, enacting the Ontario Factories Act with surprisingly little opposition. Child labour was prohibited. Women factory workers were restricted from working more than ten hours a day, for a total of sixty hours a week. Inspectors, appointed to enforce the act, could make a variety of exemptions limiting maximum hours "when the customs or exigencies" of the trade required. Where such exemptions were allowed, neither early morning nor late night work was an option. Women could not be employed before 6:00 a.m. or after 9:00 p.m. Employers had to give women factory workers an hour for lunch, but the lunch hour would not be counted as one of the ten hours. The inspectors were also authorized to order employers to provide separate lunch-rooms for women where necessary.[27]

Since the regulations did not significantly deviate from the general practice of the time, the new maximum hours of work were unlikely to have assisted women much. Many factories had already limited hours to sixty per week. And the exemptions would have offered ample room to those who wished to depart from the new law. The guaranteed meal breaks might have been more useful. But these could be added on top of the maximum ten-hour day. Women may have been reluctant to take meal breaks when this meant getting home from work an hour later in the day. There is some evidence that women workers were impatient with the provision, and bargained with their employers to waive their entitlement to the full meal break. Jean Scott, who exposed this situation in 1892, was displeased. Rejecting these workers' views, she wrote:

It need hardly be said that shortening the meal hour is poor economy in the way of preserving one's health. In this matter the girls themselves are not the best judges; for the majority of them would even prefer to take only a half hour at noon if by doing so they could stop work earlier in the evening.... It would be better if the law were more absolute in the matter....[28]

The regulations about washrooms were framed in mandatory language:

In every factory there shall be kept provided a sufficient number and description of privies, earth or water-closets, and urinals for the employees of such factory; such closets and urinals shall at all times be kept clean and well ventilated, and separate sets thereof shall be provided for the use of male and female employees, and shall have respectively separate approaches.

There were also several sections attempting to prevent occupational injury. Women could no longer clean mill-gearing machinery while it was in motion. A general provision stopped employers from allowing women to work in factories where their health was "likely to be permanently injured." Violators could receive fines of fifty to one hundred dollars, and three to six months in jail.[29]

There were some rather glaring exclusions from the legislation, and the groups excluded were often the ones in the most exploited situations. Agricultural labourers, certainly among the hardest worked, were not covered. Nor were domestic servants. The smaller factories and shops were expressly exempt, although the inspectors appointed to enforce the act insisted that these establishments were frequently the most dangerous and abusive. The statute granted total immunity to the family workshop where none but the owner's kin were employed. In some cases families contracted to do piecework from their home, and women and children would work without recess far into the night. Despite calls for a system of "family permits" that would allow inspection of these work sites, legislators adamantly refused to "intrude" into the private home.[30]

Even for the sectors that fell under the act, enforcement was anything but efficient. It was not uncommon to have years of delay before inspectors were appointed to enforce the act, and the number of inspectors was never sufficient to the task. Fines were negligible and prosecutions were few, with inspectors preferring to use persuasion rather than coercive measures. By 1900 only thirty-five charges had been laid, four of which were against parents for allowing underage children to work. The bulk of the rest were violations of the maximum hours of work in bake shops. Only eighteen convictions were obtained, and the highest fine recorded was twenty-five dollars. Most violations escaped detection entirely.[31]

There was some speculation that female workers were reluctant to confide in male inspectors. Jean Scott, a strong advocate of gender specialization, claimed: "There is not the slightest doubt that in matters where women and children are concerned, a woman will gain the confidence of her sex far sooner than a man, even in seeking general information." In response to concerted lobbying by the various branches of the National Council of Women, female inspectors were grudgingly appointed. Margaret Carlisle was named first in Ontario in 1895, and in 1896 two additional women took on inspectorships in Quebec.[32]

Margaret Carlisle was a native of Glasgow, Scotland, where she had considerable experience as an employee of a large manufacturing enterprise. After immigrating to Canada, she had worked for a manufacturing establishment for five years, and then gone into business for herself. An active suffragist, she was described as "an intelligent, active Christian woman, who will bring to the duties of her office strength of character, good judgment, sound discretion and a sympathetic disposition." Despite covering so much ground in her first year that she made her male colleagues "look like slackers" by comparison, Margaret Carlisle was paid half as much as the male inspectors.[33]

But Carlisle did not make any more use of prosecution than did the male inspectors. In her first annual report, for instance, she recorded only one prosecution. A Mr. E.M. Moffatt, manager of the Parisian Steam Laundry, 67 Adelaide Street West in Toronto, had been charged with violating the law for keeping females more than sixty hours in one week. He had pleaded guilty, and paid his fine. Carlisle reported that "time, tact and patience" would no doubt reduce the need for active enforcement. "As the law becomes better understood, the work will become less difficult," she added hopefully.[34]

Despite its shortcomings, the Ontario experiment was only the first in a series of provincial government initiatives in the area of protective labour legislation. The Conservative government of John Jones Ross in the province of Quebec was second, enacting the Quebec Factories Act in 1885. The Quebec provisions on women were almost identical to the Ontario provisions, but Quebec was more stringent in the matter of penalties. Employers could be subject to fines of two hundred dollars and up to twelve months in jail for violating certain provisions.[35]

The Maritime provinces, with their smaller industrial base and correspondingly fewer working women, did not pass similar legislation. Despite the obvious deficiencies of the Ontario and Quebec statutes, there is some evidence that eastern women felt short-changed by the refusal of their legislatures to act. Annie Marion MacLean, a graduate of Acadia College who went on to obtain her Ph.D. at the University of Chicago, was one who expressed some concern. Long interested in the conditions of women's waged labour, she had conducted some undercover investigation of women's work in several Chicago department stores while completing her Ph.D. After this she returned to Canada to serve on the staff of the Royal Victoria College for Women in Montreal. In an article in the *American Journal of Sociology* in 1899, she argued that although the number of female employees in Maritime manufacturing industries was small, estimated to be 7,191 in Nova Scotia and 5,318 in New Brunswick, "each represents a present or a future home." She reconciled herself to the absence of legislation, however, by noting that by and large the employers generally adhered to the ten-hour day, sixty-hour work week voluntarily. This MacLean attributed to their living in "small towns where public sentiment would not permit the imposition of inhuman tasks."[36]

Other Maritime women thought more should be done. Agnes Dennis, president of the Halifax Local Council of Women and a woman deeply involved in Nova Scotia organizations such as the Victorian Order of Nurses, the Children's Aid Society, and the Nova Scotia League for the Protection of the Feeble-Minded, represented Halifax at the 1897 annual meeting of the National Council of Women of Canada. At the meeting she was unequivocal in her dissatisfaction with the legislative vacuum:

I only wish that the Ontario law could have been able to apply to the whole Dominion. If it is good for the women of Ontario, it is good for the women of ... the Maritime Provinces. We have not as many factories or as many employees, but three women have as much right to be protected by law as three hundred. Here we have no Factory Act and no limit to the number of hours which women or children may be required to work if they will do so, and factories may be badly ventilated, the sanitary arrangements very poor, and accommodations very meagre.

Agnes Dennis called for Maritime legislation that would exceed the stipulations found in central Canada. She wanted the maximum hours of work for women to be set at fifty-four per week. Her demands were ignored.[37]

As industrialization edged westward, Manitoba became the third and last province to enact a Factories Act in 1900. In a turn-of-the-century gesture, the Conservative government of Rodmond P. Roblin showed off with the most progressive legislation yet. The maximum hours of work for women were reduced to eight hours a day, forty-eight hours a week. Inspectors could make the usual array of exemptions, but where they did, they had to ensure women a forty-five-minute evening meal break between 5:00 and 8:00 p.m.[38]

Factories were not the only work sites subjected to the new laws. Both Ontario and Manitoba enacted a Shops Regulation Act in 1888. Maximum hours and specified mealtimes were set for children working in retail or wholesale shops. But the protection extended to women was more selective. Esther Ryland's fertility problems had finally registered with the legislators. Charlotte Fuhrer's call for seating had been heeded. The politicians were unequivocal, requiring that employers:

shall at all times provide and keep therein a sufficient and suitable seat or chair for the use of every such female, and shall permit her to use such seat or chair when not necessarily engaged in the work or duty for which she is employed in such shop.

Violators were subject to fines of twenty dollars or one month in prison.[39]

Although the legislation insisted upon the provision of seats, there was no affirmative obligation to give the employees an opportunity to sit on them. One of the members of the National Council of Women of Canada noted the irony at the 1894 meeting: "I am told that large mercantile houses in Ottawa, with 100 to 150 employees, are not inspected, and the girls have told me that they dare not make any complaints because they would lose their positions. Seats are provided because the law demands it, but the girls told me that they dare not be found sitting if the proprietor comes round." Jean Scott reported that the "seat" problem was not confined to salesclerks in Ottawa:

Th[e] provision is, to a large extent, a dead letter. In Toronto occasionally some attempt is made at enforcement, but it is neither general nor continuous. One great objection employers seem to have to allowing girls in stores to sit down when they are not actively engaged is, that it gives the appearance of dullness of trade; and many will give a girl work to do to keep her employed when she is not serving.[40]

The Ontario legislators also seem to have been doubtful about the efficacy of this measure, and in 1897 they amended the act to add:

Nor shall any employer or occupier by any open or covert threat, rule, or other intimation, expressed or implied, or by any contrivance, prevent any such female employee using such seat or chair as aforesaid.

Contraveners were liable to a maximum fine of twenty-five dollars (with a minimum fine set at ten dollars). In default of payment, violators were to serve a minimum of one month in jail.[41]

These amendments would not achieve their goal. Margaret Carlisle reported on the situation of one particularly obstinate retailer who adamantly refused to provide seats. According to Carlisle, he declared "he would dismiss all the women he employed rather than put in seats; that he had enough to keep them busy without leaving them any time for sitting; that there was no room for seats behind the counter, and that his girls did not want seats." Inspector Carlisle stood firm. After two weeks her resolve won out and seats were provided. Yet Carlisle could not be certain that the provision of seats meant much. "Whether the employees are allowed to use their seats is another question," she conceded in her annual report.[42]

REACTION WITHIN THE WOMEN'S COMMUNITY

There is little record of what women workers thought of the legislation. Some could not read and few had the luxury of time to express their views. Working-class women seem to have been reluctant to offer their opinions even after the federal government set up a Royal Commission on the Relations of Labour and Capital in the years 1886 to 1889. Of the close to 1,800 witnesses that appeared at the hearings held across the country, only 102 were women. Forty-three of these were too frightened to reveal their names. The women workers' main interest appeared to be higher wages. On the question of hours, women testified that in Ontario they generally worked a nine-hour day, in Quebec a ten-hour day, and in the Maritimes an eleven-hour day. There were no calls for restrictions on hours of work. Women workers made no explicit comment on labour legislation at all.[43]

But as the legislatures expanded their regulatory control of women's waged work, they did so against a backdrop of heated debate among middle-class women. Two of the main protagonists were author Agnes Maule Machar and Professor Carrie Matilda Derick. Agnes Maule Machar was one of the most powerful campaigners for protective labour legislation for women in the nineteenth century. Carrie Matilda Derick, demonstrator and lecturer in botany at McGill University in Montreal, was one of her strongest opponents.

Agnes Machar was born in 1837, one of two children of Reverend John Machar and Mrs. Machar, of Sydenham Street in Kingston, themselves both descendants of a long line of Scottish ministers. Her mother was a tireless activist in women's philanthropic work and Directress of the Kingston's Orphan Home from 1859 to 1882. Historians seem to have taken little note of her and none have troubled themselves to record her full name. There are no gaps in the records on the Reverend John Machar, a founder and the second principal of Queen's College from 1846 to 1854. His often remarked-upon compassion for the poorer classes may have arisen from his work among the immigrants who passed through Kingston travelling west, many of whom became victims of the cholera epidemics. Reverend Machar believed firmly in education for women, and supervised his intellectually gifted daughter's extensive studies at home. Agnes Machar's religious upbringing found its force in a socially oriented Christianity, activated by missionary zeal. From an early age, she had been almost single-handedly responsible for maintaining the Presbyterian Church's interest in an orphan and children's mission in India.[44]

The family was well-to-do, and in addition to the Sydenham residence, they maintained a beautiful summer home, "Ferncliff," just west of Gananoque and overlooking the St. Lawrence. Agnes Machar's circle included the families of Sir John A. Macdonald and Oliver Mowat — people who would prove useful in her legislative lobbying. She wrote prodigiously from childhood, originally anonymously and eventually as a widely acclaimed professional author. She never married, and upon the death of her parents she went to live with her brother, J. Maule Machar, QC, a barrister who was the Master of Chancery in Kingston and a lecturer in law at Queen's. He too was known as a social reformer, actively concerned about the "welfare of the masses."[45]

One of Canada's nineteenth-century literary heroines, Agnes Machar has been described as "the quaintest and tiniest of women, with round face and bright bird-like eyes; a woman whose manner was at once firm and gentle, gracious and dignified." Her poems, articles, and books were widely published in Canada and the United States throughout the 1870s, 1880s, and 1890s, and she was often singled out as one of Canada's foremost authors. In *Roland Graeme*, with its heart-rending account of Lizzie Mason's demise, she turned her talents as a literary crusader upon the evils of industrialization and the squalid life of the working poor.[46]

Agnes Machar had never worked in a factory or clerked in a shop and drew her analysis from rather sporadic contacts with working-class women in Kingston. In the early 1890s, Agnes Machar had organized a branch of the Young Women's Christian Association. Her goal was to provide educational and recreational facilities for young working women in her city. She set up a series of evening lectures, but concluded the

Agnes Maule Machar.

venture was "utterly impossible" due to minimal attendance. She attributed the poor turnout to long hours and strenuous working conditions: "The effect of those long, exhausting hours of work was such as to make them so utterly wearied out in body and mind that by the evening they were unfit for any mental exertion, and seemed indisposed to do anything except rest or lounge or perhaps take some form of amusement which did not require any exertion."[47]

Machar's experience found its way into her novel. Nora Blanchard, the middle-class heroine, also attempts to start a club for working girls, "a place where they could spend the evenings when they chose, where they could have books or music, or anything else they liked." When Nora Blanchard consults with Lizzie Mason about the project, Lizzie Mason "listened without brightening very perceptibly." "It's very kind indeed, Miss Blanchard," she replied, "and I'm sure we'll be glad to come. But I'm afraid you'll be disappointed if you expect the girls to go there a great deal. You see, we're so tired out, often, we don't care to go anywheres, and them as do, likes to go to something lively."[48]

A desire for leisure activities with more flair may have deterred working-class women from patronizing Agnes Machar's lectures. But another nineteenth-century Canadian novelist, Maritimer Maria Amelia Fytche, seems to have better understood the lack of interest. In her 1895 novel *Kerchiefs to Hunt Souls*, Fytche's heroine, Nova Scotian Dorothy Pembroke, converses with Alice, an out-of-work English governess, about parties put on by philanthropic ladies of the Girls' Friendly Lodges. Alice is scathing:

Parties! We are asked to put on our best toggery and sit around a room like children, to be entertained by some swells who have "kindly volunteered their services." Grim amusement it is, and the only fun I find in it is when the entertainers get taken down a peg, which is not an unusual occurrence, I am happy to say. Such people mostly make fools of themselves when they play at being benevolent. The poor all see through it, and know it is only to amuse themselves they do it. Sometimes they want to see life, so visit the prisons and homes and other institutions; sometimes they go in for sisterhoods, or even do what they call "slumming it"; but it is always in the way of amusement to kill time.[49]

Agnes Machar stood firm in her interpretation. If she could improve upon the overly strenuous working conditions, she felt certain that working-class women would flock to self-improvement lectures. An early and energetic member of the Kingston Local Council of Women (established in 1894), she represented her chapter at the annual meetings of the National

Council of Women of Canada in 1895 and 1896. There she focused on hours of work for female employees, bolstering her case by claiming that a shortened working day was sought by women workers themselves:

I also came in contact with a number of the girls themselves and knew their own feeling in the matter.... The girls themselves felt it a grievous burden in most cases. There were some strong ones who did not, but I did not meet with one case in which the girl would not have gladly submitted to a decrease of pay if they had a decrease of hours, if that was to be obtained by opening at seven instead of half past six.[50]

Carrie Matilda Derick's background differed somewhat from Agnes Machar's, and the two women's perceptions about the best interests of working-class women diverged greatly. Born in 1862 in Clarenceville, in the Eastern Townships of Quebec, her parents were Frederick Derick, a descendant of a white, United Empire Loyalist family, and Edna Colton, a well-to-do white American. Carrie Derick showed academic distinction early, winning the Prince of Wales Medal at the McGill Normal School, and going on to study botany at McGill University in 1887.

The barriers that had denied Emily Stowe a university education had begun to fall, and Carrie Derick was one of the first generation of women students at McGill. They were never allowed to forget that their position was precarious. "We walked very warily," was how one early female student characterized the experience. Great care was taken to ensure that there would be little mingling of male and female students. The usual practice of the botany instructors, for instance, was to split the class into two, with one professor taking the young men up Mount Royal in search of plant specimens, while another would lead the women off in a different direction.[51]

At social gatherings held at the home of Principal J. William Dawson, great care was taken that the women were "precluded" from "dangerous contact" with male students. The women students assumed that the strict chaperonage was for their protection, until one day Carrie Derick had a conversation with Lady Margaret Mercer Dawson, the principal's wife, who expressed her concern that love affairs might arise between men and women who shared the same classes. Carrie Derick tried to reassure her hostess, advising her that there was little risk of romance because women tended to mature earlier than men and would be unlikely to fall in love with students their own age. She was crushed by Lady Dawson's retort: "I was not thinking of the young women, but of our sons."[52]

Despite differential treatment, Derick obtained first-class honours in natural science. Her 94 per cent average gave her first-place standing in the university and she was awarded the Logan Gold Medal in 1890. She received her initial appointment as a Demonstrator in Botany at McGill in 1891. The position of "demonstrator" was a low rank often reserved for women seeking to teach in the universities. She continued graduate research, receiving her Master of Arts in 1896, became a Lecturer in 1895, Assistant Professor of Evolution and Genetics in 1904, and in 1912, Full Professor of Comparative Botany, the first woman to achieve such a position in Canada.

Her research took her to Harvard, the University of Berlin, the University of Munich, the University of Bonn, and the Royal College of Science in London, England. Carrie Derick's brilliant academic distinction was widely acclaimed, and she was later elected a Fellow of the Botanical Society of America and a member of the American Association for the Advancement of Science. She participated extensively in women's organizations: the Montreal Women's Club, the McGill Women's Alumnae, the National Equal Franchise Union, the Montreal Suffrage Association, and the Montreal Local Council of Women.[53]

Carrie Derick's attempts to establish connections with working-class women were slightly more practical and much more successful than Agnes Machar's work with the YWCA. She was a driving force behind the founding of the Working Girls' Club and Lunch Room in Montreal in 1891. From a location at 84 and 86 Bleury Street, she organized a small band of McGill alumnae to serve as volunteers providing low-cost meals to working women. Not surprisingly, tired and impoverished factory workers came for hot meals with an eagerness they would never have shown toward Agnes Machar's evening lectures. The menu was filling, if not inspired: vegetable soup, bread, roast beef, potatoes, mashed turnips, baked beans, apple pudding, stewed prunes, tea, coffee, and milk. Attendance grew from forty a day to an average of 115 women per sitting in 1899, when the alumnae served 40,936 dinners. The Club expanded to include a library, a music and sitting room, and limited residential quarters. The lunch-room continued for almost twenty years.[54]

Tenacious and articulate, Carrie Derick strongly opposed legislation that would single women out for protection. Concerned that protective labour legislation would have severely deleterious consequences for working women, Carrie Derick took her views to the Montreal Local Council of Women. The Montreal Council was a unique body, having since its establishment in 1893 maintained a careful coalition of

Carrie Matilda Derick.

anglophone and francophone women. Carrie Derick convinced its membership to adopt her perspective, and she was delegated to represent them at the national conference. Also appearing for the Montreal Council was Lady Julia Drummond, wife of Senator G.A. Drummond, the President of the Bank of Montreal. The two Montreal women took issue with Agnes Machar's Kingston group and argued that protective labour legislation would worsen women's already-inferior working conditions.[55]

Carrie Derick claimed that women who worked fewer hours would take home lower wages. No one was calling for a minimum wage, and it was obvious that without some protection against wage reduction, restrictions on hours would threaten income. Lady Drummond argued that "hardship comes oftener from slack work than from overwork. In most trades there is a slack season and a busy season, and as in the majority of factories women are paid by the piece, it is difficult to see how they can live at all unless short hours and small pay at one season are adjusted by long hours and good pay at another."[56]

Protective labour legislation did not touch the question of wages. Everyone seemed to be well aware that women's earnings were significantly lower than men's (variously estimated at one-third to one-half less), and numbers of people, including Carrie Derick, were beginning to call for equal pay for equal work. Yet neither the proponents nor opponents of protective laws for women incorporated equal pay for equal work into their *legislative* demands, and none of the nineteenth-century statutes ever addressed it. No one used the argument of women's weakness and special needs to suggest that they should be compensated at a higher rate than men. And the concept of paid maternity leave was incomprehensible. Reforms such as equal pay and minimum wage legislation would not appear until well into the twentieth century.[57]

Agnes Machar listened to Carrie Derick's forecasts of worsened working conditions and retorted that it was precisely because of the exploitation in the labour market that women needed protective legislation. Like children, women deserved to be differentiated from men, at least temporarily, because women's working conditions were harsher:

[I]t is on the *weakest and most helpless* workers, — the women and children, — that the heaviest burden rests — the burden of the longest hours, the smallest pay, the harshest and most unreasonable exactions — simply because they are the most helpless and uncomplaining.[58]

Agnes Machar was correct. In 1884 the Ontario Bureau of Industries had conducted a study comparing male and female hours and wages. Their findings pegged the average annual wage for men at $394.34 for an average work week of 59.05 hours. The average annual wage for women was $133.09 for a work week of 59.47 hours. Furthermore, working conditions were considerably different. Machar's reference to "unreasonable exactions" encompassed fines, which she claimed were often deducted from wages for some small breach of the rules, in some cases for laughing or speaking to a fellow employee, or because of the petty spite of the overseer. Women and children were singled out for these injustices:

[F]ines are only imposed upon women and children, the most helpless class of operatives. Men will not put up with deductions from wages which they have toiled hard to obtain, and therefore the system is not applied to them.[59]

In response, Carrie Derick insisted that special privileges would ultimately mean employers would replace women with male employees, relegating women to "extreme poverty, or even to vagrancy and crime." Gender-specific legislation would seriously compromise women's ability to compete with men for equal job opportunities. Agnes Machar countered by insisting that men and women were not actively competing for the same jobs anyway, given the marked separation of the sexes in the workplace. "Very few men would consent to work for the year round at anything approaching the average pay of women ... at these mills, even if fitted for the work. There is little fear, then, of the latter being in any circumstance displaced by men...." The segregation of the work force was so complete that restrictive legislation would have had little competitive force.[60]

One obvious alternative to protective legislation was to foster collective action on the part of women workers themselves. Men had more control over their working environment, in part because some had organized unions. That few women belonged to trade unions in nineteenth-century Canada is undeniable. The reasons are more elusive. According to Jean Scott, it was because of the temporariness of their attachment to the labour market. As a consequence, women had yet to formulate that "class spirit" that was necessary to organization. Presumably the young women who worked in the factories and shops only for a few years before marriage found it difficult to forge strong, long-term ties with labour unions. Another probable reason was that most male-dominated trade unions were disinterested in, or hostile to, the inclusion of women.[61]

Agnes Machar was not adverse to the benefits of unionization, but believed the prospects of extensive success from this quarter were slim. "Men," she argued "have a capacity for organization which is entirely wanting in most girls, who can be intimidated with very little trouble." The difficulties of collective action were considerable, and the benefits from government initiative more valuable:

If we throw the burden of this on organization of the female workers for their own protection, we are proposing for them all the hardships of strikes and lock-outs, hard enough for men, but well nigh impossible for timid and inexperienced girls. I understand that a number of young women in a Union in Montreal, who "struck" against a reduction twelve months ago, have been "locked out" ever since, without employment.... But what these workers cannot do for themselves without hardship and suffering, the influential woman of Canada can do for them by urging the legislation needed to reform the system under which they work.[62]

In an odd combination of altruism and arrogance, Agnes Machar raised legitimate arguments about the barriers facing women's unionization, but not all waged women would have welcomed her designation of them as "timid and inexperienced." Some years earlier one anonymous woman had urged working-class women to organize collectively rather than to rely upon the campaigns of middle-class reformers. Writing in the *Palladium of Labor*, published in Hamilton in 1885, she had issued an open letter to "working girls." It warned against relying upon "high-born" sisters who were ignorant or forgetful of women workers' conditions and needs. "Sisters, by our dignity, co-operation, and organization, we must protect ourselves," she concluded.[63]

However, the predominantly male trade unions were frequently less than hospitable to the working-class women who sought membership. Male workers were beginning to lend their voices in support of protective labour legislation for women. By 1898, the Toronto Trades and Labour Congress, the largest grouping of organized labour in Canada, would declare its support for the "abolition ... of female labour in all branches of industrial life such as mines, factories, workshops etc." Lady Drummond was less than sanguine about the reasons for trade union support, and argued that this in itself ought to cause working women to oppose the new laws. "To protect themselves against competition is the primary motive," she declared. Protective labour legislation attracted men because it restricted women's ability to compete while at the same time saving unions from the expensive and difficult task of organizing women.[64]

Agnes Machar also founded her claim for protective legislation upon an extensive litany of health and medical concerns. First, she argued that the harshness of industrial life was too much for the delicate physical stamina of women. "The long continuous hours of work — the nervous strain of standing or walking for so many hours, tending perpetually moving machines" was intolerable:

Can we wonder that their physical health often suffers, and that anaemic conditions result, predisposing them to bronchitis, pneumonia, and heart-failure, and too often leading to an eventual collapse?

Lizzie Mason's pneumonia, fictional though it was, preyed on Machar's mind.[65]

Agnes Machar pleaded not only for the health of the women workers themselves, but also for their future progeny. Casting women's maternal role as critical was problematic, and not only because Machar, a spinster herself, was childless. Women have always resented being assigned value primarily because of their reproductive abilities. Furthermore, her goal was disrespectful of disabled people. "For the sake of Canada, as well as for the girls," Agnes Machar pleaded,

if the mothers of our coming generation are to begin enfeebled, what can we expect the coming generation to be? [I]n order to have the kind of mothers we want for the coming generation — strong in body and strong in mind — we should have a change of system that would make our Canadian people stronger and better fitted to cope with the new conditions of life in the new century to which we are all looking forward with so much hope.[66]

Coupled with the reproductive argument was the concern that working wives and mothers were not able to attend to their domestic responsibilities, and thus could not provide a proper home-life for their offspring. The point was not that women were doing work other than child care. Women had always done so, especially before industrialization had moved so much production away from the home. It was rather that in the home women had combined their productive work with child care. In the factories this was virtually impossible. The campaign to reduce women's paid hours of work was not premised on women's need for rest and leisure. Every hour spared from working in factories was intended to facilitate longer labour, without pay, in the home.[67]

Carrie Derick did not counter these offensive arguments. She did not refute Agnes Machar's position on women's physical fragility, nor her views on the responsibility of women as wives and mothers of the coming generation. She may have believed much of what Agnes Machar and her allies alleged. Carrie Derick's position was based on a quite different tack, equally offensive to our ears. Drawing upon her professional knowledge of biology and genetics, Professor Derick had become a vocal proponent of the eugenics movement. The new eugenics craze advocated Social Darwinism. The struggle for human existence was to be unimpeded, so that the truly fittest would survive. The campaign for protective legislation would only slow the inevitable by coddling the weak of the species. Carrie Derick would later advocate the segregation and sterilization of the "feeble-minded," along with restrictive immigration policies, as the only real guarantee for "race purity." Measures designed to protect factory workers would not have won support from someone seeking "survival of the fittest."[68]

Although the eugenics movement was incompatible with egalitarian principles, Carrie Derick believed herself a sincere advocate of equality. She wove her strongest arguments against protective labour laws in the language of equality:

Women have for years been contending for equality of opportunity with men, they have asserted their right to work side by side with them, and are now demanding equal pay for equal work. Is it not most inconsistent to proclaim the equality of women with men and their right to compete with them, and at the same time ask that special privileges be accorded them on account of inability to bear the same burdens?

Lady Drummond used the language of discrimination to make the same point: "We believe that such further discrimination as is hereby proposed would lend countenance to the popular assumption of an inferiority that does not exist." It was degrading and paternalistic to perpetuate the idea that women as a class needed the same protection as children.[69]

Agnes Machar found this argument profoundly disturbing. In direct response to Derick and Drummond's attack, Machar interrupted the proceedings to respond:

I should like to point out that, instead of asking for special privileges for women, we are asking that the heavy end of the burden should be lifted off those least able to bear it. The longest hours per day prevail in the factories where women chiefly are employed, — those places in which men alone are employed seldom having more than a ten hour day, while many of them have the Saturday half holiday. The amendments only aim at having that done in all cases which is now done only in some, so that there might be no discrimination and one rule for all.[70]

This marvellous exchange pointed at the heart of the problem. The concept of equality was complex. Should one campaign to eliminate discrimination by rigidly insisting that men and women be treated exactly the same? Was equality rooted in "gender-neutral" analysis? Carrie Derick believed that women should be able to compete with men on the same basis for jobs, sharing the same working conditions as men did. Otherwise women would find their work choices limited and their status demeaned. Agnes Machar, on the contrary, thought the gender-neutral analysis completely artificial. Women should not be forced to compete against a male standard that failed to take into account women's greater exploitation in the work force. Given the different working regimes, Agnes Machar had a point. Yet Carrie Derick's concern about the immediate loss of pay and job opportunities that might follow such legislation, and the long-term symbolic importance of ghettoization, were valid objections. Without minimum wage laws or prohibitions on sex discrimination in hiring, protective labour legislation held much danger.

There was no right answer to this protracted and intricate debate. The dilemma still haunts the women's movement, with little resolution in sight. The disagreement between Agnes Machar and Carrie Derick represents a fundamental sticking point for large numbers of women who held and continue to hold different perspectives. Agnes Machar was a pessimist. Having chosen a fairly conventional, white, middle-class female occupation as an author, she was trying as much as possible to protect women in the labour market as it was. Carrie Derick was an optimist. She had stormed the male bastion of the university in triumph. She urged women to establish themselves independently in farming, and called for access to all professional schools. Carrie Derick's position on protective labour legislation was derived from a vision of the labour market as it might be, taking the independent, professional woman as a model. Blinking at existing discrimination, she wanted to ensure women the widest opportunities possible in the world of the future.[71]

## WOULD-BE MINERS, BARMAIDS,
### AND PAPER-GIRLS: EXCLUSIONARY LEGISLATION

Regulatory legislation may or may not have been harmful or helpful to working-class women. There was no such dilemma about prohibitive or exclusionary labour statutes enacted in the nineteenth century. These specifically excluded women from a variety of occupations. Mines were the largest industry in this category.

Mining was a thriving enterprise in nineteenth-century Nova Scotia, Ontario, and British Columbia. Working conditions were harsh, labour intensive, dirty, and dangerous. We do not yet know whether many women worked in the mines — below ground or at the surface — but if the working situation in England was duplicated in Canada, they may have been present in small numbers, hauling out coal and other ore from the pit bottom and performing a variety of jobs above ground.[72]

The publication of a report of the Children's Employment Commission, which related scandalous working conditions of women in the mines, had caused a national furor in England in the 1840s. Hours were long, sometimes approaching eighteen a day. Women hauled out coal along low, cramped, damp spaces. Some wore harnesses of iron chains with leather belts running between their legs as they pulled tubs along the pit floor, while others pushed trams uphill. Deformed spines and swollen legs and shockingly high accident rates were occupational hazards. One could be forgiven for assuming that the harshness of working conditions would form the rationale for excluding women.[73]

Instead, femininity and morality were the chief rallying cries. The English Commission saved its most scathing critique for the attire of the female miners. In the hot and cramped atmosphere, some of the women "worked naked to the waist." Furthermore, below the waist many of the women wore trousers. Frantic recriminations followed, as commentators insisted that pants would de-sex women, rendering them coarse, unfeminine, and indecent. Although fashionable women were wearing low bodices in the drawing room and actresses short skirts on the stage, mining women were singled out for vilification. They were women who:

wore a dress more than half masculine, and who talked loudly and discordantly, and some of whom, God knows, had faces as hard and as brutal as the hardest of their collier brothers and husbands and sweethearts.[74]

In speedy response the English Parliament passed the Mines and Collieries Act in 1842, prohibiting women and girls from underground employment in the mines. In 1872, the hours of women working above ground were restricted: night work was prohibited, and women were not allowed to work on Sundays or after 2:00 p.m. on Saturdays. Specific meal breaks were set out as well. Numbers of women were apparently forced out of work by the statute, although others managed to elude inspectors. In some cases, female miners were so eager to continue their work that they agreed to have specified amounts deducted from their wages as a pool to cover fines should they be caught.[75]

There were no similar public exposés in Canada, but there was great interest in repeating the English reforms. British Columbia legislators abolished women's labour underground in their coal mines in 1877 and duplicated the English restrictions on hours and meal breaks for women employed above ground. Owners, managers, and their agents obtained a broadly worded defence, having only to prove that they had "taken all reasonable means by publishing and to the best of [their] power enforcing the provisions of this Act to prevent ... contravention or non-compliance." Fines up to one hundred dollars could be ordered for violations. In 1890 racist legislators added Chinese men to the prohibited groups, and in 1899 the Japanese. These provisions were extended to metalliferous mines as well in 1897.[76]

Ontario waited until 1890 to bar women from mines, but it went further than banning underground work. The statute stipulated that "no girl or woman shall be employed at mining work or allowed to be for the purpose of employment at mining work in or about any mine," rendering both underground and surface work off-limits. The legislation covered all mines where there were at least seven employees, except stone quarries. Owners, managers, and their agents were given the same "all reasonable means" defence found in British Columbia, but fines were set at a maximum of fifty dollars. Although Nova Scotia, whose coal mines had the worst record on the continent for major mining accidents, passed various other mining regulations, there was no attempt to bar women from mines until the middle of the twentieth century.[77]

Waitressing also became restricted. The specific concern was the serving of liquor. American legislators led the way, with Indiana passing a statute in the early 1870s barring everyone except "white males" from becoming licensed bartenders. In 1881 California denied women the right to work in any place selling alcoholic beverages, and Ohio and Washington enacted similar provisions. The stated rationale was the "preservation of morality." Selling liquor might expose women to lewd men and threaten their innocence.[78]

Members of the Woman's Christian Temperance Union, active in fighting wife and child abuse, took up the campaign against women working in bars in Canada. Along with its attack on alcohol, tobacco, gambling, and prostitution, the WCTU called for an elimination of the job of "barmaid." Manitoba was the only province to act, and in 1886 Manitoba women were prohibited from selling or delivering liquor to any guest or customer in any restaurant, tavern, or hotel. Service in the dining room, however, was permitted. Presumably customers of the class that ate in the dining room were not as fearsome as working-class drinkers. The wives and daughters of the men holding the liquor licences were also permitted to wait tables. A man's tavern was clearly as much his castle as his home.[79]

Women could hold liquor licences, and presumably this would exempt them from the waitressing ban. However, there was a pronounced reluctance to allow married women to hold licences in their own right. The 1886 Manitoba statute provided that, upon marriage, a single woman running a licensed establishment automatically transferred her licence privileges to her husband. No licence could be granted to a married woman unless she satisfied the authorities that she was the owner of the premises and that the business was "for her own use and benefit, irrespective of her husband." The barriers for married women were considerable, especially in light of the reforms to married women's property law, which was moving in the other direction. Married women could generally carry on business and own property separately from their husbands by this time, but the liquor trade was seen differently.[80]

There was something peculiar in the focus on liquor service. Restaurants, taverns, and hotels were not covered by the more general factories and shops legislation. As a result, there was no protection against excessive hours of work, prolonged standing, or occupational hazards. Presumably waitresses, working on their feet far into the night, whether they were serving liquor or not, suffered the same potential reproductive ailments as shopgirls. The narrow scope of the provisions reveals the inconsistency in the goals of the reformers.

Some municipalities also prohibited female labour. In the 1880s, Toronto City Council began to discuss licences for children who wished to peddle newspapers in the streets. John Joseph Kelso and other leaders of the "child-saving" movement were campaigning for enforced school attendance and greater recreational facilities for urban slum children. Noisy street children hawking newspapers at all times of the day or night offended their sense of decorum. Although boys held most of the news-vending jobs, there were some girls on the streets as well. In 1887 the Toronto Young Women's Christian Guild began to organize evening sewing classes for newsgirls, and "more than a score" enrolled. Over thirty turned up to attend a New Year's Eve party put on by the YWCG for female news-vendors in 1888. It was generally conceded that "the nature of their occupation expose[d] them to hardship," and that they tended to be a poorly dressed, overburdened, and weary lot. The reformers worried that these girls were particularly susceptible to sexual attack.[81]

In 1889, J.J. Kelso led a delegation from the Toronto Humane Society to Toronto City Council. He proposed a by-law to prohibit girls of any age and boys under eight from selling newspapers on street corners. There were criticisms about the proposal from the press, which depended upon children for newspaper circulation, and from families who depended upon the vendors' income. But in May of 1890 a by-law was passed, banning female news-vendors and boys under eight. The Toronto *World* noted that as of May Day, "the teasing girls who were wont to pester passers by to purchase papers found their occupation gone." The new by-law had been well publicized and the police did not anticipate any difficulties enforcing it. The older boys, continued the *World*, "said it was all the better for them." Their trade had picked up considerably. "We don't want to be bothered with the kids and the girls," they advised the reporter. "They're better at home and in school." The reporter was in-clined to share their opinion. No one interviewed the out-of-work newsgirls.[82]

The exclusionary statutes narrowed women's occupational oppor-tunities. Insofar as men were not similarly barred from well-paid women's jobs, this legislation was harmful to women. The fixation on "moral" matters is also questionable. There may have been instances of the sexual coercion of female miners, waitresses, and news-vendors. However, the isolation of this element from other matters of equal sig-nificance is disturbing. Another manifestation of the focus on women's sexuality and reproductive capacity that so tainted most discussions of protective labour legislation, it focused on women primarily as sexual objects and only secondarily as workers.

# Lawyering: Clara Brett Martin, Canada's First Woman Lawyer

"If it were not that I set out to open the way to the bar for others of my sex, I would have given up the effort long ago," announced twenty-three-year-old Clara Brett Martin on her call to the bar in Toronto, Ontario, on 2 February 1897. The first woman admitted to the profession of law in the British Commonwealth, Clara Brett Martin was the only nineteenth-century Canadian woman to challenge the all-male legal system from within.[1]

Her admission into the otherwise exclusively male domain of law was remarkable and anomalous. Throughout the nineteenth century women were forbidden to vote in provincial and federal elections, or to sit as the elected representatives for provincial legislatures or the Dominion Parliament. The laws of infanticide, abortion, and prostitution under which women were convicted and imprisoned were entirely constructed by men. The laws of seduction, rape, divorce, custody, and labour, theoretically enacted for women's protection, were male-designed. No matter how sincerely women may have lobbied for some of these statutes, they were at the mercy of men to introduce the bills, debate their significance, and enact them in a form they believed proper. The male stranglehold over the creation of law was undeniable and all-encompassing.[2]

Nor could Canadian women lend their voices or influence to the application or enforcement of the law. Not one woman sat as coroner, justice of the peace, police magistrate, or judge for the entire century. Coroner's juries and trial juries were composed solely of men. As advocates, women occasionally presented their own cases in court, arguing on their own behalf or on behalf of their husbands and families. But the female lay advocate became increasingly rare as the practice of law underwent extensive professionalization during the nineteenth century. Most women appeared in court only as witnesses, accused persons, or parties to a lawsuit.[3]

## WOMEN AND LAW: A CONTRADICTORY PROPOSITION?

Women seeking paid employment in the nineteenth century were generally relegated to the fields of domestic service, seamstressing, nursing, shop-clerking, factory work, and for women of greater means, teaching. Some women chafed at these restrictions. Those with an interest in law at times studied informally, taking advantage of the law libraries and legal expertise of male relatives. Despite their lack of formal training, Helen Gregory MacGill, who would become one of the first women juvenile court judges in 1917, and Henrietta Muir Edwards, convenor of laws for the National Council of Women of Canada, became widely acclaimed for their comprehensive knowledge of law. Others, like Ada M. Read, were diverted into law libraries. Appointed in 1886, she became the first librarian for the County of York Law Association. Still others found themselves serving as secretaries to male lawyers.[4]

Public reaction to the prospect of women practising as lawyers was highly sceptical. A journalist for the *Canadian Illustrated News*, published in Montreal in 1874, spoke scornfully:

The idea of women mingling in public affairs ... and exercising professions which necessarily banish all maiden mawkishness, is so novel, so contrary to all notion of feminine sweetness, modesty, and delicacy, that we are apt to be hilarious over it, even when most gravely advocated.

Insisting that "the human end of woman" was marriage, the periodical disparaged any form of legal apprenticeship for women as contrary to nature.[5]

Moreover, there is no indication that either Canadian women's organizations or individual advocates of women's rights had ever demanded female access to the legal profession. The National Council of Women did not champion lawyering when it campaigned for greater employment opportunities for women. Agnes Machar disparaged law in comparison to medicine in 1878, noting that law "seems a much more anomalous [profession] for women than that of medicine...." Carrie Derick, a staunch advocate of equal rights, admitted in 1900 that the learned professions were largely out of reach to women:

Started with a heritage of old world traditions, Canada has remained one of the most conservative parts of the British Empire. The ... unrestricted admission [of women] to the learned professions would be out of harmony with the spirit of the country.[6]

What possessed Clara Brett Martin to demand formal entry into the exclusively male world of lawyering? Perhaps it was the challenge, as much as anything, that provoked her interest. The profession of law would have held great allure for adventurous middle-class women in the late nineteenth century. The growing complexity of an urbanizing, industrializing Canada had furthered lawyers' status and prestige. From a small band of gentlemen who governed their affairs somewhat informally at the outset of the century, by its close the legal profession had become an entrenched, autonomous, self-governing institution, striving for monopoly control over all aspects of legal practice. Furthermore, law had become central to economic, social, and political power. To become the first woman barrister and solicitor would be an achievement of unprecedented significance.[7]

Clara Brett Martin may have kept a diary and written lengthy letters to friends and family about why she wished to pursue law, and what she encountered along the way. Literate women of her class and time were almost always the authors of voluminous and intimate correspondence. But none of these sources appears to have survived. Clara Brett Martin left no descendants who might have packed her papers away in a musty trunk and stored them in someone's attic. No one wrote her biography before her death. We are left with only scattered newspaper clippings, a few photographs, and terse Law Society minutes from which to reconstruct her life.[8]

CLARA BRETT MARTIN'S EARLY LIFE

Clara Brett Martin was born in 1874 to Abram and Elizabeth Martin. She was the youngest of twelve children of a well-to-do Anglican-Irish family. Abram Martin had immigrated from County Sligo, Ireland, in 1832, and

Clara Brett Martin.

taken up farming in Mono Township where he served as the Superinten-dent of Schools. There he married Elizabeth Brett, the daughter of an old-country acquaintance, James Brett, who owned the neighbouring property. The Bretts were a prominent banking family and James Brett was a civil engineer for York County. Either Abram or Elizabeth Martin's family may originally have come from Hungary, since Clara Brett Martin was reported to have both Hungarian and Irish ancestry. Commentators would later refer to Clara Brett Martin as "well-born" and "well-bred."[9]

By the time of Clara Brett Martin's birth, the family had moved to Toronto. She was educated at home with her siblings, under the guidance of tutors. In an era in which less than 1 per cent of the Canadian popula-tion attended university, all the Martin children received some university education. Clara Brett Martin applied for admission to the Arts program at Trinity College in Toronto in 1888. She passed the entrance examina-tion, and enrolled in a series of courses.[10]

## THE "SWEET GIRL GRADUATE"

In 1875 Grace Annie Lockhart had become the first woman to graduate from a Canadian university, with a Bachelor of Science degree from Mount Allison in Sackville, New Brunswick. Toronto's Trinity College had only begun to admit female students in 1885, and the reform was met with hostility and derision. One professor threatened to resign, the calen-dar advised women that their attendance at lectures was not required, and women students were asked to sit separately on chairs apart from the rest of the class.[11]

The debate over women's right to higher education had been extreme-ly bitter and contentious. Nineteenth-century Canadian physician William Carpenter claimed that "putting aside the exceptional cases which now and then occur — the *intellectual* powers of Woman are inferior to those of Man." Male doctors claimed that studying was dangerous for women since it "weakened their developing wombs." Other potential disorders included infertility, the inhibition of lactation in nursing mothers, serious mental disturbance, and even pelvic distortion (presumably from sitting too much).[12]

The pronounced emphasis upon damage to women's reproductive capacities was reminiscent of the debate over protective labour legislation, although the opponents were concerned with women of much wealthier classes here. Women were treated as primarily designed for childbirth, rather than for wide-ranging intellectual pursuits. The "horror" of disabled children was presumed to be the obvious consequence of female studies.

Male physicians elaborated upon alleged and apparent biological differences between men and women. The widely circulated medical journal, the *Canada Lancet*, reported the findings of American physician Dr. Edward H. Clarke in 1874. He abhorred the prospect of young women studying during menstruation:

Day after day the pupil must work with her brain, and stand and walk and exercise, just as if periodicity had no place in her system. Instead of resting both body and mind for a few days, she is expending the nerve-force which should give tone to the uterus, and exhausting menorrhagia occurs, which of course, in turn places the system in a still worse position for the next period.... This terrible routine may go on till the health is completely broken down.... Other disturbances of the uterine functions as amenorrhoea, and incomplete or non-development of the reproductive organs take place as a consequence of mental overstrain during early menstruation. The tendency to sterility ... is attributed ... to a diversion of the vital forces from the reproductive system to the brain.[13]

That journal also recounted the findings of English physician Sir James Chrichton-Browne in 1892. In an effort to prove that men and women were intellectually disparate, he noted that men had heavier brains, that this resulted in a greater specific gravity of the male brain, and that the blood supply of men was directed toward the portions of the brain concerned with "volition, cognition, and ideo-motor processes." In contrast, the doctor asserted that the female blood supply was directed toward portions of the brain concerned with sensory functions.

Chrichton-Browne's "findings" would have far-reaching implications for women who sought admission to university. Quoting directly from the English physician, the *Canada Lancet* continued: "Sir James said he regarded [female admission] as a retrograde and mischievous step, for what was decided amongst the prehistoric protozoa cannot be annulled by Act of Parliament." Chrichton-Browne belittled educated women as "sweet girl graduates," and "pantaloon-like girls," with "stooping gait and withered appearance, shrunk shanks, and spectacles on nose." Admitting that this was a "melancholy outlook," the medical editors offered the hope that in Canada "withered, shrunken-shanked girls will always be a poor miserable minority."[14]

In the face of such undisguised hostility, it took a great deal of courage for women to register for university. In 1882, Agnes Machar described the woman who might choose to do so:

Young women will always require some strong mental "vocation," some cherished and definite aim, to overcome the many "lions in the way," and the many counter attractions of life, and nerve them to submit to the somewhat rigorous discipline and steady, protracted work of a University course.

By emphasizing how extraordinary such women were, Agnes Machar minimized the potential for disruption. These were "exceptional young women who have the taste, the aptitude, the means and the perseverance, for taking a university course," she claimed. It was most "unlikely that there would ever be any very large number of female students crowding to our universities."[15]

The small number of women who did pursue university education in the nineteenth century were urged to study subjects that emphasized "development of the tastes and affections." Modern languages, music, literature, and painting were singled out as particularly appropriate. Metaphysics and mathematics were portrayed as peculiarly masculine disciplines. The 1876 *Queen's College Journal* disparaged women interested in mathematics as "logic-choppers." Agnes Machar had stated publicly that "the predominance of mathematical talent" was "much rarer among women than among men."[16]

Clara Brett Martin, however, majored in mathematics at Trinity and graduated with a Bachelor of Arts with high honours at the age of sixteen, on 27 June 1890. Years later, a Toronto newspaper would praise her achievement while at the same time stereotyping her decision as stridently masculine:

While a mere girl with Hungarian and Irish blood in her veins, she dared to beard the masculine lion by declining to take any of the admittedly feminine courses on the curriculum.... No. Miss Martin chose to take mathematics. This was in those days manifestly and palpably absurd. That was why she liked it — in addition to having a real masculine penchant for mathematics anyway. It was with great supercilious regret that the male mathematicians of those days admitted that a woman never could master the binomial theorem or the integral calculus. It was a matter of great marvel too that Miss Clara Brett Martin, with no anarchistic or revolutionary airs whatever, should quietly carry off high honors in mathematics.[17]

THE FORMAL APPLICATION FOR LAW

After graduation, Clara Brett Martin accepted a brief, one-year appointment as a school-teacher while she prepared herself to seek admission to the legal profession. One avenue of entry was to approach the Ontario Legislature for a private statute authorizing her, as an individual, to practise law. From the founding of the Law Society of Upper Canada, the provincial legislature had retained the power to admit individuals by special statute. The legislature exercised this authority rarely, but this route had been pursued successfully by the first Black lawyer in Ontario.[18]

Unable to find a white lawyer willing to hire a Black legal apprentice, Delos Rogest Davis of Amherstberg, Ontario, had petitioned the legislature in 1884 for admission by statute. He argued for admission on the basis that he had been studying law for eleven years and practising as a commissioner for taking affidavits and as a notary public. On 19 May 1885, Delos Davis was admitted to the bar as a solicitor under special statute. In 1886, again by special statute and over the protests of the Law Society, he became a barrister.[19]

For most would-be lawyers, entry was far more routine. The Law Society of Upper Canada set the general requirements for the self-regulating profession. Legal education was primarily a matter of apprenticeship, although the Law Society also operated part-time law courses, delivered from its premises at Osgoode Hall in Toronto. Candidates were required to pass an entrance examination and file a certificate of fitness and good character signed by a lawyer who had agreed to hire the student as an articled clerk. Students were required to clerk for three years, while attending lectures at Osgoode Hall. Those who passed the exams administered at the end of the three years obtained the rank of solicitor, which permitted them to conduct legal office work. To be admitted as a barrister, a rank that permitted lawyers to appear regularly in court, required two more years of articling, additional classes, and another set of examinations. However, candidates who had university degrees were permitted to skip the entrance examination, and could become both barrister and solicitor in three years.[20]

Clara Brett Martin pursued the Law Society route. Her race and class may have led her to think that, unlike Delos Davis, she would be able to obtain an articling position. Not all who watched the case were so sanguine. The Canadian Law Times speculated that it would be difficult for Clara Brett Martin to find a position, because there was "no way of compelling a solicitor to article clerks...." Clara Brett Martin did not seem to have a particular lawyer or law firm in mind in 1891, when, at the age of seventeen, she formally petitioned the Law Society of Upper Canada for registration as a student member. The "certificate of fitness" form she filed was left blank where the sponsoring lawyer was supposed to sign.[21]

The apparent omission was never raised. Instead, the Law Society voted on 18 May 1891 to refer her admission to a special committee of nine benchers, as the members elected by lawyers to govern the profession were known. The *Canada Law Journal* depicted Clara Brett Martin as a damsel at a jousting tournament: "Doubtlessly the cause of this 'mayden faire' will find some champion ready to enter the lists on her behalf." The paper predicted a "battle royal." Discussion was not restricted to Ontario law papers. The Winnipeg-based *Western Law Times* actively urged the benchers to rule against Clara Brett Martin, although the editors refrained from specifying reasons:

With no disrespect intended toward the fair sex, we hope the Benchers will refuse the application, as we do not think, all things considered, that the legal profession will be benefited by the admission of ladies to its ranks.[22]

## THE LAW SOCIETY AND THE "PERSONS" DEBATE

The special committee deliberated for more than a month, although apparently neither Clara Brett Martin nor her advocates were permitted to appear. Samuel Hume Blake, the prominent and powerful partner of the prestigious Toronto firm of Blake, Lash, Cassels, delivered the committee's report. Characterizing the question in purely technical terms, Samuel Blake undertook a detailed, legal analysis of whether the Law Society had the authority to admit women. A cautious man, he would not risk debating the broader question of whether women ought to practise law.

The statute that had first incorporated the Law Society made no reference to women, noted Samuel Blake. The language used was "persons." By the late nineteenth century, scores of common law judges in England and across the United States had been wrestling with whether women were properly included in the meaning of "persons" and ruling against women. In this, the first "persons" ruling in Canada, Samuel Blake would follow their lead. First he sought guidance from the provisions of the Ontario Interpretation Act. One section, seemingly helpful to Clara Brett Martin, provided that "words importing ... the masculine gender ... shall include ... females as well as males." A more problematic section vaguely permitted a contrary finding where there was "some thing in the context" that might "indicat[e] a different meaning or call ... for a different construction."[23]

Taking a long, historical look at the question, Blake noted that in 1797, when the Law Society statute had first been enacted, "women were not empowered in Canada or Great Britain, under any circumstances, to be entered as Members of the Legal Societies." When the legislators first penned the word "persons" then, they clearly had not contemplated the inclusion of women. As for the present, Blake reminded the Law Society that women were still far from obtaining equivalence with men. Dismissing the hard-fought campaigns for improvements in married women's property rights, Blake noted in something of an overstatement that women remained largely incapacitated under common law. What was more, he added, they could not vote.[24]

Clara Brett Martin's petition should be denied, he concluded. If women were to be admitted, the reform should be handled through legislation. "The function was legislative." On 15 September 1891, the Law Society voted to approve Blake's report, and directed the Secretary of the Society, James Hutchison Esten, "to notify Miss Brett Martin accordingly."[25]

Many in the profession were gleeful. One legal commentator applauded the decision as absolutely correct on its merits. Referring to the medical profession's comparison of male and female brains, he wrote:

[It] was ... no doubt felt that a woman can find a more suitable place in life to fill than that of a counsel. A woman does not, as a rule, arrive at a conclusion by logical reasoning, but rather by a species of instinct, which, no matter how unerring, cannot assist others to arrive at the same conclusion. Her arguments would be after the fashion of the old nursery rhyme which used to run something like this:

> "The reason why I cannot tell;
> I do not love thee, Doctor Fell,
> But this alone I know full well,
> I do not love thee, Dr. Fell."[26]

The absurdity of appealing to nursery rhymes to substantiate the argument seems to have escaped the writer.

When the Secretary of the Law Society came to deliver the negative decision to Clara Brett Martin, he was blunt. She would have to "abandon her desire for law," James Hutchison Esten declared. He offered an alternative: Clara Brett Martin could "remove to the United States." Both would have known that the barriers to women in law were toppling across the United States. In 1869, Arabella Mansfield had become the first woman admitted to the bar, in Iowa. By 1891 women had been admitted in over twenty other states and the District of Columbia.[27]

For some time, Canadian legal commentators had been watching the developments south of the border with serious misgivings. Reduced to ridiculing the women involved, the law journals had targeted Myra Bradwell. The wife of a prominent judge, Bradwell had successfully completed the Chicago bar exams in 1869, but had been denied the right to practise law by the United States Supreme Court in 1873. She had founded the *Chicago Legal News*, which would become one of the foremost legal publications in the country. The *Canada Law Journal* remarked snidely in 1868 that they hoped "Miss Bradwell w[ould] not be tempted to write her own articles."[28]

In 1879, when legislation was enacted in the United States permitting women admission to the bar of the Supreme Court, the *Canada Law Journal*'s editors noted that the "cheerful" Myra Bradwell had "contest[ed] the proposition that it will be necessary to have a nursery attached to the Courtroom." Categorically dismissing women in law, they wrote:

As conveyancers, or as compilers of text-books, there may be no reason why some women should not succeed as well as some men: but to refuse to allow them to embark upon the rough and troubled sea of actual legal practice, is, as it appears to us, being cruel only to be kind.[29]

Someone brought this broadside to the attention of Myra Bradwell. She replied in her own journal:

According to our Canadian and English brothers it would be cruel to allow a woman to "embark upon the rough and troubled sea of actual legal practice," but not to allow her to govern all England with Canada and other dependencies thrown in. Our brothers will get used to it and then it will not seem any worse to them to have women practising in the courts than it does now to have a queen rule over them.[30]

Samuel Hume Blake had conveniently omitted Queen Victoria's reign from his survey of women's historical and legal usage.

APPEAL TO THE LEGISLATURE

Clara Brett Martin was not about to remove herself to the United States. Determined to stay in Canada and to challenge the Law Society's ruling, her next step would be to seek assistance from William Douglas Balfour, an Amherstberg newspaper publisher and a member of the Ontario Legislature. Balfour had sponsored Delos Davis's successful bill in 1884, and he was becoming widely known as a progressive politician who supported legal struggles against discrimination. A strong advocate of temperance and female suffrage, he was a natural ally for Clara Brett Martin. Six months after Clara Brett Martin had been rejected by the Law Society, William Douglas Balfour introduced a bill in the legislature that would have required the lawyers to construe the word "person" in the Law Society's statute to include females.[31]

The most vocal opponent of the bill was William Ralph Meredith, then the provincial leader of the Opposition. One of the élite litigation lawyers who had represented Esther Arscott in the 1880s, Meredith came from a background strikingly similar to Clara Brett Martin's. Born into a large, aristocratic, Anglican-Irish family in London, Ontario, he had risen to prominence as a successful lawyer and Conservative politician. He supported progressive causes such as workers' compensation, the expansion of male suffrage to wider economic classes, and other social legislation, but was opposed to female suffrage, claiming that women were unfit to vote or sit side by side with men in the legislatures because they "would have to bring the babies along."[32]

A bencher of the Law Society, William Ralph Meredith had served with Samuel Blake on the committee that rejected Clara Brett Martin. Nor had the passage of a few months caused him to change his mind. He rose in the legislature to declare that the women of the province did not want to study law. One of the most obvious barriers, he assured the House, was that women concerned about the dictates of female fashion would never want to wear "the same official robes" as men. The presence of women would also wreak havoc with jury trials. Male juries would find their chivalrous instincts running out of control as they tried to compare the arguments of competing male and female lawyers. "It would upset the whole equanimity of the twelve good men and true," he warned. Appealing to the proper order of things, he closed:

Women were not intended for the position of advocate. Nature intended women should occupy a different position to men in the community. If the House were

THE BARRISTER
Caricature of a female barrister with parasol and bustle from *Punch* magazine.

carried away by gush and sentiment, it would be disastrous to the best interests of women.[33]

Clara Brett Martin sought outside support. One of her strongest backers would be Dr. Emily Stowe, then the leader of the Dominion Woman's Enfranchisement Association. A leading proponent of the contemporary women's movement, she had been lobbying for women's suffrage for years, and she immediately saw Clara Brett Martin's quest as paralleling the suffrage campaign. Her work in securing women's admission to medicine would have given her a ready appreciation of what Clara Brett Martin was up against. Working through the Dominion Woman's Enfranchisement Association, Dr. Stowe added the admission of women to law onto her agenda in 1892. She also introduced Clara Brett Martin to other women involved in women's rights activities. They received her with warmth and support, prompting one news reporter to exclaim that "Miss Martin is very popular among the Toronto women of progress."[34]

Concluding that the support of Sir Oliver Mowat, the long-term Liberal Premier of Ontario, was essential for success, women's rights advocates trained their sights on him. Mowat would have known about such women's causes as the reform of prostitutes and campaigns for greater property rights for married women. Mowat's wife, Jane Ewart Mowat, was one of the founders, along with Elizabeth Dunlop, of the Toronto Magdalene Asylum. Jane Mowat and Elizabeth Dunlop would have known one of Clara Brett Martin's aunts, Sarah J. Brett, who was also a founding member of the Magdalene Asylum. Oliver Mowat's sister-in-law, Catherine Seaton (Ewart) Skirving, had served as the secretary of the Asylum from 1863 and as its president from 1891 to 1895. But despite these examples, when asked to write a sketch of his mother, Helen Levack, for inclusion in *The Women of Canada*, Mowat would curtly decline. "In most cases a woman has no history apart from that of her husband," he replied.[35]

Despite Dr. Stowe's overtures, Premier Mowat had been lukewarm to the female suffrage campaign. Diplomatically assuring women that he did not oppose their cause but refusing to sponsor any reform, his caution had prompted Dr. Stowe to comment that she wished Mowat had been "less the politician and more the Christian." But when Dr. Stowe's organization added Clara Brett Martin's cause to their list of demands, Mowat would finally be spurred to action. Possibly he viewed the prospect of female lawyers as less threatening than votes for women. He may have seen the new demand as something he could support while still holding back the tide of female suffrage. He decided to back William Douglas Balfour's bill.[36]

With Premier Mowat's support, the bill squeaked through second reading in the legislature by a vote of forty-one to forty. The bill was sent on to the Committee on Laws, where unsympathetic politicians cut the heart out of it. First, they restricted its scope to the admission of women as solicitors. The more prestigious rank of barrister was excised. Second, they reworded the bill so that the Law Society was not required to admit women but merely given the discretion to do so. When the bill returned to the legislature for third and final reading, Premier Oliver Mowat spoke. So far as he was concerned, he said, he "would be willing to admit women to the practice of law absolutely, but as this was not the feeling of the House, a compromise was decided upon." On 13 April 1892, the radically amended statute was passed, and it received Royal assent the following day.[37]

## THE LAW SOCIETY EXERCISES ITS DISCRETION

On 13 September 1892, the Law Society met to consider how to respond to the new legislation. The benchers pondered the permissive wording of the statute, briefly deliberated how to exercise their enlarged discretionary powers, and then voted to deny Clara Brett Martin admission. Their rationale was succinct if elusive: it was "inexpedient" to frame rules for the admission of women.[38]

Clara Brett Martin again enlisted the support of Premier Mowat. Mowat was also the Attorney-General of Ontario, and as such he held an *ex officio* seat as a bencher of the Law Society. To the surprise and chagrin of the other benchers, he attended the next Law Society Convocation on 9 December 1892. Whether out of admiration for Clara Brett Martin, or out of impatience with the recalcitrant Law Society, Mowat was now determined to ensure the breakthrough of women. In front of the hushed gathering, the Premier stood up to move that the benchers should "proceed to frame Rules for the admission of women as solicitors." The seconder of the motion would be Samuel Hume Blake, who had earlier ruled against Clara Brett Martin. Possibly won over by her determination, he may also have been swayed by the new Ontario statute. Earlier he had stated that he believed reform should come from the legislature. Under Premier Mowat's stewardship, Blake declared himself prepared to advocate the admission of women.[39]

For many of those present at Convocation, the Premier's intervention had grave and sinister overtones. For some years the Law Society had been battling with Premier Mowat over the status of the legal profession. Junior members of the bar and those who worked outside of Toronto had become increasingly worried about competition from lay persons in the delivery of legal services. The non-litigation fields of bankruptcy, the drafting of wills, and the drawing of documents for the sale or mortgage of land by unlicensed conveyancers were particularly contentious. A special committee of the Law Society had met with Oliver Mowat in 1882 and 1891 to attempt to reduce the competition from non-lawyers, but the Premier had not budged. Now he was moving to admit women, yet another group of competitors.[40]

Immediately upon Premier Mowat's motion, Henry Hatton Strathy, a bencher from Barrie and one of the fiercest advocates of restricting lay competition, rose to move an amendment. He sought to postpone the discussion of the woman question until the legislature had bestowed the profession with monopoly control over entry and all aspects of conveyancing. But the senior Toronto benchers appear to have felt that this was going a bit far, and they voted down Strathy's amendment.[41]

Mowat's original motion was reread, and the question was called. The vote pitted family members, law partners, and political confrères against each other. J.K. Kerr voted against Samuel Blake, his brother-in-law, and against Clara Brett Martin. Britton Bath Osler voted with John Hoskin, his law partner, in favour of Clara Brett Martin. D'Alton McCarthy, partner to both Osler and Hoskin, voted against. Alexander Bruce and George Ferguson Shepley, both longtime Liberals, voted against Sir Oliver Mowat, their party leader. The final count would show that eleven benchers had voted against Clara Brett Martin, and twelve for her.[42]

Just as everyone thought the matter had been settled, in rushed William Renwick Riddell, a bencher who had been delayed in court and had missed the vote. Told of the count, Riddell angrily demanded the vote be held again. The chair of the meeting, Aemilius Irving, ruled that it would be most improper to vote twice. Many of the benchers were furious with his decision, and insisted that Riddell be given a chance to state how he *would have* voted. To the delight of Clara Brett Martin's opponents, Riddell declared that his vote would have been "nay."[43]

Heartened by this, a Hamilton bencher named Edward Martin moved for an adjournment, but his motion failed. Benchers Britton Bath Osler and Charles Moss, who had sided with Clara Brett Martin in the earlier vote, moved to direct the Legal Education Committee to frame the necessary rules. This time the vote came out a tie. As chair it fell to Aemilius Irving to break the tie. He voted in favour of the motion. In something of an anti-climax, the Legal Education Committee reported three weeks later. There seems to have been nothing much to deliberate about. The rules it framed for women were identical to those for male candidates. Sir Oliver Mowat had once more joined the benchers in their meeting, and he moved the formal adoption of the report. Edward Martin and Henry Hatton Strathy tried again for a six-month adjournment, but lost eleven to five.[44]

Days later the *Canada Law Journal* observed that despite the outcome, "we venture to say that a large majority both of the profession and Benchers are opposed to the change." Surmising that it had all been Premier Mowat's doing, they argued: "The Attorney-General of Ontario was the important factor on this occasion, both by his personal influence and by the shadowy suggestions that the Legislature might take the matter up and pass an Act which the Society would consider more distasteful than the rule which they were asked to swallow." The *Western Law*

*Times* agreed, and heaped scorn upon the Ontario benchers for "unmanly" behaviour:

In spite of the wishes of a large majority of the profession, and the benchers also if they only had the manliness to speak out, the Attorney General succeeded, by his political influence and vague threats of legislative vengeance on the Society, in carrying a motion so as to admit women by a bare majority of one vote....[45]

While the thought of the Ontario benchers shorn of their manliness left the editors of the *Western Law Times* "shudder[ing] in contemplating these results," the editors of the *Canada Law Journal* had a more resourceful suggestion. The Mowat statute itself might be open to legal attack, they hinted. The legislation had referred to the "Law Society of Ontario," rather than the correct title, the "Law Society of Upper Canada." Nothing further came of this, although the *Canadian Law Times* speculated that "the Act was probably drawn by ... the young woman on whose application it was passed." This was, they observed, "a bad beginning."[46]

### THE FIRST FEMALE ARTICLING STUDENT

Clara Brett Martin immediately registered with the benchers and was formally entered on the books as a student-at-law on 26 June 1893. She presented her diploma from Trinity College, which entitled her to exemption from the entrance examination. And she notified the Law Society that she had been accepted as an articling student for the required three-year term by the prominent Toronto firm of Mulock, Miller, Crowther, and Montgomery.[47]

She had obtained a first-rate articling position. Sir William Mulock, the senior partner of the firm, was a Liberal politician like Mowat, but his activity was on the federal scene. First elected as a member of Parliament in 1882, he would be appointed to Sir Wilfrid Laurier's Cabinet in 1896. Mulock was also the Vice-Chancellor of the University of Toronto. The rumour was that Clara Brett Martin's long-standing friendship with Mulock's daughter was her ticket into such a plum articling job. Her class and race had apparently brought her what Delos Davis had never secured.[48]

But her gender would continue to mark her out for isolation. One of her male fellow students, taking care to preserve his anonymity, described Clara Brett Martin as "a very odd sort of woman." Her colleagues regarded her as a "curiosity" and a "rebel." That she had a penchant for cycling only enhanced this image. Some nineteenth-century doctors forecast medical problems from bicycle-riding that rivalled even the medical side effects of post-secondary education. They predicted deformed hands, feet and legs, spinal curvatures, ruined complexions, and an ingrained tenseness caused by the anxiety of learning to ride that could result in "bicycle face." Some worried that sitting astride a bicycle seat would excite women's sexual feelings, and warned dourly of the dangers of masturbation.[49]

Despite these admonitions, middle- and upper-class young women in the 1890s took up bicycling with relish. It was a liberating form of recreation, offering wide-ranging freedom of mobility and independence. An aura of glamour and daring attached to women bicyclists, a sense of the challenge of modern womanhood. Clara Brett Martin's penchant for cycling was completely within character, but profoundly unsettling to those who preferred traditional gender roles.[50]

Her appearance and choice of attire provoked consternation as well. Female fashion had traditionally been both uncomfortable and an impediment to movement, playing an important role substantively and symbolically in the subjugation of women. From the 1820s on, the ideal waist measurement had been stipulated as eighteen inches, a circumference preposterously out of line with the natural contours of women's bodies. It could be attained only through a tightly laced corset, a dangerous undergarment that caused headaches, fainting spells, uterine and spinal disorders. Corsets, bustles, and voluminous skirts and sleeves cramped activity, and made cycling almost impossible.[51]

Dress reformers had been advocating more sensible designs for female clothing since the middle of the nineteenth century, the most controversial of their creations being the "Bloomers." This outfit was named after American feminist Amelia Bloomer, who had promoted a dress that draped to the mid-calf, worn over baggy trousers, in the 1850s. Bloomers had attracted a torrent of ridicule and abuse, subjecting women who dared to wear them to taunting and occasional stone-throwing from mobs of young men. In 1895, a bloomer-clad young woman was threatened with police arrest should she persist in wearing them in public in Victoria, British Columbia.[52]

The shirtwaist, however, was a different story. Introduced in the 1890s and worn with a long, fairly simple skirt, the shirtwaist was a blouse modelled upon a man's shirt. In deference to a culture that continued to emphasize differences between men and women, the buttons on the women's shirt remained in the back, rather than the front as on men's shirts. Nevertheless, the new design was much more comfortable than previous fashions, since the narrower sleeves, reduced amount of material, and elimination of the corset and bustle made it easier for women to move. The shirtwaist caught on, and athletic models known as the "Gibson girls" set dramatic, new fashion trends with casual blouses, skirts, and suits.[53]

As the few surviving photographs of Clara Brett Martin illustrate, she would wear elaborate, traditional dresses when the occasion warranted. But she was also something of a fashion trend-setter. Fellow articling students did not know whether to express admiration or disapproval as they watched her pedal to work in the newfangled garb. One fellow student later credited Clara Brett Martin "with the ability to wear a shirtwaist with great distinction."[54]

Yet her critics clearly outnumbered her admirers, and they seem to have combined forces to make articling a miserable experience for Clara Brett Martin. Speaking frankly but ever so politely about the problem to a reporter for the Buffalo *Express*, she admitted that for the first time she was shaken out of her accustomed optimism. Clara Brett Martin's isolation was pronounced:

You would not believe how many obstacles I have had to overcome single-handed. I was articled to one of the largest law firms in Toronto, and when I put in my appearance I was looked upon as an interloper, if not a curiosity. The clerks avoided me and made it as unpleasant for me as they possibly could (I dislike to make such a charge against the young gentlemen of Canada), and for a time it looked as if I were doomed to failure through a source with which I had not reckoned.[55]

This was clearly a low point for Clara Brett Martin, who switched articling firms. This time she selected another well-known Toronto firm, Blake, Lash, Cassels. Samuel Hume Blake, the senior partner, seems to have increasingly favoured Clara Brett Martin's bid to enter the law. Whether Samuel Blake's influence over the male articling students held their hostilities in check more than Mulock had been able to do at his firm is an open question.[56]

In September 1894, Clara Brett Martin appeared in court for the first time during her articling. Although the case was only a routine collection on a small debt, the newspapers were quick to pick up on it. A Toronto *Empire* reporter admitted that he went to watch because he "was curious to see just how unwomanly her position would be." When Clara Brett Martin entered the "musty old room assigned to the Division Court," the reporter observed that "the young men present, the majority being themselves of the profession, indulged in open smiling and underbreath comment." She rose to make her submissions only to discover that a necessary witness was missing. The case was adjourned for a week.[57]

Seven days later, she returned with all the witnesses. The press described the trial in the most patronizing terms. The accent on Clara Brett Martin's "femininity" overwhelmed the reporting of her legal prowess. As one report recounted:

A young lady, gowned in a pretty brown walking suit, came in quietly and took her seat up within the rail. The judge swept several cases rapidly off the docket. Then came one of disputed rent, the young lady removed her hat, stepped down before the stand, and in the quietest of voices asked that two witnesses be called, to each of which she put one or two questions bringing out the fact that the defendant admitted the debt he now denied. "Garnishee and costs," said the judge, briefly, and the young lady put on her hat and walked out. But it was pretty to see the colour spring to her cheeks when she heard the judge's words and knew that she had won this, the first case, for her firm.[58]

Most articling students would find their first court appearance difficult in some respects. But the additional burdens Clara Brett Martin assumed, with a throng of reporters covering her every move, were extraordinary. The press dove in to dissect everything from her clothing to her voice inflection and facial tone. Clara Brett Martin's hat would have held special meaning for nineteenth-century readers. As symbol of her femininity and status, a lady was expected to keep her hat on in public. Men, on the other hand, took their hats off when they came inside a building. Which custom Clara Brett Martin would follow assumed wide significance. Would feminine dictates fall before the male environment of the courtroom? The press strove to reassure readers that despite Clara Brett Martin's presence in a male setting, and the voluntary removal of her hat, she had behaved decorously and within the constraints of femininity.

Things were no better in the lecture halls of Osgoode Hall, where articling students had classroom instruction for several hours a day, five days a week, eight months of the year. Members of the profession had long voiced concern about admitting women to these classes, fearful of the awkwardness that might ensue when women were exposed first-hand to the discriminatory nature of many legal rules. The *Canadian Law Times* was explicit:

One can hardly imagine the grave and staid principal lecturing to a bevy of ladies on the inability of married women to contract, the measure of damages in breach of promise [of marriage] cases, the very grave necessity for corroborating their own oaths as to the promise ... and sundry other matters peculiar to themselves and their gentle sex.[59]

Clara Brett Martin's experience of classroom lectures was remarkably similar to what had confronted Emily Stowe and Jennie Kidd Trout as they sought to obtain medical qualifications. In an effort to embarrass Clara Brett Martin, some of the law instructors emphasized points involving sex. She found this treatment humiliating and described her classes as having been deliberately structured to place "unnecessary emphasis upon certain lecture points in the thousand ways that men can make a woman suffer who stands alone among them." Her alienation was compounded by mean-spirited male students, who were in the habit of hissing loudly when she entered the classroom.[60]

In response, Clara Brett Martin skipped as many lectures as she dared. Her frequent absences brought her to the attention of the benchers on 27 June 1894, when they reserved judgment on whether she should be passed through to second year in spite of her spotty attendance. She defended herself against this charge, although what she disclosed to the benchers was never recorded. On 19 November 1894 the benchers noted that Clara Brett Martin had "furnished reasons for absence from lectures," and permitted her to continue.[61]

Clara Brett Martin's forced absences from the Osgoode Hall lectures may have worried her more than she cared to admit. Upon her own initiative she would later pursue further legal education at university. Refusing to delegate any of its authority to independent institutions of higher education, the Law Society had never required lawyers to complete courses on law at university. However, a number of universities had established law courses and law degrees by the late nineteenth century. Clara Brett Martin would complete her Bachelor of Civil Law degree at Trinity College in 1897 and an LL.B. at the University of Toronto in 1899.[62]

The annual examinations administered by the Law Society, however, would pose no problems for Clara Brett Martin. "Finally," she rejoiced, "I had the satisfaction of beating them all in the examinations." This was no small feat, since at the time the failure and dropout rate throughout the course averaged about 70 per cent.[63]

## CLARA BRETT MARTIN SEEKS THE RANK OF BARRISTER

Success appeared imminent, with Clara Brett Martin eligible to be admitted as a solicitor in June of 1896. But almost all Canadian lawyers held the dual ranks of barrister and solicitor, and she had never been entirely satisfied with the legislative amendment that allowed women only to be solicitors. If she was going to become the first woman lawyer, she wanted to achieve recognition as both barrister and solicitor.[64]

In 1893, the year that the National Council of Women of Canada was formed, Clara Brett Martin enlisted its support. The founder was Lady Ishbel Marjoribanks Gordon, Countess of Aberdeen and wife of the Governor-General. Clara Brett Martin easily secured the backing of English-born Lady Aberdeen, who quickly became one of her most enthusiastic advocates. Eighteen ninety-three was also the year of the Chicago World's Fair, and representatives of various women's councils across the world met to discuss issues of mutual concern. Lady Aberdeen was elected president of the International Council of Women in Chicago, and she used her far-flung connections to great advantage. Through her efforts, resolutions supporting Clara Brett Martin flowed into the benchers from women's organizations all over the world.[65]

On the local front, the National Council of Women organized a bombardment of letters to the daily, weekly, and monthly press. These letters overwhelmingly advocated Clara Brett Martin's cause, censuring the benchers for their discriminatory behaviour. When the benchers appeared determined to stand fast regardless of the pressure, Clara Brett Martin turned once more to the legislature. Since William Douglas Balfour had died by this time, she was forced to find a new sponsor for her bill. Sir William B. Wood, the Liberal member for the District of Brant, agreed to undertake the initiative.[66]

Sir William Wood was the son of Scottish immigrants. Raised on a farm, he had achieved stature as a man of commerce, engaged in the grain trade both as a merchant and manufacturer. In April 1895 he introduced a bill that granted the Law Society the discretionary power to admit women as barristers. Why he drafted the enactment using discretionary language is not clear. Certainly it was not in Clara Brett Martin's interest to allow the final decision to rest with the Law Society. But perhaps Wood felt that the second statute should follow the first in format.[67]

Clara Brett Martin had also enlisted the support of her old ally, Sir Oliver Mowat. Well-primed to respond favourably, in March 1894 he had met yet again with pro-suffrage forces from the Dominion Woman's Enfranchisement Association, now joined by the Woman's Christian Temperance Union. One hundred and fifty delegates from the two organizations had besieged him with demands for the vote. The movement for suffrage was growing, and there were indications that a new generation was swelling the ranks. Dr. Emily Stowe's daughter, married and practising medicine as Dr. Augusta Stowe-Gullen, was now one of the leading spokeswomen. Still balking at votes for women, Mowat may have been casting about for reform measures he could live with. He had never been particularly adverse to women as barristers, even in 1892, and he was eager to declare himself on side.[68]

On the day of the bill's introduction, the public galleries in the legislature were filled to overflowing. Representatives from various women's organizations were there to see what would happen. Clara Brett Martin sat prominently among them. Sir William Wood made a "spirited appeal" for passage of the bill, arguing that it was "the logical outcome of the act which had already been passed allowing women to become solicitors." Sir Oliver Mowat rose next. While he was anxious to appear supportive, his enthusiasm for the bill was tempered with effusive reassurances to his fellow politicians that few women would be likely to seek legal careers and that the potential for large-scale disruption was minimal.[69]

The Toronto *Globe* covered Premier Mowat's speech in detail:

There was a momentary pause and some laughter and then Sir Oliver Mowat arose and said that he did not think the question required any further argument. "They had authorized women to act as solicitors, why not as barristers?" It was not necessary for barristers to appear in court and in any case he could not see why they should not appear. They went to hear women sing in public, and to speak in public. In fact the highest lady in Canada [Lady Aberdeen] speaks well and ably. Very few women, the Premier observed, would be likely to avail themselves of the privilege and the men would not be likely to be embarrassed by an overflow of women into the profession. They had for a long time been relaxing the laws with regard to women, the bitterest fight having been the admission of women to the university and no harm had resulted. They would be safe in passing the bill he said in conclusion, and on the whole he thought of the privilege as one which it would not be right to withhold.[70]

Next Nicholas Awrey, Liberal member for Wentworth County, spoke.

He confessed that he generally accepted the lead of Premier Mowat in most questions, but declared that where women were concerned he was forced by personal conviction to diverge. To great merriment and laughter he charged that if women were permitted to argue before juries of men like Mowat, who "had always had a soft spot in his heart for women," there was no telling what would result. Some of the legislators, convulsed with laughter, began to wave handkerchiefs helplessly in the air. No one suggested that women might be offered spots as jurors, thereby neutralizing any reputed chivalrous impulses.[71]

Nicholas Awrey would claim to be even more concerned about the threatened disruption of woman's role. Capitalizing upon the arguments women had been making for decades about their centrality to the family, Awrey insisted that the "homes and womanhood of Ontario" were at stake. This pointed out the dangers of maternal feminism, the main thrust of the platform of the National Council of Women. Women reformers were advocating a more companionate model of marriage, enhanced powers of child custody for women, an elimination of the worst abuses of wife battering and the sexual double standard. But their rationale for these measures, as for female suffrage, was the enhancement of the status of wife and mother. While this focus probably represented fairly the beliefs and understandings of most nineteenth-century Canadian women, it also opened the way for proponents of inequality to argue that any reform that violated the notion of "separate spheres" for women and men was intolerable.[72]

Awrey's attempt to defeat the bill failed. Laughter notwithstanding, most legislators were not inclined to take responsibility for refusing Clara Brett Martin admission — at least not while she and so many of her supporters sat watching intently from the gallery. Sixty-one members voted in favour of the bill, twenty-seven against. When the results were tallied, the legislative chamber was filled with the sound of applause. Days later, on 16 April 1895, the bill received Royal assent.[73]

## THE RECALCITRANT LAW SOCIETY

Clara Brett Martin's elation over her second legislative victory was tempered by an accident that injured her quite seriously four days later. Alighting from her carriage onto Avenue Road on 10 April 1895, she slipped against the wheel and dislocated her right shoulder. It would take until the spring of 1896 for Clara Brett Martin to file her petition to the Law Society for admission as a barrister.[74]

The benchers met on 5 June 1896 to consider the petition. Charles Moss, a longtime supporter of Clara Brett Martin, moved that the Legal Education Committee be directed to frame any additional rules necessary to give effect to the new legislation. Alexander Bruce, who had consistently voted against Clara Brett Martin since 1892, moved an amendment. It was "inexpedient to make rules for providing for the admission of women as barristers-at-law," he countered. The amendment carried, and the benchers declared the original motion lost. The Law Society had fended off Clara Brett Martin's application once more.[75]

Determined not to be defeated, she immediately alerted Premier Mowat's office. Then she sat down to compile a list of benchers who might be convinced to change their votes. The campaign would hit the benchers in their pocketbooks. Searching out some of the wealthier clients of the benchers she had designated as "swing-votes," Clara Brett Martin solicited their intervention. Some clients seem to have brought their influence directly to bear upon their legal advisors. Their combined pressure "fairly wor[e] out ... the old gentlemen," noted the Toronto-based *Woman's Journal*.[76]

At the next meeting of the benchers, on 14 September 1896, Charles Moss put his motion again. This time he announced that he did so "on behalf of Sir Oliver Mowat." The motion was seconded by Samuel Hume Blake, for whom Clara Brett Martin was now articling. The threat of Mowat's intervention may have caused some benchers to reconsider, but Clara Brett Martin's client-solicitation seems to have been the key. Overtures from clients had left many of the benchers torn with indecision. The Montreal *Daily Witness* described them as "unwilling to commit themselves and equally unwilling to offend profitable clients." They stayed away from the meeting in droves. Only twelve benchers showed up to vote. Eight voted in favour of Clara Brett Martin, four against.[77]

There was still one matter outstanding. The Legal Education Committee had yet to compile its report creating rules for the admission of women. That month the committee members met to consider the rules. The controversy centred on what a female barrister should wear to court. Male barristers appeared in long black gowns with white neckties, worn over dark trousers. But the thought of women wearing pants seems to have been too much for the benchers. The experiment with bloomers still rankled. Instead, they specified that women must wear their barrister's gowns "over a black dress."[78]

This fixation with women's dress was reflective of a concern that had haunted the members of the bar for some time. In 1892 the *Western Law*

Some Stylish Late Summer Hats.

THE DELINEATOR.            DESCRIBED ON PAGE 227                    AUGUST 1900.

**Fashion magazine layout of "Some Stylish Late Summer Hats"
from *The Delineator*, 1900.**

*Times* announced that a woman lawyer from Chicago had apparently brought her parasol into court with her, only to break it over the head of her male opponent. In 1896 the *Canada Law Journal* worried that women barristers would insist upon wearing monstrous bonnets to court:

a new and becoming headgear would have to be devised in place of the hideous horse-hair wig; some bewitching structure of dainty curls, of the particular shade of gold fashionable at the moment.[79]

The elaborate hats that fashionable middle- and upper-class women wore during the last decades of the nineteenth century were attention-catching and obstructive of vision. A Toronto reporter had followed Clara Brett Martin's every move as she took off her hat and stood forward to address the bench on her first appearance in court. The benchers went to great lengths to ensure that hats, the most visible trappings of female fashion, would not disgrace the profession. They laid down a rule that women barristers must appear "with head uncovered."[80]

When the detailed report on dress regulations for women barristers was submitted, the benchers subjected it to yet another series of delays, blocking final passage until 18 November 1896. But by now it was only a matter of time. On 4 December 1896 Clara Brett Martin filed the remaining documents required by the Law Society. On 2 February 1897, at the age of twenty-three, she was admitted as a barrister and solicitor to the Law Society of Upper Canada. After battling for more than five years, she had become the first woman in the British Empire to enter the profession.[81]

The graduating class staged its annual year-end "Mock Trial" to celebrate its call to the bar. That year women were marked out for particular ridicule. One man decked himself out as a woman of remarkable girth, complete with voluminous dress, cape, and shawl. The final touch was the hat: an ostentatious, feathered, bejewelled monstrosity. "She" was paraded into the courtroom, and against the backdrop of Osgoode Hall's stately brick arches and stained-glass windows, prosecuted her case as plaintiff in a civil trial to the uproarious amusement of the mixed audience that filled the hall to capacity.[82]

The newspapers covered Clara Brett Martin's call with fanfare. Applauding her victory, the Montreal *Witness* described Clara Brett Martin as "an attractive and earnest young lady, with a strong sincerity, an indomitable perseverance, and a splendid brain." But attention remained centred on her attire, with reporters hastening to assure their readers that Clara Brett Martin had behaved with feminine propriety, even at her

Mock trial at Osgoode Hall, Toronto, 1897.

moment of triumph. As the Toronto *Telegram* described it: "This afternoon Miss Clara Brett Martin was presented to the Judges at Osgoode Hall and was sworn in as a barrister. She wore a black gown over a black dress and the regulation white tie and bore her honours modestly."[83]

### CLARA BRETT MARTIN'S LAW PRACTICE

Now Clara Brett Martin had to prove to supporters and opponents alike that she could establish a successful law practice. The day following her call to the bar, she placed an advertisement in the Toronto *Telegram*. She had not been rehired by either of the two firms where she had articled, and she needed a new position. Publishing an "employment-wanted" notice was unusual for a young barrister and solicitor. None of her male colleagues did so. The advertisement itself was self-deprecating: "Miss Clara Brett Martin, Barrister &c., desires position in a law firm, where experience can be had in practical work, that being the object rather than salary."[84]

A small two-man law firm operated by John Shilton and William H. Wallbridge took her on. By 1901 the firm had changed its name to Shilton, Wallbridge, and Martin, in recognition of her contribution. In 1906 Clara Brett Martin left that firm to establish her own independent law office at 166 Bay Street. She went to court several times in the early years, but the fuss that always greeted her presence ultimately discouraged her, and she began to retain male barristers to act for her clients when they needed courtroom representation. Perhaps she feared that her clients' interests would suffer from having a woman advocate in court. As a result, most of her practice centred upon wills, real estate, and family law.[85]

Despite their unprecedented interest, members of the press did little to contribute to her professional status. Deeply ambivalent about whether to applaud her success or caution more traditional gender-role divisions, reporters "feminized" Canada's first woman lawyer. Irene B. Wrenshall, a reporter with the Toronto *Star Weekly* outlined in 1913 Clara Brett Martin's lengthy, wearying battle for entry. But she accompanied her copy with a full-length photograph, captioned "Charming Photo of Miss Clara B. Martin," showing her in an elegant ballgown laced with beaded trim and full-length gloves. A second caption, "Miss Clara Brett Martin: Pioneer Woman Lawyer — Special Bill Had to Be Passed by Ontario Legislature So She could Study Law — She Has Made Success of It," headed the article.[86]

Reporter Wrenshall would also insist that Clara Brett Martin had no hard feelings about her battle for admission:

A reference to Miss Martin's onerous work as a pioneer in opening the legal profession to women brought forth no trace of resentment. The long struggle seemed to be regarded with amused indifference, and was referred to in jocular vein.

The article continued, with some surprise, to recount how confidently Clara Brett Martin gave instructions to the male client she had dismissed just prior to the interview. But most important, the *Star Weekly* emphasized that Clara Brett Martin had not become "masculinized," either in her deportment or in her office decor:

The quiet varied pattern and rich subdued tints of the large rug harmonized perfectly with the general furnishings. Taste and artistic design were unconsciously suggested by the absence of obtrusiveness in furnishings, and the general harmony of arrangement. A man might thus plan and arrange an office, but he could never keep it so.

[Clara Brett Martin] also demonstrates day by day that professional success is not incompatible with the treasured feminine charms, and that a handsome woman can participate in public affairs without sacrificing the graces of a kindly nature.

Even her position on female suffrage, then only a few years from passage into law, was downplayed: "As one might expect, Miss Martin is in favour of the enfranchisement of women, though not inclined to dogmatize as to the best methods of hastening the change."[87]

It was as though the press wanted to reassure their readers, as Sir Oliver Mowat had with the legislature, that women in law would mean no real transformation. Clara Brett Martin might be practising law, but she still looked and acted like a conventional woman. Her "charming photo" and her unembittered, cheerful nature showed just how far from the stereotyped hard-bitten, abrasive, tough lawyer she was. How much the reporters were reading in their own views and attitudes and how much this was an accurate reflection of Clara Brett Martin will never be clear.

Clara Brett Martin's views about her press coverage are equally unclear. Perhaps she was pleased with a description that many would have regarded as flattering. The circumstances of her upbringing would have stressed femininity as a prerequisite for proper female behaviour. The stigma and opprobrium that attach to a woman who does not restrict herself to feminine decorum and mannerisms have always been harsh. Perhaps Clara Brett Martin consciously cultivated femininity, as a way of diminishing her anomalous position as a woman in law and of putting apprehensive clients and colleagues at ease.

But the fixation on Clara Brett Martin's dress, office decor, and graceful manners could not help but distract attention from the serious part of her personality and practice. The deliberateness of the characterizations reveal deep-seated anxiety about women in law. And such coverage was not confined to Clara Brett Martin. When American law publisher Myra Bradwell died, the obituary published by her longtime adversaries at the *Canada Law Journal* was strikingly similar:

Mrs. Bradwell was ... last, but not least, a gentle and noiseless woman, her tenderness and refinement making the firmness of her character all the more effective, a most devoted wife and mother, her home being ideal in its love and harmony.[88]

One of the taunts that had been thrown at Clara Brett Martin was that women lawyers would never find marriage partners. Whether Clara Brett Martin wanted to find a husband is another question. In 1875 Agnes Machar had retorted: "No man whose regard was worth having would be repelled" by a woman's choice of professional career. Whether Agnes Machar was wrong, and men were repelled, or whether Clara Brett Martin found no male suitor sufficiently to her liking, she remained a spinster. In this she was not atypical of many career women of her time. Neither Agnes Machar nor Carrie Derick had married. Economically and professionally independent, such women may not have faced the same degree of pressure toward heterosexual affiliation as other women. Clara Brett Martin may also have been concerned that marriage and family might force her to close down her law practice. In the early twentieth century it did not seem possible to combine professional careers with motherhood. As Canadian lawyer Ruby M. Wigle would note in 1927, approximately half of the women who were qualified gave up active practice for matrimony, something she categorized as "a regrettable fact ... but too complicated to discuss."[89]

The legal profession that Clara Brett Martin joined was viciously anti-Semitic, and she shared much of its open hostility against Jews. One of the only letters discovered from Clara Brett Martin's business files contains an anti-Semitic diatribe. Writing to the office of the Ontario Attorney-General in 1915, she accused Jewish realtors of transferring property titles improperly and misleading some of her clients about outstanding claims on certain properties. "These Jews find buying and selling property a very profitable business," she complained. "Would you kindly call the attention of the Government to this matter and try to have the Registry Act amended to prevent this scandalous work of foreigners." A solicitor in the Attorney-General's department wrote back advising that he would discuss the matter with the Registrar of Deeds, and making no comment about her anti-Semitic references.[90]

Clara Brett Martin's experience of sex discrimination had not increased her sensitivity to the injustice of anti-Semitism. Jews had been subjected to hostility throughout their years of settlement in Canada. In the first decade of the nineteenth century, Ezekiel Hart, a merchant from a small Jewish community in Trois Rivières had been elected twice to represent his riding in the Quebec Legislative Assembly. Both times he was declared ineligible to sit because he was a Jew. By the 1880s and 1890s pogroms in Russia and Romania had forced a mass exodus of Jews, several thousand of whom immigrated to Canada. To the alarm of the Jewish communities in Montreal, Toronto, and Winnipeg, incidents of anti-Semitism increased.[91]

In 1900 the Toronto *Weekly Sun* would clamour to prohibit further immigration of Polish Jews: "No invasion could be worse," it wrote, claiming that Polish Jews were "corrupter[s] of the community." In 1904 the Ottawa *Free Press* would protest the immigration of Russian Jews, a group that it described as having "drain[ed] the miserable purses of careless Russian peasants, through usury and extortions." In 1905, when the internationally famous actress Sarah Bernhardt performed in Montreal, she was pelted with rotten eggs by Laval University students shouting "Down with the Jewess!" In the 1920s and 1930s, vast sectors of the economy were closed to Jews. Banks, insurance companies, department stores, universities, and large industrial corporations would not hire Jews. There were no Jewish judges, and most law firms refused to hire Jews. Bora Laskin, later Chief Justice of the Supreme Court, could not find a job in 1937 when he returned to Toronto from Harvard Law School. The brilliant legal scholar with two master's degrees had to write headnotes for a law publisher at fifty cents a note. Anti-Semitic practices run through the heart of Canadian history, and Clara Brett Martin contributed her share.[92]

Throughout her career, Clara Brett Martin maintained her connections with some sectors of the women's community. A frequent lecturer to women's organizations on the topic of women and law, she was active in the National Council of Women of Canada, a non-denominational organization that had some Jewish women as members of local councils. Writing for the Council in 1900, Clara Brett Martin criticized the supremacy of paternal rights in matters of child custody, the double standard of sexuality in law, and the legal disabilities of married women. She hired a number of female articling students and joined with other women's rights advocates to lobby for female suffrage and for separate women's courts. Upon the prompting of Dr. Emily Stowe, she let her name stand for election as public school trustee. Successful in 1897, she served for ten years on the Toronto Board of Education, the only woman out of twenty-four trustees, and achieved a reputation as a "pioneer in the field of equal intellectual rights for women." She was narrowly defeated at the polls when she ran for alderman [sic] in 1920.[93]

Clara Brett Martin died prematurely of a heart-attack on 30 October 1923, at the relatively young age of forty-nine. Her substantial law practice was purchased in its entirety by the lawyer who probated her estate, R. Alan Sampson. Her will transferred all of her property — real estate, clothing, and jewellery — to her unmarried sister, Fanny, a school-teacher who had lived with Clara Brett Martin for many years. Extensive obituaries in the three Toronto newspapers heralded her passing as the loss of a trail-blazer for women in professional life.[94]

Others were less impressed. William Renwick Riddell, the tardy Ontario bencher who had interrupted the Law Society vote on Clara Brett Martin's application in 1892, had written sanctimoniously in 1918:

The whole number of women practicing law in Canada is very small, perhaps a dozen in all.... I do not think that the most fervent advocate of women's rights could claim that the admission of women to the practice of law has had any appreciable effect on the Bar, the practice of law, the Bench or the people. It is claimed that it was a measure of justice and fair play, that it removed a grievance and has had no other countervailing disadvantage. That claim may fairly be allowed: in other respects, the admission of women is regarded with complete indifference by all but those immediately concerned.

His characterization of the reform as "justice and fair play" was provoked largely by his assessment that women had made almost no difference to the legal profession.[95]

But even more supportive appraisers would have had to conclude that Clara Brett Martin's battle resulted in only a partial victory. Despite the heralding of her admission as a breakthrough for all women, women of other races were barred for decades. The first Black woman called to the bar in Ontario, Myrtle Blackwood Smith, would not be admitted until 1960. The first woman from the First Nations, Roberta Jamieson, would not graduate from law until 1976. In race and class Clara Brett Martin resembled the men already in the profession. Considering the many years she devoted to her fight for entry and the tenacity of the opposition, success may have been largely contingent upon the resources and connections available to Clara Brett Martin. The difficulties she encountered despite her advantages illustrate just how fundamentally gender mattered to the Canadian legal profession.[96]

# Conclusion

Nineteenth-century law provided an almost perfect example of a formally patriarchal institution. Apart from Clara Brett Martin's encroachment in the last three years of the century, women were barred from all direct control over the legal system — as voters, legislators, coroners, magistrates, judges, and jurors. They were, however, visible in court as litigants, witnesses, and accused persons. They were the subject of innumerable provincial and federal statutes. In some cases they tried to shape law in their own interests; in others they found themselves the objects of intrusive, harmful, and devastating legal actions. And women found almost every stage of their lives touched by the long reach of the law, from courtship through marriage, from consensual sexual encounters to forcible ones, throughout all aspects of fertility and reproduction, through marital breakdown, separation, divorce, and child custody, and in the field of waged and entrepreneurial labour.

Sexuality proved to be one of the broadest webs for nineteenth-century legal entanglement. When, where, and with whom women were permitted to engage sexually came under intense legal scrutiny. The major thrust of the law was to restrict sexual relations to married couples. Judicial rulings penalized parents who knowingly permitted their offspring sexual autonomy during courtship, despite evidence that the practice of bundling was the custom in rural areas. Legislation and supportive juries encouraged fathers to sue the seducers of their pregnant, unwed daughters. A maze of statutes sought to prohibit all aspects of prostitution, which was scorned as indiscriminate, extramarital sexual perversity.

Women may have perceived the tightening net of legal regulation as a mixed blessing. Various avenues of spontaneous and independent sexual expression were foreclosed to them as well as to men, the loss of which members of both sexes probably regretted. Others found their accustomed occupation as prostitutes repeatedly under attack by police. However, it was undoubtedly also risky to be heterosexually active outside of marriage. One of the major calamities that could befall a woman in nineteenth-century Canada was to become pregnant, by choice or otherwise, without a marriage partner. The economic and social prospects facing unwed mothers were stark. To the extent that the law deterred heterosexual relations that might have resulted in unwanted pregnancies, some women may even have been grateful for the restrictions.

The law of seduction provided a useful example of the ambivalence with which many women would have viewed the legal regulation of sexuality. The right to bring a seduction action for damages lay primarily with the seduced woman's father. A woman's sexuality was understood to be a form of property owned by men, and the law treated her experience — whether of mutually consensual intercourse or of rape — as irrelevant to her father's loss. Damages were owed to the father, not to the injured woman. The enforced dependency that ensued from such rules was insulting. And yet the lawsuit provided a rationale for the family of a seduced woman to seek vindication on her behalf. Many women may have welcomed the opportunity to assist their fathers as they sought to use the law of seduction to recoup financial compensation from the men responsible. Many women would have been delighted with the supportiveness offered by legislators and jurors, who exhibited acute sensitivity to the position of fathers of seduced daughters, facilitating the recovery of substantial sums for their losses.

The focus on male sexuality inherent in the seduction action was an unusual feature, and likely attributable to the fact that it was truly a man's lawsuit. The parties, both plaintiff and defendant, were men, and the actions of the woman concerned tended to slip into oblivion. This concerned some members of the judiciary, who responded to the high success rate of grieving fathers with remonstrations and muttering. Fearful that promiscuous women were benefiting unfairly, they fretted that working-class women were deliberately misbehaving sexually, in order to obtain financial redress they did not deserve. They thought it unfair that men should be penalized for responding to the seductive overtures of scheming women.

Women were the primary focus of much of the law designed to regulate sexuality. Many nineteenth-century Canadians believed that men were sexually aggressive by nature, their licentiousness spontaneously triggered by the presence of immodest and unchaste women. Thus laws that would tailor the deportment of women were designed to solve the problem of offensive sexual behaviour. Prostitution law was one highly visible example. Despite the demands of some women for an elimination of the sexual double standard, the primary target of criminal law was the female prostitute, not the male customers. The sale of sexual services, openly on the street or from brothels notorious throughout the community, spurred local police to use an intricate network of common law principles and statutory enactments to arrest, detain, and prosecute prostitutes. Prostitutes stigmatized by poverty, race, ethnicity, or religion found themselves even more harshly treated than white, economically prosperous prostitutes. Whether one views the occupation of prostitution as coercive, degrading, and dangerous, or as economically and socially liberating, this prosecutorial focus undeniably harmed women.

The late-nineteenth-century campaign of social reformers to create a new crime of seduction provides a detailed illustration of the clash of perspectives about whether women or men should be made legally responsible for extramarital heterosexual relations. As the potential for sexual exploitation of working-class women appeared to escalate due to increasing urbanization and industrialization, representatives of the National Council of Women of Canada vented their anger over what they saw as unbridled male lust. They called for severe criminal penalties to deter and punish sexually aggressive, promiscuous men. The legislators who responded argued that such initiatives were insulting to virtuous women, that women "should be made to understand that they must guard their own honour and chastity." The eventual passage of the Seduction Act in 1886 reflected an unhappy compromise between the two views, hedging the new crime with such restrictions that even the reformers acknowledged it was mainly a symbolic reform without potential for enforcement.

Some women who found themselves pregnant and unmarried took active measures of their own to correct the condition. Scores of women responded to unwanted childbirth with infanticide, frequently attempting to conceal their pregnancies and do away with the newborn infant without discovery. Harsh criminal statutes in force at the outset of the century in Newfoundland, Nova Scotia, New Brunswick, Prince Edward Island, Lower Canada, and Upper Canada consigned such women to death. But in the hands of the courts, the application of these laws was somewhat more compassionate.

The unmarried, working-class, frequently immigrant women who were caught committing infanticide would unlikely have provoked the protective instincts of judges and juries if they had come to court as rape victims. Few had families who could use the law of seduction to seek compensation. The results of their extramarital heterosexual activity were unclaimed children, without property or acknowledged lineage. The leniency that judges and juries often exhibited toward infanticide perpetrators was a safety valve, a way of creating space for desperate women who were trying to do away with the products of "illicit" sexuality. Apart from the male-controlled seduction action, the law would not intervene in any effective manner to restrict the heterosexual exploitation of women. But it would recognize the response of unwillingly pregnant, unmarried women as the rational reaction of cornered quarry. As the century progressed the legislatures reduced the criminal sanctions against infanticide. Compared to what the sentence had been, the crime of concealment provoked a relatively lenient two years' imprisonment by 1892.

Leniency was also exhibited by the judges of the higher courts toward the few economically privileged prostitutes who could afford to secure legal representation to appeal their criminal convictions. The appeal judges evidenced remarkable support of prostitutes' rights on the whole, a perspective that seems to have been quite at odds with their anti-female rulings in areas such as rape, child custody, married women's property law, and divorce. It appears that much as the judges believed in the legal regulation of sexuality, they also viewed prostitution as something of a "necessary social evil," required to accommodate male sexual needs.

An examination of the law of rape assists in clarifying the meaning behind the high court decisions on prostitution. This law should have provided protection for women subjected to forcible, involuntary heterosexual intercourse. The broad sweep of the law, as the judges were so fond of announcing, theoretically encompassed women regardless of class, marital status, or family background. But this was mostly rhetoric, for the law was applied in the narrowest of fashion by male judges and jurors who made short shrift of claims from sexually unconventional women. Women who charged they had been raped found themselves held up to extraordinary public inquiry, interrogated by malicious defence lawyers on topics from their sexual history to their minutest actions on the day of the rape. Only those who could point to irreproach-able sexual reputations and tenacious physical resistance came through this process relatively unscathed.

The systematic refusal of judges and juries to convict men who raped "immodest women" meant that they were consigning certain women to the status of public sexual property. This class of women, treated much like prostitutes, was expected to service male sexual demands. The higher courts might have been willing to uphold some freedom for prostitutes to practise their occupation unimpeded by criminal law, but they were not prepared to defend the sexual autonomy of these women. The contradic-tions could not have been more apparent. The law was applied to open sexual access for the male customers of female prostitutes, not to em-power women by freeing them from unwanted sexual attention. The enormity of the gap between the stirring speech of Ellen Rogers and the abysmally low rape conviction rates suggests how different were the perspectives of female rape victims and prostitutes from the all-male criminal justice system that adjudicated their claims.

Nineteenth-century law stepped well beyond the regulation of sexuality, into the heterosexual institution of marriage, which was central to its control over the lives of most Canadian women. Despite evidence that nineteenth-century Canadians held very diverse views about the nature of marriage, legislatures and courts seem to have been eager to set monolithic definitions. As the cases of Zoé Mignault and Susanne Pas-de-nom Connolly show, the choice of marital partner was a key concern. Who should select the spouse — the women and men involved, or their parents, relatives, and larger community? Upon what basis should the selection be made — romantic attractions, economic linkages, affinity of religion, race, and language? What exactly did marriage symbolize — an affectionate bond, reproductive partnership, an economic union?

Boldly claiming to rule upon the validity of marriage, even where this required cross-cultural analysis, lawyers and judges provided a high-profile forum for the articulation of legal rules about the boundaries of the institutions of marriage and family. Judicial rulings over marital customs among the First Nations, grudgingly supportive at the outset and an-tagonistic by the close of the century, provide a microcosm for viewing the changing dynamics between the First Nations and whites in Canada. As white dominance increased, whites increasingly assumed that European-based laws should supersede First Nations' legal systems.

As courts confronted marital disputes between parents and their children, generational loyalties tended to come to the fore. An aging judiciary, most of them parents themselves, issued rulings that not surprisingly backed parental perspectives on marital choice over those of their youthful, independently minded offspring. Enforcing statutory minimum-age requirements for autonomy in marriage, the judges confidently imposed parental authority upon runaway teenagers who had challenged family traditions by attempting to wed across cultural, economic, and linguistic boundaries.

For many couples nineteenth-century family law provided a forum for protracted and intense argument over the proper allocation of power and responsibility between husband and wife. Esther Hawley, Alberta Abell, and Nellie Armstrong refused to live with men who battered and attempted to subordinate them. But neither legislatures nor courts saw the nineteenth-century Canadian family as an egalitarian structure. The rules that divested married women of their property, prohibited tort actions against violent husbands, explicitly exempted spousal rape from criminal sanctions, and proclaimed that a "man had a right to chastise his wife moderately" all combined to construct a marked power imbalance between husbands and wives. The hierarchical, patriarchal concept of marriage enshrined in law protected tyrannical, abusive husbands and enforced servility and dependence upon many women. Access to legal divorce varied across the country, from highly restricted prospects in Quebec to a somewhat greater scope in Atlantic Canada. Adultery was generally viewed as the prerequisite for the dissolution of marriage, underscoring again the centrality of the reproductive model of marriage. Double standards, in law and in social attitudes, viewed the adultery of women as more serious than that of men.

Child custody law presented, at least in the early decades, a fathers'-rights paradise. Granted practically absolute control over their children by English common law rules, fathers took precedence over mothers regardless of parental abilities or the needs of children. Reformers found these rules particularly troubling as the century progressed and the status of motherhood and childhood began to receive growing attention. A series of statutes passed first in Ontario in 1855 and spreading to Nova Scotia, New Brunswick, and British Columbia in the 1890s, purported to grant mothers increasing rights of custody. In the hands of unsympathetic judges, however, this brought little substantive change. Mothers were typically granted custody only when they were living under the protection of some other male, usually their fathers or brothers, and only if they measured up to the idealized image of motherhood that narrowly circumscribed the range of acceptable female behaviour.

Nor were women allowed to regulate their fertility within marriage. Abortion, which was reputed to be a method frequently selected by married, Canadian-born, middle-class women who sought to reduce the number of children they birthed, came under increasing legal regulation throughout the nineteenth century. The mirror-opposite of infanticide laws, which became increasingly lenient over the century, legal prohibitions on abortion expanded greatly. From the introduction of the first statute prohibiting abortion in New Brunswick in 1810 to the wide-ranging prohibitions of abortion and birth control found in the Criminal Code of 1892, the century witnessed a consistent and protracted attempt to criminalize abortion regardless of stage of gestation, regardless of method.

Early proponents of women's rights, such as Dr. Emily Stowe, did not dispute these developments. Instead, they argued without notable success for "voluntary motherhood," the right of women to refuse heterosexual encounters that might result in unwanted pregnancies. Yet many women searched desperately for abortionists, demanding their right to prevent pregnancies where social and economic conditions made childbearing impossible. Courts that displayed compassion and understanding toward unmarried, working-class women who committed infanticide were generally heavy-handed with accused abortionists, often convicting them despite evidentiary contradictions and legal discrepancies. Emily Stowe's unusual acquittal is attributable, in all likelihood, to the gallantry of a legal system that found itself disturbed by the excesses in the testimony of male doctors against the female physician. It was much easier to discern sexism in a sister profession than within one's own ranks.

Nineteenth-century law also reached into the realm of employment, touching the lives of women who worked for wages outside their homes. Women who worked in factories, shops, mines, and restaurants found their workplaces increasingly subject to regulatory legislation. Statutes stipulating maximum hours of work, lunch-breaks, washrooms, and chairs were first promulgated in the 1880s, but vast gaps in coverage and sporadic enforcement ensured that little changed for most waged women. Whether stronger provisions would have proved useful is a more difficult question. The need for protective labour legislation directed exclusively at women sparked lengthy debate within the white predominantly middle-class women's movement. Despite protracted discussions, this was not a matter finally resolved to anyone's satisfaction. However, some legislation went beyond regulation to prohibit women from working in the mines, as waitresses in bars, and as street news-vendors. This constituted an unambiguous example of gender-biased, discriminatory lawmaking.

Clara Brett Martin's historic entry into the profession of law was by contrast, at least on the surface, a clear victory for women. An all-male stronghold had been successfully breached by a woman of vision, talent, and guts. Despite innumerable blocks and delays, Clara Brett Martin had persistently worn the benchers down until they conceded, tardily and rather gracelessly, that they could no longer bar the gates to women. But the admission of women to law in the nineteenth century was not inclusive by race or class, nor did it portend a new era of religious tolerance within the profession. Equally important, Clara Brett Martin's entry did not significantly alter the legal landscape. Catastrophic disruption had been predicted by those who opposed women in the profession. The litany was lengthy: nurseries attached to courtrooms, shrill demands to change laws perceived as discriminatory, women litigators who would use their gender to unfair advantage with judges and juries, abandoned families in unkempt homes as mothers who should have been attending to domestic duties lingered in law offices. A jocular poem attributed to "Ananias Limberjaw, QC," published in the Toronto *Grip* in 1892, claimed that women lawyers would inevitably refuse to play by time-honoured male rules:

> ... if females are
> Freely admitted to the bar,
> Could our profession long withstand
> The ruthless, innovating hand?
>
> The people have a shrewd misgiving
> That law, by which we make our living
> Is an imposture in disguise,
> A thing of quibbles, shams and lies.
>
> Now woman has perceptions bright,
> And a keen sense of wrong and right
> Her sympathies are deep and warm,
> Impatient of red tape and form.
>
> With her *esprit de corps* is lacking
> Which gives the legal shyster backing.
> Some day she'd turn, beyond doubt,
> The legal system inside out,

And, as the vulgar sometimes say,
Completely give the snap away
And stripped of technical disguise,
Expose our refuge of lies.

Praise to the benchers who have stood
Against the innovating flood,
To save us and our ample fees
From tribulations such as these.[1]

The potential that women held to transform law had been astutely probed in the *Lily*, an American feminist temperance journal published by Amelia Bloomer in 1852. The article contained two short descriptions of women purportedly arguing the same legal case against male opponents. One argued in the most traditional manner, citing with cool sophistication reams of abstract, technical legal doctrine. The other ignored precedent, forming her simple arguments upon emotional grounds and appealing solely to principles of truth and justice. In the feminist journal's account, both women triumphed over their opponents.[2]

Although the *Lily* was ambivalent about which approach was preferable, the prospect of a revolutionary, alternate vision of law was clearly recognized as an option. Women might have sought entry to law with a mission to transform it, to strip it of arcane, technical, tradition-encrusted rules. Insisting on humanizing the process and substance of law, women might have developed a more egalitarian, less emotionally detached approach, consciously diminishing the gulf between lay person and professional lawyer. Experienced in the manifold ways that sex discrimination could injure women, they might have protested laws that subordinated their sex, demanding immediate and comprehensive reform. Women might have insisted upon a full-scale restructuring of the conditions of work in law offices, so that child rearing and other familial responsibilities could be fully integrated with the practice of law.[3]

They might also have insisted upon major changes in the training of lawyers, ensuring that the needs of women students were recognized and that the curriculum and teaching methodology of legal education should be supportive and inclusive of women's issues. One route might have been to set up women-only law schools. Women doctors who had been banned from medical schools had set up their own all-female institutions in the United States, and briefly in Canada. Several all-women law schools were remarkably successful in the United States. The most prominent of these, Portia School of Law, a night-school devoted to teaching law exclusively to women, opened in Boston in 1908. The Women's Law Class of New York University, which opened in 1890 and ran until 1934, was designed to provide adult education law lectures exclusively to women.[4]

None of these potential transformations seems to have transpired. The press focus on women lawyers made much of the differences between them and their male counterparts, but only with respect to office decor, dress, and charming manners. This was not transformation, but a mere softening around the edges. Women did not set up women's law schools, nor is there evidence that, until recently, they insisted upon changes in curriculum or teaching methods in previously all-male institutions of legal education. Although Clara Brett Martin spoke and wrote about some of the legal reforms that women needed, there is little record that early women lawyers demanded wholesale removal of sexist bias in law. Nor did they insist that the legal profession welcome responsible child rearers within its midst. Instead, as the early women lawyers married and had children, they dropped out of visible practice in droves.

Women accommodated themselves to the legal profession, rather than insist upon any substantial transformation. McGill Professor Carrie Derick's perspective on equality, that women should work side by side with men under scrupulously equal conditions, seems to have been the model chosen by the first professional women. Arguments that women would add something special to the profession of law by virtue of their sex, that they would actively pursue discrimination, that by virtue of their different social acculturation they would seek to redefine advocacy and legal practice, faltered. "Lady lawyers" struggled to integrate so that their distinctive gender would fade into oblivion and they would simply be accepted as "lawyers." "You've entered a man's profession," Clara Brett Martin advised her female articling student, Lorna Brigden, in the early 1920s, "never expect them to wait on you."[5]

This may have been the only strategy that seemed possible in those early years. The undeniably difficult task of securing even a toehold for women in the profession may have taken all of the energy and resources that Clara Brett Martin and her fellow women lawyers could muster at the time. Accommodating themselves to the standards already established by a male profession undoubtedly seemed a goal that was both practical and admirable. But women looking on from outside were not enthusiastic. They voted with their feet, steering remarkably clear of the male-dominant legal profession. In 1894 Dr. Emily Stowe had spoken expectantly about the many women she hoped would soon join Clara Brett Martin within the legal profession. Yet the entrance of women was more of a trickle than a flood, and years often passed with no addition to the slim stream of female barristers and solicitors. Eva Maude Powley, the second Canadian woman, was not called to the Ontario bar until 1902. Mabel Penery French was the first woman to obtain admission in New Brunswick in 1906 and again in British Columbia in 1912. Quebec women did not enter the legal profession until 1941.[6]

No groundswell of young women followed Clara Brett Martin's lead for more than seventy years. Not until the 1970s and 1980s did gender ratios begin to alter dramatically in Canadian law schools.[7] With the public resurgence of the women's movement, large numbers of women finally began to enter law schools and the profession. Over the past few years, bolstered by such swelling of the ranks, feminist lawyers and law students have begun to confront sexist legal practices and structures somewhat more comprehensively. The earlier fork in the road — with two divergent paths of transformation and accommodation — may yet lie open again. This time women may make different choices. The strength and safety of numbers, as well as the growing maturity and vision of the women's movement, have combined to set the stage for what may ultimately be a drive to recast the legal profession and the legal system it administers in a radically more inclusive mould. But this is a story that awaits historians of the twentieth and twenty-first centuries.

CHAPTER 1: Photo of William Connolly courtesy of C. Gaudet, KC, reprinted with permission from *The Beaver*, September 1948; Photo of Amelia Douglas courtesy British Columbia Archives and Records Service, BCARS# HP3909; "Elopement à la Mode" reprinted from *Grip*, Toronto, 12 March, 1887. CHAPTER 2: "The Outcast's Return" reprinted from *Canadian Illustrated News*, Montreal, 17 January 1880; Photo of the Charltons from the National Archives of Canada, PA 33875; Photo of the National Council of Women from the National Archives of Canada, PA 28033; Photo of Lady Julia Drummond and daughter reprinted from *Canadian Men and Women of the Time*, William Briggs, Toronto, 1912. CHAPTER 3: "Scene in the Police Court" reprinted from *Canadian Illustrated News*, Montreal, 28 August 1875; "Murderous Outrage on a Lady" reprinted from *Illustrated Police News*, England, 18 March 1870. CHAPTER 4: "L'Enfant Trouvé" reprinted from *Le Monde Illustré*, 30 July 1887; Deposition of Alexandra Balo from Coroner's Inquest, Nanaimo, 16 April 1896, Archives of British Columbia, GR 1327 No. 37/1896; "Baby Farming" reprinted from *Illustrated Police News*, England, 1876. CHAPTER 5: Photo of Emily Stowe from National Archives of Canada, C9480; Photograph of Bottles of Sir J. Clarke's Female Pills from the Archives of Ontario, RG 22 Series 392, *R. v Robert Stitt*, 21 October 1878, photograph by Archives of Ontario; Photo of Augusta Stowe-Gullen courtesy The United Church of Canada/Victoria University Archives, Toronto. CHAPTER 6: "Fearful Wife Beating" reprinted from *Illustrated Police News*, England, 1868; "Le Travail" from National Archives of Canada, C108134; Letter from A.H. Abell from the Public Archives of New Brunswick, RS 58J. CHAPTER 7: "Motherly Love" reprinted from *Canadian Illustrated News*, Montreal, 19 August 1871; Cover *Canadian Illustrated News*, Montreal, 26 April 1879 from National Archives of Canada, C72064. CHAPTER 8: "No Mother at Home" reprinted from *Canadian Illustrated News*, Montreal, 31 March 1877; Photo of Magistrate Denison courtesy City of Toronto Archives, DPW54-383; Pornographic Poster from University of Western Ontario Library, Regional Collection. CHAPTER 9: "Her Day of Rest" reprinted from *Punch*, 8 April 1893; Photo of Agnes Machar from National Archives of Canada, C 51848; Photo of Carrie Derick courtesy McGill University Archives. CHAPTER 10: Photo of Clara Brett Martin courtesy Law Society of Upper Canada Archives; "The Barrister" reprinted from *Punch's Almanack*; "Some Stylish Late Summer Hats" collection of the author; Mock Trial, Osgoode Hall Law School courtesy Osgoode Hall Law School Archives.

# Notes

## Acknowledgments (pages xi to xiv)

1 The articles were published as: "Shifting Patterns in Nineteenth-Century Canadian Custody Law" in David H. Flaherty ed. *Essays in the History of Canadian Law* v. 1 (Toronto 1981) 212–48; "Nineteenth-Century Canadian Rape Law 1800–1892" in Flaherty *Essays* v. 2 at 200–247; "Involuntary Motherhood: Abortion, Birth Control and the Law in Nineteenth-Century Canada" 3 *Windsor Yearbook of Access to Justice* 3 (1983) 61–130; "Desperate Women and Compassionate Courts: Nineteenth-Century Infanticide in Canada" *University of Toronto Law Journal* 34 (1984) 447–78; "To Open the Way for Others of My Sex: Clara Brett Martin's Career as Canada's First Woman Lawyer" *Canadian Journal of Women and the Law* 1 (1985) 1–41; "The Tort of Seduction: Fathers and Daughters in Nineteenth-Century Canada" *Dalhousie Law Journal* 10 (1986) 45–80; "Pure Patriarchy: Nineteenth-Century Canadian Marriage" *McGill Law Journal* 31 (1986) 264–312; "Nineteenth-Century Canadian Prostitution Law: Reflection of a Discriminatory Society" *Social History/Histoire sociale* 18(36) (1985) 387–423; "Married Women's Property Law in Nineteenth-Century Canada" *Law and History Review* 6 (1988) 211–57.
2 The book was published as *The Secret Oppression: Sexual Harassment of Working Women* (Toronto 1979) and *Sexual Harassment on the Job* (Englewood Cliffs, N.J. 1981).

## Introduction (pages 1 to 8)

1 This wonderful reading group, named after the first book we read together, Mary Daly's *Gyn/Ecology: The Metaethics of Radical Feminism* (Boston 1978),

has been meeting monthly since 1979. The meetings and friendships that have ensued have been extraordinarily important to my energy, commitment, sense of elation around feminism, and simple sanity.

2 *The Concise Oxford Dictionary* 6th ed. (Oxford 1964): see entries for "heroine," "heroic," and "hero"; Margo Jefferson "A Vision Softly Creeping" *Vogue* (October 1984).

3 Cheris Kramarae and Paula A. Treichler *A Feminist Dictionary* (Boston 1985). The dictionary does, however, include an entry for "Great Hags," described by Mary Daly as "our foresisters ... whom the institutionally powerful but privately impotent patriarchs found too threatening for co-existence, and whom historians erase." I have no quarrel with this wonderful definition, but would prefer to see "heroine" rehabilitated in similar fashion.

4 Adrienne Rich captured this perfectly in her poem titled "Heroines" in *A Wild Patience Has Taken Me This Far* (New York 1981) 33–36. Commenting on the strictures — legal, social, economic, and otherwise — that subordinated upper-class women, as well as the privilege that kept them from appreciating the reality of working-class women and women from racial minorities, she concluded:

> you draw your long skirts
> >       deviant
> >               across the nineteenth-century
> registering injustice
> >       failing to make it whole
> How can I fail to love
> >       your clarity and fury
> how can I give you
> >       all your due
> >               take courage from your courage
> honor your exact
> >       legacy as it is
> recognizing
> >       as well
> >               that it is not enough?

5 I am indebted to Marlee Kline's "Race, Racism and Feminist Legal Theory" *Harvard Women's Law Journal* 12 (1989) 115, for providing me with a framework within which to review my own research for racism. I fear that my previous research would have provided an even more comprehensive

tool for exposition than the publications of the feminist professors that Kline used as a forum for critique.

6 For an account of Sinclair's remarks, see Toronto *Globe* 14 Nov. 1989.

7 For a brief introduction to this topic, see Sheila Jeffries *The Spinster and her Enemies: Feminism and Sexuality 1880–1913* (London 1985); Judith Schwarz *Radical Feminists of Heterodoxy* (Norwich, Vt. 1986); Lilian Faderman *Surpassing the Love of Men* (New York 1981) and *Scotch Verdict* (New York 1983); Kathy Peiss and Christina Simmons *Passion and Power: Sexuality in History* (Philadelphia 1989); Salvatore J. Licata and Robert P. Petersen *Historical Perspectives on Homosexuality* (New York 1981); Martin Bauml Duberman et al. eds. *Hidden from History: Reclaiming the Gay and Lesbian Past* (New York 1989).

## Chapter 1 (pages 9 to 39)

1 "Connolly, William" *Dictionary of Canadian Biography* v. 7 (Toronto 1988) 204–6; *Connolly v Woolrich and Johnson et al.* (1867) 11 L.C. Jur. 197 at 198–99, 232.

2 The account of the marriage ceremony was pieced together from *Connolly v. Woolrich* (1867) 225–28 and the more general descriptions found in Sylvia Van Kirk *"Many Tender Ties": Women in Fur-Trade Society 1670–1870* (Winnipeg 1980) 24, 36–37; Bradford W. Morse "Indian and Inuit Law and the Canadian Legal System" *American Indian Law Review* 8 (1980) 199; Alan D. McMillan *Native Peoples and Cultures of Canada* (Vancouver 1988) 102–3. See also *Johnstone et al. v Connolly* (1869) 17 R.J.R.Q. 266 at 283–85.

3 Morse "Law" at 215; Van Kirk *Ties* 21, 37; McMillan *Native* 102–3.

4 Van Kirk *Ties* 21, 37; McMillan *Native* 102.

5 *Connolly v Woolrich* (1867) at 198, 199, 204, 232. *Johnstone v Connolly* (1869) at 311, 322. The decision notes that Susanne was married in 1803 at the age of fifteen, hence my calculation of her birth year as about 1788.

Evidence of matrilineality among the Cree has been taken from Charles A. Bishop et al. "Matriorganization: The Basis of Aboriginal Subarctic Social Organization" *Arctic Anthropology* 17(2) 34 at 35–36. For description of the Cree lands, see McMillan *Native* 101.

Susanne's first name, not atypically in the nineteenth century, was also variously spelled Susana, Susanna, and Suzanne. For details of the naming ceremonies of the Cree, see David G. Mandelbaum *The Plains Cree* (Regina 1979) 140–42.

6 *Johnstone v Connolly* (1869) at 310–11; "Connolly, William" *DCB* v. 7 at 204–6.

7 *Connolly v Woolrich* (1867) at 198–99, 260; *Johnstone v Connolly* (1869) at 314–15; "Connolly" *DCB* v. 7 at 204–6; "Conolly, William" W. Stewart Wallace ed.

*The Macmillan Dictionary of Canadian Biography* 4th ed. (Toronto 1978) 172. On the role of First Nations' women in fur-trade marriages, see Van Kirk *Ties* and Jennifer Brown *Strangers in Blood: Fur Trade Company Families in Indian Country* (Vancouver 1980), Jennifer S.H. Brown "Woman as Centre and Symbol in the Emergence of Metis Communities" *Canadian Journal of Native Studies* 3(1) (1983) 39; "Connolly, Suzanne" *DCB* v. 9, 149 at 150.

8 Alison Prentice et al. *Canadian Women: A History* (Toronto 1988) at 38. But see also the report of *Connolly v Woolrych* found in *Canada Law Journal* 3 (1867) 14 at 15, in which Monk stated that there were nine or ten children of the marriage. See also *Connolly v Woolrich* (1867) 198–99; Jean Johnston *Wilderness Women* (Toronto 1973) 156.

9 *Connolly v Woolrich* (1867) at 200, 257–58; *Johnstone v Connolly* (1869) at 320–21. For discussion of the pattern whereby white fur traders came to seek white acculturation for their bi-racial offspring, see Van Kirk *Ties*; Brown *Strangers*.

10 *Connolly v Woolrich* (1867) at 200, 257–58; *Johnstone v Connolly* (1869) at 320–21.

11 *Connolly v Woolrich* (1867) at 199–200; *Johnstone v Connolly* (1869) 307.

12 *Connolly v Woolrich* (1867) 253, 258–59; "Conolly" Wallace *Dictionary* 172; "Connolly" *DCB* v. 7 at 150.

13 See Van Kirk *Ties* at chapters 7, 8, and 9; Kathleen Jamieson *Indian Women and the Law in Canada: Citizens Minus* (Ottawa 1978) 3–4; J.R. Miller *Skyscrapers Hide the Heavens: A History of Indian-White Relations in Canada* (Toronto 1989).

14 "Connolly" *DCB* v. 9 at 150; Brown *Strangers* 115–30, 136, 211; Sylvia Van Kirk "The Impact of White Women on Fur Trade Society" in Susan Mann Trofimenkoff and Alison Prentice eds. *The Neglected Majority: Essays in Canadian Women's History* (Toronto 1977) 27 at 35, 37.

15 *Connolly v Woolrich* (1867) 200, 236–38, 254 (emphasis in the original).

16 "Connolly" *DCB* v. 7 at 204–6; "Connolly" *DCB* v. 9 at 149–50.

17 *Connolly v Woolrich* (1867) 236, 252; *Johnstone v Connolly* (1869) at 303–4; "Connolly" *DCB* v. 7 at 204–6; "Connolly" *DCB* v. 9 at 149–50. That Susanne Connolly did not return to the Cree people may indicate that she became assimilated into white society to such an extent that a return to traditional life would have been difficult. The choice of St. Boniface was symbolic, as the Red River colony was the locus for the Métis. See Miller *Skyscrapers* 116–35.

18 *Connolly v Woolrich* (1867) at 264; "Connolly" *DCB* v. 9 at 150.

19 Montreal *Herald* 8 Sept. 1869 at 2. For discussion about the notoriety of the litigation, see Johnston *Wilderness Women* 173; Morse "Law" 222.

20 For discussion about the state of First Nations–white relations, see John Webster Grant *Moon of Wintertime* (Toronto 1984) 75, 97, 167.

21 "Cross, Hon. Alexander" George MacLean Rose *A Cyclopaedia of Canadian Biography* (Toronto 1888) 166–67; *Connolly v Woolrich* (1867) 200–201.

22 See, for example, William Pinder Eversley and William Feilden Craies *The Marriage Laws of the British Empire* (London 1910) at 279, 202–3, 290.

23 See, for example, Eversley and Craies *Marriage* 306.

24 "Monk, Hon. Samuel Cornwallis" Rose *Cyclopaedia* 537.

25 *Connolly v Woolrich* (1867) 216, 225–28.

26 *Connolly v Woolrich* (1867) at 207, 215, 247.

27 *Connolly v Woolrich* (1867) at 207, 215, 247.

28 *Connolly v Woolrich* (1867) at 225.

29 *Connolly v Woolrich* (1867) at 215, 255.

30 *Connolly v Woolrych Canada Law Journal* 3 (1867) 14 at 15.

31 *Connolly v Woolrich* (1867) at 254.

32 *Connolly v Woolrich* (1867) at 258.

33 *Johnstone v Connolly* (1869), Thomas-Jean-Jacques Loranger dissenting; "Connolly" *DCB* v. 9 at 149. For discussion of the appeal process, see Morse "Law" at 225.

34 Details of Amelia Connolly Douglas's life are found in Van Kirk, *Ties*, at 111–14, 131–32, 156, 208–9, 237; Johnston *Wilderness Women* 155–77; Derck Pethick *James Douglas: Servant of Two Empires* (Vancouver 1969) 263; Robert Hamilton Coats *The Makers of Canada: Sir James Douglas* (Toronto 1910) 103–7; Dorothy Blakey Smith *James Douglas: Father of British Columbia* (Toronto 1971) 18, 24–25, 37, 93, 108, 117.

35 Miller *Skyscrapers* 115, 152–69; Maria Campbell *Halfbreed* (Toronto 1973) 9.

36 "An Act for the gradual enfranchisement of Indians, the better management of Indian affairs, and to extend the provisions of the Act 31st Victoria, Chapter 42" 32–33 Vict. (1869) c. 6, s. 6 reads as follows:

> Provided always that any Indian woman marrying any other than an Indian, shall cease to be an Indian within the meaning of this Act, nor shall the children issue of such marriage be considered as Indians within the meaning of this Act; Provided also, that any Indian woman marrying an Indian of any other tribe, band or body shall cease to be a member of the tribe, band or body to which she formerly belonged, and become a member of the tribe, band or body of which her husband is a member, and the children, issue of this marriage, shall belong to their father's tribe only.

See Miller *Skyscrapers* 152–68; Jamieson *Citizens Minus*; Sally M. Weaver "The Status of Indian Women" in Jean Leonard Elliott ed. *Two Nations, Many Cultures: Ethnic Groups in Canada* 2nd ed. (Scarborough 1983).

37 *Fraser* v *Pouliot et al.* (1881) 7 Q.L.R. 149 (Que. Superior Ct.); *Fraser* v *Pouliot et al.* (1884) 13 R.L.O.S. 1 (Que. Superior Ct.); *Fraser* v *Pouliot et al.* (1885) 13 R.L.O.S. 520 (Que. Q.B.); *Jones* v *Fraser* (1886) 12 Q.L.R. 327 (Que. Q.B.).

One witness, Edouard Petigrew, noted that Angélique Meadows was "une sauvagesse des Hauts," although the judges seem to have taken no notice of this. *Fraser* v *Pouliot* (1884) at 30.

38 *Fraser* v *Pouliot* (1881) at 150; *Fraser* v *Pouliot* (1884) at 25; *Jones* v *Fraser* (1886) 341; "Fraser, Alexander" *Macmillan Dictionary* 4th ed. (1978) 274; Brown *Strangers* 90–94.

39 *Fraser* v *Pouliot* (1884) at 32–33; *Jones* and *Fraser* (1886) 341, 350–52; Brown *Strangers* 90–94; "Fraser" *Macmillan Dictionary* 274; Morse "Law" 225–28.

40 *Jones* v *Fraser* (1886) 334–36, 339–41.

41 Campbell *Halfbreed* 9–11; Miller *Skyscrapers* 170–88.

42 "Cross, Hon. Alexander" Rose *Cyclopaedia* 166; *Jones* v *Fraser* (1886) at 355.

43 *Jones* v *Fraser* (1886) 355–56.

44 *Jones* v *Fraser* (1886) 356–58.

45 *Jones* v *Fraser* (1886) 356–60; Brown *Strangers* 90–94; "Fraser" *Macmillan Dictionary* 274.

46 Cross was one of five judges who sat on the *Fraser* case. Justices A.A. Dorion, Ramsay, and Baby agreed that the marriage was invalid; Monk was the sole dissenter. The Supreme Court of Canada judgment was reported as *Jones* v *Fraser* (1886) 13 S.C.R. 342. See also *Re Sheran* (1899) 4 *Territories Law Reports* 83 (Supreme Court of the North-West Territories), which invalidated a mixed marriage celebrated according to the custom of the Piegan nation. The case of *Robb* v *Robb* (1891) 20 O.R. 591 (Common Pleas) also dealt with the validity of a mixed marriage between a white man and a woman of the Comox nation. In that case the court upheld the marriage, but expressly refused to rely upon the "Indian" ceremony, stating that it was "possible that a marriage according to the recognized form among Christians may also have taken place" (at 619–21, 624).

The judgment that upheld a First Nations' marriage between First Nations' partners was *The Queen* v *Nan-e-quis-a-ka* [1889] 1 Terr. L.R. 211 (N.W.T. C.A.). Judge Edward Ludlow Wetmore stated at 215:

I have great doubts if [the laws of England respecting the solemnization of marriage] are applicable to the Territories in any respect. According to these laws marriages can be solemnized only at certain times and in certain places or buildings. These times would be in many cases most inconvenient here and the buildings, if they exist at all, are often so remote from the contracting parties that they could not be reached without the greatest inconvenience.... The Indians [*sic*] are for the most part unchristianized, they yet adhere to their own peculiar marriage customs and usages. It would be monstrous to hold that the law of England respecting the solemnization of marriage is applicable to them.

47 *The Queen* v *"Bear's Shin Bone"* [1898–1901] 4 Terr. L.R. 173; (1900) 3 C.C.C. 329 (N.W.T. S.C.) at 329–30; Morse "Law" 231–32.
48 *"Bear's Shin Bone"* [1898–1901] at 173.
49 "Forget, Hon. Amédée Emmanuel" Morgan *Canadian Men and Women of the Time* 2nd ed. (1912) at 410; "Forget, Amédée Emmanuel" Stewart *Macmillan Dictionary* 2nd ed. (1945) at 208.
50 Henriette Forget "The Indian Women of the Western Provinces" in National Council of Women of Canada *Women of Canada: Their Life and Work* (Ottawa 1900) 435.
51 Forget "Indian" 435–36.
52 John McLean *The Indians: Their Manners and Customs* (Toronto 1889) at 80.
53 Forget "Indian" 435–36.
54 See Ellen M. Thomas Gee "Marriage in Nineteenth-Century Canada" *The Canadian Review of Sociology and Anthropology* 19 (1982) 311 at 320. In 1861, the average age of (first) marriage for Quebec women was 24.7; for Quebec men 26.5. Gee's data show these numbers to be relatively consistent throughout the rest of the century.
55 See Peter Ward *Courtship, Love, and Marriage in Nineteenth-Century English Canada* (Montreal 1990) 61 for discussion of the low rates of mixed marriages among nineteenth-century Catholics.
56 *Mignault* v *Bonar* (1865) 15 R.J.R.Q. 80; (1866) 1 *Lower Canada Law Journal* 97 (Que. Superior Ct.); *Mignault* v *Hapeman* (1866) 14 R.J.R.Q. 439 (Que. Superior Ct.). For information on the sleighing customs of nineteenth-century Montreal, see Edgar A. Collard *Montreal: The Days that Are No More* (Toronto 1976) 133–42.
57 (Mrs.) Rosanna Leprohon *Antoinette De Mirecourt; or, Secret Marrying and Secret Sorrowing. A Canadian Tale* (Montreal 1864) at 17, 60. See *Dictionnaire des Oeuvres Littéraires du Québec* (Montreal 1978) 34 for details of the French translation. Leprohon, who set her story in the eighteenth-century, did not profess to be writing about the Mignault–Hapinian affair, although she clear-

ly intended to mine the public fascination with secret marriages, especially those that crossed religious boundaries.

58 Leprohon *Antoinette* 40, 92.

59 Leprohon *Antoinette* 134.

60 Leprohon *Antoinette* 121–22.

61 Carole Gerson *Three Writers of Victorian Canada and Their Works* (Downsview n.d.).

62 J.B. de la Salle *New Treatise of the Duties of a Christian Towards God* (Montreal 1869) at 298–300. This text circulated throughout Canada in both languages during the last third of the nineteenth century. For discussion regarding the traditional pattern of arranged marriages and the growing tensions this would create, see Lawrence Stone *The Family, Sex and Marriage in England 1500–1800* (New York 1977) at 387–88; Alan MacFarlane *Marriage and Love in England 1300–1840* (Oxford 1986); Ellen K. Rothman *Hands and Hearts: A History of Courtship in America* (New York 1894) at 26–29, 103–7; John K'Emilio and Estelle B. Freedman *Intimate Matters: A History of Sexuality in America* (New York 1988).

63 Ward *Courtship* 124, 125, 128, 136, 171. See also Stone *Marriage* and Rothman *Courtship*.

64 *Mignault* v *Bonar* (1865) 80–81 and 97. For details on Louis A. Jetté, who would be appointed to the Superior Court in 1878, see Rose *Cyclopaedia* 432–33; M. Hutchinson *The Marriage Laws in the Province of Quebec* (1890) in *Pamphlets: Marriage and Divorce* (n.p., n.d.) at 7; "Jetté, Sir Louis Amable" *Macmillan Dictionary* 4th ed. (1978) at 391; and Henry J. Morgan *The Canadian Legal Directory* (Toronto 1878) 115. For details on the age of marriage see André Tunc "The Grand Outlines of the Code Napoleon" in Bernard Schwartz *The Code Napoleon and the Common Law World* (New York 1956) 17 at 35; Peter N. Moogk "Les Petits Sauvages: The Children of Eighteenth-Century New France" in Joy Parr ed. *Childhood and Family in Canadian History* (Toronto 1982) at 23; Civil Code of Lower Canada 29 Vict. (1865) c. 41, art. 115, 119; Frederick Parker Walton *Scope and Interpretation of the Civil Code of Lower Canada* (Montreal 1907) 19–20.

65 *Mignault* v *Bonar* (1865) 80–81 and 97.

66 See "Badgley, Francis" *DCB* v. 9 at 16; "Badgley, William" *DCB* v. 11 at 40–41; "Badgley, William" *Macmillan Dictionary* 4th ed. (1978) at 33.

67 See Moogk "Children" at 23; Tunc "Code Napoleon" 35; Micheline Dumont-Johnson "History of the Status of Women in the Province of Quebec" *Studies of the Royal Commission on the Status of Women in Canada* (Ottawa 1971) 4; Jacques Boucher et al. *Le Droit dans la vie Familiale–Livre du Centenaire du*

*Code Civil I* (Montreal 1970) 158. See also *Leveillé* v *Leveillé* (1895) 1 R.J. 443 (C.S.).

For details of the stipulations in the English-speaking common law provinces, see: Marriage Act of 1791 [*The Acts of the General Assembly of Her Majesty's Province of New Brunswick (1786–1836)* (Fredericton 1838) c. 5 of the Acts of 1791]; Marriage Act of 1832 S.P.E.I. (1843) c. 8; Marriage Act of 1899 S.N.S. (1899) c. 26; "NorthWest Territory Marriage Ordinance of 1878" *Ordinances of North West Territories Passed by the Legislative Assembly 1878–1887* (Regina 1884–87); "Marriage Ordinance of 1865 of the Colony of British Columbia" *Ordinances of British Columbia* (1865) No. 21; Marriage Amendment Act S.O. (1874) c. 6, as amended S.O. (1894) c. 40 lowering the age to eighteen.

68 *Mignault* v *Bonar* (1865) 81–82.

69 *Mignault* v *Hapeman* (1866). The type of arguments Jetté would have made are articulated in a decision he later wrote as a judge: *Larramée* v *Evans* (1880) 24 L.C.J. 235 (Que. Superior Ct.) See also *Leveillé* v *Leveillé* (1895) for a fuller articulation of the premises behind parental consent rules.

70 "Badgley, William" *DCB* 40–41.

71 See Ward *Courtship* 23 for a discussion of the problem that mixed marriages posed for the nineteenth-century Catholic Church. After his appointment to the bench, Jetté would later write a lengthy and widely acclaimed decision on the law of marriage, in which he asserted these propositions as they applied to a marriage of two Roman Catholics celebrated by a Protestant minister: see *Larramée* v *Evans* (1880) 24 L.C.J. 235 (Que. Superior Ct.). For biographical data on Fabre, see "Fabre, Most Rev. Edward C." Rose *Cyclopaedia* 446; Adam Shortt et al. *Canada and its Provinces: A History of the Canadian People and their Institutions* v. 11 (Edinburgh 1914) at 89–92; "Fabre, E. Charles" *Macmillan Dictionary* 4th ed. (1978) at 249.

72 The Quebec Act 14 Geo. III (1774) c. 83; Susan Mann Trofimenkoff *The Dream of Nation: A Social and Intellectual History of Quebec* (Toronto 1983) 33–70; Edgar McInnis *Canada: A Political and Social History* (Toronto 1982) 147.

73 McGinnis *Canada* 273, 324; J.L. Finlay et al. *The Structure of Canadian History* (Scarborough 1979) 124, 151.

74 See Hutchinson "Marriage Laws" at 1–2; Mann Trofimenkoff *Dream* 118–119; M. Jean "L'État et les Communautés religieuses féminines au Québec 1639–1840" *Studia Canonica* 6 (1972) 163–79; E.L. de Bellefeuille "Code civil du Bas–Canada. Législation sur le mariage" *Revue canadienne* 1 (1864) 602, 655, 731; *Revue canadienne* (1865) 30; Eusèbe Belleau *Des Empêchements Dirimants de Mariage* (Lévis 1889) 80, where the author states: "En principe, les mariages mites entre catholiques et protestants, doivent se faire par le

proper curé de la partie catholique....le mariage d'un catholique avec une protestante contracté devant un ministre protestant, n'est pas nul, mais simplement illicite." For biographical details on Laflèche, see *Macmillan Dictionary* 4th ed. (1978) at 426; Robert Rumilly *Mgr LaFleche et Son Temps* (Montreal 1938). It was not until 1921 that a clear separation of church and state would be pronounced in law: *Despatie* v *Tremblay* [1921] 1 A.C. 702 (H.L.).

75 Hutchinson "Marriage Laws" 6–7.
76 On 1 August 1866, the Civil Code of Lower Canada spelled out the new requirements regarding parental consent in article 119:

> Children who have not reached the age of twenty-one years must obtain the consent of their father and mother before contracting marriage; in case of disagreement, the consent of the father suffices.

It also set forth stipulations requiring the publishing of banns in the church or churches to which the parties belonged (articles 57, 58, 130).

For details of the stipulations in the English-speaking common law provinces, see: Marriage Act of 1791 [*The Acts of the General Assembly of Her Majesty's Province of New Brunswick (1786–1836)* (Fredericton 1838) c. 5 of the Acts of 1791]; Marriage Act of 1832 S.P.E.I. (1843) c. 8; Marriage Act of 1899 S.N.S. (1899) c. 26; "NorthWest Territory Marriage Ordinance of 1878" *Ordinances of North West Territories Passed by the Legislative Assembly 1878–1887* (Regina 1884–87); "Marriage Ordinance of 1865 of the Colony of British Columbia" *Ordinances of British Columbia* (1865) No. 21; Marriage Amendment Act S.O. (1874) c. 6, as amended S.O. (1894) c. 40 lowering the age to eighteen.

77 Ward *Courtship* 124, 136, 171.

## Chapter 2 (pages 40 to 80)

1 *Hogle* v *Ham* (1825) U.C.K.B.R. (Taylor) 2nd ed. 248. *The Upper Canada Herald* (Kingston) 30 Aug. 1825, 6 Sept. 1825; Kingston *Chronicle* 2 Sept. 1825.
2 For discussion of courtship practices, see Peter Ward "Courtship and Social Space in Nineteenth-Century English Canada" *Canadian Historical Review* 68(1) (1987) at 35–62; Peter Ward *Courtship, Love, and Marriage in Nineteenth-Century English Canada* (Montreal 1990).
3 For reference to the "reasonable expectation" of marriage, see *Hogle* v *Ham* 250. For discussion of the various forms of religious and community

scrutiny (encompassing public shaming from the pulpit and from church elders, as well as the tradition of charivari, which waned in influence as the century progressed) accompanying premarital sexual intercourse, see Ward *Courtship* 25–30; Bryan D. Palmer "Discordant Music: Charivaris and Whitecapping in Nineteenth-Century North America" *Labour/Le Travailleur* 3 (1978) 5. For an example of one spectacular "shotgun" wedding, see *Lawless v Chamberlain et al.* (1889) 18 O.R. 296 (Chy.). In this case the father of a pregnant woman orchestrated a marriage service while brandishing a revolver, threatening to kill both his nineteen-year-old daughter (Maud Chamberlain) and her nineteen-year-old lover (Sydney Lawless) if they refused to wed. The couple married, and Sydney's father challenged the legality of the marriage in court. The arguments that the couple were underage and that the service had been carried out under coercive circumstances were dismissed by the Ontario Court of Chancery in Ottawa.

4 In 1862 the *Upper Canada Law Journal* concluded that the loss of a woman's reputation was "destructive of domestic comfort and earthly happiness," and amounted to "a living death" (v. 8 at 309). For a more general discussion about illegitimacy, and analysis of the effect of subsequent marriage upon reputation, see W. Peter Ward "Unwed Motherhood in Nineteenth-Century English Canada" Canadian Historical Association *Historical Papers* (Halifax 1981) 34–56. Premarital pregnancy rates were much higher in the United States, where more than 20 per cent of couples had a child born less than 8.5 months after marriage. See Ellen K. Rothman *Hands and Hearts: A History of Courtship in America* (New York 1894) at 45.

5 For discussion of the family's role in shielding unmarried pregnant women, see Ward "Courtship."

6 "Hagerman, Christopher Alexander" *Dictionary of Canadian Biography* v. 7 at 365–72; David B. Read *Lives of the Judges* (Toronto 1888) 201–21.

7 William Blackstone *Commentaries on the Law of England* (Chicago 1979, orig. pub. 1768) v. 3, 142; William Holdsworth *A History of English Law* (London 1927) v. 8 at 428. For a more detailed discussion of the roots of this action, which grew out of the *actio per quod servitium amisit*, see Constance Backhouse "The Tort of Seduction: Fathers and Daughters in Nineteenth-Century Canada" *Dalhousie Law Journal* 10 (1986) 45.

8 See Backhouse "Seduction." The right of action lay exclusively with the father so long as he remained alive. In the event of his death, the widowed mother inherited the claim. Some scholars have suggested that the right of widows to litigate detracted from the patriarchal nature of the claim: see Peter Ward's review essay of Alison Prentice et al. *Canadian Women: A History* in *Canadian Historical Review* 70(3) (September 1989) 383. This argument

is not compelling, since mothers did not come by their right to litigate personally, but only by standing in the shoes of the patriarch of the family.

9 C.G. Addison *Wrongs and Their Remedies: Being a Treatise on the Law of Torts* (London 1864, orig. pub. 1860) 803–4. This text was often cited in Canadian legal circles at the time.

10 Joy Parr *Labouring Children: British Immigrant Apprentices to Canada 1869–1924* (Montreal 1980) 82–84.

11 Kingston *Upper Canada Herald* 6 Sept. 1825; *Hogle* v *Ham* 248, 251. For details regarding the essential elements of the tort, see James Edward Davis *Prize Essay on the Laws for the Protection of Women* (London 1854) 140.

12 Kingston *Upper Canada Herald* 6 Sept. 1825; Davis *Prize* 144.

13 It appears that in some cases, the women did institute breach of promise suits, or launch filiation proceedings in addition to their fathers' seduction cases. See Rosemary J. Coombe "'The Most Disgusting, Disgraceful and Inequitous Proceeding in our Law': The Action for Breach of Promise of Marriage in Nineteenth-Century Ontario" *University of Toronto Law Journal* 38 (1988) 64. But where the woman could not prove that seduction had taken place under promise of marriage, she had no claim under a breach of promise suit.

14 For a description of some of the medical and legal groups calling for reform, see Backhouse "Seduction."

For discussion of the French civil law, see Marie-Aimée Cliche "Les Filles Mères Devant Les Tribunaux dans le District Judiciare de Québec 1850–1969" unpublished manuscript; Marie-Aimée Cliche "Fille-mere, famille et société sous le Régime francais" *Histoire sociale/Social History* 41 (1988) 39–69; M. Fournel *Traité de La Séduction* (Paris 1781); P.-B. Mignault *Le Droit Civil Canadien* (Montreal 1901) 368–69. Damages under seduction actions in Quebec prior to the Civil Code were limited to loss of moral reputation and, in certain circumstances, lost wages. Lying-in expenses were the subject of a separate action, "frais de gésine."

The Civil Code of Lower Canada 29 Vict. (1865) c. 41, art. 1053, covered seduction under more general language:

> Every person capable of discerning right from wrong is responsible for the damage caused by his fault to another, whether by positive act, imprudence, neglect or want of skill.

The Civil Code assumed that a father could also bring an action because the honour of his family had been attacked. Although the Civil Code did not directly alter the legal rules concerning damages for seduction, tighter

evidentiary restrictions were placed on the parallel action of paternity decla-
rations "reconnaissance de paternité," and by the latter decades of the
nineteenth century Quebec judges would begin to demand more extensive
(frequently written) proof of promise of marriage in seduction actions.

See also André Nadeau and Richard Nadeau *Traité Pratique de la
Responsabilité Civile Délictuelle* (Montreal 1971) 201–9; Pierre Letarte
"Séduction et frais de gésine" *Revue du Barreau* 2 (1942) 251–58.

In one unusual Quebec case, the claim brought by a father was listed as a
"tort," or "action on the case," and seems to have paralleled the common
law action: *Neill* v *Taylor* (1865) 13 R.J.R.Q. 434 (C.S.). Concepts from common law could taint the civil law as jurists trained in the former discipline
attempted to administer the latter. See E. Kolish "The Impact of the Change
in Legal System" *Canadian Journal of Law and Society* 3 (1988) 1. However the
*Neill* decision, despite its language, was not an aberration since this form of
remedy had long existed in civil law.

I am indebted to Marie-Aimée Cliche, Sylvio Normand, and Victor Nabhan for their kind assistance in my research into the Quebec law of seduction.

15 "An Act to provide a Summary Remedy for Females, in certain Cases of
Seduction" 15 Vict. (1852) c. 23, s. 1 (P.E.I.) was rather clear on its face
regarding its intent to transfer the claim to the woman herself:

> In all Actions hereafter to be brought for Seduction of Females, where
> the Damages sought to be recovered shall not exceed One hundred
> Pounds, the Action shall and may be brought, if the Plaintiff so elect,
> by and in the name of the Woman seduced, whether a minor or other-
> wise, who, notwithstanding she shall be the Plaintiff in the Cause,
> shall be admitted as an Evidence therein, to and for all such purposes
> as she might or could have been before the passing of this Act, in case
> the Action had been brought *per quod servituim* [sic] *amisit*, by her
> Parent, Guardian or Master.

Judges were permitted to appoint a trustee to whom the damages could be
paid. See also 21 Vict. (1858) c. 15 (P.E.I.); 39 Vict. (1876) c. 4 (P.E.I.); 40 Vict.
(1877) c. 6 (P.E.I.); 58 Vict. (1895) c. 5 (P.E.I.).

For information on the legislation prohibiting women's right to vote, see
Prentice *Canadian Women* 99.

For details on the American legislative pattern, see M.B.W. Sinclair
"Seduction and the Myth of the Ideal Woman" *Law and Inequality* 5 (1987)

33. Both Iowa and Alabama had given seduced women their own right of action by the time of the P.E.I. enactment.

The judicial ruling was reported as *McInnis* v *McCallum* (1854) *Peter's P.E.I. Reports* 72 (S.C.).

16 *Gilmore* v *Dewar* (1838) 1 N.S.R. 101 (S.C.).

17 See also *Canada Law Journal* (1874) v. 10, N.S. 132–33, where it was recommended that the right of action be shifted, but it was also noted that "there are some who think, however, that such actions should not be maintainable, the consent of the woman taking away the right of action." For evidence that cases brought by seduced women resulted in greater scrutiny of their role in the seduction and their prior sexual morality, see Thomas Thorner et al. "A Question of Seduction: The Case of *MacMillan* v *Brownlee*" *Alberta Law Review* 20 (1982) 447 and Sinclair "Seduction."

18 "Jones, Jonas" *DCB* v. 7 at 456–61; Read *Judges* 176–87; Kingston *Upper Canada Herald* 6 Sept. 1826; *Hogle* v *Ham* 248, 253.

19 Ellen Rothman *Courtship* 46–48; Lawrence Stone *The Family, Sex and Marriage in England 1500–1800* (New York 1977) 605–7.

20 Rothman *Courtship* 47–49; Stone *Family* 606–7.

21 For the Niagara Assizes reference, see *Fuller* v *Secord* as reported in *The Colonial Advocate* 19 Aug. 1824. Ward in "Courtship" at 52 and 59 noted that upper-class, urban women were much more circumscribed in their social activities, and strict chaperonage accompanied by rigid rules of propriety would persist until the end of the century.

22 Kingston *Upper Canada Herald* 6 Sept. 1825.

23 *Hogle* v *Ham* 248–49.

24 Kingston *Upper Canada Herald* 6 Sept. 1825.

25 Kingston *Upper Canada Herald* 6 Sept. 1825.

26 Kingston *Upper Canada Herald* 6 Sept. 1825.

27 Kingston *Upper Canada Herald* 6 Sept. 1825.

28 Kingston *Upper Canada Herald* 6 Sept. 1825.

29 Kingston *Upper Canada Herald* 6 Sept. 1825.

30 Of 152 seduction actions followed during the nineteenth century, plaintiffs won 90.13 per cent of the verdicts at trial. For detailed discussion of the action, its success ratio, and damage awards, see Backhouse "Seduction."

31 *Upper Canada Law Journal* (1862) 311.

32 For a succinct articulation of this principle, see *Ross* v *Merritt* (1845) 2 U.C.Q.B. 421, where the court stated: "If the debauching of the plaintiff's servant is an injury to the plaintiff, the servant cannot give license to the defendant to commit that injury."

33 See Backhouse "Seduction" generally.

34 *Hogle* v *Ham* 251–54.
35 See, for example, the Goderich *Signal* 10 Oct. 1877, where the reporter described the trial over Elizabeth Griffith's seduction: "The courtroom was crowded when the case was called and when the young lady's counsel escorted her into the courtroom her beauty and modesty created quite a sensation. The jury seemed touched and the effect was such that the defendant immediately proposed to settle."
36 "Cartwright, John Solomon" *DCB* v. 7 at 156–59.
37 *Hogle* v *Ham* 249. See William N.T. Wylie "Instruments of Commerce and Authority: The Civil Courts in Upper Canada 1789–1812" in David H. Flaherty ed. *Essays in the History of Canadian Law* v. 2 (Toronto 1983) at 23 regarding the difficulty of satisfying civil judgments.
38 *Hogle* v *Ham* 249, 254.
39 "Macaulay, Sir James Buchanan" *DCB* v. 8, 511–13; Read *Judges* 148–57.
40 *Hogle* v *Ham* 250–52.
41 *Hogle* v *Ham* 253–54.
42 "Campbell, Sir William" *DCB* v. 6 at 113–18.
43 *Hogle* v *Ham* 258; "Campbell" *DCB* 116.
44 *Hogle* v *Ham* 258–59. Campbell's views presaged what later in the century would become accepted wisdom about proper premarital courting behaviour. One "purity manual" widely read in Canada, Dr. Henry N. Guernsey's *Plain Talks on Avoided Subjects* (Philadelphia 1882), would advise an unmarried woman that she should avoid kissing, and even the squeezing or holding of hands. To allow herself to reciprocate a suitor's loving attentions during courtship would be to fall prey to the "evils of blighted love" and to behave on a "partially animal basis." See also Michael Bliss "Pure Books on Avoided Subjects: Pre-Freudian Ideas in Canada" Canadian Historical Association *Historical Papers* (Ottawa 1970) 90; John S. Haller and Robin M. Haller *The Physician and Sexuality in Victorian America* (Chicago 1974).
45 *Hogle* v *Ham* 262; "Sherwood, Levius Peters" *DCB* v. 7 at 794–96; Read *Judges* 106; Donald R. Beer "Toryism in Transition: Upper Canadian Conservative Leaders 1836–1854" *Ontario History* 80(3) (September 1988) 207 at 215.
46 *Hogle* v *Ham* 262; Read *Judges* 105.
47 *Hogle* v *Ham* 255–56, 260.
48 Of the 152 seduction actions followed, 52 of the verdicts were subject to motions for legal review. Of these, defendants won 48.08 per cent. See Backhouse "Seduction."
49 The argument that juries were more representative is true, but should not be taken without some qualification. A typical jury for trials of this sort, em-

panelled to hear the cases up before the Assize court, would have been an all-white, all-male group of prosperous landowners from the region. For discussion of the class-bound nature of seduction actions, see Backhouse "Seduction" generally.

50 *Anderson* v *Rannie* (1862) 12 U.C.C.P. 536 at 538–39.

51 "Draper, William Henry" *DCB* v. 10 at 253–58; "Draper, William Henry" in Stewart *Macmillan Dictionary* at 222. *Snure* v *Gilchrist* (1863) 23 U.C.Q.B. 81 at 83.

52 "Actions for Seduction" *Local Courts and Municipal Gazette* 2 (1866) 35.

53 *Snure* v *Gilchrist* at 83.

54 This case was not reported, but records are available at the Archives of Ontario (hereafter AO) RG22, Wentworth County Case Files, 11 Jan. 1888.

55 Hamilton *Spectator*, Tues. 13 Sept. 1887. The spelling of Russell Blows's name was variously "Blows" and "Blowes."

56 Prentice et al. *Canadian Women* at 123, 124–25; Faye E. Dudden *Serving Women: Household Service in Nineteenth-Century America* (Middletown, Conn. 1983) 12–44, 46–60. For a legal reference to the egalitarian nature of service employment, see *Cromie* v *Skene* (1869) 19 U.C.C.P. 328 at 335–36 where the judge, John Wilson, noted that in Canada those who employed domestic servants were generally "of the same class" as those they hired, and "usually treated their servants as members of the family, and in their associations held them as equals."

57 Marjorie Griffin Cohen *Women's Work, Markets and Economic Development in Nineteenth-Century Ontario* (Toronto 1988) at 74–75. See also Parr *Labouring Children* at 82–84; Prentice et al. *Canadian Women* at 124.

58 Prentice et al. *Canadian Women* at 125; Micheline Dumont et al. *Quebec Women: A History* (Toronto 1987) at 64; Cohen *Markets* at 74–140. A typical contract of indenture can be found in a book published to assist lay farmers, John Whitley *Canadian Domestic Lawyer* (Stratford 1864) at 310–11.

59 The claim was typical for its time. The average amount claimed in a seduction action between 1885 and 1889 was $1,975. See Backhouse "Seduction" for a table compiling data on claims.

60 There is little record of Canadian commentary on the shortcomings of the seduction action, but evidence of the discussions in England and the United States suggest class-based analysis was at the heart of the reform. For information on the English debate, see *Grinnell* v *Wells* (1844) 7 Man. & G. 1044, quoted in Frederick Pollock *The Law of Torts: A Treatise on the Principles of Obligations Arising from Civil Wrongs in the Common Law* (London 1887) at 201; and Davis *Prize*. For information on the American situation, see Sinclair "Seduction" 33. For the reform legislation, see "An Act to make the remedy

in cases of seduction more effectual, and to render the Fathers of illegitimate Children liable for their support" 7 Wm. IV (1837) c. 8 (U.C.), as amended by R.S.O. (1887) c. 58 and 62 Vict. (2) (1899) c. 13 (Ont.). I am indebted to Professor Louis Knafla for his suggestion that the passage of this statute in 1837 may have been causally linked to the Rebellion. The timing and substance of the statute are highly suggestive of this theory. Unfortunately, for this time there are no Hansard debates that would shed further light upon the impetus for passage. In the closing speech for the session printed in the Upper Canada *Gazette* on 9 March 1837, the seduction bill was deemed not "proper particularly to advert to." The bill passed second reading by a majority of only one vote.

61 *Biggs* v *Burnham* (1843) 1 U.C.Q.B. 106 at 109; *Cromie* v *Skene* at 335–36.

62 "The Law of Seduction" *Upper Canada Law Journal* (1862) 309 at 310–11. For a more complete description of American law on this point, see Sinclair "Seduction" at 33. The Manitoba references are to *Hebb* v *Lawrence* (1890) 7 Man. L.R. 222 and "An Act respecting the Action of Seduction" 55 Vict. (1892) c. 43 (Man.). See Ord. N.W.T. (1903) c. 8 (Seduction), and *Simpson* v *Read* (1858) 9 N.B.R. 52 (S.C.).

63 See Backhouse "Seduction" generally.

64 The Hamilton *Spectator*, Tues. 13 Sept. 1887, reported that the jury were split eight for the Camps and four for the Blows. Inexplicably the case file indicates that the split was three for the Camps, nine for the Blows.

65 Toronto *Daily Mail* 12 Jan. 1888.

66 See Backhouse "Seduction" at 58 for a description of violent seduction cases such as *Brown* v *Dalby* (1850) 7 U.C.Q.B. 160; *Stark* v *MacDonald* AO RG22, County of Wentworth Minute Books, 22 Oct. 1888; *Urquhart* v *Zavitz* AO RG22, County of Wentworth Minute Books, 28 Oct. 1884.

67 *E.* v *F.* [1905] 10 O.L.R. 489 at 492.

68 *E.* v *F.* [1905] 10 O.L.R. 489. Chancellor Boyd, quoting from an earlier court decision, noted that "the gist of the action is the debauching of the daughter. … It would be no defence, that the crime was rape, and not seduction." The Chancellor also pointed out that section 534 of the Criminal Code provided that no civil remedy for any act should be "affected or suspended by reason that it amounts to a criminal offence."

69 For biographical data, see "Teetzel, Hon. James Vernall" Morgan *Canadian Men and Women of the Time* 2nd ed. (Toronto 1912) at 1,090; Stewart *Macmillan Dictionary* 2nd ed. (1945) at 658.

70 *Upper Canada Law Journal* (1862) 311.

71 Toronto *Globe* 12 Jan. 1888; Toronto *Daily Mail* 10 Jan. 1888.

72 The average damage award in seduction cases between 1885 and 1889 was

$663. See Backhouse "Seduction" for table regarding damage awards in nineteenth-century seduction actions.

73 For statistical details of the growing urban population in Canada, which increased from 722,343 in 1871 to 1,537,098 in 1891, see M.C. Urquhart ed. *Historical Statistics of Canada* (Toronto 1965) at 5–6. By way of comparison, the rural population increased more slowly from 2,966,914 in 1871 to 3,296,141 in 1891.

See also Rothman *Courtship* at 207. For a wonderfully detailed description of the changing patterns in leisure for working-class youth in New York at the turn of the century, see Kathy Peiss *Cheap Amusements: Working Women and Leisure in Turn-of-the-Century New York* (Philadelphia 1986) where she documents the increasing autonomy and sexual independence exhibited by working-class women within the newly commercialized dance halls, theatres, and "nickel dumps."

74 For a description of the rural exodus of young women, see Prentice et al. *Canadian Women* at 115–16. Reference to the areas of emigration come from the National Council of Women of Canada *Women of Canada* 413. Research on the historical experience of women who immigrated to Canada in the late nineteenth century is still in its infancy, but see Jean Burnet ed. *Looking into My Sister's Eyes* (Toronto 1986) for material on a slightly later period.

75 Surprisingly, although Charlton devoted many years of his political career to the passage of the seduction law, and singled the campaign out as one of the most important of his career, he failed to include any remarks on the topic in his collection of speeches and addresses published in 1904. See John Charlton *Speeches and Addresses: Political, Literary and Religious* (Toronto 1905). This may be indicative of some ambivalence or of some sense of hurt over the vituperative attack launched against him by opponents of the bill. For other biographical details, see "Charlton, John" Stewart *Macmillan Dictionary* 2nd ed. (1945) at 115.

76 *Hansard Parliamentary Debates* House of Commons v. 12 (1882) 47, 326–27; House of Commons v. 1 (1886) 441–42. See also Constance Backhouse "Nineteenth-Century Canadian Rape Law 1800–1892" in Flaherty *Essays* v. 2, 200 at 228–32.

Interestingly, the very first draft of Charlton's "Seduction Bill" contained clauses that would have extended the right of civil action to seduced women themselves. This feature was quickly dropped after the most preliminary parliamentary discussions, and reference to reform of the civil action does not appear again in the protracted debates. *Debates* House of Commons v. 12 (1882) 327.

77 *Debates* House of Commons v. 1 (1884) 143; v. 1 (1886) 441–42. The male

editors of the *Canada Law Journal* were early advocates of the bill, claiming that seduction was "one of the crying evils of the day." Their motivation for supporting Charlton seems inspired in part by guilt. "The [man who seduces] practically goes unpunished," they wrote. "He is scarcely tabooed in society; in fact, his companions think him a rather fine fellow...." Emphasizing the isolation of many seduced women, they noted: "... the unfortunate woman bears the whole burden, becomes an outcast, is driven from home, disgraced and ruined, to bear her trial alone, overwhelmed by an agony of shame, that too often ends in some hideous crime or piteous suicide" *Canada Law Journal* 18 (1882) 151.

78 Smith's comments were quoted in *The Legal News* (Montreal) v. 6, n. 13, 31 March 1883, at 97–98. For a detailed summary of his position in opposition to women's rights, see A Bystander [Goldwin Smith] "The Woman's Rights Movement" *The Canadian Monthly and National Review* (March 1872) v. 1, 3, 249–64. For a description of Smith's stature, see Ramsay Cook *The Regenerators: Social Criticism in Late Victorian English Canada* (Toronto 1985) 26–40. See also *Debates* House of Commons v. 1 (1883) 223, 284.

79 *The Legal News* v. 6, n. 18, 5 May 1883 at 137–38.

80 *Canada Law Journal* 18 (1882) 151.

81 *Debates* Senate of Canada (1886) 367–68.

82 *Debates* Senate of Canada (1886) 432.

83 For some background on the social reform campaign to criminalize sexual exploitation and prostitution, see infra chapter 8, and Graham Parker "The Legal Regulation of Sexual Activity and The Protection of Females" *Osgoode Hall Law Journal* 21 (1983) 187, where the campaigns led by D.A. Watt of Montreal are described. For Charlton's comments, see *Debates* House of Commons v. 1 (1886) 441–42. "An Act to punish seduction and like offences, and to make further provision for the Protection of Women and Girls" 49 Vict. (1886) c. 52 (Can.).

84 Seduction Act 1866, ss. 1, 2, 5, and 8. *Debates* House of Commons v. 1 (1886) 706. Convictions for seduction under promise of marriage were only obtainable against men above the age of twenty-one years. For discussion about the age limitations in previous bills, see *The Legal News* v. 7, n. 11, 15 March 1884 at 81–82.

85 *The Legal News* v. 7, n. 11, 15 March 1884 at 82.

86 "An Act to amend the Act respecting Offences against Public Morals and Public Convenience" 50 & 51 Vict. (1887) c. 48, s. 2 (Can.).

87 "An Act further to amend the Criminal Law" 53 Vict. (1890) c. 37, s. 4 (Can.); The Criminal Code, 1892 55–56 Vict. c. 29, s. 184 (Can.). Rather oddly, there was a specific defence tacked on in the 1892 provisions. An employer,

supervisor, ship-master, officer, or seaman who subsequently married the woman he seduced was to be completely exonerated from criminal prosecution.

For discussion of the debates in the House of Commons and Senate on seduction in the employment setting, see Constance B. Backhouse and Leah Cohen *The Secret Oppression: Sexual Harassment of Working Women* (Toronto 1979) ch. 3.

88 Veronica Strong-Boag *The Parliament of Women: The National Council of Women of Canada 1893–1929* (Ottawa 1976) 75–87; Appendix to *Women Workers of Canada*, Being the Reports and Discussions on the Laws for the Protection of Women and Children ... at the Third Annual Meeting of the NCWC (Montreal 1896). For discussion of "maternal feminism" see Prentice et al. *Canadian Women* at 169; Wayne Roberts "'Rocking the Cradle for the World': The New Woman and Maternal Feminism, Toronto 1877–1914" in Linda Kealey ed. *A Not Unreasonable Claim* (Toronto 1979) 15.
89 NCWC "Appendix" at 313, 320–21.
90 NCWC "Appendix" 323.
91 NCWC "Appendix" 315.
92 NCWC "Appendix" 315–16.
93 NCWC "Appendix" 321.
94 *Debates* House of Commons v. 1 (1886) 442; NCWC "Appendix" 325. For biographical details about Marion Bryce, who was also president of the Woman's Christian Temperance Union in Winnipeg, see "Bryce, Rev. George" Morgan *Canadian Men and Women* 2nd ed. (1912) at 163–64; "Bryce, George" Sir Charles G.D. Roberts and Arthur L. Tunnel eds. *A Standard Dictionary of Canadian Biography: Canadian Who Was Who* v. II (Toronto 1938) 50–53.
95 *The Queen* v *Walker* (1893) 1 *Territories Law Reports* 482.
96 Charlton *Speeches* at p. x.

## Chapter 3 (pages 81 to 111)

1 Toronto *Daily Globe* 15 Dec. 1858; Toronto *Leader* 15 Dec. 1858.
2 Toronto *Daily Globe* 15 Dec. 1858; Toronto *Leader* 15 Dec. 1858.
3 See Toronto *Daily Globe* 20 Dec. 1858; Toronto *Daily Globe* 14 Jan. 1859; Toronto *Leader* 14 Jan. 1859; Toronto City Directory (1856) 30, 72–73, 212.
4 Toronto *Leader* 20 Dec. 1858; Toronto *Daily Globe* 20 Dec. 1858.
5 Toronto *Daily Globe* 15 Dec. 1858, 20 Dec. 1858; Toronto *Leader* 20 Dec. 1858.
6 Nicholas Rogers "Serving Toronto the Good" V. Russell ed. *Forging a Consen-*

*sus: Historical Essays on Toronto* (Toronto 1984) 116–40; Paul Romney *Mr. Attorney* (Toronto 1986) 232–38.

7 For details about which rape victims initiated criminal proceedings, see Constance Backhouse "Nineteenth-Century Canadian Rape Law 1800–1892" in Flaherty *Essays* v. 2, 200 at 224–25.

8 Toronto *Leader* 18 Dec. 1858.

9 Toronto *Daily Globe* 20 Dec. 1858.

10 Toronto *Leader* 18 Dec. 1858, 20 Dec. 1858; Toronto *Daily Globe* 20 Dec. 1858; Toronto *Patriot* 12 Jan. 1859.

   For biographical details on Gurnett, see "Gurnett, George" *Dictionary of Canadian Biography* v. 9 at 345–47; "Gurnett, George" Stewart *Macmillan Dictionary* 4th ed. (1977) at 321.

   The process of appointing a Crown attorney to prosecute criminal cases was still in its infancy; see "An Act for the Appointment of County Attorneys" 20 Vict. (1857) c. 59 (P.C.); Romney *Mr. Attorney*. Richard Dempsey, the attorney for the counties of York and Peel, was assigned to the case, but he took a very inactive role. Even the press described his position as merely "watching the case for the Crown." "Richard Dempsey" Caverhill's Toronto City Directory (1859–60) at 60; Toronto *Daily Globe* 20 Dec. 1858.

11 Toronto *Leader* 20 Dec. 1858. For details about the operation of the Toronto Police Court, see Paul Craven "Law and Ideology: The Toronto Police Court 1850–1880" in Flaherty *Essays* v. 2 at 248.

12 Toronto *Leader* 20 Dec. 1858.

13 Toronto *Leader* 20 Dec. 1858.

14 Toronto *Leader* 20 Dec. 1858.

15 See Backhouse "Rape" for a description of some of the many cases in which rape complainants with "suspicious reputations" were denied protection of the criminal rape law. For good examples, see *The Queen* v *Edwin Cudmore* AO RG22, York County Minute Books, 19 Oct. 1865; *The Queen* v. *John English* AO RG22, York County Minute Books, 18 April 1866.

16 Toronto *Daily Globe* 20 Dec. 1858.

17 Toronto *Daily Globe* 20 Dec. 1858.

18 Toronto *Daily Globe* 20 Dec. 1858.

19 Toronto *Leader* 14 Jan. 1859.

20 Toronto *Leader* 20 Dec. 1858.

21 Toronto *Leader* 20 Dec. 1858.

22 Toronto *Leader* 20 Dec. 1858.

23 Toronto *Daily Globe* 20 Dec. 1858.

24 See Backhouse "Rape" for cases outlining the standard of resistance ex-

pected. Good examples included *R.* v *Fick* (1866) 16 U.C.Q.B. 379; *The Queen* v *Antoine Legacy* AO RG22, Renfrew County Minute Books, 4 Oct. 1883; *The Queen* v *Henry Waggstaff* AO RG22, York County Minute Books, 4 Oct. 1887.

25 Toronto *Daily Globe* 20 Dec. 1858. For discussion of the low frequency with which nineteenth-century lay magistrates in England dismissed charges at preliminary hearings, see Douglas Hay "Controlling the English Prosecutor" *Osgoode Hall Law Journal* 21 (1983) 165 at 169.

26 Toronto *Leader* 18 Dec. 1858; 20 Dec. 1858; Toronto *Daily Globe* 20 Dec. 1858. The latter report noted that once the accused men had been committed for trial, the two women were finally released from custody.

See also Anna K. Clark "Rape or Seduction? A Controversy over Sexual Violence in the Nineteenth Century" London Feminist History Group *The Sexual Dynamics of History* (London 1983) 13 at 26, where it is noted that English rape victims were often imprisoned after pressing charges, "if they were too poor or did not have a husband to post bond to ensure that they would prosecute."

27 Toronto *Patriot* 12 Jan. 1859.

28 Blackstone *Commentaries* v. IV at 213. Canadian legal treatises, such as W.C. Keele's *The Provincial Justice, or Magistrate's Manual, Being a Complete Digest of the Criminal Law of Canada* (Toronto 1851), espoused this view as well: "Nor is it any excuse [in a charge of rape] that the woman is a common prostitute; for she is still under the protection of the law, and may not be enforced" (at 565).

29 On corroboration, see William Eden *Principles of Penal Law* (London 1771) 236–37; Terry L. Chapman "Sex Crimes in the West 1890–1920" *Alberta History* 35 (1986) 6 at 14.

30 "The Hon. Archibald McLean" *Upper Canada Law Journal* 1 (1865) (N.S.) 281 at 282; Read *Judges* 158–75; "McLean, Archibald" *DCB* v. 9 at 512–13.

The criminal procedure of the time required that the case be heard first by the grand jury, a group of influential citizens who were empanelled at the Assizes to screen the cases before trial. The grand jury here had returned "true bills" against Robert Gregg, William Ross, Alexander Doig, John Hellam, and George Hughes for burglary, rape, and robbery. All but Hughes, who could not be found, were subsequently arraigned on the charges and set over for trial. (Toronto *Patriot* 12 Jan. 1859.)

31 For details of the appointment of Crown attorneys, see Romney *Attorney* 220–30. "Cameron, John Hillyard" *DCB* v. 10 at 118–23; "Cameron, John Hillyard" Stewart *Macmillan Dictionary* 2nd ed. (1945) at 92.

Criminal trials were typically conducted in English even in Quebec during the nineteenth century. With the reception of English criminal law after the Conquest, criminal law practice came to rest almost exclusively with the English-speaking bar. Quebec juries were typically divided between six anglophones and six francophones, but trials were conducted in English by English-speaking barristers. The one distinction was that interpretation services were generally offered for francophone witnesses and accused persons. See Andre Morel "La réception du droit criminel anglais (1760–1892)" *Revue Juridique Themis* 13 (1978) 449 at 534–38; Douglas Hay "The Meanings of the Criminal Law in Quebec 1764–1774" in Louis Knafla ed. *Crime and Criminal Justice in Europe and Canada* (Waterloo 1981) 77.

32 Toronto *Leader* 14 Jan. 1859.
33 For a more detailed analysis of the fear of false complaints, see Backhouse "Rape." For case examples, see William Henry Draper's comments in *R. v Francis* (1855) 13 U.C.Q.B. 116 at 117 and *The Queen v William Stead* as reported in the Toronto *Globe* 12 Oct. 1882. For biographical details on Eccles, see "Eccles, Henry" *DCB* v. 9 at 233; "Eccles, Henry" Stewart *Macmillan Dictionary* 239.
34 Toronto *Leader* 14 Jan. 1858; Toronto *Globe* 14 Jan. 1858.
35 Toronto *Leader* 14 Jan. 1858; Toronto *Globe* 14 Jan. 1858.
36 Toronto *Leader* 14 Jan. 1858; Toronto *Globe* 14 Jan. 1858.
37 Toronto *Globe* 14 Jan. 1858. The Toronto Directory listed Andrew Gregg under a slightly different spelling: Andrew Greig, boot and shoe-maker, 81 Sayer Street: see *Brown's General Directory for Toronto 1861* (Toronto 1861) 185.
38 Toronto *Leader* 14 Jan. 1858.
39 Paul Romney's *Mr. Attorney* at 218–19 describes the potential for bribery and extortion within the system of private prosecution. His discussion is most particularly of the English situation, where the system of private prosecution pertained much longer than in Canada. However, he notes that the Upper Canadian situation, although not as bad as in England, was not free of such pressures.

There was always, of course, a parallel civil system permitting persons victimized by crime to sue for civil damages. While there has been no systematic analysis of these sorts of lawsuits in nineteenth-century Canada, see *Gross v Brodrecht* (1897) 24 O.A.R. 687 (C.A.); *Bigonesse v Brunelle* (1883) 6 *Legal News* 270 (Que. Superior Ct.); *The Queen v Riendeau* (1900) 3 C.C.C. 293 (Que. Ct. of Q.B.) for examples.
40 Toronto *Leader* 14 Jan. 1858; Toronto *Globe* 14 Jan. 1858.
41 Toronto *Leader* 14 Jan. 1858.
42 Toronto *Leader* 14 Jan. 1858.
43 *Laliberté v The Queen* (1877) 1 S.C.R. 117.
44 For details on the common law and statutory treatment of sentences in rape,

see Backhouse "Rape." See also "An Act to Consolidate and Amend the Statute Law of England and Ireland Relating to Offenses Against the Person" 24 & 25 Vict. (1861) c. 100 (Eng.); "An Act for consolidating and amending the Statutes in this Province relative to Offenses against the person" 4 & 5 Vict. (1841) c. 27 (P.C.).

45 Macdonald Papers National Archives of Canada, MG 26A, Letterbook 11, no. 854; 8 June 1868 letter from John A. Macdonald to William Johnston Ritchie, Chief Justice, Nova Scotia. I am indebted to Jon Swainger, whose research unearthed the letter, for providing me with these details.

The failure to provide legal protection to Black rape victims has not been fully explored in Canada, but comparative American analysis indicates that "from emancipation through more than two-thirds of the twentieth century, no Southern white male was convicted of raping or attempting to rape a Black woman despite knowledge that this crime was widespread" (Susan A. Mann "Slavery, Sharecropping and Sexual Inequality" *Signs* 14(4) (Summer 1989) 774 at 788).

For analysis of the myth of the Black rapist, the anti-lynching movement, the rape of Black women by white men, see "Rape, Racism and the Myth of the Black Rapist" in Angela Y. Davis *Women, Race & Class* (New York 1981).

46 According to Prime Minister Macdonald, no execution had taken place for rape since the union of Upper and Lower Canada in 1841 (Macdonald Papers, 8 June 1868 letter). For information regarding patterns of sentencing on rape cases in Canada, see Backhouse "Rape." See "An Act to amend the Act respecting Offenses against the Person" 38 & 39 Vict. (1873) c. 94 (D.C.) and Backhouse "Rape Law."

47 Toronto *Leader* 14 Jan. 1858. For details on the practice of charging and convicting for lesser offences, see Backhouse "Rape."

48 Toronto *Globe* 14 Jan. 1858.

49 *Upper Canada Law Journal* 2 (1866) (N.S.) 234. For details of the conviction rates for rape, see Backhouse "Rape."

50 Toronto *Leader* 14 Jan. 1858.

51 Toronto *Leader* 14 Jan. 1858; Toronto *Globe* 14 Jan. 1858. The whereabouts of Ellen Rogers can be traced through the city directories, which were published in 1856, 1859–60, and 1861. She was listed in the 1856 *Brown's Toronto City Directory* (Toronto 1856) at Edward St., West of Yonge (pp. 30, 212). The *Caverhill Toronto City Directory, 1859–60* (Toronto 1860) had no listing of Ellen Rogers. Nor had *Brown's Toronto General Directory, 1861* (Toronto 1861).

52 I am indebted to Terry Chapman for bringing this unreported case to my attention in her "Sex Crimes" article in *Alberta History*. Indiana Matters of the B.C. Archives provided invaluable assistance in locating the surviving

records of the events. See Bench Book entries for *R*. v *Rabbit* [*sic*], Vernon Assizes, 11 Oct. 1897, Archives of British Columbia (ABC) GR 1727, v. 591; Assize Calendar Entries: Kamloops 4 Oct. 1897; Vernon 11 Oct. 1897, G-89-14. The Victoria *Daily Colonist* 12 Oct. 1897 reported Euphemia Rabbitt's status as the second female tried for murder.

53 Thomas Herbert Murphy "Reminiscences, 1930" ABC, E/E/M95; "Kamloops, B.C." *The Canadian Encyclopedia* v. 2 at 931; Miller *Skyscrapers* 147.

54 "Kamloops" *Canadian Encyclopedia*; "Notes of conversations with Hugh Hunter at his home, four miles east of Princeton, July 10 and 13, 1930" ABC Env.H. 169.2, EE H913.

55 Kamloops *Daily Standard* 30 Sept. 1897; Kamloops *Standard* 14 Oct. 1897; Bench Book Entries for *R*. v *Rabbitt*, heard at Vernon Assizes, 11 Oct. 1897, by M.W.T. Drake, ABC GR 1727, v. 591.

56 Kamloops *Daily Standard* 30 Sept. 1897; Kamloops *Standard* 14 Oct. 1897; Kamloops *Inland Sentinel Supplement* 28 Sept. 1897.

57 Kamloops *Inland Sentinel Supplement* 28 Sept. 1897; Bench Book Entries.

58 Kamloops *Inland Sentinel Supplement* 28 Sept. 1897; Kamloops *Standard* 14 Oct. 1897; Bench Book Entries.

59 Kamloops *Inland Sentinel Supplement* 28 Sept. 1897; Kamloops *Standard* 14 Oct. 1897; "Conversations: Hugh Hunter" 1930; Bench Book Entries.

60 Kamloops *Inland Sentinel Supplement* 28 Sept. 1897; Kamloops *Standard* 14 Oct. 1897; Bench Book Entries.

61 *R*. v *Fick* (1866) 16 U.C.Q.B. 379 (emphasis in the original).

62 Edward East, the author of an 1803 English treatise on criminal law, noted that all of the following factors aided in accepting the truth of a woman's claim: "If the witness be of good fame, if she presently discovered the offence, and made pursuit after the offender; if she shewed circumstances and signs of the injury, whereof many are of that nature that only women are proper examiners; if the place where the fact was done were remote from inhabitants or passengers; if the offender fled for it...." To the contrary, the following factors afforded a strong presumption that the testimony was feigned or contrived: "If she be of evil fame and stand unsupported by other evidence; if she concealed the injury for any considerable time after she had opportunity to complain...; if the place where the fact was supposed to be committed were near to the persons by whom it was probable she might have been heard, and yet she made no outcry...." Edward Hyde East *Pleas of the Crown* (London 1803) 445–46. See also Backhouse "Rape." Kamloops *Daily Standard* 30 Sept. 1897; Kamloops *Standard* 14 Oct. 1897.

63 Kamloops *Standard* 14 Oct. 1897; Kamloops *Daily Sentinel Supplement* 28 Sept. 1897; Bench Book Entries.

64 Kamloops *Inland Sentinel Supplement* 14 Sept. 1897.

65 For a general description of the coroner's office, see William Fuller Ayles Boys *A Practical Treatise on the Office and Duties of Coroners in Ontario and the other Provinces and the Territories of Canada and in the Colony of Newfoundland* (Toronto 1893); Christopher Granger *Canadian Coroner Law* (Toronto 1984); T. David Marshall *Canadian Law of Inquests* (Toronto 1980). For a description of the coroner's inquest in the English justice system, see Beattie *Crime* at 8–81, 91; R.F. Hunnisett ed. *Wiltshire Coroners' Bills 1752–1796* Wiltshire Record Society, v. 36 (Devizes 1980); Thomas Rogers Forbes "Crowner's Quest" *Transactions of the American Philosophical Society* 68 (1978).

66 Kamloops *Inland Sentinel Supplement* 28 Sept. 1897.

67 Kamloops *Inland Sentinel Supplement* 28 Sept. 1897.

68 Kamloops *Inland Sentinel Supplement* 28 Sept. 1897; Victoria *Daily Colonist* 28 Sept. 1897.

69 Kamloops *Daily Standard* 30 Sept. 1897.

70 "List of all prisoners confined in Kamloops Gaol, 1st Oct. 1897" ABC GR 55, Box 16, File K; Kamloops *Daily Standard* 30 Sept. 1897.

71 Victoria *Daily Colonist* 7 and 8 Oct. 1897. For biographical details on Wilson, see Morgan *Canadian Men* (1912) at 1,173–74.

72 Alfred Watts "The Hon. Mr. Justice Montague W. Tyrwhitt-Drake, Justice of the Supreme Court of British Columbia 1889–1904" *Advocate* 25 (1967) 225; "Tyrwhitt-Drake, Montague William" Wallace *Macmillan Dictionary* (1945) at 677; Joan N. Fraser *Judges of British Columbia to 1957: A Sourcebook* (Victoria 1984); *British Columbia: Pictorial and Biographical* v. 2 (Winnipeg 1914) 523–24; Victoria *Daily Colonist* 12 Oct. 897.

73 Kamloops *Standard* 14 Oct. 1897.

74 Kamloops *Standard* 14 Oct. 1897.

75 Kamloops *Standard* 14 Oct. 1897.

76 Kamloops *Standard* 14 Oct. 1897.

77 For discussion about nineteenth-century beliefs about male and female sexuality, see Haller and Haller *Physician and Sexuality*.

78 Bench Book Entries; Kamloops *Standard* 14 Oct. 1897.

79 G.W. Burbidge *A Digest of the Criminal Law of Canada* (Toronto 1890) at 216–17.

80 Burbidge *Criminal Law* 216, 219; S.R. Clarke *A Treatise on Criminal Law as Applicable to the Dominion of Canada* (Toronto 1872) 252–53.

81 Clarke *Criminal Law* 261–62.

82 Victoria *Daily Colonist* 12 Oct. 1897; *B.C. Mining Journal* (Ashcroft) 16 Oct. 1897; Kamloops *Inland Sentinel Supplement* 12 Oct. 1897.

83 See, for example, Joseph Edmund Collins *Annette. The Métis Spy; A Heroine*

*of the North West Rebellion* (Toronto 1886), in which Cree and Métis women were variously described as "minxes," "coy little maidens whom many had wooed," and "coquettish" (at pp. 51, 82, 109). Unmarried First Nations' women were portrayed as frankly interested in sexual matters, speaking among themselves of the "graceful loins" of their male compatriots, and given to repeated kissing of male lovers in public (at p. 45).

## Chapter 4 (pages 112 to 139)

1 Accounts of the trial of Angelique Pilotte were taken from AO RG22, series 134, v. 4, District of Niagara Court of King's Bench Assize Minute Book, Criminal 9 Sept. 1817; "Pilotte, Angelique" *Dictionary of Canadian Biography* v. 5 at 672–74.

None of the official records refer specifically to Angelique as Ojibwa, but merely as the "natural daughter of a Squaw and a native of the Indian Country." Professor Lisa Valentine, Department of Anthropology, University of Western Ontario, at my request generously sought to determine Angelique Pilotte's nationality. Given the geographic and time specifications, it was her opinion that the Algonkian nation of Ojibwa people was a likely choice. See also J.L. Morris *Indians of Ontario* (Toronto 1943) 63; McMillan *Native Peoples* 93–95; Grant *Moon of Wintertime* 76–77.

On the rarity of infanticide within the Ojibwa cultures, see W. Vernon Kenietz *Chippewa Village: The Story of Katikitegon* (Bloomfield Hills, Mich. 1947) 118; M. Inez Helger *Chippewa Child Life and Its Cultural Background* (Washington D.C. 1951) 33; Robert William Dunning *Social and Economic Change Among the Northern Ojibwa* (Toronto 1959) 150. See also Gilbert Malcolm Sproat *The Nootka: Scenes and Studies of Savage Life* (repub. Victoria 1987) at 68; T.R. Beck and John B. Beck *Elements of Medical Jurisprudence* (Philadelphia 1860) 458–59. For comparison with European culture, see information in this chapter.

2 A best-selling American novel, widely acclaimed in its time as the "Uncle Tom's Cabin" tale of peoples of the First Nations, *Ramona: A Story* by Helen Jackson (London and New York 1887), has as one of its prominent themes the subordinate status of interracial domestic service. For discussion about the mission of white "civilizing" efforts, see Grant *Moon of Wintertime* at 177–78.

3 For details about the construction of the new jail, see Janet Carnochan *History of Niagara* (Toronto 1914) 111, 157.

4 For general discussion of nineteenth-century infanticide in Canada, see Constance B. Backhouse "Desperate Women and Compassionate Courts: Infan-

ticide in Nineteenth-Century Canada" *University of Toronto Law Journal* 34 (1984) 447; Marie-Aimée Cliche "L'Infanticide dans La Région de Québec 1660–1969" *Revue D'Histoire De L'Amérique Française* (été 1990) 31; W. Peter Ward "Unwed Motherhood in Nineteenth-Century English Canada" Canadian Historical Association *Historical Papers* (Halifax 1981) 34; Mary Ellen Wright "Unnatural Mothers: Infanticide in Halifax 1850–1875" *Nova Scotia Historical Review* (1987) 13. For a comparative perspective, see Keith Wrightson "Infanticide in European History" *Criminal Justice History* 3 (1982) 1; Peter C. Hoffer and N.E.H. Hull *Murdering Mothers: Infanticide in England and New England 1558–1803* (New York 1981); W.L. Langer "Infanticide: an Historical Survey" *The History of Childhood Quarterly* 1 (1974) 353; R.W. Malcolmson "Infanticide in the Eighteenth-Century" in J.S.D. Cockburn ed. *Crime in England 1550–1800* (Princeton 1977) 198; J.M. Beattie *Crime and the Courts in England 1660–1800* (Princeton 1986) 113–24.

For details concerning the number of infants' bodies examined by the Toronto coroners, see Eric Jarvis "Mid-Victorian Toronto: Panic, Policy and Public Response 1856–73" unpublished Ph.D. thesis, University of Western Ontario 1978 at 134–35. With respect to Quebec City, see Cliche "L'Infanticide," Tableau 1 at 35.

5 For reference to the early French provisions, see *Recueil Général des Anciennes Lois Françaises* (Paris 1822–33) XIII at 471–73; P.G. Roy *Inventaire des Ordonnances des Intendants de la Nouvelle-France* (Beaceville 1919) I at 216–17; Ward "Unwed Motherhood" at 43. See also "An act to prevent the destroying and murthering of Bastard Children" 21 James I (1623) c. 27 (Eng.); "An Act relating to Treasons and Felonies" 32 Geo. II (1758) c. 13 (N.S.); "An Act relating to Treasons and Felonies" 33 Geo. III (1792) c. 1 (P.E.I.). The other jurisdictions adopted the statute by way of general legislation receiving English law into the colonies.

6 The wording of a typical statute was as follows: "[I]f any woman be delivered of any issue of her body, male or female, which being born alive, should by the laws of the realm of England be a bastard, and that she endeavour privately, either by drowning or secret burying thereof, or in any other way, either by herself, or the procuring of others, so to conceal the death thereof, as that it may not come to light whether it were born alive or not, but be concealed, the mother so offending shall suffer death as in the case of murder, except such mother can make proof by one witness, that the child whose death was by her so intended to be concealed, was born dead." English Act (as received into Upper Canada), s. 2; Nova Scotia Act, s. 5.

7 "Boulton, Henry John" *DCB* v. 9 at 69–72. The jurors selected were: Adam Beam, Jacob Haun, Benjamin Lam, William Buck, Andrew Miller, Robert Big-

gars, Lamur McGee, William Powell, John Applegarth, Benjamin Winter-
mute, Henry Trout, and Jeremiah Jully. There is no record of the racial or ethnic background of the jurors. AO RG22, Assize Minute Book, 9 Sept. 1817.
8 For a discussion of the development of the right to counsel, see Romney
   *Mr. Attorney* at 208. John Beattie has explained the historical reluctance to
   permit defence lawyers into the criminal justice process by quoting William
   Hawkins, whose *Pleas of the Crown* was published in England between 1716
   and 1721. Hawkins wrote that "it requires no manner of skill to make a
   plain and honest defence, which in cases of this kind is always the best."
   Beattie *Crime* 356.
9 "Beardsley, Bartholomew Crannell" *DCB* v. 8 at 69–70; "Beardsley, John"
   *DCB* v. 5 at 58–60. Reference to Angelique Pilotte's refusal to speak
   throughout the trial was found in a letter from Robert Gourlay to the
   Kingston *Gazette* 31 March 1818.
10 For discussion of the clash between First Nations' concepts of justice and
   the imposition of European criminal law, see Cornelia Schuh "Justice on the
   Northern Frontier: Early Murder Trials of Native Accused" *Criminal Law
   Quarterly* 22 (1979) 74. Schuh noted that cross-examination particularly
   bothered peoples of the First Nations, citing an 1888 case from the McLeod
   District of Alberta where the Indian [*sic*] spokesman protested that if the
   speaker were "cross-questioned by the whites she would get mixed up and
   not tell the truth" (at 102).
11 Schuh "Northern Frontier." At 102 Schuh described the typically "deferen-
   tial posture adopted by the person in a position of weakness and inferiority," noting that "colonial literature is full of peevish complaints about
   the unreliability of natives who say whatever they think will best please the
   sahib."
12 For a detailed discussion of the reluctance of judges and juries to administer
   severe sanctions against women who committed infanticide, see Backhouse
   "Infanticide."
13 The reaction of Elizabeth Hamilton was not an unusual one for upper-class
   women of the time. Anne Powell, the wife of the Chief Justice of Upper
   Canada, responded similarly when one of her servants gave birth to an illegitimate child in 1818. Labelling it as "proof of moral depravity," Powell
   dismissed the young woman and forced her to leave the home immediately
   after the birth. See Ward "Unwed Motherhood" 45–46.
14 Niagara *Spectator* 18 Sept. 1817; Kingston *Gazette* 23 Sept. 1817.
15 Upper Canada *Gazette* 15 Sept. 1817. For descriptions of the pillory and
   public treatment of those pilloried, see Beattie *Crime* at 464–68. For discussions of eighteenth-century attitudes toward the dissections of criminals, see

Peter Linebaugh "The Tyburn Riot Against the Surgeons" in Douglas Hay et al. *Albion's Fatal Tree: Crime and Society in Eighteenth-Century England* (New York 1975) 65.

16 Most written sources on First Nations' cultures are by white authors, anthropologists, or historians who necessarily, as I do, interpret information through their own cultural perspectives. Recognizing the difficulties of relying upon these accounts, I offer them as at least a partial assessment. For a general description of the indigenous birth culture in Canada, see Jutta Mason "A History of Midwifery in Canada" in Mary Eberts et al. *Report of the Task Force on the Implementation of Midwifery in Ontario* (Toronto 1987) Appendix I at 199–201. For a more detailed description of the position of women in Ojibwa culture, see Ruth Landes *The Ojibwa Woman* (New York 1938; repub. 1969); Ruth Landes "The Ojibwa of Canada" in Margaret Mead *Cooperation and Competition Among Primitive Peoples* (New York 1937); Ruth Landes *Ojibwa Sociology* (New York 1937; repub. 1969). For information on white customs, see Jo Oppenheimer "Childbirth in Ontario: The Transition from Home to Hospital in the Early Twentieth Century" *Ontario History* 75(1) (1983) 36.

17 Glyndwr Williams ed. *Andrew Graham's Observations on Hudson's Bay 1767– 91* (London 1969) 177–78. See also Anna Jamieson's similar account regarding First Nations' women in Upper Canada in 1830: Anna Brownell Jameson *Winter Studies and Summer Rambles in Canada, Selections* (Toronto 1965; orig. pub. 1838) 123. Attitudes dismissing the physical pain of women of colour, immigrant and working-class women were common. See, for example, discussions of Black women and working-class women in Beck and Beck *Medical Jurisprudence*.

18 Samuel Street, for example, had extensive trading relations with the First Nations: "Street, Samuel" *DCB* v. 5 at 781–83. Robert Nelles, who supported the petition, had a long (somewhat unsavoury) history of trade with peoples of the First Nations; see "Nelles, Robert" *DCB* v. 7 at 650–52. William Claus, who also supported the petition, had extensive ties with the Indian Department: "Claus, William" *DCB* v. 6 at 151–53. For Thomas Clark's marital information, see "Kerr, Robert" *DCB* v. 6 at 374–75. William Johnson Kerr, another petitioner, was married to Elizabeth Brant, another prominent Mohawk woman; see "Kerr, William Johnson" *DCB* v. 7 at 466–67. See also Gretchen Green "Molly Brant, Catharine Brant, and their Daughters: A Study in Colonial Acculturation" *Ontario History* 81(3) (September 1989) 235.

19 William Kirby, an Englishman who settled in Niagara in 1839 wrote in the *Annals of Niagara* (Toronto 1927; orig. pub. 1896) at 233:

The part taken by the Indians in the war ought never to be forgotten by the people of Canada.... It may justly be said that the salvation of Upper Canada was in considerable measure secured by the activity and zeal of the red men [sic] who took the field in her behalf.

Kirby noted that the Chippawas (the term used for people of the Ojibwa nation by Americans) were actively involved in the British campaign of 1812 (at 233).

For a description of interracial relations, see Miller *Skyscrapers* 83–98, where he noted that this period marked the beginning of the end for traditional military and economic alliances between peoples of the First Nations and whites. Certainly the popular view expressed in the press was that the First Nations' communities should be removed from areas of white settlement, in order to allow whites greater economic prosperity. The Niagara *Gleaner* published in full, on 26 February 1818, the following statement, apparently made by the Governor of Albany, New York:

The Indians in our territory are experiencing the fate of all savage and barbarous tribes in the vicinity of civilized nations, and are constantly deteriorating in character, and diminishing in number, and before the expiration of a century, there is a strong probability that they will entirely disappear.

It is understood that the western Indians are desirous that ours should emigrate to an extensive territory remote from the white population, and which will be granted them gratuitously. As this will preserve them from rapid destruction: as it is in strict unison with the prescriptions of humanity, and will not interfere with the blessings of religious instruction; and as their places will be supplied by industrious and useful settlers, who will augment our population and resources, it is presumed that there can be no reasonable objection to their removal.

20 Kingston *Chronicle* 28 Oct. 1825; Kingston *Gazette* 31 March 1818.
21 "Campbell, Sir William" *DCB* v. 6 113–18.
22 "An Act to prevent the destroying and murdering of Bastard Children" 43 Geo. III (1803) c. 53 (Eng.).
23 "An Act for making further provisions to prevent the destroying and murdering of Bastard Children" 50 Geo. III (1810) c. 2 (N.B.); "An Act to repeal 'An Act to prevent the destroying and murdering of Bastard Children'" 52

Geo. III (1812) c. 3 (Lower Canada); "An Act for repealing ... 'An Act relating to Treasons and Felonies'" 53 Geo. III (1813) c. 11 (N.S.).

Despite lobbying in the 1820s from powerful figures in Upper Canada who sought to revise their infanticide statute to resemble the amended English legislation, it was not until 1831 that the changes were effected. See "An Act to prevent the operation of 'An Act to prevent the destroying and murdering of Bastard Children'" 2 Wm. IV (1831) c. 1 (Upper Canada). Prince Edward Island followed suit in 1836: "An Act to provide for the punishment of Offences against the Person" 6 Wm. IV (1836) c. 22 (P.E.I.).

24 Kingston *Gazette* 21 Oct. 1817, dateline Niagara 9 Oct. 1817. On the process of obtaining pardons and commutation of sentence, see Burbidge *Criminal Law* 29–31.

25 Kingston *Gazette* 21 March 1818. For a description of the health risks facing prisoners from the First Nations, see W.A. Calder "Convict Life in Canadian Federal Penitentiaries 1867–1900" in Louis A. Knafla *Crime and Criminal Justice in Europe and Canada* (Waterloo 1981) 297 at 303–7. See Schuh "Northern Frontier" for discussion of the many occasions on which white law-enforcers tried to explain the authority of imperial leaders through phrases such as the "Big White Chief."

26 Nanaimo *Free Press* 8 April 1896.

27 Accounts of the case were taken from the Archives of British Columbia, GR 1327, No. 37/1896, Coroner's Inquest, Nanaimo, 16 April 1896; GR 419, Box 63, File 2/1896 Depositions, Brief for Crown, *R. v Balo*. See also Nanaimo *Free Press* 8 April 1896. I am indebted to Indiana Matters of the Archives of British Columbia for bringing the details of this case to my attention.

28 Nanaimo *Free Press* 8 April 1896; ABC GR 1327, No. 37/1896, Inquest.

29 E. Blanche Norcross *Nanaimo Retrospective: The First Century* (Nanaimo 1979); James Audain *Alex Dunsmuir's Dilemma* (Victoria 1964).

30 In the 1890s, the Canadian High Commissioner's office in London printed 30,000 emigration folders for distribution in Finland. Immigration routes appear to have been via Alaska, or from more established Finnish communities in the United States. See Norcross *Nanaimo* 89–91; Varpu Lindstrom-Best *Defiant Sisters: A Social History of Finnish Immigrant Women in Canada* (Toronto 1988) 22, 23, 26, 84–85. For details on the prohibition of women from the mines in British Columbia, see infra chapter 9. In 1890, racist legislators added Chinese men to the prohibited groups as well.

31 Lindstrom-Best *Defiant Sisters* at 23, 140; Norcross *Nanaimo* 90. See also Aili Gronlund Schneider *The Finnish Baker's Daughters* (Toronto 1986); Varpu Lindstrom-Best "'I Won't Be a Slave! — Finnish Domestics in Canada 1911–30" in Jean Burnet ed. *Looking into My Sister's Eyes* (Toronto 1986) at 33. For

press accounts referring to "the Finland colony," see Nanaimo *Free Press* 11 April 1896.

32 Nanaimo *Free Press* 11 April 1896, p. 1.

33 Nanaimo *Free Press* 11 April 1896. For details of the typical infanticide perpetrator in nineteenth-century Canada, see Backhouse "Infanticide."

34 See for example, the Toronto *Weekly Leader* 15 Dec. 1858, where it was reported that Mrs. Meutto of Yorkville awoke one morning to find her twelve-week-old infant lying dead in her arms. The coroner's inquest delved mainly into the reputation of the parents. As the paper recounted, "The evidence elicited at this inquest was sufficient to satisfy the jury that the parents were respectable and strictly sober persons, and a verdict was therefore returned that the child was accidentally suffocated."

35 Nanaimo *Free Press* 11 April 1896.

36 Nanaimo *Free Press* 11 April 1896. For discussion of Finnish women's working conditions and physical condition, see Lindstrom-Best *Defiant Sisters*.

37 Nanaimo *Free Press* 11 April 1896; ABC GR 419, Box 63, File 2/1896, Deposition.

38 Nanaimo *Free Press* 11 April 1896.

39 Nanaimo *Free Press* 9 April 1896, p. 4.

40 Deposition.

41 Deposition; Beattie *Crime* at 119.

42 Deposition. For discussion of the dangers of relying upon the water immersion test, see William Fuller Alves Boys *A Practical Treatise on the Office and Duties of Coroners in Ontario* 2nd ed. (Toronto 1878) 49–51.

43 Nanaimo *Free Press* 16 April 1896, p. 4.

44 Deposition; Coroner's Inquest.

45 Coroner's Inquest.

46 Lindstrom-Best *Defiant Sisters* 59–78; 111–14. Matti Kurikka, a Finnish journalist and theosophist, who advocated the abolition of marriage, attempted to found the utopian socialist community of Sointula in British Columbia in 1901 (Lindstrom-Best at 75).

47 For discussion of infanticide, abortion, birth control, and child-rearing patterns among the Finnish immigrant community between 1890 and 1930, see Lindstrom-Best *Defiant Sisters*.

48 Coroner's Inquest; Deposition.

49 Deposition; Coroner's Inquest.

50 Coroner's Inquest; Deposition.

51 Deposition.

52 Coroner's Inquest.

53 Nanaimo *Free Press* 16 April 1896. For an account of the repeal process, see
note 23 above.
54 For full details of the statutory amendments in the various jurisdictions, see
Backhouse "Infanticide." The first statute unequivocally to include married
women within the scope of the concealment offence was passed in New
Brunswick: "Offences against the Person Act" 1 Wm. IV (1831) c. 17 (N.B.).
The first federal legislation was found in "An Act respecting Offences
against the Person" 32 & 33 Vict. (1869) c. 20 (D.C.). The statute that extended this package of criminal law to British Columbia was "An Act to extend to the Province of British Columbia certain of the Criminal Laws" 37
Vict. (1874) c. 42 (D.C.).
55 The Criminal Code, 1892 55 & 56 Vict. (1892) c. 29, s. 240 (D.C.).
56 The Criminal Code, 1892 55 & 56 Vict. (1892) c. 29, s. 239 (D.C.).
57 Deposition.
58 Deposition.
59 Deposition. Clarke *Criminal Law* 467. See Beattie *Crime* at 364–66 for discussion about English rules concerning the reception of confession evidence.
60 For details about Justice Drake, see Alfred Watts QC "The Honourable Mr.
Justice Montague W. Tyrwhitt-Drake" *The Advocate* 26(6) (1967) 225 at 226.
See also Nanaimo *Free Press* 5 May 1896; ABC GR 1727, v. 589, Bench Book
Entries for *R. v Balo*, 4 May 1896, by M.W.T. Drake.
61 Nanaimo *Free Press* 6 May 1896.
62 An examination of the surviving archival court records for Ontario between
1840 and 1900 showed 66.7 per cent verdicts of "not guilty" in charges of
murder and manslaughter, and 46.7 per cent verdicts of "not guilty" in charges of concealment. (See Tables 1, 2, and 3 in Backhouse "Infanticide" at 462,
465, and 468.) Analysis of the court decisions in the judicial district of
Quebec between 1812 and 1891 showed 60 per cent verdicts of "not guilty"
in charges of murder and manslaughter, and 38.8 per cent findings *other*
than "guilty" in charges of concealment. (See Tableau 3 in Cliche
"L'Infanticide" at 49.)
63 *Upper Canada Law Journal* 8 (December 1862) at 309.
64 For details on Ontario infant mortality rates, see Ontario Registrar-General
*Report Relating to the Registration of Births, Marriages and Deaths 1880–1979* in
Oppenheimer "Childbirth" 38. See also Public Archives of Nova Scotia RG
41, Coroner's Inquest, 25 April 1861, as described in Wright "Infanticide" 24–
25.
65 Charles Arthur Mercier *Crime and Insanity* (London 1911) at 212–13.
66 For a brief discussion of baby-farming, see Backhouse "Infanticide." There
were a series of prominent cases in the late nineteenth century where the

owners of "baby farms" were charged with child murder, and legislation soon sprang up to regulate these organizations. Further research would be necessary to determine whether the accusations made against "baby farmers" were fair, or whether social reformers were motivated primarily by the taint of sexual licence that surrounded illegitimate births, and a dislike of the class of women who ran such establishments.

67 For details on La Crèche D'Youville, see Peter Gossage "Les Enfants Abandonnés a Montréal au 19e Siècle: La Crèche D'Youville Des Soeurs Grises 1820–1871" *Revue D'Histoire De L'Amérique Française* 40 (1986–87) 537. For a description of all of the institutionalized infants' homes operated in Canada at 1900, see National Council of Women of Canada *Women of Canada* 324–40.

68 National Council of Women of Canada *Women of Canada* 340. The Protestant Methodist, Congregationalist, and Presbyterian churches were actively seeking to convert "foreigners" in Canada during this period, and the Finnish Lutherans were often targets. (Lindstrom-Best *Defiant Sisters* 130.)

## Chapter 5 (pages 140 to 166)

1 Carlotta Hacker *The Indomitable Lady Doctors* (Toronto 1974); Janet Ray *Emily Stowe* (Toronto 1978). The designation "first" is somewhat problematic, for Dr. James Miranda Stuart Barry, a woman who practised as a British Army medical officer while posing as a man, preceded Emily Stowe. Barry arrived in Canada in 1857 to serve as the Inspector-General of Hospitals for Upper and Lower Canada. (See Hacker at 3–16.) For additional information on Stowe, see Joanne Emily Thompson "The Influence of Dr. Emily Howard Stowe on the Woman Suffrage Movement in Canada" unpublished thesis, University College of Waterloo Lutheran University 1963, Wilfrid Laurier University; F.C. *Gullen History* Manuscript scrapbook of Stowe, Lossing, and Gullen families, Archives, Victoria University, Toronto; *Scrapbooks* Stowe Collection, Wilfrid Laurier University Archives; Veronica Strong-Boag "Canada's Women Doctors: Feminism Constrained" in Linda Kealey ed. *A Not Unreasonable Claim: Women and Reform in Canada 1880's–1920's* (Toronto 1979) 109; Peter E. Paul Dembski "Jenny Kidd Trout and the Founding of the Women's Medical Colleges at Kingston and Toronto" *Ontario History* 77(3) (September 1985) 183.

2 Hacker *Lady Doctors* 18; Ray *Stowe* 4–8. The Jennings family converted to Methodism after settling in Canada. Emily went through a number of religious stages, later taking up Methodism, Christian Science, Unitarianism,

and Theosophy, until by the 1890s she renounced religious creeds altogether. (See Dembski "Trout" at 185.)

3 Hacker *Lady Doctors* 18–19; Ray *Stowe* 9–10.

4 Hacker *Lady Doctors* 20; Ray *Stowe* 13–14.

5 Wendy Mitchinson "The Medical Treatment of Women" in Sandra Burt et al. *Changing Patterns: Women in Canada* (Toronto 1988) 237 at 239–43; Barbara Ehrenreich and Deirdre English *Witches, Midwives and Nurses: A History of Women Healers* (Brooklyn N.Y. 1973) 3–20.

6 Mitchinson "Medical Treatment of Women" 239–43; C. David Naylor *Private Practice, Public Payment* (Kingston 1986) 8–25, 264. See also Toronto *Globe* 9, 18, 19, 25 Feb., 20 March 1874; *Canada Lancet* 6 (1874) 268; Ehrenreich and English *Women Healers* 21–32; Susan E. Cayleff *Wash and Be Healed: The Water-Cure Movement and Women's Health* (Philadelphia 1987) 6–7.

7 Mitchinson "Medical Treatment of Women" 239–43; Cayleff *Water-Cure* 12.

8 Toronto *Globe* 24 Feb. 1874. See also Ehrenreich and English *Women Healers* 21–32. For a description of the French–English debates in Quebec, see Naylor *Practice* 16–18.

9 See Charles G. Roland *Health, Disease and Medicine: Essays in Canadian History* (Hamilton 1982); Charles M. Godfrey *Medicine for Ontario: A History* (Belleville 1979); S.E.D. Shortt *Medicine in Canadian Society* (Montreal 1981); Wendy Mitchinson and Janice McGinnis eds. *Essays in the History of Canadian Medicine* (Toronto 1988). One aspect of restrictions in competition was the prohibition of midwifery. "An Act to regulate Qualification in Medicine" 29 Vict. (1865) c. 34 removed the exemption that had permitted midwives to practise without a licence for the first half of the nineteenth century. See, by way of comparison, "An Act respecting the Medical Board and Medical Practitioners" C.S.U.C. (1859) c. 40, s. 13, which provided "nothing in this Act contained shall prevent any female from practising Midwifery in Upper Canada, or require such female to take out a licence." See also C. Lesley Biggs "The Case of the Missing Midwives: A History of Midwifery in Ontario from 1795–1900" *Ontario History* 75(1) (March 1983) 21. Restrictive licensing initiatives were also evident in other provinces, beginning first in Quebec in 1788, and spreading to New Brunswick and Nova Scotia in 1816 and 1828 respectively. (See Naylor *Practice* 17–23.) See also *Canada Lancet* 3 (1871) 213; Ray *Stowe* 16: Hacker *Lady Doctors* 20. Godfrey *Medicine for Ontario* at 186 noted that Emily Stowe applied for admission to the Victoria College medical course in 1863.

10 Ray *Stowe* 17–18; Hacker *Lady Doctors* 20; Ehrenreich and English *Women Healers* 24–30. But see William Barlow and David O. Powell "Homeopathy and Sexual Equality: The Controversy over Coeducation at Cincinnati's

Pulte Medical College 1873–1879" *Ohio History* 90 (1981) 101, which noted that although the irregular sects (including homeopathy) provided much of women's early educational access to medical instruction, some homeopathic instructors displayed sexist attitudes that rivalled those at the regular medical schools.

11 *Sixth Annual Announcement of the New York Medical College for Women*; Ray *Stowe* 3, 18; Hacker *Lady Doctors* 20. Dr. Stowe stated publicly that she intended to confine her practice to the diseases of women and children. (See *Scrapbooks* Wilfrid Laurier University Archives, undated press clipping "Female Physicians: Lecture by Mrs. Doctor Stowe," probably in the late 1860s.)

12 "An Act to Amend and Consolidate the Acts relating to the Profession of Medicine and Surgery" 32 Vict. (1869) c. 45, ss. 8, 20, 25 (Ont.); *Canada Lancet* 111 (June 1871) 423. Not all doctors were as sanguine about the integration, and disagreements between the regulars and the other sects would continue to erupt for some decades: see R.D. Gidney and W.P.J. Millar "The Origins of Organized Medicine in Ontario, 1850–1869" in Charles G. Roland ed. *Health, Disease and Medicine: Essays in Canadian History* (Hamilton 1984) 65–95.

13 Ray *Stowe* 19–21; Hacker *Lady Doctors* 20–21. Whether Dr. Stowe was prosecuted for practising without a licence is unclear. Hacker speculated that Emily Stowe "was almost certainly fined at this time," but provided no reference for this statement. It is probably just as likely that the officials at the College of Physicians and Surgeons failed to launch any prosecution against Emily Stowe, uncertain of the benefits of flexing their new powers too openly.

14 Ray *Stowe* 19–20; Hacker *Lady Doctors* 22, 38–45.

15 Ray *Stowe* 20–21; Hacker *Lady Doctors* 22–23, 38–46.

16 Toronto *Globe* 15 Aug. 1879.

17 Toronto *Globe* 15 Aug. 1879; 24 Sept. 1879. For biographic details on Dr. John McConnell, see Rose *Cyclopaedia* 367–68. Like Emily Stowe, Dr. McConnell had taught school prior to his career in medicine. He was extensively involved in the military, as officer of the Oak Ridge troop of cavalry, a graduate of the Military School in 1868, and later as a Lieutenant, 12th Battalion York Rangers. His immersion in the masculinized military world may help explain some of the hostility he would exhibit toward the presence of women in the profession of medicine.

18 Toronto *Globe* 22 Aug. 1879; 24 Sept. 1879.

19 Toronto *Globe* 26 Aug. 1879.

20 Toronto *Globe* 23 Aug. 1878.

21 Toronto *Globe* 23 Aug. 1879.
22 Angus McLaren "Birth Control and Abortion in Canada 1870–1920" *Canadian Historical Review* 59 (1978) 319 at 334–35; Bernard Dickens *Abortion and the Law* (Bristol 1966) 23–26; Joseph W. Dellapenna "The History of Abortion: Technology, Morality and Law" *University of Pittsburgh Law Review* 40 (1979) 359 at 377.
23 For description of the methods of abortion used in the nineteenth century, see McLaren "Abortion" 327–30, 334–35; Patricia Knight "Women and Abortion in Victorian and Edwardian England," *History Workshop* 4 (Autumn 1977) 47–69. Some societies were much more knowledgeable about abortion techniques than others; the Nuu-Chah-Nulth people of the west coast were particularly skilled in this. See Sproat *The Nootka* 169. See also *Canada Medical Journal* 3 (1867) 225 at 231, quoting from a Boston obstetrician who spoke of the "wide-spread popular ... belief, even among mothers themselves, that the foetus is not alive till after the period of quickening."
24 For a detailed discussion of the common law and statutory positions on abortion law in nineteenth-century Canada, see Constance Backhouse "Involuntary Motherhood: Abortion, Birth Control and the Law in Nineteenth-Century Canada" *Windsor Yearbook of Access to Justice* 3 (1983) 61. See also Shelley Gavigan "The Criminal Sanction as it Relates to Human Reproduction" *Journal of Legal History* 5 (1984) 20; "An Act ... for the further prevention of the malicious using of means to procure the miscarriage of women" 50 Geo. III (1810) c. 2 (N.B.), as amended 9 & 10 Geo. IV (1829) c. 21 (N.B.); "An Act to provide for the punishment of Offences against the Person" 6 Wm. IV (1836) c. 22 (P.E.I.); and Dickens *Abortion* 20–23.
25 "An Act for consolidating ... Offences against the person" 4 & 5 Vict. (1841) c. 27 (U.C.). For detailed discussion of the legislative enactments between 1840 and 1892, see Backhouse "Abortion" 69–82.
26 Angus McLaren and Arlene Tigar McLaren *The Bedroom and the State: Changing Practices and Politics of Contraception and Abortion in Canada 1880–1980* (Toronto 1986) 38–39; James C. Mohr *Abortion in America* (New York 1978).
27 Backhouse "Abortion." For reference to married women using abortion services, see *The Queen* v *Ransom J. Andrews* AO RG22 York County Minute Books 29 Jan. 1886; (1886) 12 O.R. 184 (C.P.).
28 For reference to "race suicide" discussions, see McLaren and McLaren *Bedroom* at 17; *Canada Medical Journal* 3 (1867) 225 at 226; *Canada Medical Record* 18(8) (May 1889) at 142.
29 See Backhouse "Abortion" 76–82; *Canada Lancet* 4 (1871) 185–86; *Canada Lancet* 8 (1875) 24. See also Mohr *Abortion* for an American comparative analysis. Mohr noted that Dr. Edwin M. Hale, a leading American spokes-

man for homeopathic medicine in the mid-century, countenanced early abortions, arguing "that in no instance should the life, or even *health* of the
mother be sacrificed to save that of an impregnated ovum, before the date
of its 'viability.'" Apparently Hale reversed his position by 1867, presenting
a united front with the regular physicians (at 76–78, 173–76). Curiously, even
Canadian regular physicians believed that they should have the right to perform abortions when they diagnosed them as medically necessary. Ration-
ales for abortion in nineteenth-century medical literature ran the gamut
from the prospective death of the mother or the "child" to "pelvic deform-
ity" and "narrowing of the genital canal by tumours." See, for example,
*Canada Medical Journal* 3 (1867) 225, 233–34; *Canada Lancet* 7 (1875) 289;
*Canada Lancet* 13 (1881) 277–78, 342–43; *Canada Medical and Surgical Journal*
16 (1883) 598–99; *Canada Lancet* 27 (1894) 16–18; *Canada Lancet* 32 (1899) 113;
*Canadian Practitioners and Review* 25 (1900) 331, 334–36, 401. There was little
discussion of the legal basis for this perspective. See Backhouse "Abortion";
Shelly A. M. Gavigan "On 'Bringing on the Menses': The Criminal Liability
of Women and the Therapeutic Exception in Canadian Abortion Law"
*Canadian Journal of Women and the Law* 1 (1986) 279.

30 *Canada Lancet* 7 (1875) 289–90.

31 Mohr *Abortion* 113.

32 Toronto *Globe* 26 Aug. 1879; 24 Sept. 1879. Other drugs considered to have
abortion-producing properties in the nineteenth century included infusions
of tansy, quinine, black draught, oil of cedar, pennyroyal, rue, savin, cotton
root, and ergot of rye.

33 Toronto *Globe* 23 Aug. 1879.

34 Toronto *Globe* 23 Aug. 1879.

35 *Scrapbooks* Stowe Collection, Wilfrid Laurier Archives.

36 McLaren "Abortion"; McLaren and McLaren *Bedroom* 9–31.

37 *Canada Lancet* 4 (1871) 185–86; McLaren "Abortion"; McLaren and McLaren
*Bedroom* 9–31; Wendy Mitchinson "Historical Attitudes Toward Women and
Childbirth" *Atlantis* 4 (1979) 13 at 22.

38 Ray *Stowe* 23–43; Hacker *Lady Doctors* 23–35.

39 *Scrapbook IV* undated (c. 1877) newspaper clipping, Emily Stowe Papers,
Wilfrid Laurier University Archives. See Backhouse "Abortion" for a discussion of the "voluntary motherhood" perspective; McLaren and McLaren
*Bedroom* 12, 19. While Emily Murphy couched her condemnation within a
discussion of the social and economic factors that made women pursue
these options, her negative perspective was clear:

   Of the methods employed to keep down the birth rate of course it is impossible to speak, and unfortunately they are perhaps too well known to require more than the mention of the fact that such methods exist. [...] For those who [assist women in terminating pregnancies] for money and make it their business, there can be no sympathy except such as we feel for all malefactors when they are caught and we begin to view them simply as human beings, not as dangers to society. That all such practices are confined to low-grade physicians and unlicensed midwives would be a comforting thing to believe, for then we would think the evil much less general than it is.

All sorts of methods, as everyone knows who reads the newspapers, either the news or the advertising columns, are practised to prevent the increase of the birth rate. Those who are caught in this desperate act are severely punished. Those who are not caught are also severely punished, either physically by permanent damage to their health, or morally and mentally by the degeneracy which such a class of living must certainly bring about.

(Emily Murphy "Editorial" *Saturday Night* 22 Dec. 1900, at 1–2.) Emily Murphy's views on contraception developed in different directions over the next few decades. She became a prominent advocate of sterilization for eugenic reasons, and by the 1930s she was advocating education on birth control for similar reasons: see Terry L. Chapman "Early Eugenics Movement in Western Canada" *Alberta History* 25 (1977) 4, 9, 15; Byrne Hope Sanders *Emily Murphy: Crusader* (Toronto 1945) 335. For an American comparative analysis, see Linda Gordon *Woman's Body, Woman's Right* (New York 1976) 95–111.

40 William Caniff *The Medical Profession in Upper Canada 1783–1850* (Toronto 1894) 555–58.

41 Toronto *Globe* 26 Aug. 1879; 25 Sept. 1879.

42 Toronto *Globe* 26 Aug. 1879.

43 Toronto *Evening Telegram* 28 Aug. 1879. Dr. Archibald also appeared on behalf of Dr. Emily Stowe, but as his testimony essentially corroborated that of the other physicians, his evidence will not be discussed further here. Dr. Daniel McMichael was listed as a QC in the *Toronto City Directory 1879* (Toronto 1879) at 345, with McMichael, Hoskin, and Ogden, practising at 46 Church. The "Dr." designation, which he used with regularity, appeared to come from a doctorate of civil law (DCL), which he listed in the 1879 Directory, and/or a doctorate of law (LLD), which he listed in the 1878 Directory: *Toronto City Directory 1878* (Toronto 1878) at 245. Caniff referred to him as "the well-known barrister of Toronto": Caniff *Medical Profession* 322. See also

*The Queen* v *Robert Stitt* AO RG22, York County Minute Books 21 Oct. 1878; *R.* v *Stitt* (1879) 30 U.C.C.P. 30. Stitt was convicted and sentenced to three months in jail.

44 Toronto *Evening Telegram* 28 Aug. 1879.

45 Toronto *Evening Telegram* 28 Aug. 1879.

46 Frederick Wright graduated in medicine at the University of Toronto in 1872. See Caniff *Medical Profession* 673–74; "Rolph, John" in Wallace *Macmillan Dictionary* 3rd ed. 645.

47 Toronto *Evening Telegram* 28 Aug. 1879.

48 Toronto *Evening Telegram* 28 Aug. 1879. Dr. Berryman, who had received his M.D. in 1857 and practised in Yorkville, was a member of the medical faculty of Victoria College, who taught medical jurisprudence and materia medica. See references in Gullen *History* Archives Victoria University, Toronto; *The Medical Register for Upper Canada 1867* (Toronto 1867) 20.

49 "Ogden, Uzziel" in Morgan *Canadian Men* 1st ed. at 780–81; "Ogden, Uzziel" in Wallace *Macmillan Dictionary* 3rd ed. at 560.

50 Toronto *Evening Telegram* 28 Aug. 1879.

51 Toronto *Evening Telegram* 28 Aug. 1879, 29 Aug. 1879.

52 Toronto *Evening Telegram* 28 Aug. 1879; Toronto *Globe* 12 Sept. 1879.

53 Toronto *Evening Telegram* 27 Sept. 1879.

54 For details of the new system for appointing county Crown attorneys, see Romney *Mr. Attorney* 220–30.

55 Toronto *Globe* 12 Sept. 1879.

56 "An Act respecting Offences against the Person" 32–33 Vict. (1869) c. 20, ss. 59, 60 (D.C.).

57 Toronto *Globe* 12 Sept. 1879.

58 Toronto *Mail* 24 Sept. 1879. For details on Kenneth Mackenzie's judicial appointment, see N. Omer Coté *Political Appointments, Parliaments and the Judicial Bench in the Dominion of Canada 1867–1895* (Ottawa 1896) 335.

59 Toronto *Globe* 24 Sept. 1879.

60 For biographical details on McCarthy, see "McCarthy, D'Alton" Wallace *Macmillan Dictionary* v. 2, 2nd ed. at 379; "McCarthy, D'Alton" Rose *Cyclopaedia* 624; "The late D'Alton McCarthy" *Canadian Magazine* (1903); "McCarthy, D'Alton" *Dictionary of Canadian Biography* v. 12 at 578. See also Toronto *Globe* 24 Sept. 1879.

61 Toronto *Mail* 25 Sept. 1879; Toronto *Globe* 24 Sept. 1879.

62 Toronto *Globe* 24 Sept. 1879.

63 Toronto *Globe* 24 Sept. 1879.

64 Toronto *Mail* 24 Sept. 1879.

65 Toronto *Mail* 24 Sept. 1879; Toronto *Globe* 24 Sept. 1879.

66 Toronto *Evening Telegram* 24 Sept. 1879; Toronto *Mail* 25 Sept. 1879.

67 Toronto *Mail* 25 Sept. 1879.

68 Toronto *Evening Telegram* 25 Sept. 1879; Toronto *Mail* 25 Sept. 1879.

69 Toronto *Globe* 25 Sept. 1879; Toronto *Evening Telegram* 25 Sept. 1879.

70 Toronto *Mail* 25 Sept. 1879; Toronto *Evening Telegram* 25 Sept. 1879.
Throughout the trial there was continuing controversy over how to address Emily Howard Stowe. The papers routinely made reference to "Mrs. Stowe," or even "Mrs. Dr. Stowe," and only rarely to "Dr. Stowe." After Judge Mackenzie's interjection about his use of the phrase "Dr. Stowe," D'Alton McCarthy had immediately deferred to the judge's concern. Replied McCarthy: "Well possibly I should call her 'a prisoner.'" As late as 1888, the *Canada Medical Record* was still writing deprecatingly about "girl doctors." [*Canada Medical Record* 10 (1888) 239.]

71 Due to the paucity of abortion trials, it is difficult to draw too much from these statistics. Based on data drawn from all nineteenth-century reported cases in Canada and surviving Ontario archival records from 1840 to 1900, there were twenty charges laid. Ten resulted in guilty verdicts, nine in not guilty verdicts, and one verdict was unknown. (See Backhouse "Abortion.") Further archival research in provinces other than Ontario would be needed to extend the analysis.

72 See Backhouse "Abortion"; *The Queen v Sparham and Greaves* (1875) 25 U.C.C.P. 143; *The Queen v Robert Stitt* (1879) 30 U.C.C.P. 30.

73 *The Queen v Ransom J. Andrews* AO RG22, York County Minute Books, 29 Jan. 1886; *R. v Andrews* (1886) 12 O.R. 184 (C.P.). See also Backhouse "Abortion."

74 *The Queen v Garrow and Creech* (1896) 1 C.C.C. 246 (B.C. S.C.). See also Backhouse "Abortion."

75 Toronto *Globe* 25 Sept. 1879; Toronto *Mail* 25 Sept. 1879.

76 *Canada Lancet* 12 (1879) 61–62; Toronto *Evening Telegram* 27 Sept. 1879.

77 Ray *Stowe* 21–22, 44–46; Hacker *Lady Doctors* 22–33.

78 Toronto *Globe* 24 Sept. 1879.

79 Macdonald Papers, NAC MG 26A, Letterbook 15, pp. 20–21; 4 Jan. 1871, Private letter to Hon. James Cockburn. I am indebted to Jon Swainger whose research located this reference for sharing it with me. For legislation banning birth control, see The Criminal Code, 1892 55 & 56 Vict. (1892) c. 29, s. 179. For Charlton's comments, see *Hansard Parliamentary Debates* House of Commons v. 2 (1892) 2458–59. The doctors were strident supporters as well: see *Canada Medical Journal* 3 (1867) 226–27; *Canada Medical Journal and Monthly Record* 3 (1867) 226–28; *Canada Lancet* 4 (1871) 185–86; T. Thomas *A Practical Treatise on the Diseases of Women* (Philadelphia 1868) 58–59; J. Thorburn *A*

*Practical Treatise of the Diseases of Women* (London 1885) 525; Paul Mundé *A Practical Treatise on the Diseases of Women* (Philadelphia 1891) 562.
80 For a discussion of the different perspectives of the nineteenth-century "voluntary motherhood" feminists and the early twentieth-century birth-controllers in the English context, see Sheila Jeffreys *The Spinster and her Enemies: Feminism and Sexuality 1880–1930* (London 1985).

## Chapter 6 (pages 167 to 199)

1 Court records for this case do not survive, so all accounts of *Hawley* v *Ham*, heard at the Midland District Assizes in Upper Canada in September 1826, have been drawn from the Kingston *Chronicle* 15 Sept. 1826. The paper mistakenly gave the date of marriage twice: as 1823 and 1813. I have chosen the 1813 date as the correct one, since the account also noted that by 1826 Esther Ham had been separated and living with her father, Sheldon Hawley, for over twelve years.

2 Legal recognition of the patterns within the First Nations was noted in the *Connolly* v *Woolrich* case, discussed in chapter 1. For discussion of divorce law generally, see Constance Backhouse "Pure Patriarchy: Nineteenth-Century Canadian Marriage" *McGill Law Journal* 31 (1986) 265. Of the seven *ad hoc* petitions presented to the Legislature of Upper Canada (and later to the Legislature of the United Province of Canada) prior to Confederation, two were abandoned, four were granted, and one was granted but later disallowed; see Backhouse "Patriarchy" 270. The French law was stated by Judge René-Edouard Caron, President of the Commission responsible for drafting the Quebec Civil Code: "Le divorce n'a jamais existé pour nous comme faisant partie des lois françaises": see John E.C. Brierley "Quebec's Civil Law Codification" *McGill Law Journal* 14 (1968) 521 at 560. See also Civil Code of Lower Canada 29 Vict. (1865) c. 41, art. 185. For further details of the law of divorce in the Maritime and western jurisdictions, see infra.

3 For details of George Ham's election to the Legislature, representing Lennox and Addington in 1824, see F.A. Armstrong *Handbook of Upper Canada Chronology* (London 1967) at 90.

4 See Backhouse "Patriarchy" for examples of other cases where family, neighbours, and friends intervened in wife-battering situations.

5 Grounds for annulment under English ecclesiastical law included bodily imperfection or infirmity resulting in total incapacity for consummation, blood ties or marital connections within the prohibited degree of consanguinity, prior existing marriage, lunacy, mental incapacity, or breach of statutory re-

quirements in the solemnization of marriage: see Backhouse "Patriarchy" at 266.

The Legislature of Upper Canada heard seven petitions before Confederation. Two were abandoned. Four were granted: John Stuart (1839), William Henry Beresford (1852), John McLean (1859), James Benning (1864). A fifth, for Henry William Harris, was granted in 1845, but disallowed. (See Backhouse "Patriarchy" at 270; *Journals of the Legislative Assembly* 7–29 Nov. 1844.)

Until 1804, the English Parliament had never granted a divorce to a woman. For discussion of the English parliamentary procedure, see Mary Lyndon Shanley *Feminism, Marriage, and the Law in Victorian England 1850–1895* (Princeton 1989) 36.

6 See Shanley *Marriage* 36, for a discussion of the English situation. The paucity of records regarding the legislative divorces granted in Upper Canada makes it difficult to determine whether the English tradition was being followed exactly. Where details of the grounds survive, it appears that four of the male petitioners pleaded adultery, while one pleaded adultery as well as "great violence of temper and uncontrollable bursts of passion" on the part of his wife. That no divorces were granted to women is suggestive that the double standard was applied.

7 For a discussion of the phenomenon of "self-divorce" see James G. Snell *Controlling Divorce in Canada 1900–1939* unpublished manuscript 1988, where he states that much of this had died out by the early twentieth century in Canada, as the power and influence of the formal law increased. For details regarding Nova Scotia, see Kimberley Smith Maynard "Divorce in Nova Scotia 1750–1890" in Philip Girard and Jim Phillips eds. *Essays in the History of Canadian Law: Vol. III, Nova Scotia* (Toronto 1990). For a comparative discussion, see Marylynn Salmon *Women and the Law of Property in Early America* (Chapel Hill 1986) 58–59. Another example of an innovative response to a failed marriage was *Brennen v Brennen* (1890) 19 O.R. 327 (Q.B.), where a married woman left her husband's home and sued his father, mother, and brother for damages for false representations made to her prior to marriage. The first action of its kind, it was struck down by Judge W.G. Falconbridge as "contrary to public policy."

8 See Erin Breault "Educating Women About the Law: Violence Against Wives in Ontario 1850–1920" M.A. thesis, University of Toronto 1986 at 6, 22–23. Breault noted that an alimony action was "too expensive" for many women, who were unable to obtain legal relief until the enactment of "Deserted Wives" statutes. For example, in 1888 Ontario passed "An Act respecting the Maintenance of Wives deserted by their Husbands" 51 Vict. (1888) c. 23 (Ont.), which authorized justices of the peace to order deserting

husbands to pay weekly maintenance. In 1897 this was amended by 60 Vict. (1897) c. 14, s. 34 (Ont.), to define as a deserted wife any woman living apart from her husband due to repeated assaults or cruelty.

9 The emphasis is recorded in the account from the Kingston *Chronicle* 15 Sept. 1826.

10 For discussion of the obligation of the husband to maintain his wife and children under English common law, see Lee Holcombe *Wives and Property: Reform of the Married Women's Property Law in Nineteenth-Century England* (Toronto 1983) 30–31. See A.H. Oosterhoff and W.B. Rayner *Anger and Honsberger Law of Real Property* v. 1 (Aurora 1985) chapter 3 for an account of the reception of English common law in English Canada.

11 For details of Campbell's position, see "Campbell, Sir William" *Dictionary of Canadian Biography* v. 6 113 at 118.

12 "Campbell" *DCB* at 113–18. Hannah Hadley, of a pre-Loyalist Nova Scotia family, had married Campbell in Guysborough, Nova Scotia, in 1785. The couple had four daughters and two sons. On the matter of public views concerning wife battering, see also Katherine M. J. McKenna "The Role of Women in the Establishment of Social Status in Early Upper Canada" *Ontario History* 83(3) (September 1990) 179 at 200, where she noted that élite society in early nineteenth-century Toronto (then York) was well aware of at least one other situation of marital violence. C.B. Wyatt, the surveyor-general of Upper Canada, subjected his wife Mary Wyatt to "confinement to the bedpost, locking up in the Cellar, bruised Arms and broken head" in the middle years of the first decade of the nineteenth century. Despite the fact that leading figures wrote about the problem, including Anne Murray Powell (wife of Judge William Dummer Powell), no one intervened to try to stop the abuse.

13 This does not appear to have been the end of the litigation between Sheldon Hawley and George Ham. The Upper Canada Court of King's Bench Judgment Docketbooks noted that Hawley was successful in suing Ham for "trespass upon the case upon promises," and judgment was entered for forty-four pounds, sixteen shillings and six pence, a portion of Hawley's claim plus costs, on 20 November 1826. AO RG22 Series 131, vol. 7, 1796–1830 A-L, MS 704 (1). Further details of the litigation, which presumably involved some species of negligence, do not survive.

14 See, for example, Chancellor William Hume Blake's comments: "Happily, transactions of this sort are for the most part screened from public gaze." *Severn* v *Severn* (1852) 3 Chy. R. 431 (U.C.) at 437. For a description of some of the violence perpetrated, see Backhouse "Patriarchy" generally.

15 *Severn* v *Severn* (1852) at 448; *Rodman* v *Rodman* (1873) 20 Chy. R. 428 (U.C.)

at 430–31, 439 per Vice-Chancellor J.G. Spragge; *Bavin* v *Bavin* (1896) 27 O.R. 571 (Div. Ct.) per William Ralph Meredith.

16 Detailed research on the treatment of violence within Quebec marital jurisprudence has still to be done. A cursory examination of some of the *séparation de corps* cases reveals that standards may not have been dissimilar from those utilized by English Canadian judges. *Caissé* v *Hervieux* 5 R.J.R.Q. 14 (S.C.) serves as an interesting example, although it was not a case of *séparation de corps*, but a related action brought by the husband to compel his wife's brother to return his estranged wife. When the Civil Code of Lower Canada 29 Vict. (1865) c. 41 formalized the conditions for *séparation de corps*, it set forth the following rules:

> art. 189. Husband and wife may respectively demand this separation on the ground of outrage, ill-usage or grievous insult committed by one toward the other.

> art. 190. The grievous nature and sufficiency of such outrage, ill-usage and insult, are left to the discretion of the court which, in appreciating them, must take into consideration the rank, condition and other circumstances of the parties.

How Quebec courts interpreted this language is a matter awaiting further detailed research.

17 *Severn* v *Severn* (1852) at 448.

18 For a full discussion of the English common law rules on married women's property and their reception into English Canadian jurisdictions, see Constance Backhouse "Married Women's Property Law in Nineteenth-Century Canada" *Law and History Review* 6 (1988) 211. See also William Blackstone *Commentaries on the Laws of England* v. 1 (London 1765; repub. 1979) 430.

19 *Whibby* v *Walbank* (1869) 5 Nfld. R. 286 (S.C.) The injustice of the common law rules had become apparent as early as the late sixteenth century in England, where the courts of chancery developed a body of equitable precedents that undermined the doctrine of coverture and permitted women to retain their property separately through devices such as antenuptial and postnuptial contracts, marriage settlements, and trusts. In Canada the courts of chancery were by no means as well established, and access to lawyers experienced in equity was at a premium. The sheer expense of tying up estates in trust settlements was another major impediment. George Smith Holmested, writing at the turn of the century, concluded that for Canadians, marriage settlements were "as a rule enjoyed by the few only who could in-

dulge in [this] luxury ... to the ordinary run of married women they were a dead letter." George S. Holmested *The Married Women's Property Act of Ontario* (Toronto 1905) 1-6. For a more detailed description of common law rules and equitable precedents, and the various exceptions to them, see Backhouse "Property." For a full discussion of the English provisions, see Holcombe *Property*.

20 See Holcombe *Property* 27.

21 The wife retained property received as an inheritance or gift from her parents, although the husband had access to any profits made on these assets. For a more detailed description of the Quebec married women's property law, see Marie Gérin Lajoie "Legal Status of Women in the Province of Quebec" in National Council of Women of Canada *Women of Canada* 41–50; Dumont *Quebec Women* 68–128, 254–55; André Morel "La libération de la femme au Canada: Deux itinéraires" *Revue Juridique Themis* 5 (1970) 399–411; Michelle Boivin "L'évolution des droits de la femme au Québec: un survol historique" *Canadian Journal of Women and the Law* 2 (1986) 53.

22 Matthew Hale *Historia Placitorum Coronae: The History of the Pleas of the Crown* v. I (London 1736; reprinted 1971) 629. In 1890 Canadian criminal law commentator George W. Burbidge pointed out that Hale had given no authority for this assertion, and suggested that the position was not without some difficulty:

> It may be doubted, however, whether the consent is not confined to the decent and proper use of marital rights. If a man used violence to his wife under circumstances in which decency, or her own health or safety required or justified her in refusing her consent, I think he might be convicted at least of an indecent assault.

Burbidge *Criminal Law* 249. See also Backhouse "Rape" and The Criminal Code, 1892 55–56 Vict. (1892) c. 29 (D.C.).

23 Holcombe *Property* 26–27; Blackstone *Commentaries* v. 1 at 432–33.

24 *The Stowe-Gullen Papers* Archives, Wilfrid Laurier University, Waterloo, Ontario, "Social Problems" 1893.

25 Feminist campaigns for greater access to divorce did not appear until well into the twentieth century; Nellie McClung's work on behalf of liberalized divorce law took place in the 1920s and 1930s. See Nellie McClung *In Times Like These* (Toronto 1972), introduction by Veronica Strong-Boag at xiv; Prentice et al. *Canadian Women* 254–55. For Elizabeth Dunlop's petition, see *Journals of the Legal Council*, Index 1852–66; Toronto *Globe* "Women's Rights" 19 Jan. 1857. I am indebted to Mary Jane Mossman for bringing the petitions to

my attention. For comparative material on the divorce perspectives of American and European feminists, see Barbara Taylor *Eve and the New Jerusalem* (London 1983); Roderick Phillips *Putting Asunder: A History of Divorce in Western Society* (Cambridge 1988).

26 See Backhouse "Property" for details of the reform legislation throughout the nineteenth century.

27 See Backhouse "Property" for details of the judicial foot-dragging. See also "Married Women — Their Rights" *Canada Law Journal* 9 (1873) 41–43.

28 "Law to the Ladies" *The Novascotian* 6 July 1826. The letter was initially published in an English paper, and reprinted in the Nova Scotia press.

29 Letitia Youmans *Campaign Echoes: The Autobiography of Mrs. Letitia Youmans* (Toronto 1893) 88–91; Breault "Violence" 16–22; Wendy Mitchinson "The WCTU: For God, Home and Native Land: A Study in Nineteenth-Century Feminism" in Kealey *A Not Unreasonable Claim* 151; S.G.E. McKee *Jubilee History of the Ontario Woman's Christian Temperance Union 1877–1927* (Whitby n.d.) 87–88.

30 See Elizabeth Pleck *Domestic Tyranny: The Making of American Social Policy against Family Violence from Colonial Times to the Present* (Oxford 1987); Linda Gordon *Heroes of Their Own Lives: The Politics and History of Family Violence* (New York 1988) 254.

31 Maynard "Divorce in Nova Scotia"; Breault "Violence" 21–22.

32 Maria Amelia Fytche *Kerchiefs to Hunt Souls* (Boston 1895; repub. Sackville N.B. 1980) 40–42.

33 The account of this case has been drawn from the surviving records of *Abell v Abell*, 1883–86, New Brunswick Court of Divorce and Matrimonial Causes, PANB RS 58 J. For details of the marriage and the events that preceded the divorce, see Certificate of Marriage, 22 March 1876; "Libel" of the Plaintiff, filed 13 Feb. 1883; "Answer" of Respondent to Libel, filed 27 June 1883; Judge's Notes from the Trial.

On the myth of the "deaf-mute" see Oliver Sacks *Seeing Voices: A Journey into the World of the Deaf* (Berkeley and Los Angeles 1989) at 26:

> [Deaf people] are, of course, perfectly capable of speech — they have the same speech apparatus as anyone else; what they lack is the ability to hear their own speech, and thus to monitor its sound by ear. ... [T]he prelingually deaf have no auditory image, no *idea* what speech actually sounds like, no idea of a sound-meaning correspondence.

See also Charles H. Howe *The Deaf Mutes of Canada, A History of their*

*Education, with an Account of the Deaf Mute Institutions of the Dominion, and a Description of All Known Finger and Sign Alphabets* (Toronto 1888) and J. Scott Hutton "Outlines of History and Biography used in the Institution for the Deaf and Dumb, Halifax, Nova Scotia" (Halifax 1875) at 37–47 for discussion of various educational programs. In contrast to signing, an "articulation" system had been developed in Germany, but was little used in North America.

For discussion on the "almost universal delusion of the hearing" that Sign, the language of the deaf, is but a poor substitute for speech, see Sacks *Seeing Voices* at 20.

34 Michael Rodda, Rilla Ellis, and Philip Chaddock "A Brief History of Education of Deaf Students in the Maritime Provinces of Canada" *Association of Canadian Educators of the Hearing Impaired Journal* 9(3) (Winter 1983) 188–98.

35 Howe *Deaf Mutes of Canada* 48. See also Alexander Graham Bell's widely discussed tract *Marriage: An Address to the Deaf* (Washington, D.C. 1898), in which he explored the genetic implications of marriage between two deaf persons. Although Bell is reported to have been a fluent Signer, he denied that both his mother and wife were deaf and threw his weight behind Oralism, which by means of years of arduous and intensive training and practice would seek to integrate the deaf within the hearing world. At the 1880 International Congress of Educators of the Deaf, held in Milan, deaf teachers were not allowed to vote on the question of Sign versus Oralism. Sign was to be proscribed in schools for the deaf. For discussion of "the desire of [the hearing] to have the deaf speak," and of Sign as the natural language of deaf people, see Sacks *Seeing Voices* in general.

36 Reference to signing between Alfred and Alberta was made in the Saint John *Evening Daily Press* 7 Feb. 1879 and Saint John *Daily Sun* 15 Jan. 1879.

37 Saint John *Daily Evening News* 8 Jan. 1878; Rodda et al. "Deaf Students" 192–93.

38 Saint John *Daily Evening News* 14 Jan. 1879, 17 Jan. 1879.

39 Saint John *Daily Evening News* 14 Jan. 1879, 17 Jan. 1879; Saint John *Daily Sun* 15 Jan. 1879, 21 Jan. 1879.

40 Saint John *Daily Evening News* 17 Jan. 1879.

41 Saint John *Daily Evening News* 14 Jan. 1879; Saint John *Daily Sun* 15 Jan. 1879.

42 For details of the Stockton family background, see "Stockton, Alfred Augustus" Rose *Cyclopaedia* 116–17; Joseph Wilson Lawrence *The Judges of New Brunswick and Their Times* (Saint John 1985) at x.

43 Saint John *Daily Sun* 18 Jan. 1879.

44 Saint John *Daily Evening News* 18 Jan. 1879; 4 Apr. 1879.

45 See Backhouse "Patriarchy"; Maynard "Divorce in Nova Scotia." "An Act

concerning Marriages, and Divorce, and for punishing Incest and Adultery, and declaring Polygamy to be Felony" 32 Geo. II (1758) c. 17 (N.S.); as amended 1 Geo. III (1761) c. 7 (N.S.); 56 Geo. III (1816) c. 7 (N.S.); 29 Vict. (1866) c. 13 (N.S.). "An Act for regulating Marriage and Divorce, and for preventing and punishing Incest, Adultery and Fornication" 31 Geo. III (1791) c. 5 (N.B.); 48 Geo. III (1808) c. 3 (N.B.); 4 Wm. IV (1834) c. 30 (N.B.); 6 Wm. IV (1836) c. 34 (N.B.); 10 Vict. (1847) c. 2 (N.B.); 23 Vict. (1860) c. 37 (N.B.). See also "An Act for Regulating Marriage and Divorce, and for Prohibiting and Punishing Polygamy, Incest, and Adultery" PANB RS 24 S1-B6 (1786 New Brunswick); and PANB RS 24 S2-B5 (1787 New Brunswick) for earlier drafts that were not formally enacted. "An Act for Establishing a Court of Divorce and for preventing and punishing Incest, Adultery and Fornication" 3 Wm. IV (1833) c. 22 (P.E.I.), as amended 5 Wm. IV (1835) c. 10 (P.E.I.). There has been some difficulty determining the number of divorce applications in Prince Edward Island prior to 1900. In an earlier article I mistakenly suggested there had been none: see Backhouse "Patriarchy" 270. Maynard cited only one application in her "Divorce in Nova Scotia." Jack Bumsted and Wendy Owen uncovered three applications in their "Divorce in a Small Province: A History of Divorce on Prince Edward Island from 1833" forthcoming in *Acadiensis*. Peter Fisher's petition in 1833 spawned the passage of the 1835 legislation, although there are no further records on whether he carried through with his application after the new statute was passed. Two other divorce applications achieved success: *Collings* v *Collings* (1840–41) Public Archives of Prince Edward Island 2810/141-2 and *Capel* v *Capel* (1864) referred to in an assault decision, Public Archives of Prince Edward Island, Supreme Court Reports, Case Papers 1864 (no divorce records apparently survive on this case).

46 For a discussion of the New England laws, see Salmon *Property* 58–80; Nancy F. Cott "Divorce and the Changing Status of Women in Eighteenth-Century Massachusetts" *William and Mary Quarterly* 33 (1976) 586; Henry S. Cohn "Connecticut's Divorce Mechanism, 1636–1969" *American Journal of Legal History* 14 (1970) 35. Other possible influences include First Nations' traditions, which permitted broader access to divorce, and Scottish law, which also differed from the English. Both await further research.

47 The grounds, which also included kinship within the prohibited degrees and pre-contract, varied over the years and between jurisdictions. For more detailed discussion of the grounds, and the debates over jurisdiction at the time of Confederation, see Backhouse "Patriarchy." The British North America Act, 1867 30 & 31 Vict. (1867) c. 3, s. 91(26) (Eng.) gave jurisdiction over divorce to Parliament, but s. 129 laid the foundation for provincial

divorce courts to continue when it provided that the laws then in force, and all the courts of civil and criminal jurisdiction, should continue in Ontario, Quebec, Nova Scotia, and New Brunswick. For statistical details of the operations of the Nova Scotia and New Brunswick courts, see Maynard "Divorce in Nova Scotia" and Angela Crandall "Divorce in 19th Century New Brunswick: A Social Dilemma," unpublished manuscript 1988. Maynard noted that of the forty-four petitions in which cause and outcome were recorded, thirty-four received divorces: "Table Two: Divorces by Cause." Crandall found that approximately half of the New Brunswick applications were granted.

48 See Backhouse "Patriarchy" for a list of the parliamentary divorces (at 276), and fuller legal analysis of why individuals from these provinces adopted the practice of applying to Parliament (at 271–79). For Ontarians, there were no other options; for citizens from Manitoba and the North-West Territories (then including Saskatchewan and Alberta), it was more a matter of custom. See also John Alexander Gemmill *The Practice of the Parliament of Canada upon Bills of Divorce* (Toronto 1889) 262; "An Act to Amend the Law Relating to Divorce and Matrimonial Causes in England" 20 & 21 Vict. (1857) c. 85 (Eng.); *Hansard Parliamentary Debates* House of Commons v. 2 at 1414 (14 May 1888).

49 For descriptions of American divorce law, see E. Tyler May *Great Expectations: Marriage and Divorce in Post-Victorian America* (Chicago 1980); R.L. Griswold *Family and Divorce in California 1850–1890* (Albany 1982); W.L. O'Neill *Divorce in the Progressive Era* (New Haven 1967). See also "Divorces in the United States" *Local Courts & Municipal Gazette* 3 (1867) 163; *Hansard Parliamentary Debates* Senate at 233 (30 April 1868).

50 *Hansard Parliamentary Debates* House of Commons 641 (6 May 1868); v. 2 at 6,291 (18 July 1894); Eusèbe Belleau *Des Empêchements Dirimants de Mariage* (Lévis: 1889) 36–39; Josephine Dandurand "French Canadian Customs" in National Council of Women of Canada *Women of Canada* 22 at 24–25; for a discussion of Dandurand's status within Quebec feminism, see Marie-Aimée Cliche "Droits égaux ou influence accrue? Nature et rôle de la femme d'après les féministes chrétiennes et les antiféministes au Québec 1896–1930" *Recherches féministes* 2(2) (1989) at 101; see Backhouse "Patriarchy" (280–81) for discussion of the reaction to the few Quebec applications to Parliament.

51 The law of reception in British Columbia provided that the province should apply the law of England as of 19 November 1858: "Proclamation" by His Excellency James Douglas, Governor, Colony of British Columbia 19 Nov. 1858; English Law Ordinance, 1867 Cons. S.B.C. 30 Vict. (1877) c. 103; see also R.S.B.C. (1897) c. 62. In *M. falsely called S.* v *S.* (1877) 1 B.C.R. 25, the

British Columbia Supreme Court ruled that it had jurisdiction to apply the English divorce law. Noting that Nova Scotia and New Brunswick had been granting divorces for over a century, Judge John Hamilton Gray pronounced them "England's more practical Colonies." Manitoba and the North-West Territories were in similar legal situations, but their courts did not follow the British Columbia lead in the nineteenth century; see Backhouse "Patriarchy" 278–79.

52 Maynard "Divorce in Nova Scotia"; Gemmill *Bills of Divorce* 257; R. Pike "Legal Access and the Incidence of Divorce in Canada: A Sociohistorical Analysis" *Canadian Review of Sociology and Anthropology* 12 (1975) 115. For a discussion of the cross-border traffic, see Backhouse "Patriarchy" 275–76.

53 "Smith, Robert Barry" Rose *Cyclopaedia* 331.

54 "Libel" of the Plaintiff; "Answer of Respondent to Libel," filed 27 June 1883.

55 31 Geo. III (1791) c. 5, s. 9 (N.B.). The same statute criminalized adultery, incest, fornication, and "all acts of lewdness and unlawful cohabitation and intercourse between Man and Woman": (s. 8). For comparison, see 1 Geo. III (1761) c. 7 (N.S.).

56 It was not uncommon for women to couple claims of adultery with cruelty: see Crandall "Divorce in New Brunswick" for other examples. For information on the English adultery rules, see Shanley *Marriage*. The Civil Code of Lower Canada 29 Vict. (1865) c. 41 provided:

> art. 187. A husband may demand the separation on the ground of his wife's adultery.

> art. 188. A wife may demand the separation on the ground of her husband's adultery, if he keep his concubine in their common habitation.

The Quebec reference to concubines is intriguing, and seems to be part of a pattern of a more public discussion of kept mistresses. See, for example, the Quebec prostitution cases of *R. v Gareau* (1891) 1 C.C.C. 66 (Que. C.A.) and *The Queen v Rehe* (1897) 1 C.C.C. 63 (Que. Q.B.), discussed infra. See also John Lambert *Travels Through Lower Canada* v. 1 (London 1810) 280–93, where he reported that "the number of ... kept mistresses ... exceed[s] in proportion those of the old country."

57 The British Columbia position was a consequence of its receiving the discriminatory English legislation of 1857; see supra. The Canadian Parliament theoretically was not bound to impose a sexual double standard, and the Senators insisted that there were no arbitrary rules respecting divorce, each

case being considered on its own merits. John Gemmill proudly proclaimed that Parliament had abolished the sexual double standard in his 1889 treatise, but in reality, "An Act for the Relief of Eleanora Elizabeth Tudor" 51 Vict. (1888) c. 11 (D.C.) was the first such decision, and few others followed: Gemmill *Bills of Divorce* 22; Backhouse "Patriarchy" 284–91.

58 Gemmill *Bills of Divorce* 22. See also the judicial decisions where women attempted to equate male and female adultery in criminal conversation cases: *Quick* v *Church* (1893) 23 O.R. 262 (Q.B.); *Lellis* v *Lambert* (1897) 24 O.A.R. 653 (Ont. C.A.). While Chief Justice John Douglas Armour ruled in the first case that spouses should be treated equally, he was categorically overruled in the second.

59 For a discussion of the provisions in the American colonies, see Cott "Divorce" 605–6. Since the Canadian and Australian colonies passed comparable enactments, it would seem to be more related to the colonial setting than to identifiably American strains of thought: see H. Golder "An Exercise in Unnecessary Chivalry" in J. Mackinolty and H. Radi eds. *In Pursuit of Justice: Australian Women and the Law 1788–1979* (Sydney 1979) 42 at 44; J. M. Bennett "The Establishment of Divorce Laws in New South Wales" *Sydney Law Review* 4 (1963) 241.

Maynard, who has examined the Nova Scotia divorce records, concluded that in that province at least, discrimination on the basis of sex was not "blatant." However, of forty-four petitions she studied between 1750 and 1890, 100 per cent of the men sought divorce solely on the grounds of adultery. Only 57 per cent of the women petitioned on this basis alone: see Maynard "Divorce in Nova Scotia" Table Two.

60 These last assertions appear in a letter written by George McSorley, solicitor for Alfred Abell, 28 Oct. 1885, to F.A.H. Straton, Registrar of the Court.

61 Letter from Alfred Abell to F.A.H. Straton, Registrar of the Court of Divorce and Matrimonial Causes, 15 June 1883:

> I will have hard hill up work with my case as a great rogue such as Charles A. Stockton is interested in it and he has a habit to gain my solicitors to fool me in order to ward off trouble from himself so no wonder I am anxious. [...] I believe also C.A. Stockton is trying to do me much injury to prevent me fixing him. However I will make a hard fight with him....

62 See letter from Alfred Abell to F.A.H. Straton, 15 June 1883.

63 For details of Skinner's life, see "Skinner, Hon. Charles N." Rose *Cyclopaedia* 401–2. Alfred Abell's libel was one of the missing documents in the archival

file. Particulars have been reconstructed from the "Answer of the Respondent," filed 27 June 1883. See also Letter from Alfred Abell to F.A.H. Straton, Registrar, 15 June 1883.

64 Judgment, *Abell* v *Abell*, Court of Marriage and Divorce, 6 Nov. 1883; Moncton *Daily Transcript* 28 June 1883.

65 For details of Street's hearing impairment, see Lawrence *Judges of New Brunswick* 412, 510. There is also some evidence of deaf lawyers practising in Ontario; Hutton *Institution for the Deaf and Dumb* noted in 1875 that there were "two clever deaf-mute barristers named McLellan" practising in Belleville, Ontario (at 46).

66 The costs were apportioned at $25 for the first day of proceedings, and $15 for ten additional days: see "Abell v. Abell, Memo of Days Attendance on Matter, Allocations Allowed." Maynard "Divorce in Nova Scotia" has noted that costs in that province ranged from $30.68 to $315.20. Alberta Abell had also asked for custody of her two-year-old son. Judge Wetmore's impatience with the problems of the hearing and speaking impaired provoked him to disparage "the surroundings of the Defendant's establishment," rendering Alfred Abell an unlikely candidate for custody despite patriarchal views on such matters. Expressing his opinion that Alberta Abell was the proper person "to look after and care for [the child] during his tender years," Wetmore yet declined to make a ruling. In matters of divorce, the courts were reluctant to rule lightly, and the judge was uncertain whether there was any legal authority in his court to make orders of custody. No legal order was issued regarding custody. From affidavit evidence filed with the court in 1885, it appeared that the child lived with Alberta Abell.

67 This was the same Alfred Woodbridge that Alfred Abell would accuse of committing arson in connection with another fire at the Abell Institution in 1886. A government commission set up to investigate the charges of arson found no evidence to substantiate Abell's claim. Rodda et al. "Deaf Students" 193–96.

68 For details on the ostracism of Mrs. George E. Foster, who had obtained a divorce in Chicago from her former husband before marrying the Minister of Finance, see P.B. Waite *The Man from Halifax: Sir John Thompson* (Toronto 1985) at 391. For biographical details on Addie Chisholm Foster, see "Chisholm, Mrs. Addie" Rose *Cyclopaedia* 604–5.

69 "Affidavit of Alberta Gardner" in the Court of Divorce and Matrimonial Causes, 26 Oct. 1885; "Affidavit of Alfred Henry Abell" Court of Divorce and Matrimonial Causes, 30 June 1885.

70 "Affidavits of Dennis O'Brien, Elizabeth Surett, Mary Beatty" Court of Divorce and Matrimonial Causes, 30 June 1885; Letter from George Mc-

Sorley to Registrar Straton, 28 Oct. 1885; Order of F.A.H. Straton during the June Term 1885 regarding motion to bar Alberta Abell of her dower in Alfred Abell's lands; "Affidavit of Alfred Henry Abell" in the Court of Divorce and Matrimonial Causes, 30 June 1885.

71 "Affidavit of Alberta Lowell Gardner" Court of Divorce and Matrimonial Causes, 16 Oct. 1885.

## Chapter 7 (pages 200 to 227)

1 This account has been drawn from *In re Armstrong, An Infant* (1895) 1 *New Brunswick Equity Reports* 208 (N.B. S.C.); *In re Armstrong* PANB RS 55. After the separation, Nellie Armstrong went to reside with her father, William Love, in Glassville. William Love filed suit against William Armstrong claiming one hundred dollars in alimony, to cover the costs of Nellie's board. William Armstrong settled the case for the sum of ninety dollars: *In re Armstrong* "Transcript" at 79. There was no application for divorce on the part of either spouse.

For an analysis of nineteenth-century custody law, see Constance Backhouse "Shifting Patterns in Nineteenth-Century Canadian Custody Awards" in Flaherty *Essays* v. 1 at 212. For a comparative American perspective, see Michael Grossberg *Governing the Hearth: Law and the Family in Nineteenth-Century America* (Chapel Hill 1985).

2 *Connolly* v *Woolrich* (1867) 11 L.C. Jur. 197 at 227.

3 Clara Brett Martin "Legal Status of Women in the Provinces of the Dominion of Canada (Except the Province of Quebec)" in National Council of Women of Canada *Women of Canada* 34 at 34–35; Blackstone *Commentaries* v. I at 440–41, 449.

4 See Backhouse "Custody"; *Re Foulds* (1893) 9 *Manitoba Law Reports* 23 at 28; William MacPherson *Treatise on the Law Relating to Infants* (London 1842) 142.

5 For discussions about the impact of economic change and industrialization on the family unit, see Cook and Mitchinson *Proper Sphere* 5; Prentice et al. *Canadian Women* 116–23, 143–46. For American comparative analysis, see Barbara Ehrenreich and Deirdre English *For Her Own Good: 150 Years of Experts' Advice to Women* (New York 1978); Nancy F. Cott *The Bonds of Womanhood: "Woman's Sphere" in New England 1780–1835* (New Haven 1977); Ann Douglas *The Feminization of American Culture* (New York 1977).

6 Reverend Robert Sedgewick "The Proper Sphere and Influence of Woman in Christian Society" (November 1856) in Cook and Mitchinson *Proper Sphere* 30–32.

7 Principal Grant "Education and Co-education" *The Canadian Monthly and National Review* 111 (November 1879) 509–18.
8 See Wayne Roberts "Rocking the Cradle for the World: The New Woman and Maternal Feminism, Toronto 1877–1914" in Kealey *A Not Unreasonable Claim* 15; National Council of Women of Canada *Women of Canada*; Cheryl MacDonald *Adelaide Hoodless: Domestic Crusader* (Toronto 1986); Doris French *Ishbel and the Empire: A Biography of Lady Aberdeen* (Toronto 1988).
9 Mrs. Dr. Annie Parker "Woman in Nation-Building" in Rev. B.F. Austin ed. *Woman — Her Character — Culture and Calling* (Brantford 1890) 460. For a discussion of the changing status of childhood, see Neil Sutherland *Children in English-Canadian Society: Framing the Twentieth-Century Consensus* (Toronto 1976) 17–20; Joy Parr ed. *Childhood and Family in Canadian History* (Toronto 1982). For American comparative material, see Eli Zaretsky *Capitalism, the Family and Personal Life* (New York 1976); Christopher Lasch *Haven in a Heartless World* (New York 1977).
10 "An Act Respecting the Appointment of Guardians and the Custody of Infants" 18 Vict. (1855) c. 126 (P.C.). This statute was similar in many respects to an earlier English statute: "An Act to amend the Law relating to Custody of Infants (Lord Talfourd's Act)" 2 & 3 Vict. (1839) c. 54 (Eng.).
11 "An Act respecting the Guardianship of Minors" 50 Vict. (1887) c. 21 (Ont.). For a detailed discussion of the judicial experience under the 1855 and 1887 statutes, see Backhouse "Custody."
12 Civil Code 29 Vict. (1865) c. 41, art. 200, 214 (Quebec). Detailed historical research has not been completed on Quebec custody law prior to the enactment of the Civil Code, although preliminary assessment suggests that the codifiers intended their new code to conform to the *ancien droit*, and that custody disputes may have been resolved similarly before and after 1865. See *The Civil Code of Lower Canada: First, Second and Third Reports* (Quebec 1865) 196–97. I am indebted to Sylvio Normand for his assistance in this analysis.
13 Detailed research on this topic remains to be done, as my "Custody" article did not examine Quebec custody decisions in any depth. Marie-Aimée Cliche, who has looked at the records more closely, has formed the general impression that throughout the nineteenth century, the bulk of Quebec custody awards went to men: (personal discussions between author and Cliche). Writing in 1900, Marie Gérin Lajoie noted that the patriarchal preference found in Quebec law was, in part, modified by social custom:

> The civil law, in harmony with the natural and moral law, lays down this precept: A child, whatever may be his age, owes honor and respect to his father and mother. Their titles to respect and honor

from their descendants are in effect the same: the power and authority given them by nature are derived from the same source; but the father alone exercises this authority during marriage, the mother surrenders hers; she gives up this right along with so many others. When the husband dies she resumes it in its entirety.

We all know how far custom modifies this arbitrary and rigorous law of paternal authority, which has so little regard for the susceptibilities of a mother. Custom allows the mother to exercise, in the education and moral training of her children, a much greater influence than is given her by law.

"Legal Status of Woman in the Province of Quebec" National Council of Women of Canada *Women of Canada* 41 at 44.

14 *Bisson* v *Lamoureux* (1867) 16 R.J.R.Q. 186 (C.S.). See also *Barlow* v *Kennedy* (1871) 17 L.C.J. 253 (Q.B.), where Judge Badgley noted at 259:

As a matter of justice and of law, the father requires no provision of law to secure to him that right [to have the custody of his infant child] which no one can disturb nor force from him, nor deprive him of except on account of his own bad conduct or by his own consent. Except in the case of insanity, or some deliberate course of immorality or criminal act of his own, no father can forfeit or lose his paternal right, and even a contract by him to part with his child is so unnatural, that the law does not recognize a man's right to violate his most sacred duty....

15 "An Act to consolidate and amend the Law relating to the Custody and Care of Infants" R.S.B.C. (1897) vol. 1, c. 96 (B.C.). In Nova Scotia, courts were authorized to award custody to mothers of children up to the age of majority. The judge was to have regard to "the welfare of such infant or infants, and to the conduct or circumstances of the parents, and to the wishes as well of the mother as of the father." The additional factor, "the circumstances of the parents," was a novel feature not seen elsewhere in Canada. Maintenance orders were authorized, and separation agreements concerning custody matters were made enforceable provided they operated for the benefit of the infant: "An Act respecting the Custody of Infants" 56 Vict. (1893) c. 11 (N.S.). For a full discussion of the enforcement of this 1893 Nova Scotia statute, see Rebecca Veinott "Child Custody and Divorce: A Nova Scotia Study 1866–1910" in Phillips and Girard *Essays*. Veinott concluded that the enforcement of this legislation was fairly even-handed, an

aspect that distinguished this province from others. After the 1893 statute, in every case but one, Nova Scotia courts denied custody to adulterous fathers as firmly as they denied it to adulterous mothers.

16 "An Act respecting Practice and Proceedings in the Supreme Court in Equity" 53 Vict. (1890) c. 4, ss. 182–83 (N.B.).

17 "An Act respecting Practice and Proceedings in the Supreme Court in Equity" 53 Vict. (1890) c. 4, s. 183 (N.B.). Little is known about Judge Barker's perspectives on marriage. A New Brunswick–born lawyer and politician, Barker was known for his interest in militia matters. He was married twice himself. First, in 1865 to Elizabeth Julia Lloyd, the daughter of Edward Lloyd of the R.E. civil staff, with whom Barker had one son and two daughters. After his first wife died in 1874, he married a second time to Mary Ann Black, the daughter of B.E. Black of Halifax and niece and adopted daughter of the late Justice Wilmot, who was the first lieutenant-governor of New Brunswick after Confederation. With his second wife he had two more daughters. "Barker, Frederic Eustace" Rose *Cyclopaedia* 207–8.

18 All details of the evidence given at trial were taken from the "Transcript" *In re Armstrong* PANB RS 55.

19 "Transcript" at 20.

20 "Transcript" 54–55.

21 "Transcript" 75–76.

22 "Transcript" 30–31.

23 "Transcript" 15.

24 "Transcript" 57.

25 *In re Armstrong, An Infant* (1895) 1 N.B.Eq.R. 208 (N.B. S.C.) at 211–12.

26 *In re Annie E. Hatfield, an Infant* (1895) 1 N.B.Eq.R. 142 at 143.

27 See Backhouse "Custody" for details of the judicial reaction to the nineteenth-century custody legislation. See also Veinott "Child Custody: Nova Scotia" for details of the experience in that province, which proved to be more egalitarian than other jurisdictions during the last decade of the nineteenth century.

28 *In re Armstrong, An Infant* at 210. The English case cited was *In re McGrath* [1893] 1 Chy. Div. 143.

29 *In re Armstrong* 213–14.

30 *In re Armstrong* 214.

31 See Patricia Skidmore "Sex and Song: Roles and Images of Women in Popular Music at the Turn of the Century" *Atlantis* 2(2) (Spring 1977) at 22; "Employment for Women" *The Christian Guardian* (Toronto) 6 Sept. 1876 at 284; Jamil S. Zainaldin "The Emergence of a Modern American Family Law:

Child Custody, Adoption, and the Courts 1796–1851" *Northwestern University Law Review* 73 (1979) 1,038 at 1,051.

32 *In re Armstrong* 216.

33 See, for example, the Chinese cases of *In re Soy King, An Infant* (1900) 7 B.C.R. 291 (B.S. S.C.); *In re Ah Gway, ex parte Chin Su* (1893) 2 B.C.R. 343 and *In re Quai Shing* (1897) 6 B.C.R. 86. For a First Nations' case, see *Regina* v *Redner* (1898) 6 B.C.R. 73.

34 *In re Soy King, An Infant* (1900) 7 B.C.R. 291 (B.S. S.C.).

35 Peter S. Li *The Chinese in Canada* (Toronto 1988) 11–70; Tamara Adilman "A Preliminary Sketch of Chinese Women and Work in British Columbia 1858–1950" and Karen van Dieren "The Response of the WMS to the Immigration of Asian Women 1888–1942" in Barbara K. Latham and Roberta J. Pazdro eds. *Not Just Pin Money* (Victoria 1984) 53–97.

36 "An Act to restrict and regulate Chinese Immigration into Canada" 48 & 49 Vict. (1885) c. 71 (D.C.), as amended by 50 & 51 Vict. (1887) c. 35 (D.C.); 55 & 56 Vict. (1892) c. 25 and 63 (D.C.) and 64 Vict. (1900) c. 32 (D.C.). The latter amendment exempted the wives and children of merchants from paying head tax. Discriminatory legislation was also passed in Saskatchewan and Ontario. Li *Chinese in Canada* 27–33; Anthony Chan *Gold Mountain: The Chinese in the New World* (Vancouver 1983) 33–35.

37 Li has determined that only 5 per cent of the Chinese entering Canada between 1885 and 1903 were merchants, and less than 1 per cent were wives. In 1902 there were 92 wives among the 3,263 Chinese in Victoria, 61 of whom were married to merchants and 28 to labourers (Li *Chinese in Canada* 58). For the legislation exempting the merchants from payment of the head tax, see Chinese Immigration Act (1885) s. 4. In 1900, the class of "exempt Chinese" was expanded to include the "wives and children" of merchants (see 63–64 Vict. (1900) c. 3). For discussion of the servant situation in China, see Sue Gronewold *Beautiful Merchandise: Prostitution in China 1860–1936* (New York 1982) 32–34.

38 Victoria *Daily Colonist* 11 July 1900; Gronewold *Merchandise* 32–50.

39 Gronewold *Merchandise* 33; Scott Stephen Osterhout *Orientals in Canada* (Toronto 1929) 171–72.

40 Osterhout *Orientals* 171.

41 Osterhout *Orientals* 171–89; Van Dieren "WMS and Asian Women" 80–88.

42 Osterhout *Orientals* 172–75; Van Dieren "WMS and Asian Women" 81.

43 Van Dieren "WMS and Asian Women" 82–87; Adilman "Chinese Women" 58; Li *Chinese in Canada* 58. See Cassandra Kobayashi "Sexual Slavery in Canada: Our Herstory" *The Asianadian* I (Fall 1978) 7 for estimates of the market value of Chinese women.

44 Osterhout *Orientals* 1–68; Van Dieren "WMS and Asian Women" 82–88.

45 Van Dieren "WMS and Asian Women" 80–88; Chan *Gold Mountain* 83.

46 See Van Dieren "WMS and Asian Women" at 86 for a discussion of the Chinese community's reaction to the loss of one of their members to the Victoria Rescue Home.

47 Li *Chinese in Canada* 28; W. Peter Ward *White Canada Forever* (Montreal 1978) 8–9; Van Dieren "WMS and Asian Women" 86; *Report of the Royal Commission on Chinese Immigration* (Ottawa 1885) at 154, 266.

48 Helmcken was the son of John Sebastian Helmcken, a British-born physician of German parentage, and Cecilia Douglas, daughter of Sir James Douglas and Amelia Connolly. See also Smith *James Douglas* 117; "Hon. John Sebastian Helmcken, M.R.C.S., L.S.A." E.O.S. Scholefield *British Columbia* v. III (Vancouver 1914) 1,132–38.

49 For a description of the law regarding writs of *habeas corpus* see Blackstone *Commentaries* v. 3, 129; "An Act for better securing the liberty of the subject, and for prevention of imprisonments beyond the seas" 31 Chas. II (1678) c. 2 (Eng.), as amended by 56 Geo. III (1816) c. 100 (Eng.); "The Law as to Custody of Children" *Upper Canada Law Journal* (August 1863) 197 at 200–1; Shanley *Marriage and the Law* 133.

50 Osterhout *Orientals* 175–76.

51 Osterhout *Orientals* 176.

52 Judge Martin added cautiously in his judgment: "I say nothing as to the rights of the father, or what might be done should he see fit to assert them." *In re Soy King* 291–92, 298.

53 *In re Soy King, An Infant* 296. This statement was a direct quote from an English decision, *In re Andrews* (1873) L.R. 8 Q.B. 153 at 158. The law regarding the age at which children were permitted to choose their residence was stated in "The Law as to Custody of Children" *Upper Canada Law Journal* (August 1863) 197 at 200–1.

54 See Backhouse "Custody" 240–41 for a more detailed discussion of the trend toward removing children from parental control altogether.

55 "Of the Prevention and Punishment of Wrongs to Children" R.S.N.S. (1884) c. 95; "An Act in addition to and amendment of Chapter 70 of the Consolidated Statutes, of 'Minors and Apprentices'" 52 Vict. (1889) c. 24 (N.B.); "An Act for the Prevention of Cruelty to, and better Protection of Children" 56 Vict. (1893) c. 45 (Ont.); "An Act for the better Protection of Neglected and Dependent Children" 61 Vict. (1898) c. 6 (Man.) as amended by 62 & 63 Vict. (1899) c. 4 (Man.).

56 R.E. Kingsford *Commentaries on the Law of Ontario Being Blackstone's Commen-*

*taries on the Laws of England, Adapted to the Province of Ontario* (Toronto 1896) 380.
57 *In re Soy King, An Infant* at 292.
58 *In re Soy King* 292.
59 Li *Chinese in Canada* 11–70; Ward *White Canada* 8–9; *Report of the Royal Commission* at lix, 89, 161; Osterhout *Orientals* 77.
60 *In re Soy King* 297.
61 Ward *White Canada* 8–9; Victoria *Colonist* 14 June 1876; *Report of the Royal Commission* at 89, 161.
62 Women's Missionary Society of the Methodist Church of Canada *Annual Reports* (Toronto 1900–1901) at xcv.
63 *In re Quai Shing, An Infant* 95–96, per Chief Justice Davie in dissent.

## *Chapter 8* (pages 228 to 259)

1 Feminist historians have taken quite different perspectives over the proper interpretation of prostitution. See, for example, Judith Walkowitz *Prostitution and Victorian Society: Women, Class and the State* (Cambridge 1980); Ruth Rosen *The Lost Sisterhood: Prostitution in America 1900–1918* (Baltimore 1982); Jeffreys *The Spinster and her Enemies*; Frances Finnegan *Poverty and Prostitution: A Study of Victorian Prostitutes in York* (Cambridge 1979); Jess Wells *A Herstory of Prostitution in Western Europe* (Berkeley 1982).
2 Toronto *Globe* 17 Oct. 1860. Details of Mary Gorman's arrest record were taken from the Toronto City Jail Register (United Counties, Peel and York: 1858–69; 1862–64; 1864–70; 1871–73; 1876–78; Toronto Jail Committal and Discharge Register, 1874, 1875; Toronto City Jail Description Book 1874–75. These registers are located in the Archives of Ontario RG20 F43.
3 See Backhouse "Prostitution" for data showing the majority of convicted prostitutes in nineteenth-century Toronto were of Irish background, although Canadian-born women began to increase in numbers in the latter decades. For other descriptions of the overrepresentation of Irish women in jail, see Michael S. Cross "Violence and Authority: The Case of Bytown" in David Jay Bercuson and Louis A. Knafla eds. *Law and Society in Canada in Historical Perspective* (Calgary 1979) chapter 1 at 6; John Weaver "Crime, Public Order and Repression: The Gore District in Upheaval 1832–1851" *Ontario History* 78(3) (September 1986) 189–204; Rogers "Serving Toronto" 134; Jim Phillips "Poverty, Unemployment and the Administration of the Criminal Law: Vagrancy Laws in Halifax, Nova Scotia 1864–1890" in Philip Girard and Jim Phillips *Essays in the History of Canadian Law* v. 3 (Toronto 1990) 128.

These patterns did not show up in England, which also played host to many impoverished Irish immigrants. There was a peculiarly Canadian dimension to this experience. For discussion on this and other aspects of the lives of "Peasants in an Urban Society: The Irish in Victorian Toronto," see Murray W. Nicolson in *Gathering Place: Peoples and Neighbourhoods of Toronto, 1834–1945* (Toronto 1985) at 48–73. Nicholson notes (at 58):

> One should realize that, [in the 1860s] in Toronto, the Irish had little protection from the law. Unlike the urban centres of the United States where the police forces were made up of large numbers of Irish Catholics, Toronto's policemen were Protestant and were accused of arresting Catholics while Protestants might be warned for the same offence. Judges arbitrarily sentenced Irishmen (sic) if they were residents of any Irish Catholic area in the city, particularly if they lived in the central core.

For a comparative perspective from the City of York, England, between 1837 and 1887, where a disproportionately low number of prostitutes was drawn from the body of destitute Irish immigrants, see Finnegan *Prostitution* 32, 53–55. Comparative data on the United States are mixed. See Hasia R. Diner *Erin's Daughters in America: Irish Immigrant Women in the 19th Century* (Baltimore 1983) at 106, 114, where the author argues that Irish women in America rarely engaged in prostitution. Joel Best "Careers in Brothel Prostitution: St. Paul 1865–1883" *Journal of Interdisciplinary History* 12(4) (Spring 1982) 597 noted that Irish, Scandinavians, and Blacks were overrepresented.
4 For details of the location of brothels, see Jarvis "Mid-Victorian Toronto" 126. For the English vagrancy law, see the Vagrancy Act 17 Geo. II (1744) c. 5 (Eng.). For the reception of this law into Upper Canada, see "An Act for the further introduction of the criminal law of England into this province" 40 Geo. III (1800) c. 1 (U.C.). "An Act to authorize the Erection ... of Houses of Industry" 7 Wm. IV (1837) c. 24 (U.C.) also authorized justices of the peace to commit "all persons living a lewd dissolute vagrant life, or exercising no ordinary calling, or lawful business, sufficient to gain or procure an honest living" to provincial workhouses for confinement.
5 "An Act to amend and extend the Act of 1857, for diminishing the expense and delay in the Administration of Criminal Justice in certain cases" 22 Vict. (1858) c. 27 (P.C.) provided for the summary trial and conviction of persons charged with "keeping or being an inmate, or habitual frequenter of any disorderly house, house of ill-fame or bawdy house." Had Mary Gorman been charged with specific offences relating to her occupation, this legislation

would likely have been used. For details regarding the predominance of vagrancy and morals charges in Toronto police work, see Rogers "Serving Toronto" 132–33.

6 Toronto (York) Jail, Punishment Register 1865–70, AO RG 22, F43 Vol. I–2 recorded these classifications for hard labour, itemizing the number of inmates labouring at each task, and those in solitary confinement or unable to work because of illness. By way of contrast, hard labour for male prisoners in the jail could include stone-breaking, wood-cutting, picking oakum, digging, or gardening.

7 Toronto Jail Surgeon's Register 1858–67, AO RG20 F43 Series D19 at pp. 79, 86, 88, 91.

8 There are a number of reasons for suggesting that Mary Ann Gorman was likely Mary Gorman's daughter. Apart from the obvious similarities in name, both were listed in the Jail Register as Roman Catholic, illiterate women who were from the "lower rank in life." Mary Ann Gorman was registered as born in Canada West, in either 1857 or 1858 when Mary Gorman would have been thirty-six or thirty-seven years old. The only other Gorman listed in the Jail Register was Maria Gorman, who would have been only eleven years old in 1857. With one exception, the City Directories show no other female Gormans during this time period. A Mrs. Ann Gorman (widow of John) is listed for only one year at 62 Power in 1867: *Toronto City Directory 1867–68* (Toronto 1867) at 113. For a discussion of pregnancy inside prostitution, see Rosen *Sisterhood* 99.

9 For a discussion of child care inside prostitution, see Rosen *Sisterhood* 99. Details on Mary Ann Gorman's arrest record were taken from the Toronto Jail Register records cited above. For a discussion of the vagrancy law in the English and Nova Scotian context, see Phillips "Vagrancy Laws in Halifax." See also Judith Fingard *The Dark Side of Life in Victorian Halifax* (Porters Lake, N.S. 1989).

10 Toronto *Globe* 21 May 1868.

11 Toronto *Globe* 2 Nov. 1868. The legislation under which Mary Ann Gorman would have been convicted of larceny was probably "An Act respecting the prompt and summary administration of Criminal Justice in certain cases" C.S.C. (1859) c. 105 (P.C.). Some of the individuals released "on further examination" were sentenced at a later time, but in most cases they would be arrested on another charge before they could be sentenced for the initial offence.

12 Toronto *Globe* 14 Oct. 1868. For discussion on the occupations of young Irish Catholic women in Victorian Toronto, see Nicholson "Peasants" at 55.

13 For discussions about the reasons why women entered prostitution, see

John McLaren "Chasing the Social Evil: Moral Fervour and the Evolution of Canada's Prostitution Laws: 1867–1917" *Canadian Journal of Law and Society* 1 (1986) 125–65; Rosen *Sisterhood* 112–68.

14 Both Mary and Mary Ann Gorman served parts of the following months together in prison: May 1868, November 1868, May 1872, February 1873, July 1873. On 5 February 1873, the two were arrested together. Mary Ann Gorman paid a four-dollar fine for her release, while Mary Gorman remained behind to do thirty days in jail.

15 Toronto *Globe* 25 March 1873, noted Mary Ann Gorman's arrest as an inmate at Colenzo's Terrace, and made the reference to the grand jury concern about the area. Regarding Colenzo's prison record, see *Toronto Jail Surgeon's Register 1858–67* at 17. Colenzo was listed in the *Toronto City Directory 1873* (Toronto 1874) 67. See also Craven "Toronto Police Court 1850–1880" at 273 for a discussion of the residents of Dummer Street and their familiarity with police court. For details of the Annie Seaton house relationship, which also spawned arrests, see Toronto *Globe* 19 March 1874.

16 Rosen *Sisterhood* 97–99.

17 See, for example, "An Act for regulating and maintaining a House of Correction or Work-House within the Town of Halifax" 33 Geo. II (1759) c. 1 (N.S.) as revised (1774) c. 5; (1787) c. 6; R.S.N.S. (1851) c. 104; S.N.S. (1864) c. 81; "An Ordinance for establishing a system of Police for the Cities of Quebec and Montreal" 2 Vict. (1) (1839) c. 2 (Lower Canada) as extended to the United Province of Canada (thus including Canada West); "An Act to amend and extend the Act of 1857, for diminishing the expense and delay in the Administration of Criminal Justice" 22 Vict. (1858) c. 27 (P.C.). See Phillips "Vagrancy Laws."

18 Toronto Magdalen Asylum and Industrial House of Refuge for Females, or Female House of Refuge, Annual Reports 1854–1883, Archives of Ontario; Zoya-Claire Walsh "The Toronto Magdalene Asylum 1853–1900: The Transition from Moral Reformation to Social Service" unpublished manuscript January 1986; Jarvis "Mid-Victorian Toronto" 128–30. Although the Asylum was founded in May 1853, it was not incorporated until 1858. "An Act to incorporate the Toronto Magdalen Asylum and Industrial House of Refuge" 22 Vict. (1858) c. 73 (P.C.) listed the names of the founding women: Mesdames M. McCutcheon, Elizabeth Dunlop, Ann Baldwin, Christian Dick, Sarah J. Brett, Amelia Gilmour, E.A. Badgley, Frances Jane Baldwin, A.E. Hagerty, C.H. Blake, Mary Richardson, Jane Mowatt, Frances R. Hodgins, Ann Thompson, Caroline Watson, and Ann Mulholland. Oliver Mowat's sister-in-law, Catherine Seaton Skirving, was the secretary from 1863 and the

president from 1891 to 1895: see "Skirving, Catherine Seaton (Ewart)" *Dictionary of Canadian Biography* v. 12 at 973.

19 Walsh "Asylum" 19, 24, 25–27; Jarvis "Mid-Victorian Toronto" 128–30. For geographic location, see *Toronto City Directory* (1859–60) 112; (1861) 372.

20 Walsh "Asylum" 18; National Council of Women of Canada *Appendix to Women Workers of Canada* (Montreal 1896) 326.

21 Walsh "Asylum" has noted that the founding Board and Committee was made up of members of the various Protestant churches of the city. She has suggested that this volunteer work provided "Evangelical Protestant women with a personal role and mission in the conversion process" (at 4, 11).

As well, during the last half of the nineteenth century, Irish Catholic social action began and religious orders established self-help and other institutions, including the Refuge of the Good Shepherd to "assist with the rehabilitation of wayward women." See Nicholson "Peasants" at 66.

Religious hatred against Irish Catholics in Victorian Toronto intensified after the famine immigration. For discussion of anti-Irish Catholic sentiments in Victorian Toronto, and the Protestant crusade against Irish Catholics led by George Brown and Egerton Ryerson, as well as the role of the Protestant Orange Lodge in this crusade, which continued for nearly eighty years, see Nicholson "Peasants" at 62–64.

22 "An Act for the prevention of contagious diseases, at certain Military and Naval Stations in this Province" 29 Vict. (1865) c. 8 (P.C.). For details, see Backhouse "Prostitution." Commanders of the army and navy had pressed for similar legislation in Nova Scotia, but they were not successful in achieving enactment: Fingard *Victorian Halifax* 109.

23 See Backhouse "Prostitution" for details concerning the English and colonial legislation.

24 Toronto *Daily Telegraph* 28 Dec. 1866; 9 Jan. 1867. This position was criticized by the Toronto *Globe* 29 Dec. 1866, 9 May 1867. For discussion of the general lack of controversy over and enforcement of the statute, see Backhouse "Prostitution."

25 32 & 33 Vict. (1869) c. 28, s. 1 (D.C.).

26 Toronto Magdalen Asylum Annual Report 1855, at 20.

27 Toronto Magdalen Asylum Annual Report 1860, at 7.

28 See Halifax *Herald* 18 May, 6 Nov. 1895; Jessie C. Smith "Social Purity" in Cook and Mitchinson *Proper Sphere* 234; Prentice et al. *Canadian Women* 153.

29 For a discussion of these statistics on criminal charges, see Backhouse "Prostitution." The data were based on a sample year from the Toronto Jail Register for each decade from 1840 to 1900. There were a total of 65 charges against male customers as "habitual frequenters," "frequenters," and "found

ins." There were 2,546 charges against women for prostitution-related offences apart from "keeping."

30 For a description of the Toronto Police Court see Craven "Toronto Police Court 1850–1880" 248–307; Gene Howard Homel "Denison's Law: Criminal Justice and the Police Court in Toronto, 1877–1921" *Ontario History* 73 (1981) 171–85.

31 Craven "Toronto Police Court 1850–1880" 248–82; Homel "Denison's Law" 173–74; Colonel George T. Denison *Recollections of a Police Magistrate* (Toronto 1920) vii, 198–99. Denison's racism was remarkably explicit in this latter text, as he patronizingly and stereotypically described the "Negro element" and the "Irish element" among his cases.

32 Harry M. Wodson *The Whirlpool. Scenes from Toronto Police Court* (Toronto 1917) 26–27.

33 Wodson *Whirlpool* 28.

34 Toronto *Globe* 25 March 1873; 6 Feb. 1872. For discussion of MacNabb's reputation, see Craven "Toronto Police Court 1850–1880" 271–84. MacNabb released the Gorman women on further examination six times, compared with only one such release from Alderman John Cameron, Alderman S.B. Harriman, and Colonel George Denison.

35 Regarding the thefts, see Toronto *Globe* 19 March 1874; 19 Oct. 1877. For details concerning one assault trial, see Toronto *Globe* 21 Sept. 1877; in this case Mary Ann Gorman managed to collect four witnesses to testify to her defence in her trial for assaulting Sarah Richardson. She was discharged. For discussion of how economic recession tended to increase the incarceration rates of vagrants, see Phillips "Vagrancy Laws in Halifax" at 138, 147, 152. See also "An Act to amend 'An Act respecting Vagrants'" 37 Vict. (1874) c. 43 (D.C.).

36 For discussions about the professionalization of the Toronto police force and its main focus on moral crime, see Rogers "Serving Toronto" 123, 126–27, 132–37.

37 Toronto *Globe* 8 Oct. 1873. The *Globe* cited the fine at $1, but the City Jail Register, probably more reliable, cited $4.25. Mary Ann Gorman remained in jail until 1 November, when she was finally able to pay off the fine.

Regarding the high rates of arrest and imprisonment of Irish Catholics in Toronto, Nicholson notes in "Peasants" at 58:

> In 1863, 58.7 percent of those arrested in Toronto were Irish, as were the 59.5 percent incarcerated in the jail. Although not all of those figures represented Irish Catholics, their numbers were high enough

to prompt Bishop John Lynch to write a pastoral letter on "The Evils of Wholesale and Improvident Emigration from Ireland."

38 For details of the Fenian-Orange riot, see Rogers "Serving Toronto" 131.
39 For Halifax data between 1864 and 1873, see Judith Fingard "Jailbirds in Mid-Victorian Halifax" in Peter Waite, Sandra Oxner, and Thomas Barnes eds. *Law in a Colonial Society: The Nova Scotia Experience* (Toronto 1984) 81 at 90; Fingard *Victorian Halifax* and B. Jane Price "Raised in Rockhead, Died in the Poorhouse: Female Petty Criminals in Halifax 1864–1890" in Girard and Phillips *Essays* v. 3 at 200. For Calgary in a somewhat later period, see Judy Bedford "Prostitution in Calgary 1905–1914" *Alberta History* 29 (1981) 1 at 8. For information on Chinese and Japanese women, see Adilman "Chinese Women"; Van Dieren "The WMS and Asian Women" in Latham and Pazdro *Not Just Pin Money* 53 at 57–59 and 79–97; Chan *Gold Mountain* 80–84.
40 "An Act to amend and consolidate the laws respecting Indians" 43 Vict. (1880) c. 28, ss. 95, 96 (D.C.) specified a maximum six months' prison term for keepers of bawdy houses with "Indian women prostitutes on the premises," which matched the penalty for houses with non-First Nations prostitutes, but also added a maximum fine of one hundred dollars and a minimum fine of ten dollars. This was the statute that omitted the reference to a "common bawdy house." "An Act respecting Indians" 49 Vict. (1886) c. 43 s. 106(2) (D.C.) dealt with the conviction of First Nations' customers. This section was repealed by 50 & 51 Vict. (1887) c. 33, s. 11 (D.C.). Further amendments were made in The Criminal Code, 1892 55 & 56 Vict. (1892) c. 29, s. 190(c) (D.C.).

Research into the proportion of women of the First Nations among prison populations of prostitutes is incomplete. Preliminary work by Marjorie Mitchell and Anna Franklin "When You Don't Know the Language, Listen to the Silence: An Historical Overview of Native Indian Women in B.C." in Latham and Pazdro *Pin Money* 17 at 23–27 suggests that on the west coast women of the First Nations were not highly visible as prostitutes. But see also James Gray *Red Lights on the Prairies* (Scarborough 1971).
41 "An Act to make provision for the detention of female convicts in Reformatory Prisons in the Province of Quebec" 34 Vict. (1871) c. 30, s. 2 (D.C.). The preamble of the act stated that such reformatories should be set up "either in separate buildings or in separate portions of the common gaols for the districts of Montreal and Quebec respectively." For information on Quebec prostitution, see Dumont et al. *Quebec Women* 101, 170–72.
42 "An Act respecting certain Female Offenders in the Province of Nova

Scotia" 54 & 55 Vict. (1891) c. 55, s. 1 (D.C.), as amended by 58 & 59 Vict. (1895) c. 43, s. 1 (D.C.).

43 For information on the Sisters of the Good Shepherd, see "An Act to incorporate the Sisters of the Good Shepherd at Halifax" 54 Vict. (1891) c. 135 (N.S.); Fingard *Victorian Halifax* 146–47; and Diner *Erin's Daughters* 136.

44 Cherrier, Kervin & McGown's *Toronto Directory 1873* (Toronto 1874) showed Mary Gorman residing at 58 Dummer and 56 Dummer (at 182, 67).

45 For information on the Mercer Reformatory, see Carolyn Strange "The Criminal and Fallen of their Sex: The Establishment of Canada's First Women's Prison 1874–1901" in *Canadian Journal of Women and the Law* (1985) 79; Carolyn Strange *The Velvet Glove: Materialistic Reform at the Andrew Mercer Ontario Reformatory for Females 1874–1927* M.A. thesis, University of Ottawa 1983; Carolyn Strange "The Founding and Floundering of an Institution: Mercer 1874–1901" unpublished manuscript; Peter Oliver "To Govern by Kindness: The First Two Decades of the Mercer Reformatory for Women" unpublished manuscript. See also "An Act Respecting the Andrew Mercer Ontario Reformatory for Females" 42 Vict. (1879) c. 38 (Ont.), which authorized women convicted of provincial offences to serve their term in the Mercer, and "An Act respecting the 'Andrew Mercer Ontario Reformatory for Females'" 42 Vict. (1879) c. 43 (D.C.), which provided similarly with respect to federal offences. For comparative information on the American experience with women's prisons, see Estelle B. Freedman *Their Sisters' Keepers: Women's Prison Reform in America 1830–1930* (Ann Arbor 1981).

46 Oliver "Mercer" at 28.

47 "An act for the Prevention of Cruelty to, and better Protection of Children" 56 Vict. (1893) c. 43 (Ont.); "Of the Prevention and Punishment of Wrongs to Children" R.S.N.S. (1884) c. 95; "An Act for the Protection and Reformation of Neglected Children" 51 Vict. (1888) c. 40 (N.S.); "An Act for the better Protection of Neglected and Dependent Children" 61 Vict. (1898) c. 6 (Man.); "An Act to amend 'The Children's Protection Act of Manitoba'" 62 & 63 Vict. (1899) c. 4 (Man.).

48 For discussion about the Victorian campaign to eliminate prostitution through a preventative focus on adolescent women, see Backhouse "Prostitution."

49 Transience was a common feature of prostitution, and women would frequently travel between Canadian cities and south to the United States to escape police harassment and other unsavoury elements of their business.

50 London *Free Press* 24 Sept. 1884; 25 Sept. 1884; London *Advertiser* 29 Sept. 1884. For Arscott's residence, see *City of London and County of Middlesex Direc-*

*tory: 1884* (Toronto 1884) 224; the house was renumbered as 201 Rectory shortly thereafter: see *London City and Middlesex County Directory: 1886* (London 1886).

51 John H. Lutman and Christopher L. Hives *The North and the East of London: An Historical and Architectural Guide* (London 1982) 53–102; Frederick H. Armstrong *The Forest City: An Illustrated History of London, Canada* (Windsor 1986) 128–29; Orlo Miller *This Was London: The First Two Centuries* (London 1988) 150; Wayne Paddon *"Steam and Petticoats" 1840–1890* (London 1977) 106–10. For a very useful description of London East, see Carolyn Strange "A Profile of Prostitutes, Their Clients and Brothel Keepers in Middlesex County, Ontario 1875–1885" unpublished manuscript. Political annexation negotiations were referred to in London *Advertiser* 30 Oct. 1884.

52 Daniel Brock estimated this as the population for 1885 in "Population List for London," Regional Collections, University of Western Ontario Library; Strange "Profile of Prostitutes." See *City of London and County of Middlesex Directory 1881–82* v. 2 (London 1881) 64–65, which estimated the population for 1881 as 29,000 when the suburbs of London East, West, and South were included.

53 The London *Advertiser* 29 Sept. 1884, reporting the total receipts from the Western Fair, noted that it had been particularly successful that year. See also Strange "Profile of Prostitutes" where she considered the impact upon prostitution activity of special cultural attractions such as fairs.

54 Esther's date of birth has been calculated from her age, which was listed as forty-two in 1884 in the *Register of the Gaol for the County of Middlesex* v. 5, 21 April 1883 to 1 Oct. 1888 at 40 and 963 (Regional Collections, University of Western Ontario Library). This was corroborated by Esther's gravestone, Woodland Cemetery, London (Section "N," southeast corner), which listed her as age sixty in 1902. The place of birth was taken from her death certificate, #1902-05-016328, Office of the Ontario Registrar General. Jail records sometimes listed her birthplace as England, sometimes as Canada. The first recorded arrest was on 16 Dec. 1872, when she was charged with theft. After serving one day in jail, she was acquitted on 19 Dec. 1872: *Register of the Jail for the County of Middlesex 1872–75* at p. 17 #358, Regional Collections, University of Western Ontario Library. See Charles Lilley Scrapbook, part of Seaborne Collection, Regional Collections, University of Western Ontario Library for extracts from "Scene at the Police Court," which reported that Police Magistrate Lawrence Lawarason referred to Esther Forsyth as "this notorious character" and a "bad character." Lawarason was complaining that she had been released from jail during the night by Mayor John Campbell prior to her trial for robbery in 1872. For details of the 1874 arrest

see *Jail Register 1872–75* 11 July 1874 at p. 56 #1211. For details of the 1877 arrest, see *London Ontario Police Magistrate (Lawrence Lawarason) Minutebook 1877–79* B-16, 22 Sept. 1877. The first directory listing for Esther Forsyth was *London City Directory 1878–79* (London 1878).

Frederick Forsyth(e), named as Esther's brother in her will, was listed as a labourer living on Van Street just down the street from Esther in *London City Directory 1883* (London n.d.); *London City Directory 1884* (Toronto 1884). Other Forsyths, named Alfred, Lucinda, and Elizabeth, also lived in the Van Street residence or nearby: *London City Directory 1888–89* (London 1888); *London City Directory 1890* (London 1890). Esther Arscott's illiteracy was obvious from her will [Will of Esther Barnes, Surrogate Court, County of Middlesex, Liber "S" (1902) 136], which was signed with an "X." This appeared to be a more reliable source than the Jail Registers, which variously listed her as possessing "elementary education" (1884) and able to "read and write well" (1872, 1874). The Jail Registers also provided her religious affiliation as the Church of England (1872, 1874, 1884).

55 The date of the marriage is uncertain, although by the time of her arrest in 1877, Esther was using the Arscott name: see *London Ontario Police Magistrate (Lawrence Lawarason) Minutebook 1877–79* B-16, 22 Sept. 1877. It was not until 1879, however, that the City Directory of 1878–79 listed both Miss Esther Forsyth(e) and William Arscott as residing on the south side of Van, east of Rectory, in London East. After this, Esther was no longer listed separately until after William's death; *London City Directory: 1878–79* (London 1878) 28, 110. The London East Voter's Lists 1878–84, Regional Collections, UWO Library, Location B52, indicated that William Arscott was the owner of houses at 21 Gray as well as 19, 20, and 21 Van Street in 1878. For details of the criminal charge against William Arscott, see London *Advertiser* 23 March 1880. For details on the death of William Arscott, see London *Free Press* 27 Dec. 1883; gravestone, Woodland Cemetery, Section N, southeast corner. Strange "Profile of Prostitutes" noted that 14 per cent of the brothel keepers convicted in Middlesex County between 1875 and 1885 were widowed.

56 London *Advertiser* 29 Sept. 1884.

57 London *Advertiser* 25 Sept. 1884; London *Advertiser* 30 Oct. 1884; Lutman and Hives *London* 80–81; Paddon "Steam" 110; Miller *London* 150.

58 Charles Hutchinson Papers, Regional Collections, University of Western Ontario Library; London Police Commission Minutes, 26 June 1874, Regional Collections, University of Western Ontario Library.

59 London *Free Press* 26 Sept. 1884; London *Advertiser* 25 Sept. 1884; 26 Sept. 1884; Miller *London* 131. For discussion of the high rate of prostitution

prosecutions from the mid-1870s to the late 1880s in Middlesex County, see Strange "Profile of Prostitutes." The obscenity trial was *The Queen* v *Frank Kerchmer* London Police Court, 25 Jan. 1886; appeal dismissed 12 June 1886 Court of General Sessions. Kerchmer was convicted. I am indebted to Ed Phelps, Director of the Regional and Special Collections Library, University of Western Ontario, for bringing this case to my attention. Transcript records are with Regional Collections, University of Western Ontario Library.

60 For the English common law position, see William Oldnall Russell *A Treatise on Crimes and Misdemeanours* 5th ed. v. 1 (London 1843) 427; Clarke *Criminal Law of Canada* 198. See also "An Act for the more speedy and effectual Punishment of Persons keeping Disorderly Houses" 9 & 10 Geo. IV (1829) c. 8 (N.B.); as amended in 1840 and 1849; "Of Offences against Public Morals" R.S.N.S. (1851) c. 158; "An Ordinance for establishing a system of Police for the Cities of Quebec and Montreal" 2 Vict. (1) (1839) c. 2 (L.C.); "An Act to amend and extend the Act of 1857, for diminishing the expense and delay in the Administration of Criminal Justice" 22 Vict. (1858) c. 27 (P.C.); "An Act respecting Vagrants" 32 & 33 Vict. (1869) c. 28, s. 1 (D.C.); "An Act to amend 'An Act respecting Vagrants'" 37 Vict. (1874) c. 43 (D.C.); "An Act to remove doubts as to the power to imprison with hard labour under the Act respecting Vagrants" 44 Vict. (1881) c. 31, s. 1 (D.C.).

61 London *Advertiser* 25 Sept. 1884; 29 Sept. 1884; London *Free Press* 25 Sept. 1884.

62 London *Advertiser* 29 Sept. 1884.

63 London *Free Press* 26 Sept. 1884; London *Advertiser* 29 Sept. 1884. For details on Edmund Meredith, see Morgan *Canadian Men* 2nd ed. (1912) 796; His Honour Judge David J. Hughes and T.H. Purdom QC *History of the Bar of the County of Middlesex* (London 1912) at 33, 50. For details on Squire Murray Anderson, see Miller *London* 70–71 and comments by Lilley and Hutchinson in London *Free Press* 27 Sept. 1884.

64 London *Free Press* 27 Sept. 1884. Squire Murray Anderson also accused Lilley of being motivated by the forthcoming municipal election, and "the need of some sensation in his cause." As for Hutchinson, said Anderson: "He was paid for prosecuting the case" ("Charles Hutchinson Papers" Sept. 1884 clipping from London *Free Press*).

65 See comments of Councillor Heaman in London *Advertiser* 30 Oct. 1884.

66 London *Advertiser* 23 Oct. 1884; Petition of William Trace and forty-seven others, "Charles Hutchinson Papers" 1885–1886.

67 London *Advertiser* 23 Oct. 1884.

68 London *Advertiser* 25 Oct. 1884; 26 Nov. 1884.

69 London *Advertiser* 9 Dec. 1884 noted the date.

70 For details see *Regina* v *Arscott* (1885) 9 O.R. 541 (C.P.); *Arscott* v *Lilley and Hutchinson* (1886) 11 O.R. 153 (Q.B.).

71 London *Free Press* 6 Feb. 1885.

72 London *Free Press* 4 Feb. 1885; 9 Feb. 1885.

73 "An act for the better securing the liberty of the subject, and for prevention of imprisonments beyond the seas" 31 Chas. II (1679) c. 2 (Eng.); London *Free Press* 16 Feb. 1885.

74 The reasons for the decision of the Court of General Sessions were outlined in the London *Free Press* 21 Feb. 1885:

> 1st. The Mayor having issued his warrant there was no necessity that another should issue from the General Sessions.

> 2nd. To order the woman's imprisonment would be contrary to Mr. Justice Galt's order, which apparently declares her imprisonment to be illegal.

> 3rd. That the Habeas Corpus Act, under which the proceedings were taken to effect her liberation, prohibit her second imprisonment for the same offence.

See also *Regina* v *Arscott* (1885). For details on Mayor Lilley's activities, see correspondence from Lilley to Hutchinson 19 March 1885, "Charles Hutchinson Papers." For details on the date of arrest and discharge on bail, see *Register of the Gaol for the County of Middlesex* v. 5, 21 April 1883 to 1 Oct. 1888 at 52 (Regional Collections, University of Western Ontario Library).

75 "Meredith, Richard Martin"; "Meredith, William Ralph" Morgan *Canadian Men* 2nd ed. (1912) 797–98.

76 "Osler, Britton Bath" *Macmillan Dictionary* 4th ed. (1978) at 633–34; "Mc-Carthy, D'Alton" Rose *Cyclopaedia* 624.

77 Clarke *Of Toronto the Good* 93. Meredith described his inclination in the Toronto *Globe* 21 May 1934.

78 Curtis Cole "McCarthy, Osler, Hoskin, and Creelman, 1882 to 1902: Establishing a Reputation, Building a Practice" in Carol Wilton ed. *Beyond the Law: Lawyers and Business in Canada, 1830 to 1930* (Toronto 1990) 149–66, noted that the high-profile litigation accounted for very little of the firm's income, but produced the reputation that allowed it to establish a healthy and growing practice.

79 "Aylesworth, Sir Allen Bristol" *Macmillan Dictionary* 4th ed. (1978) at 29; Morgan *Canadian Men* 2nd ed. (1912) at 47.

80 *Regina* v *Arscott* (1885) 9 O.R. 541 (C.P.); "An Act respecting Vagrants" 32 & 33 Vict. (1869) c. 28, s. 1 (D.C.).

81 *Regina* v *Arscott* (1885) at 542–43. For details on Judge John Edward Rose, see "Rose, Hon. Justice John E." Rose *Cyclopaedia* 737.

82 *Regina* v *Arscott* (1885) 543, 547.

83 "An Act respecting Offences against the Person" 32 & 33 Vict. (1869) c. 20, s. 50 (D.C.); "An Act respecting Offences against Public Morals and Public Convenience" 49 Vict. (1886) c. 157, ss. 3, 5, 6, 7, and 8 (D.C.); "An Act to punish seduction, and like offences, and to make further provision for the Protection of Women and Girls" 49 Vict. (1886) c. 52 (D.C.); "An Act to amend the Act respecting Offences against Public Morals and Public Convenience" 50 & 51 Vict. (1887) c. 48 (D.C.); "An Act respecting Offences against Public Morals and Public Convenience" R.S.C. (1887) v. 2, c. 157 (D.C.); The Criminal Code, 1892 55 & 56 Vict. (1892) c. 29, ss. 185–88 (D.C.).

84 For a discussion of D.A. Watt's work, see D.A. Watt *Moral Legislation: A Statement Prepared for the Information of the Senate* (Montreal 1890); McLaren "Chasing the Social Evil." See also Presentment of the Grand Jury to the Judge of the Court of Oyer, and Terminer, Winter Assize 1882 *York Criminal Assize Book 1878–87*, AO RG22 at 269.

85 For discussions of the purity campaign, see McLaren "Chasing the Social Evil"; Smith "Social Purity" 234. For a general discussion of views about female and male sexuality, see Wendy Mitchinson "Medical Perceptions of Female Sexuality: A Late Nineteenth Century Case" *Scientia Canadiensis* 9 (1985) 67.

   The phrase "white slavery" was repeatedly used in this campaign, and I have long been grappling with how to interpret this. The term was apparently coined in the 1830s to describe the forcible abduction of women into prostitution, often on an international scale. Many authorities consider it to be a race-neutral concept: see, for example, Florence Rush *The Best Kept Secret: Sexual Abuse of Children* (Englewood Cliffs, N.J. 1980) 62–64. I once accepted this as an accurate characterization; see Backhouse "Prostitution" at 393 where I wrote that the term was "unrelated to skin colour, merely distinguish[ing] the traffic in women and children from the black slave trade." I now see this statement as highly problematic. Obviously Black women experienced the slavery of prostitution within the Black slave trade. Originally designed to distinguish the prostitution of women from the international slave trade in Black men, women, and children, the term could not help but emphasize that sexual status varied by race. What was new about the term "white slavery" was exactly what it implied, that the abduction of white women into prostitution was being promulgated as an abomination of a different order. The irony was, of course, that prostitution and prostitution law were rife with discrimination against racial, ethnic, and religious minority groups. Indeed, it made a mockery of the term "white slavery," and pointed up how partial was the vision of most of the purity advocates seeking reform. See also Edward J. Bristow *Prostitution and Prejudice: The Jewish Fight Against White Slavery 1870–1939* (New York 1983) 35–38 where the author has noted that virulent anti-Semites often attacked Jews as the procurers of "white" women for the prostitution trade.

86 *R.* v *Levecque* (1870) 30 U.C.Q.B.R. 509 at 513–16.

87 *R.* v *Gareau* (1891) 1 C.C.C. 66 (Que. C.A.); *The Queen* v *Rehe* (1897) 1 C.C.C. 63 (Que. Q.B.) at 65. The judicial references to "kept women" appear to have been confined to the province of Quebec during this period. This phenomenon may have been more culturally acceptable in Quebec, since in 1875 the Montreal police chief estimated that there were one hundred such women in the city. (See Dumont et al. *Quebec Women* 170.) The Civil Code of Quebec also made specific reference to the status of a concubine kept in the family dwelling. (See infra, chapter 6.)

88 *In re Polly Hamilton* (1882) *Coutlee's Supreme Court Cases* 35 at 40–43.

89 Chief Justice Cameron's judgment was unreported, but was excerpted in *Arscott* v *Lilley and Hutchinson* (1886) 11 O.R. 153 (Q.B.) at 153–58.

90 For correspondence from A.B. Aylesworth to Hutchinson, 28 Sept. 1885, see "Charles Hutchinson Papers." *Arscott* v *Lilley and Hutchinson* (1886) 11 O.R. 153 (Q.B.). Wilson's judgment was a lengthy one, composed mainly of technical recitations of previous cases regarding the legality of various warrants. Wilson did, in passing, note that he disagreed with Judge Rose's interpretation of the criminal statute, but since his was not an appeal court, he could not overrule it.

91 *Arscott* v *Lilley* (1887) 14 O.A.R. 283 (C.A.) at 286–88; *Arscott* v *Lilley* (1887) 14 O.A.R. 297 (C.A.).

92 In discussing the proper interpretation of the Vagrancy Act, Patterson expressly incorporated the earlier judgment of Adam Wilson on the matter.

93 *Arscott* v *Lilley* (1887) at 291.

94 See listings for Robert T. Barnes from 1890–1906, *London City Directories*.

95 Will of Esther Barnes, Surrogate Court, County of Middlesex, Liber "S" (1902) 136. Death notices for Esther Barnes were published in the London *Free Press* 2 July 1902; 3 July 1902; London *Advertiser* 2 July 1902.

## Chapter 9 (pages 260 to 292)

1 Charlotte Fuhrer *The Mysteries of Montreal: Memoirs of a Midwife* (Montreal 1881); repub. Peter Ward ed. (Vancouver 1984) at 86.

2 Fuhrer *Mysteries* 86.

3 Fuhrer *Mysteries* 86–87.

4 Fuhrer *Mysteries* 87.

5 Fuhrer *Mysteries* 85.

6 Testimony of Dr. Ely Van der Walker, in Louis D. Brandeis *Women in Industry* (New York 1908) at 142, emphasis added; Linda Bohnen "Women Workers in Ontario: A Socio-Legal History" *University of Toronto Faculty of Law Review* 31 (1973) 45 at 50.

7 Fuhrer *Mysteries* 85, 91. Esther Ryland Quintin succumbed to the ravages of consumption at an early age, a condition Fuhrer intimated was connected with her servitude as a shop-clerk.

8 For an account of the industrialization of Montreal, see Bettina Bradbury, "Women and Wage Labour in a Period of Transition: Montreal 1861–1881" *Social History* 17(33) (May 1984) 115; "'Pigs, Cows, and Boarders': Non-Wage Forms of Survival Among Montreal Families 1861–91" *Labour/Le Travail* 14 (Fall 1984) 9. See also Marie Lavigne and Jennifer Stoddart, "Women's Work in Montreal at the Beginning of the Century" in Marylee Stephenson ed. *Women in Canada* (Don Mills 1977) 129 at 137; Sheila M. Rothman *Woman's Proper Place: A History of Changing Ideals and Practices 1870 to the Present* (New York 1978) 52; Susan Porter Benson *Counter Culture* (Chicago 1986) 13–14.

In Ontario by 1891, about 16 per cent of the retail salesclerks were female, although in the larger department stores women could number up to half of the employees. See Marjorie Griffin Cohen *Women's Work, Markets and Economic Development in Nineteenth-Century Ontario* (Toronto 1988) 150. See also Jean Thomas Scott, *The Conditions of Female Labour in Ontario* (Toronto 1892) at 23.

9 Benson *Counter* 6, 135, 211, 266.

10 Rothman *Sphere* 52–53, 55; Benson *Counter* 26, 209. Rothman's analysis, while American, is probably suggestive of the situation in Canada as well: "Just as middle-class women preferred to employ servants of English stock or second- and third-generation Irish, so did the department stores.... Almost every Macy's employee was English or second- or third-generation immigrant. Not until 1900 did German or Eastern European girls begin to appear in the sales ranks. As late as 1909, native-born girls made up the majority of employees in Baltimore's retail stores. 'Two stores employ only

American girls,' one researcher noted. 'This preponderance is due to the fact that many customers prefer to be served by Americans, and in part to the fact that native-born girls of Anglo-Saxon stock prefer, when possible, to choose an occupation socially superior to factory work.'"

Susan Porter Benson, also writing in the American context, has noted that virtually no department store would knowingly hire a Black woman as salesclerk. "In general, department stores tried as best they could to match their selling staffs to their desired clientele; this meant always excluding Black women and weeding out as much as possible those with too-obvious immigrant or working-class demeanour."

Tamara Adilman, conducting research into twentieth-century Canadian working conditions, found that department stores such as Woodward's in British Columbia refused to consider Chinese women as clerks. ("A Preliminary Sketch of Chinese Women and Work in British Columbia 1858–1950" in Latham and Pazdro *Not Just Pin Money* 68.)

11 Scott *Labour* at 21, 26; Benson *Counter* 194.

12 Scott *Labour* at 15; Benson *Counter* 143; Lavigne and Stoddart "Work" at 137.

13 Scott *Labour* at 13, 15.

14 Agnes Maule Machar *Roland Graeme: Knight* (Montreal 1892) at 38, 65, 107.

15 Machar *Graeme* at 66, 88, 113, 116, 201, 203, 230, 274.

16 Machar *Graeme* at 66, 249, 280.

17 Machar *Graeme* at 69. Apart from her views on class, Machar's views on race have not been fully explored, although her family had been active in aiding American slaves who were travelling via the underground railway to Kingston. Slavery had existed in Canada and became abolished in stages, partially in 1793 in Upper Canada, and completely throughout the British Empire in 1833. "An Act to prevent the further introduction of Slaves and to limit the term of contracts for servitude within this Province" S.U.C. (1793) (2nd Sess.) c. 7; Emancipation Act, 3 & 4 Wm. IV (1833) c. 73. (Eng.). Yet Machar's writing frequently includes stereotyped images of Blacks and peoples of the First Nations: see *For King and Country* (Toronto 1874) at 20, 112, 147; *Marjorie's Canadian Winter: A Story of Northern Lights* (copyright 1892; Toronto 1906). Furthermore, in her advocacy of greater protection for working-class women, Machar often equates their situation with slaves, showing almost no understanding of slavery. See, for example, *Graeme* at 67, where she wrote of Lizzie:

> And so, by force of cruel fate, as it seemed, this girl was as truly chained by invisible fetters to her daily toil among those relentless wheels and pulleys, as if she were a galley-slave. The plantation

slaves, on the whole, were not so badly off. They had their regular hours of toil, but their hours of relaxation were free from care, and full of fun and frolic, and — which was another great relief — they had frequent change of labor.

18 Dumont et al. *Quebec Women* 160–63; Michael S. Cross and Greg S. Kealey *Canada's Age of Industry 1849–1896* (Toronto 1982); Greg Kealey *Toronto Workers Respond to Industrial Capitalism 1867–1892* (Toronto 1980); Cohen *Markets* 129. See also *Report of the Commissioners appointed to enquire into the working of Mills and Factories of the Dominion, and the labor employed therein* House of Commons Canada, Sessional Papers #42, 1882 at 4–5. Commissioners William Lukes and A.H. Blackeby of Galt toured Prince Edward Island, Nova Scotia, New Brunswick, Ontario, and Quebec before issuing their report. On meal breaks, the report noted:

> Some factories allow only half an hour at noon, and others three-quarters of an hour. The result of this is that the hands take their meals at the factory, and where the air is foul and vitiated from crowding or continuous occupation, [this] is liable to produce very serious results to the operatives.

Their recommendation: "Meals should not be taken in the work shops, fresh air and exercise being essentially necessary for the health of the operatives." See also Toronto *Globe* 17 Feb. 1897.

19 *Report* at 8.

20 Kealey *Toronto Workers* 221; The commissioner's *Report* noted at 9 that on the whole, factory managers cleansed their work force of "sexually promiscuous" women. Where management failed, the female employees themselves monitored the situation. "In one of these places a doubtful character had obtained entrance, and the girls, to their credit be it said, sent in a prompt and unanimous request to the manager for her removal, and with the desired effect," the commissioners noted with pride. For details of Phillips Thompson's intellectual prominence within the social reform movement, see Ramsay Cook *The Regenerators: Social Criticism in Late Victorian English Canada* (Toronto 1985) at 152–73.

21 Scott *Labour* 20–22; Dumont et al. *Quebec Women* 160–63; Lavigne and Stoddart "Work" 133; *Report* 5.

22 For descriptions of the process of manufacturing silk, see *Treatise on the Origin, Progressive Improvement, and Present State of the Silk Manufacture* (Lon-

don 1831); John D'Homerque *The Silk Culturist's Manual* (Philadelphia 1839); James Chittick *Silk Manufacturing and Its Problems* (New York 1913).

23 "Bergin, Darby" *Appleton's Cyclopedia of Biography* (New York 1856) v. 1 at 245; Eric Tucker *Administering Danger in the Workplace: The Law and Politics of Occupational Health and Safety Regulation in Ontario 1850–1914* (forthcoming University of Toronto Press, 1991).

24 Toronto *Globe* 6 Jan. 1881.

25 *Hansard Parliamentary Debates* House of Commons 1 April 1885 at 875 and 880. For details on the career of Jarvis, see Gerald N. Grob *Edward Jarvis and the Medical World of Nineteenth-Century America* (Knoxville, Tenn. 1978).

26 Brandeis *Women* at 51.

27 The question of constitutional jurisdiction over the field of labour law, and protective labour legislation in particular, was very unsettled in the nineteenth century. For an excellent discussion of the debates, and the ultimate resolution in favour of provincial powers, see Tucker *Administering Danger*.

"An Act for the Protection of Persons employed in Factories" 47 Vict. (1884) c. 39, ss. 2, 6, and 8 (Ont.). This statute was amended several times before the turn of the century. See "An Act to amend the Ontario Factories' Act, 1884" 50 Vict. (1887) c. 35 (Ont.); "An Act to amend the Ontario Factories' Act" 52 Vict. (1889) c. 43 (Ont.); "The Factories Amendment Act" 58 Vict. (1895) c. 50 (Ont.); "An Act for the Protection of Persons employed in Factories" R.S.O. (1897) c. 256.

The act defined "child" as a person under the age of fourteen years, and set up an additional category of "young girl," defined as a girl aged fourteen to seventeen. The statute permitted male children twelve and over, and female children fourteen and over to work, subject to extensive regulation. An amendment passed in 1889 set a limit on the amount of overtime an inspector could authorize in any one factory at thirty-six days a year: "An Act to amend the Ontario Factories' Act" 52 Vict. (1889) c. 43, s. 6 (Ont.).

28 Eric Tucker "The Politics of Factory Legislation: Part II" unpublished manuscript 1989 at 44–45, noted that the ten-hour day was already an existing norm. See also Scott *Labour* 13.

29 Factories Act (1884) ss. 5, 7, 11(4), 31.

30 The Ontario legislation initially exempted factories employing not more than twenty persons, but this was later reduced to five. For a critique of this exemption, see Scott *Labour* at 10–11; *Ninth Annual Reports of the Inspectors of Factories for the Province of Ontario, 1896* Sessional Paper No. 28 (Toronto 1897) 20; *Eleventh Annual Reports of the Inspectors of Factories for the Province of Ontario, 1898* Sessional Papers No. 30 (Toronto 1899) 25. Regarding the fami-

ly exemption, see *Inspectors Report* 1899 at 27. Marilyn J. Boxer argued that this type of exclusion may have been the most significant aspect of the legislation, since it functioned to redirect female workers into that realm that would always be exempt from regulation — women and children in the "home": "Protective Legislation and Home Industry: The Marginalization of Women Workers in Late Nineteenth–Early Twentieth-Century France" *Journal of Social History* 20 (1986) 45.

Domestic workers constituted another conspicuously absent group despite the fact that physicians reported frequent cases of ill health among female servants, which the physicians attributed to "long hours, lack of open air exercise, poor meals eaten too hastily and poor rooms too often in damp cellars." Wayne Roberts *Honest Womanhood: Feminism, Femininity and Class Consciousness Among Toronto Working Women 1893–1914* (Toronto 1976) 14.

Male journalists speculated that the middle-class women who were spearheading the campaign for factory legislation deliberately excluded domestic workers because they wanted no infringement on relations with their own servants. There is evidence that women such as Agnes Machar were defensive about this subject. "The hard-worked and much-tried mistress is sometimes as worthy of compassion as the undoubtedly often hard-worked servant," she wrote in the 1890s, sounding ever so much like Dr. Emily Stowe a decade earlier. To the extent that there was a problem with extended hours, Agnes Machar recommended that domestic workers simply speed up their work: "The natural incapacity and almost lack of preliminary training for their work is one cause of the unduly long hours of work, which, with greater skill and method on the part of the worker, might be greatly shortened."

Although Machar did concede that working conditions were often too harsh, she argued against the inclusion of domestic workers in legislation. Her dubious rationale was that domestic labour entailed an individualized, person-to-person relationship, which inhibited standardized rules. "There is as great a diversity in the character of domestics as there is in that of mistresses, which alone makes it impossible to deal with this question as we can with the well defined lines of factory labour." *The Week* 6 Sept. 1895, 968; 27 March 1896, 422.

31 See Eric Tucker "Making the Workplace 'Safe' in Capitalism: The Enforcement of Factory Legislation in Nineteenth-Century Ontario" *Labour/Le Travail* 21 (Spring 1988) 45. The *Report upon the Sweating System in Canada 1896* (Sessional Papers No. 61) also noted that in the smaller establishments

"women and children work many more hours daily than would be permitted in shops and factories under the regulation of the Acts" (at 8).

32 Tucker "Enforcement" 60; Lavigne and Stoddart "Work" 136; Scott *Labour* at 18.

33 Morgan *Canadian Men* (Toronto 1898) 157; Janice Acton et al. *Women at Work 1850–1930* (Toronto 1974) 223; Tucker "Enforcement" 60, 76–77.

34 *Inspectors Report 1896* 25.

35 "An Act to protect the life and health of persons employed in factories" 48 Vict. (1885) c. 32, s. 23 (Que.). See also the following amendments: Quebec Factories' Act R.S.Q. (1888) Section IV; "An Act to amend article 3026 of the Revised Statutes of the Province of Quebec, respecting persons employed in factories" 53 Vict. (1890) c. 39 (Que.).

36 MacLean received her Bachelor of Arts in 1893 and her Master of Arts in 1894 from Acadia, her Ph.M. from the University of Chicago in 1897, and Ph.D. similarly in 1899. The title of her dissertation was "The Acadian Element in the Population of Nova Scotia." She published widely, in the "Southern Educational Magazine," "Charities Review," and others. Eventually she would go on to become the head of the Department of Sociology at Adelphi College in New York City.

While completing her Ph.D. in Chicago, MacLean posed as a saleswoman and obtained employment in two department stores during the Christmas rush season. She was quite disturbed by what she found. Unpaid overtime and deplorable working situations abounded:

> Gloom, filth and weariness pervaded the first store, which paid its women employees so little as to force them to choose between starvation and shame. The second store had a more wholesome atmosphere, but still the hours there were long and the wages woefully insufficient.

MacLean was equally disturbed by some of the "ladies bountiful" who frequently tried the patience of shop-clerks with their familiarity. She recounted with relish the retort of one salesclerk after she had been asked her salary for the fifth time. She apparently answered her customer and then added: "How much do you get?" Annie Marion MacLean "Two Weeks in Department Stores" *American Journal of Sociology* 4 (May 1899) 729, 735; Annie Marion MacLean *Wage-Earning Women* (New York 1910), at pp. x and 66–67 as recounted in Benson *Counter* 135, 198, and 260; Virginia Kemp Fish "Annie Marion MacLean" Liwa Mainiero ed. *American Women Writers vol. 3* (New York 1981) 102–4.

37 *Women Workers of Canada: Being a Report of the Proceedings of the Fourth Annual Meeting and Conference of the National Council of Women of Canada* (Kingston 1897) 45. "Dennis, William" Morgan *Canadian Men* (Toronto 1912) 317.
38 "An Act for the Protection of Persons Employed in Factories" 63–64 Vict. (1900) c. 13, ss. 8 and 9 (Man.).
39 "An Act to regulate the closing of Shops and the Hours of Labour therein for Children and Young Persons" 51 Vict. (1888) c. 33, s. 3 (Ont.); "An Act to regulate the closing of Shops and the Hours of Labour therein for children and Young Persons" 51 Vict. (1888) c. 32, s. 3 (Man.). See also R.S.M. (1891) vol. II, c. 140. The hours were somewhat longer than in factories: twelve hours a day, seventy-four hours a week. On Saturdays, maximum hours were stretched to fourteen. Unlike factory workers, the young shop-clerks had their mealtimes included in these hours. They were allotted one hour for the noon-day meal, and forty-five minutes for the evening meal. Ontario later extended the provisions regarding privies to "places of business other than factories" where women or girls were employed. "An Act for the Protection of Persons employed in places of Business other than Factories" 55 Vict. (1892) c. 54 (Ont.); as amended "An Act for the further Protection of persons employed in Places of Business other than Factories" 58 Vict. (1895) c. 51 (Ont.). Excluded were places of business where only family members were employed, or where there were five or fewer employees.
 The Ontario Legislature also appears to have been worried that women, who could no longer work extended hours in the factories, were moon-lighting after hours in shops. In the 1897 Shops Regulation Act it stipulated that employers could not knowingly hire female shop-clerks who had already worked their ten hours a day/sixty hours a week allotment in a factory (s. 6).
40 *Report of the NCWC* (Ottawa 1894) 223; Scott *Labour* 17. The same situation held for Quebec. See Lavigne and Stoddart "Work" 145, where it was noted that an inquiry carried out in 1927 showed that the laws regarding seating were completely ignored.
41 "An Act respecting Shops and Places other than Factories" 60 Vict. (1897) c. 51, s. 8 (Ont.). The act also banned children under ten from working in shops, and restricted hours of work for women. Women were not to work before 7:00 a.m. or after 6:00 p.m., except on Saturdays and days before statutory holidays, when they could stay as late as 10:00 p.m. One hour was allotted for the noon-hour meal, and forty-five minutes for the evening meal (ss. 4 and 5).
42 *Inspectors Report 1898* 29.

43 Susan Trofimenkoff "One Hundred and Two Muffled Voices: Canada's Industrial Women in the 1880's" in Cross and Kealey *Industry* 212.
44 See Ruth Compton Brouwer "Moral Nationalism in Victorian Canada: The Case of Agnes Machar" *Journal of Canadian Studies* 20(1) (Spring 1985) 90 at 92, 99; A. Ethelwyn Wetherald "Some Canadian Literary Women — II 'Fidelis'" *The Week* 5(19) (5 April 1888) 300; "Machar, Agnes Maule" *Dictionary of Canadian Biography* v. 9 at 495–96; Kingston *Whig-Standard Magazine* 16 April 1983 at 7. The lack of information about Agnes's mother is unfortunate. It was not uncommon for historians to forget the names of women married to prominent men; even Agnes Machar referred to her mother only as Mrs. Machar in the volume she published about her father after his death.
45 See *The Week*; Brouwer "Moral Nationalism"; Gerson *Three Writers*; Ruth Compton Brouwer "The 'Between-Age' Christianity of Agnes Machar" *Canadian Historical Review* 65(3) (1984) 347; R.W. Cumberland "Remembering Agnes Maule Machar" *Historic Kingston* 21 (1973) 22.
46 R.W. Cumberland "Agnes Maule Machar" *Queen's Quarterly* 34(3) (1927) at 331; Brouwer "Moral Nationalism" 102.
47 *Women Workers of Canada: Being a Report of the Proceedings of the Second Annual Meeting and Conference of the National Council of Women of Canada* (Toronto 1895) 173.
48 Machar *Roland Graeme* 158–59, 175.
49 Maria Amelia Fytche *Kerchiefs to Hunt Souls* (Boston 1895; repub. Sackville, N.B. 1980) at 200.
50 *Report of the NCWC* (1895), 173–74.
51 Strong-Boag *Parliament* 159; Carol Lee Bacchi *Liberation Deferred? The Ideas of the English-Canadian Suffragists 1877–1918* (Toronto 1983) 102, 106; Jean Bannerman *Leading Ladies: Canada* (Belleville 1977) 68–69; Emily P. Weaver "Pioneer Canadian Women" *The Canadian Magazine* 49 (October 1917) 447; "Derick, Carrie" Morgan *Canadian Men* 263–64; Margaret Gillett *We Walked Very Warily: A History of Women at McGill* (Montreal 1981) 98.
52 Gillett *McGill* 98.
53 National Council of Women of Canada *Women of Canada* 65 and 406; Strong-Boag *Parliament* 159; Bacchi *Liberation* 18, 22, 38, 102, 106; Bannerman *Leading Ladies* 68–69; Weaver "Pioneer" 448; "Derick, Carrie" Morgan *Canadian Men* 263–64; Gillett *McGill* 227, 372–74.
54 Gillett *McGill* 372–74.
55 Lavigne and Stoddart "Work" at 137. In the early years, prominent French Canadians such as Thibaudeau, Marchand-Dandurant, and Gerin-Lajoie worked actively within the Montreal Council, despite the hostility of the Roman Catholic clergy. By the twentieth century, many of the French

Canadian women switched to the Fédération nationale St. Jean-Baptiste (formed 1907) in preference to the NCWC. Yolande Pinard "Les Debuts du Mouvement des femmes a Montreal 1893–1902" in Marie Lavigne et al. *Travailleuses et feministes: Les Femmes dans la Société Québécoise* (Quebec 1983) at 183; Marta Danylewycz *Taking the Veil: An Alternative to Marriage, Motherhood and Spinsterhood in Quebec 1840–1920* (Toronto 1987) at 138. Lady Drummond was the current President of the Local Council. Her work with other women's organizations was extensive; she served on the Women's History Society, the Home for Incurables, the Aberdeen Association of the Anti-Tubercular League, the Parks and Playgrounds Association of Montreal, the Victorian Order of Nurses, the Needlework Guild, the Women's Canadian Club, and the Royal Montreal Ladies' Golf Club. Morgan *Canadian Men* (Toronto 1912) 345.

56 See *Report of the NCWC* (1895) 177; *Report of the NCWC* (1896) 370.

57 Darby Bergin, M.D., noted wage differentials when he introduced his bills to the House of Commons. "Everybody knows that women and children work at lower wages than men," he stated, yet he forbore any discussion of legislative intervention: "I will not discuss this question." *Hansard Parliamentary Debates* 1 April 1885 at 874. Minnie Phelps wrote an impassioned plea for equal pay that was published in B.F. Austin ed. *Woman: Her Character, Culture and Calling* (Brantford 1890) 51–55. However, Margaret Hobbs has concluded that the decision to exclude wages was a "conscious choice" not to enter the field of wage regulation: see Margaret Hobbs "Dead Horses and Muffled Voices: Protective Labour Legislation, Education and Minimum Wage for Women in Ontario" M.A. thesis, University of Toronto 1985 at 20–21. See also Margaret E. McCallum "Keeping Women in Their Place: The Minimum Wage in Canada, 1910–25" *Labour/Le Travail* 17 (Spring 1986) 29–56.

58 Machar did not dispute that male workers might need protection as well. But she seems to have felt that this was a matter best left to reformers of the other sex. She also argued that the betterment of working conditions for women would have a salutary effect on men's: "The tendency of reform in one direction has always been to bring about reform in other directions also." Presumably the protective labour legislation for women would operate only temporarily, until the market righted any imbalance that occurred. See *The Week* 6 Sept. 1896 at 967–68. See also Machar "Unhealthy Conditions of Women's Work in Factories" *The Week* 8 May 1896 at 566. This article Machar subsequently directed to all Local Councils of the NCWC in preparation for the 1896 annual meeting. See *Women Workers of Canada:*

*Being a Report of the Proceedings of the Third Annual Meeting and Conference of the NCWC* (Montreal 1896) at 358.

59 Bohnen "Women Workers" at 49–50; Machar *The Week* 8 May 1896 at 567.

60 *Report of the NCWC* (1895) 177; *Report of the NCWC* (1896) 370; *The Week* 8 May 1896 at 568. Interestingly, Eric Tucker's recent study of the Ontario Factories Act concluded that there was no evidence that women lost jobs as a result of the legislation. It is highly unlikely that a comprehensive analysis of the results could ever be traced at this point. See Tucker "Factory Legislation: Part II" at 44–45.

61 Scott *Labour* 27.

62 Machar *The Week* 8 May 1896 at 568; *Report of the NCWC* (1896) at 359–60.

63 Gregory S. Kealey and Brian D. Palmer *Dreaming of what might be: The Knights of Labor in Ontario 1880–1900* (Cambridge 1982) 319.

64 Prentice et al. *Canadian Women* 137; *Report of the NCWC* (1896) at 362.

65 *The Week* 8 May 1896 at 567.

66 *Report of the NCWC* (1895) at 175.

67 See Cohen *Markets* 15–16.

68 Bacchi *Liberation* 97, 106–7; "Canadian Woman Professor" *Saturday Night* 17 May 1913 at 31; "Segregation of the Feeble-Minded" Montreal *Gazette* 21 Dec. 1916. In the twentieth century, Derick would also endorse the birth control ideology of Margaret Sanger. Where this fit with her eugenics perspective is not clear. See Gillett *McGill* 460.

69 *Report of the NCWC* (1896) at 361, 370.

70 *Report of the NCWC* (1896) at 419.

71 Strong-Boag *Parliament* 160. See also Nancy F. Cott *The Grounding of Modern Feminism* (New Haven 1987) 136 for a discussion of similar themes in the American context.

72 For discussion of the English situation, see Angela V. John *By the Sweat of their Brow* (London 1984). For a discussion of the dangers of the Canadian mines that does not address the question of female employment, see Donald MacLeod "Colliers, Colliery Safety and Workplace Control: The Nova Scotian Experience 1873–1910" Canadian Historical Association *Historical Papers* (1983) 226.

73 John *Sweat* 39–40; Caroline H. Dall *Woman's Right to Labor* (Boston 1860) 47–48.

74 John *Sweat* 180–88.

75 Mines and Collieries Act 5 & 6 Vict. (1842) c. 99 (Eng.); "An Act to consolidate and amend the Acts relating to the Regulation of Coal Mines and certain other Mines" 35 & 36 Vict. (1872) c. 76 (Eng.); John *Sweat* 52–55; 155–57.

76 "An Act to make Regulations with respect to Coal Mines" 40 Vict. (1877) c. 122, ss. 3, 7, 10, 55 (B.C.). See also 46 Vict. (1883) c. 2 (B.C.) and C.S.B.C. (1888) c. 84. For no apparent reason, all of these restrictions were repealed in 1892; "An Act to amend the 'Coal Mines Act'" 55 Vict. (1892) c. 31, s. 1 (B.C.). Without explanation, they were enacted again in 1897: "An Act to make Regulations with respect to Coal Mines" R.S.B.C. (1897) c. 138.

"An Act to amend the 'Coal Mines Regulation Act'" 53 Vict. (1890) c. 33, s. 1 (B.C.) added the words "and no Chinaman" to the prohibited groups. "An Act to amend the 'Coal Mines Regulation Act'" 62 Vict. (1899) c. 46, ss. 1 and 2 (B.C.) added the words "or Japanese." The wording of the latter amendment was peculiar since it was not restricted to Japanese men. Women were already excluded, but presumably the legislators did not think Japanese women fit within the generic term.

See also "An Act for securing the Safety and Good Health of Workmen engaged in or about the Metalliferous Mines in the Province of British Columbia by the appointment of an Inspector of Metalliferous Mines" R.S.B.C. (1897) c. 134, s. 12.

77 "An Act respecting Mining Regulations" 53 Vict. (1890) c. 10, ss. 2, 4, 8, and 18 (Ont.); "An Act respecting Mines" R.S.O. (1897) c. 36. See also MacLeod "Colliers" for an account of the Nova Scotian coal field accident experience; "An Act to Amend and Consolidate Chapter 3 of the Acts of 1937, The Metalliferous Mines and Quarries Regulation Act" S.N.S. (1951) c. 5.

78 For an account of some of these state enactments, and their judicial validation (except for the California statute that was struck down), see Alice Kessler-Harris *Out-to-Work* (Oxford 1982) 185–86; Judith Baer *The Chains of Protection* (Westport, Conn. 1978) 35, 51–52.

79 Wendy Mitchinson "The WCTU: 'For God, Home, and Native Land': A Study of 19th Century Feminism" in Cross and Kealey *Industry* 190 at 202. "An Act respecting the sale of Intoxicating Liquors, and the Issue of Licenses therefor" 49 Vict. (1886) c. 21, s. 27 (Man.). Maximum fines of one hundred dollars, or four months in default thereof, were set out in s. 91. See also 52 Vict. (1889) c. 15 (Man.); R.S.M. (1891) Vol. 1, c. 90.

80 Act (1886) s. 23. See also *Wishart* v *McManus* (1884) 1 M.L.R. 213 (Q.B.), interpreting 44 Vict. (1881) c. 11 (Man.).

81 Sheila Kieran *The Family Matters* (Toronto 1986) 70; "The Newsgirls' Sewing Class" Toronto *World* 19 Sept. 1887; "Those Pert Little Newsgirls" Toronto *World* 1 Jan. 1989.

82 Kieran *Family* 70; "The Small Boy and The Girl Have Quit" Toronto *World* 2 May 1890.

*Chapter 10* (pages 293 to 326)

1 For a more detailed discussion of Clara Brett Martin's admission and career, see Constance Backhouse "To Open the Way for Others of my Sex: Clara Brett Martin's Career as Canada's First Woman Lawyer" *Canadian Journal of Women and the Law* 1 (1985) 1; Theresa Roth "Clara Brett Martin — Canada's Pioneer Woman Lawyer" *Law Society of Upper Canada Gazette* 18 (1984) 323. The quote was taken from an undated clipping of the Buffalo *Express*, circa September 1896, held in the Archives of the Women's Law Association of Ontario. The only other woman admitted to the legal profession within the British Commonwealth in the nineteenth century was Ethel Rebecca Benjamin, called in Dunedin, New Zealand, on 6 April 1897. I am indebted to Henry G. Button of Cambridge for bringing the New Zealand admission to my attention.

2 See Cleverdon *Suffrage*; Bacchi *Liberation Deferred?* In contrast, the nineteenth century witnessed a marked broadening of the franchise for white men, although men from the First Nations and Chinese men were not included in the widening electoral process. There was some evidence that certain propertied white women exercised the vote despite their theoretical exclusion. But specific legislative exclusions were enacted against female voting in New Brunswick in 1791, Prince Edward Island in 1836, the United Province of Canada in 1849, and Nova Scotia in 1851. Electoral politics on local matters was more inclusive of women; unmarried women could be elected to school boards and could vote in municipal elections in many jurisdictions. See Prentice et al. *Canadian Women* 98–100, 174–88; Cleverdon *Suffrage* 5.

3 Cleverdon *Suffrage* 67, 73–74, 102 noted that Emily Murphy, appointed a police magistrate in Edmonton, Alberta, on 13 June 1916, was the first woman in the British Empire to hold such a post. Alice Jamieson, appointed in December 1916 in Calgary, was the second. British Columbia first permitted women to serve as jurors in 1922. Women often appeared as advocates for their own causes in New France, typically acting as administrator of the family estate in their husbands' absence: see Micheline Dumont-Johnson "History of the Status of Women in the Province of Quebec" *Studies of the Royal Commission on the Status of Women in Canada* (Ottawa 1971) 5. For a detailed description of the counterpart common law tradition in the United States, see Sophie H. Drinker "Women Attorneys of Colonial Times" *Maryland Historical Review* (December 1961) 335; Karen Berger Morello *The Invisible Bar: The Woman Lawyer in America, 1638 to the Present* (New York 1986). Drinker and Morello noted that the ability and expertise of some

female lay advocates eventually brought them widespread requests to act as agents for non-familial clients. The extent to which Canadian female lay advocates historically practised law outside of professional structures would be a promising avenue for further investigation.

4 Cook and Mitchinson *Proper Sphere* 166 noted that in 1901 the largest percentage of women were still employed either as domestic servants, dressmakers, or seamstresses. Jobs for women were beginning to expand, however. Nursing and teaching were most frequently mentioned, and by 1900 the National Council of Women of Canada listed the following occupational pursuits as open to women: musicians, actresses, artists, authors, journalists, printers, masseuses, midwives, stenographers, secretaries, factory inspectors, librarians, civil servants, farmers, horticulturists. A small number of women were acknowledged to have entered medicine, dentistry, and pharmacy. National Council of Women of Canada *Women of Canada* 47, 63.

For examples and details of informally acquired legal expertise, see Helen Gregory MacGill *Daughters, Wives and Mothers in British Columbia: Some Laws Regarding Them* (British Columbia 1913); Elsie Gregory MacGill *My Mother the Judge* (Toronto 1955); Henrietta Muir Edwards *Legal Status of Canadian Women* (Ottawa 1908); Mary Crawford *Legal Status of Women in Manitoba* (Winnipeg 1912).

For details of Ada M. Read's career, see John Honsberger "The Early Years" Law Society of Upper Canada *Gazette* 20(2) (June 1986) 110–21.

Additional research into the late-nineteenth-century development of specialized careers for female legal secretaries would be essential to permit a fuller understanding of the true extent of women's role in law.

5 "Woman's Rights" *Canadian Illustrated News* (Montreal) 21 Nov. 1874 at 323–24.

6 Agnes Maule Machar (Fidelis) "Woman's Work" *Canadian Monthly and National Review* 1 (September 1878) 295 at 310. Despite her reflections upon the unsuitability of law for women, Machar did endorse women's right to seek admission to the bar. She did so by noting defensively that "the publicity attending the practice of law is, after all, not nearly so great as that involved in the profession of a public singer...." Carrie M. Derick's comments, published as "Professions Open to Women" in National Council of Women of Canada *Women of Canada* 57, presumably contain a misprint: the passage as written begins, "Startled with a heritage of old world traditions." For a discussion of the restricted goals of the National Council of Women, see Strong-Boag *Parliament of Women*.

7 For analysis of the development of the professionalized Ontario bar, see Curtis Johnson Cole "A Learned and Honorable Body: The Professionaliza-

tion of the Ontario Bar, 1867–1929" unpublished Ph.D. dissertation, University of Western Ontario 1987.

8 For discussion about Clara Brett Martin's spinsterhood, see later in this chapter.

9 Abram Martin was also listed as Abraham Martin. Roth "Clara Brett Martin" at 325–26; "Mrs. E.B. Martin Dead" Toronto *Globe* 18 Feb. 1910; Isabel Bassett *The Parlour Rebellion: Profiles in the Struggle for Women's Rights* (Toronto 1975) 153; Morgan *Canadian Men* (1898) 606 and (1912) 735; correspondence with Betty L. Hall of Lockport, New York, grandniece of Clara Brett Martin, to the author, 9 Aug. 1984; Augustus Bridle "A Canadian Woman Much in Public Eye" Toronto *Star* 24 April 1914; William Renwick Riddell "Women as Practitioners of Law" (1918) 18 *Journal of Comparative Legislation* 201. The family's Anglican affiliation was obvious from Clara Brett Martin's later choice of the Anglican Trinity College and her burial in St. James Cemetery, Toronto.

10 Betty L. Hall reported that all twelve Martin children eventually secured university degrees: correspondence. In 1891 only 0.5 per cent of all Canadians aged fifteen to twenty-four attended university: Lynne Marks and Chad Gaffield "Women at Queen's University, 1895–1905: A Little Sphere All Their Own" *Ontario History* 78(4) (December 1986) 331 at 336. Different sources gave the date of Clara Brett Martin's admission to Trinity College as 1886 and 1888; the latter date is most likely the correct one: Backhouse "Clara Brett Martin" 3. See Morgan *Canadian Men* (1912) 735; Bannerman *Leading Ladies* 105.

11 Queen's granted its first degree to a woman in 1878, the University of King's College, Halifax, in 1879, Dalhousie in 1881, Acadia, McMaster, Victoria and University College, Toronto, in 1884. McGill and Manitoba followed in 1888. See Bassett *Parlour Rebellion* 112–15; Cook and Mitchinson *Proper Sphere* 120; Strong-Boag *Parliament of Women* 12; National Council of Women of Canada *Women of Canada* 112; Anne Rochon Ford *A Path Not Strewn with Roses: One Hundred Years of Women at the University of Toronto* (Toronto 1985).

12 William Carpenter *Principles of Human Physiology* (Philadelphia 1847) 911–12, 928–29. Carpenter's text was widely used in Canadian medical schools: see Wendy Mitchinson "Medical Perceptions of Healthy Women" *Canadian Woman Studies* 8(4) (Winter 1987) 42. See also Henry Lyman *The Practical Home Physician* (Guelph 1892) 842; Wendy Mitchinson "The Medical Treatment of Women" in Sandra Burt et al. *Changing Patterns: Women in Canada* (Toronto 1988) 237–60; Wendy Mitchinson "The Medical View of Women: The Case of Late Nineteenth-Century Canada" *Canadian Bulletin of Medical*

*History* 3(2) (Winter 1986) 207–24; Beth Light and Joy Parr, eds. *Canadian Women on the Move 1880–1920* (Toronto 1983) 51; Carol Dyhouse "Social Darwinistic Ideas and the Development of Women's Education in England 1880–1920" *History of Education* 5 (1976) 41–58.

13 "The Medical Aspects of Female Education" *Canada Lancet* 6(7) (March 1874) 233.

14 "Sir James Chrichton-Browne on Sex in Education" *Canada Lancet* 24(11) (July 1892) 350–51.

15 Agnes Maule Machar (Fidelis) "A Few Words on University Co-Education" *Canadian Monthly and National Review* 8 (March 1882) 313 at 314–15, 319.

16 "Sweet Girl Graduates" *Queen's College Journal* 16 Dec. 1876; Machar "Co-Education" 315. Despite her stereotyped perspective, Machar did argue that those women who might be "remarkably endowed in this respect" should be permitted to study mathematics if they so wished.

17 Archives, Trinity College, University of Toronto; Morgan *Canadian Men* 735; Bassett *Parlour Rebellion* 153; Toronto *Star* 24 April 1914.

18 Curtis Cole "Professionalization of the Bar" 87–105; Alexandra Anderson "The First Woman Lawyer in Canada: Clara Brett Martin" *Canadian Woman Studies* 2 (1980) 9 at 10; Toronto *Globe* 12 March 1955; Bannerman *Leading Ladies* 105; Backhouse "Clara Brett Martin" 7.

19 Cole "Professionalization of the Ontario Bar" 87–105; Lance C. Talbot "History of Blacks in the Law Society of Upper Canada" *Law Society of Upper Canada Gazette* 24(1) (March 1990) 65 at 65–66; Robin W. Winks *The Blacks in Canada: A History* (New Haven 1971) 328; "An Act to authorize the Supreme Court of Judicature for Ontario to admit Delos Rogest Davis to practice as a solicitor" 47 Vict. (1884) c. 94 (Ont.); "An Act to authorize the Law Society of Upper Canada to admit Delos Rogest Davis as a Barrister-at-Law" 49 Vict. (1886) c. 94 (Ont.). Davis went on to become the first Black King's Counsel in the British Empire in 1910. In 1900, his son Frederick Homer Alphonso Davis became the second Black called to the Ontario bar. Father and son practised law together in Amherstberg. For details of the first Black woman called to the bar in Ontario, see infra.

20 G. Blaine Baker "Legal Education in Upper Canada 1785–1889: The Law Society as Educator" in Flaherty ed. *Essays in the History of Canadian Law* v. 2 at 49; Brian D. Bucknall et al. "Pedants, Practitioners and Prophets: Legal Education at Osgoode Hall to 1957" *Osgoode Hall Law Journal* 6 (1968) 137; Cole "Professionalization of the Bar."

21 *Canadian Law Times* 12 (1892) 111 at 112; "Clara Brett Martin — Certificate of Fitness," Archives, Law Society of Upper Canada, Osgoode Hall, Toronto.

22 The members of the Committee were Samuel Hume Blake, D'Alton Mc-

Carthy, William Ralph Meredith, Donald Guthrie, John Idlington, Charles Moss, William Renwick Riddell, George F. Shepley, and Edward Martin (the latter, apparently no relation). Written Minutes of Convocation, Law Society of Upper Canada, 18 May 1891, 1:384. *Canada Law Journal* 27 (August 1891) 385; "Briefs" *Western Law Times* 2 (1891) 65.

23 See Albie Sachs and Joan Hoff Wilson *Sexism and the Law* (Oxford 1978) 4–146; Interpretation Act 31 Vict. (1867) c. 1, ss. 6, 7 (Ont.) as amended by 49 Vict. (1886) c. 1, s. 7(21) (Ont.).

24 Written Minutes of Convocation, 30 June 1891, 1:392; "Women as Students-at-Law" *Western Law Times* 2 (1891) 65.

25 Written Minutes of Convocation, Law Society of Upper Canada, 15 Sept. 1891, 1:407.

26 *Legal Scrap Book* 16 April 1892, 205.

27 The conversation between the Secretary and Clara Brett Martin was recounted in *Illustrated Buffalo Herald* (undated clipping, probably 1897) Archives, Women's Law Association of Ontario. Karen Berger Morello *The Invisible Bar* (New York 1986) 3–38.

28 Morello *Invisible Bar* 14–21; *Canada Law Journal* 4 (December 1868) 317.

29 *Canada Law Journal* 15 (June 1879) 146; (June 1880) 161.

30 Morello *Invisible Bar* 18.

31 "Balfour, William Douglas" *Dictionary of Canadian Biography* v. 12 at 52–53; Seventh Parliament of the Ontario Legislature, *Journals of the Legislative Assembly* 25, Toronto *Daily Mail* 6 April 1892.

32 "Meredith, William Ralph" Morgan *Canadian Men* (1898) v. 1, 623–24; Rose *Cyclopaedia* 598; R.C.B. Risk "Sir William R. Meredith, C.J.O.: The Search for Authority" *Dalhousie Law Journal* 7 (1983) 713; Richard C.B. Risk "This Nuisance of Litigation: The Origins of Workers' Compensation in Ontario" in Flaherty *Essays* v. 2 at 418; Toronto *Globe* 9 Feb. 1889.

33 "Female Students-at-Law" Toronto *Daily Mail* 6 April 1892; "Women as Lawyers" Toronto *Daily Mail* 7 April 1892.

34 Cleverdon *Woman Suffrage* 23–45; Prentice et al. *Canadian Women* 175–79. See also "Women Workers of Canada" *National Council of Women of Canada Yearbook* (Ottawa 1984) 49, where Dr. Emily Stowe noted that "in 1892 and 1893, our efforts were again elicited and successful, through the existing powers, in securing Miss Martin's entrance into the Law School — where she now is, and we hope will soon be joined by others, desiring to enter the legal profession." For another reference to this lobby campaign, see National Council of Women of Canada *Women of Canada* 54. The reference to Clara Brett Martin's popularity was from the *Illustrated Buffalo Herald*, undated but probably 1893, Archives, Women's Law Association of Ontario.

35 For reference to Jane Mowat, see Stewart *Macmillan Dictionary* (1975) v. 11 at 472; "An Act to incorporate the Toronto Magdalen Asylum and Industrial House of Refuge" 22 Vict. (1858) c. 73 (P.C.). For reference to Sarah J. Brett's involvement with the Magdalene Asylum, see AO *Magdalen Asylum Annual Reports*. For reference to Catherine Seaton (Ewart) Skirving see "Skirving, Catherine Seaton" *DCB* v. 12 at 973. For reference to Mowat's refusal to write about his mother, see Charles Robert Webster Biggar *Sir Oliver Mowat: A Biographical Sketch* (Toronto 1905) 7.

36 See Prentice et al. *Canadian Women* 178; Toronto *Globe* 9 Feb. 1889.

37 "An Act to Provide for the Admission of Women to the Study and Practice of Law" 55 Vict. (1892) c. 32 (Ont.); "Women as Solicitors" Toronto *Daily Mail* 12 April 1892; "Female Lawyers" Toronto *Daily Mail* 12 April 1892.

38 Written Minutes of Convocation, Law Society of Upper Canada, 13 Sept. 1892, 2:89. The motion was moved by George Ferguson Shepley.

39 Written Minutes of Convocation, Law Society of Upper Canada, 9 Dec. 1892, 2:109–10.

40 Cole "Professionalization of the Ontario Bar" 110–65.

41 Written Minutes of Convocation, Law Society of Upper Canada, 9 Dec. 1892, 2:109–10.

42 Written Minutes of Convocation, Law Society of Upper Canada, 9 Dec. 1892, 2:109. The benchers who voted for the admission of women were: Sir Oliver Mowat, Samuel Hume Blake, Z.A. Lash, Walter Barwick, William Douglas, John Hoskin, John Bell, Allen Bristol Aylesworth, Britton Bath Osler, Arthur S. Hardy, B.M. Britton, and Charles Moss. Those who voted against were: Edward Martin, D'Alton McCarthy, William Ralph Meredith, George H. Watson, George Ferguson Shepley, James Vernall Teetzel, Henry Hatton Strathy, Alexander Bruce, J.K. Kerr, Christopher Robinson, and F. MacKelcan. See Stewart *Macmillan Dictionary* (1975); Morgan *Canadian Men* (1898, 1912).

43 Written Minutes of Convocation, Law Society of Upper Canada, 9 Dec. 1892, 2:109–10.

44 Written Minutes of Convocation, Law Society of Upper Canada, 27 Dec. 1892, 2:111.

45 *Canada Law Journal* 28 (December 1892) 609–10; *Western Law Times* 4 (1893) 1.

46 *Canada Law Journal* 31 (May 1895) 253–54; "Women as Lawyers" *Canadian Law Times* 12 (1892) 219. The event even made headlines in legal circles in England. The *Solicitors' Journal* noted that Clara Brett Martin had been admitted as a member of the Ontario Law Society, and congratulated the English bar that they had so far escaped. "We have not yet arrived at this advanced stage of civilization," they retorted. "Current Topics" *Solicitors' Journal* 37 (1892–93) 155.

47 Written Minutes of Convocation, Law Society of Upper Canada, 27 June 1893, 2:165.

48 Bassett *Parlour Rebellion* 153; Hector Charlesworth *More Candid Chronicles* (Toronto 1928) 93–109; William James Loudon *Sir William Mulock: A Short Biography* (Toronto 1932). Reference to the girlhood friendship between Clara Brett Martin and the Mulock daughter was described by Laura Legge, QC, then Treasurer of the Law Society of Upper Canada, at a meeting with the author on 25 June 1984.

49 See Kathleen E. McCrone *Playing the Game: Sport and the Physical Emancipation of English Women 1870-1914* (Lexington, Ky. 1988); Wendy Mitchinson "The Medical Treatment of Women" in Burt et al. *Changing Patterns* 248–49; *Dominion Medical Monthly and Ontario Medical Journal* v. 7 (1896) 501; v. 8 (1897) 134–35; v. 11 (1898) 28, 30; "The Bicycle for Women" *Canada Lancet* 28(12) (August 1896) 498–99. For references to Clara Brett Martin's cycling, see Toronto *Star* 24 April 1914.

50 For a discussion of the revolutionary aspects of female cycling see Grace E. Denison "The Evolution of the Lady Cyclist" *Massey's Magazine* (Toronto) v. 3 (April 1897) 281–84.

51 Lois Banner *American Beauty* (New York 1983) 48.

52 The *London Daily Advertiser* 26 March 1895 printed the following column under the heading "Bloomers Tabooed":

> The police [in Victoria, British Columbia] have declared that bloomers are not suitable for ladies' street wear, even when worn as a bicycle costume, and have taken steps to enforce this decision. Miss Ethel Delmont is an enthusiastic wheelwoman, pretty and graceful. Last week she made her appearance in the bloomer costume and if Lady Godiva had herself essayed a repetition of her famous ride, the sensation could not have been greater. The town came forth to gaze and for the moment the police were petrified with amazement. They then aroused to action and Miss Ethel received an official visitor who informed her that a repetition of her appearance in that objectionable costume would mean a police court summons on the charge of creating a disturbance on a public street. Miss Delmont's bloomers are discarded.

53 Banner *American Beauty* 8, 86, 148.

54 For a typical example of journalistic reference to Clara Brett Martin as "attractive," see Morgan *Types of Canadian Women* (Toronto 1903) v. 1, 229, quot-

ing an undated article by the Montreal *Witness*. See also Toronto *Star Weekly* 20 Sept. 1913. See Toronto *Star* 24 April 1914.

55 Buffalo *Express*, undated clipping circa 1896, Archives, Women's Law Association of Ontario.

56 Toronto *World* 4 Feb. 1897. Samuel Hume Blake was noted for his "uncontrollable bitterness of tongue," something which may have contributed to his ability to muzzle hostile male articling students. This may have been a mixed blessing, however. Clara Brett Martin may also have found herself exposed to tongue-lashing from the senior partner on occasion. See Charlesworth *Candid Chronicles* 51.

57 "Toronto's Woman Lawyer" Toronto *Empire* 22 Sept. 1894.

58 Toronto *Empire* 22 Sept. 1894.

59 "Women as Lawyers" *Canadian Law Times* 12 (1892) 111.

60 Bassett *Parlour Rebellion* 156; Montreal *Daily Witness* 27 Nov. 1897. Even the extracurricular activities of the law students, organized under the auspices of the "Legal and Literary Society" would have been alienating for Clara Brett Martin. Male rowdiness escalated to the point that the benchers censored the students for the use of "spirituous liquors" on the Osgoode Hall premises in November 1895: Cole "Professionalization of the Bar" 128–29.

61 Written Minutes of Convocation, Law Society of Upper Canada, 27 June 1894, 2:236–37; 19 Nov. 1894, 2:259.

62 Cole "Professionalization of the Ontario Bar" 166–226; Morgan *Canadian Men* (1912) 735; Ford *Path Not Strewn* 41. Clara Brett Martin was not the first woman to obtain an academic degree in law. Eliza Orme had earned a Bachelor of Laws from the University of London, England, in 1888. Later denied admission to the English bar, she established an office in Chancery Lane where she conducted a prosperous business "devilling" for lawyers as a conveyancer and patent agent: see Leslie Howsam "Sound-Minded Women: Eliza Orme and the Study and Practice of Law in Late-Victorian England" *Atlantis* 15(1) (Fall 1989) 44.

63 Buffalo *Express*, undated clipping held in the Archives of the Women's Law Association of Ontario; Backhouse "Clara Brett Martin." The records of the Law Society do not record Clara Brett Martin as the recipient of any of its student medals, so she would likely have meant her joy was at having beaten her fellow students who had been the greatest source of torment: see Written Minutes of Convocation, Law Society of Upper Canada, volumes 11 and 12.

64 In 1891 there were 1,497 lawyers in the province. Of these, 226 (15 per cent) were qualified as solicitors only; 38 (2.5 per cent) were qualified as barristers

only. The remaining 1,233 (82.5 per cent) were qualified as both barristers and solicitors. H.R. Hardy ed. *The Official Law List, 1891* (Toronto 1891) 7–33.

65 *The Woman's Journal* (Toronto) 15(5) and 15(6), 1 and 15 Oct. 1900; Prentice et al. *Canadian Women* 180–82.

66 "A Woman at the Bar" Toronto *World* 4 Feb. 1897. For examples of the letters sent on Clara Brett Martin's behalf, see "Miss Martin's Case" Toronto *Mail* 10 Oct. 1892; "Shall Women Practise Law?" Toronto *Mail* 12 Sept. 1894. For examples of letters in opposition, see "Female Lawyers" Toronto *Mail* 13 Sept. 1892; "Women in Politics" Toronto *Globe* 12 April 1895.

67 "Wood, Sir William B." Morgan *Canadian Men* 1,102; Toronto *Globe* 5 April 1895.

68 Cleverdon *Woman Suffrage* 26–27.

69 Toronto *Globe* 5 April 1895.

70 Toronto *Globe* 5 April 1895.

71 Toronto *Globe* 5 April 1895.

72 Toronto *Globe* 5 April 1895.

73 Toronto *Globe* 5 April 1895; "An Act to amend the Act to provide for the admission of Women to the Study and Practice of Law" 58 Vict. (1895) c. 27 (Ont.).

74 Toronto *Globe* 10 April 1895.

75 Written Minutes of Convocation, Law Society of Upper Canada, 5 June 1896, 2:336–37.

76 "Women Lawyers in Canada and Elsewhere" Montreal *Daily Witness* 27 Nov. 1897; *The Woman's Journal* (Toronto) 15, 1 Oct. 1900 at 5; 15 Oct. 1900 at 6. Further details about the numbers, names, and positions of these clients have not survived.

77 Montreal *Daily Witness* 27 Nov. 1897; Written Minutes of Convocation, Law Society of Upper Canada, 30 June 1896, 2:343; 14 Sept. 1896, 2:345.

78 Riddell "Women as Practitioners of Law" 204.

79 *Western Law Times* 3 (1892) 106; *Canada Law Journal* 32 (June 1896) 784. The latter article was a reprint from an "amusing" story from India.

80 Riddell "Women as Practitioners" 204. For an example of the press interest in the rules surrounding the dress of female lawyers, see "A Woman at the Bar" Toronto *World* 4 Feb. 1897.

81 Written Minutes of Convocation, Law Society of Upper Canada, 25 Sept. 1896, 2:349; 17 Nov. 1896, 2:358; 18 Nov. 1896, 2:359; 4 Dec. 1896, 2:360; 2 Feb. 1897, 3:1.

82 Toronto *Globe* 24 Feb. 1897.

83 Montreal *Witness* undated, as quoted in Morgan *Types of Canadian Women* 229; Toronto *Telegram* 2 Feb. 1897.

84 Toronto *Telegram* 3 Feb. 1897. The *Telegram* obviously approved of this strategy, noting that the advertisement "display[ed] good judgment in her desire to now acquire practical experience in some good law firm." Toronto *Telegram* 2 Feb. 1897.

85 Bassett *Parlour Rebellion* 154; Toronto *Globe* 24 Feb. 1897, 17 Feb. 1902; National Council of Women of Canada *Women of Canada* 70; Roth "Clara Brett Martin" 335; *Toronto City Directory* (1906) at 740. For a listing of the more inclusive firm name, see entry for "Shilton, Wallbridge & Martin," *Toronto Directory* (Toronto 1904) AO B70 Series D, Reel 38 at 819. For details of Clara Brett Martin's retention of male barristers to argue her clients' cases in court, see Backhouse "Clara Brett Martin" 32–33. Clara Brett Martin's law files have not survived, but an undated, unsigned entry in the Archives of the Women's Law Association of Ontario stated: "As might be expected of a woman lawyer, she handled many cases of domestic relations, drawing settlements and agreements, though the greatest part of her business consisted of conveyancing, mortgages and wills."

86 Toronto *Star Weekly* 20 Sept. 1913.

87 Toronto *Star Weekly* 20 Sept. 1913. Some of the other portrayals were not so flattering in their stereotypes. Florence Schill's column in the Toronto *Globe* 12 March 1955, "Persistent Clara Brett Martin Won Battle with Benchers," recalled that an unnamed source had branded Clara Brett Martin "a queer old duck." In the same article, women who had been present when Clara Brett Martin addressed the inaugural dinner meeting of the Women's Law Association of Ontario in 1919 reminisced about their surprise at her demeanour and attire:

> A slightly built chestnut-haired woman dressed in a simple shirtwaist and skirt rocked gently back and forth in the cloakroom of a Toronto tea room.... The place was the Inglewood Tea Rooms, which was then at the Southwest corner of Spadina Avenue and Bloor Street.
>
> As the guests began to arrive, gaily chattering, little attention was paid to the woman in the little rocking chair tucked away in a corner of the cloakroom. Or if there was, it was a fleeting parenthetical recognition of her presence. "One of the cloakroom attendants — tired, poor dear."
>
> To those who did take note of her presence, it came as a distinct shock when they discovered later that she was the guest of honour — Clara Brett Martin, without whose persistence and determination the Women's Law Association might well have been, in 1919, merely a possibility.

A similar note was sounded in the Toronto *Globe* obituary of 2 Nov. 1923, which noted that Clara Brett Martin's funeral "was marked by a simplicity which is in perfect accord with the life of the deceased." Simplicity was surely not an accurate word to describe the protracted battles of Clara Brett Martin's life. While these belittling pronouncements appear strange in juxtaposition with the "feminizing" commentary, the characterizations are oddly in harmony. Both emphasize that Clara Brett Martin presented no threat to the male profession, and placed no serious strain upon the traditional gender roles in society at large.

88 *Canada Law Journal* 30 (April 1894) 222.

89 Agnes Maule Machar (Fidelis) "Higher Education for Women" *Canadian Monthly and National Review* 7 (February 1875) 144 at 154. In 1921, 88 per cent of all Canadian women between thirty-five and fifty-four were married or widowed: *Census of Canada, 1921* v. 2, Table 29. University graduates married at a significantly lower rate; only 58 per cent of women who entered Queen's University between 1895 and 1900 married: see Marks and Gaffield "Women at Queen's University" 343–44. See also Faderman *Surpassing the Love of Men*; Rudy M. Wigle "Sisters in Law" *Canadian Bar Review* 5 (1927) 420. Many of the first women lawyers in the United States also married, although some of these married lawyers and carried on practice with their husbands, at times formally and at times entirely behind the scenes: Virginia G. Drachman "The Perfect Portia: Women Lawyers in a Man's World," paper delivered at the Seventh Berkshire Conference of Women Historians, Wellesley, Mass., 1987; Virginia G. Drachman "My 'Partner' in Law and Life: Marriage in the Lives of Women Lawyers in Late 19th- and Early 20th-Century America" *Law and Social Inquiry Journal of the American Bar Foundation* 14 (Spring 1989) 221.

90 I am indebted to Peter Sibenik, who shared this letter with me after discovering it in the course of his Ph.D. dissertation research on the Office of the Attorney-General. The letter is held at the Archives of Ontario, Attorney-General's Department, General Correspondence, RG4-32, 1915, File 503. The complete text reads:

> Clara Brett Martin
> B.A., LL.B., B.C.L.
> Barrister, Solicitor &C.
> Notary Public
> Tanner-Gates Building
> 25 Adelaide St. West
> Toronto

March 26th, 1915

Mr. Edward Bayly
Attorney General's Department
Parliament Buildings

Dear Sir:-

I desire to call your attention to the manner in which the titles to
property in this City are being clouded.

There are it is said nearly 100,000 foreigners of which about 40,000
are Jews. These Jews find buying and selling property a very
profitable business. Through agents agreements of purchase and sale
are obtained which are not genuine inasmuch as the party selling or
buying does not understand what he is signing. These agreements or
assignments of them are registered against the lands and the innocent
party often is not aware of it until he attempts to buy or sell or
mortgage etc. again. In one case that came under my notice recently
an agreement was registered seven months after the whole matter
was apparently settled in order to hold up the party or to force the
sale to the Jew. The Jew invariably who registers the assignment will
neither sue for his deposit nor will he enter action for Specific Perfor-
mance therefore the innocent party has no immediate redress. Often
as much as $100.00 is demanded besides the deposit to obtain a quit
claim deed.

Over two years ago a client of mine not having his spectacles with
him signed an agreement which the agent read for him. A couple of
days subsequently when I read the agreement for my client he
refused to carry it out stating it was not what he understood he
signed. The sale fell through as we thought. About four months afterwards my client wished to raise a mortgage on one house but the Jew
hearing of it registered an assignment of the agreement. This action
has been in the High Court nearly two years.

A Jew bought some property on Bismark Avenue, and finding
Mrs. Lewis refused to carry out the agreement, as she held a line was
written in the offer about a mortgage which entirely changed it, he
registered an assignment of the agreement on a property on Bloor
Street East belonging to my client an innocent party. Nearly two years
after my client was selling and it took three months to remove the

cloud. The lands are not under plan in that section and an incorrect description was attached to the offer for the purpose of registration.

Another case — Mrs. Purser sold her house for $2900.00. As the mortgage for $700.00 was expiring the offer permitted the Jew to raise a new mortgage. The Vendor was to take back a second mortgage for $1500.00 and receive $700.00 cash. The Jew started to raise a mortgage of $1400.00 and offered to give her $700.00 of the mortgage money and not pay one cent on the property. I therefore called off the sale but the Jew registered an assignment of the agreement and then demanded $100.00 for his reickery [sic].

Last summer Mr. Pratt sold his house to Harris who wrote out the offer. Harris told Pratt he would give him a Mortgage of $1000. that his wife held on another house. Old man Pratt thought he was getting a first mortgage but it turned out to be a third mortgage. The first mortgagee Mr. Riches Barrister said the third mortgage was not worth a cent. I only succeeded yesterday in having a Quit Claim deed registered — although Harris received back the deposit immediately. Just think of the costs and the expense and delay caused by Harris registering an assignment to his wife.

Over twenty cases of registration of documents that in my opinion were invalid have come before my notice in one year.

It is criminal in England to cloud a title to lands. An application has to be made to the Court for leave to register agreements or assignments of same.

Would you kindly call the attention of the Government to this matter and try to have the Registry Act amended to prevent this scandalous work of foreigners. If the Government will not stop the registration of such clouds upon titles, do have the Act amended compelling the party registering to take action within thirty days or if not the agreement or assignment of same is void as in the case of Mechanics Lien.

All agreements or assignments of such *not registered should be declared void*.

> Yours truly,
> Clara Brett Martin

The response from the Attorney-General's Department reads as follows:

Toronto
March 30th, 1915

My dear Madam: -

Again referring to your letter of March 26th I beg to say that some of the proposals you make in your letter are rather drastic, especially that all agreements or assignments now registered should be declared void.

    I wish you would draft a short clause which meets your views and submit it. It may be too late for this year but there would be no harm in sending it here anyway. It is a matter which I should like to discuss with some of the Registrars of Deeds.

Yours faithfully,
Solicitor to the
Attorney General's Department

91 "Hart, Ezekiel" *Macmillan Dictionary* 3rd ed. (1963) at 303. Ezekiel Hart's son, Aaron Ezekiel Hart, became the first Jew to be called to the bar in either of the Canadas when he was admitted in Lower Canada on 6 November 1824: see "Hart, Aaron Ezekiel" *DCB* v. 8 at 363. Goldwin Smith, the prominent Canadian writer who had vigorously opposed the criminalization of seduction, was described by the *Jewish Times* as an "arch Jew-baiter" and "bitter anti-Semite." Suggesting that Jews committed "ritual murder," Smith proclaimed in the 1880s, "they have become an abhorrent tribe, antisocial and immoral." Henri Bourassa, the French Canadian parliamentarian, defended the Russian pogroms in 1905, arguing that the Jews had brought it on themselves through deception and exploitation. See David Rome *The Immigration Story I, The Jewish Times etc.* (Montreal 1986) 83–84, 89; *Canadian Jewish Times* 19 April 1907; 1 July 1910; Lita-Rose Betcherman *The Swastika and the Maple Leaf: Fascist Movements in Canada in the Thirties* (Toronto 1975) at 4.

92 Toronto *Weekly Sun*, as quoted in Rome *Immigration Story* 100; Ottawa *Free Press* as described in the *Jewish Times* 12 Aug. 1904; Montreal *Le Nationaliste* 24 Dec. 1905 as quoted in David Rome *Early Anti-Semitism: The Voice of the Media* (Montreal 1984) 72; Irving Abella "The Making of a Chief Justice: Bora Laskin, the Early Years" unpublished manuscript 1989; Jerome E. Bickenbach "Lawyers, Law Professors and Racism in Ontario" *Queen's Quarterly* 96(3) (Autumn 1989) 585 at 593–95; Stephen A. Speisman *The Jews of Toronto: A History to 1937* (Toronto 1979) 117–30; 318–35. For details of Canada's immigration policies prohibiting Jews in the 1930s and 1940s, see Irving Abella and Harold Troper *None is Too Many* (Toronto 1982). For some comparative

American material, see David A. Gerber ed. *Anti-Semitism in American History* (Chicago 1986).

93 Anderson "First Woman Lawyer" 11; J. Castell Hopkins "The Canadian Club Movement" *The Canadian Club Review* (1912); "Partial List of Lectures Delivered to the Women Teachers' Association Before 1912" *The Story of the Women Teachers' Association of Toronto* (Toronto n.d. but probably 1920s); "Laws Affecting Women in Ontario" *The Canadian White Ribbon Tidings* 1 Aug. 1912, 2,258; Clara Brett Martin "Legal Status of Women in the Provinces of the Dominion of Canada" in National Council of Women of Canada *Women of Canada* 37. The non-denominationalists within the National Council of Women of Canada, led by Lady Aberdeen, attempted to accommodate Protestants, Roman Catholics, and Jews. Outbursts of religious antagonism from various Christian members convinced the National Council of Jewish Women, first formed in 1897, to withhold affiliation, but individual Jewish women were active within local Council groups. See Veronica Jane Strong-Boag *The Parliament of Women: The National Council of Women of Canada 1893–1929* (Ottawa 1976) at 78–79, 101–2, 119. For details on Clara Brett Martin's campaigns for suffrage and women's courts, as well as her electoral record, see Backhouse "Clara Brett Martin" 34–37.

94 Last Will and Testament, Clara Brett Martin, Archives of Ontario MS 584, Reel 144, MS 583, Reel 95. Her assets included the large home she had been living in with her brother and sister at 41 Roxborough Street East, seven row houses she had purchased on Napier Street in Toronto as investment properties, clothing and jewellery. The row houses at # 2, 4, 6, 8, 10, 12, and 14 Napier Street, originally purchased in 1910, were located within the working-class area known as "Cabbagetown." Assessment rolls indicate that the value of the buildings and property was somewhat better than that of neighbouring properties. Since Clara Brett Martin had consistently maintained rents that compared favourably with those of other landlords, these row houses had attracted a stable group of tenants, most of whom were from the skilled sector of the labouring class. See *Assessment Rolls*, Ward I, Division 2, City of Toronto Archives, 1910–1924. Details of Fanny's occupation were taken from *Toronto City Directories* (see, for example, 1883, 1885, 1889, 1891). The private funeral service was conducted by Rev. William Farncombe of the Church of England, with burial in the St. James Cemetery. Toronto *Daily Star* 1 Nov. 1923; Toronto *Star* 2 April 1929; Toronto *Telegram* 1 Nov. 1923 and 2 April 1929; Toronto *Globe* 1 and 2 Nov. 1923.

95 William Renwick Riddell "Women as Practitioners of Law" *Journal of Comparative Legislation* 18 (1918) 201 at 206. An influential bencher and later a Supreme Court judge, Riddell deserves more historical attention, as Hilary

Bates Neary's *William Renwick Riddell: A Bio-Bibliographical Study* M.A. thesis, University of Western Ontario 1977, points out. Riddell seemed to have remained troubled by notions of female equality throughout his career. In one article, "An Old-Time Misogynist," published in the Toronto *Canadian Magazine* 58(5) (March 1922) at 379–80, he translated at length, and with obvious gusto, long passages from ancient Latin texts describing women variously as "a daily injury," "perpetually complaining," "a constant liar," "fondling and caressing deceit," "a filthy bedmate," "a piece of hell." Noting that the passages quoted had been "well selected," he ended on the observation that the "advance made by woman toward obtaining simple justice" meant that no modern country would allow such a book to be published.

96 Talbot "History of Blacks" 65–66. Myrtle Smith (née Blackwood), was admitted to the Law Society of Upper Canada on 22 June 1960. A Montrealer by birth, she had obtained a B.A. from Sir George Williams University. Myrtle Smith is still listed on the Law Society Rolls, but she is not in practice. Roberta Jamieson graduated from the University of Western Ontario Law School in 1976 and serves as the Ombudsman of Ontario.

## Conclusion (pages 327 to 337)

1 Toronto *Grip* 39 (September 1892) at 202.

2 For reference to the *Lily* accounts, see Elizabeth B. Clark "Religion, Rights, and Difference in the Early Woman's Rights Movement" *Wisconsin Women's Law Journal* 3 (1987) 29 at 54. For some background on the *Lily*, which was published by Amelia Bloomer, see Pleck *Domestic Tyranny* 55.

3 For a discussion in the modern setting, see Carrie Menkel-Meadow "Portia in a Different Voice: Speculations on a Women's Lawyering Process" *Berkeley Women's Law Journal* 1 (1985) 39.

4 See Morello *Invisible Bar* 70, 77–80; Clarice Feinman *Women in the Criminal Justice System* (New York 1986) 109–10; Ronald Chester *Unequal Access: Women Lawyers in a Changing America* (South Hadley, Mass. 1985) 19–52. Portia Law School opened a day division in 1922, eventually became co-educational, and changed its name to the New England School of Law in 1969.

5 Anderson "First Woman Lawyer" 11.

6 *National Council of Women of Canada Yearbook* (Ottawa 1894) 49. For details on Powley, see Cameron Harvey "Women in Law in Canada" *Manitoba Law Journal* 4 (1970) 9 at 17–18; Winnipeg *Free Press* 28 Nov. 1969 at 30. On French, see Christine Mullins "Taking the Law into Her Hands" *Horizon Canada* (9)106 (May 1987) 2,540; Christine Mullins "Mabel Penery French"

*The Advocate* 44(5) (September 1986) 676. On Quebec's belated admission,
see *Dame Langstaff* v *The Bar of the Province of Quebec* (1915) 47 Que. S.C. 131;
"An Act respecting the Bar" Geo. V (1941) c. 54 (Que.). See also Susan
Altschul and Christine Caron "Chronology of Some Legal Landmarks in the
History of Canadian Women" *McGill Law Journal* 21 (1975) 476 at 478.
7 At the Faculty of Law of the University of Western Ontario, for example,
the percentage of women entering first year rose from 22 per cent in 1978 to
44 per cent in 1989.

# Selected Bibliography

## A. Books

Acton, Janice et al. *Women at Work 1850–1930* (Toronto 1974)

Austin, Rev. B.F., ed. *Woman — Her Character — Culture and Calling* (Brantford 1890)

Bacchi, Carol Lee *Liberation Deferred? The Ideas of the English-Canadian Suffragists 1877–1918* (Toronto 1983)

Backhouse, Constance and Cohen, Leah *The Secret Oppression: Sexual Harassment of Working Women* (Toronto 1979)

Baer, Judith *The Chains of Protection* (Westport, Conn. 1978)

Banner, Lois *American Beauty* (New York 1983)

Bannerman, Jean *Leading Ladies: Canada* (Belleville 1977)

Bassett, Isabel *The Parlour Rebellion: Profiles in the Struggle for Women's Rights* (Toronto 1975)

Benson, Susan Porter *Counter Culture* (Chicago 1986)

Blackstone, William *Commentaries on the Laws of England* v. 1 (London 1765; repub. 1979)

Bordin, Ruth *Woman and Temperance* (Philadelphia 1981)

Bristow, Edward J. *Prostitution and Prejudice: The Jewish Fight Against White Slavery 1870–1939* (New York 1983)

Brown, Jennifer *Strangers in Blood: Fur Trade Company Families in Indian Country* (Vancouver 1980)

Burnet, Jean, ed. *Looking into My Sister's Eyes* (Toronto 1986)

Burt, Sandra et al. *Changing Patterns: Women in Canada* (Toronto 1988)

Campbell, Maria *Halfbreed* (Toronto 1973)

Cayleff, Susan E. *Wash and Be Healed: The Water-Cure Movement and Women's Health* (Philadelphia 1987)

Chambers-Schiller, Lee Virginia *Liberty, A Better Husband* (New Haven 1984)

Chan, Anthony *Gold Mountain: The Chinese in the New World* (Vancouver 1983)

Chester, Ronald *Unequal Access: Women Lawyers in a Changing America* (South Hadley, Mass. 1985)

Clark, Anna *Women's Silence, Men's Violence: Sexual Assault in England 1770–1845* (London 1987)

Cohen, Marjorie Griffin *Women's Work, Markets and Economic Development in Nineteenth-Century Ontario* (Toronto 1988)

Cook, Ramsay *The Regenerators: Social Criticism in Late Victorian English Canada* (Toronto 1985)

Cook, Ramsay and Mitchinson, Wendy, eds. *The Proper Sphere: Woman's Place in Canadian Society* (Toronto 1976)

Cott, Nancy F. *The Bonds of Womanhood: "Woman's Sphere" in New England 1780–1835* (New Haven 1977)

Cott, Nancy F. *The Grounding of Modern Feminism* (New Haven 1987)

Crawford, Mary *Legal Status of Women in Manitoba* (Winnipeg 1912)

Dall, Caroline H. *Woman's Right to Labor* (Boston 1860)

Danylewycz, Marta *Taking the Veil: An Alternative to Marriage, Motherhood and Spinsterhood in Quebec 1840–1920* (Toronto 1987)

Degler, Carl *At Odds: Women and the Family in America from the Revolution to the Present* (New York 1980)

Diner, Hasia R. *Erin's Daughters in America: Irish Immigrant Women in the 19th Century* (Baltimore 1983)

Douglas, Ann *The Feminization of American Culture* (New York 1977)

Duberman, Martin Bauml et al., eds. *Hidden from History: Reclaiming the Gay and Lesbian Past* (New York 1989)

Dudden, Faye E. *Serving Women: Household Service in Nineteenth-Century America* (Middletown, Conn. 1983)

Dumont, Micheline et al. *Quebec Women: A History* (Toronto 1987)

Edwards, Henrietta Muir *Legal Status of Canadian Women* (Ottawa 1908)

Ehrenreich, Barbara and English, Deirdre *Witches, Midwives and Nurses: A History of Women Healers* (Brooklyn N.Y. 1973)

Ehrenreich, Barbara and English, Deirdre *For Her Own Good: 150 Years of Experts' Advice to Women* (New York 1978)

Faderman, Lilian *Surpassing the Love of Men* (New York 1981)

Faderman, Lilian *Scotch Verdict* (New York 1983)

Feinman, Clarice *Women in the Criminal Justice System* (New York 1986)

Fingard, Judith *The Dark Side of Life in Victorian Halifax* (Porters Lake, N.S. 1989)

Finnegan, Frances *Poverty and Prostitution: A Study of Victorian Prostitutes in York* (Cambridge 1979)

Ford, Anne Rochon *A Path Not Strewn with Roses: One Hundred Years of Women at the University of Toronto* (Toronto 1985)

Freedman, Estelle B. *Their Sisters' Keepers: Women's Prison Reform in America 1830–1930* (Ann Arbor 1981)

French, Doris *Ishbel and the Empire: A Biography of Lady Aberdeen* (Toronto 1988)

Fuhrer, Charlotte *The Mysteries of Montreal: Memoirs of a Midwife* (Montreal 1881; repub. Peter Ward ed. Vancouver 1984)

Fytche, Maria Amelia *Kerchiefs to Hunt Souls* (Boston 1895; repub. Sackville N.B. 1980)

Gemmill, John Alexander *The Practice of the Parliament of Canada upon Bills of Divorce* (Toronto 1889)

Gerson, Carole *Three Writers of Victorian Canada and Their Works* (Downsview n.d.)

Gerson, Carole *A Purer Taste: The Writing and Reading of Fiction in English in Nineteenth-Century Canada* (Toronto 1989)

Giddings, Paula *When and Where I Enter* (New York 1984)

Gillett, Margaret *We Walked Very Warily: A History of Women at McGill* (Montreal 1981)

Girard, Philip and Phillips, Jim *Essays in the History of Canadian Law* v. 3 (Toronto 1990)

Goldman, Marion S. *Gold Diggers and Silver Miners* (Ann Arbor 1981)

Gordon, Linda *Woman's Body, Woman's Right* (New York 1976)

Gordon, Linda *Heroes of Their Own Lives: The Politics and History of Family Violence* (New York 1988)

Gough, Lyn *As Wise as Serpents: Five Women and an Organization that Changed British Columbia 1883–1939* (Victoria 1988)

Grant, John Webster *Moon of Wintertime* (Toronto 1984)

Gray, James *Red Lights on the Prairies* (Scarborough 1971)

Griffiths, N.E.S. *Penelope's Web* (Toronto 1976)

Griswold, Robert L. *Family and Divorce in California 1850–1890* (Albany 1982)

Gronewold, Sue *Beautiful Merchandise: Prostitution in China 1860–1936* (New York 1982)

Grossberg, Michael *Governing the Hearth: Law and the Family in Nineteenth-Century America* (Chapel Hill 1985)

Hacker, Carlotta *The Indomitable Lady Doctors* (Toronto 1974)

Haller, John S. and Haller, Robin M. *The Physician and Sexuality in Victorian America* (Chicago 1974)

Harney, Robert F. *Gathering Place: Peoples and Neighbourhoods of Toronto 1834–1945* (Toronto 1985)

Herstein, Sheila R. *A Mid-Victorian Feminist, Barbara Leigh Smith Bodichon* (New Haven 1985)

Hoffer, Peter C. and Hull, N.E.H. *Murdering Mothers: Infanticide in England and New England 1558–1803* (New York 1981)

Holcombe, Lee *Wives and Property: Reform of the Married Women's Property Law in Nineteenth-Century England* (Toronto 1983)

Holmested, George S. *The Married Women's Property Act of Ontario* (Toronto 1905)

hooks, bell *Talking Back, Thinking Feminist, Thinking Black* (Boston 1989)

Hull, N.E.H. *Female Felons* (Chicago 1987)

Innis, Mary Quale *The Clear Spirit* (Toronto 1966)

Jackson, Helen *Ramona: A Story* (London and New York 1887)

Jameson, Anna Brownell *Winter Studies and Summer Rambles in Canada, Selections* (Toronto 1965; orig. pub. 1838)

Jamieson, Kathleen *Indian Women and the Law in Canada: Citizens Minus* (Ottawa 1978)

Jeffries, Sheila *The Spinster and her Enemies: Feminism and Sexuality 1880–1913* (London 1985)

John, Angela V. *By the Sweat of their Brow* (London 1984)

Johnston, Jean *Wilderness Women* (Toronto 1973)

Jones, Jacqueline *Labor of Love, Labor of Sorrow* (New York 1985)

Kealey, Linda, ed. *A Not Unreasonable Claim* (Toronto 1979)

Kelly, Joan *Women, History and Theory* (Chicago 1984)

K'Emilio, John and Freedman, Estelle B. *Intimate Matters: A History of Sexuality in America* (New York 1988)

Kessler-Harris, Alice *Out-to-Work* (Oxford 1982)

Kieran, Sheila *The Family Matters* (Toronto 1986)

Kinnear, Mary *First Days, Fighting Days: Women in Manitoba History* (Regina 1987)

Knafla, Louis, ed. *Law and Justice in a New Land: Essays in Western Canadian Legal History* (Toronto 1986)

Lasch, Christopher *Haven in a Heartless World* (New York 1977)

Latham, Barbara K. and Pazdro, Roberta J., eds. *Not Just Pin Money* (Victoria 1984)

Lavigne, Marie et al. *Travailleuses et feministes: Les Femmes dans la Société Québécoise* (Quebec 1983)

Lebsock, Suzanne *The Free Women of Petersburg* (New York 1984)

Leprohon, (Mrs.) Rosanna *Antoinette De Mirecourt; or, Secret Marrying and Secret Sorrowing. A Canadian Tale* (Montreal 1864)

Lerner, Gerda *The Creation of Patriarchy* (New York 1986)

Li, Peter S. *The Chinese in Canada* (Toronto 1988)

Licata, Salvatore J. and Petersen, Robert P. *Historical Perspectives on Homosexuality* (New York 1981)

Light, Beth and Parr, Joy, eds. *Canadian Women on the Move 1880–1920* (Toronto 1983)

Light, Beth and Prentice, Alison, eds. *Pioneer and Gentlewomen of British North America 1713–1867* (Toronto 1980)

Lindstrom-Best, Varpu *Defiant Sisters: A Social History of Finnish Immigrant Women in Canada* (Toronto 1988)

London Feminist History Group *The Sexual Dynamics of History* (London 1983)

MacDonald, Cheryl *Adelaide Hoodless: Domestic Crusader* (Toronto 1986)

MacFarlane, Alan *Marriage and Love in England 1300–1840* (Oxford 1986)

MacGill, Elsie Gregory *My Mother the Judge* (Toronto 1955)

MacGill, Helen Gregory *Daughters, Wives and Mothers in British Columbia: Some Laws Regarding Them* (British Columbia 1913)

Machar, Agnes Maule *Roland Graeme: Knight* (Montreal 1892)

Mackinolty, J. and Radi, H., eds. *In Pursuit of Justice: Australian Women and the Law 1788–1979* (Sydney 1979)

MacLean, Annie Marion *Wage-Earning Women* (New York 1910)

Marks, Patricia *Bicycles, Bangs and Bloomers* (Lexington, Ky. 1990)

May, Elaine Tyler *Great Expectations: Marriage and Divorce in Post-Victorian America* (Chicago 1980)

McCrone, Kathleen E. *Playing the Game: Sport and the Physical Emancipation of English Women 1870–1914* (Lexington, Ky. 1988)

McKee, S.G.E. *Jubilee History of the Ontario Woman's Christian Temperance Union 1877–1927* (Whitby n.d.)

McLaren, Angus *Birth Control in Nineteenth-Century England* (London 1978)

McLaren, Angus and McLaren, Arlene Tigar *The Bedroom and the State: Changing Practices and Politics of Contraception and Abortion in Canada 1880–1980* (Toronto 1986)

McMillan, Alan D. *Native Peoples and Cultures of Canada* (Vancouver 1988)

Miller, J.R. *Skyscrapers Hide the Heavens: A History of Indian-White Relations in Canada* (Toronto 1989)

Mitchinson, Wendy and McGinnis, Janice, eds. *Essays in the History of Canadian Medicine* (Toronto 1988)

Mohr, James C. *Abortion in America* (New York 1978)

Morello, Karen Berger *The Invisible Bar: The Woman Lawyer in America, 1638 to the Present* (New York 1986)

National Council of Women of Canada *Women of Canada: Their Life and Work* (Ottawa 1900)

O'Neill, W.L. *Divorce in the Progressive Era* (New Haven 1967)

Parr, Joy *Labouring Children: British Immigrant Apprentices to Canada 1869–1924* (Montreal 1980)

446    Petticoats and Prejudice

Parr, Joy, ed. *Childhood and Family in Canadian History* (Toronto 1982)

Peiss, Kathy *Cheap Amusements: Working Women and Leisure in Turn-of-the-Century New York* (Philadelphia 1986)

Peiss, Kathy and Simmons, Christina *Passion and Power: Sexuality in History* (Philadelphia 1989)

Phillips, Roderick *Putting Asunder: A History of Divorce in Western Society* (Cambridge 1988)

Pleck, Elizabeth *Domestic Tyranny: The Making of American Social Policy against Family Violence from Colonial Times to the Present* (Oxford 1987)

Prentice, Alison et al. *Canadian Women: A History* (Toronto 1988)

Prentice, Alison L. and Houston, Susan E., eds. *Family, School and Society in Nineteenth-Century Canada* (Toronto 1975)

Rabkin, Peggy A. *Fathers to Daughters: Women, Marriage and Property in Nineteenth-Century New York* (Ithaca, N.Y. 1982)

Rasmussen, Linda et al. *A Harvest Yet to Reap* (Toronto 1976)

Ray, Janet *Emily Stowe* (Toronto 1978)

*Report of the Royal Commission on Chinese Immigration* (Ottawa 1885)

Roberts, Wayne *Honest Womanhood: Feminism, Femininity and Class Consciousness Among Toronto Working Women 1893–1914* (Toronto 1976)

Rosen, Ruth *The Lost Sisterhood: Prostitution in America 1900–1918* (Baltimore 1982)

Rothman, Ellen K. *Hands and Hearts: A History of Courtship in America* (New York 1894)

Rothman, Sheila M. *Woman's Proper Place: A History of Changing Ideals and Practices, 1870 to the Present* (New York 1978)

Sachs, Albie and Wilson, Joan Hoff *Sexism and the Law* (Oxford 1978)

Salmon, Marylynn *Women and the Law of Property in Early America* (Chapel Hill 1986)

Sanders, Byrne Hope *Emily Murphy: Crusader* (Toronto 1945)

Schneider, Aili Gronlund *The Finnish Baker's Daughters* (Toronto 1986)

Schwarz, Judith *Radical Feminists of Heterodoxy* (Norwich, Vt. 1986)

Scott, Jean Thomas *The Conditions of Female Labour in Ontario* (Toronto 1892)

Shanley, Mary Lyndon *Feminism, Marriage, and the Law in Victorian England 1850–1895* (Princeton 1989)

Speisman, Stephen A. *The Jews of Toronto: A History to 1937* (Toronto 1979)

Sterling, Dorothy, ed. *We Are Your Sisters: Black Women in the Nineteenth Century* (New York 1984)

Stone, Lawrence *The Family, Sex and Marriage in England 1500–1800* (New York 1977)

Strong-Boag, Veronica *The Parliament of Women: The National Council of Women of Canada 1893–1929* (Ottawa 1976)

Strong-Boag, Veronica and Fellman, Anita Clair *Rethinking Canada: The Promise of Women's History* (Toronto 1986)

Sutherland, Neil *Children in English-Canadian Society: Framing the Twentieth-Century Consensus* (Toronto 1976)

Taylor, Barbara *Eve and the New Jerusalem* (London 1983)

Trofimenkoff, Susan Mann *The Dream of Nation: A Social and Intellectual History of Quebec* (Toronto 1983)

Trofimenkoff, Susan Mann and Prentice, Alison *The Neglected Majority: Essays in Canadian Women's History* (Toronto 1977)

Van Kirk, Sylvia *"Many Tender Ties": Women in Fur-Trade Society 1670–1870* (Winnipeg 1980)

Walkowitz, Judith *Prostitution and Victorian Society: Women, Class and the State* (Cambridge 1980)

Ward, Peter *Courtship, Love, and Marriage in Nineteenth-Century English Canada* (Montreal 1990)

Ward, W. Peter *White Canada Forever* (Montreal 1978)

Watt, D.A. *Moral Legislation: A Statement Prepared for the Information of the Senate* (Montreal 1890)

Wells, Jess *A Herstory of Prostitution in Western Europe* (Berkeley 1982)

Wertz, Richard W. and Wertz, Dorothy C. *Lying-In: A History of Childbirth in America* (New York 1979)

White, Deborah Gray *Ar'n't I a Woman?* (New York 1985)

*Women Workers of Canada: Being a Report of the Proceedings of the Second Annual Meeting and Conference of the National Council of Women of Canada* (Toronto 1895)

*Women Workers of Canada: Being a Report of the Proceedings of the Third Annual Meeting and Conference of the NCWC* (Montreal 1896)

*Women Workers of Canada: Being a Report of the Proceedings of the Fourth Annual Meeting and Conference of the National Council of Women of Canada* (Kingston 1897)

Youmans, Letitia *Campaign Echoes: The Autobiography of Mrs. Letitia Youmans* (Toronto 1893)

Zaretsky, Eli *Capitalism, the Family and Personal Life* (New York 1976)

## B. Articles

Altschul, Susan and Caron, Christine "Chronology of Some Legal Landmarks in the History of Canadian Women" *McGill Law Journal* 21 (1975) 476

Anderson, Alexandra "The First Woman Lawyer in Canada: Clara Brett Martin" *Canadian Woman Studies* 2 (1980) 9

Backhouse, Constance "Shifting Patterns in Nineteenth-Century Canadian Custody Law" in David H. Flaherty, ed. *Essays in the History of Canadian Law* v. 1 (Toronto 1981) 212–48

Backhouse, Constance "Nineteenth-Century Canadian Rape Law 1800–1892" in Flaherty *Essays* v. 2 at 200–47

Backhouse, Constance "Involuntary Motherhood: Abortion, Birth Control and the Law in Nineteenth-Century Canada" *Windsor Yearbook of Access to Justice* 3 (1983) 61–130

Backhouse, Constance "Desperate Women and Compassionate Courts: Nineteenth-Century Infanticide in Canada" *University of Toronto Law Journal* 34 (1984) 447–78

Backhouse, Constance "To Open the Way for Others of My Sex: Clara Brett Martin's Career as Canada's First Woman Lawyer" *Canadian Journal of Women and the Law* 1 (1985) 1–41

Backhouse, Constance "Nineteenth-Century Canadian Prostitution Law: Reflection of a Discriminatory Society" *Social History/Histoire sociale* 18(36) (1985) 387–423

Backhouse, Constance "The Tort of Seduction: Fathers and Daughters in Nineteenth-Century Canada" *Dalhousie Law Journal* 10 (1986) 45–80

Backhouse, Constance "Pure Patriarchy: Nineteenth-Century Canadian Marriage" *McGill Law Journal* 31 (1986) 264–312

Backhouse, Constance "Married Women's Property Law in Nineteenth-Century Canada" *Law and History Review* 6 (1988) 211–57

Bedford, Judy "Prostitution in Calgary 1905–1914" *Alberta History* 29 (1981) 1

Bennett, J. M. "The Establishment of Divorce Laws in New South Wales" *Sydney Law Review* 4 (1963) 241

Best, Joel "Careers in Brothel Prostitution: St. Paul 1865–1883" *Journal of Interdisciplinary History* 12(4) (Spring 1982) 597

Biggs, C. Lesley "The Case of the Missing Midwives: A History of Midwifery in Ontario from 1795–1900" *Ontario History* 75(1) (March 1983) 21

Bliss, Michael "Pure Books on Avoided Subjects: Pre-Freudian Ideas in Canada" Canadian Historical Association *Historical Papers* (Ottawa 1970) 90

Bohnen, Linda "Women Workers in Ontario: A Socio-Legal History" *University of Toronto Faculty of Law Review* 31 (1973) 45

Boivin, Michelle "L'évolution des droits de la femme au Québec: un survol historique" *Canadian Journal of Women and the Law* 2 (1986) 53

Boxer, Marilyn J. "Protective Legislation and Home Industry: The Marginalization of Women Workers in Late Nineteenth–Early Twentieth-Century France" *Journal of Social History* 20 (1986) 45

Bradbury, Bettina "Women and Wage Labour in a Period of Transition: Montreal 1861–1881" *Social History* 17(33) (May 1984) 115

Bradbury, Bettina "'Pigs, Cows, and Boarders': Non-Wage Forms of Survival Among Montreal Families 1861–91" *Labour/Le Travail* 14 (Fall 1984) 9

Brouwer, Ruth Compton "The 'Between-Age' Christianity of Agnes Machar" *Canadian Historical Review* 65(3) (1984) 347

Brouwer, Ruth Compton "Moral Nationalism in Victorian Canada: The Case of Agnes Machar" *Journal of Canadian Studies* 20(1) (Spring 1985) 90

Brown, Jennifer S.H. "Woman as Centre and Symbol in the Emergence of Metis Communities" *Canadian Journal of Native Studies* 3(1) (1983) 39

Chapman, Terry L. "Early Eugenics Movement in Western Canada" *Alberta History* 25(4) (1977) 9

Chapman, Terry L. "Sex Crimes in the West 1890–1920" *Alberta History* 35 (1986) 6

Clark, Elizabeth B. "Religion, Rights, and Difference in the Early Woman's Rights Movement" *Wisconsin Women's Law Journal* 3 (1987) 29

Cliche, Marie-Aimée "Fille-mere, famille et société sous le Régime francais" *Histoire sociale/Social History* 41 (1988) 39

Cliche, Marie-Aimée "Droits égaux ou influence accrue? Nature et rôle de la femme d'après les féministes chrétiennes et les antiféministes au Québec 1896–1930" *Recherches féministes* 2(2) (1989) 101

Cliche, Marie-Aimée "L'Infanticide dans La Région de Québec 1660–1969" *Revue D'Histoire De L'Amérique Française* (été 1990) 31

Cohn, Henry S. "Connecticut's Divorce Mechanism, 1636–1969" *American Journal of Legal History* 14 (1970) 35

Coombe, Rosemary J. "'The Most Disgusting, Disgraceful and Inequitous Proceeding in our Law': The Action for Breach of Promise of Marriage in Nineteenth-Century Ontario" *University of Toronto Law Journal* 38 (1988) 64

Cott, Nancy F. "Divorce and the Changing Status of Women in Eighteenth-Century Massachusetts" *William and Mary Quarterly* 33 (1976) 586

Cumberland, R.W. "Remembering Agnes Maule Machar" *Historic Kingston* 21 (1973) 22

Dembski, Peter E. Paul "Jenny Kidd Trout and the Founding of the Women's Medical Colleges at Kingston and Toronto" *Ontario History* 77(3) (September 1985) 183

Drachman, Virginia G. "My 'Partner' in Law and Life: Marriage in the Lives of Women Lawyers in Late 19th- and Early 20th-Century America" *Law and Social Inquiry Journal of the American Bar Foundation* 14 (Spring 1989) 221

Drinker, Sophie H. "Women Attorneys of Colonial Times" *Maryland Historical Review* (December 1961) 335

Dumont-Johnson, Micheline "History of the Status of Women in the Province of Quebec" *Studies of the Royal Commission on the Status of Women in Canada* (Ottawa 1971)

Dyhouse, Carol "Social Darwinistic Ideas and the Development of Women's Education in England 1880–1920" *History of Education* 5 (1976) 41

Fingard, Judith "Jailbirds in Mid-Victorian Halifax" in Peter Waite, Sandra Oxner, and Thomas Barnes, eds. *Law in a Colonial Society: The Nova Scotia Experience* (Toronto 1984) 81

Gavigan, Shelley "The Criminal Sanction as it Relates to Human Reproduction" *Journal of Legal History* 5 (1984) 20

Gavigan, Shelly A. M. "On 'Bringing on the Menses': The Criminal Liability of Women and the Therapeutic Exception in Canadian Abortion Law" *Canadian Journal of Women and the Law* 1 (1986) 279

Gee, Ellen M. Thomas "Marriage in Nineteenth-Century Canada" *The Canadian Review of Sociology and Anthropology* 19 (1982) 311

Gossage, Peter "Les Enfants Abandonnés a Montréal au 19e Siècle: La Crèche D'Youville Des Soeurs Grises 1820–1871" *Revue D'Histoire De L'Amérique Française* 40 (1986–87) 537

Green, Gretchen "Molly Brant, Catharine Brant, and their Daughters: A Study in Colonial Acculturation" *Ontario History* 81(3) (September 1989) 235

Harvey, Cameron "Women in Law in Canada" *Manitoba Law Journal* 4 (1970) 9

Howsam, Leslie "Sound-Minded Women: Eliza Orme and the Study and Practice of Law in Late-Victorian England" *Atlantis* 15(1) (Fall 1989) 44

Kline, Marlee "Race, Racism and Feminist Legal Theory" *Harvard Women's Law Journal* 12 (1989) 115

Knight, Patricia "Women and Abortion in Victorian and Edwardian England" *History Workshop* 4 (Autumn 1977) 47

Kobayaski, Cassandra "Sexual Slavery in Canada: Our Herstory" *The Asianadian* I (Fall 1978) 7

Langer, W.L. "Infanticide: an Historical Survey" *The History of Childhood Quarterly* 1 (1974) 353

Lavigne, Marie and Stoddart, Jennifer "Women's Work in Montreal at the Beginning of the Century" in Marylee Stephenson, ed. *Women in Canada* (Don Mills 1977) 129

Machar, Agnes Maule (Fidelis) "Woman's Work" *Canadian Monthly and National Review* 1 (September 1878) 295

Machar, Agnes Maule (Fidelis) "A Few Words on University Co-Education" *Canadian Monthly and National Review* 8 (March 1882) 313

MacLean, Annie Marion "Two Weeks in Department Stores" *American Journal of Sociology* 4 (May 1899) 729

Malcolmson, R.W. "Infanticide in the Eighteenth-Century" in J.S. Cockburn, ed. *Crime in England 1550–1800* (Princeton 1977) 198

Mann, Susan A. "Slavery, Sharecropping and Sexual Inequality" *Signs* 14(4) (Summer 1989) 774

Marks, Lynne and Gaffield, Chad "Women at Queen's University, 1895–1905: A Little Sphere All Their Own" *Ontario History* 78(4) (December 1986) 331

Mason, Jutta "A History of Midwifery in Canada" in Mary Eberts et al. *Report of the Task Force on the Implementation of Midwifery in Ontario* (Toronto 1987) Appendix I

Maynard, Kimberley Smith "Divorce in Nova Scotia 1750–1890" in Philip Girard and Jim Phillips *Essays in the History of Canadian Law: Vol. III, Nova Scotia* (Toronto 1990)

McCallum, Margaret E. "Keeping Women in Their Place: The Minimum Wage in Canada, 1910–25" *Labour/Le Travail* 17 (Spring 1986) 29

McLaren, Angus "Birth Control and Abortion in Canada 1870–1920" *Canadian Historical Review* 59 (1978) 319

McLaren, John "Chasing the Social Evil: Moral Fervour and the Evolution of Canada's Prostitution Laws: 1867–1917" *Canadian Journal of Law and Society* 1 (1986) 125

Menkel-Meadow, Carrie "Portia in a Different Voice: Speculations on a Women's Lawyering Process" *Berkeley Women's Law Journal* 1 (1985) 39

Mitchinson, Wendy "Historical Attitudes Toward Women and Childbirth" *Atlantis* 4 (1979) 13

Mitchinson, Wendy "The WCTU: 'For God, Home, and Native Land': A Study of 19th Century Feminism" in Michael S. Cross and Greg Kealey *Canada's Age of Industry 1849–1896* (Toronto 1982) 190

Mitchinson, Wendy "Medical Perceptions of Female Sexuality: A Late Nineteenth Century Case" *Scientia Canadiensis* 9 (1985) 67

Mitchinson, Wendy "The Medical View of Women: the Case of Late Nineteenth-Century Canada" *Canadian Bulletin of Medical History* 3(2) (Winter 1986) 207

Morel, André "La libération de la femme au Canada: Deux itinéraires" *Revue Juridique Themis* 5 (1970) 399

Morse, Bradford W. "Indian and Inuit Law and the Canadian Legal System" *American Indian Law Review* 8 (1980) 199

Mullins, Christine "Mabel Penery French" *The Advocate* 44(5) (September 1986) 676

Mullins, Christine "Taking the Law into Her Hands" *Horizon Canada* 9(106) (May 1987) 2,540

Oppenheimer, Jo "Childbirth in Ontario: The Transition from Home to Hospital in the Early Twentieth Century" *Ontario History* 75(1) (1983) 36

Palmer, Bryan D. "Discordant Music: Charivaris and Whitecapping in Nineteenth-Century North America" *Labour/Le Travailleur* 3 (1978) 5

Parker, Graham "The Legal Regulation of Sexual Activity and the Protection of Females" *Osgoode Hall Law Journal* 21 (1983) 187

Pike, R. "Legal Access and the Incidence of Divorce in Canada: A Sociohistorical Analysis" *Canadian Review of Sociology and Anthropology* 12 (1975) 115

Roth, Theresa "Clara Brett Martin — Canada's Pioneer Woman Lawyer" *Law Society of Upper Canada Gazette* 18 (1984) 323

Skidmore, Patricia "Sex and Song: Roles and Images of Women in Popular Music at the Turn of the Century" *Atlantis* 2(2) (Spring 1977) 22

Strange, Carolyn "'The Criminal and Fallen of their Sex': The Establishment of Canada's First Women's Prison 1874–1901" *Canadian Journal of Women and the Law* 1 (1985) 79

Trofimenkoff, Susan "One Hundred and Two Muffled Voices: Canada's Industrial Women in the 1880's" in Michael S. Cross and Greg Kealey *Canada's Age of Industry 1849–1896* (Toronto 1982) 212

Tucker, Eric "Making the Workplace 'Safe' in Capitalism: The Enforcement of Factory Legislation in Nineteenth-Century Ontario" *Labour/Le Travail* 21 (Spring 1988) 45

Ward, Peter "Courtship and Social Space in Nineteenth-Century English Canada" *Canadian Historical Review* 68(1) (1987)

Ward, W. Peter "Unwed Motherhood in Nineteenth-Century English Canada" Canadian Historical Association *Historical Papers* (Halifax 1981) 34

Weaver, Sally M. "The Status of Indian Women" in Jean Leonard Elliott, ed. *Two Nations, Many Cultures: Ethnic Groups in Canada* 2nd ed. (Scarborough 1983)

Wright, Mary Ellen "Unnatural Mothers: Infanticide in Halifax 1850–1875" *Nova Scotia Historical Review* (1987) 13.

Wrightson, Keith "Infanticide in European History" *Criminal Justice History* 3 (1982) 1

Zainaldin, Jamil S. "The Emergence of a Modern American Family Law: Child Custody, Adoption, and the Courts 1796–1851" *Northwestern University Law Review* 73 (1979) 1,038

## C. Unpublished Manuscripts

Breault, Erin "Educating Women About the Law: Violence Against Wives in Ontario 1850–1920" M.A. thesis, University of Toronto 1986

Bumsted, Jack and Owen, Wendy "Divorce in a Small Province: A History of Divorce on Prince Edward Island from 1833" forthcoming in *Acadiensis*

Cliche, Marie-Aimée "Les Filles Mères Devant Les Tribunaux dans le District Judiciare de Québec 1850–1969" unpublished manuscript

Cole, Curtis Johnson "A Learned and Honorable Body: The Professionalization of the Ontario Bar, 1867–1929" unpublished Ph.D. dissertation, University of Western Ontario 1987

Crandall, Angela "Divorce in 19th Century New Brunswick: A Social Dilemma" unpublished manuscript 1988

Oliver, Peter N. *"To Govern by Kindness": The First Two Decades of the Mercer Reformatory for Women* unpublished manuscript

Snell, James G. *Controlling Divorce in Canada 1900–1939* unpublished manuscript 1988

Strange, Carolyn "The Founding and Floundering of an Institution: Mercer 1874–1901" unpublished manuscript

Strange, Carolyn *The Velvet Glove: Materialistic Reform at the Andrew Mercer Ontario Reformatory for Females 1874–1927* M.A. thesis, University of Ottawa 1983

Tucker, Eric *Administering Danger in the Workplace: The Law and Politics of Occupational Health and Safety Regulation in Ontario 1850–1914* forthcoming University of Toronto Press 1991

Walsh, Zoya-Claire "The Toronto Magdalene Asylum 1853–1900: The Transition from Moral Reformation to Social Service" unpublished manuscript 1986

# Index

PUBLICATIONS OF THE OSGOODE SOCIETY

Constance Backhouse is an Associate Professor of Law at the University of Western Ontario, London, Canada. She received her B.A. from the University of Manitoba, her LL.B. from Osgoode Hall Law School, and her LL.M. from Harvard Law School. She is the co-author, along with Leah Cohen, of *The Secret Oppression: Sexual Harassment of Working Women*, published in the United States as *Sexual Harassment on the Job*. She was the recipient of the Augusta Stowe-Gullen Affirmative Action Medal and has written extensively on women's legal history.